International Capital Markets

Systems in Transition

EDITED BY

John Eatwell
Lance Taylor

UNIVERSITY PRESS

2002

OXFORD

UNIVERSITY PRESS

Oxford   New York
Auckland   Bangkok   Buenos Aires   Cape Town   Chennai
Dar es Salaam   Delhi   Hong Kong   Istanbul   Karachi   Kolkata
Kuala Lumpur   Madrid   Melbourne   Mexico City   Mumbai   Nairobi
São Paulo   Shanghai   Singapore   Taipei   Tokyo   Toronto

and an associated company in Berlin

Published by Oxford University Press, Inc.
198 Madison Avenue, New York, New York 10016

www.oup.com

Oxford is a registered trademark of Oxford University Press

Library of Congress Cataloging-in-Publication Data
International capital markets : systems in transition / edited by John Eatwell and Lance Taylor.
p. cm.
Includes bibliographical references.
ISBN 0-19-514765-0; ISBN 0-19-515498-3 (pbk.)
1. Capital market. 2. International finance. 3. Foreign exchange market. 4. International
economic relations. I. Eatwell, John. II. Taylor, Lance.
HG4523 .I5836 2001
332'.042—dc21   2001036598

2 4 6 8 9 7 5 3 1

Printed in the United States of America
on acid-free paper

Table of Contents

Part III: Issues in Industrialized Economies

Part IV: Developing and Transition Economies

Part V: Regulatory Questions

Contributors

Robert Blecker
American University; Washington, DC, United States

Thorsten Block
New School University; New York, New York, United States

Ha-Joon Chang
University of Cambridge; Cambridge, United Kingdom

Jane D'Arista
Financial Markets Center; Philomont, VA, United States

Randall Dodd
Derivatives Study Center; Washington, DC, United States

John Eatwell
University of Cambridge; Cambridge, United Kingdom

Roberto Frenkel
Center for the Study of the State and Society; Buenos Aires, Argentina

Eric Helleiner
Trent University; Peterborough, Ontario, Canada

Jeff Madrick
Challenge magazine; New York, New York, United States

Deepak Nayyar
Jawaharlal University; New Delhi, India

Salih Nefci
New School University; New York, New York, United States

Jose Antonio Ocampo
United Nations Economic Commission on Latin America and the Caribbean;
Santiago, Chile

Gabrial Palma
University of Cambridge; Cambridge, United Kingdom

Ajit Sing
University of Cambridge; Cambridge, United Kingdom

Lance Taylor
New School University; New York, New York, United States

Philip Turner
Bank for International Settlements; Basle, Switzerland

Chul-Gyne Yoo
Seong Gong Hoe University; Seoul, Korea

PART I

Introduction

1
...
Introduction

John Eatwell and Lance Taylor

THE 1990S WERE a time of troubles for international capital markets. From the European exchange rate mechanism (ERM) crisis of 1992 through the Mexican (or "Tequila"), Asian, Brazilian, and Russian crises of mid-decade and on to the rescue of the Long Term Capital Management hedge fund in late 1998, the financial world seemed to reel from one shock to another. Though by comparison 1999 and 2000 were years of tranquility, there is no reason to believe that the underlying causes of the turbulence have gone away.

These events seemed more threatening than crises in the 1970s and 1980s (even when some, like the 1982 developing country debt shock, were devastating to the economies concerned) and led to a worldwide reappraisal of international financial arrangements. In particular, an unstated assumption among major players in both the private and public sectors that ongoing liberalization and deregulation of financial markets are invariably beneficial came under increased scrutiny. Almost all serious commentators now believe that some degree of regulation of international capital markets is both desirable and likely to happen. But there is as yet no consensus about how to analyze and specify an appropriate form of regulation or how to implement it in a proper institutional setting.

In response to these concerns (and with support from the Ford Foundation), in mid-1997 we called together a number of colleagues to analyze international financial markets and their effects on real economies throughout the world. Particular attention was paid to the impacts of the movement toward market liberalization, at the time in full swing. Our synthesis of the insights of our colleagues and others appeared in a report to the Ford Foundation, "International Capital Markets and the Future of Economic Policy," (Eatwell and Taylor 1998).

Further development of its ideas led to a book, *Global Finance at Risk: The Case for International Regulation* (Eatwell and Taylor 2000).

The book takes up the effects of capital market liberalization, evaluated both over many years (trend performance) and in the light of the recurrent financial crises that have, over the past 30 years and especially in the 1990s, disrupted both developed and developing economies. We argued that while liberalization has brought some benefits, they have been tarnished by considerable costs. Those costs could have been substantially mitigated if a key lesson had been drawn from the development of domestic financial markets—liberal markets are only efficient if they are efficiently regulated. The task of financial regulation is to manage the risks that follow in the wake of liberalization. Without regulation, the risks and associated costs can become unbearable.

The need for regulation at the international level led to our proposal for the establishment of a World Financial Authority (or WFA), to perform in the domain of world financial markets what national regulators do in domestic markets. A natural place to build the WFA is on the foundations for global financial surveillance and regulation that have already been laid at the Bank for International Settlements in Basel. But as far as our analysis is concerned, whether a WFA is actually set up is of secondary importance. The *concept* of a WFA is the key test of the regulatory needs of today's liberal financial markets. Whether a single regulator comes into being or not, *the tasks that a model WFA should perform must be performed by someone* if international financial markets are to operate efficiently.

While writing *Global Finance at Risk* and with further support from the Ford Foundation, we continued to bring people together during 1999–2000 to discuss evolving issues in financial markets and regulation. These ongoing consultations led to papers addressing questions relevant at the global level and in industrialized, transition, and developing countries. This volume draws together contributions dealing with a WFA directly, major past and future global issues in international finance, specific problems arising in different sorts of economies, and some regulatory conundrums. Brief summaries of their arguments go as follows:

Part II of the volume takes up the global capital market. Chapter 2 is an extension of our WFA proposal to take into account recent developments. It emphasizes two gaps in the current regulatory structure that sooner or later must be filled:

> *First,* the need for theory and policy that link microeconomic risk-taking to the macroeconomic propagation of systemic risk.
> *Second,* the need to develop a coherent and accountable set of institutions through which international policy may be developed and implemented.

At the moment governments and international financial institutions are beginning to address these needs, but in haphazard actions by the patchwork of players described in the chapter. The pressing challenge today is to replace the patchwork by some more coherent set of institutions that can undertake the regulatory functions of a WFA, i.e., (1) authorization and licensure of private sector financial actors, (2) the provision of comprehensive information, thus enhancing transparency, (3) surveillance of market players, (4) enforcement against any breaches of regulations that they may commit, and (5) the development of policy. One key question arising is whether the new institutions must be established by treaty or can be constructed in more administrative fashion on the basis of international "soft law." This issue is taken up in several later chapters, especially numbers 5 and 7.

Chapter 3, by José Antonio Ocampo, is a broad survey of the issues now pending on the international financial agenda, with an emphasis on developing countries. Arguments it presents have been widely discussed in light of proposals from the United Nations to deal with global financial restructuring.

Ocampo sees several features of international capital markets as crucial during the 1990s—rapid growth of private capital movements, differing degrees of instability of different forms of capital (with direct foreign investment being fairly resilient in the face of crises and other flows being highly volatile), and a pattern of unstable flows leading to crises requiring emergency rescue packages of unprecedented size which have been concentrated in a few middle income "emerging" economies.

He goes on to consider institutional barriers to financial reform—the reluctance of all countries to surrender economic and regulatory sovereignty to international organizations, the fragmentation of actors (especially developing country governments), and a lopsided policy agenda. One important imbalance has been the push for capital market liberalization mentioned above and largely orchestrated by international financial institutions and a few rich countries (notably the United States).

Against this background, the paper sets out several major themes—the need for crisis prevention and management, the role of development finance, the issues of "conditionality" as imposed by international institutions on countries in crisis and the "ownership" of policy packages by these countries, and the potential significance of regional bodies in dealing with national regulations and autonomy. This discussion complements (and in many ways goes beyond) Chapter 2 because all these are concerns that would have to be dealt with by a novel institution or institutions under the WFA template

In Chapter 4, Jane D'Arista synthesizes current regulatory concerns in a liberalized global market. She begins with a useful history of financial liberalization through its various stages—Eurocurrency markets in the 1960s, a consequent deregulation of U.S. financial markets in response, diversification of banks away from their traditional activities into fee-generating, off-balance sheet activities such as money management (an overriding theme in several later chapters), and a push toward the use of "value at risk" (VaR) measures and capital adequacy requirements as the main regulatory tools.

D'Arista next points out major holes in the current system—its likely procyclical bias, its inability to cope with opaque but increasingly prevalent over-the-counter (OTC) transactions, and its difficulty in dealing with contagion because the traditional "firewalls" that were erected to compartmentalize different segments of the financial market have been systematically broken down. She closes with several specific policy recommendations that may help overcome these problems—the use of risk-weighted charges for pooled investment funds, creation of an international investment fund for emerging markets, more effective use of public financial guaranty programs, and more effective monetary control (for example, through the use of capital controls). Harmonization of such tools across national boundaries would be essential, leading again to the question of how to organize international regulatory cooperation.

Chapter 5 by Deepak Nayyar looks in depth at potential advantages and drawbacks of capital controls, taking their use in India since World War II as a concrete point of reference. His three main suggestions are that (1) capital market liberalization is a means and not an end in itself; (2) if liberalization is done, it should be subject to safeguards and (3) should incorporate economic development as an objective. These recommendations can lead to diverse outcomes: ". . . capital controls can range from prudential controls for crisis prevention and ad hoc controls for crisis management to safeguard controls for the balance of payments and developmental controls for autonomy in the formulation of economic policies." Moreover, ". . . quantitative controls or regulatory controls should be just as permissible as price-based controls. Even asymmetries in controls, between capital inflows and capital outflows, residents and nonresidents, or individuals and corporates, which are discernible from the Indian experience, should be consistent with such a [regulatory] framework."

If a World Financial Authority emerges, one of its major chores would be to formulate a set of international rules or norms regarding capital markets, in which all countries would have the same rights but obligations would have to be graduated so that ". . . developing countries are provided with the time and space to learn so that they are competitive players rather than pushover opponents." Not necessarily an easy task!

In Chapter 6 (written in 1998) and a postscript from November 2000, Robert Blecker takes up another vexing problem—potential macroeconomic instabilities at the global level. He finds that national saving and investment levels have become less correlated since around 1980, implying that foreign funding of investment is becoming more significant at the country level. Large national net debtor and creditor positions have emerged, adding a potentially important source of instability to the global macro system.

Indeed, the world today has a "perverse" pattern of imbalances, with about two-thirds of net capital flows going into the United States and only a relative trickle into developing economies (although when trickles reverse they can rapidly destabilize an economy with a GDP in the few hundred billion dollar range, as discussed in detail below). The U.S. current account deficit serves as a source of aggregate demand for the world economy but at the same time creates significant risks: "If speculators turn against the dollar . . . , The United States could be forced to raise interest rates and contract its domestic economy, with depressing effects . . . around the world. Only better coordination of macro policies . . . can avert such an outcome."

Is this sort of macro coordination an appropriate task for a WFA? In Eatwell and Taylor (2000) we argue that such an effort would stretch a regulatory institution too far. But better regulation can help contain the systemic risks that capital market imbalances create.

Chapter 7 by Eric Helleiner takes up the politics of financial regulation, drawing lessons from the institutional apparatus that has been built up since the late 1980s to combat international money laundering. One conclusion is that such initiatives may be fairly easy to put into place if certain preconditions are met: leadership from the United States and other big powers in overcoming collective action problems and forcing noncooperators (offshore financial centers being the principal examples) to join regulatory regimes; existence of competitive pressures on countries to cooperate (for example, to adhere to "international standards" so they will not be passed over by markets); and the emergence of transnational committees operating under soft law that can undertake needed regulatory tasks.

Moreover, once structures such as the anti-money laundering apparatus are in operation, they can be used for other purposes, e.g., to monitor and regulate tax evasion or capital flight. The latter goal harks back to discussions involving the main architects of the Bretton Woods system—John Maynard Keynes and Harry Dexter White—about the necessity of international cooperation to control capital flight and destabilizing capital movements more generally. A WFA would represent the sort of institution under whose aegis such cooperation could take place.

The two chapters in Part III are devoted to issues relevant to the functioning and understanding of capital markets in industrialized nations, especially the United States. In Chapter 8, Thorsten Block takes up the question of how financial market liberalization may be affecting corporate governance and behavior. In Albert Chandler's (1990) theory of governance, managerial autonomy is essential for dynamic growth of companies and the economy as a whole. Is such autonomy possible under liberalized capital markets? There is a possibility that the imposition of financial goals on managers through hostile takeovers might induce a slowdown in investments in organization skills and firm-specific investments by employees. Such weaknesses may not be apparent in a boom but could become debilitating in a slump.

Contrasts show up in other countries. The German insider system based on committed relationships among long-term corporate stakeholders has so far proven resilient against financial liberalization while as discussed further in Chapter 13 the Korean state-led financial/industrial system recently plunged into deep crisis. Despite the apparent success of "Anglo-American" systems in the 1990s, their long-term staying power has yet to be fully tested. Harking back to Chapter 5, financial market regulation in different countries must ultimately be adjusted to the real economy's productive and institutional needs.

But are such adjustments possible in the current intellectual climate? In Chapter 9 on the influence of the financial media on the international economic policy debate, Jeff Madrick raises doubts. On the basis of textual analysis of financial reporting in leading American newspapers and magazines, he concludes that the media construct a "narrative" with a particular interpretation of a set of events, in particular the " . . . failure of economic reform, and specifically 'shock therapy,' in Russia [and] . . . the liberalization of the capital markets in developing nations in the 1980s and 1990s, which, in the view of this paper, led to the Asian financial crisis of 1997 and 1998."

In both cases, mainstream media vociferously approved of liberalization policies and only came to recognize late in the day that other points of view existed: "The job of journalism is to ferret out other points of view, but in my view, the financial press largely lost the initiative in many areas of importance."

Why do such biases endure? One reason is the desire of the media to be in tune with the "conventional wisdom" (in John Kenneth Galbraith's famous phrase). Another may be journalists' simple lack of economic sophistication. Madrick suggests the establishment of a Center for Economic Dialogue to present all reasonable points of view on major issues of public interest. World financial regulation should certainly be at the forefront of any such institution's interests.

The papers in Part IV concentrate on developing and transition economies. When their analyses are put together, Chapters 10 and 11 (respectively written by Roberto Frenkel and Salih Neftci) propose a convincing theory of financial crisis dynamics, with Frenkel describing the macro side and Neftci emphasizing microeconomic foundations.

A Frenkel-Neftci cycle begins in financial markets, which generate capital inflows. They spill over to the macroeconomy via the financial system and the balance of payments as the upswing gains momentum. At the peak, before a (more or less rapid) downswing, the economy-wide consequences can be overwhelming.

To trace through an example, suppose that a "spread" opens between interest rates in industrialized economies and developing country rates (e.g., on pre-crisis Mexican government peso-denominated bonds with a high nominal rate but carrying an implicit exchange risk) or growth in asset prices (e.g., capital gains from booming Bangkok real estate). A few local players take positions in the relevant assets, borrowing abroad to do so. Their exposure is risky but *small*. It may well go unnoticed by regulators; indeed for the system as a whole the risk is negligible.

Destabilizing market competition enters in a second stage. The pioneering institutions are exploiting a spread of (say) 10%, while others are earning (say) 5% on traditional placements. Even if the risks are recognized, it is difficult for other players not to jump in. A trader or loan officer holding 5% paper will reason that the probability of losing his or her job is close to 100% *now* if he or she does not take the high risk/high return position. Such potentially explosive behavior is standard market practice. In one description from an interview study, " . . . the speculative excesses of the international investors in the Asian financial crisis were not an exception, . . . but instead the result of normal business practices and thus to a certain degree inevitable."

After some months or years of this process, the balance sheet of the local financial system will be risky overall. It will feature "short" (indebted) positions in foreign claims and "long" positions in local assets. There may also be problems with maturity structures of claims, especially if local players borrow from abroad short-term. Nervous foreign lenders may then contrast a country's total external payment obligations over the next year (say) with its international reserves. Such comparisons proved disastrous for Mexico in 1995 and several Asian countries in 1997.

There can also be macroeconomic consequences. An upward shift in the supply of foreign exchange due to rising capital inflows tends to lead to real exchange rate appreciation—a stronger local currency—which offsets incentives for traded goods production by reducing profits from exports and making imports cheaper. Through financial markets, real appreciation is usually linked to high real interest rates (the simple reason is that investors will not want to hold securities valued in an expensive local currency unless they receive especially high returns). High rates add to production costs, penalize capital formation, and (in countries with foreign debt) increase the deficit on current account.

Higher rates may also draw in more external capital, setting off a high interest rate/strong exchange rate spiral. Via the banking system, capital inflows feed into international reserves and expansion of domestic money and credit. On the positive side, additional credit may stimulate aggregate spending through increased investment. However, it can also trigger a consumption boom (with purchases heavily weighted toward imports) or a speculative asset price bubble (typically in equity and/or real estate). The import-fed demand spurt may prove to be short-lived if the consequent widening of the external balance is unsustainable or if capital flees the economy when the bubble begins to deflate. Rolling back prudential financial regulation makes the latter outcome all the more likely.

In a typical macroeconomic paradox, individual players' risks have been shifted to the aggregate. Any policy move that threatens the overall position—for example cutting interest rates or pricking the real estate bubble—could cause a collapse of the currency and local asset prices. The authorities will use reserves and/or regulations to prevent a crash, consciously ratifying the private sector's market decisions. Unfortunately, macroeconomic factors will ultimately force their hand. The current account deficit will widen, leading at some point to a fall in reserves as capital inflows level off and total interest payments on outstanding obligations rise. Higher interest rates will be needed to equilibrate portfolios and attract foreign capital. There will be adverse repercussions for both the private and public sectors. Business saving will fall or turn negative as illiquidity and insolvency spread, threatening a systemic crisis. If the government has debt outstanding, escalating interest payment obligations as rates shoot up can provoke a fiscal crisis—witness events in Russia and Brazil in the late 1990s.

A downturn becomes inevitable, since finally no local interest rate will be high enough to induce more external lending in support of what is recognized as a short foreign exchange position at the economy-wide level. Shrewd players will unwind their positions before the downswing begins. They can even retain positive earnings over the cycle by getting out while the currency weakens visibly. But others—typically including the macroeconomic policy team—are likely to go under.

Variations around these themes are developed by Gabriel Palma in Chapter 12. On the supply side of capital markets, he joins Kindleberger (1996) in stressing the significance of the growth of liquidity in the hands of institutional investors (by 40% of GDP in the G7 countries between 1988 and 1996) and the expansion of derivatives markets as "push" factors behind the explosion of credit to emerging markets around the turn of the decade. On the recipient side, countries handled their capital inflows in differing fashions. Palma distinguishes three "routes" to crisis.

Route 1 was typically Latin American (aside from Brazil). Domestic credit expansion to the private sector sparked by the incoming external funds fed into rapid expansion of consumption and imports, accompanied by booms in equity and real estate markets. Investment tended to flow toward housing construction as opposed to more productive uses. Initially high spreads between domestic asset returns and foreign borrowing rates tended to narrow, while currency and maturity mismatches between domestic assets and foreign liabilities worsened. Withdrawals of funds became inevitable, leading to financial crises.

(South) Korea was the main traveller on Route 2. It did successfully direct the bulk of capital inflows to manufacturing investment, but with weakening regulation of "excess competition" among its industrial conglomerates and a rapid buildup of corporate debt (for more details, see immediately below). However, a shortening maturity structure of foreign debt stimulated by perverse domestic incentives, a drop-off in export growth, and low international reserves made the country a speculative target after the Asian crisis got underway. Indeed, the Southeast Asian countries combined aspects of Routes 1 and 2, running both import and investment booms, but they also proved to be vulnerable.

Brazil took a lonely journey on Route 3, keeping real interest rates high on its domestic government debt and consciously building up international reserves. But the high rates coupled with a strong exchange rate strangled the real side of the economy and led to a wave of failing banks and local governments which had to be bailed out by the central authorities. With interest rates substantially exceeding growth rates of GDP and public revenues, the ratio of debt to these aggregates grew uncontrollably, ultimately provoking a reversal of capital flows and a crisis.

Along with Ocampo in Chapter 3, Palma stresses how the changing composition and term structure of capital inflows made their management difficult. In closing, he takes up the relative effectiveness of inflow controls in Chile and Malaysia. For Chile, he concludes that "market-based" regulation helped keep down the share of short-term debt in the total and may have prevented the asset price bubble prior to the Asian crisis from becoming worse than it did.

Malaysia imposed quantity controls on inflows when they began to surge early in the 1990s. The regime was strict, and inflows dropped off rapidly but then increased again after restrictions were relaxed. Booms in real estate and stock prices were aborted, but then started again in more subdued fashion. As in Chile, the lesson seems to be that controls on inflows can be effective in deterring "hot money" at least in the short run, and may change the composition of flows toward more productive investments over time.

A view complementary to those of Frenkel, Neftci, and Palma about events in Asia is provided in Chapter 13, wherein Ajit Singh asks why "Asian capitalism" was unable to resist financial shocks. In terms of an "ideal type," he points to four major Asian institutional features, especially prior to a liberalization phase that got underway around 1990.

First, especially in the "Northern tier" of Japan, Korea, and Taiwan, relationships between business and government were historically close and mutually interactive. "Administrative guidance" was the state's chosen means for microeconomic intervention, as opposed to legislation and/or judicial proceedings such as American antitrust actions.

Second, corporate finance was largely channeled through banks, especially a "main bank" for each enterprise or conglomerate. Such durable relationships are said to allow business executives to take a long planning view because they are not threatened by hostile stock market takeovers. One implication of reliance on bank finance is that, depending on the specific country concerned, corporations carried high debt/equity ratios, at times in the range of several hundred percent.

Third, just as capital markets were far from open, product markets and investment decisions by firms were regulated. "Excess competition" in the sense of over-investment by firms and extreme cost/price cycles in sectors subject to economies of scale were avoided by the planning authorities. One corollary is that besides major investment decisions, import and export trade had to be regulated by the state. The goal was to maintain economies open to trade, but with "strategic" as opposed to "close" integration with the world economy.

Finally, social tensions never spilled over into high inflation rates, and growth was relatively stable. Communist transitions in China, Indo-China, and North Korea aside, the region did not experience macroeconomic earthquakes after World War II, in sharp contrast to Latin America. This is one reason why the events of 1997–98 were an enormous psychological shock to both economic policy makers and the general public.

A root cause of the crises was the way in which the region's macroeconomic environment was evolving. The Plaza Accord of 1985 marked a big transition when it set off substantial yen appreciation against the dollar. Japanese (along with Korean and Taiwanese) companies began to seek cheaper platforms for manufactured exports. The Southern tier was the natural place to go, especially because its economies pegged their currencies more or less tightly to the weakening dollar.

In the "long run" (that is, after about 10 years) the pegged currencies appreciated notably, leading to a region-wide crisis. The shock was also associated with a breakdown of state control over enterprises and opening of capital markets without the establishment of adequate national financial regulation. As the first and third pillars of the Asian model were removed, firms' heavily geared financial structures turned from a source of strength into a major burden as they were unable to continue borrowing. As of late 2000, the presence of these structural problems suggest that the recovery of 1999 may prove short-lived in several in the region's major economies.

One of these is Korea, analyzed by Ha-Joon Chang and Chul-Gyue Yoo in Chapter 14. They see the 1997 crisis as a watershed in Korean economic history, marking the replacement of the state-directed, industrially oriented economy put into place in the 1950s by a system much more oriented toward the interests of the financial sector and rentiers. For reasons traceable both to internal economic evolution and external pressures, the crisis was "managed" to protect financial positions. The policy thrust in earlier recovery programs after major shocks (in the late 1960s/early 1970s and late 1970s/early 1980s) was strikingly different. Emphasis was placed on debt restructuring and credit creation to spur investment demand; just the opposite happened after 1997. The pending question is whether " . . . the institutional changes made in the Korean economic system following the 1997 crisis are likely to dampen . . . investment dynamism by making the financial system much more volatile and 'conservative' than before, thus making long-term, patient capital more scarce"?

Chapter 15 by Palma goes into detail about "Route 3" financial crises in Brazil, finding sharp contrasts with the standard mainstream explanations based on "moral hazard" and "cronyism" which are supposed to underlie government subsidies via low interest rates to favored domestic borrowers. The key factors underlying the Brazilian breakdown in 1998 were extremely high interest rates on domestic government debt (exceeding 50% in the mid-1990s and over 20% late in the decade). Such high returns were a magnet for external funds, but also led to exponential growth of the fiscal deficit which was additionally pumped up by continual government bailouts of domestic financial actors (both banks and financial houses in the private sector and state and municipal governments in the public domain) which themselves got into trouble because of the high rates!

The fears of external fund managers about the instability of this vicious circle were offset for five years by the high returns they were earning in Brazil. But fear finally won out, leading to the financial crisis of January 1999. The subsequent recovery has been based on assuaging rentiers. As in Korea, there is no obvious mechanism via which financial rectitude will lead to a sustained recovery of economic growth.

Part V of the volume delves into details of regulation. Chapter 16 by Neftci and Chapter 17 by Randall Dodd concentrate on the roles derivatives have played in the past and could play in the future in provoking crises. Neftci draws on contemporary corporate finance theory to show through examples how derivative contracts can be put together to outflank many regulatory interventions including taxes on transactions, outright prohibitions of certain transactions, and so on. The prerequisite is that markets, especially forward markets, should be large and active enough to assure consistently low transactions costs. Even if markets are thin, big players are usually in a better position to undertake such maneuvers than small ones. One implication is that partially effective controls may segment the market.

Derivatives, moreover, complicate the use of VaR methods to gauge risk. They must overcome the problem that some " . . . positions themselves may look very risky, yet when put together with other positions may show no risk at all. The opposite may be true also. A position that may not look risky at all . . . may end up being very risky when combined with other positions." Although VaR measurements can grapple with such complications, they provide little direct guidance to policy makers about how to intervene to contain various forms of risk.

Dodd provides examples (drawn in part from Neftci in Chapter 11) of contract forms that became important during the Mexican and Asian crises. He observes that they had several deleterious effects on market performance: reducing transparency, allowing players to outflank regulatory safeguards; raising risk relative to capital by making it easier to construct highly leveraged or geared positions; threatening exchange rate stability by lowering the cost of speculative positions and forcing regulators to intervene in both spot and forward markets; adding to instability and contagion through proliferation of counterparty contracts; quickening and deepening crises as margin or collateral requirements began to bite after adverse swings in asset prices (including the exchange rate); and making cleanup efforts more difficult after a crisis happened.

Regulatory steps to counter these problems could involve better accounting rules and credit evaluations, surveillance of off-balance sheet positions, and more complete reporting of OTC transactions. The goals are " . . . to shape the structure of incentives for derivatives trading so that they will be used in proper ways to facilitate capital flows without their being used in destructive ways to increase risk-to-capital and outmaneuvering government safeguards." The practice may prove extremely difficult.

Finally, in Chapter 18 Philip Turner tackles the problem of the procyclicality of regulation. Regulation of the private sector proceeds predominantly by levying capital charges intended to be related to the risks taken by banks and firms. The purpose of the charge is to internalize, at least in part, the risks imposed on the rest of the economy by the actions of individual firms. When these systemic risks increase, as in a recession, the charges should increase, thus reducing the ability of the firms to lend or to invest, exacerbating the recession. Similarly, risk management techniques induce firms to react to crises in particular markets by reducing their exposure in markets deemed to be similar (all emerging markets for example) thus escalating the contagion in financial markets. Turner proposes to modify regulations to require provisions to be made for possible loan losses to cover normal cyclical risks. Provisions built up in good times can be used in bad times without necessarily affecting the capital charge. Of course, such provisions would only suffice to cover *normal* cycles. The problem of the procyclicality remains in the *abnormal* times of financial crises.

The difficulties that Turner is struggling with derive in part from the lack of a satisfactory integration of the microeconomic structure and macroeconomic consequences of regulation, i.e., it derives from the lack of a satisfactory theory of financial regulation. This lack of a satisfactory theory in turn results in institutional inadequacies. This book is an attempt to address these fundamental problems in international financial regulation.

REFERENCES

Chandler, Alfred D. 1990. *Scale and Scope*, Cambridge MA: Belknap Press.
Eatwell, John, and Lance Taylor. 1998. "International Capital Markets and the Future of Economic Policy," New York: Center for Economic Policy Analysis, New School University.
_____. 2000. *Global Finance at Risk*, New York: The New Press.
Kindleberger, Charles P. 1996. *Manias, Panics and Crises*, New York: John Wiley and Sons.

PART II

. . .

Global Questions

2

...

A World Financial Authority

John Eatwell and Lance Taylor

IN OUR 1998 Report to The Ford Foundation on international financial liberalization we recommended the establishment of a World Financial Authority (Eatwell and Taylor 1998). We argued that for efficient regulation the domain of the regulator should be the same as the domain of the market that is regulated. None of the standard tasks of a financial regulator—authorization, the provision of information, surveillance, enforcement, and the development of policy—are currently performed in a coherent manner in international markets. Indeed, in many cases they are not performed at all. In the absence of a World Financial Authority (WFA) the liberalization of international markets has resulted in a significant increase in systemic risk. In other words, it has been inefficient.[1]

Our prime objective in proposing the creation of a WFA was to assess the regulatory needs of today's liberal financial markets. Whether a single regulator is created or not, the tasks that the model WFA should perform must be performed by someone if international financial markets are to operate efficiently.

The goal of this chapter is to identify what those tasks might be and to develop proposals about how they might best be performed. In moving from our initial proposal to more concrete, policy-oriented discussion, we found that we needed to consider not only the practical developments that have taken place up to now, but also the international legal and institutional implications of our proposals. It is particularly striking that much of the criticism of the idea of a WFA has suggested that the required international cooperation will be impossible to achieve—even when a number of the necessary cooperative

---

1. Liberalization has coincided with a worldwide slowdown in the rate of growth. Whether there is a causal link between liberalization and that slowdown is, of course, a complex question. But the argument that liberalization has resulted in a higher growth rate that might otherwise be the case is even more difficult to sustain (see Eatwell 1996).

mechanisms are already in place![2] There already exists a body of international legal practice, and a cohort of institutions that would support the further development of the regime of international financial regulation. But practice and institutions need to be assembled and codified in a manner appropriate to today's regulatory needs.

While the emphasis in this chapter will be on the development of policy, a not insubstantial part of the argument will be devoted to analysis. Analysis is essential because the theoretical framework within which a new structure of international financial regulation might be formulated is lacking. Without such a framework, policy has inevitably been ad hoc, essentially responsive to pressing need, and deprived of overall coherence. In our book *Global Finance at Risk* (Eatwell and Taylor 2000) we set out the skeleton of the requisite theoretical framework. In what follows we hope to put more flesh on the bones. We first consider briefly the development of international regulation to date, and then turn to the analytical, legal, and institutional challenges that face the attempt to construct an efficient international regulatory regime for financial markets involving industrialized, transition, and developing economies.

THE EVOLUTION OF INTERNATIONAL FINANCIAL REGULATION

Observed changes in international financial regulation since 1974 have been essentially reactive.

The first major reaction was to the fact of liberalization itself. The three decades following the end of World War II had seen the refinement of the tools for managing systemic risk in *domestic* monetary and financial systems. Allied with the international commitment to the management of financial flows that was a key component of the Bretton Woods system, these domestic arrangements had resulted in 25 years of reasonable financial stability in most OECD countries. This is not to say that there were no financial crises, there certainly were. But they were predominantly of macroeconomic origin, disrupting the

---

2. For example, Will Hutton (1999) in a preview of Eatwell and Taylor (2000) argued that the authors' ". . . logic is impeccable, but it faces one insuperable obstacle. The United States at present has no intention of ceding any regulatory sovereignty to such an authority." Hutton does not take into account the degree of authority already vested in the consensual decision-making processes of the Basel G10 committees (described in more detail below). The capital adequacy requirements of banks in Iowa are determined by a committee sitting in Basel that is not accountable to the U.S. Congress. This approach has not so much involved "ceding regulatory authority" as the recognition of the advantages of collaborative decision-making. However, Will Hutton's point may become more important as the demands for accountability in international regulation become more widespread (particularly from developing countries who have, up to now, had only minor roles, if any, in development of regulatory rules and practices).

micro-economy: high inflation rates undermining confidence in monetary policy, or persistent current account deficits undermining confidence in the exchange rate. The bad old days of microeconomic instability spreading as contagion through the financial sector and destabilizing the macro-economy belonged to the prewar era of economic disaster, from which important lessons had been learned.[3] Those lessons were now embodied in appropriate policies and institutions. Important among the latter were powerful regulatory structures and interventionist central banks dedicated to the management of (indeed the minimization of) systemic risk.

There had, of course, been a partial relaxation of wartime and immediate postwar regulation through the 1950s and 1960s. But even at the end of the 1960s the regulatory regime was powerful and national. In the United States domestic money markets were particularly tightly regulated, and the interest equalization tax and other forms of exchange control introduced by Presidents Kennedy and Johnson were meant to manage international capital flows. Throughout the OECD the public authorities' international role was dedicated to the maintenance of the fixed exchange rate system. The collapse of the Bretton Woods system of fixed exchange rates in 1971 resulted in the privatization of foreign exchange risk, and the consequent necessary dismantling of international and domestic financial regulation threatened to recreate the unstable pre-War environment (see Eatwell and Taylor 2000, chapter 1).

As international barriers to financial flows disappeared, national regulators and central banks were trapped in increasingly irrelevant national boundaries. The domain of banks, investment houses, insurance companies and pension funds became international. In a rapid return to the pre-War norm, it was a microeconomic failure (of the Herstatt Bank in 1974) that threatened severe disruption of the U.S. clearing system and hence of the U.S. macro-economy. In recent years the Asian crisis also stemmed primarily from failures in the private sector reverberating through the macro-economy.

An important response to the new environment was the establishment of the "Basel committees" at the BIS, attempting, by consensual decision making in the

---

3. The distinction between crises emanating from the micro-economy and those that are macroeconomically induced is worth further consideration. Although the second phase of the Great Depression was marked by the failure of an Austrian bank, Credit Anstalt, much of the responsibility for the depression rests at the door of inappropriate macroeconomic policy—particularly adherence to the Gold Standard and domestic monetary policies associated with the Gold Standard (Temin, 1989). Similarly, the recent Korean crisis derived substantially from the decision of the Korean government to join the OECD, and to accept the required liberalization of financial markets. This led to private sector firms increasing their foreign exchange exposure to excessive levels (Chang, Park, and Yoo 1998). In both the 1930s and the 1990s, an inappropriate macroeconomic environment resulted in excessive risk taking by firms. In the 1950s and 1960s macroeconomic crises were not associated with excessive private sector risk taking, but by major macroeconomic imbalances.

Group of Ten (G10), to establish on an international scale some of the powers that had earlier been deemed necessary to stabilize national financial systems. The scope of those committees has steadily increased since 1975, usually in response to crises (Eatwell and Taylor 2000, chapter 6). A crucial development came in 1988, with the adoption of capital adequacy criteria. International financial regulation was not just about cooperation, but about the coordination of standards—standards agreed upon in committees sanctioned by international "soft law" and meeting in Switzerland.

A further important development came in response to the Mexican bond crisis of 1994. The G7 governments, responding, agreed at their Halifax summit in 1995 that the regulation of international financial markets should not be left to the G10, but should be on the agenda of intergovernmental discussions. Not much was achieved in concrete terms. Then the Russian bond crisis of 1998, coming as it did at the end of a period of extreme instability emanating from Asia, brought home to G7 governments that their economies are not immune from the contagion of third world financial turbulence. The response was the creation of the Financial Stability Forum (FSF), and establishment of the World Bank-IMF Financial Sector Assessment Program (FSAP) under the direction of the joint Bank-Fund Financial Sector Liaison Committee (FSLC).

The FSF has brought together, on the one hand, political and supervisory authorities, and, on the other hand, regulatory authorities and the macroeconomic policy makers. So, on the operational side, the supervisors are meeting with the politicians and treasury staff who can get things done. On the economic side it brings together regulation and macroeconomic policy, a vital, and up to now missing, component of effective international regulation. At the moment, while it has produced some excellent reports, the FSF is a think tank with nowhere to go. It is not at all clear what action will follow the reports, or, indeed, who will act. After a major fright in 1998, policy makers in national treasuries and central banks are now retreating from the sort of collaborative view of the world that the establishment of the FSF seemed to foreshadow.

The FSAP involves the Bank and IMF in detailed microeconomic appraisal of the financial markets and regulatory institutions of selected nations. This level of detailed appraisal of private sector structures is a significant change in the involvement of the IMF in a nation's economic affairs, and may mark a turning point in the surveillance activities of the Fund. At the same time, the Bank and Fund are under severe political pressure to simplify and streamline their operations. How these conflicting forces will influence the future development of the FSAP is unclear.

Nor is it as yet clear what will prove to be the respective roles of the Basel committees, the Financial Stability Forum, and the new Bank-Fund structures in the future management of international regulation. What *is* clear is that the issues identified in the WFA project have proved to be the fundamental issues that must be addressed if that future management is to be accountable, legitimate, and successful.

THE CHALLENGES FACING INTERNATIONAL FINANCIAL REGULATION

The challenges facing international financial regulation today may be best identified through the device of a hypothetical World Financial Authority: What tasks should be performed by such an Authority? What should be the legal foundation of WFA action? How are the tasks to be performed? Given the argument, as noted above, that for market efficiency the tasks of the WFA must be performed by someone, answering these questions in the context of the WFA provides a template for policy development.

What tasks should be performed by a WFA?

A national financial regulator performs five main tasks: authorization of market participants; the provision of information to enhance market transparency; surveillance to ensure that the regulatory code is obeyed; enforcement of the code and disciplining of transgressors; and the development of policy that keeps the regulatory code up to date (or at least not more than 10 yards behind the market in a 100-yard race). These are the tasks that now need to be performed at the international level, ideally *as if* performed by a unitary WFA.

For example, it is clear that criteria for authorization should be at the same high level throughout the international market: ensuring that a business is financially viable, that it has suitable regulatory compliance procedures in place, and that the staff of the firm are fit and proper persons to conduct a financial services business. If, in a liberal international financial environment, high standards are not uniformly maintained, then firms authorized in a less demanding jurisdiction can impose unwarranted risks on others, undermining their high standards of authorization.

Similarly, as far as the information function is concerned, the failure to attain not only transparency but also common standards of information undermines the efficient operation of international financial markets, and creates risk. The persistent inability of national regulatory bodies to agree upon international accounting standards is a prime example of just such a failure.

Surveillance and enforcement are the operational heart of any effective regulatory system. Without effective, thorough policing of regulatory codes and uniform enforcement of standards by appropriate disciplinary measures (including exclusion from the marketplace), the international financial system is persistently exposed.

Finally, the policy function is the essential driving force of effective regulation. Regulatory codes must be adapted to a continuously changing marketplace. An important component of that change is international. As national financial boundaries dissolve, and as new products are developed that transcend international boundaries by firms with a worldwide perspective, the policy function must ensure that the regulator is alert to the new structure of the marketplace, the new systemic risks created, and to the new possibilities of contagion.[4] This requires a unified policy function, capable of taking a view about the risks encountered in particular markets and by the international market place as a whole.

What should be the legal foundation of WFA action?

All these activities are necessary for the efficient operation of the new international financial order. All point to the need for a single authority determining common rules and exercising common procedures. But there are clear, in some cases overwhelming difficulties to attaining that goal, of which the problems over achieving common accounting standards are but a foretaste. All five core activities involve the exercise of authority, and hence trespass into sensitive political arenas. Nation states are naturally reluctant to cede powers to an international body, even if this might mean the acquisition of (collective) sovereignty over activities otherwise beyond their control. When this is done it is done typically by treaty, confirming collective rights and responsibilities, and, at least in principle, accountability. It is also done by the consensus and by the mutual recognition of self-interest that produces "soft law."

Article IV of the Articles of Association of the IMF empowers that organization to "oversee the international monetary system in order to ensure its effective operation." To this end the provision that "the Fund shall exercise firm surveillance over the exchange rate policies of members" has been interpreted as covering general macroeconomic surveillance, and, in the new Financial Sector Appraisal Program, *microeconomic* surveillance of the operations of the financial sectors of member states.[5] The new FSAP surveillance concentrates on the adherence of national regulation and practices to core principles developed by the Basel committees of the G10, the International Organization of Securities Commissions (IOSCO) and the International Association of Insurance Supervisors (IAIS).[6] The IMF is using a treaty-sanctioned surveillance function to examine adherence to

---

4. An important recent example was the use of "total return swaps" or credit derivatives written in Europe and the United States involving loans to Indonesia from South Korea that ultimately spread financial losses to Korean financial intermediaries and their creditors in Japan.

5. Many characteristics of domestic financial systems may be only indirectly connected to "the exchange rate" as such. Nonetheless, it is not unreasonable to link *domestic* regulation to *international* financial stability.

6. For example, the June 2000 IMF "experimental" *Report on the Observation of Standards and Codes* (ROSC) for Canada, prepared by a staff team from the International Monetary Fund in the context of a Financial Sector Assessment Program (FSAP), on the basis of information provided by the Canadian authorities, produced "an assessment of Canada's observance of and consistency with relevant international standards and core principles in the financial sector, as part of a broader assessment of the stability of the financial system. This assessment work by the IMF was undertaken under the auspices of the IMF-World Bank Financial Sector Assessment Program (FSAP) based on information up to October 1999. This has helped to place the standards assessments in a broader institutional and macro-prudential context, and identify the extent to which the supervisory and regulatory framework has been adequate to address the potential risks in the financial system. The assessment has also provided a source of good practices in financial regulation and

codes and principles that are not themselves developed by accountable treaty-based bodies. It is an activity of considerable sensitivity. Not only will comprehensive surveillance require large resources, but also the IMF could easily be drawn into the position of "grading" national financial systems, with any downward revision of grades having the potential to produce dramatic financial consequences (IMF 2000b). Nonetheless, the IMF, as an accountable body the powers of which are defined by treaty, can legitimately perform a surveillance function. Moreover, in due course the IMF may well require countries seeking its assistance to conform to international regulatory codes and standards. In other words, it will be able to enforce conformity to those standards, with severe financial penalties (withdrawal of offers of assistance) for those who do not comply. It is to be doubted, however, whether it could, other than by persuasion, effectively enforce regulatory codes when they are infringed by more powerful countries that do not require the Fund's assistance (Eatwell and Taylor 2000, chapter 7).

The rules and codes that the IMF is seeking (experimentally) to embody in its surveillance program are predominantly formulated within non-treaty, "soft-law" environments. As Alexander (2000a) explains:

> International soft law refers to legal norms, principles, codes of conduct and transactional rules of state practice that are recognized in either formal or informal multilateral agreements. Soft law generally presumes consent to basic standards and norms of state practice, but without the *opinio juris* necessary to form binding obligations under customary international law. . . . Soft law may be defined as an international rule created by a group of specially affected states which had a common intent to voluntarily observe the content of such rule with a view of potentially adopting it into the national law or administrative code.

Soft law evades some of the political difficulty of the assignment of sovereignty implicit in international regulation because it does not impose an obligation, even though there is an expectation that states will take agreed codes seriously. In financial matters the most powerful means of enforcing soft law has been the

---

supervision in various areas. . . . The assessment covered (i) the Basel Core Principles for Effective Banking Supervision; (ii) the International Organization of Securities Commissions' (IOSCO) Objectives and Principles of Securities Regulation; (iii) the International Association of Insurance Supervisors' (IAIS) Supervisory Principles; (iv) the Committee on Payment and Settlement Systems (CPSS) Core Principles for Systemically Important Payment Systems; and (v) the IMF's Code of Good Practices on Transparency in Monetary and Financial Policies. Such a comprehensive coverage of standards was needed as part of the financial system stability assessment for Canada in view of the increasing convergence in the activities of banking, insurance, and securities firms, and the integrated nature of the markets in which they operate. It should be noted that some of the standards are still in draft form, and some do not yet have a complete methodology to systematically assess compliance or consistency. This module was prepared in consultation with the Canadian authorities in the context of the IMF FSAP mission that visited Canada in October 1999, and constitutes a summary of the detailed assessments prepared by the mission. The summary was part of the Financial System Stability Assessment (FSSA) report that was considered by the IMF Executive Board on February 2, 2000, in the context of the IMF's Article IV consultation discussions with Canada" (IMF 2000a).

competitive market. A major example of this process was the rapidity with which OECD and other economies subscribed to the 1987 bilateral agreement between the United Kingdom and the United States to adopt capital adequacy standards for banks. A failure to subscribe would have undermined market confidence—too high a price to pay.

The adoption by the IMF of soft law as a criterion of surveillance suggests a process of transition from soft law to mandatory regulation, at least for those countries that are beholden to the IMF. Observation of Basel and other codes may become an IMF imposed obligation. If this happens, new questions will be raised about the accountability of the Basel rule makers and their counterparts at IOSCO and the IAIS.

Even with this potential "legalization" of international policy making and of surveillance (which includes some standardization of the information function in the drive for "transparency"), authorization and, for the richer countries, enforcement remain national activities—though even here agreements on home-host division of responsibilities inject an international dimension.

There is, in effect, a creeping internationalization of the regulatory function in international financial markets. That internationalization is federal in character, with national jurisdictions being the predominant legal actors guided by international soft law, and by the pressures of the marketplace. So some of the functions of a WFA are being performed. But they are being performed haphazardly. Authorization is still essentially national, the information function is highly imperfect, surveillance (by the IMF) is as yet "experimental," enforcement is national, and the policy function is predominantly driven by an exclusively G10 consensus. As measured against the template of a proper WFA there is a long way to go.

However, the difficulty of creating an effective framework of international regulation does not derive solely from international legal practice and from politics. An important disjuncture derives from history—from differences in national legal systems, in financial custom and practice, and in structures of corporate governance. Even within the European Union, for example, there are major differences in national legal systems and in corporate governance that make the introduction of a common regulatory code not only difficult, but potentially damaging. Regulatory codes that enhance efficiency in one jurisdiction may have exactly the opposite effect in another.

How are these tasks to be performed?

While the template of a WFA clarifies the tasks that must be performed if international financial markets are to be regulated efficiently, it does not provide much guidance as to how the tasks are actually to be performed in the (highly likely) absence of a unitary authority. In practical terms many tasks can and must be delegated to national authorities. But it is important that national authorities should operate within common guidelines. That is the importance of the WFA—not to tell national authorities what to do, but to ensure that in a single world financial market they behave in a coherent and complementary manner to manage the systemic risk to which, in a seamless market, they are all exposed. Effective international regulation will necessarily be federal, with different responsibilities at appropriate levels of the system. But there must be a coherent federation with common principles and common values, resulting in (converging) national codes enforced by national authorities to attain common goals.

The developments of the past 30 years, and more especially, the innovations of the last three years point to the recognition by member states and by market participants of the need for coherent international regulation. But the present conjuncture, in which the predominant rule making bodies are the Basel committees, IOSCO and the IAIS, while the predominant international surveillance body (in so far as there is any international surveillance at all) is the IMF, is an awkward hybrid. Moreover, it embodies the unfortunate impression that rules are made by the rich nations and enforced on the rest.

What is needed is recognition of the power of the WFA template, and the design of international institutions that can meet the demands identified by the template in an accountable, coherent, and flexible manner. A number of challenges must be met if this goal is to be attained: (1) the development and acceptance of a common theoretical framework within which to confront the tasks of international regulation; (2) the integration of macroeconomic and microeconomic aspects of international regulation; (3) the development of procedures that (at least) alleviate the tendency for risk management to be pro-cyclical and pro-contagion; (4) the harmonization of risk management in differing corporate governance structures to obtain a common international regulatory outcome; (5) solving the political challenge of accountability in a soft law regime; and (6) devising an institutional structure that performs the tasks of the template WFA.

A COMMON THEORETICAL FRAMEWORK

Over the past three decades the most difficult task of the financial regulator has been to keep up with the changing marketplace that he or she is supposed to be regulating. The speed of change has, if anything, accelerated, with the continuous development of new trading strategies and new "products," linking assets, markets, and currencies in new ways, and creating new risks. In this febrile environment the regulator needs the guidance of a coherent theoretical understanding of the propagation and management of systemic risk, as well as the pragmatic understanding and concrete tools to manage the risk.

The problem is that there is no commonly accepted theoretical understanding of what financial regulators are supposed to do. Of course, systemic risk is an "externality," but externalities are peculiarly difficult to define in other than the most abstract terms: Where exactly do costs and benefits fall? What is their scale relative to the economy as a whole? What is the relationship between particular policies to manage the externality and the performance of the economy as a whole? In the world of finance these difficulties are compounded by the fact that the externality of systemic risk is in large part manifest through a "beauty contest"—through the market participants' belief about what average opinion believes average opinion about market outcomes believes (Keynes 1936, chapter 12; Eatwell and Taylor 2000, chapters 1 and 3). Assessing the impact of regulation on average opinion is bound to be an art rather than a science, and an imperfect guide to policy. A further problem in building a coherent theory of regulation is the potential scale of the losses associated with extreme and (hopefully) rare events. Average opinion is typically very stable for long periods, dominated by convention. In these circumstances it may be comparatively easy to identify the behavioral relationships that characterize such periods of tranquillity, and to believe that they are stable and enduring. Yet these seemingly "true models" of the marketplace can be completely overwhelmed by a sharp shift in average opinion, driving markets in previously unimaginable directions, and producing potentially catastrophic disruption in the operation of the real economy.[7]

This fundamental lack of knowledge poses enormous problems for the policy maker. Are regulations to be constructed on the basis of the models of tranquillity, or are they to take account of potentially catastrophic rare events when the logic of those models is overthrown? How often do "rare" events occur, and what is the relationship between their frequency and the regulation of systemic risk in more tranquil circumstances? Are financial crises simply transitory events, oscillations around the long-run equilibrium of the real economy? Or do crises, and their reverberating impacts on average opinion and on expectations of asset price movements, play a role in determining the long-run performance of the economy?

These questions have both theoretical and empirical dimensions. Lacking generally agreed answers, international financial regulation has proceeded by trial and error, regulatory innovations following financial shocks. The device of a hypothetical World Financial Authority is designed, in part, to overcome this piecemeal approach. Starting from the perspective of a single regulator of international markets given the objective of maintaining financial stability by limiting systemic risk, the single regulator should assess the costs and benefits of particular measures against that goal. It will obviously encounter the problem of evaluating the distribution of costs and benefits. For example, measures to limit short-term capital flows to emerging markets may enhance the stability of financial markets at little cost to recipient economies, but at significant loss of income to banks in the G10. In these circumstances the WFA function must have the means to develop a coherent analysis of the overall impact on systemic risk, persuade the participants of the values of the analysis and policies, and mediate disputes.

---

7. John Meriwether, former CEO of Long Term Capital Management, commenting two years after the activities of his hedge fund had led the financial system of the West to the edge of catastrophe, said "I am not so sure we would have said this earlier - there are times when markets can be much more chaotic than one would ever predict" (quoted in the *Financial Times*, 21 August 2000).

MACROECONOMIC AND MICROECONOMIC
ASPECTS OF INTERNATIONAL REGULATION

The fact that the externality associated with the risks taken by individual firms is, in many cases, transmitted macroeconomically, requires that regulation be conceived in conjunction with macroeconomic policy. Too often today, regulation is seen as an activity that involves the behavior and interaction of firms, with little or no macroeconomic dimension. By the very nature of financial risk this is a serious error, and is likely to lead to serious policy mistakes. This is particularly true in an international setting, where a major focus of systemic risk is the exchange rate, a macroeconomic variable the changes of which can lead to rapid redistributions of the values of assets and liabilities.

An excellent example of the role of macro-linkages in the formation of regulatory policy has followed the Asian financial crisis of 1997–98. It is clear that an important component of the crisis was the excessive foreign-exchange exposure of financial and other institutions in emerging markets. In consequence, the international financial institutions have been urging the authorities in emerging markets to tighten regulation of short-term foreign-exchange exposure. The tightening is supposed to take place microeconomically by means of regulations that impact on the actions of individual firms. This is a complex task and requires a significant input of a scarce resource-trained regulators. Moreover, the quantitative measures proposed are likely to have an uneven effect, limiting the exposure of financial institutions, but missing many holdings outside the financial sector and contingent contracts or derivative instruments held "off-balance sheet" within it.

The same goal could be attained macroeconomically. Although in principle they can be evaded through the use of derivatives, in practice measures that raise the cost of short-term borrowing abroad, such as "Chilean-style" short-term capital controls, would tend to reduce the exposure of all firms, financial and otherwise (Agosin 1998). This macro approach would also economize on scarce talent. Yet although capital controls do not suffer the same level of opprobrium as they did before the Asian crisis, the relationship between the micro and macro means of attaining the same objective is not often pursued. The neglect of macromeasures is particularly puzzling given that micro-regulation tends to be quantitative and to some degree discriminatory, while Chilean-style macro controls are price based and nondiscriminatory—characteristics which might be expected to appeal to economic policy makers.

The difficulty of analyzing the macroeconomic transmission of the systemic risk generated by the actions of individual firms is illustrated by a proposal emanating from within the IMF to construct "macroprudential indicators" (MPIs) to assess the "health and stability of the financial system." As currently constructed MPIs "comprise both aggregated microprudential indicators of the health of individual financial institutions and macroeconomic variables associated with financial system soundness" (Hilbers, Krueger, and Moretti 2000; see also Evans, Leone, Gill, and Hilbers 2000).

The attempt to link micro risk to the performance of the macro economy is laudable, and is exactly where the debate on effective international regulation should be conducted. However, there are two flaws in MPIs as currently conceived. *First,* the *aggregation* of the characteristics of individual firms will not result in an indicator that accurately represents the risk to which the economy is exposed. The aggregate capital adequacy ratio of the financial sector could easily conceal major risks—a few prudent institutions with high ratios disguising the presence of the less prudent. Including data on the frequency distribution of such variables does not fully confront this problem. The characteristics of the distribution do not capture the nature of the risks taken by individual institutions.[8] *Second,* as yet there has been no attempt to link macroeconomic performance and policy to the incentives surrounding microeconomic risk-taking. Not only is the value of capital, and hence the capital adequacy ratio, directly affected by the revaluation of assets consequent upon a change in the interest rate, but also declines in the level of activity can readily transform prudent investments into bad loans. Taking these two points together, it becomes clear that in the analysis of systemic risk micro and macro factors *cannot* be treated separately. The whole is not just greater, but behaves very differently from the sum of the parts.

Effective international regulation requires a new approach to both the theory and the policy of regulation. This new approach must confront the macro-manifestation of systemic risk within the analysis of the impact of firm behavior. Building on this theoretical approach, it must be recognized that the regulator may be able to operate more efficiently in macroeconomic terms than by means of more traditional initiatives at the level of the firm.

PROCYCLICAL AND PRO-CONTAGION RISK MANAGEMENT

A further manifestation of the relationship between microeconomic risk and macroeconomic performance derives from the apparently paradoxical links between risk management, the business cycle, and financial contagion. Strict regulatory requirements will result in firms reducing lending as a result of a downturn in the economy, so exacerbating the downturn. In an upturn, the perceived diminution of risk and the availability of regulatory capital will tend to increase the ability to lend, stoking up the boom (see Jackson 1999).

This procyclicality of regulation is further amplified by the contagion-inducing techniques of risk management. During the Asian crisis, financial institutions reduced their exposure to emerging markets throughout the world. These

---

8. A further difficulty with the use of capital adequacy ratios as MPIs arises from the ambiguity surrounding the regulatory role of the ratio: is it a buffer, or is it a charge, "pricing in" the externality of systemic risk? If ratios must be maintained in all circumstances, capital cannot be a buffer to cover losses; it is needed to fulfil regulatory needs. So the size of the capital ratio merely indicates the size of the charge levied on risk-taking. If the ratio is fixed the charge will not vary significantly as between booms and depressions, yet the risk may undergo large variations.

cutbacks helped spread the crisis, as reduced lending and reduced confidence fed the financial downturn. The key to the problem is, once again, the link between microeconomic actions and macroeconomic consequences. Rational risk-management by individual firms precipitates a macro level reaction that, in a downturn, can place those firms in jeopardy, indeed could overwhelm the firms' defenses entirely. Yet because the links between regulation and macroeconomic policy are so little understood, there is no coherent policy response to this perverse consequence. In extreme circumstances regulators in developed countries have "looked the other way." At the onset of the Latin American debt crisis in the early 1980s many major U.S. banks were technically bankrupt, since Latin American assets held on their books had lost their entire market value. Nonetheless, U.S. regulators allowed those worthless assets to be evaluated in the banks' balance sheets at their value at maturity, hence boosting the banks' notional capital and preventing a sudden collapse in lending and liquidity.[9] In the autumn of 1998, many assets held on the balance sheets of financial institutions in London and New York were, if marked to market, worth nothing. Again, the regulators did not insist on an immediate (potentially catastrophic) write down.

Philip Turner (2000) has argued for a "microeconomic solution" to the procyclicality of regulation:

> The ideal response to procyclicality is for provisions to be made for possible loan losses (i.e., subtracted from equity capital in the books of the bank) to cover normal cyclical risks. If done correctly, provisions built up in good times can be used in bad times without necessarily affecting reported capital.

But he notes that even this sensible provision for "normal cyclical risks" can run foul of current regulatory procedures:

> The first stumbling block is that tax laws often severely limit the tax deductibility of precautionary provisioning and may insist on evidence that losses have actually occurred. This is important because loan loss provisions increase internal funding for the bank only to the extent that they reduce taxes.
>
> A second possible stumbling block may be the securities laws. For example the SEC in the United States has argued that precautionary provisioning distorts financial reports and may mislead investors. There may then be a trade-off between very transparent, well-documented accounting practices, on the one hand, and the need for banks to build up reserves during good times, on the other.
>
> A third possible stumbling block is that the management of banks may be too eager to report strong improvements in earnings during booms (and so too reluctant during good times to make adequate provision for losses). The present wave of takeovers in the banking industry may accentuate this eagerness: good reported earnings and high share prices serve to fend off takeovers.

---

9. This does not mean that regulatory standards were abandoned entirely: ". . . money center banks whose loans to heavily indebted countries exceeded their capital in the early 1980s were allowed several years to adjust—but there was no doubt that they would have to adjust" (Turner 2000).

But even if these stumbling blocks were overcome, Turner's proposal of extra provisioning would only serve to alleviate the problems created by the procyclicality of regulation in "normal" circumstances. It does not address the issue of the tendency of regulatory standards to deepen and widen major downturns, and to fuel booms. This tendency will become increasingly severe for developing countries as they are further integrated into international capital markets, and adopt the required risk management regulatory procedures. For all countries, there is the further difficulty that even if some sort of macroeconomic response were available to offset the procyclicality of regulation, macroeconomic policy is essentially national, whilst the problem may well be international in origin and scope. The very least that a WFA could do is assist in the coordination of macroeconomic responses. At a more general level the presence of a WFA would facilitate the international development of policies that link regulatory risk-management procedures and the needs of macroeconomic balance.

HARMONIZATION OF RISK MANAGEMENT IN DIFFERING CORPORATE GOVERNANCE STRUCTURES

A central theme of Eatwell and Taylor (2000) is that efficient regulation requires that the domain of the regulator should be the same as the domain of the market that is regulated. However, while financial markets are "seamless," they are not homogeneous. National markets are differentiated by their legal systems and institutions, by structures of corporate governance, and by business custom and practice. In consequence uniform financial regulations often do not have the same consequences, having quite different practical effects, and resulting in different systemic risks. The result is that uniform codes will expose the financial system to different systemic risks in the light of their differential impact in different jurisdictions (Alexander and Dhumale 2000).

This is the central weakness of the fixed regulatory requirements and ratios emanating from the Basel committees, and, the strength of the Basel system of codes. What is ideally required is that there should be an assessment of the relationship between the financial structure of national jurisdictions and the systemic risk emanating from each jurisdiction. That ideal is probably unattainable, since it would require detailed consideration and negotiation of each national case—an overwhelming task. A more pragmatic approach would involve:

> (a) the construction of specific rules in those cases which refer to basic institutional tenets that are universal, and are necessary for the success of any regulatory environment;
> (b) in those circumstances where national legal and governance structures predominate the development of national codes derived from common internationally agreed general principles.

In case (b) regulation is developed at two levels: *first*, a set of general principles, *second*, from these principles should be derived codes that are both flexible as circumstances change and reflect the peculiar legal and governance structures of individual countries. This is, of course, the defining characteristic of the current soft law regime. But at present many of the principles are "ideal types," to be desired rather than enforced. If principles are to be the foundation of an effective regulatory system they must be expressed through clearly articulated codes, which are regularly tested against the principles they are supposed to embody, and against the systemic risks they are supposed to manage. There will undoubtedly be differences of opinion as to whether a particular set of national codes accurately reflects shared principles, and it will be necessary to put in place powerful procedures for adjudicating disputes (another role for a WFA).

The cause of uniform adherence to principles will be reinforced by market competition, in rather the same manner as competition has led to the widespread adoption of Basel capital adequacy standards. Moreover, increasingly open markets are likely to produce competitive convergence in standards and procedures of corporate governance that will in turn permit a movement toward uniform regulatory codes, i.e., an increasing role for the universal rules referred to in (a) above.

THE POLITICAL CHALLENGE OF
ACCOUNTABILITY IN A SOFT LAW REGIME

In a liberal international financial system each nation faces risks that may emanate from behavior entirely outside its jurisdiction. Even very strong states face risks that may derive from financial crises in poor countries. The desire to manage risks may lead to two polar reactions: *first* the attempt by the rich and strong to manage the poor and weak, to protect the rich from external threat; *second*, cooperation between all countries to manage risk internationally. All procedures for international regulation will fall somewhere on a scale between these two extremes. Other than in the polar first case, international regulation will involve some pooling of sovereignty, even if only at the level of initiating proposals.

Treaties designed to establish international authority and procedures, such as the treaty agreeing the Articles of Association of the IMF, are a pooling of sovereignty in the pursuit of negotiated ends. They also typically contain procedures to ensure some accountability by the international institutions to the national signatories. As Alexander (2000a) has pointed out, the pursuit of international goals by means of treaties has high transactions costs, and may be restrained by uncertainty:

> One set of problems falls under the heading of *transaction costs*. Complexity of the issues, difficulties in negotiating and drafting, the number of participants and similar factors make it difficult for governments to agree on precise, binding and highly institutionalized commitments. . . .
> Another set of contracting problems concerns the pervasive uncertainty in which states and other international actors must operate. Many international agreements can affect national wealth, power and autonomy. Yet governments can never foresee all the contingencies that may arise under any agreement.

They are never certain that they will be able to detect cheating or other threats. They cannot even be sure how they will react to particular contingencies, let alone how others will. These problems are exacerbated by the relative weakness of the international legal system that cannot fill gaps and respond to new situations as easily as domestic legal systems can.

One way to deal with uncertainty is through soft delegation: not to courts, but to political institutions, subject to continuing oversight and control, that can produce information, monitor behavior, assist in further negotiations, mediate disputes and produce interstitial or technical rules. Another is through imprecise norms that provide general guidelines for expected behavior while allowing states to work out more detailed rules over time. A third way involves crafting relatively precise, but nonbinding, rules that allow actors to experiment by applying the rules under different conditions while limiting unpleasant surprises. All these approaches have costs, including their limited ability to regularize behavior. Yet on balance they are frequently seen as beneficial, permitting states to achieve some immediate gains from cooperation while structuring ongoing learning: this is a political process that can take states further along the path of the institutionalization of obligations.

Because treaties must overcome these difficulties they are typically a compromise, and inevitably inflexible. Moreover, because they necessarily embody some degree of accountability to their signatories, they tend to be slow moving. These are rather unattractive characteristics in the field of international financial regulation. It is therefore not surprising that developments have taken a different route, with the major role being played by the non-treaty committees housed at the BIS, together with IOSCO and the IAIS:

> The process of devising international norms and rules to regulate international banking activity involves a form of international soft law that has precise, nonbinding norms that are generated through consultations and negotiations amongst the major state regulators. This particular form of international soft law provides the necessary political flexibility for states to adopt international rules and standards into their national legal systems in a manner that accommodates the sovereign authority of the nation state. States could then move forward through the process of legalization by building on the collective intent of the major economic powers to develop binding international rules for banking supervision. States could potentially delegate the adjudication of violations to an international financial authority, but states would retain ultimate enforcement authority, including sanction (Alexander 2000a).

The problem here is, of course, the predominant role of the major states. An effective soft-law regime works by consensus, and a grudging consensus imposed by the major states upon others is likely to be less effective than a consensus in which all participate. While the existence of a legal structure does offer some protection to weaker countries, whose sovereignty is compromised by the very fact of being economically (and perhaps politically) dominated by the developed countries,[10] the fact that that structure is determined by the G10 raises the obvious question of whose interests are being protected.

The "obvious" solution of increasing the representation on the Basel committees runs the risk of overloading the decision-making mechanisms, and losing their flexibility. The partial solution adopted at the FSF of involving a wider range of countries on policy making committees is attractive, but it may not prove to be widely acceptable if the proposals contained in the reports produced by the FSF harden into concrete policy measures.

Ultimately the choice between a soft law and a formal treaty regime may come to the conclusion: "both." The treaty will lay down a method for developing general principles that should guide the regulators, and a mechanism for developing codes derived from those principles. The task of developing the codes can then be entrusted to a less formal body, akin to the current Basel committees.

DEVISING AN INSTITUTIONAL STRUCTURE THAT PERFORMS THE TASKS OF THE TEMPLATE WFA

Today an institutional structure of international financial supervision is emerging which mirrors, albeit imperfectly, the idealized structure of a WFA. The authorization function is the responsibility of national regulators, with access to markets being determined by the presence or absence of agreements specifying the terms of mutual recognition. The information function is performed partly by the international financial institutions, particularly the BIS, partly by the International Accounting Standards Committee, and partly by national regulators, stock market rules, and so on. The surveillance function is performed by the World Bank-IMF financial sector program and by national regulators.[11] The enforcement function is being developed as an implicit outcome of the World Bank-IMF financial sector program, and is otherwise the responsibility of national authorities. The policy function is in the hands of the BIS committees, IOSCO and the IAIS, the Financial Stability Forum, the IMF, and national authorities.

This list has four major features:

1. If the same list were compiled around the year 1990 most of the regulatory functions, with the exception of the policy function, would lack any international dimension. Today in all areas other than authorization, international bodies are taking up some of the regulatory tasks.

2. There is an eclectic mix of national institutions, international agreements (soft and hard) and international institutions (with varying degrees of legitimacy).

---

10. "Small states . . . may have negative sovereignty costs, since legal arrangements offer them protection from powerful neighbors. Large states, by contrast, would appear to be in less need of legalization, though in fact they might seek it as an efficient way to structure governance where they can dictate the rules and exert political control over their implementation. Soft legalization can bridge the gap between weak and strong states. This is especially true of the type of legalization . . . where norms and rules are binding and relatively precise but authority for compliance is delegated to national political institutions. In this situation weak states are protected by legal rules that fix expectations of behavior, while strong states maintain influence in political bodies where they can shape future developments" (Alexander 2000a).

11. In addition the international surveillance of financial crime, particularly money laundering, is conducted by the Financial Action Task Force (see Alexander 2000b).

Some powers are developing almost accidentally, such as the emergence of an enforcement power at the IMF via the FSAP program. Others are developing by design, such as the work of the International Accounting Standards Committee. All are developing under the pressures for effective policy exerted by the process of financial market liberalization, particularly at times of crisis.

3. The list deals only with major international regulatory developments and omits the growth of *regional* regulation, notably in the European Union. The case of the European Union is particularly interesting since it involves the attempt to develop a fully liberalized, single financial market, characterized by a wide range of different legal practices and structures of corporate governance amongst member states.

4. Measured against the template of a WFA the list displays an international regulatory structure that is limited, even incoherent. It portrays a patchwork response to crises rather than a rational response to the international development of systemic risk.

This patchy, often incoherent structure embodies significant threats to financial stability. On the one hand the growth of international institutions, such as the FSF, induces the feeling that "something has been done" to tackle systemic risk. On the other hand, the very limited powers of any of the international structures listed above suggest that such complacency is a delusion. The current threadbare patchwork cannot perform the tasks of a WFA.

ISSUES REGARDING DEVELOPING AND TRANSITION ECONOMIES

The holes in the patchwork are particularly obvious with regard to international financial regulation in transition and developing economies, which after all bore the brunt of the financial turmoil of the 1990s. Drawing on the previous discussion and other sources,[12] a number of pressing problems arise that could be addressed within the framework of a WFA:

With regard to regulatory structures, a distinction was drawn above between those that are universally based and those that rest predominantly on local legal and governance structures. The latter are likely to be especially important in economies without deeply embedded and historically proven market relationships. They have a greater need for transitional arrangements, and indeed may find it desirable *not* to move completely toward capital market liberalization.[13] At the same time, their regulatory capability is often weak and badly in need of international support. Nonindustrialized economies lack qualified personnel, and,

---

12. In particular, Dodd 2000; Nayyar 2000; Neftci 2000; Ocampo 2000a, 2000b; and the United Nations 1999.

13. As discussed in Eatwell and Taylor (2000) and elsewhere, the case for full liberalization of international capital markets is far from compelling in a world rife with unquantifiable uncertainty and destabilizing "beauty contest" market behavior.

given their small size relative to the volume of international financial transactions, the risks they confront are proportionately far greater than those of the United States, Europe, or Japan.

Indeed, as Ocampo (2000b) emphasizes, developing and transition economies are in the unpleasant position of being "business cycle/policy takers" instead of "business cycle/policy makers" (the United States is the number one example of the latter). This situation reflects basic asymmetries in financial markets: "Four must be singled out: (a) between the size of developing countries' domestic financial markets and the size of the speculative pressures they may face; (b) the nature of the currencies in which external debt is denominated, which generates significant currency mismatches between assets and liabilities; (c) significant difference in the maturities supplied by domestic and international financial institutions, which implies that there would be significant maturity mismatches for debtors unable to access international markets (e.g., small and medium-size firms) and currency mismatches for those that can; and (d) the thinness of domestic financial (particularly security) markets, which reduces the liquidity of financial instruments. Viewed as a whole, this implies that domestic financial markets in the developing world are significantly more 'incomplete' than international financial markets, indicating that some financial intermediation must necessarily be done through international markets. It also implies that integration into international financial markets is integration between unequal partners."

There are several specific forms of market intervention that recent events suggest are needed to offset these problems in poorer economies. "Market-based" capital controls of the sort employed in Chile and elsewhere have already been mentioned. But direct restrictions on certain forms of international transactions may also have a role to play. Certainly the quantitative controls on both current and capital account transactions that have historically been utilized by India and China helped those countries avoid the worst effects of the Asian crisis.

In particular, controls can help offset procyclical biases in both capital movements and their effective regulation. Much of the instability in capital flows in and out of developing and transition economies can be traced to wide spreads between foreign costs and national returns to assets. Under a fixed exchange rate regime, it is easy to see a 10% differential between local and foreign short-term interest rates or a similarly sized gap between the growth rate of the local stock market index or real estate prices and a foreign borrowing rate. Such yields are an open invitation to capital inflows that can be extremely destabilizing

Another source of potential spreads is through off-balance sheet and derivative operations, which can worsen market instabilities arising from the maturity and currency mismatches mentioned above. Local regulators can be at a major disadvantage in dealing with derivatives. It is difficult to keep up with the latest devices and most (but one hopes not all) of any nation's skilled financial operators will be on the other side, inventing still newer devices to make more money. Staying up-to-date as far as possible and inculcating a culture of probity in the local financial system are the best defenses here.

There is a serious question as to whether many developing country macro-policies and regulatory systems can meet such goals, especially when their capital markets are largely decontrolled. Another difficulty arises with timing. It is very difficult to put a stop to capital flows *after* convention has decreed that fundamentals have become adverse. At such a point interest rate increases or a discrete devaluation can easily provoke a crash. The authorities have to stifle a potentially explosive cycle early in its upswing; otherwise, they may be powerless to act. The problem with all indicators of a threatening crisis is that they often lag behind an unstable dynamic process. By the time they are visibly out of line it may be too late to attempt to prevent the crisis. Its management becomes the urgent task of the day.

Given all these difficulties, what sorts of support can an agency such as the WFA effectively provide to developing countries? One contribution would be up-to-date information on the country's international position, with appropriate interpretations and warnings. The Asian and Russian crises exploded in part because of inadequate international early warning systems on short-term debt (especially debt owed to international banks).

Second, technical assistance can be crucial. The WFA could organize technical assistance programs for the regulatory authorities. It would have been possible to build up Russia's financial regulatory capability, for example, had Russia been willing to take the politically difficult step of accepting and implementing such aid. Similar observations apply to East Asia as well.

Third, by setting best practice standards, a WFA could provide an incentive for countries to upgrade their own capabilities and standards. After all, *not* satisfying best practice would mean that a country would have to pay significantly higher costs for access to funds, and might have limited access to IMF funding.

Finally, safeguards can be maintained against potential destabilization from short-term capital flows. A return to the large-scale short-term bank lending which presaged the Asian crisis is especially undesirable. In domestic markets the risks of short-term finance are contained by the presence of a lender of last resort, tough regulation, and effective bankruptcy procedures. In the international context, short-term flows should be managed by the WFA with a combination of macroeconomic measures (agreed controls on short-term inflows) and microeconomic regulation. The WFA can form a global view in microeconomic regulation by regulating not only the borrower, but also the lender. The WFA can take into account the systemic risks being incurred by the mis-pricing of risk by the lending bank, and take steps to ensure that the full cost is internalized by imposing stringent capital adequacy requirements and other regulatory measures.

Of course, developing countries themselves can take steps in these directions. Just as in Europe, the creation of effective regional organizations that allow nations to pool their regulatory capabilities may be worthwhile. However, the European example suggests that a substantial span of time may be needed to build up the competence of regional authorities.

COPING WITH CRISES WHEN THEY STRIKE

A central goal of financial regulation is to reduce the likelihood of crisis. But when a crisis, and especially a currency crisis, strikes, a regulator, even a WFA, cannot cope on its own. International financial assistance, essentially an international lender of last resort, is required.

The first and most obvious recommendation that emerges from recent experience is to disburse rescue money quickly. Finance that is supplied only on the basis of negotiated conditions and which is released only on the basis of compliance with them is *not* liquidity. East Asian economies became highly illiquid in 1997. By 1999, their position stopped deteriorating. But their economic prospects at the end of 2000 remain precarious.

The need to inject liquidity naturally brings to the fore the question of an international lender of last resort, the task of which is to enhance confidence and stability of the international financial system and deal with abnormal risk. The natural candidate is the IMF. The IMF can only fulfill this role efficiently if there exists a complementary regulatory agency such as a WFA *operating over the same domain*. To meet the demands of the lender of last resort role the IMF's resources should be enlarged (though it must be remembered that the very existence of ample resources for the lender of last resort makes it less likely that those resources will actually be used). One obvious channel would be the reactivization of the Special Drawing Rights (SDR) mechanism set up in the mid-1960s. SDRs could be created when Fund member countries face financial difficulties. These advances would be destroyed as borrowings were repaid. Such an anti-cyclical use of SDRs to manage financial cycles should be part of a broader process aimed at enhancing their use as an appropriate international currency for a globalized world.

But as is well known, a lender of last resort increases efficiency only if there is also an effective regulator to diminish moral hazard. The WFA should provide the necessary regulatory framework within which the IMF can develop as a lender of last resort. In many countries the WFA would simply certify that domestic regulatory procedures are effective. In those countries in which financial regulation is unsatisfactory, and which would therefore not have access to the IMF in a financial crisis, the WFA would assist with regulatory reform. Many financial crises today derive from unbalanced foreign exchange exposures of private financial and nonfinancial institutions. The IMF lends only to sovereign borrowers. Sovereign borrowers use the foreign exchange acquired from the IMF to pursue their domestic lender of last resort activities. In these circumstances not only will the WFA's surveillance and enforcement of regulatory standards be necessary to reduce moral hazard and aid financial reconstruction, it will also be necessary to give confidence to the backers of the IMF operation.

The presence of the WFA permits the development of new financial vehicles that are not subject to standard IMF conditionality. Conditionality may be legitimate for drawings that a country makes when it is experiencing balance-of-payments problems originating from inappropriate macro policies, i.e., self-created adverse fundamentals. But the usual forms of conditionality are worse than useless when a country faces an externally-induced current or capital account crisis. WFA approval of national regulatory structures could be deemed a form of pre-conditionality which would allow a country threatened by financial volatility rapid access to the lender of last resort.[14] This would both increase confidence in the stability of a nation's financial system, and act as an important "carrot" inducing the acceptance of WFA best practice regulation. However, when a country's domestic financial regulation and supervision are deemed inadequate, it would be obligated to enter into an agreement with the WFA specifying reforms it should undertake.

Recent experience suggests that lender of last resort interventions can be minimized or even avoided if the rescue team "bails-in" an afflicted country's creditors in the sense of forcing them not to call outstanding loans, instead of bailing them out. Coining another term, the United Nations has proposed debtor-creditor "standstills" at times of crisis. Such a package would include an initial freeze on an afflicted country's external obligations and capital account convertibility. It would then bring borrowers and lenders together to reschedule debt, while providing financial assistance to support normal functioning of the economy. These operations would give players in the distressed country a better chance of surmounting their problems. If the crisis involves, as it often does, simultaneous international illiquidity and domestic bank insolvency, creditors would also be more likely to recover the value of their assets. The costs of adjustment would also be more equitably distributed. Again, this would probably make the cost of capital to borrowers slightly higher, and so it should. The extra cost is a measure of the now internalized risk.

To ensure that a standstill mechanism operates properly, two rules are essential. First, there should be internationally agreed "collective action clauses" in international lending (as advocated by the G7 in late 1998). Their generalized introduction is crucial to avoid "free riding." Second, renegotiations should take place within a specified time limit, beyond which either the WFA or an independent panel would have the authority to determine the conditions of the debt rescheduling. Repeated debt renegotiations have been one of the most troublesome features of the international financial landscape in recent decades and an underlying cause of the prolonged periods of crisis or slow growth in some developing and transition economies.

After a crisis, countries often have a weighty overhang of "bad debt," typically non-performing assets of the banking sector. Domestic refinancing via a bond issue to the nonbank private sector, an administratively enforced credit rollover, and price inflation are three ways of dealing with the problem. The latter two would almost certainly require reimposition of tight controls on

---

14. In April 1999, the IMF introduced Contingent Credit Lines "for countries with strong economic policies as a precautionary line of defense readily available against future balance of payments problems that might arise from international financial contagion." The CCL is "a preventative measure intended solely for members that are concerned with potential vulnerability to contagion, but are not facing a crisis at the time of commitment." The CCL is heavily buttressed by "criteria for access," a significant step toward "pre-conditionality."

outward capital movements, for which the WFA would need to secure the cooperation of the international community.

SUMMING UP

Two themes dominate this appraisal of the challenges facing the development of an efficient system of international financial regulation: *First*, the need for theory and policy that link microeconomic risk-taking to the macroeconomic propagation of systemic risk. *Second*, the need to develop a coherent and accountable set of institutions through which international policy may be developed and implemented. These two needs were met by the authorities in the immediate postwar era. They reacted to the instability of inadequately regulated markets in the 1930s by producing new procedures and institutions based on what were then new models of macroeconomic management. Internationally, the response at Bretton Woods was to put in place a set of international arrangements that permitted the pursuit of national macroeconomic policies, free from the fear of international financial disruption. The problem of accountability did not arise. Tackling the same problems on an international scale requires a reinterpretation of what both macroeconomic policy and market regulation mean, and a reassessment of the institutions required to conduct such policies. The device of a World Financial Authority provides the means of exposing both analytical and institutional questions.

REFERENCES

Agosin, M. 1998. "Capital inflows and investment performance: Chile in the 1990s," in R. Ffrench-Davis and H. Reisen (eds) *Capital Flows and Investment Performance: Lessons from Latin America*. Paris: OECD.

Alexander, K. 2000a. "The role of soft law in the legalization of international banking supervision," *Oxford Journal of International Economic Law*.

_____. 2000b. "The legalization of the international anti-money laundering regime: the role of the Financial Action Task Force," *Financial Crime Review*.

Alexander, K. and R. Dhumale. 2000. "Enhancing corporate governance for banking institutions," a paper prepared for the Ford Foundation project on "A World Financial Authority."

Chang, H-J., Park, H-J and C.G. Yoo. 1998. "Interpreting the Korean crisis: financial liberalization, industrial policy and corporate governance," *Cambridge Journal of Economics*, November.

Dodd, Randall. 2000. "The Role of Derivatives in the East Asian Financial Crisis," Revised version of a paper presented at the Center for Economic Policy Analysis, New School University; prepared for the Ford Foundation project on "A World Financial Authority."

Eatwell, J. 1996. *International financial liberalization: the impact on world development*, ODS *Discussion Paper Series*, no. 12. New York: UNDP.

Eatwell, J. and L. Taylor. 1998. "International capital markets and the future of economic policy," a paper prepared for the Ford Foundation project *International Capital Markets and the Future of Economic Policy*. New York: Center for Economic Policy Analysis; London: IPPR.

_____. 2000. *Global Finance at Risk: the Case for International Regulation*. New York: Policy Press.

Evans, O., A. Leone, M. Gill and P. Hilbers. 2000. "Macroprudential indicators of financial system soundness," *IMF Occasional Paper 00/192*. Washington: IMF.

Hilbers, P., R. Krueger and M. Moretti. 2000. "New tools for assessing financial system soundness," *Finance and Development*, September.

Hutton, W. 1999. "America's Global Hand," *The American Prospect*, December.

IMF (International Monetary Fund). 2000a. *Report on the Observance of Standards and Codes: Canada*. Washington, DC: IMF

_____. 2000b. *Experimental Reports on Observance of Standards and Codes (ROSCs)*. Washington, DC: IMF.

Jackson, P. 1999. "Capital requirements and bank behavior: the impact of the Basle accord," *Basle Committee on Banking Supervision Working Paper no. 1*.

Keynes, J. M. 1936. *The General Theory of Employment, Interest and Money*. London: Macmillan.

Nayyar, Deepak. 2000. "Capital Controls and the World Financial Authority: What Can We Learn from the Indian Experience?" revised version of a paper presented at the Center for Economic Policy Analysis, New School University; prepared for the Ford Foundation project on "A World Financial Authority."

Neftci, Salih. 2000. "Synthetic Assets, Risk Management, and Imperfections," revised version of a paper presented at the Center for Economic Policy Analysis, New School University; prepared for the Ford Foundation project on "A World Financial Authority."

Ocampo, Jose Antonio. 2000a. "Recasting the International Financial Agenda," revised version of a paper presented at the Center for Economic Policy Analysis, New School University; prepared for the Ford Foundation project on "A World Financial Authority."

_____. 2000b. "Developing Countries' Anti-Cyclical Policies in a Globalized World," Santiago Chile, Economic Commission for Latin America and the Caribbean.

Temin, P. 1989. *Lessons from the Great Depression*. Cambridge, Mass.: MIT Press.

Turner, P. 2000. "Procyclicality of regulatory ratios?" a paper presented at Queens' College, Cambridge, January 2000; prepared for the Ford Foundation project on "A World Financial Authority."

United Nations (Task Force of the Executive Committee of Economic and Social Affairs). 1999. *Towards a New International Financial Architecture*, Santiago Chile, Economic Commission for Latin America and the Caribbean.

3

. . .

Recasting the
International Financial Agenda

José Antonio Ocampo *

THE RECENT PHASE of financial turmoil that started in Asia, crossed through
Russia and reached Latin America generated a deep sense that fundamental reforms were required in the international financial architecture to prevent and
improve the management of financial crises. The crisis led, indeed, to a recognition that there is an enormous discrepancy between the sophisticated and dynamic financial world and the institutions that regulate it, that "existing institutions
are inadequate to deal with financial globalization."[1]

The crisis set in motion positive responses: a concerted expansionary effort in
the midst of the crisis, led by the United States, which was probably the crucial
step that facilitated the fairly rapid though incomplete normalization of capital
markets; the approval of new credit lines and the expansion of IMF resources; the
recognition that incentives must be created to induce adequate debt profiles in
developing countries, and that some capital account regulations may serve this
purpose and provide a breathing space for corrective macroeconomic policies; the
parallel recognition that financial liberalization in developing countries should be
carefully managed and sequenced; a special impetus to international efforts to establish minimum standards of prudential regulation and supervision, as well as of

---

*Executive Secretary, United Nations Economic Commission for Latin America and Caribbean
(ECLAC). The paper partly draws upon parallel work by the author, as coordinator of the Task Force
of the United Nations Executive Committee on Economic and Social Affairs (United Nations Task
Force 1999), as well as from Ocampo 1999, 2000a, and joint work with Stephany Griffith-Jones
(Griffith-Jones and Ocampo 1999), supported by the Swedish Ministry of Foreign Affairs.
1. United Nations Task Force (1999), Section 1.

information; the acceptance that no exchange rate regime is appropriate for all countries under all circumstances; the partial acceptance by the IMF that fiscal overkill is inappropriate in adjustment programs; the improvement of the Highly Indebted Poor Countries' (HIPC) Initiative; and the greater emphasis given to the design of adequate social safety nets in developing countries.[2]

Some responses were positive but do not seem to be leading in any clear direction (or even in a wrong one). This is the case of the adoption of collective action clauses in debt issues as an essential step to facilitate internationally agreed debt standstills and orderly workout procedures. In some cases, the responses were insufficient or clearly inadequate: IMF conditionality was overextended; the need for stable arrangements to guarantee the coherence of the macroeconomic policies of industrialized countries did not receive sufficient scrutiny; the Japanese proposal to create an Asian Monetary Fund gave rise to strong unwarranted opposition that led to its rapid dismissal (though there has been a recent revival of this idea); more generally, the role which regional institutions can play in an appropriate international financial arrangement was not given adequate attention; and no (or only very partial) steps were taken to ensure a fair representation of developing countries in the discussions on reform or in a revised international architecture.

The partial recovery of capital markets since 1999 gave way to a sense of complacency that slowed down the reform effort. Moreover, it could lead efforts in the wrong direction. One such step would be to give new impetus to discussions on capital account convertibility. The calmer environment could be taken, on the other hand, as an opportunity to broaden the agenda and to set in motion a representative, balanced negotiation process. The ongoing process for a United Nations Consultation on Financing for Development in 2001 constitutes an important opportunity in this regard. The agenda should be broadened in at least two senses: first of all, it should go beyond the issues of financial crisis prevention and resolution (which may be termed the "narrow" financial architecture[3]) to include those associated with development finance and the "ownership" of economic and, particularly, development policies; secondly, it should consider, in a systematic fashion, not only the role of world institutions, but also of regional arrangements and the areas where national autonomy should be maintained. This is the focus of this paper. As a background, the first section presents brief reflections on the nature of the problems that the system faces and the political economy of the reform effort. Then the paper deals with crisis prevention and management, development finance, the issue of conditionality vs. "ownership" which concerns both of them, the role of regional institutions, and national regulations and autonomy. The last section draws some conclusions.

---

2. See on some of these issues, the regular reports of the IMF Managing Director to the Interim, now International Monetary and Financial Committee. See IMF (1999, 2000a, 2000b).
3. Ocampo (2000a).

THE NATURE OF THE PROBLEMS THAT THE SYSTEM FACES

International capital flows to developing countries have exhibited four outstanding features in the 1990s.[4] First of all, official and private flows have exhibited opposite patterns: whereas the former have tended to decline, private capital flows have experienced rapid medium-term growth. Secondly, different private flows have exhibited striking differences in terms of stability. Thirdly, private flows have been concentrated in middle–income countries, with official flows playing only a very partial redistributive role at the global level. Finally, the instability of private financial flows has required the design of major emergency rescue packages, of unprecedented size, which have concentrated funds in a few large "emerging" economies.

The first two patterns are shown in Table 1. Both foreign direct investment (FDI) and all types of private financial flows have experienced strong medium-term growth. However, these flows have exhibited striking differences in terms of stability: whereas FDI has been resilient in the face of crises, private financial flows have experienced strong volatility and "contagion" effects. Although access to markets has tended to be restored faster than in the past, credit conditions—spreads, maturities and special options to reduce investors' risks—have

TABLE 1. Net long-term flows to developing countries,[a] 1990–1999

	1990	1991	1992	1993	1994	1995	1996	1997	1998	1999[b]
Total	98.5	124.0	153.7	219.2	220.4	257.2	313.1	343.7	318.3	290.7
Official flows	55.9	62.3	54.0	53.4	45.9	53.9	31.0	39.9	50.6	52.0
Private flows	42.6	61.6	99.7	165.8	174.5	203.3	282.1	303.9	267.7	238.7
From international capital markets	18.5	26.4	52.2	99.8	85.7	98.3	151.3	133.6	96.8	46.7
Private debt flows	15.7	18.8	38.1	48.8	50.5	62.2	102.1	103.4	81.2	19.1
Commercial bank loans	3.2	5.0	16.4	3.5	8.8	30.4	37.5	51.6	44.6	–11.4
Bonds	1.2	10.9	11.1	36.6	38.2	30.8	62.4	48.9	39.7	25.0
Others	11.3	2.8	10.7	8.7	3.5	1.0	2.2	3.0	–3.1	5.5
Portfolio equity flows	2.8	7.6	14.1	51.0	35.2	36.1	49.2	30.2	15.6	27.6
Foreign direct investment	24.1	35.3	47.5	66.0	88.8	105.0	130.8	170.3	170.9	192.0

a. Net long-term resource flows are defined as net liability transactions of original maturity greater than one year. Although the Republic of Korea is a high-income country, it is included in the developing country aggregate since it is a borrower from the World Bank.

b. Preliminary.

SOURCE: The World Bank, *Global Development Finance* 2000 (http://www.worldbank.org/prospects/gdf2000/vol1.htm), April 4, 2000.

---

4. For a full evaluation of trends, see UNCTAD (1999), Chapters III and V, and World Bank (1999, 2000).

deteriorated and significant instability in capital flows has been the rule since the eruption of the Asian crisis.[5]

In contrast to the growth of private flows, official development finance and particularly its largest component, bilateral aid, has lagged behind. Indeed, bilateral aid has fallen in real terms and currently stands at one-third of the internationally agreed target of 0.7% of GDP of industrialized countries.[6] The reduction in bilateral aid has been strongest in the case of the largest industrialized countries. This trend has been partly offset, in terms of effective resource transfers, by the increasing share of grants in official development assistance. Also, contrary to private flows, official finance has been stable and some components of it—particularly balance of payments support but also multilateral development finance—has displayed an anti-cyclical behavior.

The third pattern is shown in Table 2. Private flows have been strongly concentrated in middle–income countries. The share of low–income nations in private financing has been lower than their share in the total population of developing countries, a fact that may be expected, but it is also lower than their share in developing countries' GDP. This fact is particularly striking in bond financing, commercial bank lending and portfolio flows, if India is excluded in the latter case. In all these cases, private financing to poor countries is minimal. The share of low–income countries in FDI is also smaller than their contribution to developing countries' GDP. Moreover, a striking feature of FDI is its high concentration in China, which captures, on the contrary, a smaller proportion of financial flows. The high concentration of the most volatile flows in middle-income countries, excluding China, has implied, in turn, that issues of financial volatility and contagion are particularly relevant to them.

Low–income countries have thus been marginalized from private flows and have continued to depend on declining official resource flows. They have, indeed, been strongly dependent on official development assistance, particularly grants, coming mostly in the form of bilateral aid. If we again exclude India, this is the only component of the net resource flows to developing countries that is highly progressive, in the sense that the share of low–income countries exceeds not only their share in developing countries' GDP but also in population. This is also marginally true of multilateral financing, excluding the IMF.

The volatility of private financial flows, on the one hand, and its strong concentration in middle–income countries, on the other, have jointly generated the need for exceptional financing on an unprecedented scale, which has been concentrated in a few "emerging" countries. As a result, IMF (including ESAF) financing has exhibited both strong anti–cyclical behavior in relation to private

---

5. This was recognized by the IMF International Monetary and Financial Committee (2000) in its September 2000 Communiqué: "flows remain below pre-crisis levels, at higher spreads, and continue to show significant volatility, and market access remains extremely limited for some emerging markets."

6. World Bank (2000), p. 58.

TABLE 2. Net flow of resources, 1992–1998
(Annual averages, billion dollars and percentages)

	Foreign direct investment		Portfolio equity flows		Grants		Bilateral financing		Multilateral financing (excluding IMF)	
	Amt.	%	Amt.	%	Amt.	%	Amt.	%	Amt.	%
Developing countries	109.4	100.0	33.0	100.0	28.0	100.0	2.3	100.0	15.3	100.0
Excluding China	75.4	68.9	29.4	89.2	27.7	99.0	0.3	13.1	13.1	86.0
Low-income countries	7.4	6.8	3.0	9.0	16.2	58.0	0.8	36.7	5.8	37.8
India	1.8	1.6	2.2	6.6	0.5	2.0	-0.3	-11.2	1.0	6.4
Other countries	5.6	5.1	0.8	2.4	15.7	56.1	1.1	48.0	4.8	31.5
China[a]	34.0	31.1	3.6	10.8	0.3	1.0	2.0	86.9	2.1	14.0
Middle-income countries	68.0	62.1	26.4	80.2	11.4	40.9	-0.5	-23.6	7.4	48.2
Argentina	5.2	4.7	1.5	4.5	0.0	0.1	-0.2	-10.1	1.0	6.5
Brazil	9.8	8.9	3.6	10.9	0.1	0.2	-1.1	-49.6	0.7	4.9
Russian Federation	1.9	1.8	1.0	3.0	1.0	3.5	0.5	21.6	0.9	5.9
Indonesia	3.0	2.7	2.1	6.4	0.2	0.8	1.2	52.8	0.3	2.0
Republic of Korea[b]	2.0	1.9	3.5	10.5	0.0	0.0	0.1	3.1	1.1	7.4
Mexico	8.8	8.0	4.5	13.6	0.0	0.1	-0.7	-28.8	0.3	2.0
Other countries	37.3	34.1	10.3	31.3	10.1	36.2	-0.3	-12.6	3.0	19.6

	Bonds		Commercial bank loans		Other loans		Total		Memo:	
	Amt.	%	Amt.	%	Amt.	%	Amt.	%	GDP	Pop.
Developing countries	38.2	100.0	27.5	100.0	3.7	100.0	257.4	100.0	100.0	100.0
Excluding China	36.6	95.7	26.7	97.0	0.3	8.7	209.5	81.4	89.3	74.8
Low-income countries	1.0	2.7	0.7	2.6	1.1	29.5	36.0	14.0	11.3	40.7
India	0.9	2.4	0.5	1.6	0.2	5.9	6.8	2.6	5.3	19.4
Other countries	0.1	0.3	0.3	0.9	0.9	23.5	29.2	11.4	6.0	21.3
China[a]	1.6	4.3	0.8	3.0	3.4	91.3	47.9	18.6	10.7	25.2
Middle-income countries	35.6	93.0	26.0	94.4	-0.8	-20.8	173.5	67.4	78.0	34.1
Argentina	5.9	15.4	1.2	4.5	0.0	-1.3	14.5	5.6	4.7	0.7
Brazil	3.1	8.0	9.6	34.7	-0.5	-13.3	25.2	9.8	10.3	3.3
Russian Federation	2.3	6.0	1.1	4.0	1.1	29.0	9.8	3.8	6.6	3.1
Indonesia	1.4	3.6	0.3	1.2	0.1	2.9	8.6	3.4	3.1	4.0
Republic of Korea[b]	6.8	17.7	0.7	2.5	-0.4	-10.4	13.8	5.3	6.8	0.9
Mexico	4.8	12.6	1.6	5.8	-0.4	-10.9	19.0	7.4	6.1	1.9
Other countries	11.4	29.7	11.5	41.7	-0.6	-16.8	82.7	32.1	40.4	20.1

a. The World Bank considered China as a low-income country until 1998. Since 1999 it has been classified as a middle-income country. In this table it is considered as a specific category.

b. The World Bank classifies it as a high-income country, but it is included as a middle-income country in *Global Development Finance 2000*.

SOURCE: The World Bank, *Global Development Finance (CD-ROM), 2000 (advance release)*, Washington, DC, 2000 and *World Economic Indicators 1999*, Washington, DC, 1999 for GDP and population data.

flows and a concentration in a few countries. As Figure 1 indicates, both patterns are closely associated, as cyclical borrowing by a few countries is the major determinant of the overall cyclical pattern. The latter feature has become even more marked in recent years. Thus, whereas India and the three largest Latin American borrowers received less than half of net real flows from the Fund in 1980–1984, net real flows to only four large borrowers (Indonesia, Republic of Korea, Russia, and Mexico) accumulated close to 90% of total net real flows from the Fund in 1995–1998. As a result of this feature, the share of IMF financing going to large borrowers[7] has displayed a strong upward trend over the past two decades. Indeed, in recent years, IMF financing underestimates the magnitude of emergency financing to large borrowers, as the bilateral contributions to the rescue packages of six nations (Indonesia, Republic of Korea, Thailand, Russia, Brazil, and Mexico) are not included in the data.[8]

Strictly speaking, however, "crowding out" by the largest borrowers does not seem to have taken place, as overall Fund support has responded elastically to the needs of these large borrowers, with financing to other poorer or smaller middle–income countries remaining stagnant or even increasing marginally when they also required additional balance of payments resources. This was the case in the 1980s for much of the developing world and has also been true of the supply of financing to the smaller East Asian and Pacific nations in recent years. In any case, Fund and counterpart bilateral emergency financing have complemented private funds through the business cycle. Given the high concentration of private capital flows in middle–income countries, this has led to a similar pattern of concentration in the case of official emergency financing. In the context of a significant scarcity of official funds for low–income countries, the high concentration of balance of payments support in a few large "emerging" economies raises significant concerns as to the global rationality with which global capital, and even official flows, are distributed. It certainly raises questions about whether the problems of the largest developing countries generate specific biases in the response of the international community.

Thus, although the volatility and contagion exhibited by private capital flows, the center of attention in recent debates, are certainly problematic, no less important problems are the marginalization of the poorest countries from private capital flows and the decline in the bilateral aid on which they largely depend. International financial reforms must thus be focused also on guaranteeing solutions to all these problems. Moreover, the debt overhang of many developing countries, particularly poor ones, continues to weigh heavily on their development possibilities.

---

7. This group includes Argentina, Brazil, China, Indonesia, India, the Republic of Korea, Mexico, and the Russian Federation.

8. It must be emphasized, however, that pledged bilateral financing tends to be disbursed in smaller proportions than the multilateral shares in rescue packages.

FIGURE 1. Use of IMF credit

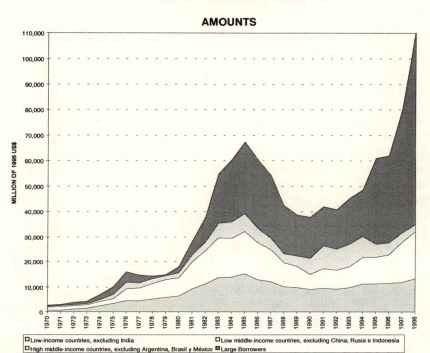

AMOUNTS

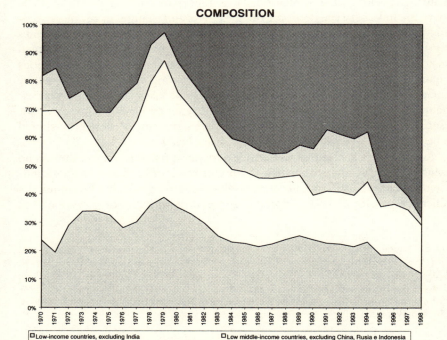

COMPOSITION

FINANCIAL CRISIS PREVENTION AND RESOLUTION

Improving the institutional frameworks in which financial markets operate

The issues associated with financial crisis prevention and resolution have received extensive attention in recent discussions.[9] The most important area of agreement relates to the need to improve the institutional framework in which financial markets operate: to strengthen prudential regulation, supervision and accounting practices of financial systems worldwide; to adopt minimum international standards in these areas, codes of conduct of fiscal, monetary and financial policies, and sound principles of corporate governance; and to improve the information provided to financial markets. From the point of view of industrialized countries, the central issues are stricter regulation and supervision of highly leveraged institutions and operations, controls on offshore centers, and the greater weight that should be given to the risks associated with operations with countries engaging in large-scale net borrowing, particularly of a short-term character, to discourage risky financing at the source. In this regard, it should be emphasized that, despite the recognition of the central role that strengthening regulations of highly leveraged institutions has, moves in this direction have been rather timid and biased towards indirect rather than direct regulations.

From the point of view of borrowing economies, greater weight should be given by domestic regulators to the accumulation of short-term liabilities in foreign currencies, to risks associated with the rapid growth of credit, to currency mismatches of assets and liabilities, and to the valuation of fixed assets as collateral during episodes of asset inflation. Most importantly, due account should be taken of the links between domestic financial risks and changes in key macroeconomic policy instruments, notably exchange and interest rates. This indicates that prudential standards should be stricter in developing countries, where such links are more important, and that they should be strengthened during periods of financial euphoria to take into account the increasing risks being incurred by financial intermediaries. Due account should also be taken of the important externalities which large nonfinancial firms could generate for the domestic financial sector, which implies that the external liabilities exposure of these firms should also be regulated. We will return to these issues below.

Nonetheless, a substantial divergence of opinion remains. Firstly, there is no consensus as to which institutions should be entrusted with enhanced responsibilities in this field. The BIS should certainly play the leading role, but this requires a significant expansion of developing-country membership in this organization. The

---

9. See, among others, IMF (1998, 1999, 2000); IMF Interim Committee (1998); Group of Seven (1998); UNCTAD (1998), Part One, Chapter IV; United Nations Task Force (1999); ECLAC (2000b); Miyazawa (1998); Rubin (1999); Summers (1999); Camdessus (1998, 2000); Fischer (1999); Akyüz and Cornford (1999); Eatwell and Taylor (2000); Eichengreen (1999); Griffith-Jones (1998); Griffith-Jones and Ocampo (1999); Ocampo (1999, 2000a); White (2000a, 2000b); and Wyplosz (1999).

more ambitious proposal to create a World Financial Authority on the basis of BIS, IOSCO, and IAIS should also be considered.[10] Secondly, the lack of adequate representation of developing countries in the definition of all sorts of international standards and codes of conduct is a basic deficiency of current arrangements[11]—which the launching of the G-20 only partly solves—and violates the central principle that G.K. Helleiner has formulated: "No harmonization without representation."[12] It also works against the necessary adaptation of rules to developing country conditions.[13]

Thirdly, although the essential role of regulation and supervision is to make financial intermediaries more risk-conscious, there are clear limits to the appropriateness of discouraging private risk-taking. Stronger prudential regulation in developing countries increases the costs of domestic financial intermediation and thus encourages the use of more external borrowing in the absence of adequate regulation of the latter. Fourthly, differences exist as to the relative merits of prudential regulations and supervision vs. alternative instruments in key areas. One particularly relevant issue in this regard, as we will in Section VI, relates to capital account regulations. Moreover, there are significant differences of opinion as to what can be expected from enhanced prudential regulation and supervision, given their inherent limitations. Regulations will tend to lag behind financial innovations, supervisors are likely to face significant information problems, and macroeconomic events may overwhelm even well-regulated systems. Finally, traditional prudential regulation and supervision tend to have pro-cyclical macroeconomic effects (they may be unable to avoid excessive risk-taking during the booms but accelerate the credit crunch during crises, when bad loans become evident and the effects of provisioning standards are thus felt), a fact which may increase rather than decrease credit risks through the business cycle.

Equally important, there is some doubt as to what can be expected from better information. Although improved information enhances microeconomic efficiency, it may not improve macroeconomic stability, which is dominated by the evolution of opinions and expectations rather than information, in the correct sense of that term (i.e., factual information). Indeed, the tendency to equate opinions and expectations with "information" is a source of confusion in the recent literature. Well-informed agents (rating agencies and institutional investors, for example) are equally subject to the whims of opinion and expectations, a fact that accounts for their inability to stabilize markets and, under certain conditions, the additional instability which they may generate.[14] To use modern terminology, more than "information cascades," what characterizes macroeconomic financial instability are

---

10. Eatwell and Taylor (2000).

11. A very strong statement in this regard has been recently been made by the Governor of the People's Bank of China: "The monopoly by a handful of developed countries on the rule-making in the international financial field must be changed" (Dai, 2000).

12. Helleiner (2000a).

13. Ahluwalia (1999).

14. See, on the former, Larraín et al. (1997); on the latter, Calvo (1998).

"opinion and expectation cascades," i.e., the alternate "contagion" of both optimism and pessimism through the business cycle. The best information system will be unable to correct this "market failure," as the whims of expectations involve "information" about the future, which will never be available.[15] Developing countries have also strongly argued for "a symmetrical application of transparency criteria between public institutions and the private sector"[16] and thus against the tendency to emphasize the former over the latter in current proposals. Heated debates still surround the advantages vs. the disadvantages of the disclosure of IMF surveillance reports, which reflect the relative virtues of greater information and transparency vs. "the importance of maintaining the Fund's role as confidential and trusted advisor."[17]

The need for coherent macroeconomic policies worldwide

The consensus on the need to strengthen the institutional framework in which financial markets operate has not been matched by a similar emphasis on the role played by the coherence of macroeconomic policies worldwide, i.e., on appropriate mechanisms to internalize the externalities generated by national macroeconomic policies.[18] A particularly crucial area, which the G-24 and other analysts have emphasized, is the high cost that fluctuations among major currencies have for developing countries.[19]

The need for coherent macroeconomic policies is crucial in relation to both booms and crises, but the need to strengthen the extremely weak existing arrangements is particularly crucial during booms, when IMF surveillance is perceived by national authorities as an academic exercise, consultative mechanisms seem less necessary and "market discipline" has perverse effects, as it does not constrain excessive private risk-taking or the adoption of national pro-cyclical policies. Indeed, the focus of current institutions—both national and international—on crises rather than booms is a serious deficiency of existing arrangements, as they underplay the preventive role that they should perform. Obviously, concerted expansionary action during crises is also essential and, as was pointed out in the introduction to this paper, moves in that direction since the Russian

---

15. For a more extensive analysis, see Ocampo (2000a). Keynes' concept of a "beauty contest" is thus much more appropriate to analyze the volatility of expectations, as Eatwell (1996) and Eatwell and Taylor (2000) have emphasized.

16. Group of 24 (1999a).

17. Group of 24 (1999b). See a more extensive discussion of this issue in IMF (1999, 2000a, 2000b).

18. See, in this regard, the emphasis of the Group of 24 (2000b) on the "imperative need for better coordination, coherence, and mutual reinforcement of macroeconomic and structural policies among the three major economies in order to reduce the risks and uncertainties in the global economy" and the absence of this topic in the parallel Communiqué of the IMF International Monetary and Committee or in the IMF (1999, 2000a, 2000b) reports on reforms of the international financial architecture.

19. See Group of 24 (1999b, 2000a). See also the different points of view on this issue in Council on Foreign Relations (1999).

crisis were probably the single most important reason for the relative though incomplete normalization of capital markets in 1999.

The lack of adequate representation of developing countries in existing organs is another deficiency of current arrangements, as the composition of the IMF's International Monetary and Financial Committee reflects. Given the more adequate balance in the representation of developing and developed countries, the United Nations could play an enhanced role in the normative area, either through an improved Economic and Social Council or an Economic Security Council.

Emergency financing

The enhanced provision of emergency financing during crises is the third pillar of the system to prevent and manage financial crises. This principle may be called the principle of the "emergency financier," to differentiate it from the role that central banks play at the national level as "lenders of last resort," which is not exactly matched by the IMF. More specifically, the Fund provides exceptional financing but certainly not *liquidity*, a fact that is reflected in the lack of automaticity in the availability of financing during crises.[20] The access to emergency financing raises, in any case, "moral hazard" issues that give rise, on the side of borrowers, to the need to define access rules and, on the side of private lenders, to the need for orderly debt workouts that guarantee that they assume a fair share of the costs of adjustment.

The main lessons from recent crises are: (1) that, as a preventive measure, wider use should be made of private contingency credit lines that are agreed during periods of adequate access to capital market, following the (partly successful) pioneering experiences of some "emerging" economies; (2) that large-scale official emergency funding may be required, though not all of it needs to be disbursed if support programs rapidly restore market confidence; (3) that funds should be made available *before*—rather than after—international reserves reach critically low levels; and (4) that, due to strong contagion effects, contingency financing may be required even by countries that do not exhibit fundamental disequilibria. At least the last two imply significant differences with respect to the traditional IMF approach, which is based on the principle of correcting fundamental balance of payments disequilibria once they have become evident. Positive measures have been adopted in this area, including a significant expansion of IMF resources through a quota increase and the New Arrangements to Borrow, which entered into effect in late 1998; the launching of the Supplemental Reserve Facility (SRF) in December 1997 to finance exceptional borrowing requirements during crises; and the creation of the Contingency Credit Line (CCL) in April 1999 to provide financing to countries facing contagion and its redesign in September 2000.

---

20. This important distinction is made by Helleiner (1999) and Eatwell and Taylor (2000). For a fuller discussion of this issue and its relation to IMF access to adequate resources, see Mohammed (1999).

The major controversies relate to inadequate funding, conditions for access, and credit terms. With respect to the first point, bilateral financing and contributions to the IMF will continue to be scarce during crises. This is a crucial issue, as the stabilizing effects of rescue packages will be absent if the market deems that the intervening authorities (the IMF plus additional bilateral support) are unable or unwilling to supply funds in the quantities required. As bilateral financing and contributions to the IMF will continue to be scarce and unreliable during crises, the best solution, according to several recent proposals, is to allow additional issues of SDRs during episodes of world financial stress; these funds could be destroyed once financial conditions normalize.[21] This procedure would create an anti-cyclical element in world liquidity management and would give SDRs an enhanced role in world finance, a principle that developing countries have advocated in the past and should continue to endorse in the future. Second-best alternatives are to make a more active use of Central Bank swap arrangements under IMF or BIS leadership, and to allow the IMF to raise the resources needed in the market.

The broad issues raised by conditionality will be discussed in Section IV below. However, the adequate mix of conditionality and other credit conditions deserves some attention here. In this regard, the idea that conditionality *cum* the provision of limited funding should be mixed with harder terms for exceptional financing—both shorter maturities and higher spreads—is controversial. This has been the pattern established in new IMF facilities (both the SRF and the CCL) and was introduced as a general principle of IMF financing in September 2000, which could only be applied, however, after a transitional period. It has eliminated the "credit union" character of the IMF but still does not reflect "market conditions." It should be recalled, in this regard, that the classical Bagehot criteria for lending of last resort relies on short-term financing at penalty interest rates, but on the basis that financing is unconditional and unlimited (or, to be precise, limited by good collaterals only). Thus, contrary to current IMF practice, Bahegot criteria consider more onerous credit terms (with unlimited funding) as a *substitute* rather than a complement for conditionality (*cum* limited funding).

Indeed, following ideas closer to these classical criteria, some of the more radical proposals in this area involve reducing conditionality significantly and moving towards short-term credit lines, at penalty interest rates.[22] These alternatives are equally controversial. First of all, they also violate one of Bahegot's criteria: unlimited funding; indeed, these proposals would restrict financing severely when compared to recent IMF credit lines. Secondly, in some of those proposals, conditionality is maintained, even including conditions that have been absent in traditional IMF financing.[23] Moreover, a basic assumption of these

---

21. See United Nations Task Force (1999), Council on Foreign Relations (1999), Group of 24(2000b), Meltzer *et al.* (2000), Camdessus (2000).

22. See, in particular, Meltzer *et al.* (2000), but also Council on Foreign Relations (1999).

23. Thus, Meltzer *et al.* (2000) would require borrowing countries, as conditions for access, fiscal soundness, minimum prudential regulation, transparent data on debt and its structure, and

proposals is that recent crises have been severe but short,[24] a fact that, as argued in Section I, is not confirmed by events since the Asian crisis.[25] More importantly, the characteristics of recent crises—including their duration—is certainly not independent of the rapid response of the international community in the form of larger and faster rescue packages than in the past (along the "lessons" previously inferred). During the Asian crisis, it was also associated, as indicated, to the rapid, concerted macroeconomic response of industrialized countries.

The recent Contingency Credit Line designed to deal with contagion has introduced similar but also some additional problems. Following, again, traditional "lending of last resort" criteria, critics have argued that such a credit line should have more onerous credit terms, but should also be automatic, based on whether countries fulfil certain ex ante criteria, and thus be detached from traditional conditionality. Even after its redesign, the CCL does not fully meet these criteria: although the "activation" process made access more automatic, and monitoring arrangements were made less intensive, the "post-activation" review still kept the character of traditional IMF financing subject to conditionality (though now subject to lower initial charges). A more important difficulty is that ex ante signaling transforms, in effect, the IMF into a credit rating agency, a fact that could generate severe destabilizing effects on countries when downgraded. It also transforms the nature of Article IV consultations, eroding its character of a dialogue with a "trusted advisor."

This discussion highlights how complex it is for an "emergency financier" (rather than a true "lender of last resort") to find the appropriate mix of conditionality, limited funding, and more onerous credit terms. The adequate solution would require: (1) large up-front financing; (2) no prequalifications but a fast review process during periods of crisis and, particularly, strong contagion; and (3) reduced conditionality in general, but particularly for those credit lines subject to harsher terms.[26]

Debt standstills and orderly workout procedures

Debt standstills and orderly workout procedures are an essential mechanism to avoid the coordination problems implicit in chaotic capital flight, to guarantee an appropriate sharing of adjustments by private lenders and, thus, to avoid "moral hazard" issues associated with emergency financing. Broad consensus on the need to create arrangements of this sort exists[27] but little action has followed. This reflects private sector opposition to non-voluntary arrangements

---

freedom of operation for foreign financial institutions. The latter is absent, not only in current conditionality but in other proposals related to IMF financing.

24. Council on Foreign Relations (1999), ch. III.

25. It must be added that commercial bank lending did not normalize in Latin America in the 1990s, despite the boom in such financing to East and Southeast Asia.

26. See a discussion along these lines in Ahluwalia (1999).

27. See the references quoted in footnote 9.

in industrialized countries, but also the practical difficulties involved in designing a mechanism of this sort.[28] As recently summarized by the International Monetary and Financial Committee, these difficulties are associated to the need to strike a balance between broad principles, needed to guide market expectations, and the operational flexibility, which requires elements of a "case by case" approach.[29] It is clear, however, that there is no substitute to the declaration of a debt standstill by the borrowing country, followed by voluntary negotiations with lenders, subject to some internationally agreed principles.

Due to the effects that the use of this mechanism could have on their credit standing, borrowing countries are unlikely to abuse it. Nonetheless, to avoid "moral hazard" issues on the side of borrowers, it must be subject to international control, by allowing countries to call a standstill unilaterally but then requiring that they submit it for approval by an independent international panel or an agreed international authority, whose authorization would give it legitimacy.[30] An alternative could be to draft ex ante rules under which debt service could be automatically suspended or reduced if certain macroeconomic shocks were experienced; such rules have sometimes been incorporated into debt renegotiation agreements.

On the other hand, debt issues and negotiations must be subject to five basic rules. Firstly, to avoid both free riding and discrimination against countries or groups of countries that adopt them, they require the *universal* adoption by borrowing countries of "collective action clauses," as indeed British rules already require. The G-7 countries must actually lead the process, as they suggested in October 1998,[31] for otherwise these clauses would become an additional source of discrimination against "emerging markets." Secondly, "bailing in" should be encouraged by giving seniority to lending that is extended to countries during the period in which the standstill is in effect and during a later phase of "normalization" of capital flows. Thirdly, IMF "lending into arrears" should continue to be considered a normal practice as long as countries are seeking to work cooperatively with private creditors. Fourthly, the phase of voluntary debt renegotiations under this framework must have a short, strictly-defined time horizon, beyond which the country in arrears could request the independent panel or international authority to intervene in the negotiations or even to determine the terms of rescheduling. Indeed, the basic deficiency of voluntary case-by-case solutions is that the negotiation periods could become extremely long, generating large costs to developing countries, as the experience of Latin America in the 1980s indicates. Finally, to avoid repeated renegotiations—another troublesome feature of voluntary arrangements in recent decades—aside from the portion that is written off (or refinanced in highly concessional terms), the service of another portion should be subject to the fulfillment of certain contingent macroeconomic conditions that

---

28. See a review of some of the controversies involved in IMF (1999, 2000a, 2000b), Boorman and Allen (2000) and Fischer (1999).

29. IMF International Monetary and Financial Committee (2000). See also Köhler (2000).

30. UNCTAD (1998), Part I, Chapter IV; United Nations Task Force (1999).

31. Group of Seven (1998).

determine debt service capacity (e.g., terms of trade, normalization of lending, domestic economic activity, etc.).

It must be emphasized, finally, that private sector involvement in crisis resolution should be seen as a *complement* rather than as a substitute or a prerequisite for emergency financing (even if only above a certain threshold level). This implies that the international agency that is given authority in this area could be given the role of advising countries on the desirability of the standstill but not the capacity to force it on debtor countries. An alternative system would significantly increase market instability and/or "solve" moral hazard issues by increasing spreads or severely rationing financing to developing countries. The recent experience indicates, indeed, that the large rescue packages of the 1990s have been served normally. This indicates that the problems faced by the emerging economies that led to large-scale emergency financing had a significant element of illiquidity rather than insolvency, a fact that argues for more rather than less emergency financing. The conditions that such financing carried are, obviously, more debatable. We will return to this issue below.

The definition of international rules on capital account regulations and exchange rate regimes has been left out of this discussion. The reason is that, under the current, incomplete international arrangements, national autonomy should continue to prevail in these areas. They are therefore considered in Section VI below.

DEVELOPMENT FINANCE

As the discussion presented in Section I indicates, although IMF financing is certainly important to low-income countries, the major issues for them are associated with the need to guarantee adequate development finance, through ODA and multilateral lending, and to generate mechanisms that will allow them to participate more actively in private capital markets. Given the relative magnitude of financing to low-income countries (see Table 2), the reversal of ODA flows, particularly those originating in the largest industrialized economies, is certainly the most important issue. Thus, it is important that efforts to accelerate HIPC should not crowd out new ODA financing. Actually, beyond a more ambitious HIPC Initiative, the world requires an even more ambitious and permanent "ODA Initiative" aimed at effectively meeting internationally agreed targets. An essential characteristic of this process, as is emphasized in the following sections, should be an effective "ownership" of policies by developing countries, a fact that requires less direction from abroad and more emphasis on national institution building. The latter requires, in turn, respect for the central role that parliaments and governments in aid-receiving nations should have in the global allocation of aid through their budgetary processes and the central role that governments in those countries should have in directing traditional areas of public policy (e.g., social policy and infrastructure), even when civil society is given a central role in execution.

Equally important, however, is the acceleration of the growth of multilateral development finance. Such lending will continue to play a central role in at least four areas: (1) to channel funds to low-income countries; (2) to correct market failures associated to the overpricing of risks, which may lead to inadequate access to long-term financing by middle income countries with insufficiently high credit rating; (3) to act as a counter-cyclical balance to fluctuations in private capital market financing; and (4) to facilitate the transition to private markets by supporting some innovations in long-term financing to developing countries and signaling creditworthiness. To these we should add the traditional "value added" of multilateral financing: lending-associated technical assistance.[32]

The first of these functions underscores the central role that financing from IBRD-IDA and the regional and subregional development banks will continue to play in the immediate future. It has received widespread support in recent debates. The second and third functions emphasize the role that official development financing will continue to play even for middle-income countries. Some authors reject, nonetheless, the validity of these arguments.[33] The high interest rates that have characterized private lending to developing countries in the 1990s, and the much shorter maturities of private vs. official financing to middle-income countries, may indicate that, on average, risk may have been overestimated (see Table 3).[34]

It must be stressed, however, that the anti-cyclical provision of funds should not be confused with the provision of emergency balance of payments financing, which is essentially a task of the IMF. However, to the extent that anti-cyclical fiscal policies are a necessary element in counter-cyclical macroeconomic management in general, there may be an argument for development financing during crisis as a counterpart to pure balance of payments financing.[35] An alternative would be to allow IMF financing—or the latitude it offers for domestic credit creation—for fiscal purposes, but this step would be suboptimal. In any case, the large-scale requirements for counter-cyclical financing to middle-income countries during crises may crowd out financing to poor countries, a point which has been made by the president of the World Bank.[36] Thus, if multilateral develop-

---

32. See, on this, Gilbert, Powell, and Vines (1999) who, nonetheless, reject the idea that market failures are an argument for development lending to middle-income countries. The idea suggested by these authors that there is some kind of "natural monopoly" in some types of development economics research is not a sensible defense of the World Bank. The parallel idea that global public goods should be provided is certainly valid, but it justifies the existence of many types of international institutions, not development banks per se.

33. The strongest argument in this regard is that of Meltzer et al. (2000) but a weaker version can be found in Gilbert, Powell, and Vines (1999), who nonetheless argue that the World Bank should be allowed to lend to middle-income countries to improve its portfolio.

34. Indeed, it is peculiar that Meltzer et al. (2000) estimate the subsidies of development financing in the 1990s by assuming that it is equivalent to only half of spreads in capital markets.

35. Such financing could be tied to broader forms of anti-cyclical management, on the basis of counterpart savings in fiscal stabilization funds during the previous boom or repayment conditions that would require acceleration of amortizations if fiscal revenues experience a strong recovery during the subsequent boom.

36. Wolfensohn (1998).

TABLE 3. Developing countries: average terms of new commitments

	1990	1991	1992	1993	1994	1995	1996	1997	1998
Average maturity (years)									
OFFICIAL									
All developing countries	22.2	20.9	21.1	21.4	22.1	19.2	21.2	20.1	18.5
Income groups									
Low income	27.0	25.9	26.8	25.4	26.2	24.4	26.8	26.2	26.6
Middle income	18.8	17.8	17.0	18.1	18.4	15.8	17.2	17.2	14.2
PRIVATE	13.9	10.2	10.0	9.4	8.9	7.4	8.3	10.0	8.8
Income groups									
Low income	13.7	11.5	12.3	11.3	11.2	8.0	7.5	7.0	7.0
Middle income	13.9	9.9	9.0	8.4	8.1	7.2	8.6	10.8	9.0
Average interest (%)									
OFFICIAL									
All developing countries	5.5	5.5	5.3	4.8	4.9	5.8	4.8	5.4	5.2
Income groups									
Low income	4.0	4.5	3.8	3.8	3.9	4.5	3.9	4.2	3.7
Middle income	6.6	6.1	6.4	5.6	5.8	6.7	5.6	6.0	6.0
PRIVATE									
All developing countries	8.5	7.8	6.8	6.3	6.3	6.4	7.3	7.3	7.9
Income groups									
Low income	7.9	7.5	6.7	6.0	5.7	6.4	6.6	6.4	6.9
Middle income	8.8	7.8	6.9	6.4	6.5	6.4	7.5	7.5	8.0

SOURCE: World Bank (2000).

ment financing is not significantly expanded, its role as a counter-cyclical device will necessarily be very limited, and it would certainly be of secondary importance relative to its first two roles, particularly the provision of long-term development financing to poor countries. This is underscored by the data from Table 2, which indicate that multilateral financing in 1992–1998 represented only 15% of that provided by the private sector, excluding FDI, and only 8% in the case of middle-income countries. Thus, a useful counter-cyclical function would certainly require a significant increase in resources available to multilateral development banks or a more active use of cofinancing and credit guarantees by these institutions (see below).

The role of development banks in supporting social safety nets, which has received a correct emphasis in recent discussions, should be seen as part of the counter-cyclical role that multilateral institutions should play. Strong social safety nets are, indeed, essential to manage the social repercussions of financial vulnerability in the developing world. The concept itself is subject to some confusion, as it has been used to refer both to the design of long-term social policies and to specific mechanisms to protect vulnerable groups during crises. The term should probably be used to refer specifically to the latter, although, as we will argue below, these arrangements should be part of stable mechanisms of social protection. Multilateral banks have been involved in the former for a long time and have also accumulated some experience with the latter.

Recent analyses have come to some basic conclusions about these programs. Firstly, safety nets must be part of *permanent* social protection schemes, as only a permanent scheme guarantees that the program coverage will respond without lags to the demand for protection of vulnerable sectors during crises.[37] Secondly, given the heterogeneity of labor markets in developing countries, a combination of several programs, with different target groups, is necessary.[38] Thirdly, these programs must be adequately financed and should not crowd out resources from long-term investment in human capital. This, it must be said, leads to a fourth conclusion: that the effective functioning of social safety nets requires that public-sector expenditure should include anti-cyclical components. This would be impossible, without generating inefficiencies in the rest of public-sector expenditure, if fiscal policy as a whole is not counter-cyclical. In the absence of this anti-cyclical fiscal pattern, external financing from development banks during crises to safety nets will be unnecessary, as overall net fiscal financing requirements will actually decrease despite the increased spending associated to such safety nets.

The fourth function is of fairly recent origin but has been rapidly gaining in importance in the 1990s and should become one of the primary focuses of multilateral financing in the future. This function has been associated in the recent past with direct financing or cofinancing to the private sector (by banks or associated financial corporations) or with the design of guarantee schemes to support private infrastructure projects in developing countries. It has also been recently used to support developing countries' efforts to return to markets after crises and could be used to support initial bond issues by developing (particularly poor) countries seeking to position themselves in private capital markets. It must be emphasized, however, that the full development of these guarantee schemes would require a radical change in the management of guarantees by development banks, as, under current practices, guarantees are treated as equivalent to lending, a fact which severely restricts the banks' ability to extend them. Such an expansion of the role of development banks in guaranteeing private financing has been criticized on the grounds that it could involve excessive risk-taking by these institutions. Nonetheless, in a world that will be dominated by private financing, it may be absolutely essential to prevent low-income countries from being left out of major developments in capital markets and to facilitate a more active anti–cyclical role for development banks. It should thus receive priority attention in current discussions.

---

37. Cornia (1999).

38. Márquez (1999). Different groups would be supported by unemployment insurance, emergency employment or emergency labor-intensive public works programs, income-support schemes in conjunction with training, and special targeted subsidies (such as some nutrition programs, subsidies to households with school-age children that are tied to school attendance, and various support programs aimed at ensuring that households with an unemployed head of household do not lose their home during crises, etc.).

CONDITIONALITY VS. "OWNERSHIP"

The most controversial issue behind international emergency and development financing is certainly conditionality. In the case of the IMF, this issue has long been a central area of contention. However, in recent years –and even decades– the issue has become increasingly troublesome for three different reasons. Firstly, the scope of conditionality has been gradually expanded to include not only the realms of other international organizations—quite often, for example, that of the WTO and the development banks—but also of domestic economic and social development strategies and institutions which, as the United Nations Task Force has indicated, "by their very nature should be decided by legitimate national authorities, based on broad social consensus."[39] The broadening of conditionality to social policy, governance issues, and private sector involvement in crisis resolution has been criticized by developing countries in the Group of 24.[40] The need to restrict conditionality to macroeconomic policy and financial sector issues is shared by a broad group of analysts with quite different persuasions as to the future role of the IMF.[41] A similar view was expressed in the external evaluation of surveillance activities of the Fund.[42] This led to the recent agreement that IMF conditionality should be streamlined, though its agreed focus is still very broad.[43]

Secondly, whereas the legitimacy of conditionality is indisputable when domestic policies are the source of macroeconomic disequilibria that lead to financial difficulties, as well as being necessary to avert "moral hazard" issues, it is unclear how this principle applies when such difficulties are generated by international crises and, particularly, by contagion effects. Thirdly, as has already been pointed out, it is even less clear why conditionality should be mixed with adverse credit terms. Finally, many observers have criticized overkill in some IMF programs, a fact that has led the Fund to allow some room for anti-cyclical fiscal policies in its adjustment programs.[44]

Even if the legitimacy of the principle of conditionality—or, as it is sometimes stated, "support in exchange for reforms"—is accepted, there are thus reasons to review the characteristics of such conditionality. Indeed, the perception that conditionality has been carried beyond what may actually be necessary in order for the Fund to perform its functions properly may be helping to undermine its legitimacy. Thus, a strong argument can be made that the way to restore

---

39. United Nations Task Force (1999), Section 5.

40. Group of 24 (1999b).

41. Council on Foreign Relations (1999), Meltzer et al. (2000), Collier and Gunning (1999), Feldstein (1998), Helleiner (2000b) and Rodrik (1999b).

42. Crow, Arriazu and Thygeseb (1999).

43. See IMF International Monetary and Financial Committee (2000) and Köhler (2000). The difficulties are associated to the fact that, although the IMF is expected to focus on macroeconomic and financial issues, it should also look at "their associated institutional and structural aspects." Such a broad definition led to the increasing scope of conditionality over the past two decades.

44. Fischer (1998).

full confidence in the principle of conditionality is by reaching a renewed international agreement on how it should be used.

Several principles can be advanced in this regard. Firstly, as noted, IMF conditionality should be restricted to the macroeconomic policies that were its purview in the past. Reforms of domestic financial regulation and supervision may also be required, but in this case parallel agreements should be made with the corresponding international authorities (a still unresolved issue, as we have seen). Secondly, low-conditionality facilities should be available in adequate quantities when the source of the imbalance is an international shock or a country faces contagion. Nonetheless, beyond and above the preestablished level of the low conditionality facilities, access to Fund resources could be subject to macroeconomic conditionality on traditional terms. Thirdly, as we have also noted, more stringent credit terms should not be used as a complement to conditionality. Fourthly, automatic rules should be agreed upon when signing an agreement with the Fund under which the restrictiveness of the adjustment program would be eased should evidence of overkill become clear. Finally, regular official evaluation of IMF programs, by an autonomous division of the Fund (a decision already adopted in 2000) and by outside analysts should be the basis for a regular revision of the nature of conditionality.

It must be emphasized that similar issues have been raised in relation to development finance. With respect to this issue, a World Bank report that analyses the success of structural lending, according to its own evaluation, comes to the conclusion that conditionality does not influence the success or failure of such programs at all.[45] Nonetheless, according to the same report, aid effectiveness is not independent of the economic policies that countries follow. In particular, the effects of aid on growth are higher for countries that adopt "good" policies, which, according to their definition, include stable macroeconomic environments, open trade regimes, adequate protection of property rights, and efficient public bureaucracies that can deliver good-quality social services. In the context of good policies, there is an additional positive effect of aid that is manifested through the "crowding in" of private financing. Neither of these effects are present, however, in countries following "wrong" policies. In terms that are now familiar in the aid literature, the *ownership* of adequate economic policies, i.e., the commitment of national authorities to them, is what really matters. Conditionality has *no* additional contribution to make in these cases, and it is obviously ineffective in the case of countries that do not follow good policies.

Curiously enough, on the basis of this study the World Bank draws the conclusion that conditionality is good after all. Hence, it claims that "Conditional lending is worthwhile where reforms have serious domestic support"[46] and, in particular, that it "still has a role—to allow government to commit to reform and

---

45. See World Bank (1998b), Chapter 2 and Appendix 2. See also Gilbert, Powell, and Vines (1999) and Stiglitz (1999).

46. World Bank (1998b), p. 48.

to signal the seriousness of reform—but to be effective in this it must focus on a small number of truly important measures."[47] This statement is certainly paradoxical if the conclusions of the report are taken at face value. Rather, this study raises serious doubts about the rationality of conditionality itself, a fact that is, indeed, implicit in the idea that policies are only effective when they are rooted in broad national consensus, the essential idea that has been captured in the concept of "ownership."[48] Indeed, the president of the World Bank has made the strongest statement in this regard: "We must never stop reminding ourselves that it is up to the governments and its people to decide what their priorities should be. We must never stop reminding ourselves that we cannot and should not impose development by fiat from above—or from abroad."[49]

Rodrik has come to complementary conclusions, which are extensive to short-term macroeconomic policies.[50] Aside from arguing that international arrangements should allow for diversity in national development strategies (different "brands of capitalism"), this author makes a strong argument that adequate institutions of conflict management, which can only be guaranteed by national democratic processes, are crucial for macroeconomic stability and that this, in turn, is vital for economic growth. To borrow the term, the "ownership" of adjustment programs is also essential to guarantee their political sustainability.

The issue of conditionality vs. ownership is, indeed, essential to the broader objectives of democracy at the world level. There is clearly no sense in promoting democracy if the representative and participatory processes at the national level are given no role in determining economic and social development strategies, as well as the particular policy mix by which macroeconomic stability is obtained. Both of them may not only be relatively ineffective but will also lack political sustainability if international institutions or the aid agencies of the industrialized countries play this role.

THE ROLE OF REGIONAL INSTITUTIONS

There are three basic arguments in support of a strong role for regional institutions in the new financial order. The first one is that globalization also entails open regionalism. The growth of intraregional trade and direct investment flows are, indeed, striking features of the ongoing globalization process. This factor increases macroeconomic linkages and thus the demands for certain services provided by the international financial system which we have analyzed in previous sections: macroeconomic surveillance and internalization of the externalities that national macroeconomic policies have on neighboring countries, and mutual

---

47. World Bank (1998b), p. 19.
48. See a full discussion of these issues in Helleiner (1999).
49. Wolfensohn (1998).
50. Rodrik (1999a).

surveillance of each other's mechanisms for the prudential regulation and supervision of the financial system.

Secondly, some of these services may be subject to diseconomies of scale and it is unclear whether others have strong scale economies to justify single international institutions in specific areas (i.e., natural monopolies). Traditional issues of subsidiarity are thus raised. For example, macroeconomic consultation and surveillance at the world level may be necessary to guarantee policy coherence among major industrialized countries, but it would certainly be inefficient to manage the externalities generated by macroeconomic policies on neighbors in the developing world (or even within Europe). Due to differences in legal traditions and the sheer scale of the diseconomies involved, surveillance of national systems for the prudential regulation and supervision of financial sectors, and even the definition of specific minimum standards in this area, may be dealt with more appropriately with the support of regional institutions. Development finance can operate effectively at different scales and, as we will see, can perform certain functions at regional and subregional levels that could not be performed at the international level. Also, although regional and international contagion implies that the management of the largest balance of payments crises should be assigned to a single world institution, it is unclear how far we should push this assertion. Strong regional institutions can serve as regional buffers, as the postwar Western European experience indicates. Regional reserve funds or swap arrangements can also play a useful role in the developing world and, if expanded, could even provide full support to the small and medium-size countries within some regions. Also, as the rising concentration of balance of payments support in a few countries indicates (see Section I), there may be biases in the response of the international community according to the size of the country, a fact which would argue for a division of labor in the provision of services in this area between world and regional organizations.

Thirdly, for smaller countries, the access to a broader menu of alternatives to manage a crisis or to finance development is relatively more important than the "global public goods" that the largest international organizations provide (e.g., global macroeconomic stability) and upon which they will assume they have little or no influence (i.e., they have the attitude of "free riders"). Due to their small size, their negotiation power vis-à-vis large organizations would be very limited, and their most important defense is therefore competition in the provision of financial services from such institutions.

The current discussion has underscored the fact that some services provided by international financial institutions, including some "global public goods," are being undersupplied. However, according to previous remarks, it would be wrong to conclude from this statement that the increasing supply should come from a few world organizations. Rather, the organizational structure should have, in some cases, the nature of networks of institutions that provide the services required on a complementary basis and, in others, should function as a system of competitive organizations. The provision of the services required for financial crisis prevention and management should be closer to the first model, whereas, in the realm of development finance, competition should be the basic rule (and, in fact, should include competition with private agents as well). But purity in the model's structure is probably not the best characteristic: it is desirable that parts of networks compete against each other (e.g., regional reserve funds or swap arrangements vs. the IMF in the provision of emergency financing) and that competitive organizations cooperate in some cases.

This implies that the International Monetary Fund of the future should not be viewed as a single, global institution, but rather as the apex of a network of regional and subregional reserve funds and swap arrangements. To encourage the development of the latter, incentives could be created by which common reserve funds could have automatic access to IMF financing and/or a share in the allocation of SDRs proportional to their paid-in resources—in other words, contributions to common reserve funds would be treated as equivalent to IMF quotas.[51] As noted, regional reserve funds or swap arrangements could provide most of the exceptional financing for smaller countries within a region, but also part of the financing for larger countries, and they could also serve to deter, at least partly, would-be speculators from attacking the currencies of individual countries.

This model should be extended to the provision of macroeconomic consultation and surveillance, as well as to coordination and surveillance of national systems of prudential regulation and supervision. Thus, regional and subregional systems, including peer review mechanisms, should be designed to internalize the externalities that macroeconomic policies generate on neighbors. This would complement, rather than substitute for, regular IMF surveillance. In the area of prudential regulation and supervision, more elaborate systems of regional information and consultation, including the design of specific regional "minimum standards," can also play a positive role. Again, peer reviews should be part of this system. Aside from other functions considered in Section III, subregional development banks can play a significant role as a mechanism to pool the risks of groups of developing countries, thus allowing them to make a more aggressive use of opportunities provided by private capital markets.

As it is well known, Western Europe provides the best example of regional financial cooperation in the post-war period. The United States, through the Marshall Plan, catalyzed the initial phases of this process, which underwent a dynamic deepening from the design of the European Payments Union to a series of arrangements for macroeconomic coordination and cooperation, that eventually led to the current monetary union of most of its members. No similar schemes have been devised in the rest of the world, although some proposals have been made, the most ambitious of which was the Japanese suggestion to create an Asian Monetary Fund. The most interesting development in recent years has been the swap arrangement among 13 Asian countries agreed in May 2000[52] and initiatives to strengthen the Latin American (previously Andean) Reserve Fund.[53]

---

51. United Nations Task Force (1999), Section 9; Ocampo (2000a).
52. Park and Wang (2000).
53. Agosin (2000) and ECLAC (2000b, ch. 2).

An institutional framework such as that suggested would have two positive features. First of all, it may help to bring more stability to the world economy by providing essential services that can hardly be provided by a few international institutions, particularly in the face of a dynamic process of open regionalism. Secondly, from the point of view of the equilibrium of world relations, it would be more balanced than a system based on a few world organizations. This would increase the commitment of less powerful players to abide by rules that contribute to world and regional stability.

THE REALMS OF NATIONAL AUTONOMY

Whatever international system is developed, it is clear that it will continue to be a very imperfect "financial safety net." Consequently, a degree of "self-insurance" by countries will continue to be essential to avoid financial crises, as well as to avoid "moral hazard" issues intrinsic to any support scheme. This raises two issues as to the national policies necessary to guarantee financial stability and the areas where national autonomy should be maintained. We will argue that the international system should continue to maintain national autonomy in two crucial areas: the management of the capital account and the choice of the exchange rate regime. The choice of development strategies is obviously an additional, essential realm in which national autonomy should prevail, as the analysis in Section IV has emphasized.

The experience of developing countries indicates that the management of capital account volatility requires: (1) consistent and flexible macroeconomic management; (2) strong prudential regulation and supervision of domestic financial systems; and (3) equally strong "liability policies," aimed at inducing good public and private external and domestic debt profiles.[54] Despite the traditional emphasis on crisis management, the focus of the authorities should instead be the management of *booms*, since it is in the periods of euphoria of capital inflows, trade expansion and terms-of-trade improvements that crises are incubated. Crisis prevention is thus, essentially, an issue of the adequate management of periods of euphoria.

In this regard, regulations on capital inflows may be essential to avoid unsustainable exchange rate appreciation during booms. Although some appreciation may be inevitable and even an efficient way to absorb the increased supply of foreign exchange, an excessive revaluation may also generate irreversible "Dutch disease" effects. The regulation of capital *inflows* thus plays an essential role in open developing economies as a mechanism for monetary and domestic credit restraint and for the avoidance of unsustainable exchange rate appreciation during booms. The nature of such regulations will be considered below.

---

54. The literature on national policies is extensive. See, among recent contributions, ECLAC (2000a, ch. 8); World Bank (1998a), Chapter 3; Ffrench-Davis (1999); Helleiner (1997); and Ocampo (1999, 2000b).

Regulations governing outflows may also play a role as a way to avoid overshooting interest or exchange rates during crises, which may have adverse macroeconomic dynamics, including the greater risk of domestic financial crises; they are also essential to put in place debt standstill and orderly debt workout procedures. It is essential, of course, that capital account regulations be used as a complement and not a substitute for fundamental macroeconomic adjustment.

As was pointed out in Section II, prudential regulation and supervision must take into account not only the micro- but also the macroeconomic risks typical of developing countries. In particular, due account should be taken of the links between domestic financial risk and changes in key macroeconomic policy instruments, notably exchange and interest rates. The risks associated with the rapid growth of domestic credit, currency mismatches between assets and liabilities, the accumulation of short-term liabilities in foreign currencies by financial intermediaries, and the valuation of fixed assets used as collateral during episodes of asset inflation must also be adequately taken into account. Depending on the operation, higher capital adequacy requirements, matching liquidity requirements, higher provisioning standards for due loans, precautionary provisioning rules or caps on the valuation of assets should be established. Moreover, given these macroeconomic links, prudential regulations should be strengthened during years of financial euphoria to take into account the increasing risks being incurred by financial intermediaries. These links also imply that the application of contractionary monetary or credit policies during booms (e.g., higher reserve requirements or ceilings on the growth of domestic credit) may be highly complementary to stricter prudential regulation and supervision. Moreover, due to the important externalities which large nonfinancial firms could generate to the domestic financial sector, particularly in the context of exchange rate depreciation, the external liability exposure of these firms should also be subject to some regulation. Tax incentives (e.g., tax on external liabilities or new borrowing, or limits on the deductibility of external interest costs or exchange-rate losses) and rules that force nonfinancial firms to disclose information on their external liabilities may thus be relevant complements to appropriate prudential regulation and supervision of financial intermediaries.

The experience of many developing countries indicates that crises are associated not only with high debt ratios but also with inadequate debt *profiles*.[55] The basic reason for that is that, under uncertainty, financial markets respond to gross—rather than only to net—financing requirements, or in other words, the rollover of short-term debts is not neutral in financial terms. This gives an essential role to "liability policies" aimed at improving debt profiles. Although improving the external debt profile should be the central role of such policies, there is a strong complementary between good external and internal debt profiles. Hence, excessive short-term domestic borrowing may force a government that is trying to rollover debt during a crisis to raise interest rates in order to

---

55. See an excellent recent treatment of this issue in Rodrik and Velasco (1999).

avoid capital flight by investors in government bonds. Also, excessively high short-term private liabilities increase the risks perceived by foreign lenders during crises, a fact that may induce a stronger contraction of external lending.

In the case of the public sector, direct controls by the Ministry of Finance are an appropriate instrument of a liability policy. Exchange rate flexibility may deter some short-term private flows and may thus partly operate as a "liability policy," but its effects are limited in this regard, as it is unlikely to smooth out medium-term financial cycles, which will be reflected in a parallel cycle of nominal and real exchange rates. Direct controls on inflows may also be an appropriate instrument to achieve a better private debt profile. An interesting, indirect price-based policy tool is reserve requirements on capital inflows, such as those used by Chile and Colombia in the 1990s. These requirements are a particular type of Tobin tax, but the equivalent tax rate (3% in the case of Chile for one-year loans and 10% or more in Colombia during the boom) is much higher than that proposed for an international Tobin tax. A flat tax has positive effects on the debt profile, as it induces longer-term borrowing, for which the tax can be spread over a longer time period, and is easier to administer. The effects of this system on the magnitude of flows have been the subject of a heated controversy. In any case, since tax avoidance is costly and short- and long-term borrowing are not perfect substitutes, the magnitude of flows—or, what is equivalent, interest arbitrage conditions—should also be affected.[56] A basic advantage of this instrument is that it is targeted at capital inflows and is thus a preventive policy tool. It also has specific advantages over prudential regulations that could have similar effects: it affects both financial and nonfinancial agents, and it uses a nondiscriminatory price instrument, whereas prudential regulations affect only financial intermediaries, are usually quantitative in nature and supervision is essentially discretionary in its operation.[57]

Simple rules are preferable to complex ones, particularly in underdeveloped regulatory systems. In this sense, quantitative controls (e.g., flat prohibitions on certain activities or operations) may be preferable to sophisticated price-based signals, but simple price rules such as the Chilean-Colombian system can also play a role. Any regulatory system must also meet an additional requirement: it must have adequate institutional backing. A *permanent* system of capital account regulations, which can be strengthened or loosened throughout the business cycles, is thus preferable to the alternation of free capital movements during booms and quantitative controls during crises. Indeed, the latter system may be totally ineffective if improvised during a crisis, simply because the administrative machinery to make it effective is not operative, and it may thus lead to massive evasion or avoidance of controls. Such a system is also pro-cyclical and leaves aside the most

---

56. Agosin (1998), Agosin and Ffrench-Davis (2000), Le Fort and Lehman (2000), Ocampo and Tovar (1998, 1999), and Villar and Rincón (2000).

57. Ocampo (2000a). Indeed, this instrument is similar to practices used by private agents, such as the sales fees imposed by mutual funds on investments held for a short period in order to discourage short-term holdings. See J.P. Morgan (1998), p. 23.

important lesson learned about crisis prevention: avoid overborrowing during booms and thus target primarily capital inflows rather than outflows.

Obviously, capital account regulations are not foolproof, and some developing countries may prefer to use policy mixes that avoid their use (e.g., more active use of fiscal and exchange rate policies, as well as alternative prudential regulations) or may prefer a less interventionist environment even at the cost of greater GDP volatility. Thus, the most compelling argument that can be derived from this analysis is the need to maintain the autonomy of developing countries to manage their capital accounts.[58]

There are actually no strong arguments in favor of moving towards capital account convertibility.[59] There is no evidence that capital mobility leads to an efficient smoothing of expenditures in developing countries through the business cycle and, on the contrary, strong evidence that in these countries the volatility of capital flows is an additional source of instability. There is also no evidence of an association between capital account liberalization and economic growth, and there are some indications that point in the opposite direction.[60] A simple way to pose the issue is to argue that, even if it were true that freer capital flows, through their effects on a more efficient savings-investment allocation process, have positive effects on growth, the additional volatility associated with freer capital markets has the opposite effect. The absence of an adequate international financial safety net is an equally important argument in this connection. Why should developing countries give up this degree of freedom if they do not have access to an adequate amount of contingency financing with well-defined conditionality rules, and no internationally agreed standstills and debt workout procedures? This is a crucial issue for countries without significant power in the international arena, for whom renouncing any possible means of crisis management is a costly alternative. Indeed, there are strong similarities between today's international financial world and the era of "free banking" at the national level: in the absence of central banks as lenders of last resort and officially managed bank rescue schemes, inconvertibility of private bank notes was a necessary legal alternative in the face of bank runs.

Similar arguments could be used to claim that there are no grounds for limiting the autonomy of developing countries to choose their exchange rate regime. There are certainly virtues to the argument that, in the current globalized world, only convertibility regimes or totally free-floating exchange rate regimes can generate sufficient credibility in the eyes of private agents. However, any international rules in this area would be unfortunate. The advantages and disadvantages of these

---

58. United Nations Task Force (1999) and Group of 24(2000b).

59. For a more extensive analysis of this subject, see United Nations Task Force (1999), UNCTAD (1998), Part One, Chapter IV, ECLAC (1998), Part III, IMF (1999), Eichengreen (1999), Griffith-Jones (1998), Grilli and Milesi-Ferreti (1995), Krugman (1998a, 1998b), Ocampo (2000a) and Rodrik (1998).

60. See, in particular, Eatwell (1996), Eatwell and Taylor (2000), Rodrik (1998) and, for Latin America, Ocampo (1999).

extremes, as well as of interventionist regimes in between the two, have been subject to extensive historical debate (and, of course, experience).[61] In practice, countries almost invariably choose intermediate regimes, a fact that can probably be traced back not only to the deficiencies of the extremes, but also to the many additional demands that authorities face.[62] The choice of the exchange rate regime has, nonetheless, major implications for economic policy that must be recognized in macroeconomic surveillance. Particularly, as we have noticed, domestic prudential regulations must take into account the specific macroeconomic risks that financial intermediaries face under each particular regime.

CONCLUSIONS

This paper has argued that the agenda for international financial reform must be broadened in at least two senses. First of all, it should go beyond the issues of financial prevention and resolution, on which the recent debate has focused, to those associated with development finance for poor and small countries, to overcome the strong concentration of private and even official financing in a few large "emerging" economies, and to the "ownership" of economic and development policies by countries. Secondly, it should consider, in a systematic fashion, not only the role of world institutions but also of regional arrangements and the explicit definition of areas where national autonomy should be maintained. These issues should be tabled in a representative, balanced negotiation process.

In the area of financial crisis prevention and resolution, a balance must be struck between the current emphasis on the need to improve the institutional framework in which financial markets operate and the still insufficient attention to or action on the design of appropriate schemes to guarantee the coherence of macroeconomic policies worldwide, the enhanced provision of emergency financing during crises, and the creation of adequate debt standstill and orderly debt workout procedures. In the area of development finance, emphasis should be given to the need to increase funding to low-income countries, including the use of multilateral development finance to support increased participation of low-income and small middle-income countries in private capital markets. The role of multilateral development banks in counter-cyclical financing, particularly to support social safety nets during crises, must also be emphasized. The enhanced provision of emergency and development financing should be accompanied by a renewed international agreement on the limits of conditionality and a full recognition of the central role of the "ownership" of development and macroeconomic policies by developing countries.

---

61. Velasco (2000) provides a recent survey of the issues involved.

62. The best conclusion on this subject is, thus, that reached by the IMF (2000a): "No single regime is appropriate for all countries or in all circumstances." See also ECLAC (2000b, ch. 2) and, for a recent defense of intermediate regimes, Williamson (2000).

It has also been argued that regional and subregional institutions should play an essential role in increasing the supply of "global public goods" and other services in the area of international finance. The required financial architecture should in some cases have the nature of a network of institutions that provide the services required in a complementary fashion (in the areas of emergency financing, surveillance of macroeconomic policies, prudential regulation and supervision of domestic financial systems, etc.), and in others (particularly in development finance) should exhibit the characteristics of a system of competitive organizations. The fact that any new order would continue to have the characteristics of an incomplete "financial safety net" implies both that national policies would continue to play a disproportionate role in crisis prevention and that certain areas should continue to be realms of national autonomy, particularly capital account regulations and the choice of exchange rate regimes. Regional institutions and national autonomy are particularly important for the smaller players in the international arena, which will gain significantly from competition in the services provided to them and from the maintenance of freedom of action in a context of imperfect supply of global public goods.

REFERENCES

Agosin, Manuel. 2000. "Fortaleciendo la institucionalidad financiera en Latinoamérica," *Temas de Coyuntura Series*, No. 9. Santiago, Chile: Economic Commission for Latin America and the Caribbean (ECLAC), October.

———. 1998. "Capital inflow and investment performance: Chile in the 1990s," *Capital Inflows and Investment Performance: Lessons from Latin America*, eds. Ricardo Ffrench-Davis and Helmut Reisen. Paris: OECD Development Centre/Economic Commission for Latin America and the Caribbean (ECLAC).

Agosin, Manuel and Ricardo Ffrench-Davis. 2000. "Managing capital inflows in Chile," in Stephany Griffith-Jones, Manuel F. Montes and Anwar Nasution, eds., *Short-Term Capital Flows and Economic Crises*. New York: Oxford University Press and United Nations University (UNU)/World Institute for Development Economics Research (WIDER).

Ahluwalia, Montek S. 1999. "The IMF and the World Bank in the New Financial Architecture," *International Monetary and Financial Issues for the 1990s*, Vol. XI. New York and Geneva: UNCTAD.

Akyüz, Yilmaz and Andrew Cornford. 1999. "Capital Flows to Developing Countries and the Reform of the International Financial System," *UNCTAD Discussion Paper*, No. 143, November.

Boorman, Jack and Mark Allen. 2000. "A New Framework for Private Sector Involvement in Crisis Prevention and Crisis Management," paper prepared for FONDAD's Conference on Crisis Prevention and Response: Where Do We Stand with the Debate on Reform of the International Financial Architecture? Ministry of Foreign Affairs. The Hague, June.

Calvo, Guillermo. 1998. "Contagion and Sudden Stops." Baltimore: University of Maryland, November, unpublished.

Camdessus, Michel. 2000. "An Agenda for the IMF at the Start of the 21st Century," *Remarks at the Council on Foreign Relations.* New York, February.

———. 1998. "Opening address at the Annual Meeting of the Board of Governors of the IMF," *IMF Survey,* vol. 27. 19 October.

Collier, Paul and John Willem Gunning. 1999. "The IMF's Role in Structural Adjustment," *Economic Journal* 109. November.

Cornia, Giovanni Andrea. 1999. "Social Funds in Stabilization and Adjustment Programmes," *Research for Action,* No. 48. Helsinki: United Nations University (UNU)/ World Institute for Development Economics Research (WIDER), April.

Council on Foreign Relations, Task Force Report. 1999. *Safeguarding Prosperity in a Global Financial System: the Future International Financial Architecture,* Carla A. Hills and Peter G. Peterson, chairs; Morris Goldstein, project director. Washington: Institute for International Economics.

Crow, John, Ricardo Arriazu and Niels Thygesen. 1999. *External Evaluation of Surveillance Report.* Washington, June.

Dai, Xianglong. 2000. "Meeting the Challenges of Globalization," *Address on the 21st Century Forum hosted by CPPCC.* Beijing, June 15.

Eatwell, John and Lance Taylor. 2000. *Global Finance at Risk: The Case for International Regulation.* New York: The New Press.

Eatwell, John. 1996. *International Financial Liberalization: The Impact on World Development,* UNDP-Office of Development Studies Discussion Paper, No. 12. New York: United Nations Development Program (UNDP), September.

ECLAC (Economic Commission for Latin America and the Caribbean). 2000a. *Equity, Development and Citizenship* (LC/G.2071(SES.28/3). Santiago, Chile, March.

———. 2000b. *Growth with Stability* (LC/G.2117(CONF.89). Santiago, Chile, October.

———. 1998. *América Latina y el Caribe: Políticas para mejorar la inserción en la economía mundial,* second version, revised and updated. Santiago, Chile: Fondo de Cultura Económica.

Eichengreen, Barry. 1999. *Toward a New International Financial Architecture: A Practical Post-Asia Agenda,* Washington, D. C., Institute for International Economics (IIE).

Feldstein, Martin. 1998. "Refocusing the IMF," *Foreign Affairs,* vol. 77, No. 2, March/ April.

Fischer, Stanley. 1999. "Reforming the International Financial System," *Economic Journal* 109, November.

———. 1998. "Reforming World Finance: Lessons from a crisis," *The Economist,* 19 October.

Ffrench-Davis, Ricardo. 1999. *Reforming the Reforms in Latin America: Macroeconomics, Trade, Finance.* London: Macmillan.

Gilbert, Christopher, Andrew Powell and David Vines. 1999. "Positioning the World Bank," *Economic Journal* 109, November.

Griffith-Jones, Stephany and José Antonio Ocampo, with Jacques Cailloux. 1999. *The Poorest Countries and the Emerging International Financial Architecture.* Expert Group on Development Issues (EGDI), Stockholm.

Griffith-Jones, Stephany. 1998. *Global Capital Flows, Should They Be Regulated?* London: Macmillan.

Grilli, Vittorio and Gian Maria Milesi-Ferretti. 1995. "Economic Effects and Structural Determinants of Capital Controls," *IMF Staff Papers,* vol. 42, No. 3, September.

Group of 24. 2000a. *Communiqué,* 15 April.

———. 2000b. *Communiqué,* 23 September.

——— 1999a. *Communiqué,* 26 April.

——— 1999b. *Communiqué,* 25 September.

Group of Seven. 1998. *Declaration of G-7 Finance Ministers and Central Bank Governors*, 30 October.

Helleiner, Gerry. 2000a. "Developing Countries in Global Economic Governance and Negotiations," in Deepak Nayyar, ed., *New Roles and Functions of the UN and the Bretton Woods Institutions*, forthcoming.

_____. 2000b. "External conditionality, local ownership and development," contribution to *Transforming Development*, Jim Freedman, ed. Toronto: University of Toronto Press.

_____. 1999. "Financial markets, crises and contagion: issues for smaller countries in the FTAA and Post-Lomé IV negotiations," paper prepared for the Caribbean Regional Negotiating Machinery. Kingston, Jamaica, January.

_____. 1997. "Capital account regimes and the developing countries," *International Monetary and Financial Issues for the 1990s*, vol. 8. New York: United Nations Conference on Trade and Development (UNCTAD).

IMF. 2000a. *Report of the Acting Managing Director to the International Monetary and Financial Committee on Progress in Reforming the IMF and Strengthening the Architecture of the International Financial System*, Washington, D.C., April.

_____. 2000b. *Report of the Managing Director to the International Monetary and Financial Committee on Progress in Strengthening the Architecture of the International Financial System and Reform of the IMF.* Washington, DC, September.

_____. 1999. *Report of the Managing Director to the Interim Committee on Progress in Strengthening the Architecture of the International Financial System.* Washington, DC, September.

_____. 1998. *Toward a Framework for Financial Stability*. Washington, DC.

IMF International Monetary and Financial Committee. 2000. *Communiqué*, 24 September.

IMF Interim Committee. 1998. *Statement*, 16 April.

J. P. Morgan. 1998. *World Financial Markets*. New York, 7 October.

Köhler, Horst. 2000. "Address to the Board of Governors of the IMF." Prague, 26 September.

Krugman, Paul. 1998a. "The Eternal Triangle." Cambridge, Massachusetts: Massachusetts Institute of Technology (MIT), unpublished.

_____. 1998b. "Curfews on Capital Flight: What are the Options?" Cambridge, Massachusetts: Massachusetts Institute of Technology (MIT), unpublished.

Larraín, Guillermo, Helmut Reisen and Julia von Maltzan. 1997. "Emerging Market Risk and Sovereign Credit Ratings," *OECD Development Centre Technical Paper*, No. 124, April.

Le Fort, Guillermo and Sergio Lehmann. 2000. "El encaje, los flujos de capitales y el gasto: una evaluación empírica," *Documento de Trabajo* No. 64, Central Bank of Chile, February.

Márquez, Gustavo. 1999. "Labor Markets and Income Support: What Did We Learn from the Crises?" Washington, DC: Inter-American Development Bank (IDB), unpublished.

Meltzer, Allan H. (chair). 2000. *Report to the US Congress of the International Financial Advisory Commission*, March.

Miyazawa, Kiichi. 1998. "Towards a New International Financial Architecture," *Speech at the Foreign Correspondents Club of Japan*, 15 December.

Mohammed, Aziz Ali. 1999. "Adequacy of International Liquidity in the Current Financial Environment," *International Monetary and Financial Issues for the 1990s*, Vol. XI. New York and Geneva: UNCTAD.

Ocampo, José Antonio. 2000a. "Reforming the International Financial Architecture: Consensus and Divergence," in Deepak Nayyar, ed., *New Roles and Functions of the UN and the Bretton Woods Institutions*, forthcoming.

_____. 2000b. "Developing Countries' Anti-Cyclical Policies in a Globalized World," *Temas de Coyuntura Series*, No. 13. Santiago, Chile: Economic Commission for Latin America (ECLAC), October.

_____. 1999. *La reforma de un sistema financiero internacional: un debate en marcha*, Fondo de Cultura Económica/Economic Commission for Latin America and the Caribbean (ECLAC).

Ocampo, José Antonio and Camilo Tovar. 1999. "Price-Based Capital Account Regulations: The Colombian Experience," *Financiamiento del Desarrollo Series*, No. 13. Santiago, Chile: Economic Commission for Latin America and the Caribbean (ECLAC).

_____. 1998. "Capital Flows, Savings and Investment in Colombia, 1960–96," in Ricardo. Ffrench-Davis and Helmut Reisen, eds., *Capital Flows and Investment Performance: Lessons from Latin America*. Paris: OECD Development Centre/Economic Commission for Latin America and the Caribbean (ECLAC).

Park, Yung Chul and Yunjong Wang. 2000. "Reforming the International Financial System and Prospects for Regional Financial Cooperation in East Asia," Department of Economics, Korea University and Department of International Macroeconomics and Finance, Korea Institute for International Economic Policy, June.

Rodrik, Dani. 1999a. *The New Global Economy and Developing Countries: Making Openness Work*, Policy Essay, No. 24. Washington, DC: Overseas Development Council.

_____. 1999b. "Governing the Global Economy: Does One Architectural Style Fit All?" paper prepared for the Brookings Institution Trade Policy Forum Conference on Governing in a Global Economy, 15–16 April.

_____. 1998. "Who needs capital account convertibility?" *Essays in International Finance*, No. 207. Princeton: Department of Economics, Princeton University.

Rodrik, Dani and Andrés Velasco. 1999. "Short-Term Capital Flows," paper prepared for the ABCDE Conference at the World Bank, *Mimeo*.

Rubin, Robert E. 1999. "Remarks of the Treasury Secretary on Reform of the International Financial Architecture to the School of Advanced International Studies," *Treasury News*, Office of Public Affairs, 21 April.

Stiglitz, Joseph. 1999. "The World Bank at the Millennium," *Economic Journal* 109, November.

Summers, Larry. 1999. "The Right Kind of IMF for a Stable Global Financial System," *Remarks to the London School of Business*, 14 December.

UNCTAD (United Nations Conference on Trade and Development). 1999. *Trade and Development Report, 1999* (UNCTAD/TDR/1999). Geneva.

_____. 1998. *Trade and Development Report, 1998* (UNCTAD/TDR/1998). Geneva: United Nations publication, Sales No. E.98.II.D.6.

United Nations Task Force of the Executive Committee of Economic and Social Affairs. 1999. *Towards a New International Financial Architecture, Report of the Task Force of the United Nations Executive Committee of Economic and Social Affairs* (LC/G.2054). Santiago, Chile: Economic Commission for Latin America and the Caribbean (ECLAC), March.

Velasco, Andrés. 2000. "Exchange-Rate Policies for Developing Countries: What Have We Learned?, What Do We Still Not Know?" *G-24 Discussion Paper Series*, No. 5. New York: UNCTAD/Harvard University, Center for International Development, June.

Villar, Leonardo and Hernán Rincón. 2000. "The Colombian Economy in the Nineties: Capital Flows and Foreign Exchange Regimes," paper prepared for the conference

"Critical Issues in Financial Reform: Latin American, Caribbean and Canadian Perspectives," organized by The Munk Centre for International Studies Programme on Latin America and the Caribbean, Toronto, University of Toronto, June.

White, William R. 2000a. "New Strategies for Dealing with the Instability of Financial Markets," in Jan Joost Teunissen, ed., *The Management of Global Financial Markets*. The Hague: FONDAD.

_____. 2000b. "Recent Initiatives to Improve the Regulation and Supervision of Private Capital Flows," paper prepared for FONDAD's Conference on Crisis Prevention and Response: *Where Do We Stand with the Debate on Reform of the International Financial Architecture?* The Hague: Ministry of Foreign Affairs, June.

Williamson, John. 2000. "Exchange Rate Regimes for Emerging Markets: Reviving the Intermediate Option," *Policy Analyses in International Economics*. Washington, DC: Institute for International Economics, September.

Wolfensohn, James D. 1998. "The Other Crisis," *Address to the Board of Governors*, Washington, D C: World Bank, 6 October.

World Bank. 2000. *Global Development Finance, 2000*. Washington, DC, May.

_____. 1999. *Global Development Finance, 1999*, Washington, DC, March.

_____. 1998a. *Global Economic Prospects and the Developing Countries, 1998–99*, Washington, DC, December.

_____. 1998b. *Assessing Aid*, World Bank Policy Research Report. New York: Oxford University Press, November.

Wyplosz, Charles. 1999. "International Financial Instability," in Inge Kaul, Isabelle Grunberg and Marc A. Stern, eds., *Global Public Goods: International Cooperation in the 21st Century*. New York: United Nations Development Program (UNDP), Oxford University Press.

4

...

Financial Regulation in a Liberalized Global Environment

*Jane D'Arista**

LIBERALIZATION AND ITS CONSEQUENCES

OVER THE LAST THREE DECADES, the use of technology has accelerated the process of innovation and brought about changes in financial markets and institutions that have undercut the effectiveness of regulatory frameworks in place in many nations since at least the immediate post-World War II period. The response of public authorities has generally been to accede to pressures from the private financial sector to dismantle the old framework. Thus, most of the changes in financial structure and regulation that have taken place have been driven by market forces rather than shaped through the deliberative processes of law and regulation. With one important exception—capital adequacy requirements for banks—there has been very little rebuilding of a rule-based foundation. And even capital adequacy standards are now being questioned by U.S. regulators as promoting evasive innovation that is making them ineffective, outmoded, and inefficient (Greenspan 1998; Meyer 1998). Their preferred strategy for ensuring soundness relies on self-regulation at the level of the individual institution through systems of internal controls. While the Basel Committee on Banking Supervision has played a critical role in providing guidelines and setting standards in many areas of supervision and regulation, the emphasis on internal controls has also been evident in

---

*This paper was prepared for the Conference on International Capital Markets and the Future of Economic Policy, Queens' College, University of Cambridge, April 16–17, 1998.

the guidelines and initiatives jointly adopted in the 1990s by its members who are central banks and banking supervisory authorities of the G-10 countries (BIS 1997). However, market practice determines the need for and content of internal controls.

This paper focuses on changes in financial markets and their implications for both the global financial system itself and the global economy. It offers a preliminary set of proposals to adapt prudential guidelines to current market structures and practices so as to moderate systemic risk resulting from liquidity crises associated with financial shocks. The ultimate goal of these or any other proposals for financial reform must be to avoid further falls in real output like those experienced by heavily indebted countries in the 1980s, Mexico in 1995, and East Asian countries in 1997. In addition, they must contribute to reducing the level of perceived risk in the system that, as Eatwell (1996) points out, produces a bias toward short-term investment in the private sector and a bias toward deflationary policies on the part of the public sector.

Liberalization: what and when

Two developments have dominated how financial markets were liberalized: the rise on the Eurocurrency markets in the 1960s and the shift from banks to portfolio investment in the 1980s.

The role of external (Eurocurrency) markets

The pattern of financial liberalization was established in its initial phase with the acquiescence of regulatory authorities—notably the Bank of England and the U.S. Federal Reserve Board—to the creation of external credit markets denominated in the major national currencies where transactions were conducted outside existing national regulatory and monetary policy frameworks. By the early 1960s, U.K. banks were accepting deposits and making loans denominated in dollars in London, and U.S. banks soon began to do the same. For both U.K. and U.S. banks, it was an escape from capital controls and permitted because transactions in dollars in London did not affect the balance of payments accounts of either country. It was also an escape from monetary and prudential restrictions—quantitative controls on the growth of credit in the case of U.K. banks; reserve requirements, interest rate ceilings, and deposit insurance premiums in the case of U.S. banks.

By the middle of the 1960s, however, the balance-of-payments effects of the so-called Eurodollar market became clear as credit tightening by the U.S. central bank in 1966 and 1969 pulled dollars out of offshore balances in Europe for investment in New York. As the Federal Reserve (Fed) lost control of the credit supply and pushed interest rates to (then) historically high levels to dampen demand, differences in the impact that domestic credit restraints have on different sectors of the economy when they attract sizeable capital inflows also became apparent. Large corporate borrowers that could afford to pay higher rates for short-term credit continued to borrow, operating at high levels of capacity and charging higher prices. Small businesses, the housing sector, consumers, and other borrowers that could not pass on the higher cost of credit stopped borrowing. Those that were customers of small and regional banks without external sources of funds lost all access to credit in the disintermediation that followed as domestic investors withdrew deposits from institutions subject to interest rate ceilings and moved funds into government securities (D'Arista 1976).

These waves of capital flows into the United States and subsequently into Germany, Switzerland, and other European countries in the late 1960s and early 1970s demonstrated how effectively the Eurocurrency markets could circumvent capital controls by making it possible for participants to change the currency denomination of loans and investments outside national markets in response to changes in interest rates and, subsequently, changes in exchange rates. While the abandonment of fixed exchange rates was certainly not desired by continental European countries, their inability to preserve effective control over interest and exchange rates as the Eurocurrency markets expanded resulted in acquiescence to the U.S. decision to float the dollar in 1973 and end the Bretton Woods system.

After the 1969 credit crunch, the Fed took the first of many successive steps in dismantling the existing regulatory framework by removing interest rate ceilings on large, negotiable CDs to make them competitive with Eurodollar deposits and minimize incentives for damaging flows between the domestic and external dollar markets. One effect of this action, however, was to enhance opportunities for interest rate arbitrage between the two markets and increase incentives for capital flows. Moreover, as the role of the Euromarkets in recycling OPEC current account surpluses further expanded offshore institutions' share in global lending, the cost of capital in U.S. markets rose to reflect the requirement that domestic borrowers compete with Third World governments in obtaining dollar loans (D'Arista 1994).

It is likely that their role in recycling OPEC surplus funds contributed to the U.S. government's willingness to overlook these and other negative aspects of the Euromarkets throughout the 1970s. The attraction of the Eurodollar market for U.S. investors—its freedom from exchange rate risk and the higher interest rate paid on deposits absent interest rate restrictions, reserve requirements, and deposit insurance premiums—was largely unnoticed as was the degree to which outflows from the United States fed liquidity into the external market. Rising inflation was attributed to the oil price increase and overly expansive U.S. monetary policy that was seen as reflecting the government's decision to fight unemployment. By the end of the decade, however, the falling dollar called attention to the excessive growth in external dollar liabilities and to the fact that the "round-tripping" of dollar deposits—their investment by U.S. residents in the unregulated market as deposits and reinvestment by foreign branches of U.S. banks as loans to domestic borrowers—had made the Fed's monetary policy operating targets obsolete.

In 1978, the Fed imposed reserve requirements on balances loaned by foreign offices of U.S. banks to U.S. residents. In the early 1980s, the Fed attempted to persuade other central bank members of the Basel Committee on Banking Supervision to join in imposing reserve requirements on all Eurocurrency liabilities of banks. The effort's failure put U.S. banks at a significant competitive disadvantage. Reserve requirements determine the ratio of total deposits that can be loaned out by a bank for profit. Since U.S. banks were subject to reserve requirements on lending within the domestic market from both domestic and (from 1978 to 1990) offshore offices, while foreign banks were only subject to U.S. reserve requirements if loans were made by offices located in the United States, a new channel for inflows opened in the 1980s—loans to U.S. businesses by foreign banks from their offshore offices—that was not even captured in balance of payments data until the end of the decade (McCauley and Seth 1992). Foreign banks could (and did) lower rates on credits to U.S. corporate customers, forcing U.S. banks to expand lending to other, more risky sectors, such as commercial real estate, and for highly leveraged transactions that financed changes in corporate control.

Meanwhile, U.S. banks were also experiencing a loss of competitiveness because their exposure to heavily indebted countries had lowered their credit ratings and raised their cost of funds. Moreover, Congress had added a provision to legislation increasing IMF funding in 1983 that required U.S. banking authorities to impose explicit capital requirements on banks as a cushion against losses and as protection for the deposit insurance fund. With other national banking systems operating with significantly lower capital requirements and lower funding costs, U.S. banks reshaped their operations, securitizing assets and moving away from traditional banking activities, expanding their fee-generating, off-balance sheet activities such as money management, and providing financial insurance against the interest and exchange rate volatility now embedded in the system.

The Fed's response to these developments was to shift its regulatory approach. It was a major player in negotiating the capital adequacy standards adopted by the members of the Basel Committee in 1988 and in promoting the adoption of a supervisory framework that placed responsibility on banks themselves to develop and monitor internal controls. In 1990, it eliminated reserve requirements on domestic time deposits and reduced the level of reserves required for demand deposits from 12% to 10% (FRS *Bulletin*). Given that capital requirements covered banks' consolidated operations and that all external deposits were time deposits, the only cost advantage remaining for Eurodollar operations was the relatively small premium paid to insure domestic deposits.

While the above narrative illustrates the ways in which liberalization was propelled by the decision to permit an unregulated external market for dollar assets and liabilities to function as a substitute and counterpoint for a regulated market, similar developments took place in other national markets. The continued existence and expansion of the Euromarkets underscored the costs of regulation—e.g., that there is more profit if a bank can lend out 100% of a deposit rather than only the 90% (or less) allowed under reserve requirements; that a given level of lending limits or liquidity or capital requirements similarly restrict growth and profits. Moreover, funding and lending in the Euromarkets made clear that differences in regulation that applied to banks in their national markets could affect their competitive positions in external markets and, thus, the competitiveness of national banking systems. As conditions for attracting capital to and retaining savings in national markets were increasingly affected by global developments, the competitiveness of a country's banking system became more important. As a result, pressures for financial deregulation intensified in tandem with competition in the global economic environment.

Pressures for liberalization came from many quarters—including the harmonization efforts of the European Community in later years—and had a strong ideological component. Nevertheless, concerns about monetary control, balance of payments positions, and the effects of changes in exchange rates on competitiveness also encouraged monetary authorities in industrialized countries to view reducing the cost advantages of external markets as a means to remove incentives for destabilizing capital flows. By the early 1990s, most of the regulatory restrictions that had made the cost advantages of the Eurocurrency markets so attractive —interest rate restrictions, lending limits, portfolio investment restrictions, and reserve and liquidity requirements—had been reduced or eliminated, as had the capital controls that were the original impetus for the creation of the external markets.

The shift to portfolio investment

In the 1980s, international credit flows shifted away from loans through large international banks to securities markets, there were larger flows between national markets, markets became "far more closely integrated worldwide," and capital "much more mobile" (BIS 1986). By the end of the decade, these developments had intensified as a result of the removal of capital controls by many developed and developing countries, a wave of privatizations of state enterprises initiated by the Thatcher government in the United Kingdom in the early 1980s (culminating in the restructuring of Third World economies and formerly centrally planned economies in the 1990s), and the dramatic increase in foreign portfolio investment that these developments facilitated.

The increased dominance of foreign portfolio investment that became apparent in the mid-1980s reflected significant changes in saving and investment patterns in the national markets of the major industrialized countries. These changes were largely due to the growth of private pension plans. Because pooled funds held by such plans are invested primarily in securities, institutional investors—e.g., pension funds, life insurance companies, mutual funds, and investment trusts—became more important in channelling savings than banks and other depository institutions in some of the major industrial countries. In the United States, for example, the share of total financial sector assets held by institutional investors rose from 32% in 1978 to 52% in 1993, while the share of depository institutions fell from 57% to 34% over the same period (FRS *Flow of Funds*).

Although the rising dominance of pooled funds as channels for savings is particularly pronounced in the U.S. and U.K. financial markets, the growth in the assets of institutional investors in Canadian, German, and Japanese markets is no less significant. Measured as a percentage of GDP, their assets doubled over the period from 1980 to 1994 in four of these countries and almost doubled in Canada. In 1993, the assets of U.K. institutional investors rose to 165% of GDP and those of U.S. investors to 125% of GDP (IMF 1995). As their assets expanded, institutional investors' diversification strategies increasingly included cross-border investments. Cross-border transactions in bonds and equities among the G-7 countries (excluding the United Kingdom) rose from 35% of GDP in 1985 to 140% of GDP in 1995 (BIS 1996). For the United States, foreign portfolio investment accounted for over 65% of total U.S. net private capital outflows in 1990, rising to 77% in 1993 and falling to 38% in 1994 (FRS *Bulletin*), with more than 30% of new international investment by U.S. mutual funds going to emerging markets during 1990-1994 (World Bank 1997). The rise in total industrialized country foreign securities investment flows to emerging markets—from 0.5% in 1987 to 16.2% in 1993 (IMF 1995)—was equally dramatic.

Increased capital mobility, the liberalization of domestic financial markets, and shifts in credit flows to securities markets outside the direct influence of monetary policy have made implementing monetary policy more difficult in all countries (Federal Reserve Bank of Kansas City 1993). They have eroded central banks' ability to control the supply of credit, forcing them to rely more on their ability to change interest rates through open market operations to influence the demand for credit. However, as early as the 1969 U.S. credit crunch, it became apparent that efforts to control aggregate demand through open market operations would require that "…interest rates generally have to become higher and more variable" (BIS 1995). In the process, these three factors become powerful inducements for procyclical surges of foreign portfolio investment that undermine the policy objectives sought by the change in interest rates. Thus, the most damaging effect of the liberalization of global financial markets may be the loss of central banks' power to implement countercyclical policies.

The gaps in regulation

The shift to portfolio investment as the primary channel for savings has also further undermined regulatory strategies, including capital adequacy standards. Regulatory authorities still give primary attention to traditional banking activities, and banks remain the focus for capital adequacy and other prudential requirements. But the shift of savings to pension funds, mutual funds, unit trusts, annuities, etc. has left the average saver without adequate protection or a safety net comparable to that provided by deposit insurance programs. And the corollary role for deposit insurance in protecting the payments system is also inadequate because the limits on insured balances are based on assumptions about the balances of small savers rather than those of, say, the local hospital with daily payments on a much larger scale.

Effective oversight of payments systems and traditional banking activities is and will remain an important focus for regulation. Nevertheless, money management and trading are now the primary activities in the global system in terms of the volume of instruments and transactions. The extraordinary increase in banks' trading activities since the 1970s reflects this shift. The largest, most active and globally integrated markets are not national equity and bond markets but the over-the-counter (OTC) markets for foreign exchange and financial derivatives dominated by banks. Bank dominance of these markets poses particularly difficult questions in terms of regulatory standards because they have imposed their institutional culture on these markets, adapting market practices to the style of portfolio lenders. Thus, as dealers in these markets, they "hold" instruments even if the "portfolio" in which they are held is "off balance sheet."

As the style of trading in which banks engage becomes more pervasive across a wider spectrum of assets and institutions, the market system is being pushed backward, recreating conditions like those that prevailed in the United States before enactment of the securities laws. OTC markets are opaque, not transparent; they do not conform to the concepts or requirements for the disclosure necessary if investors are to make informed decisions. They are not public markets. There is no surveillance of trading practices and no system for making information on prices and the volume of transactions routinely and continuously available to the public. Above all, many of the instruments themselves are not readily tradable—a critical factor that undermines liquidity and contributes to concentrations of contracts within a relatively small circle of dealers. Concentrations necessarily occur when exposures must be hedged with new contracts because existing positions cannot be sold. Despite efforts to mitigate the potential repercussions of disruptions through netting agreements in derivatives contracts, these particular characteristics of the OTC markets increase the potential that disruptions resulting from inaccurate assessments of credit or market risk will escalate into systemic crises. However, can inaccuracy be avoided without transparency?

The proliferation of non-public markets prompted regulators to privatize monitoring and surveillance at the level of the individual firm. Beginning in the United States in the 1970s, with the requirement that banks devise effective checks in systems for recording foreign exchange transactions and positions (D'Arista 1976), these requirements are now a major component of the Basel Committee's core principles of regulation and apply to all OTC trading markets in which banks participate. The weakness in the strategy is its emphasis on the individual firm. It reinforces the lack of market transparency and increases the likelihood that, in the absence of effective external checks through clearing houses, systems for routing transactions that permit ongoing surveillance, or other forms of systemic oversight, gaps in a firm's recording and monitoring system may go unnoticed, resulting in large losses (Daiwa) or failure (Barings) and increasing the potential for systemic repercussions.

The increase in the trading activity of banks is an outgrowth of the rising importance of money management and its requirements for ancillary services. Derivatives, standby letters of credit, and commercial paper guarantees are all innovative instruments devised by financial institutions to provide a privatized system of financial insurance to their customers. Banks are the major players in providing guaranties because they have the power to create deposits by making loans when the guaranty is activated. It would appear that the credibility of these guaranties is supported by the application of risk-based capital requirements to off-balance-sheet positions of banks. However, support would only be effective in situations involving one or a few customers. In a wider liquidity crisis, banks' ability to raise new capital to support an expansion of assets and liabilities on their balance sheets would be limited or, possibly, nonexistent. Central banks would still be required to provide the backup needed to contain a downward spiral in asset prices.

The limited ability of capital adequacy requirements to support the vast system of private financial guaranties created by banks and other financial institutions points up one of the weakness of relying on capital adequacy as the new cornerstone for prudential regulation: like internal controls, they are a rational tool for regulating individual institutions but irrational in a systemic context. Capital requirements are not only likely to prove useless in a liquidity crisis but are also a dangerously procyclical instrument of macroprudential policy. The market will supply capital to the banking system in a boom and withhold it in a downturn. Thus, capital requirements will tend to act as a barrier to the effective implementation of countercyclical monetary policies. Efforts either to dampen economic activity by raising interest rates or to jump-start the economy in a downturn by lowering rates will not succeed if this asymmetry between banks' ability to raise capital and policy objectives persists.

Capital adequacy standards apply to banks' traditional business and to some off-balance-sheet activities, but they do not apply to the money management activities that are now a primary function of almost all segments of financial systems in developed market countries—banks, securities firms, insurance companies, mutual funds, and unit trusts. All these institutional segments are competing for opportunities to manage a larger share of pooled savings but there are differences in the products they offer and much larger differences in the ways they are regulated both within and between national markets. While those differences have important consequences for investors in the various national markets, the common thread is the absence of any effort to apply an across-the-board emphasis on soundness regulation to the regulatory structure for money management. Disclosure and the prevention of fraud are the primary objectives of regulation in developed securities markets; prudence, diversification, and suitability are the guidelines applicable to individuals and institutions that manage securities investments. But with so large a share of global savings invested rather than deposited—including those of the most vulnerable: the small or lower-income saver whose principal financial assets tend to be held in pension funds—the impact of a loss of confidence on market liquidity will affect larger and more diverse shares of the populations of many countries and cause greater economic dislocation.

There is also concern about the ability of central banks to find an appropriate channel to exercise their functions as lenders of last resort to contain market disturbances and halt a free-fall in prices. In the case of the OTC derivatives markets, finding a channel through which central banks can supply liquidity may be particularly difficult. It is likely that the Fed's role in providing liquidity to the foreign exchange market in 1975 by assuming and executing (at a loss) Franklin National Bank's foreign exchange book is the model that would need to be used again (D'Arista 1976).

Henry Kaufman pointed out in 1985 that the pendulum had swung toward an emphasis on the entrepreneurial responsibilities of financial institutions to reward shareholders by increasing profits and away from their previous emphasis on exercising their fiduciary responsibilities to depositors and borrowers and the economies in which they operate. The relevance of his remarks became even more apparent as the OTC derivatives markets expanded over the subsequent decade. Undermining the mutuality of the traditional banking relationship that links the profitability of the financial institution to the prosperity of its customers, many contracts sold in these markets are based on the premise that either the financial institution or its customer will accept the losses that result in the other's gain. However, as even isolated losses accumulate, the ultimate loss may be public confidence in the financial system.

These issues point to the final and most difficult issue involved in liberalization: the consequences of institutional failure. Capital adequacy standards rely on market forces to discipline banks by withholding capital and curtailing new lending. The market also determines the cost of institutions' funding in the global wholesale markets. A bank—or even a national banking system such as Japan's—will find these forces difficult to counter. Restoring soundness and confidence clearly takes longer and, in some cases, may not be possible. The higher cost of capital and funding for banks in which markets have lost confidence lowers their profitability and impedes their ability to grow out of problem loans and to compete in attracting better borrowers. As these conditions continue, banks—and even national banking systems—stagnate and many eventually will fail.

This outcome should come as no surprise. The market does not discipline only by withholding rewards. Its ultimate effectiveness rests on its ability to threaten or cause failure. While most national governments have adopted systems of regulation that include reliance on market forces, most nevertheless still view their financial systems as key industries in their economies and understand the disruption that financial failures cause. As Japan continues to cope with a financial system that, like savings and loan institutions in the United States in the 1980s, was not restructured to bear the brunt of global market forces, and East Asian countries confront sudden, dramatic collapses in their systems, there may be renewed interest in reconstituting an institutional and regulatory framework that can either reduce the number and frequency of financial failures or help insulate economies against their impact.

In the meantime, the most dangerous threat to the global financial system—its vulnerability to contagion—is not being addressed. In the past, the primary strategy to deal with contagion was compartmentalization. In countries with developed securities markets such as the United States, the United Kingdom, and Japan, restrictions on functions and products helped insulate different markets from spillover effects. Thus, as late as the 1987 market decline, funds withdrawn from equity and derivatives markets in the United States could be recycled through banks and loaned back to dealers and institutional investors (with the support of the Fed) to halt price declines. The effectiveness of this strategy in containing the crisis depended on the fact that banks were not significantly involved in trading or holding equities and not subject to the contagion that spreads as confidence is lost.

Compartmentalization also characterized the structure of so-called universal banking systems up through the late 1980s in the sense that these institutions operated in countries with relatively small or underdeveloped securities markets where traditional banking operations were the dominant financial activity. However, as discussed above, securities markets have become more important components of financial systems in almost all developed and many developing countries over the last decade. Thus, the activities of universal banks have taken on some of the characteristics of the U.S. financial conglomerates owned by commercial enterprises such as General Electric and the three major automobile manufacturers. While an informal group of banking, securities, and insurance supervisors has made recommendations (BIS 1995) for the improvement of supervisory practices in the area of information sharing among the various authorities and consolidated reporting by firms, the emphasis, again, is on capital adequacy and the adequacy of internal controls within components of the conglomerate. Thus, as in the case of banking, the initial focus of the regulatory framework for conglomerates is structured to address problems at the level of the individual financial function.

The interconnection risks that arise because of the melding of multiple functions within individual firms have already been made explicit by complex derivative contracts that link performance across several markets. It is a new source of risk and one that poses a uniquely powerful threat to systemic stability. The absence of strategies to deal with the risk of contagion that is inherent in tighter linkages between markets and products constitutes the major gap in regulation in the liberalized global environment.

REGULATORY PROPOSALS TO REDUCE THE NEGATIVE IMPACTS OF LIBERALIZATION

Four measures would greatly reduce the adverse effects of liberalization: risk-weighted capital charges on pooled funds, creating a public emerging market international investment fund, reforming savings and transaction deposit insurance, and increased reserve requirements and other steps designed to improve monetary control.

Risk-weighted capital charges for pooled funds

As noted above and discussed more fully in a previous paper (D'Arista and Griffith-Jones 1998), certain soundness strategies for regulating savings held in pooled funds and invested in securities now seem more appropriate than in the past. While requirements for diversification do apply to mutual funds, explicit liquidity requirements such as levels of cash reserves or provisions for insurance coverage to promote confidence do not apply. Nor, until recently, has attention been paid to the impact of national macroeconomic developments—known by securities regulators as "market risk" and including variables such as exchange rates and interest rates—on securities markets. However, as institutional investors have assumed a dominant role in financial markets, and as differences between banks and pooled funds blur, some of the strategies used to promote public confidence in banks are beginning to be adapted to the needs of mutual funds in the United States.

The most important of these adaptations is contained in legislation enacted in the United States in 1991 (12 CFR, 201.3(d)), that permits any individual, partnership, or corporation to borrow from Federal Reserve Banks using U.S. government securities as collateral if the failure to lend would adversely affect the economy, and permits loans against collateral other than U.S. government securities with the affirmative vote of five of the seven members of the Federal Reserve Board of Governors. In short, the 1991 Act not only gives securities markets explicit access to the lender of last resort, it also expands the types of collateral against which the Fed can lend in an emergency to include corporate stocks and bonds—securities in which banks cannot invest depositors' funds under current U.S. law.

The enactment of this measure resulted largely from the 1987 and 1989 market declines and reflected concern about their potential to damage the U.S. economy. Certainly, as former Federal Reserve Board Chairman Marriner Eccles had already noted in the 1930s, in an emergency there is no source of liquidity "…except that liquidity which can be created by the Federal Reserve or the central bank through its power of issue . . ." (U.S. Congress, 1935). Nevertheless, central banks historically have used their emergency powers sparingly and the requirement that five members of the Board approve loans collateralized by assets other than U.S. government securities suggests that interventions to halt a market disruption would be weighed carefully and occur infrequently.

Meanwhile, market participants are concerned about assuring that sources of liquidity are available under volatile conditions that may not be seen as damaging to the U.S. economy and would not activate the Fed to supply resources. Gaps between the timing of outflows for redemptions of shares and the receipt of funds from sales of securities are frequent and have raised concerns about redemption and settlement risks among U.S., U.K., and international organizations and regulators. Particularly in the United States, the industry itself has been involved in putting in place backup sources of liquidity such as interfund lending using repurchase agreements within a family of funds, the creation of money market "funds of funds" within a family of funds, and committed lines of credit from banks. "With the increased specialization and internationalization of mutual fund portfolios," one large family of funds explained, "the industry is appropriately giving greater attention to alternative methods for funding redemptions during periods of market volatility" (SEC March 1995). The U.S. Securities and Exchange Commission (SEC) has also indicated greater concern about liquidity in this context. It now "urges money funds to monitor carefully their liquidity needs in light of the shorter settlement period" and to consider the percentage of the portfolio that will settle in three days or less, the level of cash reserves, and the availability of lines of credit or interfund lending facilities when doing so (SEC March 1996).

The time gap between redemptions of shares and settlement of securities sold has also focused investor interest on the level of cash reserves of individual funds or types of funds (McGough 1997). This concern has been heightened by the potential for increased redemptions during a market decline (Kinsella 1996). In such a period, gaps between the timing of redemptions and settlement would create a scramble for funds that might exacerbate price declines. As these developments and discussions involving U.S. mutual funds indicate, finding alternative sources of liquidity for securities investment funds is a priority issue even when a fund's portfolio is invested in domestic assets. The problem becomes larger when cross-border holdings are involved, particularly holdings in emerging market countries.

The U.S. experience to date suggests two potential solutions to the problem. One would be purely market based, using the "fund of funds" created by the enormous—$416 billion in assets at that time (Gasparino and Jereski 1996)—Fidelity family of funds (SEC August 1996) as a model for the industry as a whole. This would allow all mutual funds to buy shares in an "umbrella," or "top," fund whose shares would not be sold to the public. The "fund of funds" would invest in highly liquid money market instruments that would be sold to redeem the shares of mutual funds seeking liquidity to fund redemptions by public shareholders. In addition, the "fund of funds" would be authorized to invest for short periods in the shares of funds that had exhausted their redemptions, up to a given amount (proportional to the size of their portfolios), if other means for funding redemptions were not available.

One problem with using the Fidelity model is that market declines and disruptions may affect all participating institutions at the same time. Moreover, its contribution to maintaining public confidence in markets may be limited. Unlike deposit insurance for banks, this type of liquidity facility will not guarantee that shares can be redeemed without losses. Nevertheless, if it were seen as contributing to public confidence that a market recovery would occur, it could reduce shareholder redemptions and cushion the downward spiral of price declines that make a market recovery and the restoration of confidence more difficult. It might also give the central bank more time to assess the situation, making it less likely to miss the point at which prompt action could halt the downward spiral of redemptions, securities sales, and price declines.

Another potential solution to the problem of providing liquidity to mutual funds and other pooled funds is to require that some portion of their cash reserves be placed in the form of interest-bearing deposits in commercial banks as a prudential capital charge. The immediate availability of such deposits would reduce market volatility associated with the timing of settlement, particularly in situations involving large redemptions. They would also constitute a first line of defence for access to liquidity in the event of a significant market decline. As a pre-assessment vehicle, the capital charge proposal is preferable to post-assessment arrangements such as bank credit lines, in that deposit withdrawals by pooled funds would likely be redeposited in banks by sellers of securities rather than trigger a credit expansion that would require validation by the central bank without regard to current monetary policy objectives.

The use of the term "capital charge" in discussions of liquidity facilities for mutual funds and other pooled funds refers to their particular structure as inter-mediaries for direct investment. Because shareholder capital backs 100% of the invested assets, neither the capital nor provisioning requirements applicable to banks are directly applicable to these funds. Nevertheless, the need for defined sources of liquidity for pooled funds has become more apparent as their role in financial markets has expanded and concern about the potential for shareholder withdrawals to precipitate serious market disruptions in the form of sharp de-clines in asset prices has increased.

Imposing capital charges on pooled funds in the form of required, segre-gated cash reserves deposited in commercial banks to ensure defined sources of liquidity may also contribute to removing distortions in the financial industry by reducing the cost advantage pooled funds now enjoy in competing with banks to attract savings. Making the capital charge comparable to the capital adequacy requirements that apply to banks under the Basel Accord would somewhat lower earnings for some pooled funds that do not maintain adequate levels of cash reserves since interest bearing deposits may earn less than other financial assets in which funds invest. However, bank deposits are payable at par and that, to-gether with the introduction of an industry-wide standard, might increase inves-tor confidence and lower the potential for runs.

A capital charge requirement would also provide a structure that would make risk weighting—another essential element in capital adequacy regulation for banks—applicable to pooled funds. Risk weighting would require that money managers perform a more rigorous analysis of their investments—particularly cross-border investments—and of market and other risks than have been under-taken to date. Such a requirement should also be linked to increased disclosure, so that central banks would be able to monitor investment flows for monetary policy purposes, assess systemic concentrations of investment that result in "bubbles," and change weights as needed to reflect changes in risk.

Creating a public international investment fund for emerging markets

Given the immense growth in the assets of institutional investors in industri-alized countries and the fact that several developing countries—Chile, Malaysia, Singapore and, prospectively, Mexico—have adopted compulsory saving schemes involving funded pension plans, it is clear that foreign portfolio investment will continue to be an important channel for international capital flows. It is also obvious that emerging markets will continue to need the support of foreign investment even if these countries increase the amount of domestic savings. Thus, efforts must be made to address the problems associated with foreign portfolio investment flows—in particular, large and rapid changes in asset prices and the speed with which outflows can precipitate a crisis affecting both securities and exchange markets—and to assert control over the procyclical surges in flows that have weakened central banks' ability to implement monetary policy.

Establishing an investment fund for emerging markets managed by a public international financial agency would make a substantial contribution toward stabilizing foreign portfolio investment flows. Structured as a closed-end investment fund, it would issue its own liabilities to private investors and buy stocks and bonds of private enterprises and public agencies in developing countries in consultation with their governments. The proposed fund could be capitalized by purchasing and holding government securities of the major industrial countries in amounts determined by the percentage of shares in the fund held by residents of those countries. This would provide a basic guaranteed return to investors, denominated in their own currencies, in addition to their share of dividends or returns on investments in emerging-market securities.

As a closed-end fund, the proposed fund's shares could be bought and sold freely in many markets and many currencies. Although the value of the fund's shares would fluctuate, it would not have to sell the underlying portfolio in response to a fall in the price of its shares. This would protect emerging markets from the abrupt fluctuations in capital flows that have been associated with foreign portfolio investment in the 1990s and would help moderate changes in the prices of securities in their domestic markets caused by external developments. The proposed fund's investment objectives would focus on the longer-term economic performance of enterprises and countries rather than short-term financial performance. Meanwhile, the value of the fund's capital would be explicitly guaranteed by the institutional investors' own governments because it would be invested in their obligations. This would add stability by providing a floor against losses for the beneficiaries of pension and other pooled funds whose savings are at risk.

The creation of a public international investment fund would reduce the need for capital controls to moderate inflows, especially in countries that choose to accept foreign portfolio investment solely through the proposed fund. It would also provide an appropriate channel for capital outflows from developing countries when the objective is a reasonable level of diversification of savings, particularly those held in newly established pension funds. Moreover, investments in shares of the proposed public international investment fund could help minimize problems that may emerge as public or private institutional investors in developing countries acquire the skills needed to manage large pools of funds. The creation of such a channel could significantly reduce the cost of information needed to put together a balanced and diversified portfolio and contribute to solving the problems associated with lack of disclosure by domestic issuers in these markets.

The powers and functions incorporated in the charter of the World Bank—including its mandate to facilitate private investment in developing countries and its ability to issue its own liabilities in global capital markets—make this institution the most appropriate existing agency to manage the operations of the proposed fund. Creating a public international investment fund is entirely consistent with the original and ongoing objectives of the Bretton Woods institutions and, given the shift in channels for international capital flows and the effects of this shift on the economies of developing countries, a review of current programs for extending assistance to these countries is long overdue.

Reforming and reconstituting public financial guaranty programs

Federal deposit insurance for commercial banks and thrift institutions was authorized in the United States in the 1930s after decades of debate and experimentation with state programs. The success of these funds in restoring confidence in depository institutions after the wave of bank failures in the early years of the Depression was seen by economists as the "most important structural change in the banking system" (Friedman and Schwartz 1963) and a fundamental contribution to U.S. monetary and financial stability (Galbraith 1975). The growing perception of deposit insurance as the cornerstone of financial stability and its record in providing protection at minimal cost led to the creation in 1970 of federal insurance funds for credit unions and securities firms (the Securities Investor Protection Corporation), state guaranty funds for insurance companies, and the Pension Benefit Guaranty Corporation in 1974.

The adoption of deposit insurance programs in other industrial counties began in the 1960s with West Germany's creation of a voluntary private system based on contributions from participating institutions. A compulsory semiofficial program was created in Japan in 1971, followed by a series of compulsory, officially administered programs inaugurated in Holland (1979), Great Britain (1982), Belgium (1985), and Ireland (1989). Spain instituted a voluntary officially administered program (1977), and France (1980) and Italy (1987) covered customers of their state-owned banking systems under private programs—compulsory for France, voluntary for Italy (Dufey and Giddy 1994).

One of the common elements in all these programs is that they insure institutions rather than their customers. Therefore, they have become a procyclical influence within the regulatory framework in an environment of increasing financial fragility. With the focus of these programs on protecting the deposit insurance funds and minimizing losses to taxpayers, charges for premiums are lowered or eliminated in a boom when few banks fail and raised in a recession when the number of problem banks rises. In the United States, for example, bank failures and rising ratios of nonperforming loans in the early 1990s prompted a sharp increase in deposit insurance premiums from 12 cents to 19.5 cents per $100 of deposits in January 1991 and then to 23 cents by midyear 1992. These increases fell most heavily on community and regional banks without access to non-insured foreign deposits, reducing their profitability and/or lowering the interest rates they paid to depositors. The lower interest rates on deposits not only limited banks' ability to attract funds, but also encouraged outflows to Euromarkets where rates on non-insured deposits were higher. Thus, they contributed to the stagnation in bank lending that was a factor in prolonging the recession (D'Arista 1994).

The system of insuring institutions has led to distortions in regulatory emphasis as well. Regulatory objectives have tended to move in the direction of fostering institutional profitability. Profitability is certainly an important measure of the soundness of institutions and, in the normal course of events, constitutes an additional umbrella of protection for depositors. However, insuring institutions in periods of financial and economic instability or weakness means that institutional profitability is the only source of protection, short of the taxpayer, as profitability becomes the major determinant of the viability of the insurance fund itself. Thus, priority status is given to the entrepreneurial activities of depository institutions in pursuit of earnings. At the same time, their depositors and shareholders have been assumed to have primarily entrepreneurial objectives as well—to be more concerned with interest earnings and the rising values of shares than with the safety of principal or the possible consequences of failure for tax liability.

The search for stable profits in an unstable financial and economic environment necessarily requires an unending game of innovation. Financial institutions and their regulators have focused on guessing what new products, powers, or markets are most likely to ensure continued profitability. However, financial innovation, whatever else it has done, has not lowered the level of fragility in the system and has not demonstrated that it can guarantee profits in periods of economic weakness.

Constructing a system that will minimize taxpayer liability in the context of financial and economic instability requires shifting insurance coverage and its cost from institutions to individuals. Posing a choice as to who pays the premiums for deposit and other forms of financial insurance clarifies the issue of who gets protection. If the financial institution pays the premiums, it is insured. It is the client of the insurance agency, and its depositors are relegated to the role of nominal beneficiaries. This has tended to encourage a save-the-institution mentality on the part of insurance agencies and governments. Of course, depositors too are protected in this process. But only up to a point—the point at which the losses of institutions exceed the pool of funds their premiums have created. At that point, the depositors lose because the benefit of their protection will be taxed away.

An alternative proposal for protecting savings

A fair and rational system for protecting savings would include several essential elements outlined here in a U.S. context that could be adapted to the needs and systems of other countries as well:

• All individuals and households would be required to purchase financial guaranty insurance to cover savings up to a given amount. They would do this by accepting a lower rate of interest on insured assets than could be earned on uninsured assets. The lower rate would reflect the deduction for the insurance premium. A compulsory system is necessary to ensure that all savers are covered, reserves are adequate, and liability for losses is fairly distributed.

• Covered assets could be held in a variety of accounts in federally regulated institutions: bank, thrift, or credit union deposits; mutual funds, annuities, and pension plans. A financial guaranty program must focus on all channels for savings if it is to offer adequate protection for the average saver, whose primary savings are deferred income that may be invested in pools or other vehicles chosen by employers.

• Premiums would be collected from the interest or gains on covered savings assets, offset by a full tax deduction. The amount of the premium would be deducted by the institution and paid directly into the insurance fund before the accrued interest or gains are credited to the saver's account. Statements on premiums paid would be added to reports on earnings and filed with the individual's tax return as a deductible item. A compulsory system involving individuals will work only if paying premiums is relatively automatic and painless; that is, if it does not involve earned income.

• The amount of savings in the various accounts of individuals would be reported to the Internal Revenue Service by financial institutions, as is currently done. Records of aggregate savings of individuals and households based on social security numbers would be maintained by the insurance fund.

• Insurance reserves would be invested in U.S. government obligations as they are now in the United States. Continuing this practice under a regime in which individuals pay premiums clarifies the relationship between their roles as savers and as taxpayers. Because the assets of the fund are those for which savers-taxpayers are already liable, savers' premiums will reduce their tax liability if failures are contained. If failures exceed acceptable levels and seriously deplete reserves, the impetus for action to address problems will be enhanced by a tax liability that kicks in earlier in the slide.

This basic framework could be elaborated or modified to add flexibility to meet the needs of individuals and households rather than those of institutions. For example, coverage could be expanded for households on the basis of the number of dependents; small savers could be relieved of all but nominal premium payments for accounts under a certain amount. Obviously, the savings of individuals and households will grow over time and may exceed the maximum amount covered by insurance. This should not be a significant problem for older or more affluent households except in a period of rising inflation. The amount of coverage should be reviewed periodically to ensure that there has been no significant erosion in purchasing power. If there has been, raising the level of coverage will automatically increase the flow of premiums into the insurance fund and maintain the needed ratio of reserves to liabilities.

Protecting transactions balances

Before considering a financial guaranty program that protects funds needed for current transactions, one must accept a fundamental premise: it is unrealistic to limit insurance coverage for accounts that are necessary to sustain economic activity. The current limits on coverage in all countries with deposit insurance programs are inadequate in the case of employers, whether it be for large or small businesses, farmers, nonprofit organizations, or state and local governments. If payrolls are not met, the interruption of payments down the line will result in a widening circle of losses. In the case of regional or money center banks that have large customers and hold clearing balances for other financial institutions, inadequate coverage of transactions balances can result in even broader repercussions, causing dislocations to any number of communities or to whole nations. Because these repercussions are so destructive, the too-big-to-fail approach has become a reality under the current system.

But the current system fails to take into account the differences in protection needed for savings and transactions balances and the fact that, in the case of transactions accounts, the criterion for too-big-to-fail responses should be the size and economic functions of depositors. A more effective and, in the context of economic disruption, affordable means for safeguarding transactions balances requires that coverage be unlimited regardless of the multimillion dollars involved; that insured transactions balances be clearly defined as non-interest bearing demand deposits in federally regulated depository institutions that are payable at par with no limit on the number of withdrawals; that interest foregone would be assumed to be equivalent to that on Treasury bills and would be paid by institutions into the insurance fund after deducting a reasonable percentage of profits on the assets in which these funds are invested; that, like the fund for savings, premiums would be invested in U.S. government securities and transactions balances invested in segregated pools of loans and investments that meet the highest standards in terms of quality, liquidity, and diversity.

One of the more important benefits of transferring insurance coverage from institutions to customers is that it better accommodates the current framework in which market forces play a substantial role in regulating institutional behavior and outcomes. With individual savers and the payments system adequately and independently protected, markets can exercise discipline in precipitating failure without interference from government. Indeed, in the United States, the government itself is assumed to have a role in precipitating failures as it exercises its responsibility under current law to take prompt corrective action to close institutions whose capital has fallen below a statutory minimum level. That responsibility could be incorporated into the reform proposal offered here by requiring that any institution that fails to meet accepted standards within a set period of time would no longer be licensed to accept transactions balances or insured funds of savers. Customers would be notified to withdraw funds and would, in effect, participate in an organized run on the institution.

Admittedly this could be seen as an effect of the proposed reform that might damage institutions' ability to attract shareholder capital as compared with the current system of insuring institutions which encourages the too-big-to-fail protective responses of regulators and thus reassures shareholders. However, withdrawing an institution's license to accept insured funds will heighten awareness of the need for effective regulation to promote the stability and continuity in financial systems that sustains the confidence of customers, taxpayers, and share-holders alike.

Strategies to improve monetary control

Among the more radical outcomes brought about by liberalization is that procyclical forces have reemerged as determinants of developments in financial markets after half a century of public sector commitment to moderating their effects. The evolution and refinement of effective tools to moderate the supply and demand for money and credit in the post-World War II era contributed to financial stability by preventing excessive increases/decreases in debt and wide fluctuations in interest and exchange rates, and supported other public and private sector initiatives that contributed to the remarkable increase in economic growth that characterized that period. As the effectiveness of these tools has weakened, the ability of monetary authorities to implement countercyclical policies has been undermined, eroding the stability of financial markets and creating conditions that impede economic growth. To reinstate the degree of monetary control necessary to reestablish financial stability in both national and global markets, central banks will need to recreate or adapt existing tools that directly influence the supply side of money and credit markets.

As discussed, liberalization has weakened central banks' leverage in implementing policy objectives by removing quantitative restrictions on bank lending—reserve requirements, lending limits, and interest rate ceilings. In the United States, for example, monetary strategies included substantial reliance on reserve requirements to influence both the supply of and demand for bank credit and thus banks' ability to create money. Since the volume of aggregate reserves in the banking system could only be changed by actions of the central bank in paying sellers or charging buyers for government securities in transactions conducted in the open market or, less frequently, through discount operations, the Fed exercised considerable influence over the availability of bank credit and the deposits it created as well as their cost. Moreover, since its open market purchases and sales changed the composition of portfolios of bank and nonbank investors and the price of Treasury bills, they also had the effect of changing demand for private securities and their price. With the removal of reserve requirements on savings deposits and a lower reserve rate for demand balances, reserve requirements are obviously a less important component of the monetary mechanism now than before these changes were completed in 1990 (FRS *Bulletin*).

However, the removal of reserve requirements is not the only development that has eroded the effectiveness of policy initiatives. Innovations such as repurchase agreements and cash management accounts have been used for many years to evade reserve requirements on demand balances, and the increased volume of offshore transactions also made banks a less reliable channel for the transmission of policy over the last several decades. Finally, the decline in the importance of bank credit in financing the economy as savings flows shifted to securities markets administered the final blow to the supply side of monetary control in the United States. Now, the Fed must rely on its ability to influence the demand for credit, using open market purchases and sales to induce changes in interest and exchange rates.

In the U.S. case, these changes initiate capital flows that move in the same direction as policy initiatives—that is, inflows in periods of rising interest and exchange rates; outflows as interest rates fall and the dollar declines. In countries whose currencies are not widely used in international transactions and are more subject to loss of confidence than the major OECD currencies, the reverse may occur—that is, rising interest rates may result in capital outflows and a falling exchange rate, while falling interest rates may signal increased financial stability, inducing inflows and currency appreciation. However, for many OECD countries, procyclical capital flows have resulted in surges in credit expansion and contraction, and in bubbles in asset prices followed by price deflation such as the widespread collapse in real estate values in the early 1990s.

Moreover, the procyclical inducements to capital flows in the major market countries have also influenced the direction of flows to and from emerging markets. As discussed above, the fall in interest rates in the United States in 1990 prompted outflows that reflected a substantial increase in foreign portfolio investment by U.S. residents, a rising share of which was invested in emerging markets over the next several years. In 1994, however, rising U.S. interest rates slowed that flow, helping to set the stage for the Mexican peso crisis at the end of the year (FRS *Bulletin*).

After the 1995 crisis, recognition of the damaging effects of capital flows for emerging markets prompted reconsideration of the appropriateness of the use of capital controls for these countries by the Bank for International Settlements (BIS 1995) and the International Monetary Fund (IMF 1995). However, the 1995 BIS view—that "it is now widely agreed that prudence in liberalizing capital inflows implies that short-term operations should not be free until the soundness of the domestic financial system is assured"—was dismissed by the private global financial sector which continued to press for liberalization.

While the use of capital controls by developing countries may offer some protection and should not be dismissed as a tool of stability, it is doubtful that global stability would be regained by attempts to reimpose capital controls in the major market countries. Only the reassertion of monetary control—defined as influence over both the supply and demand for money and credit—will create the conditions necessary for global financial stability. Reimposing quantitative restrictions on the growth of money and credit is a necessary beginning for that process. It is clear, however, that central banks must begin to identify and influence monetary and credit aggregates within the context of global—not national—credit markets. They must also create new policy tools that take into account the shift in investment and borrowing from banks to securities markets and ensure that they have better control over total credit by expanding their direct influence over the supply of credit provided by all major sectors of the financial system.

A proposal that would achieve these objectives would undoubtedly require a greater degree of harmonization of monetary policy tools and strategies among

OECD countries. Since most central banks now conduct open market operations in foreign exchange markets as well as national money markets, it would be reasonable to propose that reserve requirements be reinstated as the primary tool for influencing the supply of money and credit. However, requirements must apply to financial institutions' consolidated balance sheets, including offshore and foreign currency liabilities. This would ensure that the effectiveness of reserve requirements would not be eroded again by the transfer of intermediation to offshore markets. It would also give central banks a far more effective tool for stabilizing exchange rates than intervention alone can provide, given the limited amounts of foreign exchange reserves available to central banks for use even in concerted actions.

Reserve requirements must also apply to a wider variety of institutions—not just banks—to broaden the so-called "transmission belt" for policy implementation. All financial institutions or sectors whose operations result in flows or holdings of instruments that aggregate more than a given percentage of total financial assets/liabilities—5% to 10%, for example—would be required to hold reserves with central banks and in cash deposits with banks as described above. Thus, reserve requirements would cover all existing activities of both universal banks and financial conglomerates—banking and nonbank finance, securities and other trading operations, insurance, and pooled funds—and could be extended to cover new, innovative instruments or activities as they emerge and assume importance in national and global markets.

In summary, the objective of this proposal is to set a global standard for effective policy tools, increase the leverage of monetary authorities, and prevent evasions of policy constraints by some institutions and markets at the expense of others. Such a proposal is justified by the fact that the increasingly integrated and deregulated global financial marketplace that now dominates national markets and policy initiatives responds only to market performance. Its procyclical bias has a destructive potential that undermines stability and impedes sustainable growth. Efforts to restore stability can only succeed in an environment in which monetary policy regains its effectiveness as a countercyclical influence on financial markets.

REFERENCES

Bank for International Settlements. 1985. *Recent Innovations in International Banking*. Basel.
_____. 1992. *62nd Annual Report*. Basel.
_____. 1995. *65th Annual Report*. Basel.
_____. 1995. *The Supervision of Financial Conglomerates*. Basel.
_____. 1996. *66th Annual Report*. Basel.
_____. 1997. *67th Annual Report*. Basel. Board of Governors of the Federal Reserve System [FRS]. Table 1.15. "Reserve Requirements of Depository Institutions." *Federal Reserve Bulletin*. Washington. Various years.

_____. Table 3.10. "U.S. International Transactions." *Federal Reserve Bulletin*. Washington. Various years.

_____. *Flow of Funds Accounts*. Washington. Various years.

Dam, Kenneth W. 1982. *The Rules of the Game: Reform and Evolution in the International Monetary System*. Chicago: The University of Chicago Press.

D'Arista, Jane. 1994. *The Evolution of U.S. Finance, Vol. II*. Armonk, NY: M.E. Sharpe, Inc.

_____. 2000. "Globalization of Financial Markets," in Ray Marshall, ed., *Back to Shared Prosperity*. Armonk, NY: M.E. Sharpe, Inc.

_____. 1996. "International Capital Flows and National Macroeconomic Policies," Working Paper, Institute of Economic Research, Otaru University of Commerce, Otaru, Japan.

_____. 1976. "U.S. Banks Abroad," in *Financial Institutions and the Nation's Economy*, Book II. US House of Representatives, Committee on Banking, Currency and Housing. Washington: US Government Printing Office.

_____ and Stephany Griffith-Jones. 1998. "The Boom of Portfolio Flows to Emerging Markets and its Regulatory Implications", in Manuel Montes, ed., *Short-term Capital Movements and Balance of Payments Crises*. Helsinki: World Institute for Development Economics Research, forthcoming, 1998.

_____ and Tom Schlesinger. 1996. "Financial Restructuring and the U.S. Regulatory Framework," in Todd Schafer and Jeff Faux, eds., *Reclaiming Prosperity: A Blueprint for Reform*. Armonk, NY: M.E. Sharpe, Inc.

Dufey, Gunter and Ian Giddy. 1994. *The International Money Market*. Englewood Cliffs, NJ: Prentice-Hall, Inc.

Federal Reserve Bank of Kansas City. 1993. *Changing Capital Markets: Implications for Monetary Policy*, Proceedings of a Symposium Sponsored by the Federal Reserve Bank of Kansas City, Jackson Hole, WY, August.

_____. 1997. *Maintaining Financial Stability in a Global Economy*, Proceedings of a Symposium Sponsored by the Federal Reserve Bank of Kansas City, Jackson Hole, WY, August.

Friedman, Milton, and Anna Jacobson Schwartz. 1963. *A Monetary History of the United States, 1867–1960*. Princeton, NJ: Princeton University Press.

Galbraith, John K. 1975. *Money: Whence It Came, Where It Went*. Boston: Houghton Mifflin Co.

Gasparino, Charles and Laura Jereski. 1996. "Mutual Funds Tell Investors Not To Worry About Cash." *The Wall Street Journal*, July 16, p. C1.

Greenspan, Alan. 1998. "The Role of Capital in Optimal Banking Supervision and Regulation," remarks before the Conference on Capital Regulation in the 21st Century, Federal Reserve Bank of New York, February 26.

Griffith-Jones, Stephany. 1996. "The Mexican Peso Crisis," mimeo, Institute of Development Studies, University of Sussex, Brighton.

International Monetary Fund. 1995. *International Capital Markets: Developments, Prospects, and Policy Issues*. Washington.

Kaufman, Henry. 1985. Testimony before the Subcommittee on Telecommunications, Consumer Protection and Finance, U.S. House of Representatives Committee on Energy and Commerce, June 5.

Kinsella, Eileen. 1996. "Debate Rages: Would Mutual Fund Holders Jump?" *The Wall Street Journal*, December 11, p. C1.

McCauley, Robert N. and Rama Seth. 1992. "Foreign Bank Credit to U.S. Corporations: The Implications of Offshore Loans." *Quarterly Review, Spring,* Federal Reserve Bank of New York, New York.

McGough, Robert. 1997. "Quarterly Mutual Fund Review: How Much Cash Is Enough?" *The Wall Street Journal,* January 9, p. C1.

Meyer, Laurence H. 1998. "Financial Globalisation and Efficient Banking Regulation." Remarks before the Annual Washington Conference of the Institute of International Bankers, March 2.

U.S. House of Representatives, Committee on Banking and Currency. 1935. *Banking Act of 1935: Hearings on H.R. 5357, 74th Cong., 1st Sess.* Washington: US Government Printing Office.

U.S. Securities and Exchange Commission [SEC]. 1996. *Investment Company Act* Release No. 22107; 812-9956. August 5.

———. 1995. *Letter to SEC from T. Rowe Price Funds* (1995 WL 498696 [SEC]), July 31.

———. 1996. *Revisions to Rules Regulating Money Market Funds* (1996 WL 137266 [SEC]), March 21.

5

. . .

Capital Controls and the World Financial Authority

What Can We Learn from the Indian Experience?

Deepak Nayyar*

THE OBJECT OF THIS PAPER is to analyze the Indian experience with capital account liberalization and its regulatory structure of capital controls, to explore the interface between national regulation for cross-border capital movements and international norms that would be an integral part of the proposed World Financial Authority.

At the outset, it is essential to contextualize this exercise in a historical perspective. The reason is simple. India is a special case. For one, less than a decade after independence, India introduced a complex web of controls on trade flows and on other current account transactions. And even if the capital account was a negligible residual, controls were widespread. For another, private capital inflows into, or outflows from, India were no more than a trickle for almost three decades thereafter. Until 1980, concessional development assistance was almost the only form of foreign capital inflows. During the 1980s, India resorted to commercial borrowing in international capital markets and borrowing on commercial terms

---

*I would like to thank Gerry Helleiner and Lance Taylor for comments and suggestions on a preliminary draft. And I am particularly grateful to Venugopal Reddy, not only for meticulous comments and constructive suggestions on an earlier version but also for sharing his understanding which clarified my ideas on the subject. For perceptive questions on presentations of the ideas developed in this paper, I would also like to thank Ha-Joon Chang, John Eatwell, Edward Nell, José Antonio Ocampo, and participants in the discussion at the workshops for this volume.

from nonresident Indians.[1] Other forms of private foreign capital flows came only in the 1990s. Yet, there are several lessons that can be drawn from the Indian experience, particularly because there were extensive capital controls until not so long ago. And, even if private capital flows to some developing countries became significant earlier, such flows to the developing world have witnessed a phenomenal growth beginning in the early 1990s.

The structure of the discussion in the paper is as follows. The first section sketches the contours of capital account liberalization in India and presents available evidence on capital flows during the 1990s. The second section analyses the regulatory structure of capital controls that is discernible even if it is not explicit. Section three examines some exchange rate policy dilemmas that arise as a consequence of capital account liberalization, to consider their macroeconomic implications. The final section discusses the interface between actual national regulatory structures and potential international regulatory norms, to contemplate a framework for capital controls in the proposed World Financial Authority.

CAPITAL ACCOUNT LIBERALIZATION

The process of capital account liberalization in India needs to be situated in its wider context, for it was shaped by the reality in the national context and the conjuncture in the international context. In response to the external debt crisis, which surfaced in 1991, the government set in motion a process of stabilization, adjustment, and reform. Economic liberalization and structural reforms sought to increase the degree of openness of the economy through trade flows, investment flows, technology flows, and capital flows.[2] The process began with the introduction of convertibility on trade as quantitative restrictions on imports, except for consumer goods, were dismantled and tariff levels were reduced. It was combined with a liberalization of the regimes for foreign investment and foreign technology. And restrictions on international economic transactions, including capital movements, were progressively reduced. This process was also influenced by the gathering momentum of globalization which was associated with increasing economic openness in trade flows, investment flows and financial flows.

The introduction of convertibility in trade transactions was a first step towards the current account convertibility. In August 1994, India accepted Article VIII status, giving up its right to transitional arrangements under Article XIV at the IMF. This acceptance of convertibility obligations, however, was more de

---

1. It is worth noting that this borrowing was not done by the government. In effect, however, it carried a sovereign guarantee and was used almost entirely for balance of payments support. The commercial borrowing in international capital markets was mostly through state-owned public enterprises. The borrowing from nonresident Indians was through the mostly state-owned commercial banking system.

2. For a description and evaluation of structural reforms in India, see Nayyar (1996). And, for a somewhat different perspective, see Joshi and Little (1996).

jure than de facto. Some restrictions continued. The divergence between principle and practice was, in part, attributable to history and to inertia. But it was also attributable to a concern about capital outflows in the guise of current account transactions. Safeguards were, therefore, introduced in the form of regulations to govern transactions in the current account.[3] The requirement that export earnings should be repatriated and surrendered to the central bank was continued. This was not inconsistent with Article VIII obligations. Authorized dealers were allowed to sell foreign exchange only for underlying transactions that were identifiable and supported by some evidence. Indicative value limits were specified for different categories of transactions, particularly for invisibles, so that for any sale of foreign exchange above these limits banks, or authorized dealers, had to approach the central bank. And the central bank was assigned a proactive role in developing, as also monitoring, markets for foreign exchange. These were supportive safeguards. The fungibility between current account transactions and capital account transactions was substantively preempted by two restrictions. First, dollar denominated transactions between residents were prohibited. Second, offshore rupee transactions were prohibited. The object was to ensure that there would be no dollarization of the domestic economy and no internationalization of the domestic currency.[4] For such liberalization of transactions in the current account would, in effect, have meant a liberalization of transactions in the capital account.[5] And the Latin American experience highlights the macroeconomic problems that arise in even partly dollarized systems.

The approach to capital account liberalization in India was much more cautious. What was liberalized was specified. Everything else remained restricted or prohibited.[6] The contours of liberalization of the capital account were, in large part, shaped by the salutary lessons of the external debt crisis which surfaced in early 1991 and brought India close to default in meeting its international obligations. The balance of payments situation, then, was almost unmanageable. The vulnerability was accentuated by two factors: it became exceedingly difficult to roll over short-term debt in international capital markets and there was capital flight in

---

3. For a more complete discussion on the logic, as also nature, of these safeguards, see Reddy (1999).

4. Cf. Reddy (1999). Onshore dollar transactions between residents are an offense that is punishable under the legislation for the regulation or management of foreign exchange. Offshore rupee transactions are outside the jurisdiction of national laws but constitute an offense under the legislation if the settlement is done in India.

5. Such changes have been a common feature of economic liberalization in developing countries with profound implications for macroeconomic management. For, in dollarized systems, capital flight simply takes the form of speculating against national currency and converting it into dollars. And the central bank cannot act as a (dollar) lender of the last resort, beyond the limits set by its foreign exchange reserves, should there be a run on dollar deposits in the commercial banking system. These implications of dollarization are emphasized by Helleiner (1997).

6. This was, in fact, the opposite of the more common approach to capital account liberalization, elsewhere, in which restricted or prohibited transactions were specified while everything else was liberalized.

the form of withdrawals from deposits held by nonresident Indians.[7] This experience dictated the parameters of capital account liberalization.[8] It prompted strict regulation of external commercial borrowing, especially short-term debt. It led to a systematic effort to discourage volatile capital flows associated with repatriable nonresident deposits. Most important, perhaps, it was responsible for the change in emphasis and the shift in preference from debt creating capital flows to non-debt creating capital flows. To some extent, the liberalization that was introduced was also influenced by the perceived needs of the economy: financing the current account deficit, mobilizing resources for investment, and attracting international firms. But capital account convertibility remained, fortunately, in the realm of rhetoric. The Mexican crisis in late 1994 was, ironically enough, a blessing in disguise for India. It was not just an early warning signal. It dampened the enthusiasm of those who advocated capital account liberalization with a big bang. It lent support to those who questioned the wisdom of capital account convertibility that would have been premature in every sense.

The contours of capital account liberalization in India were determined by these factors. In sketching these contours, it is necessary to distinguish between different forms of private capital inflows and outflows, as there are important differences between these categories in the nature and the degree of liberalization. A complete description would mean too much of a digression. For our purpose, it would suffice to consider the contours of liberalization in the following categories of capital account transactions: direct investment, portfolio investment, external commercial borrowing, nonresident deposits, commercial banks, and capital outflows.[9]

The liberalization of the policy regime for *direct foreign investment* began in July 1991 with two major decisions. First, direct foreign investment with up to 51% equity was to receive automatic approval in selected high priority industries subject only to a registration procedure with the Reserve Bank of India. Second, a Foreign Investment Promotion Board was constituted to consider all other proposals for direct foreign investment where approval was not constrained by predetermined parameters and procedures. In effect, this created a dual route for inflows of direct foreign investment. The approval was automatic, within the specified parameters, from the Reserve Bank of India, while all other inflows were subject to approval through the Foreign Investment Promotion Board. The access through the automatic route has been progressively enlarged over time. Needless to add,

---

7. The factors underlying this capital flight from nonresident deposits and its macroeconomic implications are discussed, at some length, in Nayyar (1994). For an analysis of the external debt crisis, see Nayyar (1996).

8. Cf. Reserve Bank of India (1993).

9. The description that follows in this section is selective rather than exhaustive. It draws upon a wide range of sources. See, in particular, Government of India (1993), Nayyar (1996), Joshi and Little (1996), Bhaumik (1997), Reserve Bank of India (1997) and Reddy (1999). The changes in policies are also reported, in some detail for every year, in the *Economic Survey* published by the Ministry of Finance and the *Report on Currency and Finance* as also the *Annual Report* published by the Reserve Bank of India.

outflows associated with direct foreign investment are not subject to any restrictions, but this was so even in the era of capital controls.

The liberalization of the policy regime was extended to *portfolio investment* in September 1992. To begin with, foreign institutional investors such as pension funds or mutual funds were allowed to invest in the domestic capital market subject simply to registration with the Securities and Exchange Board of India. Guidelines issued by the Reserve Bank of India permitted such foreign institutional investors to invest in the secondary market for equity subject to a ceiling of 5% (subsequently raised to 10%) for individual foreign institutional investors in a single Indian firm with an overall limit at 24% of equity (later relaxed to 30% of equity at the option of the firm) for total foreign institutional investment in a single Indian firm. Similar access was provided to foreign institutional investors in the secondary market for debt. Soon thereafter, foreign institutional investors were also allowed investment or placement in the primary market, subject to approval from the Reserve Bank of India, with a maximum limit of 15% of the new issue. It was some time before foreign institutional investors were permitted investment in government securities in the primary and secondary markets. This came in 1996–97 and was subject to the ceiling for external commercial borrowing. Subsequently, in 1998–99, foreign institutional investors were also permitted to invest in treasury bills. There are no reserve requirements stipulated for, or taxes imposed on, these capital inflows. It also needs to be said that foreign institutional investors are allowed to repatriate the principal, the capital gains, the dividends, the interest, and any other receipt from the sale of such financial assets, without any restriction, at the market exchange rate. The income tax rate for dividends on such portfolio investment for foreign institutional investors is 20%, which is much lower than the corporate income tax rate for domestic or foreign firms. But foreign institutional investors are subject to a higher short-term capital gains tax at 30% compared with 20% for domestic investors, while the long-term capital gains tax is the same at 10%. Sales of such financial assets for the purpose of repatriation are absolutely unrestricted, provided the sales are through stock exchanges. However, disinvestment through any other route, or in any other form, requires approval from the Reserve Bank of India.

The option of portfolio investment was also made available to domestic corporate entities from September 1992. Indian firms were allowed access to international capital markets through global depository receipts or Euroconvertible bonds which converted debt into equity after a stipulated period. This access, however, was not automatic. Individual applications, drawn up in conformity with the general guidelines of the government, were subject to approval. This process remains unchanged.

Similar facilities for portfolio investment were subsequently extended to nonresident Indians (as individuals) and overseas corporate bodies, only for investment in shares or debentures through stock exchanges, on the same terms as foreign institutional investors, but subject to a ceiling of 5% for individual nonresident Indians or overseas corporate bodies in a single Indian firm.

Capital account liberalization in the sphere of *commercial borrowing* in international capital markets has been limited. If anything, commercial borrowing in the 1990s has been much more restricted than it was in the 1980s. It would seem that the experience of the external debt crisis in 1991 has left a lasting impression. There is a small component of commercial borrowing, for limited amounts or specified maturities, which is based on a simplified procedure of automatic approval by the Reserve Bank of India. However, the bulk of commercial borrowing requires case by case approval from the government where the decision depends upon the amount borrowed, the maturity period and the proposed utilization. Short-term debt, including trade-related credits for a period of more than 180 days, is subject to the most strict regulation and is approved case by case where approval depends upon the purpose, the amount, and the terms. In addition, there is an indicative overall annual ceiling on the total approvals for all such debt creating capital inflows which is decided upon by the government at the beginning of every financial year.

During the 1980s, there was a conscious effort to attract capital inflows in the form of *nonresident deposits*, through interest rates that were significantly higher than those in international capital markets or those in the domestic capital markets of industrialized countries from where these deposits originated.[10] The capital flight from nonresident deposits at the time of the external debt crisis in 1991 precipitated an already difficult balance of payments situation and brought India close to default. The lesson of this experience was not lost on the policy makers. During the 1990s, an attempt was made to exercise some control on capital inflows in the form of repatriable deposits held by nonresident Indians. The interest rate differentials which had characterized the 1980s have more or less disappeared, while interest rates ceilings are specified for different maturities. What is more, the exchange rate risk is no longer underwritten by the Reserve Bank of India and has to be borne either by the depositors or, subject to prudential limits, by the commercial banks. Thus, in the latter case, an exchange rate depreciation could impose losses on commercial banks so that their willingness and ability to accept such deposits is significantly reduced, unless there is a confidence that the exchange rate would be stable. In addition, from time to time, the Reserve Bank of India has sought to use variable reserve requirements, stipulated for commercial banks, to discourage or encourage these capital inflows.

Commercial banks, as a rule, are not allowed to accept deposits or to extend loans which are denominated in foreign currencies. There are a few exceptions. Deposits from nonresident Indians can be accepted, just as foreign currency accounts for exporters are permissible. Similarly, loans can be extended from the bank's corpus of nonresident deposits, just as foreign currency loans for exporters are permissible. As authorized dealers in foreign exchange, commercial banks are allowed to borrow up to $10 million, or 15% of their unimpaired capital (whichever is higher), without any conditions on end-use or repayment terms.

---

10. For a detailed discussion, see Nayyar (1994).

Similarly, commercial banks are allowed to invest up to $10 million, or 15% of their unimpaired capital (whichever is higher) in money markets abroad. Borrowing or lending abroad is almost prohibited for non-banking financial intermediaries, unless it is for specified end-uses stipulated in guidelines. The public sector financial institutions have somewhat more freedom to borrow abroad subject to prior approval from the government and prudential requirements specified by the Reserve Bank of India.

Apart from capital outflows associated with direct investment, portfolio investment, commercial borrowing, and repatriable nonresident deposits, the regime for *capital outflows* has not witnessed any significant liberalization. For individuals who are residents, capital outflows are prohibited. For individuals who are nonresidents, capital outflows are almost prohibited. For domestic corporate entities, capital outflows are possible but within strict limits that are stipulated. For Indian firms which wish to set up joint ventures or subsidiaries abroad, proposals for investments up to $15 million are cleared by the Reserve Bank of India through a near automatic route, but any investment in excess thereof is subject to a case by case approval and there is an aggregate annual ceiling for such approvals. For Indian firms which execute projects abroad, specific approval is needed from the Reserve Bank of India. And, for Indian firms which wish to establish offices abroad there is an entitlement for exporters but all others require approval from the Reserve Bank of India.

It is important to recognize that the structure of capital account liberalization, as also the nature of capital controls, has been shaped by history and influenced by experience in independent India. There has been a traditional concern about capital outflows. This is not surprising in a country that experienced persistent, almost chronic, balance of payments difficulties. It was also motivated by a desire to utilize domestic savings for domestic investment. It was reinforced further by a belief that the payments situation, as also the exchange rate, were vulnerable to volatile private expectations which could cause capital flight. The prohibitive controls on transactions in the capital account by residents or individuals were an integral part of this world view which extended much beyond India.[11] Similarly, controls on inflows of foreign investment were characteristic of most countries that were latecomers to industrialization, particularly those with a colonial past. In contrast, the approach to other forms of foreign capital inflows was much more open in India, as also elsewhere, for such inflows were seen as a means of easing macroeconomic constraints on growth. After some time, concessional development assistance was progressively replaced by borrowing on commercial terms in international capital markets.

The experience with debt-creating capital inflows during the 1980s, however, which led to the external debt crisis in 1991, reshaped attitudes to capital inflows. And, there was a significant shift as controls sought to limit the size and

---

11. Until not so long ago, the literature argued that capital account outflows should be the very last to be liberalized (Williamson, 1991).

change the composition of inflows. Short-term inflows were curbed and minimized. Medium-terms inflows through commercial borrowing came to be strictly regulated. Capital inflows associated with repatriable deposits from nonresident Indians, which had proved volatile, were systematically discouraged. The revealed preference for long-term over short-term capital inflows and for equity inflows over debt inflows makes perfect sense. It constitutes learning from recent experience in India. But the unqualified openness to what are described as non-debt creating capital inflows is puzzling. It suggests an absence of learning, at least so far, from recent experience in other countries.

It is widely accepted that portfolio investment flows are prone to surges, inward as well as outward, and may be highly volatile. But this reality does not appear to have exercized any influence on the mix of capital account liberalization and controls in India. What is more, controls on inflows of direct foreign investment have been progressively reduced to minimal levels.[12] There is, in fact, a common presumption that direct investment is clearly preferable to portfolio investment not only because it is longer-term and less volatile but also because it combines access to capital with access to technology, markets, and management. These presumed differences can be overdone. It is not sufficiently recognized that direct foreign investment inflows may not provide either equity or stability.[13] For one, such investment is often intra-firm lending rather than equity. Much of it, when permitted, is financed by local banks or domestic investors. For another, the management of liquid funds by transnational corporations is extremely sophisticated. When necessary, what appears to be fixed investment disappears abroad as quickly as portfolio investment, through borrowing from local banks against the security of physical assets. In some countries, capital account liberalization facilitates such hedging against exchange rate risk as also other forms of risk.[14] Even in countries such as India, where there are capital controls, transnational corporations probably have the capacity to evade or avoid controls via sophisticated financial management of liquid funds and the use of derivatives in financial markets.

It is clear that the nature and the pace of capital account liberalization, outlined above, exercised an influence on the dimensions and the composition of private foreign capital inflows to, and outflows from, India. Table 1 presents available evidence on capital inflows to and outflows from India, for the principal components of the capital account, during the period 1990–91 to 1998–99. The comparison with average annual inflows and outflows during the 1980s highlights the

---

12. In February 2000, the government decided to dispense with case-by-case approval, so that, except for a small negative list, all direct foreign investment would be approved through the automatic route.

13. For a discussion of this issue, see Helleiner (1997).

14. In situations where direct foreign investment is treated more leniently than portfolio investment, there is a strong incentive to *relabel* essentially portfolio flows as direct investment. In Brazil, for instance, when domestic interest rates were high in 1998, direct foreign investment increased suddenly, if mysteriously, as the authorities moved to discourage unwanted interest-responsive capital inflows.

consequences of capital account liberalization for the magnitudes of inflows and outflows. Table 2 outlines the changes in the composition of net foreign capital inflows during the 1990s. It clearly shows a shift from debt creating to non-debt creating capital flows. It also reveals the increasing significance of portfolio investment and the continuing significance of nonresident deposits, which represent liabilities that can be withdrawn on demand.[15] Table 3 sets out the evidence on foreign investment flows into India during the 1990s. It makes a distinction between direct investment and portfolio investment. It disaggregates direct foreign investment into four categories: the Reserve Bank of India automatic route, the Foreign Investment Promotion Board approval route, nonresident Indians, and the acquisition of shares, to show that an overwhelming proportion of foreign investment flows came through approval route. It also disaggregates portfolio investment into two categories: foreign institutional investors and global depository receipts. It shows that both forms of portfolio investment peaked during the mid-1990s and dropped sharply during the late 1990s in the aftermath of the Asian financial crisis. In fact, portfolio investment by foreign institutional investors turned into a net outflow in 1998–99.

It should be stressed that, in sharp contrast with most developing countries, particularly those in Asia but also elsewhere, described as emerging markets, the integration of the Indian economy into international capital markets has been both slow and limited. For instance, during the period from 1992 to 1997, India's share of direct foreign investment in developing countries was just 2% while India's share of portfolio investment in developing countries was in the range of 6%.[16] The proportion of gross domestic capital formation in India financed by foreign direct investment and portfolio investment, taken together, was about 5.5%.[17] Yet, India was not untouched by the problems associated with capital account liberalization which have surfaced in most developing countries. It had to manage surges of capital inflows. It had to cope with pressures on the exchange rate. It had to contend with instability of capital flows. It had to worry about contagion and possible capital outflows.

---

15. The stock of outstanding nonresident deposits increased, moderately, from $10.2 billion at the end of March 1991 to $12.3 billion at the end of March 1999. But, at the end of March 1999, $6.8 billion was in the form of non-repatriable deposits, held in the Rupee Deposit Scheme, introduced in late 1992, where the principal is not repatriable but the interest is repatriable and the interest rates are significantly higher than in international capital markets. All the same, repatriable nonresident deposits ($5.5 billion) together with short-term debt ($4.3 billion), which are liabilities that can be withdrawn on demand, were the equivalent of one-third of foreign exchange reserves ($29.5 billion) at the end of 1998–99. The par value of outstanding portfolio investment, without allowing for capital gains realizable and repatriable, was $15.5 billion: the equivalent of more than one-half of foreign exchange reserves at the end of 1998–99. These figures are from the Reserve Bank of India, *Annual Report, 1998–99*.

16. Calculated from data reported in UNCTAD (1998).

17. This proportion, which is an average for the period 1992–93 to 1997–98, has been calculated from data on direct investment and portfolio investment from the Reserve Bank of India and data on gross domestic capital formation from CSO *National Accounts Statistics*.

TABLE 1. Capital Inflows to and Outflows from India (US $ million)

Item	1980s	1990–91			1991–92			1992–93			1993–94			1998–98		
	Net	Inflows	Outflows	Net	Inflows	Outflows	Net	Inflows	Outflows	Net	Inflows	Outflows	Net	Inflows	Outflows	Net
Foreign Investment	140	113	10	103	151	18	133	589	32	557	4611	376	4235	5743	3331	2412
(a) Direct	80	107	10	97	147	18	129	345	30	315	651	65	586	2518	38	2480
(b) Portfolio	60	6	0	6	4	0	4	244	2	242	3960	311	3649	3225	3293	-68
External Assistance	1487	3397	1193	2204	4366	1335	3031	3302	1446	1856	3476	1580	1896	2726	1927	799
External Commercial Borrowings	1044	4282	2028	2254	3152	1689	1463	1179	1545	-366	3015	2330	685	7231	2864	4367
Banking Capital*	7	2758	3612	-854	3263	2989	274	2810	985	1825	2650	1592	1058	2897	3159	-262
Non Resident Deposits	1135	7347	5811	1536	7695	7405	290	9188	7187	2001	8850	7645	1205	5300	3558	1742
Rupee Debt Service	0	0	1193	-1193	0	1240	-1240	0	878	-878	0	1053	-1053	0	802	-802
Short Term Capital	-3	1752	677	1075	1898	2413	-515	4190	5269	-1079	3480	4249	-769	4814	5562	-748
Indian Investment Abroad	0	0	0	0	0	0	0	0	0	0	0	0	0	149	249	-100
Other Capital (net)	165	3117	1186	1931	2809	2335	474	1359	1399	-40	2873	1235	1638	3958	2801	1157
IMF	76	1858	644	1214	1245	459	786	1623	335	1288	321	134	187	393	393	-393
Total	4051	24624	16354	8270	24579	19883	4696	24240	19076	5164	29276	20194	9082	32818	24646	8172

Item	1994–95			1995–96			1996–97			1997–98		
	Inflows	Outflows	Net	Inflows	Outflows	Net	Inflows	Outflows	Net	Inflows	Outflows	Net
Foreign Investment	5753	831	4922	5629	824	4805	7816	1663	6153	9169	3779	5390
(a) Direct	1351	8	1343	2173	29	2144	2863	22	2841	3596	34	3562
(b) Portfolio	4402	823	3579	3456	795	2661	4953	1641	3312	5573	3745	1828
External Assistance	3193	1675	1518	2933	2066	867	3056	1955	1101	2885	2000	885
External Commercial Borrowings	4249	3125	1124	4262	2977	1285	7579	4723	2856	7382	3372	4010
Banking Capital*	1215	1721	-506	1524	1865	-341	1243	2364	-1121	1378	3396	-2018
Non Resident Deposits	5805	5633	172	4929	3826	1103	6775	3425	3350	7532	6407	1125
Rupee Debt Service	0	983	-983	0	952	-952	0	727	-727	0	767	-767
Short Term Capital	3488	3095	393	4137	4088	49	7085	6247	838	7034	7130	-96
Indian Investment Abroad	10	125	-115	14	204	-190	8	198	-190	97	134	-37
Other Capital (net)	2201	224	1977	748	3285	-2537	2629	2883	-254	3815	2463	1352
IMF	0	1143	-1143	0	1715	-1715	0	975	-975	0	618	-618
Total	25914	18555	7359	24176	21802	2374	36191	25160	11031	39292	30066	9226

NOTE: The figures in the first column, for the 1980s are average-of-period per annum.

SOURCE: Reserve Bank of India

*Excluding Nonresident Deposits.

TABLE 2. Composition of Net Foreign Capital Inflows in India

Item	1990–91	1991–92	1992–93	1993–94	1994–95	1995–96	1996–97	1997–98	1998–99
Total Capital Inflows (net)	7056.0	3910.0	3876.0	8895.0	8502.0	4089.0	12006.0	9844.0	8565.0
(US $ million) of which: (in percent)									
1. Non-debt Creating Inflows	1.5	3.4	14.4	47.6	57.9	117.5	51.2	54.8	28.2
a) Foreign Direct Investment	1.4	3.3	8.1	6.6	15.8	52.4	23.7	36.2	29.0
b) Portfolio Investment	0.1	0.1	6.2	41.0	42.1	65.1	27.6	18.6	-0.8
2. Debt Creating Inflows	83.3	77.5	39.9	21.2	25.1	57.7	61.8	52.5	62.7
a) External Assistance	31.3	77.7	48.0	21.4	17.9	21.6	9.2	9.2	9.6
b) External Commercial Borrowings	31.9	37.2	-9.2	6.8	12.1	31.2	23.7	40.6	50.9
c) Short Term Credits	15.2	-13.1	-27.8	-8.6	4.6	1.2	7.0	-1.0	-8.7
d) NRI Deposits	21.8	7.4	51.6	13.5	2.0	27.0	27.9	11.4	20.3
e) Rupee Debt Service	-16.9	-31.7	-22.7	-11.8	-11.6	-23.3	-6.1	-7.8	-9.4
3. Other Capital	15.3	19.1	45.8	31.2	17.0	-75.2	-13.0	-7.3	9.1
4. Total (1 to 3)	100.0	100.0	100.0	100.0	100.0	100.0	100.0	100.0	100.0
Total Capital Inflows (net) as a percentage of GDP	*2.4*	*1.6*	*1.7*	*3.2*	*2.6*	*1.2*	*3.0*	*2.3*	*2.1*

SOURCE: Reserve Bank of India, *Annual Report, 1998–99.*
NOTE: Other Capital includes delayed export receipts, advance payments against imports, and banking capital.

TABLE 3. Foreign Investment Flows into India (US $ million)

	1991–92	1992–93	1993–94	1994–95	1995–96	1996–97	1997–98	1998–99
A. Direct Investment	129	315	586	1314	2144	2821	3557	2462
a. RBI Automatic route	—	42	89	171	169	135	202	179
b. FIPB approval route	66	222	280	701	1249	1922	2754	1821
c. NRIs	63	51	217	442	715	639	241	62
d. Acquisition of Shares					11	125	360	400
B. Portfolio Investment	4	244	3567	3824	2748	3312	1828	-61
a. FIIs	—	1	1665	1503	2009	1926	979	-390
b. GDRs	—	240	1520	2082	683	1366	645	270
c. Offshore funds	4	3	382	239	56	20	204	59
Total (A+B)	133	559	4153	5138	4892	6133	5385	2401

SOURCE: Reserve Bank of India, *Annual Reports*.
NOTE: FIIs: Foreign Institutional Investors. RBI: Reserve Bank of India. GDRs: Global Depository Receipts.
FIPB: Foreign Investment Promotion Board. NRIs: Nonresident Indians

REGULATORY STRUCTURE OF CAPITAL CONTROLS

It is important to distinguish between exchange controls and capital controls, for they often coexist and can overlap.[18] Exchange controls are applicable to all transactions in foreign exchange. The object is to regulate the demand for foreign exchange, in different uses, so that it can be met by the available supply of foreign exchange. Thus, exchange controls can be imposed on transactions irrespective of whether these are in the current account or in the capital account. In contrast, capital controls are limited in their scope and different in their purpose. For one, capital controls are applicable only to transactions in the capital account on the balance of payments. For another, capital controls seek to restrict or to prohibit cross-border movements of capital.

The regulatory structure of capital controls in India is complex. It is, however, possible to discern a pattern. The *degree of control* is a function of the transactors. The *form of control* depends upon the transactions. The *nature of control* is determined by its effectiveness.

There are three sets of asymmetries in India's capital controls, which suggest that the degree of control is a function of the transactors. First, there is an asymmetry between capital outflows and capital inflows. There are extensive controls on capital outflows but there has been considerable liberalization in the

---

18. Cf. Rangarajan and Prasad (1999). The articles of Agreement of the International Monetary Fund, however, make a clear distinction between exchange controls (provided for as transitional arrangements in Article XIV Section 2) and capital controls (provided for in Article VI Section 3).

sphere of capital inflows.[19] Second, there is an asymmetry between residents and nonresidents. There are strict controls on capital account transactions by residents but there is some relaxation for capital account transactions by nonresidents. Third, there is an asymmetry between individuals and corporates. There are prohibitive controls on transactions in the capital account by individuals but there has been a significant liberalization for transactions in the capital account by corporates (and, to a limited extent, by banks).

This is, obviously, an oversimplification. There are exceptions. What is more, no one distinction is enough. Indeed, all three distinctions are necessary to define a transactor. Yet, highlighting these sets of asymmetries serves an important analytical purpose. If we think of cross-border movements of capital, from and to India, maximum controls are likely for capital outflows on the part of individuals who are resident, while maximum freedom is likely for capital inflows on the part of corporates that are nonresident. In this manner, it would be possible to construct a hierarchy, with different combinations of the three attributes of transactors, in which the degree of control increases or decreases as a function of the transactors.

There are different forms of capital controls in India, as elsewhere, which are imposed on different capital account transactions.[20] The forms of capital controls are manifold. There is a complete prohibition on some transactions. Other transactions require prior approval. And yet other transactions are subject to limits specified in terms of either value or time or both. It is also possible that discriminatory taxes may be imposed on some transactions. Similarly, reserve requirements may be stipulated or interest penalties may be imposed to regulate the execution or the conclusion of some transactions. In turn, transactions in the capital account can also be classified, for the form of control often depends upon the economic nature of the transaction.[21] There are transactions in capital markets or money markets associated with a cross-border sale or purchase of financial assets such as shares, bonds, debentures, government securities or money market instruments, which may also extend to derivatives. There are transactions arising from direct foreign investment and from portfolio investment on the part of foreign institutional investors. There are transactions attributable to cross-border borrowing or lending on the part of commercial banks and non-banking financial intermediaries. There are, in addition, transactions on the part of individuals in the form of cross-border loans, deposits, gifts, inheritances or settlement of debts. There are transactions related to a cross-border sale or

---

19. It would seem that this asymmetry characterizes a large proposition of the regimes for capital controls in developing countries. In 1995, for example, 119 developing countries maintained some form of capital controls, among which 67 developing countries had comprehensive controls. Of these 67 countries, all had comprehensive controls on capital outflows, whereas only 17 had comprehensive controls on capital inflows (Helleiner, 1997).

20. For a survey of the literature on capital controls, see Dooley (1995).

21. For a systematic classification of capital account transactions that are subject to controls, see IMF *Annual Reports on Exchange Arrangements and Exchange Restrictions*.

purchase of physical assets, in particular real estate. Needless to add, in each of these transactions it is possible to draw a distinction between outflows and inflows, residents and nonresidents, as also individuals and corporates.

It would seem that there are three broad categories of capital controls: quantitative controls, price based controls, and regulatory controls.[22] There are quantitative controls on specified transactions which range from complete prohibition at one end to some liberalization subject to limits at the other end. This means an explicit moratorium or stipulated limits on such transactions. In addition, there are quantitative controls which require prior approval for specified transactions on the capital account. Such controls are, in effect, discretionary. But all of them seek to regulate cross-border capital movements through quantitative limits on their value. In contrast, price based controls seek to introduce disincentives to discourage some categories of capital flows or incentives to encourage other categories of capital flows. Thus, discriminatory taxation or differential interest rates may be used to stimulate or to dampen capital inflows just as they may be used to discourage capital outflows. Similarly, multiple exchange rates may, in principle, be used as an incentive or a disincentive for specified capital account transactions. The essential object of such price based controls is to alter the costs or the benefits associated with specified transactions so as to discourage or to encourage capital flows in these categories. There are, in addition, regulatory controls on specified transactions in the capital account which seek to use a mix of quantities and prices to restrict capital flows. The most common example of such regulatory controls is unremunerated reserve requirements that are stipulated to restrict capital inflows. In India, capital controls are essentially quantitative, although there are some examples of price based controls or regulatory controls. The preference for quantitative controls is probably attributable to the fact that outcomes are more certain and more predictable. The nature of control, then, is shaped by the perceived effectiveness of capital controls.

EXCHANGE RATE POLICY AND MACROECONOMIC DILEMMAS

The macroeconomic implications and consequences of capital account liberalization are most clearly discernible in the dilemmas and the conundrums associated with the exchange rate. The discussion that follows begins with a consideration of India's exchange rate regime in retrospect, examines the management of the exchange rate and analyzes the impact of capital account liberalization on the exchange rate. In doing so, it seeks to focus on the emerging dilemmas in exchange rate policy and limits on degrees of freedom in macroeconomic management.

For almost a quarter of a century, India was on a regime of fixed exchange rates. Indeed, between 15 August 1947 when India became independent and 15

---

22. Cf. Rangarajan and Prasad (1999). See also Dooley (1995).

August 1971 when the United States announced that the dollar was no longer convertible into gold, the parity of the rupee was adjusted only twice: in September 1949 and in June 1966. In this experience, India was not very different from the outside world, although moderate rates of inflation compared with most developing countries may have meant that exchange rate adjustments were neither frequent nor large. During this phase, exchange controls were widespread. And there was almost no market for foreign exchange.[23] Following the collapse of the gold exchange standard, in June 1972, the rupee was pegged to the pound sterling which in turn was afloat. This continued until September 1975. Thereafter, the rupee was pegged to a basket of currencies: possibly the U.S. dollar, the pound sterling, the Deutsche Mark and the Japanese yen. But the currencies and their weights in the basket were not disclosed. Under this regime, the Reserve Bank of India announced, daily, buying and selling rates to authorized dealers in foreign exchange for transactions. Given its obligation to buy and sell unlimited amounts of the intervention currency (the pound sterling until March 1993) on a day-to-day basis arising from purchases and sales by commercial banks, the Reserve Bank of India performed a market clearing role. It was, essentially, a managed float where the pound sterling was the intervention currency and exchange rate policy was determined by the government through the central bank.

The program of macroeconomic stabilization and structural reform, which was introduced in response to the external debt crisis in early 1991, led to changes in the management of the exchange rate and the development of a market for foreign exchange. In July 1991, there was a substantial exchange rate adjustment when the rupee was depreciated in two steps by almost 20 percent vis-à-vis the U.S. dollar. There was a further depreciation of the rupee implicit in the introduction of a dual exchange rate system in March 1992 and the subsequent unification of the exchange rate in March 1993 at the market determined rate.[24] Consequently, between end-June 1991 and end-June 1993, in nominal terms, the rupee depreciated by about 33 percent vis-à-vis the U.S. dollar. It was the beginning of a transition from an entirely managed exchange rate towards a market based system.

The development of a market for foreign exchange, thus, gathered momentum during the 1990s.[25] The average monthly turnover rose from $17 billion in

---

23. Indeed, until 1978, authorized dealers in foreign exchange were allowed to undertake only cover operations and maintain "square" or "near-square" positions *at all times*. This stipulation was relaxed in 1978 permitting authorized dealers to maintain "square" or "near-square" positions *at the close of business every day*, thus allowing commercial banks to undertake intra-day trading in foreign exchange.

24. Under the dual exchange rate system, 40% of current account receipts had to be surrendered to the Reserve Bank of India at the official exchange rate and this was utilized to meet essential imports at lower cost. During this period, the difference between the official rate and the market rate was in the range of 10%. For an account of exchange rate management in India, during the 1990s, see Reddy (1997) and Rangarajan (1998).

25. The brief description of the structure of the foreign exchange market, outlined in this paragraph, is based on information provided in the Reserve Bank of India *Annual Reports*.

1987–88 to $50 billion in 1993–94 and $110 billion in 1998–99. The transactions in this market can be classified in terms of two distinctions between: (i) merchant transactions and interbank transactions, and (ii) spot transactions and forward transactions. In the late 1990s, merchant transactions made up less than one-fifth of the total turnover, while interbank transactions constituted more than four-fifths of the total turnover. Spot transactions accounted for somewhat less than one-half of the total merchant turnover, whereas forward transactions accounted for a little more than two-fifths of the total interbank turnover. It is worth noting that the forward market for foreign exchange is mostly active up to six months, where two-way prices are quoted. This maturity profile is essentially determined by the norm period for receipts and payments in trade transactions. For some transactions, it has recently been lengthened and prices are also quoted for twelve months into the future. In spite of these developments, however, the foreign exchange market is neither wide nor deep. It comprises authorized dealers, money changers, customers, and the central bank. The authorized dealers are essentially commercial banks. The customer segment of the spot market is dominated by the requirements of public sector enterprises (e.g., for the import of crude oil and petroleum products) and the government sector (e.g., for debt servicing), although foreign institutional investors have also emerged as significant players because of transactions related to portfolio investment.

The present exchange rate system, in principle, seeks to determine the exchange rate through forces of supply and demand in the market. In practice, it is a quasi-managed float where the central bank plays the role of a big brother in terms of management. The objectives of exchange rate policy, according to the Reserve Bank of India, are: to reduce volatility in the exchange rate so that market corrections for overvaluation or undervaluation are orderly and calibrated; to help maintain an adequate level of foreign exchange reserves; and to assist in the development of a healthy market for foreign exchange by eliminating market constraints.[26]

Under this system, the exchange rate is strongly influenced, even if not entirely determined by market forces. There is an explicit intervention on the part of the Reserve Bank of India whenever there is a high degree of volatility or instability in the market. But there is also an implicit management of the market for foreign exchange by the Reserve Bank of India. As a rule, transactions in foreign currency can take place essentially for financing identifiable underlying transactions supported by documentation. Genuine hedging of exposures is allowed through forward exchange contracts, foreign currency-rupee swaps, cross-currency options and other derivates, subject to Reserve Bank of India guidelines, provided there is matching exposure to exchange rate risk in permissible and identifiable transactions.[27] And some flexibility is provided to reduce the cost of

---

26. See Reddy (1997) and (1999).

27. It is worth citing some examples. Authorized dealers can enter into contracts for forward purchase and sale of foreign currency with residents who have a crystallized exposure to exchange risk in respect of genuine (permissible) transactions. Authorized dealers can also arrange foreign-

hedging. The idea is to facilitate transactions at the market exchange rate. But, at the same time, the object is also to prevent destabilizing speculation. Thus, as far as possible, the central bank attempts to ensure that the market rate is determined by the transactions demand rather than the speculative demand for foreign exchange. The Reserve Bank of India makes sales and purchases of foreign currency in the market, it is said, basically to even out lumpiness, or mismatches between demand and supply, in what is a thin market.[28] However, contrary to the pronouncements or the claims made by the Reserve Bank of India, the exchange rate is managed as much as possible, except on occasions when the market leaves no room for manoeuvre. It is plausible to suggest, though impossible to establish, that exchange rate management is guided by the notion of a monitoring band with respect to the real effective exchange rate. In this management, longish periods of nominal exchange rate stability are interspersed with short periods of nominal exchange rate depreciation. The latter, however, is a creeping adjustment over the period rather than a discrete adjustment at one point in time. Since end-June 1993, there has been such a creeping downward adjustment only twice: once in the first quarter of 1996 and once in the first quarter of 1998. This management of the exchange rate has turned out to be possible only because extensive capital controls have meant a limited integration into international financial markets which has enabled the Reserve Bank of India to intervene in a thin market for foreign exchange. The task has also been easier than in some other developing countries because of manageable current account deficits and comfortable foreign exchange reserves.

Yet, capital account liberalization, limited though it has been, has reduced degrees of freedom in exchange rate policy. It has done so in three ways: by forcing an appreciation of the real effective exchange rate of the rupee over some periods, by creating a pressure for a nominal appreciation of the rupee in other periods, and by mounting a pressure for a nominal depreciation of the rupee in yet other periods.

Capital account liberalization is often thought of as a means of stimulating non-debt creating capital flows. However, when capital inflows such as portfolio investment become an important source of financing the current account deficit

---

currency-rupee swaps between corporates which run long-term foreign currency exposures, but this swap route is not available as a surrogate for those who do not qualify for forward cover. Authorized dealers can offer cross-currency options to residents to cover their genuine exposures including contingent exposures like tender bids, but regulations require that such an option should be written on a fully covered back-to-back basis. Authorized deals can offer interest rate swaps, currency swaps, coupon swaps and interest rate caps, on a back-go-back basis, for hedging of loan exposures where the loan transaction has been approved by the Reserve Bank of India and the amount/maturity of the hedge does not exceed that of the loan.

28. The demand for foreign exchange from public sector enterprises (for their imports) and from the government (for its debt servicing) tends to be lumpy and uneven over time. The consequent demand-supply mismatches can lead to some volatility or even destabilizing speculative activity. This provides the rationale for intervention, through sales and purchases of foreign exchange, by the Reserve Bank of India (Reddy, 1999).

in the balance of payments, problems may arise over a period of time. For the economy then needs a high interest rate and a strong exchange rate regime to sustain such inflows in terms of both profitability and confidence. The consequent appreciation of the real effective exchange rate erodes the competitiveness of exports over time and enlarges the trade deficit. It is important to recognize the macroeconomic implications. Larger trade deficits, hence current account deficits, require larger portfolio investment inflows which, beyond the point, undermine confidence and create adverse expectations even if the government wants to keep the exchange rate pegged. This story line materialized in India during the mid-1990s as portfolio investment flows at more than $3 billion per annum sustained by nominal exchange rate stability led to a considerable appreciation in the real effective exchange rate because the inflation rate in India then was significantly higher than in the world outside. The pressure on the exchange rate ultimately surfaced in late 1995 and early 1996. Driven by concerns about confidence, the Reserve Bank of India resisted this pressure through intervention in the spot market, which was supported by the imposition of an interest surcharge on import finance, the tightening of concessions on export credit, and the withdrawal of liquidity from the money market to prevent speculative attacks on the rupee.[29] But this resistance did not last long. For monetary policy and administrative measures could only postpone the adjustment. And, even in a thin market, the adjustment became inevitable during the first quarter of 1996. The exchange rate depreciated from Rs.31.50 to Rs.35.50 for one U.S. dollar.

The capital account liberalization also created pressure for an appreciation of the rupee, in nominal terms, whenever there was a surge in capital inflows. This was experienced during the second half of 1996–97 and the first half of 1997–98.[30] Large surpluses on capital account led to a rapid accumulation of foreign exchange reserves. In a thin market for foreign exchange, excess supply was immediately discernible. Concerned about an appreciation of the rupee, which seemed most likely at the time, the Reserve Bank of India stepped into the market for foreign exchange with large purchases of U.S. dollars both in the spot market and in the forward market, so much so that net purchases of U.S. dollars by the Reserve Bank of India were more than $6 billion during the second half of 1996–97 and almost $4 billion during the first quarter of 1997–98. This was combined with an increase in reserve requirements and some attempt at sterilization through open market operations. The problem of exchange rate management during this period in India, as also elsewhere, was coping with surges in capital inflows which created upward pressures on the nominal rate.

The financial crisis in Southeast Asia and East Asia led to a dramatic transformation in the situation. The second half of 1997–98 witnessed a mounting pressure for a depreciation of the rupee, in nominal terms, since there was an expectation of capital outflows arising from contagion effects as the financial

---

29. Cf. Reddy (1997) and Rangarajan (1998).
30. For a discussion, as also some evidence, see Reddy (1997) and Rangarajan (1998).

crisis spread through several countries in Asia. The problem was exacerbated by the appreciation in the real effective exchange rate of the rupee over time that had been reinforced by the surge in capital inflows during the preceding year. There was also a sharp slowdown in capital inflows as confidence in international financial markets took a beating. And there was considerable volatility in the foreign exchange market between November 1997 and February 1998. The Reserve Bank of India sought to manage the situation by large sales of U.S. dollars in the spot market and in the forward market, combined with monetary policy and administrative measures to stem adverse market expectations.[31] This intervention had some impact on a nervous market. It is no surprise, however, that the efforts met with only limited success. For, in a short span of nine months, during the last two quarters of 1997–98 and the first quarter of 1998–99 (between end-September 1997 and end-June 1998), the exchange rate depreciated from Rs.36.40 to Rs.42.50 for one U.S. dollar.

The preceding discussion highlights some exchange rate policy dilemmas associated with capital account liberalization. It is important to stress their macroeconomic implications. The strong exchange rates and the high interest rates needed to sustain private foreign capital inflows erode the competitiveness of exports and stifle domestic investment. A progressive integration into international financial markets also means that exchange rates can no longer be used as a strategic device to provide an entry into the world market for manufactured goods, just as interest rates can no longer be used for guiding the allocation of scarce investible resources in a market economy. Deliberately undervalued exchange rates, maintained over a period of time, have been known to provide a competitive point of entry into markets for differentiated manufactured goods, particularly where quality is perceived in terms of established brands but lower prices of unknown brands allow initial access to markets. Similarly, interest rates are not simply the scarcity price of borrowing finance determined by market forces. The structure of interest rates has been used as a strategic instrument for channelling credit in a market economy in accordance with a long term perspective of comparative advantage or national priorities. But that is not all. Countries which are integrated into the world financial system are also constrained in using an autonomous management of demand to maintain levels of output and employment. Expansionary fiscal and monetary policies, whether large government deficits to stimulate aggregate demand or low interest rates to encourage domestic investment, can no longer be used because of an overwhelming fear that such measures could lead to speculative capital flight and a run on the national currency.[32]

The problem is not confined to fewer degrees of freedom in macroeconomic management. It extends to an accentuation of vulnerability which can have far reaching macroeconomic implications. In a world where capital account

---

31. Cf. Rangarajan and Prasad (1999) and Reddy (1999).
32. These issues are discussed further in Nayyar (2000).

liberalization proceeds some distance and gathers momentum, the exchange rate is an asset price that is determined by expectations, as in the "beauty-contest" parable set out by Keynes, and not by macroeconomic fundamentals.[33] Such expectations can change—and change rapidly—in thin markets for foreign exchange. The problem of instability and volatility is compounded whenever capital flows assume the form of short term capital movements or portfolio investment flows. Short term capital movements, driven by interest rate differentials and in search of capital gains, are obviously most sensitive to expectations about the exchange rate. Similar problems arise with portfolio investment flows for they represent an intersection of two inherently unstable markets: stock markets and currency markets.[34] And, in emerging markets such as India, stock markets are just as thin as foreign exchange markets. It needs to be said that both short term capital movements (in money) and portfolio investment flows (in financial assets) constitute short term liabilities or liabilities that can be withdrawn on demand and are therefore susceptible to capital flight. In situations where there is an erosion of confidence, herd behavior and contagion effects, which are characteristics of panic in financial markets, compound the problem further.

It should be obvious that the exchange rate policy dilemmas, the much reduced degrees of freedom in macroeconomic management and the boom-bust cycles in financial markets associated with capital account liberalization, are serious problems that cannot be wished away. And it would be a mistake to believe that prudent macroeconomic policies combined with appropriate financial standards would be sufficient safeguards in the pursuit of capital-account convertibility.[35] These can, at best, reduce the risks but cannot eliminate them. It must also be recognized that the orthodoxy about the virtues of convertibility on capital account is open to serious question.[36] Indeed, theory and experience provide

---

33. Cf. Eatwell and Taylor (2000).

34. This point is emphasized by Singh (1997).

35. The report of the committee on capital account convertibility in India (Reserve Bank of India, 1997), for example, specified three such conditions to be satisfied in a period of three years: (i) a reduction in the gross fiscal deficit of the central government from 5% of GDP to 3.5% of GDP; (ii) an inflation rate not to exceed an average of 3 to 5% per annum over the three years; and (iii) a reduction in the cash reserve ratio of commercial banks from an average effective rate of more than 9% to 3% and a reduction in gross non-performing assets of the banking system from about 17% to 5%. In addition, the committee suggested a sustainable current account deficit, a monitoring band of ± 5% around the real effective exchange rate, adequate foreign exchange reserves, and a strengthened financial system. Even if such criteria are satisfied, the risks are reduced but not eliminated. The real problem with this approach is that it does not recognize the macroeconomic dilemmas associated with capital account liberalization and thinks of capital account convertibility as an objective in itself instead of situating it in the wider context of economic development.

36. See, for example, Cooper (1998) and Rodrik (1998). Cooper argues that capital account convertibility might not even lead to an efficient allocation of scarce capital. Further, he reaches the strong conclusion that, except in large and diversified countries with well developed and sophisticated financial markets, free movements of capital and floating exchange rates are basically incompatible. Of course, he recognizes that free movements of capital are also incompatible with

a rationale for capital controls, particularly in countries that are latecomers to industrialization and development.[37] And the reasons are straightforward enough. A stable and appropriate real exchange rate, an effective monetary policy, and an autonomous fiscal policy are critical components of any macroeconomic management that is shaped by development objectives, instead of being driven by international capital markets. In any case, capital account convertibility is not a matter of all or nothing. The mix of liberalization and controls is a strategic choice in the process of economic development.

DOMESTIC REGULATIONS AND INTERNATIONAL STANDARDS

The interface between actual national regulatory structures and potential international regulatory norms for cross-border movements of capital is a relatively unexplored theme in the literature on the subject. In exploring this theme, it is necessary to begin with a consideration of existing or emerging international regimes which relate to international capital movements. It may then be possible to set out a suitable model which could provide some conceptual basis for a framework on capital controls in the proposed World Financial Authority.

The mood of the moment and the ideology of the times, reinforced by the gathering momentum of globalization, has been such that there was an almost unilateral capital account liberalization on the part of countries during the 1990s. There were, of course, pressures from the IMF as also from the United States. But there were no multilateral obligations. And this was entirely in the domain of national economic policies. At the same time, however, the process of creating international regimes which would impose a discipline on countries seeking to restrict cross-border movements of capital was also set in motion. The financial crises, which surfaced in Southeast Asia and East Asia with Russia and Brazil as the most recent casualties, have dampened the enthusiasm for capital account liberalization. The most advanced developing countries, which are an integral part of the process of globalization, have been ravaged by such crises. This has set in motion the search for an international financial architecture which would inter alia govern international financial markets. But the attempt to create international regimes which would facilitate the liberalization of capital movements across national boundaries continues in parallel, even if most of it is still on negotiating tables.

There are three such international regimes which are on the anvil. First, there is the General Agreement on Trade in Services, in the WTO, which seeks to liberalize international trade in financial services. The framework has already

---

fixed but adjustable exchange rates. Thus, unless countries are prepared to fix the values of their currencies to a leading currency, he believes it would be sensible to preserve the right to control at least some forms of capital movements across their borders.

37. For a discussion on the economic logic of capital controls, as also their necessity in the context of development, see Helleiner (1997). See also Rodrik (1998).

come into existence. It sets the rules on bargaining for market access. The sectoral negotiations, essentially among the key players, may then be multilateralized through the MFN principle. This process of liberalization, which is a follow-up of the Uruguay Round agreement, is not affected by the stalemate at Seattle. Second, there is the prospective Multilateral Agreement on Investment, which seeks free access and national treatment for foreign investors with provisions to enforce commitments and obligations to foreign investors. A similar agreement among the OECD countries was negotiated. But it could not be put in place because of a stalemate. Ironically enough, it is possible that such an agreement may now be lodged in the WTO, at the initiative of the major industrialized countries. The collapse of the Ministerial Meeting at Seattle, however, was a setback to this process. But it is almost certain that pressure will mount once again and soon. Third, there is a proposed amendment to the Articles of Agreement of the IMF, which seeks to make the promotion of capital account liberalization a specific objective of the Fund.[38] In doing so, it proposed to give the IMF appropriate jurisdiction over capital movements across borders. In the aftermath of the financial crises across the world, however, the proposed IMF amendment looks dead for the present, of if still alive, it will relate to jurisdiction rather than to liberalization.

The objective of these international regimes if and when created, in their respective spheres, is to ensure a progressive liberalization of capital movements across borders through international institutions and rules. The object of the proposed World Financial Authority, in sharp contrast, is to manage systemic risk associated with international financial liberalization, coordinate national action against market failure or abuse, and act as a regulator in international financial markets.[39]

In the pursuit of this objective, the interface between national regulatory structures and international regulatory norms is bound to be critical. And this interface is likely to be not only important but also complex in the sphere of capital controls. In the proposed World Financial Authority, the basic premise must be that capital controls are neither temporary devices nor exceptions to the rule which must ultimately disappear but are essential instruments of policy that would have to be used, from time to time, to govern international financial flows. Yet, it would be necessary to evolve some international norms for domestic regulations which would facilitate the coordination of national action on the part of the World Financial Authority.

In contemplating this task, there is a fundamental distinction that should be drawn between countries where capital controls exist and countries where capital controls do not exist. In countries where capital controls exist, mostly developing countries or transitional economies, capital account convertibility is limited.

---

38. See Fischer (1998), who outlines the rationale of the proposed amendment and considers the role of the IMF in the context of capital account liberalization.

39. For a detailed discussion, see Eatwell and Taylor (2000).

The essential issue would be the conditions under which such controls can be strengthened or diluted and the conditions under which new controls can be introduced or old controls dispensed with. In countries where capital controls do not exist, mostly industrialized countries but also some developing countries, capital account convertibility is complete. The essential issue would be the conditions under which controls should be introduced, or retained after introduction, on capital inflows or capital outflows. Controls on capital inflows may be necessary in response to surges, so as to retain autonomy in monetary policy, to minimize costs of sterilization, to restrain appreciation of the exchange rate and so on. Controls on outflows may be necessary in response to dwindling foreign exchange reserves, so as to ward off speculative attacks on the currency for, given the enormous size of international transactions in foreign exchange, central banks may be unwilling or unable to defend the exchange rate. There is perhaps another distinction which is just as important in thinking about capital controls: that between cross-border movements of capital and cross-border movements of money. The case for controls on the latter is obviously much stronger and more persuasive. However, it is easier to make this distinction in theory than in practice. For there is a fungibility between money and financial assets, particularly those which have short maturities or easy liquidity. Thus, in this context, it would be appropriate to consider short-term liabilities or liabilities that can be withdrawn on demand as near-money.[40]

In constructing a suitable model that could provide a framework for capital controls in the World Financial Authority, we can learn something from existing institutional arrangements or international institutions which developed an interface between national policies and international obligations. The IMF and the erstwhile GATT, now incorporated in the WTO, are the obvious models to examine.

The IMF began life at a time when there was no convertibility even in trade transactions, let alone current account transactions. Exchange controls were widespread. Article VIII, which stipulated current account convertibility, was enshrined as a fundamental obligation. But Article XIV allowed for transitional arrangements in the most flexible manner because no transition periods were specified. Of course, the IMF thought of exchange controls as undesirable. All the same, it was recognized that exchange controls on current account transactions could be phased out only over time. And, for a large number of countries the transition to current account convertibility stretched over decades. The issue, however, is not transition time. The IMF model is simply not suitable as a basis for any framework on capital controls. There are two reasons. For one, the World Financial Authority should think of capital controls as a means of governing international financial flows. In the IMF, with the passage of time, exchange controls came to be thought of as restrictions that were temporarily necessary but had to

---

40. In designing such capital controls on the cross-border movements of money and near-money, it is important to recognize the possibilities of avoidance through the use of derivatives in international financial markets.

be dismantled over time, even though the founding fathers may have had a different view.[41] For another, the World Financial Authority discipline on capital controls should be applicable not only to capital importing countries but also to capital exporting countries. It should, of course, be recognized that controls on capital inflows are much easier and perhaps more effective than controls on capital outflows. In the IMF, surveillance and conditionality were, in effect, imposed only on deficit countries that were borrowers but not on surplus countries that were lenders.

The GATT also began life at a time when restrictions on trade between countries were widespread. In its quest for trade liberalization, essentially in the sphere of manufactured goods, the GATT sought to transform all quantitative restrictions into tariffs and then to reduce tariffs progressively over time. The reduction in tariffs was brought about through bilateral bargains between major trading partners which were multilateralized through the MFN principle. The GATT model is also not suitable as a basis for any framework on capital controls. The reasons are simple. In the GATT, quotas were seen as worse than tariffs, while high tariffs were seen as worse than low tariffs. The same logic cannot be extended to capital controls in the context of the World Financial Authority. For, contrary to conventional wisdom, there is no reason to presume that price based controls are better than quantitative controls or that fewer controls are better than more controls. In the context of cross-border capital movements, it would perhaps be appropriate to think of price based controls and quantitative controls as complements rather than substitutes. In the GATT, the modus operandi of trade liberalization was characterized by a near mercantile reciprocity. The same logic cannot be extended to capital account liberalization. Indeed, any progressive relaxation of capital controls on the basis of bilateral bargains which are multilateralized would be altogether inappropriate.

The lessons from these models, both positive and negative, suggest three fundamental principles for any framework on capital controls in the World Financial Authority. First, it should recognize that capital account liberalization is a means and not an end in itself. In other words, capital account convertibility should not be seen as the ultimate objective for which transitional arrangements need to be made. Second, it should provide for safeguards, not only to protect the balance of payments but also to manage the macroeconomic vulnerability associated with cross-border capital movements. Such safeguards would be nec-

---

41. In this context, it needs to be stressed that capital controls were an integral part of the conception and design of the IMF. Indeed, Article VI Section 3 states: "Members may exercise such controls as are necessary to regulate international capital movements, but no member may exercise these controls in a manner which will restrict payments for current transactions or which will unduly delay transfers of funds in settlement of commitments...." What is more, the use of IMF resources to support financing on capital account was explicitly forbidden. Article VI Section 1 states: "A member may not use the Fund's general resources to meet a large and sustained outflow of capital... and the Fund may request a member to exercise controls to prevent such use of the general resources of the Fund. If after receiving such a request, a member fails to exercise appropriate controls, the Fund may declare the member ineligible to use the general resources of the Fund."

essary not only in capital importing countries but also in capital exporting countries. Third, it should incorporate development as an objective. For it is absolutely essential to recognize, even more than it was half a century earlier, that there are vast differences in levels of development between countries. And, capital controls, which enable countries to sustain low interest rates or weak but stable exchange rates, may be an integral part of strategies of development. Thus, international regimes should be conducive to the pursuit of national development objectives instead of reducing degrees of freedom for countries that are latecomers to development. In addition, any such framework in the World Financial Authority should be based on the premise that capital controls are just another form of regulation of markets, where domestic financial regulations and cross-border capital controls are analogues in a world where there is an increasing integration of national and international capital markets.

It is clear that the nature of international financial flows and the problems associated with development require structural flexibilities rather than structural rigidities in capital controls, particularly because there are specificities in time and in space. Thus, any framework for capital controls would need to be flexible. Different controls, whether general or selective, should be usable for different transactions in the capital account. Similarly, quantitative controls or regulatory controls should be just as permissible as price based controls. Even asymmetries in controls, between capital inflows and capital outflows, residents and nonresidents, or individuals and corporates, which are discernible from the Indian experience, should be consistent with such a framework. But that is not all. The regime for capital controls in the World Financial Authority would have to recognize that the underlying objectives can differ between countries and can change over time. Therefore, capital controls can range from prudential controls for crisis prevention and ad hoc controls for crisis management to safeguard controls for the balance of payments and developmental controls for autonomy in the formulation of economic policies.

In a world of unequal partners, where economic disparities between countries are vast, it is only reasonable that developing countries should be allowed more time to implement the rules or exceptions to the rules. But the concept of special and differential treatment is *passe*. Indeed, the emerging rules of the game for international economic transactions assume that everybody has graduated. The time has come to think of a somewhat different paradigm for the World Financial Authority. For countries at vastly different levels of development, there should be some flexibility, instead of complete rigidity, in the application of uniform rules. For we should be concerned with the desirability of the outcomes and not with the procedural uniformity of rules. It is, in principle, possible to formulate general rules where application is a function of country-specific or time-specific circumstances, without resorting to exceptions. It implies a set of international rules, or norms, in which every country has the same rights but the obligations are a function of its level or stage of development.[42] In contemplating any interface

---

42. For a discussion of this set of issues, in the wider context of rules of the game for globalization, see Nayyar (2000).

of national policies and international obligations, it is important to remember that fair rules are necessary but not sufficient. For a game is not simply about rules. It is also about players. And, if one of the teams or one of the players does not have adequate training and preparation, it would simply be crushed by the other. In other words, the rules must be such that newcomers or latecomers to the game, say the developing countries, are provided with the time and the space to learn so that they are competitive players rather than pushover opponents. This must be the starting point for any framework on capital controls in a World Financial Authority.

REFERENCES

Bhaumik, S.K. 1997. "Convertibility of the Rupee: Implications for Trade and Policy," *Money and Finance*, No. 2, pp.18–41.

Cooper, R. N. 1998. "Should Capital-Account Convertibility be a World Objective?" in P. B. Kenen, ed., *Should the IMF Pursue Capital-Account Convertibility?* Princeton: Essays in International Finance, No. 207, May.

Dooley, M. P. 1995. "A Survey of Academic Literature on Controls over International Capital Transactions," *NBER Working Paper Series 5352*, November.

Eatwell, J. and Taylor, L. 2000. *Global Finance at Risk: The Case for International Regulation*. New York: The New Press.

Fischer, S. 1998. "Capital-Account Liberalization and the Role of the IMF," in P. B. Kenen, ed., *Should the IMF Pursue Capital-Account Convertibility?* Princeton: Essays in International Finance, No. 207, May.

Helleiner, G. K. 1997. "Capital Account Regimes and the Developing Countries," in UNCTAD, *International Monetary and Financial Issues for the 1990s*, Volume VIII. New York and Geneva: United Nations.

Government of India. 1993. *Economic Reforms: Two Years After and the Task Ahead*, New Delhi: Ministry of Finance.

Joshi, V. and Little, I. M. D. 1996. *India's Economic Reforms: 1991–2001*, New Delhi: Oxford University Press.

Nayyar, D. 1994. *Migration, Remittances and Capital Flows*, New Delhi: Oxford University Press.

_____. 1996. *Economic Liberalization in India: Analytics, Experience and Lessons*. Calcutta: Orient Longman.

_____. 2000. "Globalization and Development Strategies," *High-Level Round Table on Trade and Development at UNCTAD X*, TD X/RT.1/4. Geneva: United Nations.

Rangarajan, C. 1998. "Foreign Exchange Management: A Brief Review and Directions of Enquiry," *Money and Finance*, No. 7, pp. 13–18.

Rangarajan, C. and A. Prasad. 1999. "Capital Account Liberalization and Controls: Lessons from the East Asian Crisis," *Money and Finance*, No. 9, pp. 13–45.

Reddy, Y. V. 1997. "Exchange Rate Management: Dilemmas," *Reserve Bank of India Bulletin*, September, pp. 701–708.

_____. 1999. "Managing Capital Flows," *Reserve Bank of India Bulletin*, January, pp. 95–116.

Rodrik, D. 1998. "Who Needs Capital-Account Convertibility?" in P. B. Kenen, ed., *Should the IMF Pursue Capital-Account Convertibility?* Princeton: Essays in International Finance, No. 207, May.

Reserve Bank of India. 1993. *Report of the High-Level Committee on the Balance of Payments.* Bombay: Reserve Bank of India.

_____. 1997. *Report of the Committee on Capital Account Convertibility.* Bombay: Reserve Bank of India.

Singh, A. 1997. "The Stock Market, Industrial Development and the Financing of Corporate Growth in India," in D. Nayyar, ed., *Trade and Industrialization.* New Delhi: Oxford University Press.

UNCTAD. 1998. *World Investment Report 1998.* New York: United Nations.

Williamson, J. 1991. "On Liberalizing the Capital Account," in R. O'Brien, ed., *Finance and the International Economy*, Volume V. Oxford: Annex Bank Review.

6

. . .

International Capital Mobility, Macroeconomic Imbalances, and the Risk of Global Contraction

*Robert A. Blecker**

IN THE WAKE of the Mexican and East Asian financial crises of the 1990s, economists of various persuasions have noted the increasing international mobility of financial capital as a major new aspect of the contemporary global economy. It is now well known that the volume of international financial transactions far exceeds what is necessary to finance ordinary trade in goods and services, and that the lion's share of those transactions are driven by purely financial considerations such as hedging strategies, arbitrage opportunities, and currency speculation. Opinion is more divided, however, on exactly how this financial globalization impacts on real activity in national economies and to what extent it constrains macroeconomic policies in individual nations.[1] Even some economists who are

*This author is Professor of Economics, American University, and Research Associate, Economic Policy Institute. This paper was prepared for the Project on International Capital Markets and the Future of Economic Policy, Center for Economic Policy Analysis, New School University. The author would like to acknowledge helpful comments from Dean Baker, Alan Isaac, Robert Scott, and participants in seminars at Queens' College, University of Cambridge, and the Economic Policy Institute, as well as research assistance by Juan Fernandez and Jesse Rothstein. The author is solely responsible for the contents and for any remaining errors.

1. See Mussa and Goldstein (1993), Marston (1995), D'Arista (1996), and Bhaduri (1998) for analyses of the increasing importance of international capital flows. See Wachtel (1990) and Eatwell (1996) for the argument that international financial liberalization has significantly constrained domestic economic policy, and needs to be re-regulated in order to make progressive economic policies more feasible. See Glyn (1998) and Pollin (1998) for the contrary view, that domestic constraints are more important than international constraints in preventing more expansionary macroeconomic policies.

ardent supporters of free trade and other forms of economic liberalization have come out in opposition to the free mobility of short-term financial capital (e.g., Bhagwati 1998; McKinnon and Pill 1996).

This paper seeks to inform this debate by examining three related aspects of international capital mobility in the contemporary global economy. First, we review the literature that has attempted to measure the degree of international capital mobility. Although some early research around 1980 seemed to show that capital was far less mobile than was commonly believed, the preponderance of evidence now supports the finding of a very high degree of international financial integration. However, the integration of financial markets has not led to the fulfillment of some of the traditional expectations about capital mobility, and to a significant extent flows of saving and investment are still contained within national borders.

Second, we examine the pattern of international lending and borrowing that has emerged since the liberalization of international financial markets in the 1970s. We investigate how international capital flows have been linked to differences in fiscal policies and growth performance across countries. In particular, we highlight the perverse pattern of international lending among the major blocs of countries, in which the surplus regions (Japan, other East Asian countries, and western Europe) largely lend to the United States to cover the latter's chronic trade deficits.[2] The U.S. trade deficits are the mechanism by which the United States transfers its relatively strong aggregate demand growth to the rest of the world, while absorbing the excess savings of countries that are relying on export-led growth and repressing their own consumer demand. The United States absorbs far more capital inflows than the developing nations, and in fact the latter have often transferred resources to the industrialized nations rather than the other way around in the past two decades.

This then leads into our third topic, the sustainability of the current pattern of international capital movements, which rests upon continued U.S. net borrowing to sustain global demand and prevent an international contraction. We shall show that at the present rate, U.S. international borrowing is likely to lead to the build-up of a significant foreign debt problem over the next several years, and that the reaction of international investors to this growing debt burden—or any other "trigger" of a financial panic causing a massive exodus of funds from the United States—could potentially force painful adjustments on the United States that would also have depressing effects on other economies around the world.

---

2. The European Union (EU) overall trade surplus is now larger than Japan's, but the EU bilateral surplus with the United States is only about half as big as the latter's, indicating that the EU largely lends to other areas of the world. This point is discussed in more depth in section 4, below.

EVIDENCE ON CAPITAL MOBILITY AND
SAVING-INVESTMENT IMBALANCES

Standard economic theory teaches that, if capital funds are mobile internationally, those funds should flow from high-saving countries (defined as countries whose national saving exceeds their domestic investment) to low-saving countries (defined conversely).[3] Assuming that real interest rates are equalized across countries by international capital flows[4] and that saving and investment functions are independent of each other, national saving and investment rates should be "uncorrelated" in a world of perfect capital mobility, i.e., countries should be free to save more or less than they invest at home, with any excess lent out abroad and any deficiency made up by international borrowing. Moreover, there is an expectation (although no theoretical necessity) that such international capital flows should go primarily from the richer ("capital-abundant") countries to the poorer ("capital-scarce") countries, in which case international capital flows would help to promote greater equality in the world economy.

This benign view of international capital mobility has received a number of challenges in the last two decades. One important anomaly—that a significant portion of international capital flows has gone in the "wrong" direction, from poorer to richer countries—will be addressed in the next section. In this section, we focus on another anomaly, originally uncovered by Feldstein and Horioka (1980). Feldstein and Horioka showed that, in the 1960s and 1970s, the saving and investment rates of the industrialized countries were highly correlated. In other words, the industrialized countries were behaving as if, in the long run,[5] their domestic investment was largely (if not entirely) financed by their own national saving, implying that they were not significant net lenders (or net borrowers) of funds on international capital markets. Feldstein and Horioka concluded from this that capital was actually relatively immobile internationally, and that therefore increased national saving in individual countries would stimulate higher domestic investment rather than flow into a global "pool" of capital funds to be invested mainly abroad.

After the publication of Feldstein and Horioka's pioneering study, an enormous literature arose testing the robustness of their conclusions and providing explanations for their findings (see Frankel 1991, Mussa and Goldstein 1993, and Blecker 1997 for surveys). For the most part, Feldstein and Horioka's chief empirical

---

3. "National saving" in this context equals the sum of private saving plus the government budget surplus (or minus the budget deficit).

4. Recent work on international capital mobility emphasizes that the free flow of funds does not necessarily equalize real interest rates across countries, for reasons that will be discussed later in this section (see the discussion of "real interest parity," below).

5. Feldstein and Horioka's findings were based on data averaged over long periods of time (1960–1974 in their original study), and thus did not imply that there were no significant international capital flows in the short run. Rather, their findings implied that any such net capital inflows or outflows in the short run generally offset each other and "washed out" in the long run.

finding—that the major industrialized countries had highly correlated saving and investment rates, and hence had negligible long-run net capital outflows (or inflows) in the 1960s and 1970s—was found to be robust. However, this result turns out to have been true only for a relatively narrow range of countries and years. Subsequent studies found that: the saving-investment correlation is much weaker for developing countries than for industrialized countries (Dooley, Frankel, and Mathieson 1987; Summers 1988); the saving-investment correlation is also weaker for the smaller industrialized countries than for the seven largest countries (Murphy 1984); and the strong saving-investment correlation for the major industrialized countries weakened considerably in the 1980s, mostly as a result of persistent U.S. current account deficits (requiring net borrowing) and persistent Japanese surpluses (indicating net lending) (Frankel 1991; Bayoumi 1990; Tesar 1991; Feldstein and Bacchetta 1991).

While the empirical support for the Feldstein-Horioka proposition was already weakening, theoretical explanations for it were still being produced in generous quantities. Starting with the suggestions of Tobin (1983) and Westphal (1983), a number of economists proposed explanations of why saving and investment rates might be correlated even if capital funds are, in fact, highly mobile across national boundaries. Most of these explanations fall into two broad groups, which may be called "endogenous policy responses" and "common factor" (or "endogenous saving") arguments.

The endogenous policy responses explanation starts by noting that any imbalance between national saving and domestic investment is equivalent to the current account surplus (or deficit) in the balance of payments, which in turn indicates a country's net international lending (or borrowing) activity. Furthermore, sustained international lending leads to a build-up of international assets or a net creditor position, while sustained international borrowing leads to a net debtor position. Several authors have argued that governments are not indifferent to such current account imbalances and the attendant creation of substantial net creditor or debtor positions, especially in a world in which there are no enforcement mechanisms that can compel international debtors to be able to meet their debt service obligations to creditor countries. As a result, governments act to offset current account imbalances by actions that effectively bring total national saving back into line with domestic investment (see Summers 1988; Bayoumi 1990; Artis and Bayoumi 1990; and Epstein and Gintis 1992). These policy responses could entail fiscal policy adjustments, which raise (or lower) public saving to offset any shortfall (or excess) of private saving, but could also include monetary policy adjustments that either raise or lower private sector activity and private saving. The fact that such policy responses weakened in the 1980s and 1990s—especially in the United States and Japan—is one of the chief explanations for the emergence of greater international saving-investment imbalances in these two decades.

The "common factor" explanations all rest on the idea that the saving and investment rates of a country are not necessarily independent of each other, but may be simultaneously influenced by some of the same causal factors, thus implying that they may rise or fall together even if capital funds are highly mobile internationally. In effect, this means that the saving rate is not an exogenous constraint on investment, as presumed by Feldstein and Horioka, but rather the saving rate itself is an endogenous variable influenced by some of the same variables that determine domestic investment. Some neoclassical economists have offered "common factor" explanations based on the supply-side variables emphasized in neoclassical growth models, such as the rate of population growth, the age composition of the population, and the rate of productivity growth (e.g., Obstfeld 1986; Finn 1990). There is no empirical support in the literature for the population growth or productivity growth explanations, although there is some limited support for a life-cycle explanation based on the percentage of working-age people in the total population (see Summers 1988; Feldstein and Bacchetta 1991; Tesar 1991).

An alternative common factors view, which is more consistent with some strands of Keynesian theory, focuses on the importance of the internal finance of corporate investment in the private sector (e.g., Murphy 1984; Liu and Woo 1994; Blecker 1997). Since the corporate saving that is used for internal finance of investment counts as part of national saving, there is necessarily a correlation between saving and investment in the corporate sector to the extent that corporations finance a significant portion of their investment internally. Moreover, a large literature on financial constraints on investment suggests that total investment spending (including the part that is externally financed) is linked to the availability of internal funds in corporations, because robust internal funds ("cash flows") are a signal to lenders (whether banks or bondholders) of the ability of firms to service their debts.[6] Empirical support for the internal finance explanation is strong for the United States and certain other industrialized and developing countries, but the evidence is very sensitive to the particular countries studied.[7]

Thus, by the 1990s, it became clear that the saving-investment correlation discovered by Feldstein and Horioka in 1980 was limited to a relatively small group of countries (the larger industrialized nations) and had been weakening even among those countries after 1980. It was also established that such a correlation, even if it existed, did not necessarily imply international immobility of capital funds, since the correlation could be explained by endogenous policy responses of governments to current account imbalances combined with common factors that cause both private saving and private investment to vary in the same direction.

Moreover, the traditional notion that international capital mobility would lead to equalization of real interest rates across countries—a key assumption underlying the prediction of uncorrelated saving and investment rates—has now

---

6. The importance of internal finance of corporate investment was emphasized by Kalecki (1971), Steindl (1976), and Minsky (1986). Similar notions of financial constraints on investment and the importance of internal finance for relieving those constraints are found in some recent neoclassical literature such as Stiglitz and Weiss (1981) and Fazzari, Hubbard, and Petersen (1988).

7. For example, Liu and Woo (1994) find evidence that financial constraints are important in Taiwan, while Blecker (1997) and Bayoumi (1997) report that Australia is an exception among the industrialized countries.

been recognized to be flawed. Since real interest rates (i.e., nominal interest rates adjusted for inflationary expectations) pertain to returns on assets denominated in different currencies, international investors cannot arbitrage differences in real interest rates without having to be concerned about the risk of exchange rate changes over the life of the investments. Thus, in a world of volatile exchange rates, one cannot expect that the liberalization of international capital flows alone would be sufficient to equalize real interest rates in different countries. Taking exchange rate fluctuations into account, there is now a standard categorization of different definitions of the international mobility of financial capital (see, e.g., Frankel 1991).[8] In ascending order from the weakest to the strongest, these definitions are: (1) covered interest parity, (2) uncovered interest parity, (3) real interest parity, and (4) uncorrelated saving and investment rates (the Feldstein-Horioka definition).

Covered interest parity (1) can be defined by the well-known approximation

$$i - i^* = f \qquad (1)$$

where i is the home country interest rate, i^* is the foreign interest rate, $f = (F-E)/E$ is the forward premium on the foreign currency (with the forward exchange rate F and the spot exchange rate E both defined as the home currency price of foreign exchange). Condition (1) holds if short-term portfolio investment is mobile enough to arbitrage away any difference between a country's interest rate premium (on comparable assets of the same maturity) and the forward premium on foreign exchange (or, equivalently, the forward discount on the home currency). This requires only the free mobility of funds into and out of a country (i.e., the absence of political barriers plus minimal transactions costs) and the absence of country risk (i.e., the country's short-term government bonds are regarded as riskless assets and there is no perceived threat of the imposition of capital controls).

Each of the other definitions requires one additional assumption in addition to those required for the preceding definition. Uncovered interest parity (2) holds if the interest rate premium on a country's short-term bonds equals the expected rate of depreciation of the currency:

$$i - i^* = x \qquad (2)$$

where x is the expected rate of depreciation. This condition requires covered interest parity (1) *plus* the absence of an exchange risk premium. In effect, this means that domestic and foreign bonds must be regarded as "perfect substitutes" in terms of their risk characteristics, so that they differ only in their interest rates and in the currencies in which they are denominated.

Real interest parity (3) requires that real interest rates (nominal interest rates adjusted for expected inflation) are equalized across countries.

---

8. It should be noted that all of these conditions pertain to the mobility of financial or portfolio capital; no one claims that "real" or productive capital is perfectly mobile across countries.

$$i-p^e=i^*-p^{*e} \qquad (3)$$

where p^e is the expected rate of inflation (and a $*$ denotes a foreign variable). This condition holds only if uncovered interest parity (2) holds *and* the expected rate of real depreciation of the currency is zero. This last condition is known as "ex ante relative purchasing power parity," which implies that the expected rate of nominal depreciation equals the difference between the expected rates of inflation at home and abroad, i.e., $x=p^e-p^{*e}$. It should be noted that, since real interest parity concerns expected rates of returns on assets *denominated in different currencies*, there is no direct arbitrage activity that can be expected to enforce this condition if ex ante relative purchasing power parity does not hold. To put it another way, condition (3) requires effective integration of goods markets (so that purchasing power parity is expected to hold) as well as of capital markets. Finally, the Feldstein-Horioka definition (4) holds only if there is real interest parity *and* if there are no common factors or endogenous policy responses causing saving and investment to be correlated, as discussed earlier.

There is now firm evidence that covered interest parity (CIP) holds for all the major industrialized and for many developing countries that have liberalized their capital markets since the late 1970s. A classic study finding that covered interest differentials were smaller than transactions costs was Frenkel and Levich (1975). Later studies using different methodologies, and correcting some deficiencies in Frenkel and Levich's methods, have generally reached similar conclusions.[9] Frankel (1991, 1993) and Marston (1995) show definitively that covered interest differentials are negligible in both industrialized and developing countries that have liberalized their capital markets (especially by eliminating exchange controls).[10] By this criterion, all the major players in the international economy have highly integrated financial markets—at least for the types of highly liquid, money-market assets covered in these studies (typically, short-term treasury bills).

With regard to the other two interest rate parity conditions (uncovered and real), although there is no unanimity in the literature, there is a broad professional consensus that they are not satisfied in practice (see Mussa and Goldstein 1993; Hallwood and MacDonald 1994; and Marston 1995 for surveys). Early studies of uncovered interest parity (UIP) by Cumby and Obstfeld (1981), Fama (1984), Mark (1985a), and others assumed that expectations of exchange rate changes were "rational," which implies that ex post, actual exchange rate changes can be used as unbiased measures of ex ante expected depreciation. These studies rejected the hypothesis of UIP and found that there are significant, time-varying risk premiums on holding

---

9. M. P. Taylor (1987, 1989) and Taylor and Fraser (1991) found evidence mostly supportive of covered interest parity using contemporaneous data on exchange rates and interest rates at specific times when dealers could have conducted covered interest arbitrage operations. However, their use of interest rates for Eurobonds sold in London but denominated in different currencies means that their results do not really tell us anything about capital mobility across national borders (Frankel, 1991, p. 256 n. 38). See also Hallwood and MacDonald (1994, pp. 42–44) for a broader survey.

10. These authors also report that exceptions sometimes occur when countries are going through unusual financial market turmoil, at which time country risk presumably becomes non-negligible.

foreign currencies that cause interest rate differentials to differ from expected rates of depreciation. Later studies (e.g., Froot and Frankel 1989; Frankel and Froot 1990; MacDonald and Torrance 1990; and Marston 1995) used survey-based measures of expected exchange rate changes and came to the same conclusion. These later studies show not only the existence of a time-varying risk premium, but also that there are persistent errors in agents' expressed expectations of exchange rate changes.[11] Although there been some dissents,[12] the vast majority of the literature concludes that UIP does not hold in the data.

With regard to real interest parity (RIP), early studies that rejected it include Cumby and Obstfeld (1984), Cumby and Mishkin (1986), Merrick and Saunders (1986), and Mark (1985b). These studies all found that there are significant differences between real (inflation-adjusted) interest rates across countries.[13] Frankel (1991, 1993) concludes that persistent real interest rate differentials are caused by to the failure of expected purchasing power parity to hold. Ex ante (or expected) purchasing power parity is a dubious proposition in a world in which ex post purchasing power parity does not generally hold: real exchange rates are not stationary, and tend to "drift" away from their long-run means at least in the short and medium runs (although there is some evidence for mean-reversion over long time horizons of 20 years or more).[14]

Marston (1995) concludes that real interest differentials are significant and are also "systematic" in the sense that they are statistically related to information available to market participants at the time that inflationary expectations are formed. However, Marston notes that real interest differentials, while statistically significant, are actually quite small on average for most major industrialized countries.[15]

---

11. Defenders of "rational expectations" (e.g., McCallum 1994) counter that the expectations stated by agents in surveys may not correspond to the expectations that motivate their actual behavior in the market.

12. Reinhart and Weiller (1987) found evidence in favor of UIP using survey data. McCallum (1994) suggests that endogenous policy responses by the monetary authorities, which use interest rate instruments to try to smooth exchange rates, cause forward exchange rates to be biased predictors of future spot rates, and that taking this factor into account the data are consistent with UIP. McCallum, however, uses a somewhat unusual definition of UIP, which allows for an error term that incorporates excess returns (the difference between the forward exchange rate and the ex post future spot rate). I am indebted to Alan Isaac for this point.

13. In a typical methodology, these authors ran econometric regressions of the form

$$r_{i,t} = a + b r_{j,t} + e_t$$

where r is the real interest rate, i and j index countries, t is the time period, and e is a random error, and real interest parity is modeled as the hypothesis that $a=0$ and $b=1$.

14. If real exchange rates followed a pure random walk around their long-run average values, then the (rationally) expected rate of real depreciation would be zero, and ex ante purchasing power parity could still hold even if ex post real exchange rates deviated from their long-run averages. However, the evidence suggests that investors' expected real exchange rate changes are not zero (see, e.g., Froot and Frankel 1989).

15. A partial exception is the Japanese-U.S. real interest differential, the measurement of which is very sensitive to the specific interest rates and price indexes used. In particular, this differential is much smaller using manufacturing or producer prices, which more closely reflect traded goods prices, rather than a consumer price index that includes large proportions of non-traded services.

He attributes these small deviations from RIP to the fact that deviations from purchasing power parity are also small in the long run, even though they can be quite large over shorter time periods. Moreover, Marston finds that deviations from RIP are highly correlated with deviations from UIP, suggesting that the same underlying factors—exchange risk premiums and systematic exchange rate forecast errors—account for the failure of both of these interest parity conditions.

Although the evidence seems to indicate that UIP and RIP do not hold, it is important to recognize that whether these conditions hold is *not* a test of whether financial markets are integrated per se. The integration of financial markets is well-established by the fact that CIP holds. Furthermore, there is another type of evidence that supports this conclusion. That is, even if international interest rates differ in ways that violate some of the interest parity conditions, they may nevertheless still *move together* over time in ways that indicate a substantial degree of capital mobility.

Obstfeld (1986, pp. 63–64) cites studies of differences in interest rates on "onshore" and "offshore" assets *denominated in the same currency* (so as to avoid issues of exchange risk), such as U.S. dollar-denominated large certificates of deposit issued by New York and London banks (the latter constituting "Eurodollar" CDs). Such studies generally find that these interest differentials can be accounted for by bid-ask spreads and regulatory differences (e.g., in reserve requirements and deposit insurance) and that the rates are highly correlated over time, when the countries have liberalized their capital markets. Also, Goodwin and Grennes (1994) found strong evidence that different countries' real interest rates are "cointegrated," i.e., they have a long-run link to each other, and cannot move too far away from each other.[16]

Thus, the empirical failures of uncovered and real interest parity must be attributed to other factors, particularly the existence of currency risk premiums, systematic errors in exchange rate forecasting, and the absence of expected purchasing power parity, and not to the absence of capital mobility. As Frankel puts it,

> Only the *country premium* has been eliminated; this means that only *covered* interest differentials are small. Real and nominal exchange rate variability remain, and indeed were larger in the 1980s than in the 1970s. The result is that a *currency premium* remains, consisting of an exchange risk premium plus expected real currency depreciation. This means that, even with the equalization of covered interest rates, large differentials in *real* interest rates remain. (Frankel, 1991, p. 252, emphasis in original)

---

16. Goodwin and Grennes interpret this as evidence in support of real interest parity. They assume that real interest rates can differ internationally within narrow bands due to transactions costs, but tend to revert to these bands because arbitrage occurs once real interest rate differentials exceed the "neutral bands" attributed to transactions costs. The authors do not have any explicit measures of transactions costs, however, which could be compared with interest rate differentials, and they do not explain what type of "arbitrage" could avoid exchange risk. Thus, their results are better interpreted as showing that capital markets are highly integrated rather than as supporting real interest parity per se.

Frankel's comment about exchange rate variability being higher in the 1980s than in the 1970s suggests that some of the reasons for the persistence of real interest differentials—the currency risk premiums and the failure of expected purchasing power parity—may have been *exacerbated* by financial market liberalization and the prevalence of floating exchange rates. Thus, paradoxically, financial market liberalization may be preventing the convergence of real interest rates that is usually associated with the idea of capital mobility, at least under a floating exchange rate regime. But the traditional presumption that perfect capital mobility would lead to RIP basically ignored exchange rate volatility in the first place. In any case, the failure of RIP and UIP to hold does not imply the immobility of financial capital across national borders any more than Feldstein and Horioka's finding of a correlation of saving and investment rates did.

This brings us full circle back to the issue this section started with. Feldstein and Horioka's study was widely cited as showing that capital was far less mobile internationally than often assumed. The conclusion of this brief survey of the post-Feldstein and Horioka literature is that their own results did not really carry that implication, since their finding of a high degree of correlation between saving and investment rates across countries could be explained by many other factors besides immobility of capital. Moreover, their empirical results have not proved to be robust to more recent (post-1980) time periods and larger samples of countries. The evidence shows that portfolio capital today is close to being "perfectly" mobile between the major industrialized countries and many leading developing nations in the sense that financial markets are integrated enough to eliminate covered interest differentials on short-term government bonds. The evidence is much less clear on the degree to which markets for other types of financial instruments have become internationally integrated, however, since longer-term and more complex financial instruments do not have simple arbitrage conditions that are easily amenable to straightforward empirical testing.

The world still does not fit the traditional model of perfect capital mobility, in which all national savings flow into one global "pool" of savings, with equalized real interest rates and domestic investment completely uncorrelated with national saving in each country. This, however, is not due to a lack of integration of financial markets, but rather to other features of the contemporary global economy, which were ignored in the traditional model. These features include: the presence of exchange risk, which causes uncovered interest parity not to hold; expectations of real exchange rate changes (violations of expected purchasing power parity), which cause real interest parity not to hold; and the existence of "common factors" and endogenous policy responses that continue to make a large proportion of national saving flow into domestic investment in most countries (albeit to a lesser extent today than in the 1960s and 1970s). Nevertheless, the degree of capital mobility has clearly reached a point where changes in domestic saving and investment rates do spill over into significant and persistent current account imbalances, even for the large industrialized countries. This suggests a need for an examination of international trends in current account balances, to which we now turn.

THE PATTERN OF GLOBAL IMBALANCES
AND GLOBAL GROWTH

As discussed earlier, the 1980s witnessed a breakdown in the correlation of saving and investment rates across the major industrialized countries, particularly
the United States and Japan, while this correlation was never very strong among
the smaller industrialized nations or in the developing world. Since the difference between saving and investment equals net lending to the rest of the world
(or its net borrowing, if negative), a nation's saving-investment gap is equivalent
to the current account surplus (or deficit) on its balance of payments.

Table 1 shows the current account balances as percentages of gross domestic
product (GDP) for the major industrialized countries (the G-7) and selected
developing countries for the years 1970–96 (or the longest period after 1970 for
which data are available for each country). The United States went from having
alternating (but small) surpluses and deficits in the 1970s to persistent, larger
deficits in the 1980s and 1990s. The U.S. current account deficit peaked at 3.6%
of GDP in 1987 and then fell to only 0.1% in 1991, through the combined effect
of a depreciated dollar, a domestic recession, and transfer payments received for
the Gulf War. But this deficit recovered to 2.1% of GDP by 1997 and is projected to be even larger in 1998.[17]

The other side of the coin among the G-7 countries, of course, is the Japanese surplus, which peaked at 4.3% of GDP in 1986 but has remained persistently high in the 1990s, never falling below 1.4%. Germany also had large
surpluses in the 1980s, peaking at 4.8% of GDP in 1989 on the eve of reunification. But after reunification, Germany's current account quickly swung into a
deficit that has persisted at roughly 1% of GDP for most of the 1990s. The
United Kingdom had large deficits that reached 4.3% of GDP in 1989, but returned to balance on the current account in the mid-1990s. France was somewhat of an exception in the 1980s, without any major imbalances in either direction
except in Mitterrand's first year (1982) when there was a 2.2% of GDP deficit.
However, France did not eliminate foreign exchange controls until 1990, and by
1996 its current account surplus had climbed to a non-negligible 1.3% of GDP.
Italy and Canada both achieved balanced current accounts or surpluses in the
mid-1990s, after running persistent deficits throughout most of the previous 20
years.

Among the four major Latin American countries shown (Mexico plus the
"ABC" countries, Argentina, Brazil, and Chile), one finds a persistent pattern of
large current account deficits, as one would expect for countries with chronic
debt problems. However, some of these countries have occasionally run significant surpluses, usually immediately after a major financial crisis and devaluation
episode when international lending was cut off (e.g., Mexico in 1983–85 and

---

17. The 1997 figure was computed from data in Bach (1998). Table 1, which uses data from
the International Monetary Fund, only goes through 1996.

TABLE 1. Current Account Balances, as Percentages of Gross Domestic Product, G-7 Countries Plus Selected Developing Countries, 1970–1996

	United States	Japan	United Kingdom	France	Germany	Italy	Canada	Mexico	Argentina	Brazil	Chile
1970	0.3		1.6		0.0	0.8	0.6				
1971	-0.1		1.9		0.1	1.4	-1.1				
1972	-0.4		0.3			1.5	-2.2				
1973	0.5		-1.3		1.2	-1.7	-1.6				
1974	0.1		-3.8		2.4	-4.4	-2.9				
1975	1.1		-1.5	0.8	0.7	-0.3	-4.9			-5.4	-6.8
1976	0.2		-0.6	-0.9	0.8	-1.4	-3.8		1.2	-4.3	1.5
1977	-0.7	1.6	0.1	-0.1	0.8	1.0	-3.4		2.2	-2.9	-4.1
1978	-0.7	1.7	0.7	1.5	1.5	2.0	-3.9		2.8	-3.5	-7.1
1979	0.0	-0.9	-0.2	0.9	-0.7	1.6	-3.6	-4.0	-0.5	-4.8	-5.7
1980	0.1	-1.0	1.3	-0.6	-1.6	-2.3	-2.3	-5.4	-2.3	-5.4	-7.1
1981	0.2	0.4	2.8	-0.8	-0.5	-2.6	-4.2	-6.5	-2.8	-4.5	-14.5
1982	-0.4	0.6	1.6	-2.2	0.7	-1.8	0.6	-3.4	-2.8	-5.9	-9.5
1983	-1.3	1.8	1.1	-1.0	0.7	0.2	-0.8	3.9	-2.3	-3.5	-5.7
1984	-2.5	2.8	0.4	-0.2	1.6	-0.8	-0.4	2.4	-2.1	0.0	-11.0
1985	-3.0	3.8	0.7	0.0	2.8	-1.0	-1.6	0.4	-1.1	-0.1	-8.6
1986	-3.4	4.3	-0.2	0.3	4.6	0.4	-3.0	-1.1	-2.7	-2.0	-6.7
1987	-3.6	3.5	-1.2	-0.5	4.2	-0.3	-3.2	3.0	-3.9	-0.5	-3.6
1988	-2.5	2.7	-3.5	-0.5	4.2	-0.9	-3.0	-1.4	-1.2	1.3	-1.0
1989	-1.9	2.2	-4.3	-0.5	4.8	-1.5	-3.9	-2.8	-1.7	0.3	-2.5
1990	-1.6	1.5	-3.3	-0.8	3.2	-1.6	-3.4	-3.0	3.2	-0.9	-1.8
1991	-0.1[a]	2.0	-1.4	-0.5	-1.0	-2.2	-3.8	-5.1	-0.3	-0.4	0.3
1992	-0.9	3.0	-1.7	0.3	-1.0	-2.5	-3.7	-7.3	-2.4	1.6	-1.6
1993	-1.4	3.1	-1.6	0.7	-0.7	0.8	-3.9	-5.8	-2.9	0.0	-4.5
1994	-1.9	2.8	-0.2	0.5	-1.0	1.3	-2.7	-7.0	-3.5	-0.2	-1.2
1995	-1.8	2.2	-0.5	1.1	-1.0	2.3	-0.9	-0.6	-0.9	-2.5	0.2
1996	-1.9	1.4	-0.0	1.3	-0.6	3.4	0.5	-0.6	-1.4		-4.1

	Korea	Thailand	Indonesia	Malaysia	Philippines	Singapore	P.R. China
1970							
1971							
1972						-17.1	
1973						-12.5	
1974				-5.7		-19.8	
1975		-4.1		-5.3		-10.4	
1976	-1.1	-2.6		5.3		-9.6	
1977	0.0	-5.5		3.4	-3.6	-4.5	
1978	-2.2	-4.8		0.8	-4.5	-5.8	
1979	-6.4	-7.6		4.4	-5.1	-7.8	
1980	-8.4	-6.4		-1.1	-5.9	-13.3	
1981	-6.6	-7.4	-0.6	-9.9	-5.9	-10.6	
1982	-3.4	-2.7	-5.6	-13.4	-8.6	-8.5	2.1
1983	-1.8	-7.2	-7.4	-11.6	-8.3	-3.5	1.4
1984	-1.4	-5.0	-2.1	-4.9	-4.1	-2.1	0.7
1985	-0.8	-4.0	-2.2	-1.9	-0.1	0.0	-3.7
1986	4.4	0.6	-4.9	-0.4	3.2	1.8	-2.4
1987	7.4	-0.7	-2.8	8.1	-1.3	-0.8	0.1
1988	8.0	-2.7	-1.7	5.4	-1.0	7.3	-0.9
1989	2.4	-3.5	-1.2	0.8	-3.4	9.7	-1.0
1990	-0.7	-8.5	-2.8	-2.0	-6.1	8.3	3.1
1991	-2.8	-7.7	-3.7	-8.7	-2.3	11.3	3.3
1992	-1.3	-5.7	-2.2	-3.7	-1.9	11.4	1.3
1993	0.3	-5.1	-1.3	-4.7	-5.5	7.6	-1.9
1994	-1.0	-5.6	-1.6	-6.2	-4.6	17.2	1.3
1995	-1.8	-8.1	-3.5	-8.4	-2.7	17.0	0.2
1996	-4.8					15.2	

SOURCE: International Monetary Fund, *International Financial Statistics*, CD ROM, December 1997, and author's calculations.
a. Includes transfers received from U.S. allies for Operation Desert Storm of approximately +0.7% of GDP.

1987). Indeed, one of the striking things about the Latin American countries has been the instability of the net capital inflows and outflows represented by these current account balances. Rather than having a steady net inflow of capital at a sustainable rate, these countries have tended to fluctuate between surges of capital inflows that proved to be unsustainable and sudden withdrawals of capital inflows forcing painful adjustments in exchange rates and domestic growth.

The East Asian countries are an even more diverse group and, despite their recent common problems (the so-called "Asian flu" in financial markets) have markedly different patterns of current account imbalances over the past two decades. Indonesia and Thailand—two of the countries worst hit by the 1997–98 financial crisis—have had chronic current account deficits, which increased in the years just before the outbreak of the current crisis. The Philippines has also had more or less chronic deficits. South Korea and Malaysia both had surging current account deficits in the mid-1990s, but in these cases the deficits represented a marked change from large surpluses in the late 1980s. Singapore has had substantial surpluses throughout the 1990s, even in the last few years (although these are somewhat exaggerated as a share of GDP due to the fact that Singapore is a small city-state). Historically, however, Singapore had large deficits in the late 1970s and early 1980s. Finally, the People's Republic of China (hereafter P.R. China) has had a roughly balanced current account, with comparatively small deficits and surpluses approximately offsetting each other over the period shown (data are available only for 1983–95).[18] This is as expected, since China has never liberalized its capital markets as most of the other East Asian countries have, and the Chinese government has avoided becoming a major international debtor.

These data show the perverse pattern of international borrowing and lending since the 1980s that has frequently been commented on. In a well-functioning world capital market, a significant share of net outflows of savings would flow into the developing nations that need external finance for investment in order to be able to grow more rapidly without unduly sacrificing current consumption. But in fact, net resource transfers into developing countries have been relatively modest at best and negative at worst in recent decades. This can be seen more clearly in the data on the "resource transfer balance," which takes out the net investment income (interest payments and profit repatriation) from the current account balance, as shown in Table 2.

The data in Table 2 show that developing regions—especially Latin America and the leading East Asian exporters of manufactures—have often made significant net transfers of resources to the rest of the world since the mid-1980s. Latin America alone transferred out a cumulative $145.7 billion between 1985 and 1991. In the early 1990s, net resource transfers into Latin America became positive and reached $14.3 billion by 1993, before falling to almost zero in 1995 in the aftermath of the Mexican crisis. The Four Tigers (Hong Kong, Korea, Taiwan, and

---

18. Comparable data for Hong Kong and Taiwan are not available from the same database (the International Monetary Fund, *International Financial Statistics*).

TABLE 2. Net Transfer of Financial Resources[a] of Groups of Developing Countries, 1985–1995, in Billions of U.S. Dollars

	1985	1986	1987	1988	1989	1990	1991	1992	1993	1994	1995[b]
Total Africa	-7.4	2.1	-3.3	3.5	0.4	-10.8	-6.4	-1.4	1.3	6.3	5.8
Sub-Saharan Africa[c]	3.1	6.0	6.0	7.8	6.3	8.1	8.7	10.8	8.7	6.6	7.7
Latin America and Caribbean	-30.6	-11.9	-18.1	-21.8	-27.3	-27.1	-8.9	8.4	14.3	6.4	0.4
West Asia	18.3	34.4	22.1	27.3	19.1	4.3	51.9	39.8	34.3	17.2	10.1
Other Asia	4.1	-11.1	-29.9	-18.2	-11.0	-8.6	-7.2	-7.3	9.1	0.8	14.6
China	12.5	7.4	-0.3	4.1	4.9	-10.7	-11.6	-5.0	11.5	-7.6	-5.5
Four Tigers[d]	-12.1	-22.7	-3.0	-26.4	-21.7	-11.5	-7.1	-8.6	-12.6	-13.0	-7.1
All Developing Countries	-17.6	11.0	-32.7	-16.6	-24.7	-38.5	30.1	38.7	66.6	35.6	38.4

SOURCE: United Nations, *World Economic and Social Survey 1996: Trends and Policies in the World Economy.* New York: United Nations, 1996, Table III.1, p. 70.

a. Net resource transfers are defined as the negative of the balance of payment on goods, services (excluding net investment income), and unilateral transfers. Conceptually, this is equivalent to net capital inflows less net outflows of investment income. A positive number indicates a net inflow of financial resources and a negative number indicates a net outflow.

b. Data for 1995 are preliminary.

c. Excluding Nigeria and South Africa.

d. Hong Kong, South Korea, Singapore, and Taiwan.

Singapore) transferred another $145.8 billion cumulatively to other countries between 1985 and 1995. For developing countries as a whole, these large net outflows are counterbalanced by large net inflows into some other regions (western Asia and sub-Saharan Africa). Nevertheless, all developing countries together had negative net resource transfers (i.e., net financial outflows) for most of the late 1980s, peaking at $38.5 billion in 1990. After that, net resource transfers became positive in the 1990s, but they peaked at $66.6 billion in 1993 before declining to under $40 billion per year in 1994–95 after the peso collapse in Mexico.

While the developing nations as a group have had small or negative net inflows of resources, the world's richest nation—the United States—has been soaking up the lion's share of the world's net capital outflows from other countries. As can be seen in Figure 1, in 1996 the U.S. current account deficit of nearly $150 billion dwarfed the net capital inflows of all other capital-importing regions combined.[19] Among the developing nations that do receive significant net inflows of capital, only a mere handful account for most of the capital received. Thus, instead of going primarily to finance capital accumulation in developing nations, international capital flows are mostly financing U.S. trade deficits.

---

19. The data in Figure 1 are somewhat skewed to the left (i.e., toward bigger current account deficits or smaller surpluses) by the misreporting of international transactions that gives the world as a whole a $40 billion deficit on current account.

FIGURE 1. Current Account Balances, Selected Countries and Regions, 1996, in Billions of U.S. Dollars

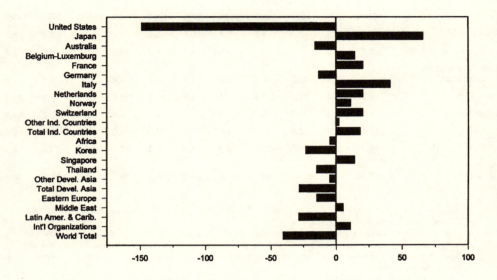

Source: International Monetary Fund, *Balance of Payments Statistics Yearbook 1997, Part 2: World and Regional Tables*, pp. 10–11, and author's calculations.

Note: The individual countries shown separately are those that had current account surpluses or deficits of at least $10 billion in 1996. Regional totals include other countries not shown separately.

Next, we examine how these patterns in current accounts have been linked to domestic growth and fiscal policies in each country. Data on government budget balances as percentages of GDP and growth rates of real GDP are presented in Tables 3 and 4, respectively. For the United States, the chronic current account deficits have allowed the country to finance chronic federal budget deficits and sustain moderate but steady growth of at least 2–3% annually for most of the period since 1983. While this is not exceptionally rapid growth by U.S. historical standards, it has been the most stable growth among the major industrialized countries during the last 15 years.

There are several qualifications to this apparently rosy U.S. picture, however. First, while the trade and budget deficits appeared to be "twins" in the 1980s, when they generally moved in the same direction, the trade deficit has worsened while the budget deficit has improved in the 1990s.[20] As of fiscal year 1998, the U.S. government is running a budget surplus, and hence continued net capital inflows in 1998–99 are likely to be entirely financing the excess of

---

20. For skeptical views on the so-called "twin deficits" in the United States see Blecker (1992) and Morici (1997).

private investment over private saving. Second, the chronic trade deficits had a devastating effect on the U.S. manufacturing sector in the 1980s and, while this sector has recovered somewhat in the 1990s through a lot of "downsizing" and restructuring, the picture has remained bleak for manufacturing workers whose wages and living standards have continued to erode (Mishel, Bernstein, and Schmitt 1997). Since most of the trade deficit is in manufactures, the continued excess of imports over exports has contributed notably to a decline in high-paying industrial jobs and their replacement by lower-paying jobs in the service sector (see Scott, Lee, and Schmitt 1997), which in turn has contributed to increasing inequality between highly-educated professional and technical workers on the one hand, and less-educated blue-collar and white-collar workers on the other (two groups that are often, rather misleadingly, referred to as "skilled" and "unskilled" workers, respectively).

Third, there are increasing concerns about the sustainability of the current U.S. growth path. The chronic U.S. current account deficits have turned the country into the world's largest debtor, with potentially destabilizing consequences down the road if the country's growing net debtor position and attendant net outflows of interest payments become too large or if foreign investors lose confidence in the United States and seek to withdraw their funds. We shall return to this set of issues in section 5, below.

Interestingly, few other industrial countries have exhibited the same sort of "twin-deficit" connection that the United States appeared to have in the 1980s. In the United Kingdom, the two deficits have been more like mirror images.[21] The United Kingdom had trade surpluses with fiscal deficits in the early 1980s, followed by the reverse pattern in the late 1980s. Both balances have been in deficit in the 1990s, but with the trade deficit improving and the fiscal deficit worsening. France has had minimal current account imbalances, as noted earlier, in spite of chronic large fiscal deficits. Germany has had more or less continuous budget deficits since the mid-1970s, but only in the 1990s (with the rebuilding of the eastern region) did a worsening of the budget deficit coincide with a turn toward trade deficits. Italy has managed to contain its current account deficits in spite of chronically enormous budget deficits (in the range of 10–15% of GDP), partly by devaluing the lira and partly by maintaining sluggish growth and high unemployment. Canada has had persistent deficits in both its trade and budget balances, and of similar orders of magnitude, but their movements have not generally been positively correlated over time. Japan has gone from large budget deficits in the 1970s and early 1980s to surpluses in the 1990s, coinciding with (and, indeed, contributing to) the slowdown in Japanese growth to a virtual standstill, but the current account surplus has remained relatively steady at roughly 2–3% of GDP in spite of a reduction of the fiscal deficit amounting to about 7% of

---

21. See Poloz (1992) for an international test of the so-called "twin deficit" hypothesis and Blecker and Hamam (1997) for a comparison of the budget-trade linkage and other macro relationships in the United States and the United Kingdom.

TABLE 3. Government Budget Balances, as Percentages of Gross Domestic Product, G-7 Countries Plus Selected Developing Countries, 1970–1996

	United States	Japan	United Kingdom	France	Germany	Italy	Canada	Mexico	Argentina	Brazil	Chile
1970	-1.1	-0.4	1.8	0.5	1.0	-4.8	-1.1			-0.6	-2.8
1971	-2.2	-0.2	-0.7	-0.4	0.9	-6.6	-2.0	-1.0		-0.9	-7.9
1972	-1.5	-1.6	-2.7	0.7	0.7	-7.4	-1.6	-3.0		-0.4	-12.8
1973	-1.2	-1.6	-3.4	0.4	1.4	-8.3	-1.3	-4.0	-2.9	0.3	-7.3
1974	-0.3	-1.3	-4.6	0.4	-0.7	-7.4	-1.3	-3.5	-12.2	1.2	-5.4
1975	-3.3	-5.2	-7.4	-2.6	-3.6	-12.1	-3.3	-3.8	-11.9	-0.5	0.1
1976	-4.1	-5.7	-5.8	-1.0	-2.8	-8.4	-3.2	-4.1	-8.8	-0.2	1.4
1977	-2.6	-6.4	-3.4	-1.2	-2.1	-10.4	-4.3	-3.0	-4.3	-0.8	-1.1
1978	-2.6	-7.5	-5.2	-1.4	-2.1	-13.5	-4.9	-2.9	-3.8	-1.7	-0.1
1979	-1.4	-7.4	-5.6	-1.5	-2.0	-9.8	-3.8	-3.0	-3.0	-0.6	4.8
1980	-2.7	-7.0	-4.6	-0.1	-1.8	-9.6	-3.5	-3.0	-3.1	-2.5	5.4
1981	-2.5	-6.5	-4.8	-2.3	-2.4	-11.5	-2.4	-6.5	-5.4	-2.5	2.6
1982	-3.9	-6.5	-3.4	-3.4	-2.0	-13.4	-5.6	-12.0	-4.2	-2.6	-1.0
1983	-5.8	-6.7	-4.4	-3.5	-2.0	-14.0	-6.2	-8.2	-7.5	-4.3	-2.6
1984	-4.6	-5.8	-3.2	-2.7	-1.8	-13.2	-6.5	-7.2	-3.8	-5.1	-3.0
1985	-5.1	-4.9	-2.9	-2.7	-1.1	-15.1	-6.0	-7.6	-5.3	-11.1	-2.3
1986	-4.8	-4.8	-2.4	-3.4	-0.9	-12.3	-4.0	-13.1	-2.4	-13.3	-0.9
1987	-3.1	-3.5	-0.7	-1.2	-1.1	-11.6	-2.5	-14.2	-2.7	-12.0	1.9
1988	-3.1	-2.6	1.5	-2.3	-1.7	-11.6	-2.2	-9.6	-1.3	-15.2	1.0
1989	-2.6	-2.9	1.5	-1.9	-0.2	-11.2	-2.5	-5.0	-0.7	-18.6	1.4
1990	-3.8	-1.6	0.7	-2.1	-1.6	-11.1	-3.1	-2.8	-0.3	-6.1	0.8
1991	-4.6	1.7	-1.0	-1.3	-2.2	-10.5	-3.6	-0.2	-0.5	-0.4	1.5
1992	-4.6	0.3	-5.0	-3.9	-2.4		-4.3	1.5	0.0	-3.9	2.2
1993	-3.9	-1.5	-6.4	-5.7	-2.5		-4.4	0.3	-0.6	-9.3	1.9
1994	-2.9		-5.2	-5.6	-1.4		-3.7	-0.7	-0.7		1.7
1995	-2.1		-5.3	-6.6	-1.8			-0.6			2.5
1996	-1.5			-5.4	-2.1						2.2

	Korea	Thailand	Indonesia	Malaysia	Philippines	Singapore	P. R. China
1970	-0.8	-3.7	-3.0	-3.9	0.1	1.6	
1971	-0.3	-4.7	-2.5	-8.1	-0.4	0.6	
1972	-3.9	-4.2	-2.6	-9.6	-2.0	1.3	
1973	-0.5	-3.2	-2.4	-5.6	-1.2	-0.1	
1974	-2.2	0.9	-1.6	-6.0	0.4	1.6	
1975	-2.0	-2.1	-3.7	-8.5	-1.2	0.9	
1976	-1.4	-4.0	-4.5	-6.1	-1.7	0.2	
1977	-1.7	-3.2	-2.1	-7.7	-1.8	1.0	
1978	-1.2	-3.6	-3.3	-5.9	-1.2	0.8	
1979	-1.7	-3.7	-2.4	-3.3	-0.2	2.3	
1980	-2.2	-4.9	-2.4	-6.9	-1.4	2.1	-2.8
1981	-3.3	-3.4	-2.0	-15.6	-4.3	0.7	-0.5
1982	-3.0	-6.4	-1.9	-16.7	-4.5	3.4	-0.6
1983	-1.0	-4.0	-2.4	-9.9	-2.0	1.8	-0.8
1984	-1.1	-3.4	1.4	-6.0	-1.9	4.1	-0.6
1985	-1.1	-5.2	-1.0	-5.7	-2.0	2.1	0.2
1986	-0.1	-4.2	-3.5	-10.5	-5.0	1.4	-0.8
1987	0.4	-2.2	-0.8	-7.7	-2.5	-2.7	-0.5
1988	1.5	0.7	-3.1	-3.6	-2.9	6.7	-0.9
1989	0.2	2.9	-2.0	-3.3	-2.1	9.9	-0.9
1990	-0.7	4.5	0.4	-3.0	-3.5	10.6	-0.8
1991	-1.6	4.7	0.4	-2.0	-2.1	8.6	-1.1
1992	-0.5	2.8	-0.4	-0.8	-1.2	12.6	-1.0
1993	0.6	2.1	0.6	0.2	-1.5	15.5	-0.8
1994	0.3	1.9	0.9	2.3	1.1	16.0	-1.2
1995	0.3	2.9	2.2	0.9	0.6	14.3	-1.0
1996	0.1		1.2		0.3		

Source: International Monetary Fund, *International Financial Statistics*, CD ROM, December 1997, and author's calculations.

TABLE 4. Actual Growth Rates of Real Gross Domestic Product,
G-7 Countries Plus Selected Developing Countries, 1970–1996

	United States	Japan	United Kingdom	France	Germany	Italy	Canada	Mexico	Argentina	Brazil	Chile
1970	0.0	9.4	2.3	5.7		5.3	2.6	6.9	2.6	2.6	2.1
1971	3.1	4.2	2.0	4.8		1.9	5.8	4.2	3.4	11.3	9.0
1972	4.8	8.4	3.5	4.4		2.9	5.7	8.5	1.9	12.0	-1.2
1973	5.2	7.9	7.4	5.4		6.5	7.7	8.4	3.2	13.9	-5.6
1974	-0.6	-1.2	-1.7	3.1		4.7	4.4	6.1	6.3	8.1	1.0
1975	-0.8	2.6	-0.7	-0.3		-2.1	2.6	5.6	-0.7	5.2	-12.9
1976	4.9	4.8	2.8	4.2		6.5	6.2	4.2	-0.2	10.2	3.5
1977	4.5	5.3	2.4	3.2		2.9	3.6	3.4	6.2	4.9	9.9
1978	4.8	5.1	3.5	3.3		3.7	4.6	8.3	-3.3	5.0	8.2
1979	2.5	5.2	2.8	3.2		5.7	3.9	9.2	7.3	6.8	8.3
1980	-0.5	3.6	-2.2	1.6	1.0	3.5	1.5	8.3	1.5	9.2	7.8
1981	1.8	3.6	-1.3	1.2	0.1	0.5	3.7	8.5	-5.7	-4.2	5.5
1982	-2.2	3.2	1.7	2.5	-1.0	0.5	-3.2	-0.6	-3.1	0.8	-14.1
1983	3.9	2.7	3.7	0.7	1.7	1.2	3.2	-3.5	3.7	-2.9	-0.7
1984	6.2	4.3	2.3	1.3	2.8	2.6	6.3	3.4	2.4	6.4	6.4
1985	3.2	5.0	3.8	1.9	2.3	2.8	4.8	2.2	-7.0	7.5	2.5
1986	2.9	2.6	4.3	2.5	2.3	2.8	3.3	-3.1	7.1	7.0	5.6
1987	3.1	4.1	4.8	2.3	1.4	3.1	4.3	1.7	2.5	3.4	6.6
1988	3.9	6.2	5.0	4.5	3.6	3.9	4.9	1.3	-2.0	-0.1	7.3
1989	2.5	4.7	2.2	4.3	3.7	2.9	2.4	4.2	-7.0	4.0	9.9
1990	0.8	4.8	0.4	2.5	5.7	2.2	-0.2	5.1	-1.3	-4.3	3.3
1991	-1.0	3.8	-2.0	0.8	13.2ª	1.1	-1.8	4.2	10.5	0.0	7.3
1992	2.7	1.0	-0.5	1.2	2.2	0.6	0.8	3.6	10.3	-0.9	10.7
1993	2.2	0.3	2.1	-1.3	-1.2	-1.2	2.2	2.0	6.3	4.6	6.6
1994	3.5	0.6	4.3	2.8	2.9	2.2	4.1	4.5	8.5	6.1	4.2
1995	2.0	1.4	2.7	2.1	1.9	2.9	2.3	-6.2	-4.6	4.1	8.5
1996	2.8	3.6	2.3	1.5	1.3	0.7	1.5	5.1	4.3		7.2

	Korea	Thailand	Indonesia	Malaysia	Philippines	Singapore	P. R. China	Hong Kong
1970	8.8	10.5	7.5		4.6	13.7		9.4
1971	9.2	5.0	7.0	7.1	4.9	12.5		7.3
1972	5.9	4.1	9.4	9.4	4.8	13.4		11.0
1973	14.4	9.9	11.3	11.7	9.2	11.5		12.7
1974	7.9	4.4	7.6	8.3	5.0	6.3		2.2
1975	7.1	4.8	5.0	0.8	6.4	4.1		0.2
1976	12.9	9.4	6.9	11.6	8.0	7.5		17.1
1977	10.1	9.9	8.8	7.8	6.1	7.8		12.5
1978	9.7	10.4	7.8	6.7	5.5	8.6		9.5
1979	7.6	5.3	6.3	9.3	6.3	9.3	7.6	11.9
1980	-2.2	4.8	9.9	7.4	5.2	9.7	7.8	10.4
1981	6.7	5.9	7.9	6.9	2.9	9.6	4.5	9.4
1982	7.3	5.4	2.2	5.9	3.6	6.9	8.3	2.7
1983	11.8	5.6	4.2	6.3	1.9	8.2	10.4	6.3
1984	10.1	5.8	7.0	7.8	-7.3	8.3	14.6	9.8
1985	6.2	4.6	2.5	-1.0	-7.3	-1.6	16.2	0.2
1986	11.6	5.5	5.9	1.1	3.4	2.3	8.9	11.1
1987	11.5	9.5	4.9	5.4	4.3	9.7	11.6	13.0
1988	11.3	13.3	5.8	8.8	6.8	11.6	11.3	8.0
1989	6.4	12.2	7.5	9.2	6.2	9.6	4.1	2.6
1990	9.5	11.6	7.2	9.7	3.0	9.0	3.8	3.4
1991	9.1	8.4	7.0	8.6	-0.5	7.3	9.2	5.1
1992	5.1	7.8	6.5	7.8	0.3	6.3	14.2	6.3
1993	5.8	8.3	6.5	8.3	2.1	10.4	13.5	6.1
1994	8.6	8.9	7.5	9.2	4.4	10.4	12.7	5.4
1995	8.9	8.7	8.2	9.5	4.8	8.8	10.6	3.9
1996	7.1		8.0		5.7	7.0		4.9

SOURCE: International Monetary Fund, *International Financial Statistics*, CD ROM, December 1997, and author's calculations.
a. Year of German reunification.

GDP over the 10-year period from 1983 to 1992. The explanation for this anomaly is that Japanese domestic investment has also fallen off, rather than being "crowded-in" by a reduced fiscal deficit as one might expect from neoclassical theory.

The growth rate data in Table 4 clearly show the stagnation of most of the major European economies and Japan in the 1990s. Among the G-7 countries shown here, only the United States and the United Kingdom have had steady, positive growth rates of 2% or higher every year since 1993. In this respect, the United Kingdom seems to have benefitted from its decision to withdraw from the European Exchange Rate Mechanism (ERM) in 1992 and to allow the pound to depreciate. In contrast, countries like Germany and France that have been committed to the path of fiscal austerity and high interest rates in order to qualify for the European Monetary Union under the Maastricht agreement have exhibited weak growth performance. With Japan also stagnated, the United States has been the only major "engine of growth" among the industrialized nations in the past five years (although Europe is finally showing signs of recovery in the late 1990s).

Among the Latin American nations shown here, only Chile has achieved steady, high rates of growth, and it has done so with conservative fiscal policies (the budget has been in a surplus every year since 1987). Chile's net capital inflows (current account deficits) have been somewhat erratic, but have generally been modest for a developing country (no more than 4.5% of GDP any year since 1987) and have not reached the levels that seem to have stimulated financial crises in Mexico, Thailand, and other countries. In contrast, while Argentina, Brazil, and Mexico have all reduced their budget deficits and/or run budget surpluses in the 1990s (with different timing and some setbacks), and while they have all had payoffs in the form of containing formerly high (even hyper-) inflation rates, none of them have achieved the kind of stable, rapid growth that Chile has exhibited. Mexico's recovery in the early 1990s was aborted by the 1994–95 peso crisis, after which real GDP fell by 6% in 1995 before recovering by 5% in 1996—a recovery that was almost entirely fueled by a rise in net exports and an oil-revenue funded increase in government spending, with private domestic absorption (consumption plus investment) barely recovering (Lopez Gallardo 1998). Argentina joined Mexico in a recession in 1995 and Brazil's growth has also been uneven.

Among the East Asian countries shown, only the Philippines has traditionally exhibited Latin American-style unstable growth, while the others all earned their designation as "tigers" for their exceptional growth performance right up to the eve of the 1997–98 financial crisis. The fiscal stances of the East Asian countries have been much more mixed. Singapore and Thailand have both run chronic budget surpluses, while P.R. China has had steady but small deficits of about 1% of GDP. The Philippines, Malaysia, Korea, and Indonesia all had chronic budget deficits until the mid-to-late 1980s—the exact year varies by country—but all four of these have moved toward budget surpluses at some point in the last 10 years. Certainly, fiscal profligacy cannot be blamed for these countries' recent financial turmoil, and the International Monetary Fund (IMF) conditionality that requires them to increase their budget surpluses seems like especially inappropriate advice in these cases (Sachs 1998). At a minimum, the East Asian record suggests that fiscal rectitude is neither necessary for steady growth nor sufficient to prevent a financial crisis in the private sector.

This brief tour through the data on international macro imbalances and growth rates should suffice to demonstrate the importance that net international capital flows have acquired since the 1970s. It also illustrates the frequently perverse pattern of international lending and borrowing, with the largest and richest industrialized nation, the United States, absorbing most of the net capital outflows from the surplus countries. The question then is what this pattern implies for international economic growth and macroeconomic stability, to which we now turn.

INTERNATIONAL ADJUSTMENT, MACRO INSTABILITY, AND THE RISK OF A GLOBAL CONTRACTION

The pattern of net capital flows, growth rates, and budget deficits detailed in the preceding section illustrates the dilemmas currently confronting the global economy. Among the industrialized countries, there are three major players: the United States, the European Union (EU), and Japan. The United States has been running chronic, large current account deficits, absorbing a large share of the world's net capital outflows, but at the same time transferring a significant aggregate demand stimulus to the rest of the world—including developing countries as well as the other industrialized nations. The United States is the only one of the three major areas with steady, moderate growth for the last five years (1992–97), and is close to full employment with the unemployment rate below 5% in 1997–98. Japan, on the other side, has been running chronic, large current account surpluses, supplying roughly half of the foreign savings flowing into the United States. Japan's economy has been in a protracted period of stagnation in the 1990s, with low growth rates and the threat of a recession in 1998. Europe is somewhere in between these two extremes, with—for the most part—large current account surpluses, slow and unsteady growth, and high unemployment.[22] Thus, the industrialized world is in a situation in which two of the three major regions have trade surpluses with generally sluggish growth, while the third region has a large trade deficit and relatively higher (if not extremely rapid) growth.

When one examines U.S. bilateral trade imbalances with the rest of the world, the picture looks somewhat different (see Figure 2). Japan still looms large, as the single country with which the United States has the largest current account deficit ($60.4 billion in 1997). However, the developing countries in Asia collectively

---

22. Notable exceptions include post-reunification Germany, which has had current account deficits since 1991, and Britain, which has had relatively robust growth, as discussed in the previous section.

FIGURE 2. U.S. Bilateral Current Account Imbalances with Japan, Other Asia, and the European Union, 1997

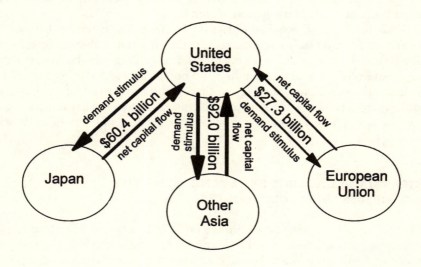

Source: Christopher L. Bach, "U.S. International Transactions, Fourth Quarter and Year 1997," *Survey of Current Business*, April 1998, Table 10, pp. 92–97.

Note: Arrow thicknesses show approximate magnitudes of the bilateral imbalances. Data for other Asia include Africa.

have an even larger current account surplus with the United States ($92.0 billion in 1997), even though they have an overall current account deficit with all other nations (contrast "total devel. Asia" in Figure 1 with "Other Asia" in Figure 2).[23] The reason, evidently, is that the other Asian countries have large deficits with other major countries, particularly Japan and the European nations, which more than compensate for their surpluses with the United States. Also, the EU accounted for only $27.3 billion of the U.S. current account deficit in 1997, in spite of having a projected $114.9 billion overall current account surplus with the rest of the world for that year (Organization for Economic Co-operation and Development 1997, p. A53). Evidently, a large proportion of the EU's total

---

23. Actually, the U.S. current account deficit with "Other Asia" shown in Figure 2 also includes Africa as well as all countries in Asia except Japan. Unfortunately, the source (Bach 1998) does not present separate figures for current account balances with Asia and Africa. However, one suspects that Africa accounts for only a small portion of the total for both continents combined. The U.S. merchandise trade deficit with Asia (excluding Japan) is reported separately in the same source, and is very similar ($90.0 billion) to what is reported for the current account deficit with other Asia and Africa together.

net lending is going to other parts of the world, such as Asia, Africa, and Latin America.

Putting all these figures together, what one sees is that the entire U.S. trade deficit today is accounted for by slow-growing nations in Europe and Asia. Sluggish as the latter economies may be, their growth prospects would be notably worse if it were not for the continual injection of roughly $200 billion of aggregate demand annually from the United States. The risk of a global economic contraction arises from the difficulties that the United States must face over the next several years in seeking to continue its economic expansion in spite of growing trade deficits and rising external debt. If the United States is forced to adjust by contracting its aggregate demand in order to reduce its trade deficit, the effects will be felt by other economies around the world. With no other major region or country currently pursuing expansionary policies, the next U.S. recession has the potential to bring on a global economic crash. In order to prevent such a scenario, it is essential for the surplus countries to bear more of the adjustment burden (a point emphasized by Davidson 1996). Given that most of the surplus countries have sluggish growth already, it would be in their interest as well to adopt stimulative policies that would reduce their surpluses and contribute toward reducing the U.S. deficit.

In particular, the world desperately needs Japan, as the largest surplus country, to stimulate its domestic economy, open its markets, and provide more demand for the products of other nations. But the Japanese government has been gripped by a combination of political paralysis and policy inertia that has prevented any serious response to the country's stagnant growth. Moreover, Japan is caught in a genuine bind, insofar as its rapid growth between the 1960s and the 1980s was highly export-led, and hence the reduction of Japan's trade surplus threatens what has long been its main source of demand stimulus. The appreciation of the yen in the late 1980s contributed heavily to Japan's subsequent stagnation, as it forced many industries to relocate offshore in order to remain internationally competitive. Indeed, fear of the consequences of further yen appreciation led to intervention to prevent the yen from rising further in the mid-1990s, but this prevented progress in eliminating Japan's trade surplus (Morici 1997). At this writing (June 1998), the yen is depreciating without intervention to push it down, due to a crisis of confidence in the Japanese economy and financial system. This can only worsen Japan's trade surplus and also puts competitive pressure on other Asian countries to devalue further, thus exacerbating the trade imbalance between Asia as a whole and the United States.

Japan cannot escape from this dilemma unless it relies more on domestic consumer demand, which requires major reforms of the country's internal as well as external policies to cheapen consumer goods and services and induce consumers to spend more and save less. Tax cuts and government spending can play a role in this process, but are unlikely to do a lot of good unless accompanied by deeper structural reforms to encourage consumer spending—otherwise, the extra disposable income (especially from tax cuts) may largely be saved, leading to small or negligible "multiplier effects." As one noted observer of Japan has written,

> Desirable as they may be, conventional tax cuts and other fiscal stimuli will not
> be nearly enough to do the job that needs to be done in Japan [in order to clean
> up its own financial mess and at the same time become a major buyer of the
> world's exports]. It will require extensive deregulation and restructuring mea-
> sures such as: open skies in aviation and complete deregulation of inland trans-
> portation, telecommunications, and distribution; drastic reduction of taxes on
> the buying and selling of land along with removal of most land use restrictions;
> . . . introduction of standard international accounting rules; the breakup of
> major government ministries; . . . and cessation of implicit government loan
> guarantees. . . . (Prestowitz 1997, p. C4.)

Ultimately, what is required is for Japanese consumer living standards to catch
up with Japan's potential income and productivity levels (at full employment). In this
respect, what Bayoumi and MacDonald (1995) call Japan's "consumption smoothing"—really, the failure of its consumer spending to keep up with its productive
capabilities—may be seen to impart a contractionary bias into the entire global
economy. Japan's policy failures create a negative externality for the entire world
economy and especially for the United States, which faces a greater burden of
adjustment in the absence of expansionary action by Japan. Furthermore, this problem is now being replicated in other Asian countries, which have been compelled
to contract their own domestic expenditures by their financial crises and the IMF
conditionality imposed as a condition for their bailouts. As Prestowitz argues,

> Asia's 'sound fundamentals' are counterproductive. The Asian system compels
> citizens to save too much, which results in too much investment (often in the
> wrong things) and too little consumption. . . . The IMF bailouts may be neces-
> sary, but because they have been primarily aimed at shoring up financial sys-
> tems and include large doses of austerity, they could wind up simply perpetuat-
> ing the old system and even exacerbating its flaws of excessive savings and ex-
> port-oriented investment. (Prestowitz 1997, p. C4)

Europe's situation today is dominated by the formation of the European Monetary Union (EMU), which will transfer control over monetary policy to a unified
central bank, combined with the continued existence of separate national governments with some (increasingly limited) policy autonomy. For the last several years,
the countries that are seeking to qualify for the EMU have been forcing themselves to reduce their budget deficits and maintain tight monetary policies. As a
result, unemployment has persisted at very high levels, and stagnant aggregate
demand has contributed to large trade surpluses in most (although not all) western
European countries. The primary objective of policy seems to be to control inflation and to guarantee that the new "Euro" will be strong currency, rather than to
promote full employment or rapid growth. A shift toward more expansionary macro
and monetary policies in Europe is also essential for boosting global demand and
lessening the pressure on the United States to adopt contractionary adjustment
policies. Moreover, since the EU's trade surplus is mainly with other countries
besides the United States, faster growth that reduces the EU's overall trade surplus would have a major, positive impact on other regions of the world such as
Africa, the Middle East, Latin America, and East Asia.

At present, the U.S. trade deficit (and the dependency of the rest of the world on demand stimulus from the United States) seems to be getting worse rather than better. As Table 5 shows, the U.S. merchandise trade deficit has worsened in each of the last several years. In part, the widening U.S. trade deficit results from the coincidence of faster growth at home than in many leading U.S. trading partners—especially when some of its leading trading partners still have relatively closed internal markets, especially in East Asia. But a rising dollar has also played a role. If traditional adjustment mechanisms were at work, in a world of mostly flexible exchange rates, one would expect the U.S. dollar to be depreciating against the currencies of those countries with which the United States has large trade deficits. However, such traditional adjustment mechanisms can be (and have been, in reality) suspended by capital movements into the United States and/or by foreign intervention in currency markets.

As Table 5 shows, the U.S. trade deficit has been highly concentrated with a relatively small number of countries. In recent years, the largest merchandise deficits by far have been with Japan and China[24] (each about $50 billion per year as of 1997), while large deficits have also been recorded with Canada, Mexico, the EU, Taiwan, other Pacific Rim countries, and OPEC. Yet, as can be seen in Table 6, the dollar has generally been appreciating and not depreciating against the currencies of most of the countries with which the United States has the largest trade deficits, such as the Japanese yen, the European currencies (ECU), and many newly industrializing countries' currencies, during most of the period from 1993 to 1998. (In some cases, the dollar initially depreciated in 1993–95, but in almost all cases it appreciated in 1995–98 and it also generally appreciated over the whole period 1993–98.)

Why is the dollar rising in spite of such large and growing trade deficits? In some of these cases (e.g., Japan and China), foreign governments have deliberately intervened to prevent their currencies from appreciating or even to make them depreciate against the dollar, as emphasized by Morici (1997).[25] Such intervention appears in the form of large net increases in foreign official assets in

---

24. The reported U.S. deficit with China may be somewhat exaggerated by the fact that a significant amount of U.S.-Chinese trade passes through Hong Kong, and such entrepôt trade is not well accounted for in the official statistics (e.g., some U.S. exports destined for China but shipped through Hong Kong may show up as exports to Hong Kong rather than to China). For the same reason, however, the reported U.S. surpluses with Hong Kong may also be misleading. A more reliable figure may be the total U.S. trade balance with China and Hong Kong combined, which was a deficit of $44.9 billion in 1997. See Huang and Broadbent (1998) for further analysis of problems in the U.S.-China bilateral trade data.

25. In Morici's words:

In the 1990s, the Japanese, the Chinese, and other governments have dramatically increased their purchases of U.S. government securities, propping up the value of the dollar against other currencies. This has helped to sustain both their trade surpluses and U.S. trade deficits, even as the United States has put its fiscal house in order. In most cases, these purchases are not market-driven decisions, made in response to higher interest rates. Rather, they often reflect policy decisions to block exchange rate adjustments, and reduce internal pressures on national governments to revise protectionist trade policies and the reliance on export-led growth. (Morici 1997, p. v.)

TABLE 5. U.S. Merchandise Trade and Trade Balances with Selected Countries and Regions, 1994–1997, in Billions of U.S. Dollars

Country or Region	1994			1995			1996			1997		
	Exports	Imports	Balance	Exports	Imports	Balance	Exports	Imports	Balance	Exports	Imports	Balance
Canada	114.4	128.4	-14.0	127.2	145.3	-18.1	134.2	155.9	-21.7	151.5	168.1	-16.6
Mexico	50.8	49.5	1.4	46.3	61.7	-15.4	56.8	74.3	-17.5	71.4	85.8	-14.5
South/Central America	41.7	38.5	3.2	50.0	42.3	7.7	52.6	49.5	3.1	63.0	53.7	9.4
European Union	107.8	119.5	-11.7	123.7	131.8	-8.2	127.7	142.9	-15.2	140.8	157.5	-16.7
E. Europe/former USSR	5.3	5.8	-0.5	5.7	7.0	-1.3	7.3	7.0	0.3	7.7	8.4	-0.7
Australia	9.8	3.2	6.6	10.8	3.3	7.5	12.0	3.9	8.1	12.0	4.6	7.4
Japan	53.5	119.2	-65.7	64.3	123.5	-59.1	67.6	115.2	-47.6	65.7	121.4	-55.7
China	9.3	38.8	-29.5	11.8	45.5	-33.8	12.0	51.5	-39.5	12.8	62.6	-49.7
Hong Kong	11.4	9.7	1.7	14.2	10.3	3.9	14.0	9.9	4.1	15.1	10.3	4.8
Singapore	13.0	15.4	-2.3	15.3	18.6	-3.2	16.7	20.3	-3.6	17.7	20.1	-2.3
Taiwan	17.1	26.7	-9.6	19.3	29.0	-9.7	18.5	29.9	-11.4	20.4	32.6	-12.2
Korea	18.0	19.6	-1.6	25.4	24.2	1.2	26.6	22.7	4.0	25.1	23.2	1.9
Indonesia	2.8	6.5	-3.7	3.4	7.4	-4.1	4.0	8.3	-4.3	4.5	9.2	-4.6
Other Pacific Rim	15.6	28.6	-13.0	19.4	34.4	-14.9	20.9	36.7	-15.8	25.1	40.3	-15.2
OPEC	17.9	31.7	-13.8	19.5	35.2	-15.7	22.3	44.3	-22.0	25.6	46.1	-20.5
Total World[a]	512.6	663.3	-150.6	584.7	743.4	-158.7	625.1	795.3	-170.2	688.9	870.7	-181.8

SOURCE: U.S. Department of Commerce, Economics and Statistics Administration, *U.S. International Trade in Goods and Services*, various issues. Data are measured on a Census basis.

a. Includes other countries and regions not shown separately.

TABLE 6. Selected Exchange Rates, in Foreign Currency per U.S. Dollar
(end of period, except as noted)

	1993	1995	1997	May 1998
SDR	0.72804	0.67273	0.74115	0.74870
ECU	0.8918	0.7609	0.9068	1.1053
Japan (yen)	111.85	102.83	129.95	138.57
Germany (mark)	1.7263	1.4335	1.7921	1.7828
Canada (dollar)	1.3240	1.3652	1.4291	1.4550
Mexico (new peso)	3.1059	7.6425	8.1360	8.8160
Australia (dollar)	1.4769	1.3423	1.5321	1.5966
China (yuan)	5.8000	8.3174	8.2798	8.2793
Hong Kong (dollar)	7.7260	7.7320	7.7460	7.7490
Taiwan (dollar)	26.77[a]	27.32[a]	31.79[a]	33.98
Korea (won)	808.10	774.70	1695.80	1407.50
Singapore (dollar)	1.6080	1.4143	1.6755	1.6740
Thailand (baht)	25.54	25.19	47.25	40.39
Indonesia (rupiah)	2,110.0	2,308.0	5,625.0	11,300.0

Sources: Exchange rates for 1993, 1995, and 1997 are for December 31 of each year, from International Monetary Fund, *International Financial Statistics*, February 1998, plus author's calculations for the ECU/dollar rate, except as noted for Taiwan. Exchange rates for May 1998 are for May 29 (the last business day in the month) and are taken from the *Financial Times*, June 1, 1998. p. 24.

a. Data for Taiwan for 1993, 1995, and 1997 are period averages for December 1993, December 1995, and November 1997, respectively, from U.S. Board of Governors of the Federal Reserve System, *Federal Reserve Bulletin*, various issues.

the United States, which rose to over $100 billion per year in 1995–96 before falling to only $18 billion in 1997 (see Table 7). In the cases of Mexico and several East Asian countries (Thailand, Korea, Indonesia, and Malaysia), the sharp depreciations of their currencies resulted from their financial crises (in 1994 and 1997, respectively), which led to large withdrawals of speculative capital, rather than deliberate policy actions (if anything, policymakers tried to keep nominal exchange rates too rigid, which invited speculative attacks on currencies perceived to be overvalued).

———

While Morici is right about foreign manipulation of exchange rates in the mid-1990s, by the late 1990s these official purchases of U.S. assets were swamped by the much larger private purchases, as discussed in the next paragraph.

But foreign exchange-rate management is only a part of the story of the rising dollar, and a less important one in the last few years (since about 1996). In the last few years, the United States has been flooded with soaring private capital inflows as international portfolio investors have fled "emerging markets" in developing countries that were suddenly perceived as more risky. As shown in Table 7, annual net foreign portfolio investment in the United States rose almost tenfold from $59.2 billion in 1990 to $564.4 billion in 1997, and more than doubled between 1995 and 1997 alone. These massive purchases of U.S. financial assets have contributed to the increasing value of the dollar in the last few years, which in turn has helped to push up the U.S. trade deficit (along with booming domestic expenditures financed in part by the foreign capital inflows).

TABLE 7. Net Increases in Foreign Assets in the United States,1990–1997, in Billions of U.S. Dollars

	Foreign Official Assets	Direct Foreign Investment	Portfolio Investment[a]
1990	33.9	47.9	59.2
1991	17.4	22.0	70.2
1992	40.5	17.9	110.4
1993	71.8	49.0	158.9
1994	40.4	45.7	211.3
1995	110.7	67.5	273.0
1996	122.4	77.0	348.2
1997	18.2	107.9	564.4

SOURCES: U.S. Department of Commerce, Bureau of Economic Analysis, "U.S. International Transactions, Revised Estimates for 1974–96, *Survey of Current Business*, vol. 77, no. 7 (July 1997), Table 1, pp. 64–65, and "U.S. International Transactions: Fourth Quarter 1997," Statistical Release of March 12, 1998; and author's calculations.
   a. Portfolio investment is defined as "other foreign assets in the United States, net" minus "direct investment."

The present capital inflow-driven rise in the value of the U.S. dollar is only the latest example of the power of international capital movements to dominate current account balances and exchange rate fluctuations in today's global economy. In the early 1980s, one reason for the U.S. dollar appreciation at that time was the search of portfolio investors for a "safe haven" in the face of the Latin American debt crisis, falling oil prices, sluggish European growth, and other problems in the global economy, which led to a boom in demand for U.S. assets. The liberalization of capital outflows from Japan released a pent-up supply of excess savings that came pouring into the U.S. capital market and helped to drive up the dollar's value at that time. While there were many other factors at work, including the unusual mix of loose fiscal policy and tight monetary policy at home (see Blecker 1992, Bosworth 1993), the surge of relatively autonomous portfolio capital into U.S. asset markets was an important reason for the dollar's rise at that time.

The recent crises in several major developing countries have also been driven largely by booms and busts in their liberalized capital markets. In Mexico, for example, huge inflows of portfolio capital into newly liberalized financial markets contributed to a real overvaluation of the peso and sharply rising trade deficits in 1991–93. Then, a sudden loss of confidence due to a combination of political events (a guerilla uprising by impoverished peasants, the assassination of the leading presidential candidate) and economic realities (recognition of the unsustainable character of Mexico's current account deficit and international debt position) led to massive withdrawals of capital in 1994, culminating in the devaluation of the peso at the end of that year. With net capital inflows suddenly reduced from about 7% of GDP to nearly zero, and under pressure from the United States and the IMF to adopt austerity measures, interest rates soared, and domestic expenditures were cut drastically. Mexico then fell into a severe economic crisis with depression-level unemployment and renewed high inflation in 1995.

To be sure, there were inconsistencies in Mexico's macroeconomic and trade policies in the early 1990s that made some adjustments inevitable (see Blecker 1996, 1997). The export-led growth anticipated from the North American Free Trade Agreement could not materialize with an overvalued peso being used as a lever to suppress domestic inflation, and deficit spending during the 1994 presidential campaign fueled an unsustainable boom in domestic spending. In this respect, Mexico's "fundamentals" were flawed and required some corrections (see Dornbusch and Werner 1994). But the severity of the 1994–95 crisis in Mexico far exceeded anything that could be directly attributed to the requisites of ordinary macroeconomic adjustment. As argued by Sachs, Tornell, and Velasco (1996), there was a "sudden shift to a panic equilibrium . . . in December 1994 after the announcement of a 15% devaluation," which set in motion a set of "self-fulfilling expectations [that] became decisive in generating a panic only after the government ran down gross reserves and ran up short-term dollar debt" (p. 266).[26] Such a "self-fulfilling panic" was made possible by Mexico's openness to volatile flows of portfolio capital, without which the dimensions of the macroeconomic crisis might have been more easily contained. Moreover, one could argue that the "fundamentals" were allowed to deteriorate excessively prior to the 1994 crisis by the ability of Mexico to cover such enormous current account deficits with international borrowing.

Similar dynamics were played out in the epidemic of East Asian financial crises in 1997–98. Starting with Thailand and then spreading to other countries, investors suddenly lost confidence in countries that had previously been

---

26. For another version of the self-fulfilling panic story for Mexico's financial crisis see Calvo and Mendoza (1996).

seen as offering golden investment opportunities. The large current account imbalances that were built up in some of these countries in the mid-1990s (especially Thailand, Malaysia, and Korea) became unsustainable as capital inflows turned into outflows, forcing painful adjustments in exchange rates, incomes, and employment. As in the case of Mexico, the crises were aggravated beyond what was needed to correct the fundamental disequilibria by speculative attacks that unleashed self-fulfilling panics in the financial markets, and by the adoption of IMF-promoted austerity policies for "stabilization" purposes.

The details of these financial crises in Latin America and Asia will be covered in other papers for this project (especially those by Roberto Frenkel, Salih Neftci, and Ajit Singh) and need not be discussed further here. What is important for present purposes is the potential for capital movements to suspend the traditional adjustment mechanisms or even make them work in the "wrong" direction, causing current account imbalances to persist or to grow more severe. In a sense, capital mobility seems to introduce what might be called "nonlinearities" into the international adjustment process. Instead of the smooth adjustments promised by traditional models of exchange rates and the balance of payments, disequilibria in the "fundamentals" are allowed to escalate as a result of the elastic nature of short-term international capital flows. Debt-financed excesses of government spending, private investment, or consumer spending can grow larger, continue longer, and create more fragile financial positions as a result of international capital inflows.

The perverse adjustments permitted by international capital flows do not last forever. As the cases of Mexico and Thailand illustrate, eventually the "bubbles" in the financial markets that attract large capital inflows are punctured, and traditional macro correctives reassert themselves: currencies are devalued, expenditures are slashed, and balance of payments equilibrium is restored with a reduced current account deficit (or possibly a surplus) adjusted to a lower level of net capital inflows (or possibly net outflows). By the time this happens, the requisite adjustments have become far more onerous and painful as a result of the magnitude of the disequilibria that were built up during the heady days of the foreign investment-led boom—and as a result of the self-fulfilling panics that can ensue. "Hot money" then rushes out of a country even faster than it came in and leaves the country broke and its economy depressed. The capital that has fled moves on to the next attractive market, threatening another boom-bust cycle in its wake.

Eventually, then, the "fundamentals" reassert themselves, but only after the magnitude of the required corrections has been greatly enlarged by the erstwhile availability of foreign capital to finance positions that, over time, become more and more unsustainable, as well as by the potential for financial panics to become self-fulfilling prophecies.[27] Indeed, in the data discussed in the previous section, the developing countries with the most steady, sustained

---

27. It must be emphasized that capital *inflows* per se do not necessarily seem to impart a contractionary bias into a nation's economy. While such mobility seems to promote greater instability, the countries that are on the receiving end of net capital inflows are able to grow faster as

growth (especially China and Chile) were countries that did not allow unfettered capital inflows, but rather regulated and managed such inflows—and these countries have been largely untouched by the financial turmoil among their neighbors in the 1990s.

As long as the instability fostered by international capital mobility can be contained in relatively small economies, as it has been so far, the damage to the world economy as a whole will remain limited. For the future, the major systemic risk lies in the structure of capital flows and macroeconomic positions among the major trading regions, the United States, Europe, and East Asia (including Japan), as outlined earlier in this section. As we have seen, the large U.S. current account deficits have served as an "engine of growth" for other countries, while serving as an outlet for the excess savings of the surplus nations. The issue, then, is whether the U.S. current account deficits that underlie this regime are sustainable, and what are the consequences for the United States and the rest of the world if the United States can no longer act as the "market of last resort" for other countries' exports.

THE SUSTAINABILITY OF THE U.S. INTERNATIONAL POSITION

In mid-1998, the U.S. economy is the envy of the world, with moderate but steady growth, low unemployment, and low inflation. There is much happy talk of a "new economy" that has made business cycle instability a thing of the past. Yet all the evidence is that the U.S. economy is having nothing more than a fairly normal but prolonged business cycle expansion, aided by some special factors that have suppressed inflationary pressures (e.g., the high dollar, weakened labor unions, and falling computer prices) (see Krugman 1998).

Moreover, the U.S. boom increasingly appears to be resting on a "bubble economy" of inflated asset values, mounting debt burdens, and an overvalued currency—not unlike what was observed in Mexico and the East Asian countries before their financial collapses, albeit with different nuances and a stronger set of underlying institutions.[28] For purposes of this paper, we shall focus in this

---

long as the inflows continue. This occurs, in spite of the trade deficits that are the other side of the coin of the net capital inflows, because of the stimulus given to domestic spending (either for consumer expenditures, private "real" investment, or government spending) when the latter can be financed (directly or indirectly) by foreign savings (see Bhaduri 1998 for a simple model of this phenomenon). Whether long-run average growth rates are higher or lower in the presence of high capital mobility, after controlling for other factors, is not obvious, and is a question that needs more research. If capital mobility does cause an overall contractionary bias in macroeconomic outcomes, this would seem to be mainly the result of the pressures of international financial interests on macroeconomic policymakers, rather than a result of capital movements per se as argued by Eatwell (1996).

28. The *Financial Times* of London referred to "the U.S. bubble" in a recent editorial, which warns that "the lessons of the Japanese bubble economy of the 1980s are surely that a failure to restrain a bubble can lead to an excessive accumulation of debt that debilitates the economy and paralyses the financial system" ("Addressing the U.S. bubble," April 22, 1998, p. 15).

section on the linkage between the U.S. current account deficit, which is financed by net borrowing from abroad, and the U.S. international debt position created by the cumulation of that borrowing over time. But this international dimension of the U.S. "bubble economy" is closely linked to domestic problems such as the overvalued stock market and the increasing reliance on consumer debt, and we shall highlight those linkages below.

Persistent current account deficits have turned the United States from the world's largest creditor nation in the early 1980s to the world's largest debtor today. By the end of 1996 (the last year for which data are currently available), the U.S. net debt position was $870.5 billion for all assets (including direct foreign investment valued at current cost and U.S. gold reserves valued at market prices) and $1,209.0 billion for portfolio investment alone (excluding direct foreign investment and U.S. gold reserves), as shown in Figure 3.[29] The U.S. net debtor position is worse for portfolio investment than for total investment because the United States has a large net creditor position in direct foreign investment (DFI) by multinational firms, which reached $241.7 billion in 1996, and because official gold reserves (valued at $96.7 billion in 1996) are included in total U.S. international assets.

The U.S. trade deficit is likely to become even larger in 1998–99 due to the repercussions of the East Asian financial crisis and the rising value of the dollar. Japan, Korea, Thailand, and other Pacific Rim countries are likely to increase their net exports to the United States, because of both the collapse of their domestic demand and the depreciation of their currencies. The U.S. merchandise trade deficit was $199 billion in 1997, while the current account deficit was $166 billion, and many forecasts imply that these numbers could worsen by $100 billion or more in 1998.[30] A $300 billion trade deficit would represent nearly 4% of U.S. GDP (which is currently about $8 trillion), and while this might not be a large percentage for a developing country, it would certainly be large by U.S. historical standards (see Table 1).

Over time, an increasing net international debt position creates an endogenous drag on a country's balance of payments by increasing debt service obligations—net interest outflows plus the need to refinance principal as it comes due. Surprisingly, the U.S. net investment income account (the net inflow or outflow of interest and other capital income from international assets and debts, which is counted in the current account of the balance of payments) had not turned negative as of 1996 (see Figure 4), even though the United States had become a net debtor overall by the late 1980s (in 1986 with DFI valued at current cost, as

---

29. All data in this paragraph are from Scholl (1997) and author's calculations. The U.S. net debt position was $831.3 billion with DFI measured at market value in 1996.

30. Preliminary data for 1997 are from Bach (1998). Scott and Rothstein (1998) cite predictions by David Hale and C. Fred Bergsten regarding likely increases in the U.S. trade deficit for 1998. The total merchandise trade deficit for 1997 reported in Table 5 (about $182 billion) differs from the figure cited here because it is measured on a Census basis, whereas the International Transactions data cited here are measured on a balance-of-payments basis.

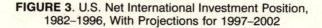

FIGURE 3. U.S. Net International Investment Position, 1982–1996, With Projections for 1997–2002

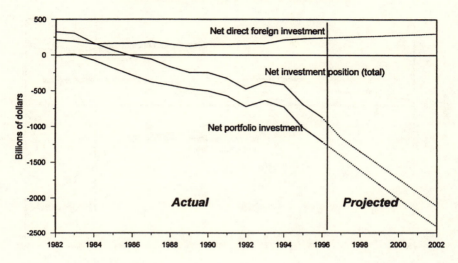

SOURCE: Russell B. Scholl, "The International Investment Position of the United States in 1996, *Survey of Current Business*, July 1997, Table 3, p. 33, and author's calculations. See text for explanation of the assumptions made in the projections.

NOTE: Direct foreign investment is measured at current cost. The total net investment position includes direct foreign investment measured at current cost. The net portfolio investment position is defined as the net position for all assets excluding direct foreign investment and U.S. official gold reserves.

shown in Figure 3, and in 1988 with DFI valued at market value). The main reason for this discrepancy is that net income from DFI continued to be large enough to offset net interest payments on portfolio debt, although the latter were rising faster than the former.[31] As can be seen in Figure 4, this meant that the U.S. surplus on total net investment income fell from about $30 billion per year in the early 1980s to just $3 billion in 1996.

Current trends indicate that this delicate balancing act has begun to collapse. Preliminary U.S. balance of payments data for 1997 indicate a deficit on net investment income of $14.3 billion, consisting of a net outflow of $82.0 billion of portfolio investment income (interest, dividends, etc.) only partially

---

31. Godley and Milberg (1994) explain this phenomenon by noting that the implicit rate of return on U.S. net DFI is higher than on U.S. net portfolio debt, which is why the net income from the former has until recently been large enough to counterbalance the net outpayments on the former. They argue that this may be somewhat misleading if foreign companies operating in the United States tend to bring their income home more in the form of "transfer pricing" (high prices for semi-finished goods they import into the United States from their home countries) rather than in profit remissions. This has no effect on the overall balance of payments or current account, but tend to make the merchandise trade balance look worse and the net investment income balance look better than would be the case if the income were brought home more in the form of repatriated profits.

FIGURE 4. U.S. Net International Investment Income,
1970–1996, With Projections for 1997–2002

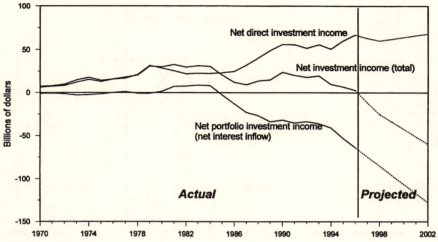

Source: Christopher L. Bach, "U.S. International Transactions, First Quarter 1997," *Survey of Current Business*, July 1997, Table 1, pp. 64–65, and author's calculations. See text for explanation of the assumptions made in the projections.

Note: Net portfolio investment income includes all net investment income inflows (receipts) and outflows (payments) *except* for direct foreign investment; both "U.S. government" and "Other private" receipts and payments are included.

offset by a net inflow of $67.7 of DFI income.[32] With a current account deficit headed upwards of $200 billion per year, U.S. borrowing is likely to increase steadily and the net debtor position for portfolio investment is likely to deteriorate sharply in the next few years. This in turn will entail a rising outflow of net interest payments, which will grow much more rapidly than DFI net income. Furthermore, the rising value of the dollar in the last few years (as shown in Table 6) implies a negative valuation effect for the dollar value of U.S. investments abroad (both DFI and portfolio), and hence the income on those investments will be also be worth less in dollar terms as foreign currencies depreciate. This implies that the dollar value of net inflows of repatriated income from U.S. investments abroad (both DFI and portfolio investments) will fall in 1997–98. As a result of these trends, the net outflows of interest payments are going to rise much more rapidly than the net inflows of income from DFI, giving the United States a growing deficit for total net investment income over the next several years.

To make these predictions more concrete, some projections of the trends in the U.S. net international investment position and net investment income flows

---

32. Bach (1998), Table 1, p. 79, and author's calculations. Net "portfolio" income includes U.S. government receipts less U.S. government payments.

for the years 1997 to 2002 are shown in Figures 3 and 4, respectively.[33] Figure 3 assumes that the U.S. DFI position improves gradually (by about $10 billion per year, which is consistent with recent trends), as U.S. multinational firms take advantage of the high dollar to invest abroad. It is also assumed (conservatively) that the U.S. portfolio investment position worsens by $200 billion per year due to continued large current account deficits (and, at least in 1997–98, the valuation effect of the higher dollar). Based on these projections, the U.S. net investment position declines to a net portfolio debt of $2.4 trillion and a net total debt of $2.1 trillion by 2002, representing roughly 20% of GDP at that time (which should be on the order of about $10 trillion in nominal terms).

Figure 4 shows the corresponding projections for net investment income flows. Net income from DFI is assumed to fall from $67 billion in 1996 to $60 billion in 1998, due to the rising dollar, and then to recover gradually by $2 billion per year thereafter (again, based on extrapolation of recent trends). It is also assumed that the net interest outflow on portfolio investment equals 5.3% of the value of the net portfolio debt in each year from 1997 through 2002 (essentially, assuming a nominal interest rate approximately equal to the current level[34]). On these assumptions, the net interest outflow doubles from $64 billion in 1996 to $128 billion in 2002, and the total net investment income deficit rises to about $60 billion by 2002.[35]

This baseline forecast is essentially just an extrapolation of current trends: it tells us the likely outcome if there are no changes in current patterns in U.S. international borrowing, interest rates, and other variables over the next few years. In reality, change should be expected, and the actual outcome could differ in either direction. If interest rates rise or the current account balance worsens further, then the U.S. net debt position and U.S. net outpayments of interest income will become correspondingly larger. On the other hand, adjustments that could lower the U.S. current account deficit (e.g., dollar depreciation, a U.S. recession, or increased foreign growth) would lessen the amount of new borrowing and ameliorate the increase in debt service obligations. Since international financial conditions can change very rapidly, these forecasts are intended only to be indicative of the possible order of magnitude of the future U.S. international debt problem.[36]

---

33. The forecasts start with 1997 because complete data for that year are not yet available. Preliminary data on net investment income flows are found in Bach (1998), but data on outstanding stocks of international assets and debts for 1997 will not be available until later in 1998.

34. In 1996, the last year for which complete data is available, U.S. net payments of interest were $63.9 billion relative to a net portfolio debt position of $1,209.0 billion, representing an implicit interest rate of about 5.3%.

35. The projected net investment income outflow for 1997 is $11.7 billion, slightly lower than the actual $14.3 billion net outflow reported in preliminary data for that year by Bach (1998). This indicates that the present estimates can be regarded as conservative.

36. A net investment income deficit on the order of about $60 billion per year (as shown for 2002 in Figure 4) would nearly cancel out the benefit that the United States currently receives from its much-touted surplus in nonfactor services (which was about $80 billion in 1996 and rose to $85

One obvious question that emerges from this discussion is how sustainable is the U.S. net international debt position in terms of its own dynamics. The international finance literature contains various models of the conditions for a country's net international debt position to stabilize or explode. One conventional sort of analysis shows that a net debt position can be stabilized as a constant ratio to GDP if the growth rate of the debt (which, with a constant ratio of debt to GDP, must equal the growth rate of GDP) exceeds the interest rate.[37] At present, the United States is still out of such a steady state, but could be converging into one. The country's net debt position was increasing at a 20% annual rate in 1996, which is projected to slow to about 8% per year in 2002 in the forecasts depicted in Figure 3. If nominal GDP growth continues at about 5% per year, and if the growth rate of the net debt position eventually slows to about 5% (this would occur when the net debt position reaches $4 trillion, which would be around 2012 assuming continued net borrowing of $200 billion per year), the U.S. debt position could stabilize at a constant proportion of GDP—but *only if* the interest rate is held below 5%. A higher interest rate would spoil this scenario and imply a destabilizing explosion of debt payments in the future.

Although an unstable debt dynamic could potentially generate a balance-of-payments crisis for the United States, that is probably not likely to occur in the immediate future *unless* there is some other shock that triggers a financial crisis. However, there are a number of possible "triggers" of a financial panic that could, in one way or another, make it difficult for the United States to finance its current account deficit and put the country on an unstable debt trajectory. One scenario is that "news" of large current account deficits and/or an increased international debt position over the next few years could spook investors and diminish confidence in the United States, much as occurred in Mexico in 1994 or Thailand in 1997. Of course, such news should not really be a surprise, but for short-sighted investors who are currently overoptimistic about the U.S. economy (and who are "rationally" participating in the bubble economy by buying assets that they expect to continue to appreciate in value over a short time horizon), an accumulation of bad economic news could engender a belief that current trends are unsustainable—and hence make them actually unsustainable, by inducing a sell-off of U.S. assets.

---

billion in preliminary data for 1997). Coupled with net unilateral transfers that are typically negative (to the tune of almost $40 billion annually in recent years), this would imply that the U.S. current account deficit would begin to exceed the merchandise trade deficit (which, up to the present, has been larger) by the early 2000s. Moreover, rising net outflows of interest income generate a negative feedback onto the U.S. net debtor position, since a worsened current account balance requires further increases in U.S. net borrowing. However, the dynamic interaction of debt accumulation, interest payments, and increased net borrowing is not explicitly incorporated into the forecasts shown in Figures 3 and 4.

37. See Hallwood and MacDonald (1994, pp. 369–70) for a standard exposition. See L. Taylor (1997) for a theoretical model examining the stability (or instability) of debt dynamics under a variety of scenarios. See also Bhaduri (1987) for an analysis of the consequences of interest rates, saving rate, and propensities to export and import for debt dynamics.

A trigger for a financial crisis could also emerge from the domestic economy or domestic politics. Banks that have overlent to consumers could encounter trouble if consumers begin to have problems servicing their debts. The stock market bubble could be punctured and asset markets could take a nosedive. A political crisis could make the United States appear to be less of a "safe haven." Whatever the trigger, anything that would cause investors' expectations about the U.S. economy or financial system to be revised downward could potentially induce massive withdrawals of portfolio capital from the country, which in turn would make the United States unable to continue financing current account deficits of upwards of $200 billion per year.

A financial crisis for the U.S. economy would put the Federal Reserve in an uncomfortable policy bind. On the one hand, the standard response of a central bank to a withdrawal of foreign funds and a run on the currency is to raise interest rates in the hope of stemming the outflow of funds and bolstering the exchange rate. But, as we have seen repeatedly in recent years, such a response tends to cripple the domestic economy and to undermine the stability of domestic banks. On the other hand, to stabilize the banking system and prevent major financial institutions from failing, the Fed's natural response would be to inject liquidity into the system by pumping reserves into the banks, as the Fed did after the stock market crash of 1987. Such a response would mean lower interest rates and a depreciated dollar, which could help to reduce the trade deficit and thus curtail the U.S. economy's need for international borrowing. But low interest rates and a falling dollar might only heighten investors' panic, causing more capital to flee and putting more pressure on the Fed to reverse course and raise interest rates. Moreover, dollar depreciation could potentially stimulate a revival of inflation,[38] which in turn could induce the Fed to raise interest rates (and precipitate a recession) in pursuit of its paramount objective of price stability.

It is at this point that the dynamics of the U.S. international debt become important. Even if the rising U.S. foreign debt is not itself a trigger of a financial crisis, a response to such a crisis that entailed higher interest rates would make it more expensive to service the debt, since much of the debt consists of short-term instruments that have to be rolled over frequently. This means that the debt places an additional constraint on U.S. policy makers, which they did not face the last time there was a run on the dollar in 1979.[39] At that time, then-Fed chairman Paul Volcker raised interest rates through the roof in order to stem inflation and rescue

---

38. The dollar depreciation of 1985–87 did not unleash a large increase in inflation, contrary to fears at the time. However, the U.S. economy is more import-dependent today than ten years ago, and the high dollar is now widely cited as a factor containing inflationary pressures. Even a modest inflationary effect of a depreciated dollar could induce a contractionary policy response of the Fed, which is all that matters for the present argument.

39. Although the dollar depreciated more in 1985–87 than in 1978–79, the 1985–87 depreciation was much more orderly and in fact was welcomed by policy makers who were trying to talk the dollar down. Thus, the 1985–87 episode cannot be regarded as a "run" on the dollar, at least not in the usual sense of a crisis calling for a policy response.

the dollar. But the United States did not have a large outstanding international portfolio debt to service at that time. In contrast, by 2002 we project a net U.S. portfolio debt on the order of $2.4 trillion. If the interest rate were to double from (say) 5% to 10% at that time, the net interest payments deficit would increase by up to $120 billion (depending on how much of the debt was variable rate or short-term), which in turn would worsen the current account by the same amount. Since the higher current account deficit would require yet more international borrow-ing, the debt could begin to rise explosively, virtually assuring that a painful con-traction in national income would be needed in order to curtail the U.S. appetite for imports and keep the current account deficit from widening too much.

One could object that the amount of foreign assets in the United States is too small for its withdrawal to cause a major crisis, or that foreign investors have no other "safe haven" to which they can flee. With regard to the first point, foreign assets in the United States are far from negligible, especially in terms of ownership of highly liquid assets such as Treasury securities. By the end of 1997, foreigners (including foreign central banks) owned fully one-third of outstand-ing U.S. Treasury securities, up from less than one-fifth in 1993.[40] Thus, a large-scale sale of U.S. Treasury securities by foreign owners could virtually force the Federal Reserve to raise interest rates as bond prices would be depressed.[41] Over-all, gross foreign portfolio assets in the United States (excluding central bank official assets and foreign DFI in the United States) reached $3.1 trillion by 1996 (Scholl 1997, Table 1, p. 31, and author's calculations), an amount clearly large enough to have a significant impact on domestic financial markets if large parts of it were sold off. Furthermore, it is not only foreign money that would flee the United States in a financial crisis; domestic investors could also engage in "capital flight." Much domestic investment has returned to the United States from "emerging markets" since the Mexican crisis of 1994 and the Asian crisis of 1997, but such funds could go abroad again.

With regard to the second point, it is true that the amount of money that would have to flee the United States to foster an external financial crisis for the United States probably could not be absorbed in a lot of small markets and would need a large, stable financial center to which to go. In this respect, the creation of the Euro as a new strong currency could prove to be a significant factor, by providing another "safe haven" for international investors. The Euro could create an alternative to the dollar for use as a reserve currency and for conducting international transactions.

---

40. Author's calculations, based on data in U.S. Board of Governors of the Federal Reserve System, *Flow of Funds Accounts*, Release of March 13, 1998, Table L.209, from website: www.bog.frb.fed.us/releases/Z1/Current. At yearend 1997, the "rest of the world" owned $1,256.6 billion out of a total of $3,778.3 billion of outstanding U.S. Treasury securities.

41. This point suggests that the globalization of financial markets constrains the Fed's ability to set interest rates, an ability that is taken for granted in some theories of "endogenous money." See Pearlstein (1998), who reports that large foreign purchases of U.S. Treasury securities have made it difficult for the Fed to raise interest rates in the last few years. The same could be true in reverse, if foreign investors and central banks began to dump U.S. Treasury securities.

If the European economies have a boom in the early 2000s, Europe could become a new center of attraction for global finance. The Asian economies could also recuperate in the next several years, and again become an attractive location for investors.

Thus, the outbreak of a financial crisis in the United States has the potential to make the U.S. international debt position unsustainable, even if it could be sustained in the absence of such a crisis. An exodus of portfolio capital from the United States could force interest rates to rise and destabilize the country's debt dynamics, even if the country's international debt would be serviceable as long as the net capital inflows continued. Thus, one cannot conclude from the fact that the U.S. net international debt would still be "only" about 20% of GDP by 2002 (according to the projections in Figure 3) that the country would be immune to an international financial crisis.

While such a crisis scenario bears some resemblance to the recent financial crises in Mexico and East Asia, there are also some important differences. One key difference is that the United States does not have a fixed exchange rate regime. Thus, the U.S. government would not be forced to defend an indefensible currency peg, as the governments of Mexico, Thailand, and several other countries felt obligated to do. Nevertheless, a massive sell-off of U.S. assets and a flight into other currencies would cause the dollar to lose value very abruptly. Moreover, although the U.S. government is not obligated to defend the dollar's value, it could choose to do so via extensive exchange-market intervention, which would invite the same sort of speculative attack that can be launched on a fixed exchange rate.

Another key difference is that the United States can borrow in its own currency. This means that a currency depreciation does not instantly raise the domestic-currency cost of debt service, as it does in a country that has to borrow in a foreign currency. While this is an advantage for the United States today, if there were sufficient perceptions of exchange rate risk by foreign investors in the future, they could begin to demand that loans to the United States be denominated in (or indexed to) foreign currencies. The U.S. government has considered issuing foreign currency-denominated bonds in the past and could be forced to do so in the future.

To summarize, the real problem is not that the U.S. international debt will necessarily become unserviceable in the immediate future. A net debt upwards of $2 trillion could conceivably be serviced well into the 2000s. Of course, U.S. domestic incomes would have to be squeezed to some extent to allow for the net transfer of interest payments abroad, and our forecasts of the net interest outflow imply that it will amount to just over 1% of GDP by the early 2000s. But the most likely risk in the not-too-distant future is the threat of a financial crisis causing a sudden withdrawal of funds from the United States, which would force the country to adjust to a much lower level of net capital inflows and a lower current account deficit—an adjustment that could have serious depressive repercussions for the entire global economy, for reasons argued earlier. Even if this risk is small, it is real, it is not negligible, and the possibility of a significant global contraction cannot be ruled out.

CONCLUSIONS AND POLICY IMPLICATIONS

The evidence reviewed in this paper confirms that international financial markets have in fact become tightly integrated in the past two decades. The most basic international financial arbitrage condition—covered interest parity—holds for all the major industrialized countries and many developing countries as well. Somewhat paradoxically, however, the world still does not completely fit the traditional model of "perfect capital mobility"—a model that ignored the implications of exchange-rate uncertainty. While portfolio capital is clearly mobile enough to eliminate covered interest differentials, neither uncovered interest parity nor real interest parity holds. Moreover, financial market liberalization and floating exchange rates may actually have contributed to preventing these latter two conditions from holding, insofar as they increase exchange risk premiums and cause expected deviations from purchasing power parity.

Much national saving still flows through restricted channels to finance domestic investment in most countries. Still, saving and investment rates have become less correlated since 1980 as a combined result of financial market liberalization and a greater tolerance for current account imbalances by policy makers (a tolerance that in turn is encouraged by the greater ease of international capital flows). As a result, current account imbalances have become larger and have led to new forms of interdependency between borrowing and lending nations. Current account imbalances also lead to the build-up of large net creditor and net debtor positions, which add an important source of instability to the global macroeconomy on the eve of the 21st century.

The world today has a perverse pattern of global imbalances, with most of the world's net capital flows going into the richest and most powerful nation, the United States, and only a relative trickle of funds going into poorer, developing countries. At the same time, the U.S. current account deficit serves a useful function by transferring an aggregate demand stimulus to the countries that have trade surpluses with the United States. With growth stagnant or slowing down in many of these surplus regions, and with a rising net debt position making the United States more vulnerable to a financial crisis in the not-too-distant future, there is a vital need for the surplus countries (especially Japan and other Asian countries, and Europe) to adopt more expansionary domestic macro policies and wean themselves from dependency on trade surpluses with the United States. Otherwise, the adjustments that the United States will eventually have to make will be even more draconian, and will have the potential to cause a global collapse in demand. If speculators turn against the dollar in the late 1990s or early 2000s, the United States could be forced to raise interest rates and contract its domestic economy, with depressing effects on other nations around the world. Only better coordination of macro policies, with the adoption of much more expansionary fiscal and monetary stances by the surplus nations, can avert such an outcome.

But such macro policy coordination—difficult as that may be to accomplish—will not be enough on its own. Financial liberalization has greatly increased the ability of speculative capital movements to destabilize national economies. Sometimes speculators exploit genuine contradictions in economic "fundamentals," but at other times they create "self-fulfilling panics" in situations that are otherwise fundamentally sound (or at least, in situations where fairly modest macro policy corrections would suffice, in the absence of the speculation-induced panic). This problem has been most acute in certain developing nations that have only recently liberalized their financial markets, without having adequate regulatory structures in place, such as Mexico, Thailand, Indonesia, and Korea. But developed countries with better regulated financial systems may not be immune to such speculative pressures.

At this writing (June 1998), the huge inflows of capital coming into the United States are keeping interest rates down and financing buoyant consumer spending and business investment in the private sector, thus keeping the economic recovery going in spite of a contractionary fiscal policy that has succeeded in balancing the federal budget (aided by the private-sector growth, of course). Recent history shows that such capital inflows can leave a country even more rapidly than they entered and that the result can be soaring interest rates and collapsing real activity. When this happens in a small, developing country, the damage is limited. If this happens in the United States, whose deficits are at the center of international capital flows, the damage could be much greater. Adopting new kinds of controls on international financial mobility—especially, efforts to discourage or restrict speculative movements of short-term portfolio capital—are therefore necessary to prevent destabilizing speculation in the United States and other countries, as well as to prevent financial interests from undermining the kind of expansionary macro policy coordination advocated here.

POSTSCRIPT, NOVEMBER 15, 2000

This chapter was written in the spring of 1998, at the height of the Asian financial crisis. Although the analysis in the chapter remains valid, there have been some changes in the international financial situation and global macroeconomic imbalances described in sections 3–5 since that time. The following update was written as the book goes to press in the fall of 2000.

Starting with the United States, strong economic growth continued in the late 1990s, with annual growth rates of over 4% from 1997 through the first three quarters of 2000.[42] The budget balance swung into a large surplus, but—contrary to the "twin deficits" view of the 1980s—the trade deficit only widened. By 1999, the U.S. merchandise trade deficit reached $345.6 billion and the current account deficit totaled $331.5 billion; both deficits are projected to top $400 billion in 2000. These deficits are more than double the figures for 1996–97 reported in the chapter (e.g., in Table 5 and Figure 1). The U.S. net international debt reached

---

42. All data in this paragraph are from the website of the U.S. Department of Commerce, Bureau of Economic Analysis (www.bea.doc.gov).

$1.1 trillion ($1.3 trillion excluding direct investment) at the end of 1999,[43] and net interest outflows (i.e., net investment income excluding returns to direct investment) were $75.7 billion during 1999.

The huge surge in the U.S. trade deficit between 1997 and 2000 was driven by two factors: faster growth in the United States compared with its trading partners, and a continued rise in the value of the dollar. In particular, the growth slowdown in Asia after the 1997–98 crisis cut U.S. exports, while the devaluation of the Asian currencies made their exports more competitive, leading to large or increased trade deficits of the United States with several Asian countries in addition to China and Japan. Although the dollar fell relative to the yen, it rose in relation to the new euro currency after it was inaugurated on January 1, 1999, in spite of the fact that the United States already had a significant trade deficit with Europe. This continued the rising trend of the dollar relative to the former ECU in 1995–98 shown in Table 6. The fall in the dollar/euro exchange rate was effected by massive capital flows from Europe to the United States, thus validating the argument in the chapter that capital flows often cause perverse changes in exchange rates that exacerbate trade imbalances.

By 2000, Europe had begun a notable recovery from its slow growth of the mid-to-late 1990s. Contrary to the intentions of its creators, however, the euro has failed to become a strong currency and instead has depreciated steadily. The euro's fall is partly driven by investors responding to faster growth in the United States, but it is also driven by self-fulfilling speculative expectations. As a result of the falling euro, the European expansion is fueled by improved external competitiveness, and hence does not give much of a stimulus to the rest of the world economy. Japan fell into a recession in 1998 and has barely resumed positive growth as of 2000; Japanese domestic investment and consumption continue to be weak.[44]

Thus, the United States with its large and growing trade deficit remains the global "consumer of last resort." A reduction in the U.S. private saving rate has more than offset the rise in U.S. public sector saving (the budget surplus), with the gap between robust investment and low saving filled by ever-rising net capital inflows into the United States.

In the developing world, Latin America had a growth slowdown in the late 1990s as a result of contagion from the Asian crisis. Brazil had a recession in 1998, but then recovered after the real was finally devalued and then allowed to float in early 1999. Meanwhile, Argentina had a more severe recession in 1999 and continues to be depressed in 2000 as a result of its commitment to a permanently fixed exchange rate with a currency board, which prevents Argentina from matching the Brazilian depreciation. Mexico managed to avoid a repeat crisis in the late 1990s thanks to its managed floating exchange rate.

---

43. Due to extensive revisions in the historical data series for the U.S. net international investment position, these figures for the net international debt in 1999 are not comparable to the older data used in writing this chapter.

44. See International Monetary Fund, *World Economic Outlook*, September 2000, available at www.imf.org.

Most leading emerging market countries in Asia had sharp economic downturns during the financial crisis in 1997–98. Most of these countries began to recover in 1999 and showed strong growth rates by 2000, although they differed in the precise timing and strength of their recoveries.[45] However, in most cases the impressive-looking aggregate growth rates of 1999–2000 mask continued structural problems in the emerging market economies. Generally, their rapid aggregate growth is due mainly to improved trade balances as a result of depreciated exchange rates and repressed domestic demand. Domestic consumption and investment spending have yet to recover fully in most of the countries affected by the financial crisis. Real wages and middle class incomes remain depressed.

Moreover, the crisis exposed serious structural problems in these countries' domestic finances, including weak banking sectors saddled with large portfolios of bad loans and unprofitable corporate sectors burdened with huge debt obligations—problems that were exacerbated by the overlending which occurred during the emerging market bubble of the early 1990s. The ongoing process of restructuring banks and industries is still causing painful adjustments throughout East Asia and is likely to continue well into the early 2000s. As part of this restructuring process, some of the post-crisis countries are receiving a new form of capital inflows: equity investment for acquisitions of financially troubled national enterprises by foreign corporations (including banks, where allowed) at "fire sale" prices.

Thus, in spite of some changes especially in the Asian and European situations between 1998 and 2000, the basic pattern of global growth, capital flows, and trade imbalances remains similar to what is described in the chapter as of 1998. If anything, the core imbalance between the U.S. trade deficit and the European and Asian surpluses has only become more extreme. The surplus countries still have not adopted the kinds of *domestic* economic stimuli required to reduce these imbalances and to wean the global economy away from its dependence on U.S. demand. The dollar is still overvalued in relation to trade flows and its rise in relation to the euro shows evidence of a bubble. Developing countries are no longer overwhelmed by volatile inflows of short-term capital, but neither are they receiving adequate amounts of more stable, long-term investment. If foreign investors become nervous about lending the United States $400 billion a year, or if speculators begin to doubt that the euro can fall any further, the possibility of a hard landing—i.e., a dollar crisis, a U.S. recession, and a global contraction—still cannot be ruled out.

---

45. Ibid.

REFERENCES

Artis, Michael, and Tamim Bayoumi. 1990. "Saving, Investment, Financial Integration and the Balance of Payments," in *Staff Studies for the World Economic Outlook 1990*. Washington, DC: International Monetary Fund, pp. 19–34.

Bach, Christopher. 1998. "U.S. International Transactions, Fourth Quarter and Year 1997," *Survey of Current Business* 78, no. 4 (April), pp. 52–97.

Bayoumi, Tamim. 1990. "Saving-Investment Correlations: Immobile Capital, Government Policy, or Endogenous Behavior?" *International Monetary Fund Staff Papers* 37 (June), pp. 360–87.

_____. 1997. "'Comment' on 'Policy Implications of the International Saving-Investment Correlation,'" in Robert Pollin, ed., *The Macroeconomics of Finance, Saving, and Investment*. Ann Arbor: University of Michigan Press, pp. 243–50.

Bayoumi, Tamim, and Ronald MacDonald. 1995. "Consumption, Income, and International Capital Market Integration," *IMF Staff Papers* 42, no. 3 (September), pp. 552–76.

Bhaduri, Amit. 1987. "Dependent and Self-reliant Growth with Foreign Borrowing," *Cambridge Journal of Economics* 11 (September), pp. 269–73.

_____. 1998. "Implications of Globalization for Macroeconomic Theory and Policy in Developing Countries," in Dean Baker, et al., eds., *Globalization and Progressive Economic Policy: What Are the Real Constraints and Options?* Cambridge, UK: Cambridge University Press, forthcoming.

Bhagwati, Jagdish. 1998. "The Capital Myth: The Difference between Trade in Widgets and Dollars," *Foreign Affairs* 77, no. 3 (May/June), pp. 7–12.

Blecker, Robert A. 1992. *Beyond the Twin Deficits: A Trade Strategy for the 1990s*. Armonk, NY: M.E. Sharpe, Inc., Economic Policy Institute Series.

_____. 1996. "NAFTA, the Peso Crisis, and the Contradictions of the Mexican Economic Growth Strategy," Working Paper No. 3, Center for Economic Policy Analysis, New School for Social Research, New York (July).

_____. 1997. "Policy Implications of the International Saving-Investment Correlation," in Robert Pollin, ed., *The Macroeconomics of Finance, Saving, and Investment*. Ann Arbor: University of Michigan Press, pp. 173–229.

Blecker, Robert A., and M. Mehdi Hamam. 1997. "All in the Family? The 'Cousin Deficits' and Other Causal Relations in the United States and the United Kingdom," mimeo, American University, February.

Bosworth, Barry P. 1993. *Saving and Investment in a Global Economy*. Washington: Brookings Institution.

Calvo, Guillermo A., and Enrique G. Mendoza. 1996. "Mexico's Balance-of-Payments Crisis: A Chronicle of a Death Foretold," *Journal of International Economics* 41, nos. 3/4 (November), pp. 235–64.

Cumby, R. E., and F. S. Mishkin. 1986. "The International Linkage of Real Interest Rates: The European-U.S. Connection," *Journal of International Money and Finance* 5 (March), pp. 5–23.

Cumby, R., and Maurice Obstfeld. 1981. "Exchange Rate Expectations and Nominal Interest Rates: A Test of the Fisher Hypothesis," *Journal of Finance* 36, pp. 697–703.

_____. 1984. "International Interest-rate Linkages under Flexible Exchange Rates: A Review of Recent Evidence," in J. F. O. Bilson and R. C. Marston, eds., *Exchange Rate Theory and Practice*. Chicago: University of Chicago Press.

D'Arista, Jane. 1996. "International Capital Flows and National Macroeconomic Policies." Discussion Paper No. 32, Institute of Economic Research, Otaru University of Commerce, Otaru, Hokkaido, Japan (October).

Davidson, Paul. 1996. "Reforming the International Payments System," in Robert A. Blecker, ed., *U.S. Trade Policy and Global Growth*. Economic Policy Institute series. Armonk, NY: M. E. Sharpe, Inc.

Dornbusch, Rudiger, and A. Werner. 1994. "Mexico: Stabilization, Reform, and No Growth," *Brookings Papers on Economic Activity*, 1:1994.

Dooley, Michael, Jeffrey Frankel, and Donald J. Mathieson. 1987. "International Capital Mobility: What Do Saving-Investment Correlations Tell Us?" *International Monetary Fund Staff Papers* 34 (September), pp. 503–30.

Eatwell, John. 1996. "International Financial Liberalization: The Impact on World Development." United Nations Development Programme, Office of Development Studies, Discussion Paper Series, September.

Epstein, Gerald A., and Herbert Gintis. 1992. "International Capital Markets and the Limits of National Economic Policy," in Tariq Banuri and Juliet B. Schor, eds., *Financial Openness and National Autonomy: Opportunities and Constraints*. Oxford: Oxford University Press.

Fama, Eugene F. 1984. "Forward and Spot Exchange Rates," *Journal of Monetary Economics* 14, pp. 319–38.

Fazzari, Steven M., R. Glenn Hubbard, and Bruce C. Petersen. 1988. "Financing Constraints and Corporate Investment," *Brookings Papers on Economic Activity*, 1:1988, pp. 141–95.

Feldstein, Martin, and Philippe Bacchetta. 1991. "National Saving and International Investment," in B. Douglas Bernheim and John B. Shoven, eds., *National Saving and Economic Performance*. Chicago: University of Chicago Press.

Feldstein, Martin, and Charles Horioka. 1980. "Domestic Saving and International Capital Flows," *Economic Journal* 90 (June), pp. 314–29.

Finn, Mary G. 1990. "On Savings and Investment Dynamics in a Small Open Economy," *Journal of International Economics* 29 (August), pp. 1–21.

Frankel, Jeffrey A. 1991. "Quantifying International Capital Mobility in the 1980s," in B. Douglas Bernheim and John B. Shoven, eds., *National Saving and Economic Performance*. Chicago: University of Chicago Press.

———. 1993. "International Financial Integration: Relations Between Interest Rates and Exchange Rates," in Dilip K. Das, ed., *International Finance: Contemporary Issues*. London: Routledge.

Frankel, Jeffrey A., and Kenneth Froot. 1990. "Chartists, Fundamentalists, and the Demand for Dollars," in A. S. Courakis and M. P. Taylor, eds., *Policy Issues for Interdependent Economies*. Oxford: Oxford University Press, pp. 73–126.

Frenkel, Jacob A., and Richard M. Levich. 1975. "Covered Interest Arbitrage: Unexploited Profits?" *Journal of Political Economy* 83, pp. 325–38.

Froot, Kenneth, and Jeffrey A. Frankel. 1989. "Forward Discount Bias: Is It an Exchange Risk Premium?" *Quarterly Journal of Economics* 104, pp. 139–61.

Glyn, Andrew. 1998. "Internal and External Constraints on Egalitarian Policies," in Dean Baker, et al., eds., *Globalization and Progressive Economic Policy: What Are the Real Constraints and Options?* Cambridge, UK: Cambridge University Press, forthcoming.

Godley, Wynne, and William Milberg. 1994. "U.S. Trade Deficits: The Recovery's Dark Side?" *Challenge* (November-December), pp. 40–47.

Goldstein, Morris, David Folkerts-Landau, and a Staff Team from the International Monetary Fund. 1994. *International Capital Markets: Developments, Prospects, and Policy Issues*. Washington, DC: International Monetary Fund.

Goodwin, Barry K., and Thomas J. Grennes. 1994. "Real Interest Rate Equalization and the Integration of International Financial Markets," *Journal of International Money and Finance* 13 (February), pp. 107–24.

Hallwood, C. Paul, and Ronald MacDonald. 1994. *International Money and Finance*, second edition. Oxford: Blackwell.

Huang, Chao-Dong, and Simon Broadbent. 1998. "Trade with China: Do the Figures Add Up?" *International Review of Applied Economics* 12, no. 1 (January), pp. 107–27.

International Monetary Fund. 1997. *International Financial Statistics*, CD ROM, December.

Kalecki, Michal. 1971. *Selected Essays in the Dynamics of the Capitalist Economy*. Cambridge, UK: Cambridge University Press.

Krugman, Paul. 1998. "America the Boastful," *Foreign Affairs* 77, no. 3 (May/June), pp. 32–45.

Liu, Liang-Yn, and Wing Thye Woo. 1994. "Saving Behaviour Under Imperfect Financial Markets and the Current Account Consequences," *Economic Journal* 104 (May), pp. 512–27.

Lopez Gallardo, Julio. 1998. "Economic Crisis and Recovery in Mexico: A Post-Kaleckian Perspective," Paper presented at Allied Social Sciences Associations meetings, Chicago, January.

MacDonald, Ronald, and T. S. Torrance. 1990. "Expectations Formation and Risk in Four Foreign Exchange Markets," *Oxford Economic Papers* 42 (July), pp. 544–61.

Mark, Nelson C. 1985a. "On Time Varying Risk Premia in the Foreign Exchange Market," *Journal of Monetary Economics* 16, pp. 3–18.

_____. 1985b. "Some Evidence on the International Inequality of Real Interest Rates," *Journal of International Money and Finance* 4 (June), pp. 189–208.

Marston, Richard C. 1995. *International Financial Integration: A Study of Interest Differentials Between the Major Industrial Countries*. Cambridge, UK: Cambridge University Press.

McCallum, Bennett T. 1994. "A Reconsideration of the Uncovered Interest Parity Relationship," *Journal of Monetary Economics* 33, pp. 105–32.

McKinnon, Ronald I., and Huw Pill. 1996. "Credible Liberalization and International Capital Flows: The Overborrowing Syndrome," in T. Ito and A. Krueger, eds. *Financial Deregulation and Integration in East Asia*. Chicago: University of Chicago Press, pp. 7–42.

Merrick, J. J., Jr., and A. Saunders. 1986. "International Expected Real Interest Rates: New Tests of the Parity Hypothesis and U.S. Fiscal-policy Effects," *Journal of Monetary Economics* 18 (November), pp. 313–22.

Minsky, Hyman. 1986. *Stabilizing an Unstable Economy*. New Haven: Yale University Press.

Mishel, Lawrence, Jared Bernstein, and John Schmitt. 1997. *The State of Working America, 1996–97*. Economic Policy Institute Series. Armonk, NY: M. E. Sharpe, Inc.

Morici, Peter. 1997. *The Trade Deficit: Where Does It Come from and What Does It Do?* Washington: Economic Strategy Institute, October.

Murphy, Robert G. 1984. "Capital Mobility and the Relationship between Saving and Investment in OECD Countries," *Journal of International Money and Finance* 3, pp. 327–42.

Mussa, Michael, and Morris Goldstein. 1993. "The Integration of World Capital Markets," in Federal Reserve Bank of Kansas City, ed., *Changing Capital Markets: Implications for Monetary Policy*. Proceedings of a Symposium Sponsored by the Federal Reserve Bank of Kansas City, Jackson Hole, WY, August.

Obstfeld, Maurice. 1986. "Capital Mobility in the World Economy: Theory and Measurement," *Carnegie-Rochester Conference Series on Public Policy* 24 (Spring), pp. 55–103.

Organisation for Economic Co-operation and Development (OECD). 1997. *OECD Economic Outlook, December 1997.* Paris: OECD.

Pearlstein, Steven. 1998. "The Greenback Is Golden Again: Economic Troubles in Asia Spur Resurgence of U.S. Dollar," *Washington Post,* January 15, pp. C1-C6.

Penati, Alessandro, and Michael Dooley. 1984. "Current Account Imbalances and Capital Formation in Industrial Countries, 1949–81," *International Monetary Fund Staff Papers* 31 (March), pp. 1–24.

Pollin, Robert. 1998. "Can Domestic Expansionary Policy Succeed in a Globally Integrated Environment? An Examination of Alternatives," in Dean Baker, et al., eds., *Globalization and Progressive Economic Policy: What Are the Real Constraints and Options?* Cambridge, UK: Cambridge University Press, forthcoming.

Poloz, Stephen S. 1992. "Fiscal Policy and External Balance in the G-7 Countries." Bank of Canada, Technical Report No. 60, June.

Prestowitz, Clyde. 1997. "Retooling Japan is the Only Way to Rescue Asia Now," *Washington Post,* December 14, pp. C1–C4.

Reinhart, V., and K. Weiller. 1987. "Increasing Capital Mobility: Evidence from Short-Term and Long-Term Markets," in Federal Reserve Bank of New York, *Research Papers on International Integration of Financial Markets and U.S. Monetary Policy* (December).

Sachs, Jeffrey D. 1998. "The IMF and the Asian Flu," *The American Prospect* (March-April), pp. 16–21.

Sachs, Jeffrey D., Aarón Tornell, and Andrés Velasco. 1996. "The Mexican Peso Crisis: Sudden Death or Crisis Foretold?" *Journal of International Economics* 41, nos. 3/4 (November), pp. 265–83.

Scholl, Russell B. 1997. "The International Investment Position of the United States in 1996," *Survey of Current Business* 77, no. 4 (July), pp. 24-33.

Scott, Robert E., Thea M. Lee, and John Schmitt. 1997. "Trading Away Good Jobs: An Examination of Employment and Wages in the U.S., 1979–94." Briefing Paper, Economic Policy Institute, October.

Scott, Robert E., and Jesse Rothstein. 1998. "American Jobs and the Asian Crisis: The Employment Impact of the Coming Rise in the U.S. Trade Deficit." Briefing Paper, Economic Policy Institute, January.

Steindl, Josef. 1976. *Maturity and Stagnation in American Capitalism.* New York: Monthly Review Press.

Stiglitz, Joseph E., and Andrew Weiss. 1981. "Credit Rationing in Markets with Imperfect Information," *American Economic Review* 71 (June), pp. 393–410.

Summers, Lawrence H. 1988. "Tax Policy and International Competitiveness," in Jacob A. Frenkel, ed., *International Aspects of Fiscal Policies.* Chicago: University of Chicago Press.

Taylor, Lance. 1997. "Growth in Two Countries with International Debt," mimeo, New School for Social Research, April.

Taylor, M. P. 1987. "Covered Interest Parity: A High-frequency, High-quality Data Study," *Economica* 54 (November), pp. 429–38.

_____. 1989. "A DYMIMIC Model of Forward Exchange Risk, with Estimates for Three Major Exchange Rates," *The Manchester School of Economic and Social Studies* 56 (March), pp. 55–68.

Taylor, M. P., and P. Fraser. 1991. "Some 'News' on Covered Interest Arbitrage," in M. P. Taylor, ed., *Money and Financial Markets.* Cambridge, MA: Blackwell.

Tesar, Linda L. 1991. "Savings, Investment and International Capital Flows," *Journal of International Economics* 31, 55–78.

Tobin, James. 1983. "Comment on 'Domestic Saving and International Capital Movements in the Long Run and the Short Run,'" *European Economic Review* 21, 153–56.

Wachtel, Howard M. 1990. *The Money Mandarins: The Making of a Supranational Economic Order*, second edition. Armonk, NY: M. E. Sharpe, Inc.

Westphal, Uwe. 1983. "Comment on 'Domestic Saving and International Capital Movements in the Long Run and the Short Run,'" *European Economic Review* 21, 157–59.

7

· · ·

The Politics of Global Financial Regulation
Lessons from the Fight Against Money Laundering

Eric Helleiner *

REFORM OF THE GLOBAL financial system has emerged as one of the central issues on public policy agendas around the world. In normal times, the public rarely shows much interest in global financial issues. Seemingly arcane and technically complex, the subject is left to specially trained economists, practitioners in the markets, and financial journalists to debate. But these are hardly normal times. Developments during the last few years have highlighted to all some of the costs associated with the dramatic globalization of financial markets: diminished national policy autonomy, volatile exchange rates and a new vulnerability to systemic financial crises. Indeed, it was the desire to avoid these costs that led the architects of the Bretton Woods system over 50 years ago to endorse the use of capital controls and a much more regulated international financial system than we now live in.

Particularly prominent in the new debate on global financial reform is the widespread interest in the reregulation of global financial markets. Gone is the rhetoric of a few years ago that governments are powerless in global finance and that the financial globalization trend is inevitable and irreversible. The new conventional wisdom asserts that global financial markets will survive and flourish only if public authorities are actively involved in promoting this outcome through various regulatory activities. Some analysts call for the strengthening of international

---

*Acknowledgements: For their research assistance, I am grateful to Vince Sica, Matt Griem, Melissa Harnett, and the Social Sciences and Humanities Research Council of Canada. I am also grateful for comments from John Eatwell, Lance Taylor, and other participants in workshops associated with the preparation of this book.

prudential supervision and regulatory standards for banking and securities markets. Others propose greater international information-sharing, the harmonization of accounting and auditing practices, and mechanisms to encourage private financiers to assume greater portion of the risk in international lending. Still others suggest restrictions on short-term speculative flows of money either by individual countries or cooperatively through proposals such as the Tobin tax.[1]

Many of these proposals will require a high degree of international cooperation and coordination between national regulators and perhaps even a strengthening of public international financial institutions. Economists are usually the authors of these proposals and, despite their reputation as dismal scientists, they are usually optimistic about the prospects for cooperation and coordination. By contrast, their political science colleagues often have the more dismal perspective. They recall that political barriers inhibited international cooperation during the interwar years, bringing down the global financial system of the 1920s. In the contemporary period, they highlight that successful international cooperation and coordination in the regulatory arena has been rare, with the 1988 Basel Accord being the main exception.[2]

There are many reasons why political scientists think cooperation and coordination are difficult in the financial regulatory sector, but two arguments are particularly common. First, "realists" highlight that international regulatory initiatives may serve global economic welfare, but are often scuttled as states see them in a more political light as serving one country's national interests over others. Second, even if each state shares the same goal, cooperation and coordination may still fail because of collective action problems. For example, all states may see new international regulatory standards as desirable, but some may be tempted not to follow them as a way of attracting footloose financial capital and business to their less-regulated financial markets. Their "free riding" behavior—one thinks especially of the numerous offshore financial centers—undermines the effectiveness of the regime as a whole. Indeed, more generally, many political scientists argue that the heightened mobility of financial capital has unleashed powerful competitive deregulation pressures that inhibit not just collective reregulatory initiatives at the international level but even unilateral ones in each country's own markets. Any reregulatory initiative is likely to be opposed—particularly by the domestic financial sector—on the grounds that it will render the national financial system uncompetitive.

These arguments highlighting the political difficulties of international regulatory cooperation and coordination in the financial sphere are important ones. In this paper, however, I question the pessimism of many political scientists by examining a case where international regulatory cooperation and coordination have developed quite substantially: the international fight against money laundering. Over the last decade, states around the world have begun to construct an

---

1. For a recent overview of these proposals, see Eichengreen (1999).

2. For two prominent "pessimistic" arguments from political scientists, see for example Strange (1998) and Cerny (1993, 1994).

elaborate "global prohibition regime" that seeks to curtail money laundering.[3] The creation of this international anti-money laundering regulatory regime has been neglected almost entirely in the literature on the politics of international financial regulation. This neglect is unfortunate because, as I argue in this paper, the case is important in two ways.

First, it provides us with a second example—alongside the Basel Accord—with which we can examine how political barriers to regulatory cooperation and coordination might be overcome. I do not want to overstate the success of the anti-money laundering regime—it is still very much a regime in formation—but I will show how many of the political circumstances that enabled cooperation and coordination to develop in this case were similar to those that existed with respect to the Basel Accord. The two cases together may help us to identify important political conditions that can foster collective regulatory initiatives in the international financial area.

Second, I argue that the anti-money laundering regime may be useful more directly in pursuing some other regulatory goals. Specifically, the kinds of international cooperation and coordination that have been introduced to combat money laundering may help to strengthen international regulatory initiatives aimed at curbing tax evasion and capital flight. Indeed, as I will demonstrate, this potential is already beginning to be recognized by the leading financial powers in ways that the original Bretton Woods architects in fact originally intended. Before turning to these two points, however, let me begin by providing a brief description of the emergence of the anti-money laundering regime.

THE EMERGING INTERNATIONAL ANTI-MONEY LAUNDERING REGIME

It is widely recognized that economic globalization has encouraged the growth of a wide variety of illicit international economic transactions.[4] Hardly surprising is the fact that money laundering activities—that is, activities which hide the origins and ownership of money earned through criminal means—should be a particularly prominent aspect of this phenomenon. Money has always been one of the commodities that is most mobile and easiest to hide from state authorities. The financial sector is also where globalization has been most dramatic in recent years. As technological developments and financial liberalization have made money more mobile, the opportunities for money laundering have grown dramatically. Criminals have taken particular advantage of the proliferation of offshore secrecy havens as places to hide their origins of their illegal earnings.[5]

As money laundering activity has grown dramatically (to as much as $500 billion per year[6]), states have responded with an increasingly strong set of initiatives

---

3. For the term "global prohibition regimes" see Nadelmann (1990).
4. Friman and Andreas (1999).
5. See especially Blum et al. (1998)
6. Tanzi (1997)

designed to curtail it. These initiatives began in a serious way in the late 1980s and have been pursued in a variety of forums including the United Nations (especially the 1988 Convention Against Illicit Traffic in Narcotic Drugs and Psychotropic Substances, or "Vienna Convention"), the Bank for International Settlements (its 1988 recommendations to banks on the issue), IOSCO, various regional bodies (e.g., the EU, the Council of Europe, the OAS, the Commonwealth) as well as many bilateral legal assistance treaties. Playing the leadership role during the last decade, however, has been the Financial Action Task Force (FATF), a free-standing body set up by the G-7 in 1989 to address the money laundering issue. In 1990, it issued 40 recommendations which incorporated many of the other initiatives of the time and subsequently became a kind of standard promoted in other multilateral, regional, and bilateral settings. Because the various initiatives within the FATF and elsewhere have complemented each other closely, analysts refer to them collectively as an increasingly cohesive anti-money laundering "regime" at the international level.[7]

What are the key features of this regime?[8] To begin with, it does not focus on controlling illicit financial movements at the border. Indeed, its regulatory initiatives are often designed explicitly to prevent governments from being tempted to use capital controls to control money laundering.[9] This does not mean that borders have been neglected entirely as "intervention" points to curtail money laundering, however. Some countries—namely the United States and Australia—have begun to *monitor* cross-border capital flows as a way of gathering information about money laundering activities.[10] The FATF recommendations also ask countries to consider implementing this kind of monitoring system, although "without impeding in any way the freedom of capital movements."[11]

---

7. See for example MacDonald (1992). Many of the procedures developed in Interpol for handling the issue, for example, were adopted in the UN's 1988 Vienna Convention and supported by FATF. Compliance with the UN Vienna Convention is also advocated or required in most of the other agreements. In addition, many of the regional initiatives attempt to persuade governments to adopt the FATF recommendations. Both the Vienna Convention and the FATF also encourage the various kinds of regional and bilateral initiatives.

8. For a more detailed overview, see the FATF's Annual Reports and also Savona (1997).

9. See for example the EU's 1991 anti-money laundering directive (Gilmore (1992, 244).

10. Australia has done this since 1988 and the United States since 1970. Initial U.S. efforts to monitor cross-border money movements were very limited, focusing only on the requirement that people fill out reports if they were bringing in or out of the country currency or monetary instruments over $5000. A 1992 U.S. law, however, requires the U.S. government to develop ways of monitoring cross-border financial movements taking place via wire transfers as well. This requirement has finally been implemented in 1996 (Sultzer, 1995, 223–31).

11. The quotation comes from FATF recommendation #22 (FATF 1990, 20). Quirk (1997, 7) reports that some governments have told the FATF that implementing this recommendation "would require adopting regulations contrary to the IMF's advice for liberalizing financial markets." Member governments have also been asked by FATF to "consider recording in at least the aggregate, international flows of cash in whatever currency, so that estimates can be made of cash flows and reflows from various sources abroad, when this is combined with central bank information. Such information should be made available to the IMF and BIS to facilitate international studies." (FATF, 1990) The

Instead of controlling flows at the border, the anti-money laundering regime seeks to bolster the ability of each government to crack down on money laundering activity within its borders. It does this in two ways. First, it actively promotes the international harmonization of domestic laws and practices that are designed to combat money laundering. The FATF recommendations call on governments to criminalize money laundering (as required under the Vienna Convention), to require financial institutions in their territory to report all "suspicious" transactions to domestic authorities,[12] and to refuse to engage in transactions where the identity of the customers involved is unknown by the institutions. By pushing governments around the world to introduce these measures, the regime aims not only to reduce money laundering directly in each country but also to lessen the likelihood of all countries being vulnerable to the growth in money laundering activities in a less regulated financial center.

Second, the regime encourages extensive international information sharing and legal cooperation between governments with respect to investigation, prosecution, confiscation, and extradition in money laundering cases. A key pillar of this approach has been a commitment that participating governments have made (since the Vienna Convention) *not* to allow bank secrecy provisions to interfere with these forms of international cooperation. This important provision eliminates a key barrier to international cooperation that has existed in other areas such as the fight against tax evasion. Another interesting feature of international information-sharing—to which I will return later—has been the FATF recommendation that countries consider providing information *proactively* to foreign governments regarding suspicious flows to and from those foreign countries that take place under its jurisdiction.[13]

The construction of these key features of the anti-money laundering regime is still very much in progress. Although levels of compliance with the FATF's 40 recommendations among member countries has been quite impressive (especially

---

quotation comes from FATF recommendation #22 (FATF 1990, 20). Quirk (1997, 7) reports that some governments have told the FATF that implementing this recommendation "would require adopting regulations contrary to the IMF's advice for liberalizing financial markets." Member governments have also been asked by FATF to "consider recording in at least the aggregate, international flows of cash in whatever currency, so that estimates can be made of cash flows and reflows from various sources abroad, when this is combined with central bank information. Such information should be made available to the IMF and BIS to facilitate international studies." (FATF, 1990).

12. Within the FATF, there is some disagreement about how best to operationalize this notion of "suspicious reporting." The United States and Australia have pressed for financial institutions to be required to report all currency transactions above a certain threshold. Other countries have preferred to allow financial institutions to report only those transactions that the institutions have thought to be of a suspicious nature. See FATF (1990, 21; 1991, 42).

13. As the FATF's recommendations put it, "If a country discovers an unusual international shipment of currency, monetary instruments, precious metals, or gems, etc., it should consider notifying, as appropriate, the Customs Service or other competent authorities of the countries from which the shipment originated and/or to which it is destined, and should co-operate with a view toward establishing the source, destination, and purpose of such shipment and toward the taking of appropriate action." Interpretative Notes on Recommendation #22.

given that the recommendations have no binding force on governments), some states are still in the process of implementing them. Regulators have also been forced to adopt a dynamic approach to regulation as their initial initiatives have often encouraged diversion of illicit financial activity away from financial sectors that were initially targeted (e.g., banks) towards others (e.g., securities markets).

FATF members are also still in the process of extending the geographical coverage of the regime. The FATF itself has 26 member governments (as well as the European Commission and Gulf Cooperation Council) including most of the major financial centers of the world.[14] FATF members have also been quite successful in encouraging many non-member states to adopt the 40 recommendations through various missions, seminars and the fostering of regional groupings with an associative relationship to the FATF. For example, the 1988 Vienna Convention has been ratified by over 75 countries. Similarly, the FATF's 40 recommendations have been endorsed by countries that belong to the Caribbean Financial Action Task Force which includes all the key offshore financial centers in that region. FATF countries are now working hard to extend the regime further (as discussed below) to include Eastern Europe and countries such as the Seychelles and Russia where money laundering has grown in recent years.

Because this anti-money laundering regime is still in formation, it is difficult to evaluate its effectiveness at this point. In this paper, I make no effort to undertake such an evaluation. Instead, I am more interested in analyzing the political process that has enabled states to begin to work together in such extensive ways to construct a new international regulatory regime in the financial sector. Given the skepticism of many political scientists about the possibilities of this kind of regulatory cooperation and coordination taking place, we need to ask how this regime has begun to be able to be built. How were the different political interests of states overcome? And why haven't collective action problems and competitive deregulation pressures scuttled the initiative to a greater degree? Answering these questions should prove useful to current policy debates because the kinds of international regulatory initiatives being promoted in the anti-money laundering regime are broadly similar to that being proposed by advocates of a "new international financial architecture" today. In both cases, two kinds of international activity are prominent: 1) the push for harmonization of domestic standards across the world and 2) the fostering of extensive information sharing between national regulatory authorities.

THE POLITICAL CONDITIONS FOR INTERNATIONAL REREGULATION

The politics of cooperation and coordination in the anti-money laundering regime are especially interesting because of their similarity to those that accompanied the construction of the Basel Accord. Among political scientists who are

---

14. This includes the G-7, the rest of EU, Australia, New Zealand, Norway, Switzerland, Iceland, Singapore, Hong Kong, China, and Turkey.

skeptical of the prospects for international regulatory initiatives in global finance, the Basel Accord is often portrayed as an exceptional agreement, unlikely to be duplicated. In fact, however, the political difficulties associated with regulatory cooperation and coordination have been overcome in quite similar ways in both cases, suggesting some broader lessons about how international regulation can take place.

To begin with, in both instances, the United States used its dominant position in the international financial system to push states to work together to regulate international finance. In the case of the Basel Accord, Ethan Kapstein shows how the United States pressured foreign governments by threatening to cut off their access to the U.S. financial system unless they complied with the new standards. Because of the centrality of U.S. financial markets in the global financial system, this threat was very effective in encouraging foreign governments to comply.[15]

A similar threat was made—and even more explicitly—by the United States in its efforts to encourage foreign states to begin to crack down on money laundering. The Kerry Amendment to the 1988 Anti-Drug Abuse Act empowered the U.S. government to cut foreigners off from access to the U.S. financial system, including its clearing systems, if their governments refused to reach specific anti-money laundering agreements with the U.S. Treasury. Foreigners had to take this threat seriously, especially since the U.S.-based clearing systems CHIPS and Fedwire handle the vast portion of all wire transfers sent and received in the world.[16] In Mario Possamai's words, the threat was thus "a hefty club, since those systems are the underpinning of world trade and finance. A haven that was not plugged in would not survive long."[17] In fact, no country has yet had its access to the U.S. financial system cut off under this provision and the Treasury has only negotiated a few agreements of the precise kind that the Amendment requires.[18] Still, the threat has been effective—as it was in the Basel Accord negotiations—in focusing foreign governments' attention on the seriousness with which the United States viewed the issue.[19]

---

15. Kapstein (1994). The United States was also assisted by Britain in this instance who made a similar threat with respect to access to its markets. Porter (1993, 68–71), however, takes a more skeptical view than Kapstein of the importance of the U.S. role in this case.

16. Wyrsch (1992, 518).

17. Possamai (1992, 136).

18. These agreements were supposed to require foreign governments to get their own banks to record all U.S. dollar transactions above $10,000 and make them available to the United States on request. Several agreements of this kind have been negotiated with Latin American countries, but even they allow foreign governments to withhold information with minimal justifications. See Sultzer (1995, 209 fn. 404), Possamai (1992, 136-7). Beaty and Hornik (1989, 50) note that the U.S. government has been reluctant to enforce the Kerry Amendment "for fear of hampering the U.S. Banking industry."

19. See, for example, Friman (1994, 258) on its role in encouraging Japan to adopt anti-money laundering legislation. Discussing the power of U.S. threats of retaliation against non-complying states, Senator John Kerry (1997, 153) notes: "Administration officials tell me that the very hint of such an approach by the United States has already pushed several countries in the Caribbean and Western Europe to begin imposing real regulations to combat the launderers." The United States has also used other forms of power in pushing foreign governments to cooperate in combating money laundering. In the early 1980s, the United States flirted briefly with the use of extra-territorial application of its

U.S. leadership, thus, has been crucial in fostering regulatory cooperation and coordination in global finance. But political scientists have often questioned the prospects of such leadership being forthcoming in the future, particularly given the fragmented nature of the U.S. state.[20] In both of these instances, however, U.S. policy makers have been able to act decisively and with a strong unity of purpose, suggesting that skepticism of U.S. leadership potential in finance is easily overstated. In the case of the Basel Accord, the Federal Reserve took the lead, responding to a perception of systemic risk in global financial markets that had been highlighted by the international debt crisis of the early 1980s. In the money-laundering case, decisive U.S. action to regulate global finance stemmed in large part from the way the issue was linked to a cause that had been declared a "national security" issue: the war on drugs.

In both instances, U.S. leadership can also be attributed to one further factor that also challenges some political scientists' assumptions. Although competitive deregulation pressures are often said to inhibit reregulatory international initiatives, they have played the opposite role with respect to U.S. policy towards capital adequacy standards and the anti-money laundering regime. In the capital adequacy standards case, once the U.S. Congress made clear its intention to impose such standards on domestic banks, those same banks and various U.S. state officials were encouraged by competitive concerns to press for these standards to be imposed on foreign banks through an international agreement. Without a "level playing field" internationally, they feared the new domestic standards would drive financial business and capital away from U.S. markets and institutions. The same dynamic has encouraged the United States to play a lead role in pushing for international regulation of money laundering. In other words, the very competitive pressures that are said to work against reregulation internationally have actively encouraged the United States to promote it once the tide turned against deregulation domestically.

A further way in which competitive dynamics can encourage reregulation instead of deregulation is outlined by Kapstein in his analysis of the Basel Accord.[21] He notes that international financial markets themselves have played an important role in encouraging compliance with the standards. Financial institutions and financial centers that are not abiding by the new standards have been perceived within the markets to be less stable and secure than those that have

laws, particularly with respect to the Caribbean offshore havens. As part of a drug investigation in 1983, the U.S. government demanded access to financial information from branches of the Bank of Nova Scotia in the Bahamas and the Cayman Islands. When the bank refused, a U.S. court assigned it heavy contempt of court charges (that reached $1.8 billion) and threatened to seize its U.S. assets. International protests made the United States more wary of pursuing this tactic again, but it did have the effect of encouraging not only the bank to give up the information requested, but also the Cayman Islands (and the Bahamas) to sign a mutual legal assistance treaty with the United States to combat money laundering. More recently, the United States made its aid and tariff concessions under the Caribbean Basin Initiative conditional on their cooperation in helping to trace money laundering (Naylor 1994, 299–304). Foreign bankers who have not been fully cooperative with U.S. government authorities in this area have also had their visas revoked (Andelmann 1994, 97).

20. See Strange (1998) and Cerny (1993, 1994).

21. Kapstein (1994).

adopted the standards. This, in turn, has encouraged the exact opposite of the competitive deregulation dynamic: financial institutions and governments have been keen to adopt the new regulations in order to maintain their reputation within the financial markets. This "competitive *re*-regulation" dynamic has also encouraged financial institutions and governments to comply with the new anti-money laundering regulations. A growing number of financial scandals and crises involving money laundering have drawn the attention of "clean" market actors to the risks of doing business with financial institutions and jurisdictions that have not complied fully with the standards and regulations outlined in the new anti-money laundering regime. Once again, "reputational effects" have driven a kind of upward harmonization process that has encouraged the adoption of money-laundering regulations.[22]

Of course, there remain offshore financial centers (as well as specific institutions) that still anticipate benefits from a "regulation-free" reputation in both the capital-adequacy standards and money laundering cases. Their compliance with international standards can only be obtained through more coercive means. But the difficulties involved in forcing these "free riders" to introduce internationally agreed standards should not be overstated. I have already outlined how the United States has threatened to use access to its markets and clearing systems as a bargaining card in these situations. Increasingly, however, there is talk of the leading financial powers as a group pursing a similar strategy of denying access to the Western-controlled international financial system for states that are outside of the "international consensus."

Some limited action along these lines has, in fact, already been taken in the money laundering case. As part of its effort to encourage financial institutions to know the identity of their customers, the FATF pressed the electronic messaging system SWIFT to broadcast a message on July 30, 1992 to all its users asking them to include the names and addresses of all senders and receivers of electronic messages who were not financial institutions. This was an important move since SWIFT is a central body in the "plumbing" of the international financial system, transmitting instructions for a very large portion of the financial transactions that move through clearing houses such as Fedwire, and CHIPS.[23] Initiatives of this kind may signal the first step along a potential route of transforming CHIPS, Fedwire and SWIFT into "closed-circuit systems" that can be used only by those willing to adopt certain responsibilities vis-a-vis the regulation of money laundering. Such a move would be very effective in controlling money laundering around the world. In Stephen Zamora's words: "If the world community adopts a closed-circuit system, it will be essential to enter that system in order to take part in the Western financial system."[24]

---

22. Quote from Kapstein (1994, 190 fn.40). See also Kapstein (1994, 13; 126), Porter (1993, 78; 157), and Eatwell and Taylor (1999, ch.4 p.2) for the Basle Accord, and Helleiner (1999) for the anti-money laundering regime.

23. SWIFT's two operating centers are in the Netherlands and near Washington, DC. Close to 140 countries are linked by the SWIFT network

24. Zamora (1992, 203–4).

Members of the FATF have also raised the prospect that financial movements between them and non-FATF members might be treated in a special way. One of the FATF's 40 recommendation states: "Financial institutions should give special attention to business relations and transactions with persons, including companies and financial institutions, from countries which do not or insufficiently apply these recommendations."[25] This kind of special monitoring would not only help to detect money laundering activities deriving from these non-complying jurisdictions but also, in FATF's words, "increase the cost of transactions with them and thus compensate for the competitive advantage of the financial institutions located in the non-cooperative country or territory."[26]

FATF countries appear increasingly willing to consider the implementation of this recommendation. Back in 1994, David Andelman reported that: "FATF officials believe that they will have in place by 1998 or 1999 the core of a global regulatory and enforcement mechanism considerably more rigid than any now in place. After a critical mass of countries has adopted and implemented laws consistent with the FATF's 40 points, the governments that have taken these steps will be in a position to recommend actions against those governments that have not."[27] Sure enough, in September 1998, the FATF created an Ad Hoc Group on Non-Cooperative Countries or Territories whose objective was to identify jurisdictions that were not cooperating with the FATF recommendations and to recommend steps to be taken to encourage such cooperation.[28] In February 2000, the FATF published criteria that defined "non-cooperating" countries or territories, and it advocated the consideration of various courses of action against them including: 1) customer identification requirements for financial institutions dealing with people or legal entitites which have accounts in "non-cooperative" jurisdictions, 2) requirements that financial institutions pay special attention to, or report, financial transactions conducted with people or legal entities having accounts at financial institutions established in non-cooperative jurisdictions, 3) "conditioning, restricting, targeting or even prohibiting financial transactions with non-cooperative jurisdictions."[29]

The last recommendation is particularly interesting since it raises the prospect of financial movements involving non-FATF members being not just monitored

---

25. Recommendation #21 quoted in FATF (1990, 20).

26. FATF (1991, 49).

27. Andelman (1994, 107).

28. In its 1991 report, FATF noted that a special meeting had been held to consider whether a "black list" of non-complying countries should be drawn up. At that time, this idea was rejected in favor of continued public and peer pressure, although individual states were allowed to do more as long as FATF was kept informed of their activities (FATF, 1991, 41; 48). The G-7 finance ministers (1999) have been very supportive of the new approach: "The Financial Action Task Force should take concrete steps to bring OFCs [Offshore Financial Centers], and underregulated and non-cooperating jurisdictions, into compliance with the 40 recommendations against money laundering and to protect the international financial community from the adverse impact of those that do not comply."

29. FATF (2000, 8).

but also controlled. This raises the prospect of Western financial powers forming a kind of "zone of exclusion" within which capital movements take place freely but which is open only to those states which have agreed to police money laundering. As the head of the IMF's fiscal affairs division, Vito Tanzi puts it, the international financial market "should become an exclusive club with benefits and obligations for those who wish to belong to it." Indeed, he has suggested that a "kind of quarantine" be created in which such flows were taxed or international legal recognition was denied to financial operations conducted in such locations.[30] These sorts of moves would likely be very effective in encouraging compliance with the FATF standards since the various financial centers outside of FATF would find it difficult to attract significant financial business to their territories in these circumstances. These moves are also similar to the threats that the BIS central bankers have made with respect to those countries that do not supervise their financial systems according to BIS standards.[31]

Some might argue that moves of this kind will ultimately be ineffective because market actors will always find places to move and store money that are beyond Western regulators. But as Saskia Sassen has noted, it is important to recognize the extent to which global financial markets depend on complex legal, informational, and technical infrastructures which are concentrated in the leading financial centers of the world. Indeed, contrary to the popular image of the "end of geography" in global finance and "stateless money," she and others have highlighted how the degree of geographical concentration of these infrastructures in leading "world cities" has actually increased with globalization and the information technology revolution.[32] As long as the markets are reliant on these concentrated locations, they are subject to regulation by the Western financial powers that regulate those sites.[33]

The growing discussions about how Western financial powers as a group might collectively enforce and uphold international regulatory standards raise one final point about the basis of political support for international financial regulation. Consensus among financial policy makers in the leading financial

---

30. Tanzi (1997, 101).

31. There is, however, one important difference. BIS members have threatened to prevent financial *institutions* from entering their markets if the institution's home government does not follow BIS supervisory practices (Porter, 1993, 61; 72). FATF members are threatening instead to monitor or curtail financial *transactions* from jurisdictions that do not adopt the FATF recommendations. The latter strategy has also been raised as a possible way of implementing the Tobin tax. For example, Stanley Fischer of the IMF has recently suggested, in the words of *IMF Survey* (January 22, 1996, p.32), "that the Tobin tax could be implemented if the major money center countries favored it and found a way of penalizing transactions in offshore markets—perhaps as part of the trend towards uniform regulatory requirements for financial institutions."

32. Sassen (1998). See also Thrift (1994).

33. Indeed, the FATF's February 2000 report explicitly seeks to use this fact to its advantage. In discussing its third recommended course of action against non-cooperative jurisdictions, it suggests that: "FATF members should also examine ways to prevent financial institutions located in identified non-cooperating countries or territories from using facilities (for example, information technology facilities) located in the FATF members' territory." (FATF 2000, 8).

powers has been easier to reach than "realist" political scientists predict with their models of governments being driven only by political perceptions of national self-interest. What these realists neglect is the extent to which policy makers in these countries find themselves working in increasingly tight transnational networks of officials who share similar world views. Kapstein, for example, explains how international support for the Basel Accord was bolstered by the common cognitive frameworks which central bankers working within the BIS share in analyzing problems of international finance.[34]

In the case of money laundering, the transnational networks of officials involved in policymaking are wider, including not just central bankers but also other financial and law enforcement officials. Like central bankers, however, these latter two groups are also involved in quite cohesive transnational policy networks which are associated with the kinds of bodies that were involved in the construction of the anti-money laundering regime such the G-7, IOSCO, the UN, Interpol, and various regional forums.[35] It was within these transnational policy networks that various officials—especially from the United States—began to promote the idea that money laundering was a problem requiring regulation. And the rapid manner in which an international consensus emerged on the issue can be attributed at least in part to the shared values and world views that are held by officials within these transnational networks. The high degree of compliance with such voluntary rules such as the FATF recommendations and the BIS code of conduct can also be attributed partly to the same factor.[36]

To summarize, the politics associated with the construction of the anti-money laundering regime should be scrutinized closely by those who seek to strengthen regulatory cooperation and coordination as part of building a "new international financial architecture." Alongside the Basel Accord, the anti-money laundering regime represents a second example of how extensive international action of this kind is in fact politically realistic. As suggested above, the two cases together highlight four specific reasons why regulation cooperation and coordination may be less politically difficult than it is sometimes portrayed. First, because of its dominant position in global finance, the United States can play a key leadership role in helping to overcome collective action problems as well as political opposition abroad. Second, leading financial powers as a group have important tools at their disposal for forcing non-cooperative offshore financial centers to join international regulatory regimes. Third, competitive considerations need not always scuttle international reregulatory initiatives but in fact may sometimes strengthen them by 1) encouraging domestic interests for press for new international regulations as a way of offsetting the impact of new domestic regulation and 2) encouraging compliance for "reputational" reasons. Finally, the increasingly

---

34. Kapstein (1992).

35. For this phenomenon with respect to law enforcement officials, see Anderson (1989, 13).

36. Moreover, the influence of the norms may have been enhanced by the consensual way in which they have been enforced through practices such as the mutual evaluation procedure used in the FATF since 1991.

important role of transnational policymaking communities in finance helps to foster collective action in the regulatory arena.

These four factors help to explain not only why regulatory cooperation and coordination have been possible but also an interesting feature of it: the fact that it has not been accompanied by the creation of strong international institutions or many binding treaties to ensure compliance or enforcement. The international institutions at the center of both regimes—the Bank for International Settlements in the case of the Basel Accord and the Financial Action Task Force (FATF) in the case of money laundering—have little power over member states (and the FATF is not even intended to be a permanent body). In both cases, regulatory initiatives have been pursued instead through intensive interaction between sovereign states. And even in that respect, this cooperation and coordination have been characterized by voluntary agreements and few binding rules. The lack of formal enforcement mechanisms may seem unusual, but is more easily understood in the context of the role of the United States and other Western financial powers, the way competitive pressures have worked in favour of reregulation, and the consensual pattern of policymaking among leading financial powers.

Whether this pattern of cooperation and coordination will remain in the coming years is an open question. In the area of prudential supervision and regulation, there is growing sentiment that the effectiveness of this approach may have reached its limits. John Eatwell and Lance Taylor, in particular, argue that the severity of global financial problems today requires a more powerful international institution to be created. They suggest the creation of a new "World Financial Authority" that could act as both a policy making body to develop common international regulatory standards and an institution capable of ensuring that states actually comply with these standards.[37] In a more limited way, the recent creation of the Financial Stability Forum also reflects the growing sentiment that existing institutions and procedures need to be reformed and strengthened.

A similar sentiment seems to be emerging in the fight against money laundering. The recent decision of the G-7 to extend the FATF's life a further five years reflects a recognition of the need for a more permanent international institution in this area. Although it has no enforcement powers, the FATF is valued as a forum for discussing policy development and coordinating peer review exercises. With respect to enforcement, FATF members seem increasingly willing to use more formal coercive mechanisms to target non-cooperating "outsiders" of the FATF regime. Within the IMF, Vito Tanzi has gone further to argue strongly that the next step in the fight against money laundering must involve the setting of *binding* minimum worldwide standards for anti-money laundering laws.[38] Eatwell and Taylor also suggest that their proposed WFA could be used in the fight against money laundering.[39]

---

37. Eatwell and Taylor (1999).
38. Tanzi (1997).
39. Eatwell and Taylor (1999).

USING THE MONEY LAUNDERING FRAMEWORK FOR
OTHER REGULATORY PURPOSES

In highlighting the politics that have helped to construct the anti-money laundering regime, I am not suggesting that this case *proves* that regulatory cooperation and coordination will be possible in other areas. My objective is a more limited one of drawing on the money-laundering case—and that of the Basel Accord—to argue that international reregulatory initiatives may be less difficult than is sometimes suggested. Skeptics might dismiss this analysis, stating that many unique political circumstances enabled cooperation and coordination to take place in these cases which will be difficult to replicate in other areas. Even if this were true, it would still be wrong to dismiss the significance of the money laundering case for current debates about the prospects for global financial regulation. For even if *new* international regulatory arrangements will prove difficult to construct in other areas, the *existing* anti-money laundering regulatory regime may turn out to be useful for broader regulatory purposes than the fight against money laundering.

Indeed, this potential has already being recognized by the G-7 finance ministers in new initiatives announced in 1998 to counter international tax evasion. Alongside money laundering, international tax evasion has grown in recent years as global financial markets have provided new opportunities to hide money from state authorities. In the past, efforts to curb this phenomenon have been hindered greatly by difficulties in devising cooperative ways to collect and share financial information internationally between different national authorities. In 1998, however, the G-7 recognized the potential of the anti-money laundering regime—where cooperation on information-gathering and sharing is much better developed—to help address this weakness. They stated that domestic agencies involved in the fight against money laundering should now be permitted to share financial information with both domestic and foreign tax authorities. They also agreed that suspicious reporting requirements should include money laundering activities associated with the crime of tax evasion.[40]

One can understand why this initiative has been undertaken. As part of the fight against money laundering, many states have begun to develop very sophisticated information gathering procedures that draw on the latest information technologies. In the United States, for example, a body called FinCEN (Financial Crimes Enforcement Network) was created in 1990 within the U.S. Treasury to collect and analyze information that might be relevant primarily to drug money laundering. With the help of an artificial intelligence (AI) computer program, it analyzes an enormous amount of data relating to domestic and cross-border financial transactions as well as other kinds of data in government, private, and foreign databases. In Bercu's words, it is a kind of "hybrid between a data base

---

40. An interpretative note was also added to the FATF's Recommendation 15 concerning suspicious reporting in 1999 which required financial institutions to report suspicious transactions associated with money laundering *even if* the client claimed the transactions related only to tax evasion.

and a focused surveillance tool."[41] Already, FinCEN has been used to collect information for criminal activity relating to tax evasion.[42] And significantly, FinCEN is also empowered to share information with foreign governments. Indeed, former U.S. Treasury Secretary Nicholas Brady initially described FinCEN as "a system that will be used to consolidate, analyze and disseminate data concerning financial crimes throughout the world."[43]

As a side note, it is interesting that the activities of FinCEN and other countries' recent initiatives to curtail money laundering can call into question the common view that information technology weakens the regulatory power of the state in the financial sector.[44] As I have argued elsewhere, the experience of money laundering regulation suggests that information technology may in fact strengthen this power in three ways. First, as just mentioned, artificial intelligence programs can help authorities analyze enormous amounts of information collected relating to financial transactions in new sophisticated ways. Second, in contrast to old fashioned forms of money, electronic money flows usually leave some kind of electronic record that can be tracked by state authorities. And finally, electronic money tends to flow through centralized payments systems—such as Fedwire or CHIPS—that can also be monitored.[45]

In addition to fighting tax evasion, the anti-money laundering regime might also be useful in the dealing with the problem of capital flight. "Capital flight" is a notoriously difficult term to define precisely, but it refers generally to an outflow of capital from a country where capital is relatively scarce that is not part of normal commercial transactions. Like tax evasion and money laundering, capital flight has grown alongside the financial globalization trend as citizens from many poorer countries have found it increasingly easy to send their money abroad.

This flight of capital has been an important contributor to international financial crises over the last two decades. During the international debt crisis of the 1980s, the private assets of citizens of many Latin American and African countries held abroad were often equal to, or even greater than, the size of the country's external official debt. These countries were, in other words, creditors to the world economy at the very moment they were experiencing "debt crises." If the foreign private assets of their citizens could have been mobilized somehow to help pay off the public liabilities of the country, there would have been no

---

41. Bercu (1994, 397).

42. Bercu (1994, 391 fn. 37). Similarly, in Australia, the government efforts to track money laundering led it to introduce an AI system which analyzes financial data relating to cash transactions and wire transfers in and out of the country within 24 hours of those transactions having taken place. The computer system is a very sophisticated one that had been initially developed by a U.S. defense contractor to track incoming missiles. As in the United States, Australian procedures set up to track money laundering have already been used to monitor for tax evasion. Indeed, in the Australian case, the majority of suspicious transactions that have been identified in recent years have in fact related to tax evasion (Jensen 1993).

43. Quoted in Bercu (1994, 397). Kimery (1993, 5).

44. For this common view, see for example Eichengreen (1999, 2).

45. Helleiner (1998).

debt crisis.[46] More recently during the 1994 Mexican crisis and the 1997 Asian crisis, it was often domestic citizens pulling their money out of their countries first that triggered the crises, despite all the attention on the volatile role of foreign investors. And massive capital flight from post-Soviet Russia has been a major cause of that country's ongoing financial difficulties. Like many Latin American and African countries during the 1980s, the size of flight capital held abroad by Russian citizens today is estimated to be roughly the size of the country's external debt and the annual outflows in recent years have been more than four times the country's annual external debt servicing costs.[47]

Many economists argue that capital flight can only be stopped by changing the afflicted countries' economic policies that are said to have caused the exodus of "hot money" such as overvalued exchange rates or inflationary monetary policies. This view, however, ignores the extent to which capital flight—especially in a context such as contemporary Russia—is also related to factors more difficult to correct by economic reforms, such as political instability or corruption. Furthermore, deflationary stabilization programs may encourage further flight of money which is escaping the low returns on capital in the country's depressed economy.[48] Finally, some analysts critique the focus on economic stabilization on more political grounds that it does not call into question whether domestic elites should have the right to take their money abroad in the face of domestic difficulties. In Manuel Pastor's words, "What is essentially being said is that wealthy individuals . . . be allowed veto power over the direction of national policy."[49]

For some or all of these reasons, many analysts argue that capital controls have a role to play—usually alongside various economic stabilization measures—in stemming capital flight.[50] This is also the conclusion that many governments have come to during the last few years of international financial upheavals. The Malaysian government was one prominent example, introducting capital controls in 1997. Another was Russia when it dramatically tightened its capital controls after the August 1998 crisis.[51] Even many Western governments, which had been supporting financial liberalization abroad over the last decade, have become more

---

46. See for example, Lissakers (1991), Felix (1985), Naylor (1994), Helleiner (1995), Lessard and Williamson (1997).

47. Abalkin and Whalley (1999). See also Baker (1999).

48. See for example Felix (1985, 50), Lissakers (1991, 159), Baker (1999).

49. Pastor's (1990, 14). This was also a point made by the chief U.S. negotiator at Bretton Woods, Harry Dexter White, in his defense of the need for controls on capital flight in an early draft of the Bretton Woods agreement. He argued that capital flows should not be permitted to "operate against what the government deemed to be the interests of any country" even if this involved restricting "the property rights of the 5 to 10 percent of persons in foreign countries who have enough wealth or income to keep or invest some of it abroad" (Horsefield, 1969, 67).

50. See for example Eatwell and Taylor (1999). Eichengreen (1999, 56) is generally more skeptical of the role of controls on capital outflows, but he accepts the case for them if investors seem to be involved in an irrational panic and he also acknowledges that his preferred form of controls—Chilean-style controls only on inflows—"will make no difference when it is residents who are fleeing the currency" (p.90).

51. See for example Whitehouse (1999).

sympathetic to the role that capital controls might play in stemming capital flight during the recent financial upheavals. In February 1999, for example, U.S. President Clinton expressed his concern about the difficulties Russia was having to "control the flow of its money . . .across its borders."[52] At their report to the G-8 Summit meeting in Cologne in June 1999, the G-7 Finance Ministers also noted that controls on capital outflows "may be necessary in certain exceptional circumstances." As they explained: "In exceptional circumstances, countries may impose capital or exchange controls as part of payments suspensions or standstills, in conjunction with IMF support for their policies and programmes, to provide time for an orderly debt restructuring."[53] One of the key supporters of such internationally-legitimated standstill arrangement has been Canada's Finance Minister Paul Martin, who recently argued: "The point is that we need to stop condoning capital flight—by either international or domestic investors."[54]

Interestingly, the principal Bretton Woods architects, John Maynard Keynes from Britain and Harry Dexter White from the United States, also endorsed the idea that capital controls had a major role to play in curtailing capital flight.[55] At that time, their fear was of large-scale capital flight from war-devastated Europe to the United States and Switzerland in the postwar period. This fear was a key reason for their insistence that all countries have the right to introduce capital controls under Article 6 of the IMF's Articles of Agreement. Without such controls, they worried that European countries' policy autonomy would be undermined, stable exchange rates and international trading patterns would be disrupted, and that the meager resources of the IMF would be exhausted trying to finance payments imbalances caused by the flight capital.

But Keynes and White also recognized the difficulties that countries would have in making their controls on capital outflows fully effective because of the fungibility and mobility of money. Indeed, it is these very difficulties that have led some analysts today to be skeptical of the role that controls on capital outflows could play in the new international financial architecture.[56] What is often forgotten, however, is that Keynes and White addressed this issue directly with a further proposal. They argued that controls on capital flight would be much more effective if the countries *receiving* that flight capital assisted in their enforcement.

In White's early drafts of the Bretton Woods agreements, he argued that receiving countries should refuse to accept capital flight altogether without the endorsement of the sending country's government. Strong opposition from the U.S. banking community, however, watered down this proposal and the final IMF Articles of Agreement simply *permitted*, rather than required, cooperation between countries to control capital movements (Article 8-2b). The only requirement was

---

52. Clinton (1999).
53. G-7 Finance Ministers (1999).
54. Martin (1999, 6). UNCTAD (1998) also endorsed the idea of capital controls and standstill clauses in crisis situations as do Eatwell and Taylor (1999).
55. For a more detailed discussion, see Helleiner (1994, Ch.2).
56. See for example Eichengreen (1999, 55).

a more limited one that IMF members had to ensure that all exchange contracts which contravened other members' exchange control were "unenforceable" in their territory (Article 8-2b).[57] In their initial drafts, both Keynes and White also sought to require receiving countries of capital flight to share information with countries using capital controls about foreign holdings of the latter's citizens. Again, this proposal was weakened by U.S. bank opposition and the final IMF Articles of Agreement state that countries are *required* to provide information on capital movements and holdings only to the IMF on request (except to the extent that such information would disclose the affairs of individuals or companies) (Article 8-5a).[58]

Keynes and White's proposal to use international cooperation to strengthen national efforts to control capital flight may be worth revisiting today, especially in light of the creation of the new anti-money laundering regime. A number of analysts have noted that the information-collecting and sharing procedures developed to fight money laundering could be used not just to counter tax evasion but also capital flight. Among the first to make this point prominently was Karin Lissakers, now U.S. Executive Director to the IMF, in her important 1991 book *Banks, Borrowers and the Establishment.* After lamenting the fact that the United States did nothing during the 1980s to discourage inflows of flight capital from Latin America (and indeed actually encouraged them with some regulatory changes), she suggested briefly that the new anti-money laundering regulations might help to enable future U.S. governments to take a different approach: "The potential of the new record-keeping and client-identification requirements as a tool for tracking flight capital is obvious."[59]

It is perhaps in the current Russian context that this potential is most likely to be realized in the near future.[60] One reason is that a considerable portion of Russian capital flight (as much as 25% according to one estimate[61]) is reported

---

57. Helleiner (1994, ch.2). A 1942 draft of White's stated: "It would seem to be an important step in the direction of world stability if a member government could obtain the full cooperation of other member governments in the control of capital flows. For example, after the war a number of countries could request the United States not to permit increases in the deposits or holdings of their nationals, or to do so only with a license granted by the government making the request. Or, some governments greatly in need of capital might request the United States to supplement their efforts to attract capital back to the native country by providing information or imposing special regulations or even special taxes on the holdings of the nationals of the foreign countries" (Horsefield, 1969, 66). In one 1942 draft of White's, governments were required: "a) not to accept or permit deposits or investment from any member country except with the permission of the government of that country, and b) to make available to the government of any member country at its request all property in the form of deposits, investments, securities of the nationals of that member country" (Horsefield, 1969, 44).

58. Helleiner (1994, Ch.2).

59. Lissakers (1991, 158). For another early recognition of this point, see Zamora (1992, 202).

60. Abalkin and Whalley's (1999, 438) important study on Russian capital flight also recently recommended that a key priority for the international community should be the initiation of "international cooperation on information exchange and other devices to better track Russian assets abroad." Although they suggest that the negotiation of new international tax treaties may be the forum to pursue this, more immediately useful is likely to be the information collecting and sharing mechanisms of the existing anti-money laundering regime.

to be linked to criminal groups. There may thus be natural overlap between the fight against capital flight and that against money laundering in this context. A second reason is that Western governments have already indicated their support for Russia's efforts to curtail flight capital. In early 1992, the G-7 and IMF applauded the decision of the Russian government to hire the U.S. private investigations bureau Kroll Associates to track down flight capital. (I have been unable to discover whether Western governments at that time provided concrete support for this investigation, which was abandoned a year later in the face of what Kroll Associates said was a lack of support from key Russian authorities. But one press report notes that President Yeltsin did request the help of FinCEN in tracking stolen Communist Party funds abroad.[62]) More recently, as I noted above, Clinton signaled his concern in February 1999 about the difficulties Russia was encountering in making its capital controls effective. And most importantly, at its June 1999 summit in Cologne, the G-8 made an important commitment in speaking of its support for Russia's reform: "We agreed to deepen our cooperation on law enforcement, fighting organized crime and money laundering, *including as they relate to capital flight*" [emphasis added].[63]

This last statement seems to indicate that the G-7 governments have now formally agreed to cooperate with the Russian government in curtailing capital flight and that they may also be prepared to draw on the anti-money laundering regime as part of this initiative. If so, it may be interesting for contemporary policy makers to know that there is a precedent for this kind of cooperation during the period of the Marshall Plan. As Keynes and White had predicted at Bretton Woods, there was enormous capital flight from European countries to the United States immediately after World War Two, and it contributed greatly to the region's economic crisis in 1947–8. When the prospect of a large U.S. aid package was raised to address this crisis, some members of the U.S. Congress wondered whether the cost to the U.S. taxpayer might be reduced by helping European governments to track down the flight capital of their citizens. Many European governments were in fact requesting exactly this kind of assistance, with the French government going so far as to ask the U.S. government to force U.S. financial institutions to hold assets of French citizens subject to instructions from the French government. In the end, the U.S. government chose not to collect information on the flight capital that had entered the United States since the end of the war—this was seen as too burdensome a task and was also opposed by the U.S. banking community. But it did agree to share information with European governments about European private assets that the government had been seized during wartime (which represented flight capital from the 1930s and early war years) which had not yet been claimed by European citizens.[64]

---

61. Galeotti (1998). See also Tikhomirov (1997, 595).

62. For this initiative, see Tikhomirov (1997) and Burns and Tett (1994). For Yeltsin's request, see Kimery (1993).

63. G-8 (1999).

64. The Congressional Act authorizing the Marshall Plan also included a clause requiring any government receiving Marshall aid to "locate and identify and put into appropriate use" the foreign

Although the initiative fell short of what many were calling for, it represented an interesting example of the kind of idea that Keynes and White had floated, and that may be pursued today in the context of the Russian crisis. Indeed, some might argue that the case for international assistance for tracking Russian flight capital is greater than in late 1940s Europe. Eatwell and Taylor suggest that the Russian state's capacity to control capital flight on its own is probably more limited than was that of Western European governments in the late 1940s because of problems associated with corruption and the eroding authority of the state.[65] Moreover, there seems to be no appetite among Western aid donors at the moment to provide enormous aid packages of the Marshall Plan kind, especially after they saw a huge capital outflow immediately after the IMF loan in 1998.[66] Much cheaper to Western governments than providing more IMF money or U.S. aid might be to help Russia in its fight against capital flight at this point by mobilizing the information available through the anti-money laundering regime.

The possibility of using the money laundering regime to curtail flight capital has also begun to appear in a different context: the growing U.S. interest in cracking down on government corruption in developing countries. In September 1999, bills were introduced into both the U.S. Senate and House of Representatives that aim to widen the definition of unlawful money laundering activities to include fraud committed against a foreign government and misuse of funds of international institutions such as the IMF. The early Congressional committee hearings on the bill made clear that this initially was being driven by allegations of improper use of IMF loans to Russia as well as dramatic cases of corruption-related capital flight among Third World leaders such as General Abacha of Nigeria.[67] Although the bill addresses only these specific elements of the phenomenon of "capital flight," its provisions are interesting because they go beyond simply sharing information as a way of curtailing capital flight. If these bills pass (and they reportedly have the support of the Clinton administration), they would prevent U.S. banks from handling money involved in these activities altogether.

With these developments taking place, now may also be an interesting moment to consider more generally whether some kind of international cooperation relating to capital flight could be embedded within the new international financial architecture, as Keynes and White initially intended. The most ambitious initiative would be to widen the definition of money laundering activities used by the FATF to include capital flight. Some FATF members have in fact seemed quite open to this idea in the past. In 1993, for example, then president of the FATF, Tom Sherman, wrote that he thought it necessary to recognize that

---

assets of its citizens. There was some debate immediately after the Act's passage as to whether this clause implied that the United States was obligated to help European efforts to mobilize flight capital. (Helleiner 1995, 91).

65. Eatwell and Taylor (1999, ch.5 p.23).

66. See for example Sanger (1999).

67. See also Baker (1999).

"money laundering" could be associated not just with drug money but also "in the case of developing countries, offenses relating to capital flight."[68] This kind of initiative might also receive support in a more limited way from those concerned about capital flight related to governmental corruption. Indeed, in October 1999, a G-8 ministerial conference on combatting transnational organized crime agreed "on the importance of extending predicate offenses of money laundering beyond drug-related offenses to other serious crimes, such as bribery or corruption."[69]

A less ambitious initiative might involve only the use of information-sharing from the money laundering regime to pursue flight capital. Here, I am not thinking of the kind of wide-sweeping proposal that Keynes and White had in mind in which countries be required to share all information about foreign private holdings with any foreign government that requested it as part of its effort to enforce capital controls. Instead, what may be more politically palatable today is a more limited and targeted proposal in which information-sharing could be provided only in instances where countries were introducing capital controls as a way of coping with a severe financial crisis, such as the current Russian situation (or that experienced in 1947-48 by European countries).

Like the proposals for the activation of standstill clauses on cross-border contracts, the IMF could be empowered to declare when such a crisis moment existed. And when the declaration was made, the information-collecting and sharing mechanisms developed to fight money laundering could be mobilized to track capital flight from the crisis-struck country and to share the relevant information with that country's government. The information about capital flight might be provided only in response to a request from the country experiencing the crisis, or alternatively all countries might be required to provide information to that country independent of such a request during the crisis moment. (With respect to the latter, recall the FATF recommendation that countries consider providing information *proactively* to foreign governments regarding suspicious flows to and from those foreign countries that take place under its jurisdiction). Whatever the specifics, my point is that the information-collecting and sharing obligations would not be considered part of the normal functioning of the global financial system (as Keynes and White had imagined) but rather simply part of its crisis-management procedures.

This proposal might have several advantages in helping the resolution of financial crises. First, as noted already in the Russian context, it might help to reduce the costs of financial bailouts to Western taxpayers and international organizations. This is not just because capital flight might be slowed. It is also because existing flight capital abroad might be mobilized either by the country experiencing the crisis or by the international community. For example, during the discussions in the late 1940s, a number of interesting proposals of this kind were considered by the U.S. government, including one IBRD proposal that would

---

68. Sherman (1993, 13).
69. G-8 (1999).

have seen a portion of the European flight capital invested in either U.S. or IBRD bonds with the proceeds used for aid or loans to European governments.[70] Similar proposals were made by some analysts during the Latin American debt crisis of the 1980s for flight capital to be mobilized either to help service the external debt or as collateral for further borrowing.[71]

Second, this proposal might help spread the distribution of the adjustment burden within the country experiencing a financial crisis in a more equitable fashion. During the international debt crisis of the 1980s and more recent crises, there has been pressure from international creditors for debtor governments to assume the private foreign debt of their citizens as part of crisis-management procedures. There are important reasons why this has been seen as necessary, but it has had the side effect of shifting the burden of adjustment for private borrowing behavior—usually that of more wealthy citizens—onto the nation as a whole. By mobilizing flight capital in crisis moments to help service the external debt of the country, the international community would ensure that it was not just the foreign debts of wealthier citizens in these countries that were socialized but also their foreign assets.

Third, the existence of this kind of procedure at the international level might discourage flight capital in the future. At the moment, the prospect of financial crisis creates a strong incentive for wealthy domestic asset holders in poorer countries to engage in capital flight. Not only do they protect their money from a prospective devaluation or imposition of capital controls this way, but they also have the prospect of "round-tripping" the money after a devaluation and stabilization program to buy up domestic assets at bargain prices.[72] If domestic asset holders were aware that their foreign assets might be controlled or even mobilized for public purposes as part of a financial rescue plan, they might be less inclined to flee at the first sign of a possible crisis. In this way, the existence of this kind of procedure might help to discourage speculative flows and contribute to a more stable international financial order.

What are the prospects for these kinds of reforms to bolster international cooperation in curtailing capital flight? In a legal sense, they would require little change to IMF rules, since several parts of its Articles of Agreement—the legacies of Keynes and White's original proposal—allow international cooperation of this kind.[73] And with respect to money laundering regulations and procedures, it might

---

70. Helleiner (1995).

71. See for example Felix (1985). In an interesting although less ambitious proposal, Carlos Diaz-Alejandro (1984) proposed that the U.S. government impose a tax on the interest earned from Latin American deposits in the United States and donate the proceeds to the InterAmerican Development Bank. See also discussion in Lessard and Williamson (1987).

72. See especially Naylor (1994).

73. Tanzi (1997) points out more generally that Article 8 empowers the organization to require members to furnish information necessary for the discharge of its mandate. As Tanzi points out with respect to the control of money laundering, the IMF could monitor capital movements more as part its surveillance function in order to support a formal international agreement to combat money laundering.

be necessary simply to expand the definition of "money laundering" to include capital flight, as discussed already.

In a more political sense, opposition may come in Northern countries from the financial community and those who oppose capital controls more generally—what Jagdish Bhagwati has called the "Wall Street-Treasury complex" in the U.S. context[74]—if the experiences of the Bretton Woods negotiations, the Marshall Plan, and the 1980s debt crisis are any guide.[75] Opposition can also be expected from groups in poorer countries whose involvement in capital flight is the target of the initiative. In the 1980s debt crisis, for example, David Felix suggests that elite opposition was a key explanation for the fact that Latin American governments did little to request foreign assistance in tracking down capital flight.[76] Vladimimir Tikhomirov also suggests that this kind of opposition seems to have played a role in dampening the initial enthusiasm of the Russian government in the early 1990s to track down flight capital.[77]

On the other hand, the proposal may attract support from some important quarters. In many poorer countries, the issue of capital flight is a highly politicized one and the governments of these countries may see this reform as an important one for them to promote for this reason. In Russia, for example, Tikhomirov notes that the issue is "socially explosive"and "one of the most hotly debated in Russian politics," with capital flight being "seen by the majority of the Russian people as a gross economic crime being committed in the process of redistribution of the national property inherited by all of the population from the Soviet era."[78]

Equally important may be Western politicians who are wary of providing more funds for international aid and financial rescue packages but who are concerned about political and economic stability in poorer countries experiencing severe financial crises. Some of these may be politicians on the political left who are attracted more generally to the idea of capital controls and also to the way the proposal promotes greater equity of burden-sharing in the debtor countries. But support is also likely to come from more conservative, even isolationist, quarters. In 1947–48, for example, the greatest support for the proposal to help European governments track down flight capital in the United States came from Republican

---

74. Bhagwati (1998).

75. See Helleiner (1995) for these experiences. An interesting example of the importance with which the principle of free capital movements is defended even in crisis situations such as Russia was provided in March 1999 by then U.S. Treasury Secretary Robert Rubin. After telling a Congressional panel that he suspected much of the $4.8b IMF loan to Russia last year "may have been siphoned off improperly," he later qualified his testimony saying "it may have been careless to use the word 'improper'" because "there is nothing improper about moving money out of Russia or any other country." Quoted in Sanger (1999).

76. Felix (1990, 761).

77. Tikhomirov (1997, 592). Interestingly, during the late 1940s, this kind of opposition among European elites was quite limited, perhaps given the extent to which they had been discredited by the wartime experience in many of the key countries (e.g., France) pursuing capital flight.

78. Tikhomirov (1997, 595; 599; 595).

congressmen. As the powerful and traditionally isolationist Republican Senator Henry Cabot Lodge argued at the time: "It seems to me that you cannot defend either before an American audience or a foreign audience, for that matter, a proposition whereby the people of moderate means in this country are being taxed to support a foreign aid program which the well-to-do people abroad are not helping to support." He continued: "In a lot of these countries it is a well-known fact that there is a small, bloated, selfish class of people whose assets have been spread all over the place and that that is a very bad thing for the morale of those countries and it is a bad thing for the morale over here." Former U.S. president Herbert Hoover also defended the proposal to mobilize European flight capital saying "If there is protest that taking over these privately held resources is a hardship to the owners, it may be pointed out that the alternative is a far greater hardship for the American taxpayer."[79] The regulation of capital flight may thus be one of the few causes in which U.S. isolationist sentiments can be mobilized to support stronger international regulatory cooperation.

CONCLUSION

I have argued in this paper that studying the experience of the international fight against money laundering over the last decade provides two important lessons for current debates about the prospects for international reregulatory initiatives in the financial sector. First, the case suggests that these initiatives may be easier to achieve politically than skeptics argue. Indeed, the case may help us to begin to understand political conditions that help to enable and encourage regulatory cooperation and coordination in global finance. Specifically, I have suggested that the construction of the anti-money laundering regime was made possible by many similar conditions to those that fostered the 1998 Basel Accord: 1) strong U.S. leadership has helped overcome collective action problems and political opposition abroad, 2) Western financial powers as a group have been increasingly willing to identify tools at their disposal for forcing non-cooperative offshore financial centers to join international regulatory regimes, 3) competitive pressures have sometimes strengthened, rather than weakened, the move for international reregulation, and 4) regulatory cooperation and coordination has been helped by the increasingly important role of transnational policy making communities. Whether these same conditions may help to encourage international reregulatory initiatives in other parts of the financial sector is a question that needs further study.

An examination of the international anti-money laundering regime also provides a second, more direct lesson for debates about the prospects for international reregulatory initiatives. Even if the politics encouraging reregulation in the money laundering case are not replicable in other financial areas, policy makers

---

79. All quotes taken from Helleiner (1995, 87; 90).

are recognizing that this existing anti-money laundering regime has created co-operative structures at the international level which can be useful for other regulatory purposes. The G-7 have already made clear their intention to take advantage of these mechanisms with respect to the regulation of tax evasion. And they show signs of recognizing that it may also be relevant for the project of regulating capital flight in specific situations.

If policy makers were to use this kind of international cooperation to regulate capital flight, I have noted that they would in fact be returning to an idea that the principal negotiators of Bretton Woods endorsed. Keynes and White both argued that this kind of international cooperation could play a major role in making controls on capital outflows more effective, and the Bretton Woods agreement endorses this kind of practice in a limited way.[80] But such international cooperation was rarely forthcoming in the postwar period—the experience of the Marshall aid period was the one exception. With the creation of the anti-money laundering regime, however, the international community is putting in place an important set of structures that could finally allow this idea to be operationalized. Coincidently, these structures are being built at the very time when there is growing interest in many quarters in the control of capital flight. It thus seems an important moment to give serious consideration to the idea of reviving Keynes and White's proposal, although probably in the more limited ways that I have discussed. In this way, the fight against money laundering may play an unintended role of enabling the "new international financial achitecture" to be built more closely on foundations laid by the architects of Bretton Woods.

REFERENCES

Abalkin, A. and Whalley, John. 1999. "The Problem of Capital Flight from Russia." *The World Economy* 22(3) (May): 421–44.

Andelman, David. 1994. "Drug Money Maze." *Foreign Affairs* (July/August): 94–108.

Anderson, Malcolm. 1989. *Policing the World.* Oxford: Clarendon.

Baker, Raymond. 1999. "The Biggest Loophole in the Free-Market System." *The Washington Quarterly* 22(4): 29–46.

Beatty, Jonathan and Richard Hornik. 1994. "A Torrent of Dirty Dollars." *Time*, Dec. 18.

Bercu, Steven. 1994. "Toward Universal Surveillance in an Information Age Economy: Can We Handle Treasury's New Police Technology?" *Jurimetrics: Journal of Law, Science and Technology* 34: 383–449.

---

80. Among those supportive of capital controls playing a larger role in the new international financial architecture today, it is interesting to see this idea beginning to be revived. In their proposal for a new World Financial Authority (WFA), Eatwell and Taylor (1998, 18) support the idea of a country's using capital controls and they add: "Once particular conditions for the management of capital movement have been agreed then member states of the WFA should be required to provide assistance to fellow members in their operation."

Bhagwati, Jagdish. 1998. "The Capital Myth" *Foreign Affairs* 77(3): 7–12.

Blum, Jack, Michael Levi, Thomas Naylor and Phil Williams. 1998. *Financial Havens, Banking Secrecy and Money Laundering*. New York: United Nations.

Burns, Jimmy and Gillian Tett. 1994. "Probe Into Flight of Capital From Former Soviet Union Abandoned." *Financial Times* Feb.7.

Cerny, Phil. 1993. "American Decline and the Emergence of Embedded Financial Orthodoxy," in P. Cerny, ed., *Finance and World Politics*. Aldershot: Elgar.

_____. 1994. "The Dynamics of Financial Globalization."*Policy Sciences* 27(4): 319-42.

Clinton, President Bill. 1999. "Remarks by President Clinton on Foreign Policy, Grand Hyatt Hotel, San Francisco, February 26, 1999." Office of the Press Secretary, White House, February 26.

Diaz-Alejandro, Carlos. 1984. "Latin American Debt: I Don't Think We Are in Kansas Anymore." *Brookings Papers on Economic Activity* 2: 335–403.

Eatwell, John and Lance Taylor. 1998. "International Capital Markets and the Future of Economic Policy." CEPA Working Paper Series III, Working Paper No. 9, August 1998. Center for Economic Policy Analysis, New School for Social Research, New York.

_____. 1999. *Global Finance at Risk: The Case for International Regulation*. Mimeo.

Eichengreen, Barry. 1999. *Toward a New International Financial Architecture*. Washington: Institute for International Economics.

Felix, David. 1985. "How to Resolve Latin America's Debt Crisis." *Challenge* 28 (November/December): 44–51.

_____. 1990. "Latin America's Debt Crisis." *World Policy Journal* 7(4): 733–71.

Financial Action Task Force on Money Laundering (FATF.) 1990. "Report—February 6, 1990," in W. Gilmore, ed., *International Efforts to Combat Money Laundering*. Cambridge: Grotius Publications, 1992.

_____. 1991. "Report—1990–91," in W. Gilmore, ed., *International Efforts to Combat Money Laundering*. Cambridge: Grotius Publication, 1992.

_____. 2000. *Report on Non-Cooperative Countries or Territories*. Paris: FATF.

Friman, H. Richard. 1994. "International Pressure and Domestic Bargains: Regulating Money Laundering in Japan." *Crime, Law, and Social Change* 21: 253–66.

Friman, H. Richard and Peter Andreas, eds. 1999. *The Illicit Global Economy and State Power*. New York: Rowman and Littlefield.

Galeotti, Mark. 1998. "The Three Faces of Russian Crime." *The Times of London*, Nov.9, p.31.

Gilmore, William, ed. 1992. *International Efforts to Combat Money Laundering*. Cambridge: Grotius Publications.

Group of Seven (G-7) Finance Ministers. 1999. "Strengthening the International Financial Architecture," report to the Cologne Economic Summit, June 18–20. www.g8cologne.de/.

Group of Eight (G-8). 1999. *Ministerial Conference of the G-8 Countries on Combating Transnational Organized Crime, Communique*. Moscow, October 19–20.

_____. 1999. Press Communique, Cologne Summit, June 18–20. www.g8cologne.de/.

Helleiner, Eric. 1994. *States and the Reemergence of Global Finance: From Bretton Woods to the 1990s*. Ithaca: Cornell University Press.

_____. 1995. "Handling 'Hot Money': U.S. Policy Toward Latin American Capital Flight in Historical Perspective." *Alternatives* 20: 81–115.

_____. 1998. "Electronic Money: A Challenge to the Sovereign State?" *Journal of International Affairs* 51(2): 387–410.

_____. 1999. "State Power and the Regulation of Illicit Activity in Global Finance" in H. R. Friman and P. Andreas, eds., *The Illicit Global Economy and State Power*. New York: Rowman and Littlefield.

Horsefield, J. K. 1969. *International Monetary Fund.* Washington: IMF.

Jensen, Neil. 1993. "International Funds Transfer Instructions: Australia at the Leading Edge." *Journal of Law and Information Science* 4:304–29.

Kapstein, Ethan. 1992. "Between Power and Purpose: Central Bankers and the Politics of Regulatory Convergence." *International Organization* 46: 265–87.

_____. 1994. *Governing the Global Economy: International Finance and the State.* Cambridge: Harvard University Press.

Kerry, Senator John. 1997. *The New War: The Web of Crime that Threatens America's Security.* New York: Simon and Schuster.

Kimery, Anthony. 1993. "Big Brother Wants to Look in Your Bank Account" *Wired* (December 1993).

Lessard, D. and J. Williamson, eds. 1987. *Capital Flight and Third World Debt.* Washington: Institute for International Economics.

Lissakers, Karin. 1991. *Banks, Borrowers and the Establishment.* New York: Basic Books.

MacDonald, Scott. 1992. "Frontiers for International Money Regulation After BCCI: International Cooperation or Fragmentation?" *Proceedings of the 86th Annual Meeting of the American Society of International Law.* Washington.

Martin, Paul. 1999. "International Financial Architecture Reform: Completing Bretton Woods," statement by the Honourable Paul Martin, Minister of Finance for Canada to the Chicago Council on Foreign Relations, June 7, 1999. Department of Finance Canada, Ottawa.

Nadelmann, Ethan. 1990. "Global Prohibition Regimes: The Evolution of Norms in International Society." *International Organization* 44: 479–526.

Naylor, Tom. 1994. *Hot Money and the Politics of Debt.* Montreal: Black Rose Books.

Pastor, Manuel. 1990. "Capital Flight from Latin America." *World Development* 18 (January).

Porter, Tony. 1993. *States, Markets and Regimes and Global Finance.* London: MacMillan.

Possamai, Mario. 1992. *Money on the Run* Toronto: Viking.

Quirk, Peter. 1997. "Money Laundering: Muddling the Macroeconomy." *Finance and Development* 34(1): 7–9.

Sanger, David. 1999. "U.S. Official Questions How Russia Used Loan." *The New York Times*, March 19, p.8.

Sassen, Saskia. 1998. *Globalization and Its Discontents.* New York: New Press.

Savona, Ernesto, ed. 1997. *Responding to Money Laundering: International Perspectives.* Amsteldijk: Harwood Academic Publishers.

Sherman, Tom. 1993. "International Efforts to Combat Money Laundering: The Role of the Financial Action Task Force," in David Hume Institute, *Money Laundering.* Edinburgh: Edinburgh University Press.

Strange, Susan. 1998. *Mad Money.* Ann Arbor: University of Michigan Press.

Sultzer, Scott. 1995. "Money Laundering: The Scope of the Problem and Attempts to Combat It." *Tennessee Law Review*, v.63 pp.143–237.

Tanzi, Vito. 1997. "Macroeconomic Implications of Money Laudering," in E. Savona, ed., *Responding to Money Laundering: International Perspectives.* Amsteldijk: Harwood Academic Publishers,

Thrift, Nigel. 1994. "On the Social and Cultural Determinants of International Financial Centres," in S. Corbridge et al., eds., *Money, Power and Space.* Oxford: Basil Blackwell.

Tikhomirov, Vladimir. 1997. "Capital Flight from Post-Soviet Russia." *Europe-Asia Studies* 49(4): 591–615.

UNCTAD. 1998. *Trade and Development Report.* Geneva: United Nations.

Whitehouse, Mark. 1999. "In Russia, Capital Flight Continues Unabated." *The Wall Street Journal*, April 19, p.A19.

Wyrsch, Gerard. 1992. "Treasury Regulation of International Wire Transfer and Money Laundering." *Denver Journal of International Law and Policy* 20: 515–35.

Zamora, Stephen. 1992. "Remarks," in *Proceedings of the 86th Annual Meeting of the American Society of International Law*. Washington. April.

PART III

...

Issues in Industrialized Economies

8

. . .

Financial Market Liberalization and the Changing Character of Corporate Governance

*Thorsten H. Block**

CORPORATE GOVERNANCE is concerned with the implementation of monitoring and disciplining devices that will ensure the efficient use of available resources by private corporations. It became a popular topic in the United States during the 1970s and 1980s, when observers lamented the apparent loss of industrial leadership to companies in Germany and Japan. Today, the U.S. economy appears to be vigorous again and issues of corporate governance systems and their reform are widely discussed in the stagnant economies of Europe and Japan. This paper will attempt to contribute to this discussion by examining the impact of the ongoing transformation of international capital markets on governance and its effectiveness.

We will start by providing different definitions of the nature and scope of corporate governance. Governance issues are conventionally discussed in the context of principal-agent (PA) models, which presuppose a distinction between ownership (shareholders) and control (managers) (Berle and Means 1932). The agency problem exists because managers might misuse their position, and there are costs associated with prevention of abuse. According to this view of governance, the crucial problem is to subordinate managers' interest to that of shareholders. Shareholders are put into this superior position because they have the greatest incentive

* This paper was prepared for a conference on "International Capital Markets and the Future of Economic Policy" sponsored by the Ford Foundation. I would like to acknowledge very helpful discussions with Ute Pieper and Lance Taylor as well as their comments on earlier drafts. The usual disclaimers apply.

to guarantee the company's success. This is the case due to the fact that they are the *residual claimant*, i.e., they receive the profit that is left over after lenders, suppliers, and employees are paid. Similarly, they alone bear the *residual risk* because shareholders, in contrast to lenders or suppliers, lose everything should bankruptcy occur. The following section will discuss Michael Jensen's approach to the agency problem.

Blair and Stout (1997) propose an alternative to agency theory with its narrow focus on shareholders as owners and managers as their agents. Following Alchian and Demsetz's (1972) seminal contribution, they argue instead that public corporations evolved primarily as a solution to the "team production" problem. Team members face the problems of shirking and rent seeking that cannot easily be resolved by contracts, especially when team production processes are increasingly continuous and complex. Through a mediating hierarchy, members give up important property rights as well as inputs, such as financial capital and firm-specific human capital, to the fictional legal entity created by incorporation. According to the authors, the mediating hierarchy approach suggests that managers should not be under direct control of any particular stakeholder group—including shareholders. The corporation is then best seen not as a nexus of implicit and explicit contracts, but as a solution to complex decision-making processes. Many and varied individuals give up control over their firm-specific investments to an independent third party in hopes of sharing in the economic gains that can flow from team production. Blair and Stout thus dispute that shareholders are the only group that assumes the residual risk. Employees who invest in firm-specific assets also stand to lose from the company's bankruptcy.

Alfred Chandler's model of managerial capitalism is similar to Blair and Stout's view in that he also identifies a crucial role for managerial autonomy. In contrast to the principal-agent model as developed by Berle and Means, which interprets managerial autonomy as a passive response to dispersed stock ownership patterns, Chandler argues that managerial discretion develops in order to accumulate the organizational knowledge as a crucial ingredient for the growth and sustainability of the corporation and especially so, in capital-intensive industries (Hikino 1997, 483). The distinction between managers and owners is thus not just a nuisance, which is costly to overcome, but a necessary competitive asset in modern capitalism. The next section will present a more detailed description of Chandler's managerial model.

The choice of governance mechanisms is by no means only a reflection of economic incentives, however. It is also inherently political, shaped by a regulatory framework that is set by the state. Moreover, it is subject to historical change. Fligstein (1990), for example, provides a historical account of corporate transformation based on a sociological framework for the case of the United States. For Fligstein, organizations are embedded in organizational fields defined in terms of product line, industry, and firm size or suppliers, distributors, or owners. The state sets the rules of behavior within which corporations employ strategies, structures, and technologies that shape and constrain their patterns of growth. These organizational fields are not benign but are set up to benefit their most powerful members. Thus, Fligstein introduces the power dimension that is missing from the previously discussed approaches.

He argues that corporate strategy in the nineteenth century consisted of predatory competition. The manufacturing and managerial conception of control was developed by absorbing suppliers and marketing functions into their own organization in an attempt to stabilize the production process through oligopolistic pricing. Finally, the currently dominant conception of the corporation emphasizes the use of financial tools, which measure performance according to profit rates. Fligstein demonstrates that corporate control mechanisms are not adopted because they are most efficient but rather they have come into existence because of a social and political process that defines and redefines the character of markets.

This paper will adopt a similar historical perspective on changes in the nature of corporate governance systems. We will argue, in particular, that the deregulation and internationalization of financial markets has changed the macroeconomic incentive system by raising the real interest rate. Higher interest rates are an expression of the increased power of creditors over borrowers in liberalized financial markets. In the United States, this has lead to a shift from a corporate governance system with relative managerial autonomy to a system dominated by the financial interests of shareholders. Financial considerations are beneficial in some instances but damaging in others.

The argument will proceed in several steps. We will first compare and contrast the managerial with the agency view of governance. Secondly, the liberalization and deregulation of financial markets will be linked to higher real interest rates. Thirdly, it will be shown how higher real interest rates put pressure on managerial autonomy, thus shifting incentives towards financial market dominance in the United States. Fourthly, we will examine the rise of the large institutional investors and discuss their ability to provide a solution to the governance problem. Lastly, we will present a brief overview of other countries' experience with financial liberalization and its impact on corporate governance.

MANAGERIAL AUTONOMY vs. FINANCIAL MARKET DOMINANCE

The following section will compare the agency view of governance as proposed by Michael Jensen with Alfred Chandler's managerial model of capitalism. The former stresses the efficiency of financial markets as disciplinary whereas the latter sees a need for the relative autonomy of managers who are, in turn, kept in check by Schumpeterian competition in product markets.

Michael Jensen (1986, 1997), one of the foremost proponents of agency theory, assumes the efficient market hypothesis (EMH), according to which financial markets process information efficiently thereby generating optimal asset prices. The strong form of the EMH states that security prices fully reflect all available information and thus makes the assumption of no information costs. In the weak version, preferred by Jensen, prices reflect information to the point where the marginal benefits of acting on the basis of information—i.e., the profits from this action—do not exceed the marginal costs.

Based on this belief in the efficiency of financial markets, Jensen defends the role of capital markets in product market restructuring. In particular, he has been a staunch supporter of the Leverage Buy-Out (LBO) and Merger & Acquisition (M&A) activity of the 1980s. According to this view, the market for corporate control is a fast and efficient mechanism by which firms are forced to exit mature markets where overcapacity persists. Product markets will also provide similar pressures if companies cannot produce the products customers desire and therefore will eventually be unable to generate sufficient profits. However, according to Jensen, the disciplinary effect of product markets operates much more slowly and therefore is socially wasteful. Bankruptcy procedures in the United States, for example, are a long and drawnout process, which strives to maintain the operation of the firm in order to protect creditors as well as employees. Furthermore, internal control systems are also too slow to respond to market challenges. He cites the example of General Motors, where the board intervened too late to change GM's high cost production structure, leading to substantial losses in the early 1990s (Jensen 1997, 31).

What he fails to mention is the success of GM and, in fact, the entire U.S. auto industry to regain market share from the Japanese and their ability to design new products and streamline their production facilities over the last decade. In addition, the early 1990s were characterized by a severe business cycle downturn in the United States, which certainly contributed greatly to the losses. The problem with Jensen's account of the U.S. auto industry is his conception of the nature of product market competition. The appropriate strategy for Jensen would have been simply to cut costs by closing plants and firing managers and workers in order to adjust to existing worldwide overcapacity. However, this assumes that costs and thus prices are the principal competitive assets in the automobile business. Instead, one could argue that the success is based on adopting a more long-term perspective, which took time to develop and implement. It is also reasonable to argue that the success was dependent on the Cupertino of workers and their unions. Managerial capabilities, innovation, and stable labor relations might go a long way in explaining the success of the U.S. auto industry in regaining competitiveness.

There is also the case of the attempted takeover of Chrysler by a group of investors in 1994–95. The investors were after the cash that Chrysler had accumulated in the previous business upswing. The takeover group argued in typical Jensen style that the cash should be disbursed to shareholders instead of invested in substandard investment projects. Chrysler managers, on the other hand, were planning to invest the cash in costly new model development in order to strengthen the company's long-term competitive position, especially vis-à-vis their Japanese rivals, and to use it as a financial cushion for the next downturn. The management position eventually won out, not the least because management could convince larger institutional investors of the strategy's benefits to long-term shareholder value (Brancato 1997). Chrysler's remarkable comeback from near bankruptcy in the early 1980s based on an innovative product line certainly speaks for allowing management to pursue this forward-looking strategy. The question also arises at what stage a market is matured enough so that exit becomes necessary. The automobile example has shown that a relatively mature product like the automobile presents ample possibilities for innovation and growth (minivans, SUVs, etc.). By stripping Chrysler of its cash flow, the investor group might have damaged the company's ability in maintaining its competitive position.

There is also evidence that the recent downsizing wave in a variety of industries might have gone too far—in some cases depriving companies of valuable managerial knowledge. A study by Wayne Cascio (cited in Blair 1996) on the effects of massive downsizing shows that three years after downsizing, sample companies had subsequent earnings increases of 183%. Comparison firms in the same industries that did not downsize had earnings increases of 422%; cumulative stock returns over three years were 4.7% vs. 34.3%. The study concludes that pension fund managers would be justified in encouraging a second look at possibly premature downsizing and "exit" tactics.

Stock markets, of course, are always enthusiastic about such corporate restructurings because they promise more future cash flow that can be distributed to shareholders. This is also the main reason to explain the evidence that takeover activity is positively correlated with the business cycle; there is simply more cash flow available, to be targeted by corporate raiders. The threat of hostile takeovers can thus act as a corrective device only in business cycle upswings when liquidity is abundant, as in the takeover frenzy in the later half of the 1980s. Similarly, the occurrence of merger activity in waves again suggests the cyclical nature of takeovers as disciplining device. This suggests that other incentives were at play, which activate the market for corporate control. We will see in the next section that high real interest rates play a large role in the changed incentive structure.

In contrast to agency theory, another strand of corporate governance theory focuses less on capital market discipline. Alfred Chandler's framework of managerial capitalism starts from the existence of an information asymmetry between managers who run the company and outside evaluators like shareholders or financial institutions (Hikino 1997). To succeed in constantly changing product market conditions management needs to accumulate knowledge about product and factor markets as well as production technology in the industries in which they operate. Management is in a superior position to gather and utilize such knowledge compared with shareholders, debt holders, customers, employees, and government because management not only constantly gathers and evaluates information, it also continuously has to apply this information in order to run the firm. Outsiders simply do not have the time and resources to collect and utilize this type and amount of information (Taylor 1990).

For Chandler ownership per se is not necessarily the issue. The critical element is the long-term commitment and capacity of management, including the compatibility of the managerial structure with the structure and business of the firm. The Chandlerian story is especially applicable to the growth of dynamic capital-intensive industries—Chandler's "engines of growth." Because firms in capital-intensive industries often face critical decisions of large-scale investments that are discontinuous and uncertain, they must create an organizational learning device to minimize risk and maximize the benefits of such investments (Chandler 1990). Hence, the ability of managers to exert discretionary power in strategic decision-making is the essential ingredient for the success of managerial capitalism.

However, who controls these managerial decisions in order to avoid waste and corruption? Who ensures that managers will continuously invest in the accumulation of organizational capabilities? Given the tacit, fungible, and non-patentable nature of this internal organizational knowledge of technology and markets, such knowledge does *not* realize its full potential in external market transactions (Hikino 1997; Winter 1993). The ability of capital market institutions to match this information-processing activity is limited because it requires actual and ongoing experience of production processes, whereas external actors' knowledge will always be conceptual and theoretical. Technical knowledge of financial institutions will be helpful in devising investment strategies but cannot substitute for the accumulated, firm-specific knowledge of the manufacturing firm. Taking these fungible assets into account, Jensen-style restructurings may damage companies in a way that is not measured by conventional financial indicators. Jensen, therefore, implicitly has to assume the existence of a conventional production function according to which factor inputs are turned into products by means of a given technology. Chandler's framework, on the other hand, incorporates the idea of learning and technological changes as endogenous processes with investment characteristics (Winter 1993).

In the Chandlerian model, the ultimate disciplinary of management is the constant pressure from Schumpeterian competitors in domestic and international product markets. These markets decide whether managers have invested wisely and adopted the right strategy, or whether the company is unable to provide the right product for their customers at a competitive price. While Jensen might have a point in that this type of restructuring takes longer and incurs higher "measurable" cost, it nevertheless ensures that crucial managerial, or otherwise firm-specific, knowledge is maintained during the restructuring process. In fact, since organizational capabilities do not show up in conventional accounting numbers, the flow of resources into maintaining them may be confused with truly wasteful expenditure which does not add value to the firm. Hence, the amount of free cash flow that triggers Jensen-type restructurings is not easily determined and might be overestimated. The observable shareholder gains resulting from takeovers might thus simply result from cuts in investment in intangible, non-marketable assets or wage concessions.

Similarly, Blair (1995) argues that owners view employee wages as a cost to be reduced, yet, the return on firm-specific human capital is part of what society as a whole should want to see maximized. Employees are much more likely to participate in cost cutting and innovation if they are confident they will share in the wealth created. Corporate governance discussions need to recognize the importance of employees to wealth creation. Kreps (1990) develops a model in which the firm's sole asset is its reputation not to exploit business partners. Owners have an interest in maintaining this reputational capital because it allows for profitable transactions based on mutual commitment of the transactions partners. This model underscores Blair's previous point that firms have to induce employees to share some of the costs of firm-specific training, due to the uncertainty about future returns on this investment. The point again is that these fungible assets play a large role in creating firm competitiveness but are absent from financial accounting and other conventional performance measures.

Hikino (1997, 490–1) interprets the differences between Jensen's agency approach and Chandler's model of managerial capitalism as resulting from differences in their analysis of economic change. Chandler focuses on the ability of the large managerial enterprise to enter new markets by building upon accumulated organizational knowledge in medium and high-tech sectors. In contrast, Jensen emphasizes the ability to shift capital out of maturing industries in order to shed overcapacities. Capital market discipline thus assures timely exit from low-tech sectors in which the importance of organizational skills is likely to play only a minor role. This interpretation suggests that one perfect all-purpose governance mechanism does not exist, but that its design and efficiency is dependent on the character of the industry and, in particular, the share of intangible assets such as organizational competence.

DEREGULATION, INTEREST RATES, AND THE CHANGING NATURE OF CORPORATE GOVERNANCE

The previous section attempted to show that there is no single optimal governance mechanism. Instead, governance is dependent on the nature of the production process and the character of technological change. However, it is also likely that the relationship between shareholders and managers is influenced by a number of macroeconomic incentives. In this section, we will identify the real interest rate as a crucial macroeconomic variable influencing the nature of governance. Financial liberalization has created an environment that raised interest rates, leading to a shift from relative managerial autonomy to a proliferation of financial goals in the 1980s. The awakening of the market for corporate control in the 1980s is a direct response to this shift rather than a response to managerial failure.

We start by investigating the link between financial globalization and rising interest rates. The process of financial globalization is not simply the outcome of technological change, as many observers seem to assume implicitly. Technological advances in information and transport technologies, according to the conventional story, have lowered the transaction cost of international market transactions, which created the basis for the growing integration of our economies. The challenge for market actors—governments, enterprises, and workers alike—is to adapt to these new technology-driven opportunities in order to reap their full benefits (OECD

1997). A free market environment is generally identified as the best institutional arrangement to achieve the full potential of globalization. In that view, the capital-market based governance system in the United States is an optimal institutional response to the challenges and opportunities presented by more efficient international financial markets.

In an alternative, institutional account, the proliferation of new technologies has gone hand in hand with the conscious creation of global markets through market deregulation over the last 25 years. Eatwell (1996), for example, argues that pressures for deregulation mounted after the collapse of the Bretton Woods system. Under the Bretton Woods rules, the United States pegged the U.S. dollar to gold and all other all countries pegged their currencies to the U.S. dollar, with the governments bearing the implicit foreign exchange risks. Most of the time, businesses did not have to be concerned with fluctuating values of their asset holdings, costs, and sales in different currencies, because they were tied securely to one another by the fixed exchange rate system.

A period of fluctuating exchange rates ensued after the United States de-linked the dollar from gold, and both nonfinancial and financial enterprises were forced to cope with the resulting risks. For financial interests, volatile exchange rates provided an important playing ground for profit-seeking speculation. Regulatory structures, however, inhibited flows of capital and were consequently challenged as inefficient and against the national interest; they were dismantled and the "infrastructure of speculation" was constructed (Eatwell 1996). Speculation, while certainly possible in a system of fixed exchange rates, became more lucrative after 1973 under the new regime of deregulated currency prices. Since its objective is to earn short-term capital gains from correct guesses about future price movements, this activity thrives on market volatility.

The incentive to deregulate international capital flows was powerfully reinforced by the need to hedge against the costs which fluctuating exchange rates imposed upon the private sector (Edey and Hviding 1995). The need to absorb and cover foreign exchange risk demanded the creation of new financial instruments (derivatives such as currency swaps, options, and futures contracts) which, in turn, required the removal of the regulatory barriers limiting the possibilities of laying off risk. There had to be a restructuring of financial institutions. The various new instruments also attracted speculators by allowing them to trade large amounts of currency with little capital. This is why today currency speculation is a significant source of profits for many banks and corporations.

In the United States, mounting pressures for deregulating financial markets can also be interpreted as the financial sector's response to falling profits and stagnant securities markets during the volatile 1970s. The squeeze on banks intensified when negative real interest rates prevailed in the United States. During the 1970s, ease of credit maintained spending levels but increased the level of overall inflation. This process sustained real capital accumulation but at the direct cost of financial capital (Guttmann 1997). Stock and bond markets, for example, remained stagnant between 1968 and 1982. Inflation involves two opposite price movements, rising output prices in industry and, by pushing up nominal interest rates, falling prices for financial securities. Inflation also hurt lending activity because borrowers could repay their debts with devalued dollars.

The new situation contributed to higher interest rates as banks saw themselves competing for deposits with other intermediaries. Banks then tried to maintain profits by investing these funds in higher-yielding but riskier assets like junk bonds, real estate, developing countries, and so forth. Deregulation is also one of the main reasons behind the rise in real interest rates since it shifted the balance of power from borrowers to lenders. One indicator for this shift is the fact that banks have tended to move aggressively into variable interest rate loans, which shift the interest rates risk to the borrower.

Free capital markets also severely restricted the ability of governments to pursue independent monetary policies, which could be used to lower interest rates and boost activity. Sensible monetary policies arguably contributed to stability in the pre-1973 period. After the deregulation of interest rates, there has been a shift from targeting monetary aggregates to interest rate targeting as the dominant monetary policy instrument in OECD countries. In a liberal financial environment, according to Felix (1996), monetary authorities are confined to manipulate the short-term rate. The effect that interest rate policy will have on nominal income is then largely dependent on how the foreign exchange and long-term bond markets respond. The general market response to lower short rates has been to move funds from long-term bonds into domestic equities and foreign securities. This raises share prices and depreciates the exchange rate but increases longer-term interest rates, which runs counter to the initial attempts to stimulate activity.

In contrast, during the era of capital controls, long bond holders, correctly or incorrectly anticipating higher inflation from a credit easing, could shift to shorter-term domestic bonds and equities, but not easily into foreign securities. The reactions of long bondholders thus helped lower short-term rates, reinforcing the effectiveness of manipulating the short-term rate. In the era of financial globalization, however, shifts between domestic and foreign bonds identify and document causal links from financial globalization to these real economic trends (Felix 1996).

The behavior of the bond market is a good example of the increasing dominance of financial market considerations in designing economic strategies. As we have just pointed out, the bond market appears to determine its operations based on a presumed link between activity and accelerating inflation. This behavior is based on the idea of a natural rate of unemployment, which suggests that the economy exhibits a persistent tendency to gravitate towards its equilibrium position at the natural rate. Only if we assume that this theoretical model does indeed represent the adjustment mechanism of the economy, will a systematic upswing in activity cause accelerating inflation. The frequent re-estimations of the natural rate for the case of the United States seem to imply that the "natural" rate simply shadows the actual unemployment rate. If the natural rate hypothesis does not hold, macroeconomic policy might well be successful in stimulating activity in order to raise employment levels. However, the possibility of a short-term increase in inflation alarms the bond market and negates the expansionary effect.

How and why do higher interest rates effect governance? Blair (1995, 108–10) points to the relationship between the increased activity in the market for corporate control and the high real interest rates in the decade of the 1980s. High real interest rates drive up the opportunity cost to investors for investing in corporate equities while simultaneously reducing the number of attractive investment opportunities for corporations. In the presence of low interest rates, companies have an incentive to retain cash flow and reinvest it quickly. When real interest rates are high, however, investing the cash flow is less likely to be optimal for shareholders who put their cash into safer, high-yielding securities. Graph 1 plots the relationship between profit and real interest rates.

In discussing Chandler's model of managerial autonomy, we have seen that he justifies the built-in growth drive of managerial enterprises as long as it results from the application of accumulated organizational skills in new but related markets. This model thus has a strong explanatory power in the context of growing markets and in sectors in which technological change is endogenous to the large enterprises (Hikino 1997, 491). We have already mentioned the importance of low interest rates relative to profit opportunities in providing a macroeconomic incentive system to sustain this growth orientation. In addition, the rate of growth of demand in general can be identified as a variable representing the desirability of reinvesting company cash flow instead of distributing it to shareholders. The early 1980s, therefore, not only put financial pressure on managers via higher real interest rates but also because of slowing output growth. In fact, comparing real output growth rates to real interest rates might serve as a proxy for the viability of the growth-oriented managerial model. Graph 2 plots this relationship for the period 1960–1997. There is an apparent break in the early 1980s: growth rates were generally above real interest rates before 1981 and have been consistently below real interest rates since then. In spite of the fall in nominal interest rates and the recovery of profits shown in Graph 1, the macroeconomic incentive system continues to put pressure on the managerial model of governance in favor of financial interests.

The merger threats of the 1980s can thus be interpreted as the shareholder response to a changed incentive structure brought about by high real interest rates and low growth. Clearly, macroeconomic factors play a role and should, therefore, be part of a systems approach to corporate governance. Blair and Stout (1997) argue that "[T]he shift in the balance of power in boardrooms toward shareholders is the result not of directors' sudden recognition that shareholders are 'owners' of the corporation, but from changing economic and political forces that have improved shareholders' relative bargaining power vis-à-vis other coalition members." This interpretation is also compatible with Fligstein's (1990) historical account mentioned in the introduction.

Blair and Schary (1993) present sectoral evidence on the relationship between profits and cost of capital as a proxy for investment opportunities. In order to test Jensen's free cash flow hypothesis, this proxy is compared to the rate

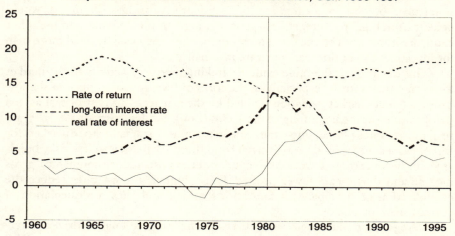

Graph 1: Rate of return and real interest rates, USA 1960-1997

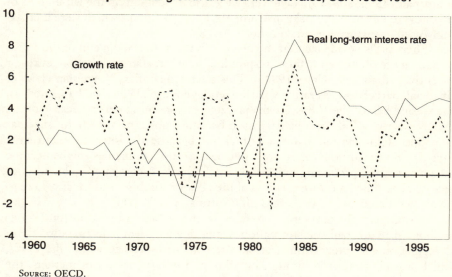

Graph 2: Real growth and real interest rates, USA 1960-1997

Source: OECD.

of cash generation in these industries. The authors conclude that free cash flow was present largely due to the steep rise in the cost of capital in combination with stable or slowly falling cash generation. Their findings also complement other empirical studies, which found higher takeover and merger activity in low tech sectors. Higher real interest rates put more pressure on mature industries with a broad base of revenues from past investments but little room for expansion (tobacco, food processing, retail). Equity prices for these companies would benefit from higher leverage. Fast-growing, high-tech companies, on the other hand, are not subject to the same pressure, because they usually need more cash for investment than they can generate internally.

There is also considerable evidence linking increased activity in the market for corporate control—especially in the form of leverage buy-outs—to the low q-ratios (stock market valuation divided by the replacement cost of real assets) that prevailed at the beginning of the 1980s (Long and Ravenscraft 1993). Again real interest rates play an important role in explaining stagnant stock markets for three reasons. First, funds are diverted from the stock market to less risky bonds as yields become more attractive. Second, interest costs reduce companies' gross income and thus create lower profits. Third, higher interest rates reduce the capitalization of anticipated income flows, which underlies the calculation of current share prices.

Deregulation of financial markets also contributed to finance-driven governance in a different way. After consolidation in the early 1980s, the major Wall Street securities firms began to look aggressively for new profit opportunities. Merger activity became an important source of profits for the financial sector (Guttmann 1994, 308–10). Takeovers were also dependent on the willingness of investors to buy new and risky instruments, like junk bonds, which were increasingly used to finance these takeovers.

There is also evidence that the merger frenzy towards the end of the 1980s took on a life of its own without responding to any real underlying pressures or incentives (Blair and Schary 1993a). This seems to confirm Keynesian views of financial markets as generating volatility endogenously. What had happened? In the second half of the 1980s, stock markets were booming partly because of the takeover activity. Takeover activity itself became a powerful vehicle for speculation. Speculators started to invest in stock, not because of positive expected earnings or other traditional measures, but because the companies might become takeover targets, promising quick and large rewards. A company's value was not assessed based on its future earnings ability, but by valuing its assets if it were to be dismembered and its parts sold off (Guttmann 1994, 311).

In summary, the pressures generated by the collapse of the Bretton Woods system led to a broad transformation of the financial sector in two directions: deregulation and internationalization. After the turbulent decade of the 1970s, which was characterized by high inflation and bearish securities markets, the 1980s saw what Smithin (1996) calls the "revenge of the rentier," a broad-based re-empowerment of financial interests. This shift, and not managerial failure, caused the frantic activity in the market for corporate control, especially via the channel of high real interest rates and low growth. In the following section, we will look at another development in deregulated financial markets, the growth of the institutional investor and its impact on corporate governance.

THE RISE OF INSTITUTIONAL INVESTORS

The growth of the institutional investor (pension and mutual funds, insurance companies, investment companies) is one of the driving forces behind structural changes in both the process of corporate governance and the structure and character of capital markets in the OECD. One of the leading factors behind the growth of financial investors is the deregulation of the banking and securities industries, which has heightened the competition between banks and other financial institutions. Under these pressures, banks have increasingly moved into the insurance and investment fund business in search of new activities that generate earnings in the form of commissions and fees.

In the United States, the growth of the institutional investor has also been encouraged by the aging population in combination with the existence of capital-based pension schemes. This development is contributing to the creation of an equity culture, including greater scope for the market for corporate control and direct control via equity. Henwood (1997), for example, points out that institutional investors frequently supported and financed hostile takeovers in the 1980s.

What is the evidence that institutional investors have the incentive and ability to intervene to correct corporate governance failures? Why should they "voice" rather than "exit"? Institutional investors are likely to hold only small share stakes in individual companies (around 1–3%) in order to spread risk in their portfolios. Under these circumstances, any direct involvement depends on the ability to marshal additional support from other investors and the required costs of doing so. There is also obviously a free-rider problem, which works against these collective shareholder actions. Increasing use of indexed funds, however, tends to limit the shareholders' options for exit and forces them to play a more active part.

There is also the question of "who monitors the monitor"? Jenkinson and Mayer (1992, 2) rightly ask: "Why precisely managers of institutional funds are supposed to be so much better at administrating nonfinancial enterprises than the management of these enterprises themselves, or why similar problems of corporate governance do not afflict the funds themselves are questions that are never clearly answered." Coffee (1991), for example, argues that there are reasons to believe that institutional investors are more accountable to their owners than are corporate managers to their shareholders, and argues that traditional governance mechanisms are limited. Self-administered pension funds are immune from takeover mechanisms. The shareholders and the company's or public employees are for obvious reasons unable to sell their stakes in the fund if its performance is below average.

This is especially relevant in the context of recent allegations against CalPERS, the nation's largest public pension fund, and a leader in promoting shareholder activism. The *Los Angeles Times* (2/2/98) reports of investment decisions that apparently hinged on individual board members being lobbied by investment firms. Examples include a $60 million investment in a real estate partnership that employed the son-in-law of a board member as well as a $75 million investment to a Los Angeles firm cofounded by the mayor. The problem with the latter is that a pension fund trustee was also a top deputy in Mayor Richard Riordan's administration.

Brancato (1997), a supporter of more institutional shareholder involvement, proposes that companies define their strategic targets first and then target a specific shareholder segment. Markets, in this view, might not generate the best results for companies. She specifically differentiates between traders with a short-term horizon and investors looking for a more long-term commitment. Traders have only a short-term interest in the company and do not exercise any voting rights, but provide liquidity to the market. Investors, on the other hand, are attracted by the compatibility between their goals and those of the companies in which they invest. She provides evidence to support her claim of differences in strategy and time horizon among the diverse group of institutional investors.

Because of the variety of investors and their goals, Brancato (1997, 102) concludes that

> Investor targeting challenges the conventional wisdom that markets are efficient and that management should just tell their story and let market forces operate. Rather, it forces companies to clarify their strategy and enables them to communicate their goals to those investors who share their objectives. Companies that successfully employ their investor targeting enjoy less stock price volatility and a lower cost of capital, enabling them to make the in-depth investments necessary to achieve sustained growth.

Like Chandler, she therefore acknowledges the importance of managerial autonomy in devising an appropriate business strategy and then forming ties with actors in financial markets.

COMPARATIVE COUNTRY EXPERIENCE

The previous discussion has focused narrowly on the case of the United States. Financial systems, ownership structures, and therefore corporate governance mechanisms are, however, different across countries (Zysman 1983; Franks and Mayer 1997; Pollin 1995). Thus, it is likely that the transformation of international capital markets will have different effects depending on the existing financial system. We will now turn to a brief discussion of this hypothesized differential impact focusing on the cases of Germany and Korea.

Germany

In the financial systems literature, the German economy is typically characterized as a bank-based system (Zysman 1983) in which banks play a dominant role in financial intermediation as well as in the monitoring of corporations. In contrast, in the U.S. economy, both corporate finance and control are market-based. Recent evidence, however, suggests that this view of the German system has to be modified. First, empirical studies based on flow-of-funds data have shown that private investment in Germany is internally financed to a similar degree as in the United States (Corbett and Jenkinson 1996). In fact, U.S. banks have provided a larger share of finance than their German counterparts since the 1970s. Second, in a comprehensive investigation of the monitoring role of banks, Edwards and Fischer (1994) conclude that German banks play only a minor role in management shake-ups, especially when compared to the active role of Japanese banks. This has led some observers to suggest that the crucial difference between the American and German systems of governance can be traced to the different ownership structures and not to the role of banks per se (Franks and Mayer 1997; Mayer 1996; Edwards and Fischer 1994).

According to Mayer (1996), the German system of ownership and control is best described as an *insider system* compared to the *outsider system* in the United States. As we have seen during the previous discussion, the U.S. system is characterized by dispersed ownership and sophisticated financial markets including an active market for corporate control. In Germany's insider system, financial markets are relatively underdeveloped and stock market capitalization is low relative to GDP. In addition, there simply does not exist a market for corporate control, and hostile takeovers are almost unheard of. The essential feature of this arrangement is a concentrated ownership structure in which a large share of corporate equity is retained within the sector through a sophisticated system of cross-equity holdings creating large corporate groupings (Franks and Mayer 1997). These groupings are reinforced by representation on each other's supervisory boards. Banks are part of these groupings via their direct ownership stakes as well as their proxy voting rights (Edwards and Fischer 1994). In the context of intercorporate shareholdings, the application of the principal-agent problem does not make sense: firms are more appropriately viewed instead as coordination devices for aligning self-interest with the collective good of several parties (the stakeholders). Arguably, this system has generated relative managerial autonomy from financial interests and has allowed firms to pursue a strategy of strengthening their long-term competitive position (Porter 1992).

The strength of this system is the committed relationship among company stakeholders, including suppliers, banks, workers, and the larger community. Commitment and trust are more easily sustained under concentrated ownership structures compared to the Anglo-Saxon outsider systems, where shareholders can sell out anonymously and without costs. According to Mayer (1996), commitment and trust are particularly important where productive activities depend on the involvement of and investment by a large number of stakeholders (including workers' investment in firm-specific human capital). Complex manufacturing processes, which require several different supplier and purchaser arrangements, may be particularly dependent on ownership patterns that promote commitment and trust.

Based on this analysis, Mayer (1996) argues that it is likely that neither the German insider nor the American outsider system is universally better. They are each to be viewed as being designed to accommodate specific circumstances and industries, with insider systems better suited to cases where commitment to other stakeholders is important. Outsider systems are more appropriate in cases where there is rapid and radical technological progress, which also rapidly devalues the stock of intangible assets as an important competitive asset. This suggests that governance mechanisms be not only affected by macroeconomic incentives but also by the character and speed of technological change.

This interpretation is compatible with the managerial model, which as Chandler (1997, 1990) has always stressed, argues for the superior position of the managerial enterprise in applying its managerial resources to new products in *related* sectors. It could be argued that the current period is characterized by radical technological change brought about by computer technology, software, and biotechnology. Here success might not be dependent on accumulated organizational knowledge but on entrepreneurial talent and serendipity. In radically new technologies, capital markets might be superior to managerial talent in assessing the value of the new enterprise precisely because of their ability to compute large amounts of information (Allen and Gale 1995), spread risk, and provide venture capital. Sophisticated financial markets might thus provide the flexibility to respond to these challenges.

There is still the question of what mechanism ensures that committed relations do not invite collusion and inefficiency in the absence of financial market control as well as direct bank monitoring. As in the Chandlerian model, the answer seems to be relentless product market competition. In the German case, firms are exposed to strong competitive pressures, in particular in export markets. Compared to its size, the German economy is relatively open and has traditionally been export-oriented in capital- and/or skill-intensive sectors such as electrical machinery, industrial chemicals, and luxury cars (Wengenroth 1997; Carlin and Soskice 1997).

Its success is likely to be one of the reasons for the remarkable stability of this system in spite of the financial globalization pressures that we talked about in Section 2. Like in the United States, the early 1980s in Germany were characterized by rising interest rates and falling rates of return. Similarly, real growth rates started to fall below real interest rates at around the same time. However, Germany has been one of the laggards among OECD countries in adopting financial liberalization measures. Equity markets, in particular, remain underdeveloped, due to high securities transfer taxes as well as weak disclosure and insider trading rules (Edey and Hviding 1995). Germany has, therefore, not been subject to the increasing securitization, i.e., the increased use of securities in the intermediation of finance, which has been one of the major implications of financial liberalization in the United States.

In other areas, the German financial system has always been relatively unregulated. Germany abolished capital controls early in the 1960s and did not implement regulation Q-type interest rate controls as in the United States. Again in comparison to the United States, the German system has kept real interest rates positive even in the turbulent period of the 1970s mainly due to low rates of inflation. Smithin's (1996) "revenge of the rentier" in response to negative interest rates has not been a factor in Germany. Furthermore, the stability of the system has also been supported by stable and high spreads between lending and interbank rates, which have bolstered banks' profits. The spreads have been consistently around 4% since 1960 compared to differentials of around or even below zero in the United States under regulation Q. They have since then edged up to 2.4% in the early 1990s (Edey and Hviding 1995, 41).

In spite of the system's stability, there are signs of change associated with the process of financial liberalization. German banks have started to reduce their equity stakes in nonfinancial enterprises in order to adopt a more "value-oriented" approach. Deutsche Bank, for example, is keen on selling part of its 23% stake in Daimler-Benz, Germany's largest industrial conglomerate. At present, high German capital gains taxes prevent Deutsche Bank from making this move. In a *Financial Times* (FT 2/16/1998), interview Deutsche Bank chairman Rolf Breuer expresses his dissatisfaction with the bank's share portfolio in so far as it is primarily German and heavily biased toward automobile production. This attitude change is driven by investor pressures on bank management to increase the value of the shares of the banks. It is not clear what impact this change will have on German corporate governance structures in the light of the previously mentioned evidence that banks do not play a large role in corporate restructurings and that bank finance does not amount to a large share of corporate financing in Germany.

Similarly, a number of large German corporations have started to list their shares on the New York Stock Exchange, beginning with Daimler-Benz in 1993. Hoechst, the chemical giant, wanted such a listing in order to tap into the liquid U.S. capital market in support of its global strategy (*Financial Times* 11/5/97). The company CEO is well aware that this move will go hand in hand with a greater emphasis on shareholder values.

In Germany, the pay-as-you-go pension system has so far restricted the availability of funds to be invested in pension and mutual funds and is thus the main factor in explaining the relative underdevelopment of such institutions. Blommestein (1997, 49) argues that a switch to a funded pension system would probably give a big boost to both the development of capital markets and equity-based corporate governance channels. In short, such a major institutional change would contribute to the proliferation of shareholder value culture in Germany. In fact, there are signs of a change in corporate pension plans. At present, most German companies provide for their employees' pension by putting money into book reserves (Pensionsrückstellungen) to cover accrued benefits. This money is typically invested in the company's plant and equipment in order to raise profits to allow the company to pay pensions from existing cash flow. These reserves have facilitated continued investment and have smoothed earnings even in hard times. Taking the reserves off the balance sheet would mean a sudden drop in free cash flow, forcing companies to rely on more expensive forms of finance in the stock and bond markets.

According to a Deutsche Bank report, these pension liabilities account for nearly one-fifth of total ancillary personnel costs in the mid-1990s (*Global Investor*,

June 1996). Fund managers are eager to get their hands on the estimated $200 billion in corporate pension funds to stimulate the fund management industry, which in 1994 had funds amounting to $124 billion (about one-third of the per capita fund ownership in the United States). Fund managers are also eager to scrap the existing limitations on equity investment, which is currently at only 25% of total assets for pension funds. Note that the large banks support these changes, since they are all major players in this emerging sector with various subsidiaries. Equity investments is attractive because management fees on equity-oriented funds are normally 20 to 30 basis points higher than the meagre 10 basis point management fee levied on bond funds. At present, however, a typical portfolio has 80% invested in bonds and only 20% in equity. Several factors limit the expansion of equity finance besides regulation. Germans are traditionally risk adverse and are unwilling to accept high volatility patterns of their investments. They are also very wary about investing overseas, even in equity portfolios.

Korea

Amsden (1989) provides a managerial model of governance updated for the case of late industrialization in Korea. She argues that the state has to play an active role in late industrialization to overcome the challenges of backwardness; the state needs to nurture domestic companies to give them the time to accumulate the necessary "Chandlerian" managerial assets to eventually become competitive in world markets. According to her and others (see, for example, Wade 1990), the Korean state played a pervasive role in the country's industrialization drive in the form of protecting and subsidizing industry. In particular, the government channelled cheap credit to capital-intensive enterprises it perceived as crucial for long-term growth and competitiveness; it literally "picked the winners."

This model presents serious governance problems for obvious reasons. Why should Korean companies invest in managerial assets and otherwise invest efficiently, if they are shielded both from international product market competition through protective tariffs and from the monitoring role of financial markets? The answer Amsden provides is that the state also assumed the role of disciplinary. Financial support and protection from foreign competitors came at a price. Nurturing was offered only in exchange for specific, easy-to-monitor export targets. In addition, the government allowed a number of domestic *chaebol* to enter the same sector so that they each faced stiff domestic competition. What is now sometimes called "crony" capitalism provided an incentive system that turned Korea into one of the leading industrial economies in record time. In terms of our governance focus, the crucial ingredient for the success of this model is the state's selective use of market forces to provide necessary disciplinary pressures while at the same time circumventing markets, especially foreign competition and market-based credit supply, if they are deemed destructive, or insufficient, for the development of industrial capacity.

A tight government control on financial markets is an essential element of this strategy. Bank-based finance of industry will necessarily lead to high debt-equity ratios compared to Western conventions. This causes a certain amount of fragility for the financial system, since firms will be vulnerable to shocks that disturb cash flow or bank finance because debt payments have to be made at a fixed level whereas dividend payments are a residual after cost (Wade 1998).

A theoretical model developed by Peterson and Rajan (1995) might serve to explain the fact that financial market competition might be counterproductive under these circumstances. Their model refers to the case of new small firms, which tend to have low cash flow but the potential for high future profits. However, it might as well be applied to fast-growing companies in developing countries when retained earnings are also insufficient to finance this level of growth. Creditors might be inclined to lend to these companies only if they are guaranteed a share of their future profits. This guarantee is unlikely under the assumption of competitive markets. Firms will simply not have an incentive to remain with their initial provider of funds if they can access cheaper resources from competitors. In fact, because of the higher risks associated in investing in these new (or developing country) firms, interest rates in competitive markets will be very high. In the presence of committed relationships, however, banks have the assurance to spread the gains over time—making a loss at the early stages of firm growth and larger gains when the firm is able to generate more cash flow.

Based on these assumptions, Peterson and Rajan (1995) develop a formal model and provide an empirical analysis for a sample of small U.S. firms. They conclude that "credit market competition imposes constraints on the ability of the firm and creditor to intertemporally share surplus. This makes lending relationships less valuable to a firm because it cannot expect to get help when most in need (1995, 845)." We have seen earlier that in Korea the state assumed the role of bank *and* disciplinary in order to let firms accumulate competitive assets and subsequently share surplus intertemporally.

Wade (1998) argues that financial market liberalization and especially the recent financial crisis present a severe shock to this "commitment-and-trust" system of governance. The refusal of international banks to roll over loans to Korean banks has forced them, in turn, to call in their loans to the heavily exposed *chaebol*. This breakdown in lending, in combination with extremely high interest rates to protect the currency, has led to widespread insolvency and bankruptcy. The IMF-imposed adjustment measures prohibit any cushioning of the shock by continuing to provide subsidized credit to companies. Instead, Korean companies are increasingly forced to sell assets to foreigners to lower debt levels. According to Krugman (1998), this sell-off has already reached "fire-sale" dimensions. Wade (1998, 22) argues that the "combination of massive devaluations, IMF-pushed financial liberalization, and IMF-facilitated recovery may even precipitate the biggest peacetime transfer of assets from domestic to foreign owners in the past fifty years anywhere in the world."

Is this a beneficial reallocation of ownership titles? The answer to this question depends on the favored interpretation of the state-led development model. Observers who now discredit the Korean system as "crony" capitalism will welcome the ownership transfer as efficiency enhancing. In this view, the crisis will also have the cleansing effect of finally "getting the prices (especially the interest rate) right." High debt-equity ratios, subsidized credit, and close state-bank-industry relations were unsustainable and are rightly supplanted by more market-based allocation mechanisms. Another view, derived from the work of Amsden and Wade, suggests that the highly successful Korean model was derailed by premature financial liberalization (Chang 1997). Deregulation did not only raise interest rates but also sharply reduced the government's control over the banking system. Consequently, banks were able to increase their short-term borrowing abroad at low interest rates and re-lend it at a sizeable profit to the local *chaebol*. The now frequent accusations of overinvestment might not be a result of too much state involvement, as the crony capitalism view would suggest, but of diminishing state-imposed discipline as a result of financial deregulation. The financial crisis was thus also accompanied by a crisis of governance.

CONCLUSION

This paper attempted to link changes in international capital markets to changes in the character of corporate governance structures. It was argued that financial deregulation and rising interest rates have led to a shift from relative managerial autonomy to a predominance of financial interests in the United States since the early 1980s. While this tendency might have been beneficial in redirecting funds from stagnating companies and sectors to more dynamic ones, it arguably did not improve corporate governance mechanisms in general. Alfred Chandler's managerial model of capitalism assigns a crucial role to managerial autonomy in the dynamic growth of companies and the economy as a whole. The imposition of financial goals on managers through the threat of hostile takeovers or the linking of managers' remuneration to stock performance might have induced a slowdown in investments in important fungible assets such as organizational skills and firm-specific investments by employees.

We then turned to a discussion of governance systems in other countries to assess their changes due to financial liberalization. The German insider system, which is characterized by committed relationships among long-term stakeholders, was shown to exhibit a remarkable stability in spite of similar macroeconomic pressures to those in the United States. The Korean system, on the other hand, has recently plunged into a severe crisis. It is still too early to fully assess the changes brought about by the continuing financial crisis, but it seems certain that the previous, highly successful model of state-led finance and governance will be substantially modified to accommodate greater financial openness and foreign ownership. Our discussion raised some doubts about the expected benefits that this change will generate for the Korean economy.

REFERENCES

Alchian, Armen A., and Harold Demsetz. 1972. "Production, Information Costs, and Economic Organisation," *American Economic Review*, 62, pp. 777–795.

Allen, Franklin, and Douglas Gale. 1995. "A Welfare Comparison of Intermediaries and Financial Markets in Germany and the U.S.," *European Economic Review*, 39, pp. 179–209.

Amsden, Alice. 1989. *Asia's Next Giant: South Korea and Late Industrialisation*. Oxford: Oxford University Press.

Blair, Margaret. 1995. *Ownership and Control*. Washington, D.C.: The Brookings Institution.

_____. 1996. *Wealth Creation and Wealth Sharing: A Colloquium on Corporate Governance and Investments in Human Capital*. Washington D.C.: The Brookings Institution.

Blair, Margaret, ed. 1993. *The Deal Decade: What Take-overs and Leveraged Buyouts Mean for Corporate Governance*. Washington, D.C.: The Brookings Institution.

Blair, Margaret, and Lynn. A. Stout. 1997. "A Theory of Corporation Law as a Response to Contracting Problems in Team Production," mimeo, The Brookings Institution, September.

Blair, Margaret, and Martha A. Schary. 1993. "Industry-Level Indicators of Cash Flow," in Blair, ed., *The Deal Decade: What Take-overs and Leveraged Buyouts Mean for Corporate Governance*. Washington, D.C.: The Brookings Institution.

_____. 1993. "Industry-Level Pressures to Restructure," in Blair, ed., *The Deal Decade: What Take-overs and Leveraged Buyouts Mean for Corporate Governance*. Washington, D.C.: The Brookings Institution.

Blommestein, Hans J. 1997. "The New Financial Landscape and its Impact on Corporate Governance," in Keasey and Wright, eds., *Corporate Governance: Responsibilities, Risks and Renumeration*. Chichester and New York: John Wiley and Sons.

Brancato, Carolyn. 1997. *Institutional Investors and Corporate Governance: Best Practices for Increasing Corporate Value*. Irwin Professional Publishers.

Carlin, Wendy, and David Soskice. 1997. "Shocks to the System: The German Political Economy Under Stress," *National Institute Economic Review*, 1, pp. 57–76.

Chandler, Alfred D. 1997. "United States: Engines of Economic Growth in the Capital-intensive and Knowledge-intensive Industries," in Chandler, Hikino and Amatori, eds., *Big Business and the Wealth of Nations*. Cambridge, New York: Cambridge University Press.

Chandler, Alfred D. 1990. *Scale and Scope*. Cambridge: Belknap Press.

Chandler, Alfred D., and Takashi Hikino. 1997. "Large Industrial Enterprises and the Dynamics of Modern Economic Growth," in Chandler, Hikino and Amatori, eds., *Big Business and the Wealth of Nations*. Cambridge, New York: Cambridge University Press.

Chang, Ha-Joon. 1997. "Perspective on Korea: A Crisis from Underregulation," Los Angeles Times, December 31.

Coffee, John. 1991. "Liquidity Versus Control: The Institutional Investors as Corporate Monitor," *Columbia Law Review*, 91(6), pp. 1277–1268.

Corbett, Jenny, and Tim Jenkinson. 1996. "The Financing of Industry 1970–1989: An International Comparison," *Journal of the Japanese and International Economies*, 10, pp. 71–96.

Crotty, James A. 1990. "Owner-Manager Conflict and Financial Theories of Investment Instability: A Critical Assessment of Keynes, Tobin, and Minsky," *Journal of Post Keynesian Economics*, 12(4), pp. 519–542.

Crotty, James A. and Dan Goldstein. 1993. "Do U.S. Financial Markets Allocate Credit Efficiently? The Case of Corporate Restructuring in the 1980s," in Gary A. Dymski, Gerald Epstein, and Robert Pollin, eds., *Transforming the U.S. Financial System*, Economic Policy Institute Series. Armonk, NY: M. E. Sharpe.

Deutsche Bundesbank. 1997. "Shares as Financing and Investment Instruments," *Monthly Report*, No. 1.

Deutsche Bundesbank. 1992. "Longer-term Trends in the Financing Patterns of West German Enterprises," *Monthly Report*, No. 10.

Dimsdale, Nicholas and Martha Prevezer, eds. 1994. *Capital Markets and Corporate Governance*. Oxford: Clarendon Press.

Dymski, Gerry A., Gerald Epstein and Robert Pollin, eds. 1993. *Transforming the U.S. Financial System: Equity and Efficiency for the 21st Century*. Armonk, NY: ME Sharpe.

Eatwell, John. 1996. "International Capital Liberalisation: An Evaluation," Center for Economic Policy Working Paper, New School for Social Research, New York.

Edey, Malcolm, and Ketil Hviding. 1995. "An Assessment of Financial Reform in OECD Countries," Economics Department Working Paper No. 154, OECD, Paris.

Edwards, Jeremy and Klaus Fischer. 1994. *Banks, Finance and Investment in Germany*. Cambridge: Cambridge University Press.

Felix, David. 1996. "Financial Globalisation Versus Free Trade: The Case of the Tobin Tax," UNCTAD *Review*.

Fligstein, Neil. 1990. *The Transformation of Corporate Control*. Cambridge, MA: Harvard University Press.

Franks, Julian, and Colin Mayer. 1997. "Corporate Ownership and Control in the UK, Germany and France," in D. Chew, ed., *Studies in International Corporate Finance and Governance Systems*. New York: Oxford University Press.

Guttmann, Robert. 1997. "The Transformation of Financial Capital," paper presented at the Center for Economic Policy Analysis Workshop on Globalisation and Social Policy, New School for Social Research, New York.

Guttmann, Robert. 1994. *How Credit Money Shapes the Economy: The United States in a Global System*. Armonk, NY: M. E. Sharpe.

Henwood, Doug. 1997. *Wall Street*. London and New York: Verso.

Hikino, Takashi. 1997. "Managerial Control, Capital Markets, and the Wealth of Nations," in Chandler, Hikino and Amatori, eds., *Big Business and the Wealth of Nations*. Cambridge, New York: Cambridge University Press.

Holland, John. 1994. "Bank Lending Relationships and the Complex Nature of Bank-Corporate Relations," *Journal of Business Finance and Accounting*, 21(3), pp. 367–93.

Jenkinson, Tim, and Colin Mayer. 1992. "The Assessment: Corporate Governance and Corporate Control," *Oxford Review of Economic Policy*, 8(3), pp. 1–10.

_____. 1994. *Hostile Take-overs*. New York: McGraw-Hill.

Jensen, Michael. 1997. "The Modern Industrial Revolution, Exit, and the Failure of Internal Control Systems," in Donald Chew, ed., *Studies in International Corporate Finance and Governance Systems*. New York: Oxford University Press.

Jensen, Michael. 1986. "Agency Cost of Free Cash Flow, Corporate Finance, and Take-overs," *American Economic Review*. 76(2), pp. 323–29.

Kreps, David. 1990. "Corporate Culture and Economic Theory," in J. Alt and K. Shepsle, eds., *Perspectives on Positive Political Economy*. Cambridge, MA: Cambridge University Press.

Krugman, Paul. 1998. "Fire-Sale FDI," mimeo, MIT, Cambridge, MA.

Long, William F., and David J. Ravenscraft. 1993. "Decade of Debt: Lessons from LBOs in the 1980s," in Blair, ed., *The Deal Decade: What Take-overs and Leveraged Buyouts Mean for Corporate Governance*. Washington, DC: The Brookings Institution.

Mayer, Colin. 1988. "New Issues in Corporate Finance," *European Economic Review*, 32, pp. 1167–89.

———. 1990. "Financial Systems, Corporate Finance, and Economic Development," in R. G. Hubbard, ed., *Asymmetric Information, Corporate Finance, and Investment*. Chicago: Chicago University Press.

———. 1996. "Corporate Governance, Competition and Performance," Economics Department Working Papers No. 164. Paris: OECD.

Modigliani, Franco, and Merton Miller. 1958. "The Cost of Capital, Corporation Finance, and the Theory of Investment," *American Economic Review*, 48, pp. 261–97.

O.E.C.D. (various), *Financial Statistics*, Paris.

Peterson, Martin, and Raghuram Rajan. 1995. "The Effect of Credit Market Competition on Lending Relationships," *Quarterly Journal of Economics*, 110, pp. 407–43.

Pollin, Robert A. 1995. "Financial Structures and Egalitarian Economic Policy," *New Left Review*, November/December, pp. 26–61.

Porter, Michael. 1992. "Capital Disadvantage: America's Failing Capital Investment System," *Harvard Business Review*, September–October, pp. 65–82.

Prowse, Stephen. 1995. "Corporate Governance in an International Perspective: A Survey of Corporate Control Mechanisms Among Large Firms in the U.S., U.K., Japan and Germany," *Financial Markets, Institutions & Instruments*, 4(1), pp. 1–63.

Shleifer, Andrei, and Robert W. Vishny. 1997. "A Survey of Corporate Governance," *Journal of Finance*, LII(2):737–83.

Smithin, John. 1996. *Macroeconomic Policy and the Future of Capitalism: The Revenge of the Rentier and the Threat to Prosperity*. Cheltenham, UK: Edward Elgar.

Taylor, William. 1990. "Can Big Owners Make a Big Difference?" *Harvard Business Review*, September–October, pp. 70–82.

Wade, Robert. 1998. "The Asian Debt-and-Development Crisis of 1997–9?: Causes and Consequences," *World Development*, August.

———. 1990. *Governing the Market: Economic Theory and the Role of Government in East Asian Industrialisation*. Princeton: Princeton University Press.

Wengenroth, Ulrich. 1997. "Germany: Competition Abroad—Cupertino at Home, 1870–1990," in Chandler, Hikino and Amatori, eds., *Big Business and the Wealth of Nations*. Cambridge: New York: Cambridge University Press.

Winter, Sidney G. 1993. "Routines, Cash Flows, and Unconventional Assets: Corporate Change in the 1980s," in Blair, ed., *The Deal Decade: What Take-overs and Leveraged Buyouts Mean for Corporate Governance*. Washington, D.C.: The Brookings Institution.

Zingales, Luigi. "Corporate Governance," in *The New Palgrave Dictionary of Economics and the Law*, forthcoming.

Zysman, John. 1983. *Government, Markets, and Growth: Financial Systems and the Politics of Industrial Change*. Ithaca, NY: Cornell University Press.

9
· · ·

The Influence of the Financial Media
over International Economic Policy

*Jeff Madrick**

IN A RECENT REVIEW of books about the Whitewater and Monica Lewinsky allegations, the writer Joan Didion concluded that the Washington political press had become insiders who were now part of the nation's "permanent professional political class." The members of the press claimed that they "did not think ideologically," but Didion shows how they essentially formed a single "narrative" that was antagonistic towards the president, sympathetic towards the special prosecutor, and failed to convey the questionable motives of their news sources. "I had relied on the elves for information at critical junctures—even while they concealed from me their role in bringing the Lewinsky allegations to the Jones lawyers and later to Ken Starr," wrote the journalist who broke the story. However one feels about President Clinton's transgressions, the inability of prosecutor Kenneth Starr to come up with even a single criminal charge makes the press's one-sidedness hard to justify.

"What we now know occurred during the last year was, in other words, a covert effort to advance a particular agenda by bringing down a president," says Didion. But we didn't know this by reading the day-to-day reporting of the political media ("Uncovering Washington," *The New York Review of Books*, June 24, 1999).

I begin this paper with an example from the world of politics because bias is easier to detect there. But, in many respects, there are similar damaging tendencies in the financial press. The members of the mainstream financial media have developed their own ideological "narratives" about important issues, which are

---

*I am grateful for the excellent research assistance of Mona Ahmad.

sympathetic to some causes and antagonistic to others, and rarely question or make clear the vested interests of their news sources. Like the Washington press corps, they have increasingly become insiders. Rather than challenge their sources, as they once regularly did, they increasingly seem to accept them and adopt their values. In the coverage of economics, the financial press too readily believes that their sources are objective because they are "expert."

The one-sidedness of the financial media has been, in my view, an integral part of the formation of public opinion as well as the development of public policy in international economics. The absence of pluralistic voices in the financial press has been increasingly damaging. The purpose of this paper is to demonstrate how narrowly the media's reporting on globalization and the development of free markets has been, and how this narrow reporting has contributed to the failure of international economic policies. (A subsidiary purpose is to offer recommendations and encourage further discussion about how a more diverse set of views concerning economic policies can be communicated to the media.)

Recent events in international economics and finance provide two general examples of the one-dimensional nature of the financial press that are extremely useful for our purposes. *The first is the failure of economic reform, and specifically "shock therapy," in Russia. The second is the liberalization of the capital markets in developing nations in the 1980s and 1990s, which, in the view of this paper, led to the Asian financial crisis of 1997 and 1998.* In both cases, the conventional wisdom of the mainstream economics profession as portrayed, and moreover espoused, in the financial press was proven wrong or simplistic. As crises broke, the financial media reversed almost completely the tenor of their coverage in both cases.

Such a public discourse, led by the financial media, has been forbidding to any alternative discussion of international financial regulations, controls, and a more effective international financial architecture. Only crisis has shaken the faith of the financial media in the dominant points of view in recent years, which have generally been an unmitigated enthusiasm towards reduced international regulation and increased freedom for participants in markets. Few economists oppose these values in principle, and one needn't be an extremist to propose that the speed of change be slowed, the potential for fraud be reduced, the sweep of deregulation be informed by a sense of human frailty, and the fever of speculative excess be occasionally dampened. One needn't be an extremist to be determined that the plight of workers not be ignored when adopting financial policies as well, nor that the table of regulations not be tilted too far in the direction of the developed nations against the less developed. But the press rarely reported even the most moderate versions of these views.

Our methodology was to do a comprehensive search of all articles published on these subjects since 1990 in the major U.S. financial media, including the financial pages of major general interest publications. We used such keywords and phrases as "shock therapy," "gradualism," "reform" and "capital controls" to make these searches. Thus, we believe we probably read most relevant articles over these years on the subject, although we cannot say definitively that we canvassed all such articles. The publications we included were *The Wall Street*

Journal, The New York Times, Business Week, Fortune, Time Magazine, and *Newsweek.* We also searched less exhaustively *The Washington Post, The Economist,* and a handful of other newspapers, including *The Los Angeles Times, The Manchester Guardian* and *the Detroit Free Press.* (I would like at this point again to thank Mona Ahmad for her diligent effort in unearthing a voluminous quantity of articles. This required not merely long hours but considerable judgment on her part.)

Both of these international issues have provided us ideal laboratories from which to generalize. Economic reform in Russia was a constant theme in the nation's press since Gorbachev's early economic reforms and the famed but ill-fated 500-day plan. All issues concerning the fall of the Iron Curtain attracted considerable attention in those years. As for the globalization of international markets, it gained increasing attention over these years from two points of view. During a period in which average American wages fell, there was a great deal of concern about how foreign competition might displace American jobs or place downward pressure on wages in general. The second area was financial. Cross-border financial flows grew dramatically, and the media paid *increasing* attention to them. Globalization also interested personal finance editors as equity investing around the world gained attention.

A comprehensive reading of these articles yields several conclusions.

• As we have noted, the financial media essentially accepted basic ideological tenets of the mainstream opinion of the period about the advantages of rapid and unmitigated market liberalization. The assumptions underlying this view were almost never challenged. In fact, it was rarely recognized that there were assumptions that could be questioned.

• There were few truly sophisticated analyses of economic issues from any point of view in the American press. One may disagree with *The Economist's* point of view on many matters, but it writes in a depth that is usually absent from the equivalent U.S. publications.

• The success of the U.S. stock market increasingly influenced financial reporting in two ways. It reinforced the general acceptance of free-market ideas, thus enhancing skepticism of any proposals that suggested a slowing of deregulation or privatization, and it placed increasing emphasis on the personal investment perspective (as opposed to, say, the worker perspective). If globalized markets were good for investors, than they were increasingly considered good in general.

• For similar reasons, there was increasing approbation accorded business in general over this period, even as profits increased significantly as a proportion of national income. "There is much more glorification of business than suspicion today than there once was," says David Wessel, economics reporter for *The Wall Street Journal.* "This reflects society as a whole. Remember, at least until recently, Bill Gates was the true American hero."

• Once, the financial press thought one of its key roles was to serve as a watchdog for its readers—an outsider protecting the public interest. Increasingly, it sees itself as one of the participants in the economy, with the same views and even the same values as its sources.

In terms of our two specific case studies—Russian reform and the liberalization of the capital account—I believe the prevailing "narrative" of the financial press had a crucial part in the adoption of government policies and the widespread support of over-simplified attitudes. Let me draw two major conclusions, which we will amplify later in the paper.

• In general, the press was almost uniformly in favor of shock therapy for Russia. At worst, the press was neutral. The financial press rarely reported on alternative policies for economic reform in Russia, and then only passingly. *They typically precisely equated economic reform with democratic reform.*

• In the articles we surveyed, *there was not one warning about the potential risks of a rapid liberalization of capital accounts around the world* (until after the Asian crisis), despite the long history of financial market bubbles and their consequences. This is perhaps our most stunning single conclusion.

THE RECENT EVOLUTION OF THE FINANCIAL MEDIA

Coverage of business news by the financial media—both newspapers and television—expanded dramatically beginning in the early 1970s. Rarely these days does a newscast on radio or television go by without an update of the Dow Jones industrials average. This was not true even in the 1970s. These updates now often also include the day's gains or losses for the benchmark Treasury bond. When I was a regular television reporter as recently as the early 1990s, the long Treasury bond was considered too technical to mention. Now, even on general news broadcasts we hear about housing starts and auto sales, monthly personal income and savings rates, corporate profits and wages. The only economic data that were regularly included in general news broadcasts a decade ago were the unemployment rate, inflation, and occasionally the price of gold. Major corporate mergers are now included among the day's top stories in general newscasts and often receive front-page treatment by the newspapers. Before Paul Volcker's tenure, it is doubtful many people knew who the Federal Reserve chairman was. Today, Alan Greenspan is as visible in the news as any politician or diplomat save the president. Robert Rubin, the Treasury Secretary, is almost as well known.

Many of us forget that *The New York Times* did not have a separate financial section (Business Day) until 1978. The business staff of the *Times* has risen by roughly 30 to 40% over these years. In the early 1980s, the Associated Press had only four reporters on its business staff; today it has 22. Personal finance magazines have especially proliferated. When I was a columnist for *Money* magazine in the mid-1970s, it was a struggling and even dubious enterprise. Now, with two million subscribers (and an estimated eight million readers), it is one of Time Warner's most successful publications.

Television dedicated to finance has become a commonplace. In 1985, FNN, "Business Times" on ESPN, and a handful of other programs at most reached a couple hundred thousand people a day. Now, at 6:30 p.m., CNBC, CNN and CNN FN, Public Broadcasting's "Nightly Business Report," and Bloomberg's syndicated news services may well reach two million or so viewers, excluding those who watch in their offices. Over the week, a popular program such as "Nightly Business Report" claims 3.25 million unduplicated viewers. The growth of the Bloomberg financial news services, which includes a news wire, a 24-hour business news service, and other news outlets, may be most representative of these changes. Started in 1990 with one employee, it now has nearly 700 reporters and editors, many of them assigned to regular beats such as the markets and banking.

This more intense interest in business news started with the OPEC oil price hikes of 1973, the ensuing recession which was to be the worst of the post World War II period (until 1982), and the rise of inflation. Before this, business coverage was for the most part restricted to financial publications, and was rare on TV or the radio. Rising interest rates later in the 1970s, along with their deregulation, forced savers to search through new money market funds and certificates of deposit to get the best rate possible. Even ordinary savers could no longer be passive in a time of high inflation and interest rates.

In 1982, the nation had the worst recession of the post-World War II period and unemployment rates reached 10%, adding still further to the intensifying interest in business. Wages discounted for inflation continued to fall even as the economy recovered later in the decade, and incomes grew more unequal. Average weekly wages, for example, fell from about $270 in 1980 to $260 in 1990. Tight monetary policy and the Reagan tax cuts led to a soaring federal budget deficit, which became a major political issue.

In general, then, the past 25 years of slow-growing GDP and productivity (until only recently) and high inflation took their toll on Americans through historically high unemployment rates, falling average wages, and negligible gains in family income. According to the Census Bureau, median family income in 1999 stands only slightly higher than its 1989 level, which in turn was only a few thousand dollars higher than it was in 1980. One of the most dramatic consequences of slow real economic growth is that both spouses must now work to make ends meet.

The dramatic rise in both the stock market and the bond market, and the proliferation of investment vehicles also increased interest in financial news. Some 40% of America's personal financial assets are now equities compared to only 20% or so in 1990. In aggregate, stocks are of greater value than homes.

Americans must now manage their own retirement funds, through IRAs and other tax-deferred vehicles, or through "defined contribution" plans offered by their employers who no longer guarantee retirement benefits. One of the more extreme manifestations of the public interest in investment is that an increasing number of people now trade intra-day over the Internet.

In sum, business is now front-page news. In the past 25 years, business issues such as the federal deficit were always among the top 10 issues for Americans. In the 1990s, concerns over globalization also grew. Most telling, I think, a *Wall Street Journal* survey asked a random selection of Americans just what characterized America best. First were free markets. Democracy was only third.

Not only did the media expand its coverage in these years, it began to hire reporters with an economic education, including those with master's degrees and Ph.D.s, and new pride was taken in the sophistication of the coverage. There were obvious benefits to a more technically trained reporting staff. But there were sometimes disadvantages because empirical reporting—which is to say, "go out and get the facts"—was often neglected in favor of the prevailing mainstream ideological view. These better-educated reporters often wanted to maintain their membership in good standing with the mainstream economics departments. Nevertheless, the financial press is often subject to what I would call "expert bullying." In a recent small meeting organized by Harvard's Shorenstein Center, for example, both Treasury Secretary Rubin and FDIC's Franklin Raines couched their criticism of the press as an inability to *understand* the issues. This is an easy and effective way for sources to be censorious. The press has increasingly accepted such criticism as true. In my view, the financial press should report many sides of an issue, not make choices about who is "correct" in a debate that may be more ambiguous and value-laden than typical reporters are able to assess.

ECONOMIC REFORM IN RUSSIA AND EASTERN EUROPE

After the fall of the Iron Curtain

The fall of the iron curtain raised a momentous question. How does a nation the size of Russia make the transition from socialism to a market economy? Shock therapy, primarily ushered into the public discourse by Harvard's Jeffrey Sachs, quickly filled a seeming vacuum. Sachs was an effective spokesman for the point of view and claimed success in South America and also in Poland. The general program consisted of rapid and even immediate decontrol of prices, opening of trade, stabilizing of macroeconomic fiscal and monetary policies, and privatizing of state-run businesses and collective agricultural institutions.

Ask academic observers what the press reaction to this radical policy was in the 1990s and they are largely unanimous in believing that press attitude towards shock therapy was uniformly positive. "As long as Washington was speaking with one voice," says Dani Rodrik of Harvard, "the press reflected it. There was a sense of inevitability that it was the next step." Says political scientist Susan Woodward of Brookings: "There was one theme, and you didn't really hear anything else." Columbia's Padma Desai was in favor of a more gradualist approach. "There were instant experts everywhere," she says. "Gradualism became such a pejorative word that you didn't have a chance. If I sent in some piece, I didn't have a chance of being published."

In our comprehensive reading of the major periodical and newspaper publications about economic reform in Russia since 1990, there are several observations that I think are especially telling.

• We found only a handful of positive references to "gradualism" over the entire period in all the publications combined. Ironically, the press expressed most skepticism about shock therapy in the early years. Even so, the criticism was generally mild and short-lived, and we found no article in the press that called for abandonment of shock therapy; criticism was more in the form of pointing out the obstacles it faced. There were periodic reports on how ordinary people suffered in Russia and elsewhere.

• We found only one reference to China's successful economic reforms as a possible guide to reform measures in Russia.

• If serious attention was paid at all to reform proposals other than shock therapy, it was usually to dramatic conservative proposals (partly because of the dogged influence of *The Wall Street Journal*'s op-ed page, of which there is no alternative equivalent), such as ending all aid to Russia completely or tying the currency to a package of commodities, rather than to gradualism or a more practical sequencing of reforms such as in China.

• We found literally no credible attention paid to the possibility of postponing *privatization*. The word itself contained strong ideological implications and few dared criticize the process.

To understand fully the nature of the media coverage, and how it forestalled other constructive approaches to reform in Russia, we will analyze a sample of pertinent articles more closely. The evident lack of pluralism has been damaging to economic policies, and also suggests a dangerously narrow set of views in a democracy that prides itself on open debate and depends more crucially than other democracies (which have alternative institutions to protect weaker interests) on a vital free press.

The early reaction to economic reform

The Western press generally greeted the possibility of reform in Russia and Eastern Europe with extraordinary enthusiasm. Rarely will the press embrace what they repeatedly called "radical" change so readily in any other area. Two editorials from *The New York Times* in November 1991 characterize the general reaction, and probably broadly influenced it as well. The *Times* is seldom as bold when it comes to policy changes in the United States.

"The Russian President, Boris Yeltsin, has announced a program of genuinely radical reform, just about everything outsiders could have hoped for—yet nobody in the West seems to notice," wrote the *Times* editorialists (November 12, 1991). "The plan would rein in subsidies to inefficient businesses, tighten control over the money supply, decontrol most prices and rapidly privatize state-owned enterprises." The *Times* professed that such shock therapy should not be diluted; gradualism was a mistake. "Though not even shock therapy guarantees success," the *Times* insisted, "slow reform would almost certainly produce failure."

Any supporting analysis of so provocative a proposition, as opposed to a handful of quotes from economists, cannot be found in any *New York Times* article that I have read. In general, the press in these years took as an article of faith that shock therapy was the only alternative to Russia's former command economy. In large part, I believe, this was attributable to the articulate and passionate espousal of

Jeffrey Sachs. His credibility was no doubt aided, in the minds of the press, by his association with Harvard. In the many articles I have read from this period, Sachs was almost the only economist cited in support of this point of view.

In fact, Sachs was also part of a group organized by the Harvard Kennedy School that included Stanley Fischer of the World Bank and Graham Allison of the Kennedy School. The program offered by the group was more tempered than the undiluted Sachs view, though the shock therapy program implemented in Poland was still the basic model. These other men were cited relatively rarely in the press.

Perhaps the clearest indication of the one-sidedness of the reporting about the early shock therapy proposals was the following early assertion by one *New York Times* reporter (emphasis mine): "Despite the obstacles and prospect of public resistance, *a striking measure of consensus* is emerging among officials and economists in Eastern Europe about the strategies necessary to move these societies from their current economic stagnation to a more prosperous future. More than two dozen East European officials and economists interviewed were virtually in agreement on which basic steps were needed. All Eastern European nations should follow the steps being taken by Poland, they said . . . ("Slow Pace For Reform in Eastern Bloc," dateline Warsaw, January 29, 1990). By contrast, Dani Rodrik thinks that if one scratched hard enough, most economists probably believed in a far more gradualist approach.

Coincidentally, I also reported from Warsaw only a few months earlier than did the above-cited reporter. I found significant differences of opinion among the leading economists and business people of Poland over the course of economic reform, many of whom were opposed to the harsher forms of shock therapy. But there was a strong impetus in the Western press to insist that a consensus had formed. Reporters seemed to believe that shock therapy ran more or less unopposed in an election among economists.

Returning to the *Times* editorials, the newspaper was clearly bent on influencing President Bush to supply aid to Russia in 1991. An editorial only two weeks after the one cited above stated the following (November 26, 1991): "The situation cries out for intervention. And according to Jeffrey Sachs, an economics professor at Harvard who advises the Russian government, it won't take much sacrifice by the West. He outlines a Western aid package costing $15 billion a year, about $3 billion of it from the United States."

Thus, the *Times* favored conditionality, on which all future U.S. aid was predicated. The United States would give money—and private investors would invest—as long as "radical reform" was undertaken and maintained. In such an environment, there was little room for talk of more gradual reform or the sequencing of pieces of the plan. "In the Sachs plan," wrote the *Times*, "aid would be targeted and conditioned on market reforms."

The *Times* was also especially articulate about the heroic sacrifice ordinary Russians had to make in order to right their economy. I think John Maynard Keynes once warned against advice that required sacrifice on the part of the common people first. "The initial stages of shock therapy can be brutal, as Poland has discovered," the *Times* wrote, "when prices and unemployment soar . . . The West will doubt Mr. Yeltsin's resolve until the plan is carried out. But . . . to preserve jobs and check inflation, Mr. Yeltsin refused to index wages to prices. That insures that workers' living standards will plummet—hardly the goal of a politician pandering to the masses."

It must be conceded that *The New York Times* was well aware of the pain of economic reform in Eastern Europe and frequently reported it in the early years of reform. "Integration into the Western economy will take years, and getting there will almost certainly involve real pain," wrote one *Times* reporter (January 7, 1990). Later in 1990, the *Times* reported that, "the huge drop in output resulting from Poland's shock therapy caused officials elsewhere to think twice about tough economic reforms (December 30, 1990)" The *Times* article even quoted some outside economists as claiming the Polish experiment was failing: "'Poland's program is unsuccessful,' Mr. Klacek, the Czechoslovak economist said."

There were similar warnings from other publications. To take one of many examples, *Time* magazine warned about how difficult it was for the Polish people under shock therapy: "Rising prices and tight curbs on wages have sliced the purchasing power of some families as much as 40%" ("Living With Shock Therapy," June 11, 1990).

But neither the *Times* nor *Time* nor any other publication we read sought out alternatives to shock therapy in recognition of the pain it would cause, or the political dangers that it would engender. Quite the contrary, they typically insisted even more strenuously that shock therapy was necessary, no doubt subscribing to the theory that pain is a necessary purgative if there is to be any gain. "Ironically, these somber facts may be indicative of success more than failure," continued *Time* magazine, after a recitative on the suffering of the Poles. In another article some 18 months later, *Time* continued: "The secret of success for such radical reform is the courage to stick with it until the program works" ("More Pain than Gain," January 13, 1992).

Under the weight of such pain, shock therapy as it was originally proposed was not maintained in Poland, a fact that was rarely reported in the American press. Rising inflation and unemployment necessarily resulted in a slower approach to economic reform in Poland. Furthermore, some contend that by not privatizing state-owned industries right away, in contrast to the plan for Russia, the Polish government was able to assure itself a source of hard currency in these years. In Russia, of course, privately owned businesses often refused to pay taxes and sent capital overseas. We found no article in which the slowing of the reform approach in Poland was reported. In the end, it took Poland five or six years to restore production to former levels. You would not know this by generally reading the American press. The framers of shock therapy in Poland had originally promised the economy would turn around in only six months.

The widespread calls for rapid reform in Russia were no doubt linked to Cold War fears. But they were also stimulated by the increasingly poor performance of the Soviet economy under Mikhail Gorbachev. It was a simple reflex to ascribe this to the stop-and-go attitudes of Gorbachev towards change (he did not carry through the 500-day plan, among other proposals). It is not as if gradualist approaches were not raised as possibilities in Russia. The attitude seemed to develop in America that anything but rapid-fire, simultaneous reforms across all fronts was tantamount to a betrayal of free-market principles. One of Mikhail Gorbachev's early reformers, for example, Leonid I. Abalkin, proposed that market reforms be extended over five or six years. But the Soviet economy of the time was doing poorly. The *Times* published a guest column by Ed Hewett of Brookings (March 25, 1990), one of the few "experts" called upon other than Sachs, who urged that rapid Polish-style reform be implemented.

This attitude grew in ideological power. Article after article in the following years more or less equated rapid economic reform in Russia with democratic reform. If one opposed such reform, one was characterized as anti-democratic. Ironically, Gorbachev may have felt just the opposite. I do not presume any expertise on the true motives of the Russian leaders, but he and others seemingly feared that the economic pain of shock therapy could undermine democracy and bring back dictatorship. Their go-slow attitude was, in their minds, an attempt to save democracy.

The economic basis of shock therapy was itself rarely treated in the press. This paper is not the place to criticize theories of economic development, but the light analysis in the press may well have reflected the new and seemingly almost instant analyses emanating from academia. On the other hand, we certainly found no article in the financial press of the 1990s that seriously challenged the skimpy analysis that supported the shock-therapy approach, or how little it was based on empirical research, former case studies, or any serious growth models. In fact, there was no single article we found in the American press that clearly presented an analytical case about why rapid economic reform was necessary.

By contrast, several early articles in *Fortune* suggested how ideological attitudes underlay support for rapid and painful economic reform. For example, proponents of rapid economic reform were usually referred to as "courageous" in the press. The *Times* editorials cited above did this. So did other *Times* articles. Consider this 1991 headline (October 23, 1991): "Moscow's Brave Entrepreneurs." Just as Yeltsin was taking over fully from Gorbachev, a *Fortune* reporter wrote (emphasis mine), "Can Yeltsin exhibit the same *courage* in pushing economic reform as he did in climbing atop a tank last summer to face down the coup plotters? ("Russia Starts All Over Again," January 13, 1992)" Theoretically, of course, it could take as much courage, or even more, to go slow in light of the pressure from the West, and the financial press, to link monetary aid to reform.

The same *Fortune* article took Sachs's extraordinary optimism at face value. He is the only economist cited in this piece, as was frequently the case in other publications. "He (Sachs) thinks the Yeltsin plan will have a fast payoff in one area," wrote *Fortune*. "After a few months of sharply rising prices, he expects prices to stabilize and stores to fill up with goods, ending the long waiting lines." Sachs warned that industry would remain in recession, but *Fortune* quoted him as saying further, that "private businesses could develop rapidly, 'if the reforms go through in as radical a way as they should.'"

In the first year of Russian reform, matters went badly. Production fell and inflation soared. Crime rates rose. Yeltsin dismissed his free-market reformer, Yegor Gaidar. Dismissals of free marketers were greeted with almost unanimous derision in the American press. Another *Fortune* article ("Russia 1993: Europe's Time Bomb," January 25, 1993) revealed how rapid economic reform became equated with the future of democracy, and how the dominant "narrative" among the press became ideological. Most important, consider *Fortune's* use of value-laden adjectives: "Barely 12 months after launching a dramatic bid to create a dynamic, market-oriented democracy," wrote *Fortune*, "Yeltsin seems to be backing down.... The blatant compromise bought Yeltsin some time, but it also threatened to bury his fragile reforms under a morass of half measures that would intensify the economic crisis and could ultimately cost Yeltsin his job." Note how democracy and markets were explicitly linked: a "market-oriented democracy." Note also how words like 'dynamic' were used to convey positive connotations about reforms and words like 'half measures' negative connotations.

I will quote further from this article to illustrate the ideological point of view (emphasis mine). "Then Yeltsin appointed as Prime Minister Victor Chernomyrdin, 54, a *hardworking but unimaginative* petroleum minister. With *his barrel chest and gray complexion*, Chernomyrdin seemed the archetypal Soviet era command-system manager," wrote *Fortune*. How do we know he was unimaginative? I assume because he wanted to go more slowly on reforms. In fact, Chernomyrdin professed to want a market economy. Perhaps he was talking through the side of his mouth, and he remained a controversial figure in ensuing years, of course, but *Fortune* would certainly have none of it. They quoted him as follows: "'I am for a market,' he said, adding *grimly*, in an apparent reference to the free traders now flooding Russia's streets, 'but not for a bazaar.'"

This kind of black-and-white reporting of economic reform characterized the press at the time—and, disturbingly, ever since. Reformers were knights in shining armor with "impeccable credentials," non-reformers had "gray complexions" and spoke *grimly*. *Fortune* thus provided among the most graphic examples of ideological reporting. *The Wall Street Journal*, whose reporting I generally admire, was somewhat more circumspect but nevertheless continually betrayed a point of view. Writing about the same events (December 16, 1992), the *Journal* reported, "Mr. Chernomyrdin isn't opposed to economic reform . . . he lacks Mr. Gaidar's vision of a market economy that reassured foreign supporters and kept harsh reforms moving forward." The *Journal* found some sources who actually praised Chernomyrdin, unlike *Fortune*, but noted that only its white knights—unmitigated reformers— have the "vision-thing." (Ironically, the often and maybe justifiably reviled Chernomyrdin was recently appointed head of Gazpom to widespread praise because he may pay the legal taxes to the government unlike his predecessors.)

In this same article, the *Journal* again quoted Jeffrey Sachs, who said Gaidar's loss was "potentially catastrophic." At least the *Journal* also found an economist other than Sachs to quote, though he was Anders Aslund, long famous for his criticism of Sweden's welfare state. Aslund was an adviser to the Russian reformers and, predictably enough, he worried that shock therapy would be slowed down. The general theme of the *Journal* article was just that. The article expressed fears that some prices would be re-fixed, that the currency may no longer be convertible, and most of all that privatization would be delayed. The *Journal* assumed that all such steps were more or less anathema. It found no Western economist who might agree that in some respects a slowing of reform would make sense. This characterized virtually all the articles we read.

Later coverage of economic reform

The seeming failure of economic reform in 1992 and 1993 led to generalized criticism of economic reform in the U.S. press. The decontrol of prices resulted in soaring inflation, which hurt most Russians. By 1992, output in many industries fell sharply and unemployment was generally high by former standards. "To hear some businessmen, economists and factory managers tell it, everything has gone wrong with reform," reported *The Wall Street Journal* (April 1, 1992). By 1993, Jeffrey Sachs felt obliged to defend himself vigorously. He published a reply to critics in *The Wall Street Journal* at the end of 1993 (December 30, 1993), which largely attributed Russian economic problems to the country's domestic politics and the thwarting of liberal programs by conservatives and former "apparatchiks."

As noted, however, the tenor of criticism in the American press was highly general. The theme was usually the following. The economic reforms proposed by Sachs and others and supported by Washington were not flawed; rather, the problems in Russia were nearly insurmountable and, indeed, there were enemies of reform in Russia who simply blocked the purer shock therapy programs that may have worked had they not been diluted. The Administration no doubt stimulated this view by persistently lobbying in favor of reform candidates in Russia and implicitly tying promises of aid to their appointment. They promoted a good guy-bad guy portrayal of Russian politicians that was typically reflected in press accounts. As a writer in the *Manchester Guardian* noted several years later, "At times it seemed western governments believed as long as there was someone under forty in charge of one of the main economic ministries who talked the market talk and walked the market walk (to the IMF for another handout), then reform must be on track ("Catching Up with the West Finally Takes its Painful Toll," August 18, 1998)."

Perhaps the greatest irony of the press coverage in the mid-1990s was that the press consistently cited privatization as evidence of economic progress in Russia and other East European nations. In the case of Russia, of course, early privatization allowed oligarchs to take over the nation's major businesses and divert their profits into their own pockets and out of the country altogether. This stood in sharp in contrast to the ability of China, which has delayed major privatization, to retain capital. *The Economist* was an early forceful advocate of immediate privatization. "Building an environment in which market forces can do their job should start with a massive transfer of assets from the state to private ownership," wrote the magazine in 1990 ("And Now for the Hard Part," April 28, 1990). A few years later, *The Wall Street Journal* reported that, "Privatization, the transfer of state assets to private hands, is generally viewed as one of the few success stories of President Boris Yeltsin's government (July 1, 1993)." Jeffrey Sachs and Anders Aslund were strong supporters of early privatization. In his 1993 defense, Sachs wrote, "The reformers have done extraordinarily well. More than 80,000 enterprises have been privatized, setting the basis for a new middle class and entrepreneurial class, as well as setting in motion real restructuring of many enterprises."

This is not a brief against privatization. One can make a plausible case, however, that privatization should have been delayed until other reforms were well underway so that the economy could have been stabilized without running down state revenues. We found no article advocating such a position in the American press. (Again, we cannot be certain that our search was 100 percent exhaustive, but surely any such article was rare.) There were a handful of op-ed pieces or letters to the editor casting doubt on privatization, including two in *The New York Times* by Columbia's Padma Desai. Moreover, there were occasional claims in some op-ed pieces (in *The Wall Street Journal*) that Russia was actually doing very well and that privatization and other reforms were indeed working.

In sum, then, no serious alternative ideas to shock therapy-type reforms were discussed except on a literal handful of occasions—and then only briefly. There were several calls for a reduction in Russian tax rates to encourage businesses to pay. But as noted, after 1992, we found no article that took gradualism seriously (except in the one passing case cited below). There was no discussion of a sequencing of particular reforms, which in academia is now getting a wider hearing. The most interesting article, perhaps, was published by *The Wall Street Journal* in the fall of 1994 about a meeting of the Mont Pelerin Society. Gary Becker was quoted as saying that "chaos (in Russia) was not all that bad." The brief, 745-word article went on about Becker's thoughts: "He suggests that Russia's infamous corruption and organized crime may even be providing the valuable service of easing market development by getting around state rules that often hamper what should be routine activities—such as importing goods ("Free-Market Group is Divided on How to Bring Capitalism to Ex-Soviet Bloc," September 30, 1994)."

On the other hand, Ronald Coase was quoted as saying that "you can only move gradually." This was one of the few remarks in favor of gradualism to appear in the financial press in a decade of reporting on the issue. "He (Coase) cites the example of China's economy building up small enterprises based on the cultural unit of the family. 'To imbibe the principles of a market society takes a long time,' says Mr. Coase, 'because knowledge travels with great difficulty.'" This is the only article we found that reported on such ideas.

The about face

Only after the financial crises of 1997 and 1998 did the financial press turn harshly critical of shock therapy and economic reform. An article in *Newsweek* towards the end of the year reflected a new tone—indeed, a new "narrative"—that was virtually impossible to have read even a year earlier. "Harvard economist Jeffrey Sachs and (Anatoly) Chubais advocated 'shock therapy' for Russia . . . the elimination of most price controls and speedy privatization of state companies. But the recipe didn't work very well. The freezing of prices initially led to hyperinflation, wiping out savings of average Russians. And privatization resulted mostly in what Russians called the 'great grab'—bankers, managers and outright criminal gangs taking control of the country's most important assets for prices well under market value." Now, allegations of corruption against Chernomyrdin and Chubais among others also surfaced.

Although as we noted, Russia bolted from economic crisis to crisis throughout the 1990s, it took the 1998 default for the press finally to do an about-face on shock therapy. Even the former good guys—the reformers with "impeccable credentials"—were now at last susceptible to criticism. "Washington's most significant blunder was a failure to recognize that Yeltsin's reformers were introducing a system that only worsened endemic corruption, crime, and cynicism," *Newsweek* went on. Another *Newsweek* article reported that, "Yeltsin's Russia is a certified economic basket case, unable to meet its most basic financial obligations (whether to international bondholders in London or ambulance drivers in Vladivostok ["An Early Russian Winter," August 24, 1998])." The *Manchester Guardian* had a field day: "Russia has no legacy of free-market capitalism and attempts to short-circuit the transition process ignore the fact that it has taken two centuries for the West to develop its modern economic infrastructure (ibid)."

We could cite similar examples in much of the press coverage. The fact that it took a crisis for the press to criticize shock therapy directly, and how quickly they did once the crisis ensued, is a sure sign of how dominant a "narrative" the pure market solutions had been. It was reinforced not merely by Washington but by Wall Street and business interests. "Experts" were consistently chosen from both areas. Michael McFall, a foreign policy specialist who spent time in Russia and is now with the Carnegie Peace Endowment, says he was always surprised at how the press would quote investment bankers who had a vested interest in bolstering the Russian reformist regime.

Again, this is not a brief against most of the tenets of Russian economic reform. But it is a brief for a variety of points of view, for the recognition of the true interests of news sources, and for the courage to go against the dominant "narrative" of the time, even if it means losing friends in Washington and Wall Street, and maybe among readers. Alternative views were simply not aired. As noted, there was little serious and in-depth discussion of more gradual adoption of some reforms, the order and sequencing of reforms, the absence of required institutions and industries, or intelligent ways to provide a social net for the Russian people. Despite China's success at transforming its economy slowly, for all intents and purposes, there was no discussion of China as a model—no doubt for ideological reasons. Thus, the American press repeatedly mistook economic reform for democratic reform. But slower economic reforms were indeed compatible with democratization, and may have even helped make it more durable.

One important point still not recognized in the press is how both the Administration and the Russian reformers were urged to make reforms because it would raise the confidence of the investment community, whether or not those reforms were required. Washington was often perturbed when Yeltsin dismissed a well-known Russian reformer more by its immediate effect on the financial markets and the willingness of banks to lend money than for what it might mean for the future of the Russian economy itself. The IMF had a similar influence over Russian reform, largely subscribing to rapid economic reform and not nearly as divorced from political matters as it insisted it was. As the Oxford political scientist Ngaire Woods points out, the IMF made a large loan to support Yeltsin's presidential campaign in 1996 when he was most threatened by the Communist Zyuganov.

THE LIBERALIZATION OF CAPITAL ACCOUNTS

The absence of reporting

The Asian financial crisis marked a turning point in financial reporting about deregulated global financial markets. Moreover, what became known as the Washington consensus was at last open to criticism. Consider the following lengthy excerpt from a *New York Times* article.

> . . . some economists also say that if those (Asian) countries had weak foundations, it is partly because Washington helped supply the blueprints. They argue that the Clinton Administration pushed too hard for financial liberalization and freer capital flows, allowing foreign money to stream into these countries and local money to move out. In many cases, foreign countries were happy to open up in this way because they thought it was the best road to economic development, but a wealth of evidence has shown that overhasty liberalization can lead to banking chaos and financial crises.
>
> Even some former Administration officials acknowledge that they went too far. Mickey Kantor, the former trade representative and commerce Secretary, now says that the United States was insufficiently aware of the kind of chaos that financial liberalization could provoke. "It would be a legitimate criticism to say that we should have been more nuanced, more foresighted that this could happen," he said.
>
> Speaking of the risks of financial liberalization as the best thing for other countries, it is also clear that it pushed for free capital flows in part because this was what its supporters in the banking industry wanted. "Our financial services industry wanted into these markets," said Laura D'Andrea Tyson, the former chairwoman of President Clinton's Council of Economic Advisers and later head of the National Economic Council ("How U.S. Wooed Asia to Let Cash Flow In," February 16, 1999).

This is excellent reporting—as good as it gets, in my view. But it would have been far more useful had it been published before the Asian financial crisis, not in the winter of 1999, nearly two years after the crisis had begun. In fact, we found no article in the press we surveyed that questioned the liberalization of capital flows into developing nations until late in 1997, after the Thai baht had plummeted. Further, there was no article in a mainstream U.S. publication in the 1990s in which the implementation of capital controls drew favorable coverage until the Asian crisis was well underway.

This is a rather stunning finding. It partly reflects a simple lack of sophistication on the part of American financial journalism. These were complex, technical matters for which there is little tradition of reporting even in the best of America's financial publications. In Europe in general, capital controls and the movement of currencies were of more general interest. Of the publications we surveyed (we did not survey *The Financial Times)*, only *The Economist*, ironically enough, published articles on capital controls before 1998 that were even mildly open to their adoption. *The Economist's* interest had partly to do with crisis in the European pegged rated system at the time, which short-term capital flows helped undermine. *The Economist* reported on the possible resurrection of capital controls in 1992 in a piece entitled "The Way We Were (October 3, 1992)." But *The Economist* did not abandon the matter. In an article in early 1995, the magazine surprisingly wrote in partial favor of Chile's controls: "For all these reasons, it would be wrong to conclude that capital controls are a sensible long-term policy, although some restrictions may be appropriate for countries in the early stages of economic reform, or as a temporary measure when large amounts of foreign capital flood in unexpectedly. Many developing countries would indeed do well to copy the Chilean model (Capital Punishment, February 4, 1995)."

A lack of tradition cannot completely explain the lapse on the part of the American press to address such issues. The Tobin tax had been under wide discussion in the late 1970s and in the 1980s, for example. Moreover, there were some prominent academic experts who were discussing the issues rather volubly, including Barry Eichengreen of the University of California at Berkeley. Robert Wade of Brown was also an articulate voice in the field from a mainstream university, though he is a political scientist. In retrospect, it is clear that such mainstream figures as Joseph Stiglitz and Jagdish Bhagwati had their doubts as well.

In the fall of 1995, in fact, *The Economist* ran a long piece citing Eichengreen's (et al.) work. "The authors concluded that the scope for self-fulfilling attacks on currencies has increased as capital flows have become more mobile," the magazine wrote. It further noted that the authors "would require banks to make compulsory non-interest-bearing deposits with the central banks in some proportion to all their domestic-currency lending to non-residents ("Not-so-divine Intervention," October 7, 1995)."

Over these same years, fears of globalization were addressed only in the most general ways in the financial press. Non-financial issues usually attracted the most attention. There were reports of sweatshop labor, for example. The debate over NAFTA raised concerns over undiluted free trade and its effects on jobs. Similarly, the risks of the international flow of capital stimulated stories about job losses. But the dangers of speculative excess due to unregulated capital flows were, in our reading, never raised. As for the need for more regulation of these capital flows, this too was rarely raised. When it was, the argument was quite general. *The New York Times* occasionally reported on the lost power of governments as multinational companies and global trading superseded domestic authorities. But the conventional wisdom of the time about capital controls was that they were utterly impracticable. In 1992, after the European currency crisis, *The New York Times* at least raised the fears when it wrote, "A generation ago, in the late 1960s, countries with currencies under attack by speculators could and did resort to capital controls, making it harder to move money into or out of the country in question. Now, such actions by major industrial countries are almost unthinkable, and are seldom even mentioned. 'Governments have lost power to control capital, and they probably have lost it forever,' said David C. Roche, a global strategist for Morgan Stanley ("Why Currencies Move Faster Than Policies," September 23, 1992)."

The *Times* cited a number of investment bankers who made the same comments about the lost domestic power of governments. The newspaper essentially took for granted that given the volume of cross-border transactions, controls were no longer possible, as did most publications. The Tobin tax, though discussed, was generally seen as a dinosaur of earlier years. But of course such an attitude reflected the views, and indeed the profit-making objectives, of Wall Street and other financial participants. It also well reflected the view of the Clinton administration and the Federal Reserve. In these sophisticated and technical fields, the financial press in America was more dependent on its principal sources—Wall Street and Washington—than in most other areas. Increasingly abandoning its watchdog posture, and increasingly becoming an insider, the financial press was especially vulnerable in these areas. Timothy Metz, a reporter for *The Wall Street Journal* for 23 years, also says pithy stories are no longer the first priority. "Entertainment value is so important these days," says Metz. "Now breezy feature stories are on the front page. More serious stories are in the back."

In general, then, the financial press was fully in the camp of the liberalization of capital controls. The stage had been set in the early 1990s. The ideology had veered sharply towards the thinking of an economist like John Rutledge, who wrote in *Forbes* in 1992 that, "the responsibility of the new president will be to create more attractive conditions for capital. Trying to reverse the trends with protectionism and capital controls is not the answer. With today's technology, capital controls would be entirely ineffective ("The Right Kind of Industrial Policy?" July 6, 1992)."

The Clinton Administration, under the guidance of Robert Rubin, had essentially adopted this line, and the financial press generally accepted it. Again, this is not a brief for the reversal of capital flows. But amelioration deserved consideration. Berkeley's Eichengreen believed fully in the opening up for capital markets around the world and in the importance of foreign capital in developing nations. But he also believes in the occasional adoption of controls.

The financial press did not understand how aggressive the administration was in liberalizing capital accounts. I believe it generally assumed that such liberalization was simply inevitable. Certainly no one on Wall Street demurred, and few prominent academics other than those mentioned considered the problem urgent. They probably would not have gotten a hearing, anyway. (One unexplored theme that keeps arising as we researched this paper is that economists, too, increasingly seemed to tailor their views according to what the market would bear.)

A former Treasury official told me that a few colleagues in the department would raise questions about the unbridled opening of markets, but many believed vigilance in this area was the province of the Federal Reserve. After all, it was the Fed who was chartered with responsibility for strength and sobriety of financial institutions. But Alan Greenspan, of course, had no predisposition to consider controls. As late as 1998 in the midst of the financial crisis, Greenspan published the following in the *Cato Journal*: "It should be recognized that if it is technology that has imparted the current stress to markets, technology can be used to contain it. Enhancements to financial institutions' internal risk-management systems arguably constitute the most effective countermeasure to the increased potential instability of the global financial system. Improving the efficiency of the world's payment systems is clearly another."

Greenspan goes on: "The resort to capital controls to deal with financial market disturbances of the sort a number of emerging economies have experienced would be a step backwards from the trend toward financial market liberalization, and in the end would not be effective. The maintenance of financial stability in an environment of global capital markets, therefore, calls for greater attention by governments to the soundness of public policy ("The Globalization of Finance," Winter 1998)."

How the Asian fnancial crisis turned the press

As with shock therapy, a crisis was required to change the "narrative" about capital liberalization that the press had so uniformly adopted in the 1990s. But so ingrained was the Washington-Wall Street point of view that even after so many developing economies were brought to the brink by the chain of events that began in Thailand in 1997, many prominent publications retained the view. Consider the *Newsweek* columnist Robert Samuelson, one of the more thoughtful conservative commentators in the nation: "Countries became overdependent on foreign capital, which, having entered in huge amounts, is trying to leave the same way... What initially triggered the reversal was the recognition that much foreign money had been squandered through 'crony capitalism' or misguided industrial policies ("Global Capitalism R.I.P.?" September 14, 1998)." According to Samuelson, then, the causal direction did not flow from unwise speculators but from unwise borrowers. Crony capitalism didn't exist on Wall Street but only in the treasuries of developing nations. It was tampering with the market—cronyism and industrial policy—not the speculative market itself that was to blame.

But nowhere was evidence of the embeddedness of this "narrative" so obvious than in a cover story *Time* magazine did on Robert Rubin, Lawrence Summers, and Alan Greenspan entitled "The Three Marketeers" (February 15, 1999). In *Time*'s breathless style (his intellect "never fails to dazzle"), the piece lionized the three as saviors of the financial system. While some publications correctly asked who lost Russia, *Time* loudly proclaimed that these three saved the world economy. The attitude about who caused the crisis was similar to the quieter Samuelson's of *Newsweek*. ". . . those economies had trundled billions of dollars into useless real estate and industrial development." No American or Japanese bankers were cited to share even part of the blame here.

Perhaps such simplifications are understandable. These are not simple issues. But *Time* went much further. "Rubin, Greenspan and Summers have outgrown ideology," the magazine insisted. "Their faith is in the markets and in their own ability to analyze them." The conversion of some of the financial press is nowhere clearer. Beginning with Daniel Bells' *End of Ideology*, which saw ideology only as Marxist, and Fukuyama's *End of History*, which saw free-market theory as purely pragmatic, much of the American press failed to see that there could be ideological underpinnings in free-market reforms.

In the cover story cited above, *Time* almost offers us a caricature. "The pragmatism (of Rubin, Summers and Greenspan) is a faith that recalls nothing so much as the objectivist philosophy of the novelist and social critic Ayn Rand, which (sic) Greenspan had studied intently," wrote *Time*. I know of few philosophers who would call followers of Ayn Rand ideology-free, other than perhaps followers of Ayn Rand.

Most of the financial press, however, followed another course after the ramifications of the financial crisis became clear. They at last became critical of unbridled liberalization of markets and the role of the IMF. But even in these cases, the press did not lead but follow the urgent writings of a few prominent mainstream economists. One exception was a *New York Times* story towards the end of 1997 (December 29, 1998). The reporter Louis Uchitelle followed up with an inside-page story from the World Economic Forum in Davos on the same subject in February, 1998 (February 2, 1998). But it was the pronouncements of prominent economists that turned most of the press towards a more critical attitude. In a front-business page profile later that spring on Joseph Stiglitz, chief economist of the World Bank and the former Clinton administration economist, spoke in favor of the occasional use of capital controls, which put him at odds with the U.S. Treasury's viewpoint (May 31, 1998).

Outright criticism of the IMF was led, ironically, by Jeffrey Sachs, who wrote several op-ed pieces for various publications. It was followed by an article in *Fortune* in August by Paul Krugman of MIT, which proclaimed the value of exchange controls. When Malaysia finally invoked exchange controls, the issue at last became front-page material. A story in the *Times' News of the Week in Review* on September 12 was headlined, "The Invisible Hand's New Strong Arm." The reporter, David Sanger, went on to write, "Suddenly, many believe that the best way to practice capitalism is to make sure that once the capital pours in it can't pour out all at once." Sanger then quoted Morgan Stanley's Asian operations chief as saying, "It's only a bit of an overstatement to say that the free-market-IMF-Bob Rubin-and-Larry Summers model is in shambles."

This was an extraordinary about-face in the thinking of market participants, and one in which the press at last joined. In ensuing weeks, many stories, including a fine four-part series about the limitations of markets by *The Wall Street Journal*, at last made the front pages. As one reporter for a major newspaper noted, "This crisis really has people scared here that the markets aren't working." But if so, the financial media should ask themselves why they weren't better prepared? If economists like Stiglitz, Sachs, and Krugman (and also Bhagwati) hadn't come forward, the financial press's reaction to events may have changed far less.

The most impressive piece of journalism was the four-part series by *The New York Times*, from which we cited the earlier excerpt. The reporter, Nicholas D. Kristof, along with David Sanger, closely documented how the Administration was determined to liberalize markets. "Referring to Mr. Rubin, Mr. Kantor and the late Commerce Secretary Ron Brown, Mr. Garten (Jeffery Garten, a former Commerce official and now dean of Yale School of Management) said, 'there wasn't a fiber in those three bodies—or in mine—that didn't want to press as a matter of policy for more open markets wherever you could make it happen. . . . In retrospect we overshot and in retrospect there was a certain degree of arrogance.'" The reporters cite a particular example where the administration pressed Korea to liberalize markets faster in order to become a member of the OECD.

As refreshing as this reporting is, it also reminds us of the deeper concern that is the theme of this paper. This reporting would probably never have made the light of day if there had been no severe crisis. Furthermore, despite the persistent and intelligent toiling of non-mainstream economists about these issues, and even a few mainstream economists, the press only turned its attention to these matters when a few especially prominent economists publicly criticized the prevailing views. The job of journalism is to ferret out other points of view, but in my view, the financial press has largely lost the initiative in many areas of importance.

CONCLUSION AND SUGGESTIONS

The financial press had an enormous part in the policies developed in America concerning economic reform in the former Soviet Union and the liberalization of international financial markets. The power of the financial press has not been lost on business. Public relations is now a vast and growing industry in America, which is far larger and most sophisticated than it was only 20 years ago. "The degree of promotion is more powerful than I've ever seen it," says an editor of *Business Week*, Chris Welles. "Even the academics now have consulting arrangements with business."

I have not addressed the dominance of much of the academic community by what is conveniently called mainstream economics. The most influential academic departments in the nation increasingly speak with only one voice. Moreover, it is arguable that that voice also bends to desires of its audience. Barry Eichengreen argues that that those who favored gradualism in Russia never presented a cohesive case. But it could well be that, if this is so, it is because there was no obvious outlet for such a case—no demand for the product.

In such an environment, I believe new institutions are needed to convey alternative points of view. When Milton Friedman faced what he believed was a similar bias in the press in the 1960s—this time in favor of a moderate Keynesianism—he used his own university effectively to forge a national counter-argument. By the 1970s, economic events, principally inflation, became an ideal environment in which to expand his influence. The conservative establishment in America has made extraordinary progress in creating institutions—think tanks, academic departments, journals and other media—to disseminate its point of view.

Although there are indeed liberal publications and a handful of alternative academic departments, they are less effective at getting their views across. I believe there should be a more concerted effort to diversify academic institutions and to criticize on a consistent and specific basis the financial media's coverage of events. The Century Foundation, for example, has accomplished this admirably concerning the Social Security debate. Should the United States enter a recession, or the stock market collapse, the environment would be more conducive to alternative views, just as it has been since the financial crises in Asia. Friedman and his acolytes, as noted, benefited from inflation and slow growth. But it would be a mistake to believe that the financial press's recent receptivity to capital controls or slower economic reforms in Russia will be long lasting. There are already signs that old biases are rising again—a recent article on Nigeria in *The New York Times*, which excoriated the leadership for not making early market reforms, is a good example. The influence of the markets will remain powerful.

In my view, the highest priority should be something entirely different than partisan economics, however. I would propose a Center for Economic Dialogue that regularly presents all responsible points of view on major issues of public interest— including with equal emphasis serious alternative views to the prevailing conventional wisdom about liberalizing markets. It would be both a debating forum and a publications institution that in equal part is targeted to the economics profession and to the financial press.

At the very least, the influence of the financial press must be recognized by those who seek to affect national and international economic policy. The tendency by the press towards single "narratives" should no longer surprise. If the tendencies of the financial press are understood, those with alternative ideas can make themselves heard, but not without effort and determination. It will not happen automatically, and surely not simply based on the strength of one's argument.

PART IV

Developing and Transition Economies

10

. . .

Capital Market Liberalization and Economic Performance in Latin America

Roberto Frenkel*

SOME SPECIFIC FEATURES OF CAPITAL MARKET LIBERALIZATION IN LATIN AMERICA

IN THIS SECTION, we review Latin America's experience with capital market liberalization and comment on features of the process shared by most economies in the region. Some of these resulted from external conditions and the policy context in which market reforms were implemented. We consider them first. Other features were determined by the specific historical circumstances that marked the reforms. To highlight these, we briefly review the past two decades of Latin American macroeconomic history.

The financial reforms in Latin America have not been isolated policy initiatives, but were generally implemented as components of Washington Consensus structural reform packages and in conjunction with major macroeconomic stabilization programs.
     It is never simple to explain observed economic performance as the result of a determined policy. Contexts change and the measures we attempt to evaluate are often part of a wider set of initiatives with overlapping effects. These vague considerations are highly relevant in the case of capital market reforms in Latin America (or LA).

---

*This paper was prepared for the conference on International Capital Markets and the Future of Economic Policy, Queens' College, University of Cambridge, April 16–17, 1998.

In the first place, with respect to the overlapping of effects, financial liberalization and opening have always been implemented in LA as components of wide-ranging structural reforms and stabilization policies. Packages of this kind were practiced in the region in the second half of the 1970s and their implementation became generalized in the 1990s. For this reason, the outcomes of financial reforms have always emerged in combination with the effects of trade opening and public-sector reforms, as well as with the measures and results of macroeconomic stabilization policies. Both in the case of the 1970s and in the more important ones of the 1990s, a fixed exchange rate was an important first-order ingredient in stabilization packages.

In the second place, regarding the external context of the policies, financial reforms coincided with boom periods in international financial movements. They were always accompanied by massive capital inflows with their own significant effects on the working of the economy.[1] Because of this correlation, the effects of liberalization in LA are not easily distinguishable from those of drastic changes in the size and composition of capital flows.

Since the first half of the 1970s, there has been a global trend toward financial liberalization and a parallel growth in the international capital flows to developing countries. Both trends were interrupted in Latin America by the 1980s external debt crisis. During those years, LA capital markets were segmented from international markets.

In the first boom of capital flows into developing economies—the period that followed the 1973 oil shock—the region pioneered drastic financial reforms. (The Argentine and Chilean cases are the most notable experiences.) This phase came to an abrupt end with deep financial and external crises. They were followed by the nationalization of private external debts and the establishment of an institutional arrangement in which external financing had to be intermediated by negotiation with the international banks and the IMF. Apart from this link of permanent negotiation, the region remained practically isolated from international capital markets for the rest of the decade. If we were to date that period more precisely, we could say that it lasted between the 1982 Mexican moratorium and the signing of the first Brady Plan to restructure external debt (for Mexico, in 1990). During that time, the region operated under a regime characterized by two stylized facts: external financing was rationed and negotiations with creditors and multilateral financial organizations generally imposed macroeconomically significant transfers abroad.

The constraints set by external financial rationing and these transfers dominated policy design and economic performance during the 1980s. In the initial years, control over external debt burdens and financial crisis took absolute policy

---

1. Cases in which liberalization has not been followed by massive capital inflows are rare but do exist. Bolivia, in the second half of the 1980s, did not receive private inflows despite having deregulated and fully opened its financial markets in 1985. There are cases in both the 1970s and the 1990s of significant capital inflows without major liberalization measures. Brazil is the most important example in both periods.

priority and the institutional setting of financial markets was subordinated to this target. For instance, private external debt was nationalized through massive interventions such as the nationalization of the banking system in Mexico, the generalized refinancing of private debts in Argentina, and a total bailout of the banking system in Chile. In this phase, the priority given to external adjustment and the need to gain control of the economic performance often led to the reversal of previously adopted liberalization and opening policies. Emergency measures such as the reintroduction of exchange controls to block capital flight, interest rates regulations to ease the management of the financial crisis, and new regulations on intermediaries were implemented.

Although the urgency of the early 1980s removed financial liberalization from the immediate policy debate, it reappeared on the agenda of conditionality that accompanied the external debt negotiations. This link became clear in the mid-1980s with the appearance of the adjustment-cum-growth Baker Plan. Since then, coordination between the IMF, the World Bank, and other agencies has increased and the Washington Consensus has become more clearly defined. Even so, capital market decontrol was of secondary relevance in the 1980s. The history of the economic performance during that period—especially in Argentina, Brazil, and Mexico, the largest economies in the region—is basically about a sequence of attempts and failures of comprehensive macroeconomic stabilization programs. Inflation and the balance of payments were stabilized for some time before new destabilizing trends required further adjustments and stabilization measures. There were huge real fluctuations around a stagnant trend. Variations in the institutional financial setting were of secondary importance compared to these cycles.

The 1980s' stabilization programs attempted to reconcile the external financial constraint with the achievement of three conflicting targets: debt service, inflation reduction, and recovery of a positive rate of growth. While some countries—Chile and Colombia, for example—could resolve this conflict in the second half of the period and stabilize the performance of their economies,[2] the biggest were unable to do so until the end of the decade. In Argentina, Brazil, and Mexico stabilization was only achieved in the 1990s, when transfers abroad reversed abruptly and the region became the recipient of strong capital inflows. Financial liberalization gained new relevance under these conditions. The external constraint ceased to bind.

The market segmentation of the 1980s, the instability that lasted until the end of the decade, and the joint effects of both circumstances on the domestic financial markets determined other specific features of the experiences of the 1990s. Similar circumstances characterize the Chilean and Argentine liberalization experiments of the 1970s.

---

2. Chile and Colombia, for different reasons, were cases of minimal transfers abroad. In Colombia, this was because its external debt was relatively small. Chile showed the highest regional debt/GDP ratio, but its transfers were minimal because it received a relatively greater proportion of multilateral support. See Mario Damill, Jose Maria Fanelli, and Roberto Frenkel (1994).

Among the "initial conditions" of the Southern Cone experiments during that period were the particular situation of domestic financial markets. They had recently undergone deep crises and restructuring (Chile 1971–76, Argentina 1974–77), were emerging from a long period of segmentation from international markets, and had adapted to a high inflation environment. The financial markets of the biggest economies in the region found themselves in similar conditions at the end of the 1980s. Especially in the three larger countries, the "second wave" of financial liberalization and capital inflows, like the first, generally took the form of a shock in economies that until then had shown low levels of monetization and financial deepening, weakly developed banking systems, a poor menu of financial assets, and scarce credit for the private sector.[3]

Such conditions imply a particular inability of the financial systems to allocate efficiently a strong injection of funds. The small size and poor diversification of financial markets gave rise to a natural tendency for capital flows to induce major disturbances. Their magnitude was large compared to the existing stocks of money, credit, and domestic financial assets. Such high flow/stock ratios implied strong appreciation pressures in the exchange rate market and/or high credit and liquidity expansion rates according to the degree of intervention of the monetary authority. They also generated a swift appreciation of financial and real assets, such as land and real estate. Those tendencies were enhanced under the fixed exchange-rate regimes found in the majority of experiences. More generally, the shock implied the emergence of important expansionary financial effects in domestic demand. That is why the initial phase of a real and financial boom and the propensity to generate speculative bubbles—widely observed in developing countries associated with financial liberalization and massive capital inflows—were closely linked to these "initial conditions" in the LA cases.

Lastly, the region's passage from the 1980s to the 1990s signified the transition from a situation of external financial rationing and transfers abroad to one of abundant financing. This change, in itself, could only have had beneficial effects on macroeconomic performance. The stabilization programs could succeed; there was a generalized drop in inflation. GDP and domestic absorption grew—the latter more than the former. This has two implications. On the one hand, as already mentioned, the impact of this fundamental change is difficult to distinguish from the effects of liberalization policies. On the other, no evaluation could see the conditions of the 1980s as either the contrasting case or the policy alternative to the current setting. The painful experience of the "lost decade" teaches us that policy should seek to preserve fluid access to international financial markets, a goal which economies in LA have unsuccessfully pursued for many years.

---

3. The relatively deeper development of Chile's financial system in the late 1980s makes it a relevant exception to this observation. Chile did not undergo inflation rates of the order registered in the biggest economies, and its macroeconomic performance was stable in the second half of the 1980s. Colombia's macroeconomic performance was also stable, but its financial system was small and poorly diversified.

Synthesis

The history of Latin America suggests that we evaluate the regional processes of financial liberalization, not as policy initiatives that can be isolated from their context, but rather as a set of experiences that comprise all the specific features mentioned above. This paper looks at recent experience from two points of view. First, we focus on sustainability of the growth process. Second, we examine the quality of the patterns of growth as they are mainly defined by their employment and income distribution characteristics.

The "Southern Cone liberalization experiments"—the cases of Argentina and Chile that we analyze here—are for these purposes closed episodes with well-defined beginnings and ends.[4] They were short-lived, but can still enrich our understanding of the effects of liberalization measures. With respect to the 1990s, our view is particularly influenced by five national cases: Argentina, Brazil, Colombia, Chile, and Mexico. These are the biggest economies in the region. They make up more than three-quarters of the regional product and were the main recipients of the capital inflows. They also provide good examples of a variety of policies and economic performances.

THE LIBERALIZATION EXPERIENCES IN THE 1970S

In the mid-1970s, Argentina and Chile were undergoing similar political and economic processes. The Peronist and *Unidad Popular* governments had been succeeded by military dictatorships in the midst of deep economic crises. The first phase of the macroeconomic policy of the military administrations did not deviate significantly from the traditional stabilization recipes that both countries had repeatedly put into practice since the 1950s. Price controls were lifted, wage increments were repressed, and the exchange rate was devalued. After that, a crawling-peg regime was adopted. Fiscal adjustment was mainly based on contraction of wage expenditures. Real wages fell dramatically in both countries and employment made a strong drop in Chile. The fiscal adjustment was deep and

---

4. There is surely no cause for objection in the case of Argentina, although it could be so in the case of Chile. The more commonly told story about the evolution of reforms there considers the process as a somewhat continuous sequence in which the first steps were completed in the 1970s. In this narrative the external and financial crisis of the 1980s and its real consequences have secondary significance and do not represent a discontinuity. Certainly, Chile was the country in Latin America that most preserved the reforms implemented in the 1970s during and after the crisis. Therefore, the point is debatable. However, there is no room in this paper for a detailed analysis of Chile's history. For our purposes, the Chilean crisis in the 1980s closes a period whose performance can be evaluated by itself. With this, we do nothing more than recover the perspective from which the Southern Cone experiments were observed in the years following the debt crisis. The story mentioned above was constructed later on in the late 1980s, when Chile was constituted as the prime LA example of the Washington Consensus's success.

permanent in the Chilean case and less significant and lasting in the Argentine. An innovation in economic policy was domestic financial reform: the interest rate was freed and most regulations on financial intermediaries were removed.

Both economies had been isolated from international financial markets in the first half of the 1970s. The Eurodollar bank market was already booming in that period, particularly after the 1973-oil shock. (Brazil, for instance, was utilizing this source of external financing intensively.) In the mid-1970s, the Argentine and Chilean economies did not have sizeable external debts. Their balance of payments had already been equilibrated by the stabilization packages. The orthodoxy of the military administrations gained credibility with the IMF and international banks, despite the fact that both economies were experiencing high rates of inflation. High domestic financial yields attracted capital inflows, even before the capital account had been opened. Confronted with these pressures, the authorities initially gave priority to the control of the domestic monetary supply and attempted to curb inflows by imposing regulations.

In the second half of the 1970s, first Chile and shortly later Argentina implemented new and similar policy packages. Liberalization of the foreign exchange market and deregulation of capital flows were added to the domestic financial reform that had previously been implemented. Trade liberalization programs were launched simultaneously. Tariff reductions were scheduled to converge in a few years to a flat and low tariff.[5] Exchange rate policy was the anti-inflation component of the package. Exchange rates were fixed by announcing predetermined paths for monthly devaluation rates, converging to a nominal constant exchange rate (the "tablitas"). This macroeconomic stabilization package was inspired by the "monetary approach to the balance of payments."

The following features characterize the external and real performances after the packages were launched. There were massive capital inflows and a first phase of reserve accumulation, and high rates of growth of money and credit. There was a strong expansion in domestic demand, led by consumption, as well as the emergence of bubbles in financial and real assets. The real exchange rate appreciated continuously because domestic inflation was systematically higher than the rate of devaluation plus the international inflation rate. Current account deficits rose fast and persistently and the external debt soared. When U.S. monetary policy drove up the international interest rate in late 1979, both economies were already showing huge current account deficits and external debts. From then, the increased international rate contributed its own effect to their external fragility. The crisis broke soon afterward. The exchange rate regime collapsed in Argentina in early 1981 and in Chile in 1982. External market finance closed for both economies in 1982, and massive bailouts were implemented to confront the resulting financial crises. Both economies fell into deep recessions.

How can we evaluate economic performance in these cases? The depth and

---

5. The tariff reduction schedules were considered rapid at the time. They would be perceived as gradualist under the current conventional criteria.

duration of the real consequences is well known. The essential question is about sustainability of growth during and after the crises. The negative external shock played a fundamental role in the genesis of the LA debt crisis. The rise in the international interest rate not only had a direct financial impact, but also other indirect negative effects caused by world recession and a fall in the terms of trade. (In the case of Brazil, a highly dependent oil importer at the time, higher import prices added to the effects of the 1979 second oil shock.)

Secondly, the crisis encompassed the entire region. In the highly liquid and low interest rate context of the 1970s, many economies had major current account deficits and accumulated important debts. At one end of the spectrum of institutional and policy regimes were the Argentine and Chilean liberalization and opening packages. At the other was the indebtedness policy of Brazil's plan for deepening import-substituting industrialization (or ISI), whereby capital flows were mediated and administrated by the government. Mexico lay somewhere between these two ends, with a combination of programmed policy indebtedness and market effects. The crisis involved all of the highly indebted economies and others by contagion, such as Colombia. In the 1970s, this country had explicitly refused to join the newly developed international financial market by changing its policy regime and had reduced its external debt/GDP ratio by a half.

Taking into account this diversity, one way of evaluating Argentina's and Chile's liberalization policies is to compare their performances with those of the countries that reached the crisis with other policy settings. Were the real effects less important in the Southern Cone? Did market-cushioning mechanisms operate as had been foreseen to limit the extent of the crisis and to reduce its social cost?

About the real effects, Chile experienced the deepest recession in the region and Argentina's contraction can be counted among the largest. In the first half of the 1980s, GDP in both countries contracted more than Mexico's and Brazil's and more than the regional average. In Chile, the adjustment fell mainly on jobs as unemployment rates reached 30%. In Argentina, the adjustment took place principally through a drastic fall in real wages, and a sustained three-digit inflation ensued. The extension, depth, and social costs of the Southern Cone's financial crises also surpassed the relative importance they attained in the other countries facing a negative external shock.[6] Market stabilizing mechanisms—i.e., price and interest rate flexibility and real resources allocation and portfolio flexibility—either did not work as had been foreseen or gave rise to perverse effects such as the deepening of the crisis due to a rise in domestic interest rates. Be it for the greater relative importance of capital flight (Argentina), for worse previous external debt indicators (Chile), for higher financial fragility (both countries), or for fewer available policy instruments (both countries), the Chilean and Argentine policy regimes showed low ability to defend themselves against the

---

6. In Argentina, the fiscal direct cost of the post-crisis bailout is estimated at $5 billion. (At that time, the private external debt was $14 billion.) In Chile, the issue of public domestic debt to finance the bailout amounted to one-third of GDP. See Mario Damill, Jose Maria Fanelli, and Roberto Frenkel (1994).

volatility of international financial markets. An intercountry comparison does not favor financial liberalization.

An alternative way to evaluate the policy packages is to analyze the macro-economic dynamics they generated while attempting to weigh the significance of the jump in the international interest rate. Was growth on a sustainable path prior to the external shock, or did local macroeconomic dynamics already show signs of instability? One important fact is that both countries' domestic financial crises preceded their external crises and devaluations by over one year. In Argentina, the collapse of the exchange rate regime occurred one-and-a-half years before the Mexican crisis.

In fact, both countries show strong evidence of an endogenous cycle with a turning point and contraction phase that emerged independently of the evolution of the international interest rate. It was jointly driven by domestic financial developments and the evolution of the balance of payments. Cross effects were positive in the first phase and negative in the second. The cycle affected the real economy mainly through financial linkages: the evolution of credit, asset holders' portfolio decisions, and the financial situation of firms. Its evolution can clearly be seen in the current account, the level of international reserves, and the domestic interest rate. The stylized facts go as follows:[7]

The opening of both the trade and capital accounts was accompanied by the predetermination of the nominal exchange rate. From that moment on, there was persistent exchange rate appreciation. The inflation rate tended to fall but was systematically higher than the sum of the programmed rate of devaluation plus the international rate of inflation.

The launching of the package was followed by an injection of funds from abroad. The monetary base, bank deposits, and credit grew swiftly, as did the number of financial intermediaries. There was rapid appreciation of domestic financial and real asset prices. Domestic demand, production, and imports tended to expand. The increment in imports caused by trade opening, exchange rate appreciation, and expansion in domestic demand steadily widened the trade deficit. Likewise, the current account deficit showed a gradual increase because the external debt was initially small. Initially, capital flows were higher than the current account deficit, and reserves accumulated. Its increment led to the domestic money expansion mentioned above.

The evolution of the external accounts and reserves marked one aspect of the cycle. There was a continuous but gradual increase in the current account deficit, while capital inflows could shift abruptly. At a certain moment, the deficit surpassed the level of inflows. Reserves reached a maximum and then contracted, inducing monetary contraction overall. However, the cycle was not exclusively determined by this mechanical element: the size of capital flows was not an exogenous datum. Portfolio decisions regarding assets denominated in

---

7. We presented a formal model in Frenkel (1983). It is sketched in Williamson (1983) and restated by Taylor (1991).

domestic currency and dollars were not independent of the evolution of the balance of payments and finance. Both played a crucial role in the process.[8]

The domestic interest rate was a clear indicator of the financial aspects of the cycle. It fell in the first phase and then turned upward after a certain point. Because the exchange-rate rule initially enjoyed high credibility, arbitrage between domestic and external financial assets and credit led at the beginning to reductions in the domestic interest rate and the expected cost of external credit. The latter became negative in both countries. The real domestic bank-lending rate became negative in Argentina and fell dramatically in Chile (to one-fourth its previous value). Lower interest rates helped spur real and financial expansion. However, financial fragility in the sense of Hyman Minsky (1986) increased significantly.

In the second phase, rising domestic interest rates and episodes of illiquidity and insolvency appeared, first as isolated cases and then as a systemic crisis. What explained the increase in nominal and real interest rates? The nominal domestic interest rate can be expressed as the sum of the international interest rate, the programmed exchange-rate devaluation rate, and a residual accounting for exchange rate and financial risks. This was the main variable explaining the increase in the interest rate. On the one hand, financial risk rose in conjunction with financial fragility. But, more importantly, the increase in the risk premium was associated with the evolution of the external sector. The persistent increment in the current account deficit—and at some point the fall in reserves—reduced the credibility of the exchange rate rule. Higher interest rates were needed to equilibrate portfolios and attract foreign capital. In turn, illiquidity and insolvency spread a la Minsky, threatening a systemic crisis. Episodes of bankruptcies in banks and firms further contributed to reducing the credibility of the exchange rate rule. This dynamics proved to be explosive in both Argentina and Chile. At the end of the process, no interest rate was high enough to sustain the demand for domestic assets. There were runs on Central Bank reserves, leading finally to the collapse of the exchange rate regime. The resulting devaluations further deepened the financial crisis.

This analysis highlights the relatively minor role of the international interest rate in the domestic financial developments, at least directly. Its increase in the late 1970s surely contributed to a more rapid deterioration of the current account, but this seems to have been its principal impact on the domestic cycle. As pointed out

---

8. Neoclassical models based on different "adjustment speeds" of the trade and capital accounts following a simultaneous trade and financial opening were constructed to interpret the cycle. These models replicated the initial expansionary phase but neither the contractionary one nor the crisis. The symmetry of neoclassical models suggested a second phase in which downward price flexibility could correct exchange-rate appreciation and the current account deficit, leading the economy to a new equilibrium. There was no such deflation in the cases we are considering here. In addition to the complete implausibility of a deflation of the size and velocity that would be necessary to re-equilibrate the current account, these models ignored financial relations. In the financial system, there is no symmetry between the expansionary and contractionary phases. In any case, the supposed deflation would aggravate the liquidity and insolvency problems that characterize the contractionary phase.

earlier, the exchange rate and financial risk premium were the main contributors to the upward trend in domestic interest rates in the second phase.

We should also mention that neither the fiscal deficit nor the existence of public guarantees on bank deposits played significant roles. Both were present in Argentina, but Chile had a fiscal surplus and deposit guarantees had been eliminated with the explicit purpose of making the working of the financial system more efficient and less risky. The more important destabilizing factors were the rudimentary nature of the financial system and weaknesses in banking supervision norms and practices. Those are generic features of liberalization and opening processes in Latin America. If financial opening packages had been postponed until the systems were robust, diversified, and well monitored, then none of them would have been implemented, either in the 1970s or the 1990s.[9]

THE EXPERIENCES OF THE 1990S

In this section, we do not enjoy 100% hindsight. LA experiences in the 1990s are not far-off closed cases, but rather current history. However, enough time has passed for some features to be discerned. With respect to sustainability, in particular, the Mexican and Argentine 1994–95 crises mark a watershed and delimit a period—the early 1990s—which can be analyzed as a fait accompli. In the first part of this section, we examine macroeconomic performance early in the decade, contrasting Mexico's and Argentina's stylized facts with those of other economies in the region whose dynamics proved to be more stable. We then turn to employment and the income distribution, which have been more adversely affected than macroeconomic sustainability per se.

Sustainability problems[10]

The region's macroeconomic performance in the early 1990s

Stabilization efforts in the 1980s confronted the impossible task of reconciling external debt-service obligations with the preservation of basic macroeconomic balances—both external and fiscal. Destabilizing shocks from these two sources were the main sources of recurring instability. This situation reversed in the 1990s. Almost every country closed its fiscal and external gaps.

---

9. Liberalizing and opening capital markets only after the economy is stabilized, open to trade, and financially robust is precisely the recommendation of the "sequencing" literature, developed in the 1980s after the evaluation of the Southern Cone experiments, among other cases. These orthodox prescriptions were lost along the roads to the Washington Consensus as actually applied.

10. The following discussion draws on Roberto Frenkel (1995).

This important difference underlay the lower inflation rates and higher rates of growth observed region-wide. Changing international financial conditions and their impact on the evolution of the external sector are the main causes of the improvement.

With the relaxation of the external constraint, macroeconomic performance improved because most of the mechanisms feeding instability could be deactivated. Firstly, the availability of external resources allowed domestic absorption and activity to expand. Capital inflows were of such a magnitude that many countries experienced an excess supply of foreign currency, despite the rapid growth of imports. There was generalized reserve accumulation and exchange rate appreciation.

Higher economic activity and exchange rate appreciation favored stability. The latter contributed significantly to the reduction in inflation and improvement in the fiscal accounts by diminishing the real value of interest payments on external debt. At the same time, tax receipts improved with the rise of activity and sales. Lower inflation rates also helped raise tax collection, directly by increasing the real value of taxes and indirectly by easing the implementation of tax and administrative reforms. Additionally, fiscal equilibrium was facilitated in some countries through the implementation of massive privatization schemes, partly financed with foreign capital.

The Mexican crisis and its repercussions

Until mid-1994, Brazil was the main and important exception to these regional trends. The Real Plan stabilization program, launched in July 1994, then put the economy in line with the rest of the larger countries, with respect to inflation, the balance of payments, and appreciation of the exchange rate.

Paradoxically, only a few months after the Brazilian economy was synchronized with its neighbors, Mexico and Argentina were hit by external and financial crises and confronted another round of adjustments. Official and multilateral support to both countries in 1995 prevented default on external payments and the reemergence of a scenario like that in 1982. In contrast to that experience, financial markets rapidly reopened for Latin America.

Mexico had been at the forefront of the region's stabilization and structural reform processes. It led international investors' expectations about Latin America as a whole. Its evolution in the early 1990s was assessed as a stable development process, with increasing international trade and financial integration, particularly with the United States. Mexico was placed in the vanguard for similar changes elsewhere in LA. The Mexican crisis abruptly changed perceptions by showing that the good performance of the 1990s was not immune to a resurgence of instability. In this sense, the crisis marked a watershed for the region as a whole. It ended a period whose beginning can be situated in 1990, when Mexico signed the first Brady agreement.

Both the Mexican and the Argentine crises, triggered by the Tequila Effect, suggest we explore the region's sustainability problems in the early 1990s by comparing these two cases—with proven difficulties—with other countries which demonstrated more robust performances.

Capital flows, the exchange-rate appreciation and the external fragility

In 1991–93, net inflows of financial resources into the region amounted to about $166 billion, while current account deficits added up to $98 billion. In every country, net capital inflows were higher than current account gap, giving rise to the accumulation of reserves. Of total inflows, $75 billion went to Mexico, $29 billion to Argentina, $20 billion to Brazil, and $8 billion to Chile. These four countries received 80% of the total regional inflow in 1991–93, and Mexico alone absorbed about 45%. Outside these countries, capital inflows were also significant in Peru and Venezuela.

Exchange-rate appreciation was universal, but its magnitude differed across countries. Mexico and Argentina experienced the greatest appreciation in comparison with the real exchange rate prevailing in the second half of the 1980s. In 1994, Chile and Colombia were at the other end of the spectrum. The degree of relative appreciation was determined by the level of the exchange rate at the beginning of the 1990s and its subsequent dynamics. In Mexico, where the stabilization program dated from late 1987, a significant appreciation had taken place in 1988. The process persisted at a slower pace until 1990 and accelerated from 1991. In Argentina, the exchange rate experienced an important appreciation in 1990 and was nominally fixed at that already appreciated real level in 1991. Further appreciation continued into the early 1990s. In contrast, Chile and Colombia entered the 1990s with relatively depreciated exchange rates. Chile's subsequent rate of appreciation was lower than in the rest of the countries. In Colombia, the process accelerated in 1994. Brazil maintained a depreciated exchange rate until 1993. The exchange rate appreciated strongly after the Real Plan was launched, most intensively in the first year.

The different evolution of exchange rates was associated with the macroeconomic policies each country followed. Mexico and Argentina implemented stabilization policies in which a fixed nominal exchange rate was a crucial ingredient, fully deregulated their capital accounts, and adopted a passive attitude vis-à-vis capital inflows. On the other hand, Colombia, Chile, and Brazil (until 1994) included real exchange rate targets in their exchange rate, fiscal, and monetary policies.[11] Chile and Colombia adopted crawling-band exchange rate regimes, regulations on capital inflows by imposing differential taxes according to types of flows—which required the maintenance of some control over the foreign exchange market—and implemented sterilization policies. These packages did not always completely fulfil their objectives, but did lead to less fragile performances.[12]

---

11. Some capital flow regulations were implemented in Brazil after the launching of the Real Plan according to the changing circumstances of capital flows. However, the set of exchange, monetary, and capital account policies resembles those of Argentina and Mexico more than it resembles those of Chile and Colombia.

The region's trade deficit showed an increasing trend, reaching $15 billion in 1993. However, this total is biased by Brazil. During 1991–94, Brazil accumulated a $50 billion trade surplus, despite the jump in imports induced by the Real Plan in 1994. By contrast, Mexico's trade deficit was $63 billion in 1991–93. The Argentine deficit was $8 billion. In both cases, the deficit resulted from rapid growth of imports. This trend persisted in 1994, when the deficit of the two countries totalled $29 billion. Imports also grew fast in Colombia, where the trade balance passed from a $2.3 billion surplus in 1991 to a $2.1 billion deficit in 1994. In Chile, the trade account was in surplus in the early 1990s, except for 1993.

The region's annual growth rate in imports went from 10.3% in the second half of the 1980s to 16.1% in the 1990s, while the rate of growth of exports declined (except in Brazil). In Mexico, growth of imports had already tripled that of exports in the second half of the 1980s and this ratio persisted into the 1990s. In Argentina, exports increased by 5.5% per year in 1991–94, while imports grew by 55.6% per year in the same period.

Overall, the Current Account Deficit/Exports ratio (CAD/X) for Latin America was 27.5% in 1993 and slightly lower in 1994. This regional average is biased by the more favorable results of Brazil's external sector, where the current account was practically in equilibrium. With this in mind, the regional average indicator of external fragility can be used as a standard for the comparison of the national cases.

It is interesting to underline the situation in 1993 because it constitutes the most immediate antecedent to the changes that took place in 1994 and which we describe below. In 1993, the order of the external fragility indicators showed a clear pattern. Chile and Colombia had ratios lower than the regional average, while Mexico and Argentina doubled it. The external debt/exports ratio exhibited a similar pattern, although Brazil's high relative external indebtedness pushed its level close to that of Mexico and Argentina. In 1994, Colombia's CAD/X ratio rose slightly—but remained lower than the regional average—and the ratio fell in Chile. Meanwhile, the ratios worsened in Mexico and Argentina, increasing by 20% with respect to 1993.

The turning point in 1994

At the end of 1993, Mexico and Argentina were the economies with the most unfavorable indicators of external fragility in the region. Difficulties in

---

12. Mexico and Argentina, on the one hand, and Chile and Colombia, on the other, entered the 1990s with different economic realities and varying degrees of freedom to define their policies. Chile and Colombia had stabilized their economies in the mid-1980s and were growing at relatively high rates in the second half of the decade. It is understandable that their macroeconomic policies were oriented in the direction of preserving stability in the face of capital inflows. In contrast, Mexico had only recently implemented its stabilization program, while Argentina began in 1991. Both programs used a fixed exchange rate as the main "anchor" for inflation. Their sustainability depended fundamentally on continuing capital inflows.

sustaining the macroeconomic performance of the early 1990s were foreseen. The dynamics resembled the initial phases of the Southern Cone experiences analyzed in the previous section; a turning point with a subsequent contraction was to be expected. Signs of such a change emerged in 1994, well before Mexico's December devaluation. One indicator was a shift in the trend in the international reserves in Mexico and Argentina. The inflection in the trend was associated with adjustments in international financial conditions.

It was triggered in February 1994, when the U.S. Federal Reserve began to raise the federal funds rate. Following the Fed's decision, long-term bond prices fell and the long-term interest rate increased, together with the short-term rates. Both movements had a more than proportional impact on LA bond prices and the interest rates that countries faced. Along with the increment in interest rates, there was an increase in the region's country-risk premiums. They rose significantly more for Mexico and Argentina than other countries, in line with their relative levels of external fragility. The relative performance of financial assets is symptomatic: important drops had been observed in the cases of Argentina and Mexico early in 1994, a slightly smaller decline occurred for Brazil, and prices stabilized for Chilean assets.

How can this rise in the country-risk premium be explained? A plausible hypothesis is that international investors perceived an increase in external fragility as a result of the impact of the higher interest rate that the debtors had to confront. But, by reducing their exposure to higher risk—i.e., demanding higher compensation for the risk—financial market players accentuate the unfavorable impact of an international interest rate as a self-fulfilling prophesy. The signal provided by the change in the federal funds-rate policy of the Federal Reserve set off a reaction similar to the one that would later coordinate the Mexican devaluation. In this sense, the Mexican and Argentine crises did not erupt suddenly, but were the last episodes in a period of increasing financial tension.

Together with the increase in country-risk premiums came a decline in capital flows to Argentina and Mexico, which significantly modified the trend in the regional aggregate. In 1994, total inflows amounted to $47 billion, compared to an annual average of $55 billion in 1991–93 and a maximum of $70 billion in 1993. The reduction was fully explained by the two countries, and particularly by Mexico, whose capital inflows dropped from $30 billion in 1993 to $10 billion in 1994. In contrast, Brazil and Colombia's capital inflows augmented in 1994, and the rest of the region's were similar to the preceding year.

The fall in capital inflows in Mexico and Argentina was concomitant with an increase in the current account deficit in both cases. In 1993, the deficits had amounted to $23.5 billion in Mexico and $7.5 billion in Argentina. They grew to $30.6 billion and $11.1 billion in 1994, respectively. As the joint outcome of lower capital inflows and higher current account deficits, both countries recorded reductions in their reserves in 1994 for the first time in the 1990s. In Argentina, because of its currency board regime, falling reserves induced contractionary monetary effects before the tequila effect triggered the crisis.

The Tequila Effect

The initial turbulence generated by the Mexican devaluation affected Latin America and other more distant markets for some time. But after a relatively brief period, the economies of Chile and Colombia did not register further perturbations. In the case of Brazil, the abrupt balance-of-payments effects of the Real Plan had already placed the economy in a fragile external position and in the first half of 1995 the country had capital outflows. Nevertheless, Brazil countered with abundant reserves, and the turbulence only brought about a deceleration in growth.

In contrast, the Tequila Effect hit Argentina with full force. The contagion effect in this episode appears to be a continuation of the common trends mentioned above and was associated with the similarities of the Mexican and Argentine macroeconomic situations. In Argentina, the Mexican crisis triggered a financial crisis and a strong outflow of private capital in the first half of 1995—partially compensated for, as in Mexico, by the increase in the public external debt. Both economies experienced deep recessions. In 1995, GDP contracted by 6.6% in Mexico and by 4.6% in Argentina. Both countries' 1995 unemployment rates doubled those of 1993.

Synthesis and conclusions

Latin American macroeconomic experience in the 1990s was similar in many ways to that of the 1970s. The combined effects of liberalization and opening of financial markets, massive capital inflows, trade opening, and exchange-rate appreciation generated growing external and financial fragility. Economies became prone to perverse financial cycles and vulnerable to changes in international conditions. The similarity with the experience of the 1970s is closest in the cases of Mexico and Argentina. They showed strong parallelism between the real, financial, and external developments of the 1991–94 period and the initial expansionary phase of the Southern Cone experiments. It was particularly associated with the role played by exchange-rate policy and capital inflows in the design of the macroeconomic scheme and the goal of achieving full integration with international financial markets. Capital inflows were encouraged through various means (including complete deregulation) but policy was predominantly passive with respect to their domestic monetary and financial effects.

In the Southern Cone experiences, the turning point was reached in a relatively short time via domestic financial developments. For this reason, the real dimension of the cycle was mainly a reflection of the financial cycle. The expansionary phase of the financial cycle lasted longer in the Mexican and Argentine experiences in the 1990s, giving rise to deeper real effects of the combination of trade opening and exchange-rate appreciation.[13] We will discuss this point in the following section.

---

13. Emerging out of a very deep recession in 1990, Argentina's GDP grew swiftly in the early 1990s. Instead, Mexico's slow growth suggests that depressing real effects were important from the beginning of the 1990s. We have already mentioned that trade opening and exchange-rate appreciation were operating in this case for some years beforehand. See Jose Maria Fanelli and Roberto Frenkel (1998) on Argentina and Rudiger Dornbusch and Alejandro Werner (1994) on Mexico.

The analysis we presented above highlights the 1994 increment in the international interest rate as the external factor which triggered the change of trends in capital inflows and reserves observed that year in Mexico and Argentina. Obviously, this increment is not comparable in magnitude and duration to the 1979 increase. Besides, its incidence on external fragility took a different form because of the distinct external financing mechanisms that predominated in the 1970s and the 1990s. Floating-rate bank credit predominated in the 1970s, so that the increase in the international interest rate affected external fragility mainly by raising the current account deficit. In Mexico and Argentina in the 1990s, debt in bonds predominated and the increase in the international rate affected external fragility by reducing capital inflows and augmenting the country-risk premium. In the 1970s, the current account was more sensitive to variations in the international interest rate. In the 1990s, the current account was less sensitive, but financial flows were more volatile.

Lastly, let us consider the comparison between Mexico and Argentina and the countries showing paths that are more robust. It is clear that the different performances could not be exclusively explained by the elements examined in this paper. With this caveat in mind, the above analysis suggests two types of factors differentiating the countries' performances.

First, differences in macroeconomic policy stand out, particularly with regard to the exchange rate. Greater fragility is associated with more exchange-rate appreciation and this, in turn, with the different exchange-rate regimes and monetary policies the countries adopted. The other important difference lies in the conception that ruled the interaction between the domestic financial system and the international capital markets. Both aspects appear to be associated, so that policies relating to the capital account are congruent with a country's macroeconomic orientation. Mexico and Argentina implemented an unrestricted opening of the capital account. In contrast, the countries that attempted to preserve some monetary and financial autonomy implemented regulatory norms aimed at cushioning the capital flows and influencing their composition. As we have seen, these orientations were not always entirely successful in their objectives, but they did result in a better relative performance.

Employment and income distribution

There have been widespread negative effects on employment and the income distribution in LA in the 1990s. The stylized facts linking macroeconomic and distributional developments are the following:

- There was a recovery of growth as GDP growth rates improved significantly.
- There was a reduction in inflation. In the high inflation countries (Argentina, Brazil, Mexico, and Peru), the new conditions made successful stabilization plans possible. In the moderate inflation countries (Colombia, Chile, and Uruguay), a gradual reduction in inflation took place.
- International trade was liberalized. All countries either implemented or

completed trade policy reforms aimed at reducing tariffs and eliminating non-tariff restrictions on imports.

• Public-sector deficits were reduced. The public sector deficit dropped due to lower inflation and higher activity, in part, from administrative and tax reforms and, in part, from adjustment of public expenditures.

• Important privatization programs were implemented, in terms of both the magnitude of the resources and the volume of employment involved.

• There was a significant appreciation of real exchange rates in comparison with levels prevailing in the second half of the 1980s.

• High trade deficits arose because of the strong increment in imports, implying a marked increase in the share of domestic demand covered by imports.

These stylized facts cannot be exclusively attributed either to the changes in the international financial conditions and capital inflows, or the policies implemented by the countries in this new context. They were the result of a combination of these factors and had significant effects—some positive, others negative—on the labor market, employment, income distribution, and poverty.

Positive effects can undoubtedly be attributed to higher levels of activity and the reduction in inflation. Higher activity implied greater demand for labor. The reduction in inflation had positive effects on the purchasing power of wages and reduced the "inflation tax," which falls mainly on the lowest-income sectors. Those positive effects were particularly important in the exchange-rate anchored "shock" stabilizations, where the launching of the program was followed by a strong recovery in demand and activity, a rise in labor demand, and an improvement in the purchasing power of low-income sectors. Similar but weaker benefits were observed elsewhere.

Other effects have negative impacts. Privatizations of state enterprises were usually preceded or followed by rationalization processes and thus with a plunge in the employment level. Analogous effects followed expenditure adjustments at various levels of the public sector, because they generally imply contractions in employment and wages. These effects on employment and wages were "once-and-for-all." Their relative importance differed across countries. Although they did not have a significant global impact in some cases, they were important in specific regions or segments of the labor market.

Lastly, there were the joint repercussions of trade opening and exchange rate appreciation. This combination had persistent negative effects on employment in the traded goods sector, particularly in manufacturing.

By increasing competition in the domestic market exerted by imported goods and by easing domestic firms' access to cheaper and better quality inputs and capital goods, the decrease in tariffs and elimination of non-tariff restrictions were aimed at increasing the efficiency and productivity of the tradable sector. Trade opening thereby implied the displacement of firms and employment in the less efficient areas of the tradable sector. In the simplest version of the theory on which the policy is based, the simultaneous creation of new employment in activities gaining competitiveness through increases in productivity should compensate for those negative effects. More complex versions admit a somewhat extended period of falling employment and negative redistributional effects, which can and should be alleviated by public policies. Beyond those assertions, the fact is that trade opening took place in Latin America in the 1990s together with the appreciation of the exchange rates.[14] This combination worsened the loss in competitiveness of existing activities and inhibited incentives for new export or import substituting ventures, thereby accentuating negative effects on employment.

All of the above-mentioned effects, both positive and negative, were observed in all countries in the region. From their relative intensity resulted the signs and magnitudes of aggregate effects. The evolution of employment and income distribution over time also depends on the different velocities of the processes involved. One highly relevant case, because of the importance of the countries involved—notably Argentina, Brazil and Mexico—rested on the dynamics generated by exchange-rate anchored stabilizations, in contexts that simultaneously involved trade opening, privatization, and fiscal adjustment. Typically, a cycle in employment and low-income-sector earnings emerged. There was an initial upward trend in which the positive effects of reactivation and the reduction in inflation predominated. A downward phase followed in which the initial effects tended to attenuate and the negative effects predominate, particularly the persistent results of the combination of trade opening and exchange-rate appreciation.

We can illustrate those circumstances with Argentine data on employment. The employment rate (employment/population) tended to grow between 1991 and 1993, and then to fall systematically until its 1996 level reached a figure that was well below the 1990 observation. It should be stressed that in 1993, when the employment rate began to drop, Argentina was still undergoing an output expansion. The contraction in employment particularly affected males, heads of household, and full-time jobholders. Two-thirds of the contraction corresponded to the manufacturing sector. Although privatization and fiscal adjustment in the provinces had adverse effects on employment, the most important negative impact came from the restructuring and concentration in activities producing tradable goods.[15] Similar outcomes were also observed in Brazil and Mexico.[16]

The combined effects of trade opening and exchange-rate appreciation

This issue deserves a more detailed analysis. The behavior of labor demand in manufacturing can be disaggregated into three components. In the first place, a positive component originates in the increase in aggregate demand. The higher the increase in demand, the larger is the effect on manufacturing production and

---

14. These circumstances contradicted conventional recommendations about the macroeconomic policy that should accompany trade opening.

15. Cf. Roberto Frenkel and Martín Gonzalez Rozada (1997).

16. Cf. Mario Damill, Jose Fanelli, and Roberto Frenkel (1996) and Edward Amadeo (1996).

employment. In the second place, given the increase in aggregate demand, there is a negative effect on production and employment derived from the degree of penetration of imports serving this demand. The higher the share of aggregate demand covered by imports, the lower is the domestic production and employment. In the third place, the need to gain competitiveness, on the one hand, and the change in relative prices favoring imported inputs and machinery, on the other, can lead firms to reduce employment per unit of production. This increase in the productivity of the labor force results from changes in product composition (for instance, lower product diversity, and greater imported input components), efficiency gains through restructuring, and substitution of machines for the labor force.

As was already mentioned, the observed outcome of those processes has generally been a contractionary trend in manufacturing employment. That is, the increase in the aggregate demand for manufacturing goods—even in its expansionary phase—was not sufficient to compensate for the negative components: the direct displacement of domestic production by imports and the process of labor reduction per unit of production in the surviving firms. It should be mentioned that small- and medium-sized enterprises (SMEs) found it the most difficult to remain open. The closing of SMEs was an important cause of the contraction in employment.

How does exchange-rate appreciation affect each of these components? With regard to growth of aggregate demand, a stronger exchange rate operates as a constraining factor, directly by inhibiting exports and indirectly by limiting the growth in domestic demand. External and current account balances register deficits and a high import elasticity is observed. External fragility tends to deepen when the economy accelerates its expansion. In 1995, Mexico and Argentina were examples of sudden cuts in growth imposed by their crises. Brazil was forced to make contractionary adjustments in 1995 and late 1997. In early 1998, Argentina again confronted the issue of forcing output reduction to improve its external accounts (explicitly suggested by the IMF). External fragility associated with an appreciated exchange rate clearly operates as a constraint on the potential rate of growth.

The role of the exchange-rate appreciation is also clear via the second channel mentioned above. It amplifies the effects of the trade opening by further reducing the competitiveness of local activities. Consequently, given the aggregate demand level, it tends to increase the direct displacement effects of domestic production and employment by imports. It inhibits manufacturing activities for exports and the domestic market which, even in an open trade setting, would be competitive with a more depreciated exchange rate.

Lastly, the negative effect of exchange-rate appreciation is also significant for the process of labor reduction per unit of output that takes place within firms. A strong exchange rate enhances incentives to reduce the labor force because it additionally lowers the relative price of imported inputs and machines with respect to labor costs.

The macroeconomic configuration and trends in employment and income distribution

The macroeconomic configuration underlying the combination of trade opening and exchange rate appreciation can be synthesized in three characteristics: fragility of growth, high unemployment, and a trend toward increasing inequality. External fragility creates difficulty in sustaining high rates of growth. Behind external fragility and unemployment lies the low international competitiveness of domestic activities. Overall, competitiveness did not improve in the 1990s despite important gains observed in labor force productivity because relative price changes neutralized their effects.[17] The third characteristic was mainly a consequence of the first two. High unemployment and the pressure it exerted on wages generated a persistent trend toward higher inequality.

THE DIAGNOSIS AND THE PROPOSED REMEDIES

The accumulated experience of the 1990s appears to be driving economists from differing schools of thought to agree on the diagnosis sketched above. The most negative features regarding competitiveness, employment, and income distribution, as well as the most severe sustainability problems are associated with policy regimes that lose sight of the real targets of macroeconomic policy and open the capital accounts without any restrictions.

Despite a greater consensus about the diagnosis, in Latin America there is a marked cleavage regarding the orientation of policies that might reverse these negative features. Instead of pragmatically revising the macroeconomic scheme and the conditions of financial opening, the dominant view attributes the problems to a supposed incompleteness of liberalizing reforms. It uses this (essentially Utopian) line of reasoning to explain why the economy does not behave as the theories behind the already implemented reforms predicted it would. In a permanent escape into the future, this orientation recommends further reform in the face of any difficulty arising in economic performance. So, a "second generation" succeeds the first, and future generations can surely be expected.

With regard to competitiveness and employment problems, in particular, this orientation seems to believe that the remedies are embodied in the very development of present trends. The pressure unemployment exerts on wages should lead to a reduction of labor costs and, through this mechanism, to the simultaneous "solution" of the fragility, competitiveness, and employment problems. This orientation sees the most important obstacle as being the institutional rigidity of the labor market and advocates "flexibilization" as the main policy instrument to resolve employment problems.

---

17. Calculations with a common methodology for various countries can be seen in Víctor Tokman and Daniel Martínez (1997).

Faced with this issue, an academic comment might be that there seems to be no successful cases involving this kind of model in the development experience. Losses of competitiveness associated with financial opening and massive capital inflows have *not* been offset by reductions of real wages. Even if processes of this kind were viable, they would surely be long and painful stories. We believe, nevertheless, that the main criticism of the mainstream orientation is not derived from an analytical point of view but from a normative one, since the "solution" implies promoting a social structure that is even more unequal and unfair than the one we currently find in Latin America.

This opinion should not be interpreted as a defense of existing labor legislation —which in many countries is obviously obsolete and inefficient—but rather as a criticism of the prevailing idea that the "cause" of employment performance is located in the rigidity of labor market institutions and that, consequently, flexibilization is the most important policy orientation in this regard, if not the only one.

Perhaps the cleavage over policy recommendations can be better understood if we express it in more technical terms. As such, it becomes clear that its deep roots date back to the origin of macroeconomics as a discipline. It is worth remembering that the discipline was born with Keynes' analysis of the causes and remedies of the Great Depression's unemployment. Also, that the unemployment diagnosis was at the center of the debate Keynes sustained with his contemporaries.

The orientation we are criticizing asserts that there is only one equilibrium price configuration in every economy, which includes full employment (or better, unemployment at its natural rate) in the labor market. When high rates of unemployment or employment generation problems are observed, these problems must be attributed to imperfections in the labor market. That is, institutional obstacles inhibit the working of competition in this market, preventing the price of labor from falling to the point at which the unemployment rate equals the natural rate. This diagnosis, which is implicit most of the time, can be submitted to a test by the following question.

Consider the economic situation in Latin America at two points in time: the second half of the 1980s and first half of the 1990s. In the first, the international interest rate was high; economies were financially rationed and made significant transfers abroad; absorption was lower than output; production was stagnant and productivity decreased. In the second period, the international interest rate was lower; economies had access to international financial markets and received transfers from abroad; absorption was greater than output; production was growing and productivity went up. There seems to be no doubt that there was a positive shock between the first and second points. Why then should real wages have to fall to preserve equilibrium conditions in the labor market? Certainly, there is no reason for that. Nevertheless, employment in the second period was lower than in the first.

The paradox we reach from the idea of a unique equilibrium configuration highlights the inadequacy of this perspective. The alternative means considering the possibility of multiple equilibrium configurations depending, among other circumstances, on the factors imposed by the external context and economic policies as actually implemented. Some configurations are more favorable to employment and growth. Others imply that the economy is being driven to low-growth and low-employment traps. The observed changes between the 1980s and the 1990s do not appear to be paradoxical from this perspective. The conjunction of massive capital inflows and the implementation of the liberalization and open policies drove some LA economies to low-growth and low-employment macroeconomic configurations.

The art of economic policy making does not consist in merely discovering the equilibrium point and promoting all the deregulation needed for market forces to conduct the economy spontaneously there. The art consists in managing economic policy in an international context that is more influential and volatile than ever before to induce relative prices and incentives that favor growth, employment, and a rise in real wages to accompany improvements in productivity. These configurations do not depend on only one instrument, but on the persistent implementation of every policy instrument focusing on these real targets.

REFERENCES

Amadeo, Edward. 1996. "The Knife-Edge of Exchange-Rate-Based Stabilisation: Impact on Growth, Employment and Wages." *UNCTAD Review*. Geneva.

Damill, Mario, José María Fanelli and Roberto Frenkel. 1994. *Shock Externo y Desequilibrio Fiscal: La Macroeconomía de América Latina en los Ochenta*, CEPAL. Santiago de Chile.

_____. 1996. "De México a México: el desempeño de América Latina en los noventa." *Desarrollo Económico*, número especial, vol. 36. Buenos Aires, verano.

Dornbusch, Rudiger and Alejandro Werner. 1994. "Mexico: Stabilisation, Reform and No Growth," *Brookings Papers on Economic Activity*, I.

Fanelli, José María, and Roberto Frenkel. 1998. "The Argentine Experience with Stabilization and Structural Reform," in Lance Taylor, ed., . . . , Michigan University Press.

Frenkel, Roberto. 1983. "Mercado Financiero, Expectativas Cambiarias y Movimientos de Capital," *El Trimestre Económico*, No. 200. Mexico.

_____. 1995. "Macroeconomic Sustainability and Development Prospects: Latin American Performance in the 1990s." *UNCTAD Discussion Papers*, No. 100. Geneva, August.

Frenkel, Roberto and Martín González Rozada, "Apertura, productividad y empleo. Argentina en los años noventa." CEDES, mimeo, Buenos Aires, 1997.

Minsky, Hyman P. 1986. *Stabilising an Unstable Economy*. Yale University Press, New Haven, Conn.

Taylor, Lance. 1991. *Income Distribution, Inflation and Growth*. MIT Press, Cambridge, Mass.

Tokman, Víctor, and Daniel Martínez. 1997. "Costo laboral y competitividad en el sector manufacturero de América Latina," in Edward Amadeo et al., *Costos laborales y competitividad industrial en América Latina*. OIT, Peru.

Williamson, John. 1983. *The Open Economy and the World Economy*. Basic Books, New York.

11

. . .

FX Short Positions, Balance Sheets, and Financial Turbulence
An Interpretation of the Asian Financial Crisis

Salih N. Neftci*

ONE OBVIOUS ASPECT of financial crises is the violence of movements observed in prices and valuations.

This is best seen in the record exchange rate movements observed during the years 1997–1998, where within one day the dollar-yen exchange rate exhibited a movement of 8%, in the absence of any major event. Another example is the ratings of sovereign credits.[1] For example, during the month of October 1997, South Korea was rated as AA- by S&P. Certainly a solid *investment grade* rating. After barely 6 months, South Korea's Rating had fallen 9 steps to B+. Such a steep, mass downgrading in such a short period of time was unprecedented, and completely unpredictable just a few months earlier.

This paper discusses a framework that may make the explanation of such dynamics easier. In the framework that we develop below, market participants start taking risky positions due to an initial mispricing. The positions weaken the balance sheet of the financial sector. This fragility then imposes constraints on the central bank's policies and makes sure that the mispricing is perceived as "long-term," which in turn leads to an increase of the risky positions.

---

*Paper presented at the conference on International Capital Markets and the Future of Economic Policy, Queen's College, Cambridge, April 15–16, 1998.

1. Using the criteria of S&P, these ratings are grouped under symbols such as AAA, AA, A, BBB, BB, B, and C. Agencies also distinguish between borrowers by attaching "+" or "-" signs to these letter grades. The ratings below BBB- are considered to be speculative grade, in contrast to being investment grade.

In a sense, we argue that many precarious-looking market conditions may turn into some sort of equilibrium that may last for years, making the balance sheet of the financial sector progressively worse and worse. Yet, given the right "circumstances," these worsening balance sheets may be interpreted by market participants as a short-term guarantee that the mispricing that is at the root cause of such risky positions will continue unchanged.

The discussion below will be conducted in terms of the Asian crisis of 1997. The mispricing under consideration will be exchange rate pegging. The risky positions will be represented by open FX positions of the banking sector. Yet, the discussion is general enough and any type of mispricing can potentially lead to the similar "equilibria" given the right circumstances.

Hence the paper will first develop the parameters and the conditions that are needed in order for such a dynamics to start taking place. In doing this we will use the environment of the Asian financial crisis, and base the examples on East Asian data.

Second, the paper will describe various stages of this process in more detail.

There is some recent research that deals with some of the issues that we discuss below in more formal models. Cavalleri and Corsetti (1997) and Corsenti, Pesenti and Roubini (1998) are two very good examples. A good background reading for the Asian crisis is Claessens and Glaessner (1997).

The paper is organized as follows. In the next section we briefly summarize various approaches to financial crises. Next, we develop the institutional parameters of the framework that we have in mind. In the following section we discuss the necessary conditions for such dynamics to take place. The third section will describe the process itself. The final section concludes.

SOME APPROACHES TO FINANCIAL CRISES

There are several explanations for financial crises. For a recent review, see Flood and Marion (1998). Briefly, these can be grouped as follows:

Speculative attack interpretation

Expansion of domestic credit eventually leads to a breakdown of a pegged exchange rate system. In heuristic terms, excessive money supply leads to an attack by speculators, who "bet" that the currency will collapse. This joint action leads to a steep devaluation; a crisis follows.

Credibility issues and the risks of pegged exchange rate models

The experiences of failed Latin American stabilization programs have complemented the speculative attack models with notions of policy credibility. One example is as follows.

At the time of their introduction, stabilization packages have to peg the exchange rate in order to lower inflationary expectations.

In a nutshell, the argument goes like this. In the midst of an inflationary period, the currency depreciates. Policy makers think that pegging the currency will convey the message that the government is now committed to lowering the inflation rate.

If the "reforms" and other stabilization measures are credible, players in financial markets will adjust their inflationary expectations downward. Yet, if the measures are not perceived as credible, or if the government is not sufficiently determined, inflation will not decrease very much, the peg becomes doubtful and leads to an overvalued currency. Agents react, leading to a collapse. Again, financial crisis follows.

Bank runs literature

These interpretations deal with the 19th and early 20th century Western banking crises. It is not clear at the outset if these are directly related to episodes such as the Asian Financial Crisis, yet careless or even negligent credit expansion was one of the main factors behind the bank runs. Also, during the bank runs one witnessed the existence of lax regulatory rules and overly optimistic assessment of economic conditions, parameters certainly not very foreign to the Asian markets of 1995–97.

It should also be emphasized that the late 19th and the early 20th centuries had also seen international capital flows that were in excess of the present case. Bank runs literature had emphasized the role of such factors as well.

In all these models, the existence of some "fixed or managed price" and "factors leading to the fragility of the banking system" play a prominent role. The *excessive* expansion of credit or of some other (capital) flow is also critical.

Most of these effects will be present in our discussion as well. However, we discuss these issues within the context of the Asian financial crisis.

Clearly, there are significant structural and financial differences among various economies in Asia, and this played a significant role in the dynamics of the crisis. Yet, the similarities in terms of some "fixed price" and the presence of heavy short term capital flows are well known.

In the case of the Asian financial crisis, the fixed prices in question were the exchange rates of Asian countries, all pegged one way or another to the U.S. dollar. The excessive valuation in question was real estate prices or was the factors that led to heavy real investment. Careless lending practices and to some extent careless use of financial derivatives also played a role. Non-transparent data reporting processes complicated things further.

The essential idea of this paper is that these conditions created what at the beginning was short term above normal profit opportunities for a banking sector that was operating in a badly-regulated environment. This led to balance sheet fragility. Once the system became fragile, it was too late to change the exchange rate pegging, since this would lead to the insolvency of the banking system.

A key argument of this paper is that the way these positions develop, and the way they make the concerned institutions "too big to fail" played an important role in episodes such as the Asian financial crisis. Financial derivatives, although essential for sound risk management and financial engineering, can nevertheless facilitate this process if used solely for the purposes of leverage.

Hence, in many ways the Asian financial crisis has aspects similar to those emphasized in the speculative attack literature and the models of bank runs. But there are some differences as well.

Below we first describe an environment where the discussion can proceed further.

THE ENVIRONMENT

The health of an institution should be visible from its balance sheet. Yet, in effect there is not one, but (at least) *two* balance sheets. The first is the visible one displaying the on-balance sheet items. The second is the one that incorporates the effect of the off-balance sheet items. We call this the "true" balance sheet.[2]

Asian countries had, and still have, financial systems where the environment is ripe for these two balance sheets to diverge significantly. And what is more important, this divergence is non-transparent.

What are some of the major characteristics of such environments which are believed to have played an important role in the Asian financial crisis? We begin by describing the plausible parameters of such an environment.

Environmental parameters

A brief summary of the environmental parameters is as follows:

1. Imperfect *flow of information*, *non-transparent* books, non-transparent final exposures (in contrast to exposures on balance sheets).

Even in closely regulated, mature financial markets the accounting standards for off-balance sheet items are newly developing. In Asian countries such standards were non-existent.[3]

What were the true liabilities of Asian banks? What was the level of Asian

---

2. A brief definition of on and off-balance sheet items will be appropriate. Any asset acquired by paying "hard cash," or any liability that has generated "hard cash" is an on-balance sheet item. But there are many other transactions that have neither generated cash nor were the result of cash payments. Many contracts are just contingencies at the time they are entered into and may result in cash receipts or payments only if certain contingencies are realized. They are legally enforceable promises, yet until the time they generate cash or lead to cash payments, they will be off the balance sheet. An example may help. When a household buys a new car this will be included among the households assets - regardless of how the car is purchased, by cash or by bank loans. Hence the car will be on the balance sheet of the household. Yet, the purchase of a collusion insurance on this car does not add another car to the household balance sheet. At least, not until some accident occurs. Yet, by writing an insurance policy the insurer has committed himself in some very precise way and must take the necessary measures.

3. Poor regulation is not a very critical factor in explaining the Asian financial crisis. If somebody wants to cut corners, regardless of the level of supervision/regulation, with modern instruments, they can. The key is the desire to obey rules. As an example, note that Asia had better supervision than Latin America.

countries' short-run debt? What were the maturities involved? To what extent was the banking system supported by government credit?

And more importantly, were banks involved in previously unsuspected derivatives deals?

The non-transparency of the balance sheets in Asia was at such a level that these questions were not asked.[4]

2. Undercapitalized banks and the *concentration of ownership* in relatively few hands.

In many Asian economies individuals or families dominated in making policy decisions in the banking sector. Thailand and Indonesia were the primary examples. The same phenomenon was true in the Philippines and to some extent in Malaysia. South Korea banks were reasonably managed, yet they were under the influence of the Ministry of Finance and were not able to follow market criteria fully in making loans.

Besides making decisions based on their personal experience, owners of banks in economies such as in Thailand or Indonesia are able to form *informal groups*, where decisions can be coordinated and "weak" members can be "supported" during periods of need.[5] Such collusive attitude leads to sustain weak members much longer than, say a Western banking system would permit. In the short run this behavior can be regarded as a strength. It may even "work" for many years and sustain precarious equilibria. Yet, in the long run, such equilibria are likely to collapse much more suddenly than a banking system that is subject to market competition on a regular basis.

3. Limited experience with *past* banking crises.

Latin America has had financial crises since the 19th century. Yet, apart from similar problems experienced by China before and during the Maoist revolution, severe financial crises are to a large extent new to Asian societies.[6] Given today's communication and electronic trading technologies, financial crises could spread much more rapidly than in the past. Markets that have very limited experience with such episodes are much more prone to panic selling (buying). The response of the public is likely to be quite severe.

4. Finally, we should mention the vague notion of *corrupt public institutions* as a factor with some significance.

It is interesting to note that Singapore and Taiwan, which are known to have less corrupt institutions, were affected less by the Asian financial crisis. At the

---

4. An example of the non-transparency of balance sheets is Table I given in the Appendix. In Table I we list the total foreign debt of various Asian countries as given before the Asian crisis. According to this Table short-run debt of South Korea is shown to be only $70.2 billion. Yet, after the turbulence in South Korean markets the true short-term debt of South Korea was determined to be close to $100 billion. Similarly, in Table I Indonesia is shown before the crisis, with a total debt of 55 billion dollars. After the turbulence the same number turned out to be over $80 billion.

5. This is in fact the case of the so-called convoy system used in Japan.

6. Of course, here the issue is one of severity. For example, during 1980 the Thai banking system did go through a financial crisis. So did the Philippines on several occasions. During the Mexico crisis in 1994 Thailand was affected. Yet, these were not full blown crises and had limited effect.

other extreme, there was Indonesia and then Thailand, where the corruption was endemic.[7]

This environment provides a very fertile ground for financial crises. Yet, the weaknesses it introduces in the financial system are not in general *sufficient* for a crisis of the magnitude we observed. After all, this environment also creates its own forces to protect the system against failures of its weaker members.[8]

We need further conditions.

Some necessary conditions

In order for a financial crisis similar to the one in Asia to develop, one needs some further conditions. First, some sort of *exchange rate pegging* is needed. Second, it appears that some significant non-transparency of risk exposures has to be assumed.

We discuss these briefly before dealing with the dynamics leading to a crisis.

Pegged exchange rate

The basic argument that we are trying to develop starts with an initial mispricing and continues with ways in which the balance sheet of the financial sector progressively worsens as a result of this.

The initial mispricing can be in any asset's price. But in order to maintain that the mispricing persists a sufficiently long period of time, it needs to be related to some price set by policy. Say, either an interest rate or an exchange rate. Since the 1970s, while interest rates are "assumed" to be market determined, there has been a significant Central Bank pegging of exchange rates, especially within emerging market economies.

Hence, we work with exchange rate pegging. This could either be a constant peg to dollar, or a version of crawling peg. For our purposes, the essential role played by the peg is that it will make the short-term behavior of the nominal exchange rate *easy to forecast*.

The ability to accurately forecast the behavior of the nominal exchange rate in the very short term is in fact a key element of our discussion. As long as financial players can forecast, or rather, as long as they *think* they can accurately forecast the immediate future of the exchange rate behavior, the "peg" will, given

---

7. South Korea was on the positive road in terms of establishing a corruption-free public administration. So, in this respect one might think that it forms a counter-example to the importance of corruption factor. Yet, as will be discussed below, South Korean banks had carelessly exposed themselves to Indonesian risk during the previous period.

8. The reader should notice the absence of any comments about the real economy. In fact, the real side of economies that possess such environments is not very important. Such economies may in fact experience very high growth and very fast transformation towards a modern society. This will not prevent the onset of a crisis. It may however delay it. On the other hand, if the real side has problems of its own, then this would make the crises occur earlier.

enough time, lead to a crisis in an environment such as the one described above. But, with (approximately) floating exchange rate regimes the arguments below are difficult to justify.

Non-transparency of exposures

The second important condition has to do with the issue of non-transparency. Given that the reader may be less familiar with some of the practices here, we prefer to spend a little bit more time on this point.

First we note that there are (at least) two ways of acquiring a credit: namely, on-balance sheet, and off-balance sheet. For example, in South Korea, short term off-balance sheet loans secured by banks were around $20 billion. This number is to be compared with total short-term liabilities of South Korea that in November 1997 was estimated to be $80 billion.

Off-balance sheet credit exposures may lead to significant non-transparency effects in a environment described earlier in the paper. We would like to discuss two examples.

The role of SPVs

How can a bank borrow off-balance sheet?

We illustrate the idea using the mechanism of Special Purpose Vehicles (SPV). The use of an SPV is a relatively new practice in financial markets.

A South Korean bank that wants to borrow in international credit markets indirectly forms an SPV, an entity established offshore and fully owned by the bank. Next, the parent company can "give" some its stock to the SPV, which in turn issues short-term paper, or borrows, using these stocks as collateral. These funds can then be used to take any position desired by the parent bank.

In a deeper sense, it is the bank that borrowed. Yet, if we look at the bank's balance sheet, these liabilities will not be visible.

In Asia, the use of SPVs in order to borrow *off*-balance sheet was facilitated by the existence of controls on the proportion of stocks foreigners could buy. For example, in South Korea foreigners are prevented to own more than 20% of the market. Using SPVs established by South Korean banks, international banks can obtain exposure to South Korean risk indirectly, circumventing these controls.

Role of derivatives

A second mechanism by which the liabilities of a bank can be taken off the balance sheet is through financial derivatives. There are many derivatives that can accomplish this. A recent and, during 1995–1997, very popular one in Asia was the Total Return Swaps (TRS). These swaps seem to have played some role in the contagion of the Asian financial crisis.

Total return swaps are a significant innovation that is likely to play a very important role in pricing credit correctly in the future. These instruments will certainly be essential in hedging and trading credit risk. But, as is the case with any asset, when they are mispriced, they can cause problems.

Major investment banks used Total Return Swaps in Asia, in order to facilitate the issuance of Indonesian paper during the years 1995–97. As a result of this process South Korean banks were heavily exposed to Indonesian credit. A nutshell description follows.

During the 1995–97 period a significant portion of Indonesian credit was swapped out to Korean banks, who were in search of higher yields due to the high funding cost that they started to pay on their existing loans beginning 1996.[9] But, given the difficult situation and the long-term nature of the loans to *chaebol*, these higher funding costs could not be passed on. As a result, many South Korean banks saw their profit margins shrink or even turn negative. They started to look for a way out of this situation.[10]

At the other end, Indonesian companies were in need of new funding, given the high growth of the economy. But the credit standing of Indonesia was not the same as South Korea or Singapore. It appears that there was not adequate demand for low quality Indonesian corporate paper *if issued according to standard market practices*. But, by using the TRS such demand could be created.

Total Return Swap is described in Figures 1 and 2. We see that the derivative consists of the exchange of two types of cash flows. An international bank swaps a LIBOR+280bp return involving Indonesian corporate risk against a LIBOR+75 return involving South Korean bank risk. This exchange of cash flows are regular, made every six months or every year.[11]

The second exchange involves any capital gains or losses that the paper generates during the year. In particular, in the event of bankruptcy of the Indonesian corporate, the South Korean Bank would compensate the international bank for the loss. This is shown in Figure 1.

According to Figure 1, in return for a higher predictable annual return, the South Korean bank is selling default-protection to the international bank, the default in question being that of an Indonesian corporate.

The spread of 60 basis points that the international bank obtains from the CD return of LIBOR+340 is a compensation for various risks involved in the

---

9. The funding costs of South Korean banks were increasing during 1996–1997. South Korean banks had floating rate liabilities that they used to finance capital investments of the *Chaebol*. These investments were long term and their expected rates of return were declining during this period. At the same time, various scandals and the ensuing democratization process had exposed the questionable accounting standards of these industrial conglomerates and had increased the South Korean risk. Korean banks saw their funding cost increase. Another factor was the Japan premium that Japanese banks had started paying on the dollar loans that they secured. Some Japanese banks passed the higher funding costs to Korean banks.

10. Note that given the special relationship between banks-chaebol and the policies followed by the South Korean ministry of finance, the loans to *chaebol* could not be sold in the secondary market. If this was possible, the banks would have taken a one time hit and then continued their operations in a more efficient manner. But the special relationship forced them to carry these long-term loans on their balance sheet.

11. One percent is 100 basis points. In other words, 280 basis points can also be expressed as 2.8%. The LIBOR on the other hand is the rate of interest quoted by an average of five London banks in "selling" dollar loans. It is a benchmark interest rate used in floating rate loans.

FIGURE 1. Annual Cash Flow Exchanges With No Capital Gains or Losses

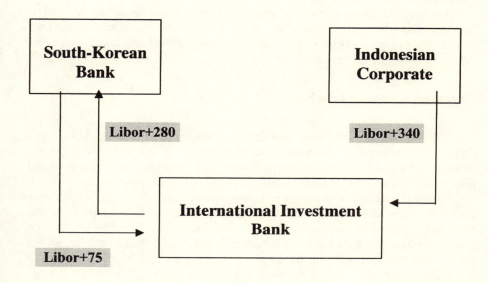

FIGURE 2. Cash Flow Exchanges In the Event of an Indonesian Default

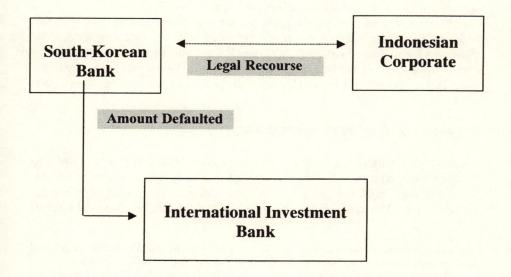

deal. The major component of this is, of course, the default-risk of the South Korean banks involved in the TRS.[12]

But note that at the end of this process, Korean banks are being exposed to Indonesian credit. This however was not visible on their balance sheets. This situation not only created the possibility for contagion but also made the contagion unpredictable and severe.

Contagion effects: an example

The discussion above also provides an example of contagion. This is not directly related to our main point, so we note it only in passing.

As a result of such TRS (mostly) European investment banks that swapped the Indonesian credit to Korean banks faced the following situation:

• Korean banks that took over Indonesian default risk could be insolvent during a potential financial crisis in Indonesia. A South Korean bank in this situation could not be expected to generate a payment of $100 million to pay the international investment bank, especially during a period where liquidity would dry up in international credit markets.

• This means that the credit risk of Indonesia is eventually born by the large international banks, who originally thought they eliminated this exposure by buying protection from South Korea.[13]

• Because Korean banks may default on their commitments to international banks, they are more likely to default on their loans obtained from Japanese banks.

• Thus, a financial crisis in Indonesia would be transmitted to South Korea first, and then through South Korea would be transmitted, in terms of higher spreads, to Japan second. It would become "contagious."

Another way of putting the same problem is to say that throughout this process, Indonesian risk was not properly priced. Also the risk was not diversified and allocated to a broad investor base. It was concentrated in relatively few hands. Instead of a broad body of investors who would have purchased the Indonesian CDs, a small number of Korean, European, and Japanese banks are hurt.

DYNAMICS OF SUSTAINED MISPRICINGS

These elements are now used in a somewhat more formal framework in order to bring an interpretation to the dynamics of crises such as the one observed in Asia.

Consider a small economy. Let e denote the percentage change in the exchange rate of domestic currency per one USD, during an infinitesimal interval

---

12. Competition among international banks for a share of the Asian market later drew this spread to almost zero. There is in fact another mispricing here, but it is not essential for our purposes.

13. Foreign bank lending in Indonesia is as follows: Japanese banks $23 billion, German banks $5.6 billion, French banks $4.8 billion, U.S. banks $4.6 billion.

dt. Let *r* be the return received from some investment in some domestic currency asset during the same infinitesimal interval. Let r^f be the cost of funds in USD, secured from a foreign bank and finally, let *m* be the risk premium associated with the domestic currency assets.

Then, arbitrage arguments will require:

$$r = r^f + e + m$$

with *m* being the "normal" risk premium. According to this, local investment would pay a known (predictable) return equaling the cost of foreign funds, plus depreciation of the local currency, plus a risk premium. The risk premium should be sufficiently high, but not higher than what is required by the risk associated with the investment.

The fair value of *m* is difficult to estimate. Hence the analysis will treat as a residual:

$$r - r^f - e = m$$

The main point of this section is the following.

We intend to show that in an environment similar to the one described above, the value assumed by *m* can remain *very high* during periods as long as three or four even five years. We then argue that this *process* will eventually make the *true* balance sheet of a banking system insolvent, given the environmental parameters discussed earlier. Being unsustainable, the "equilibrium" is bound to collapse.

Below, we discuss the case of Thailand. But similar calculations can be made for other Asian economies as well. The so-called *domestic asset*, utilized in the case of Thailand, may be different for other countries. For example, in Thailand and Malaysia it could be the property sector or dollar-yen short positions in Japan. In South Korea it could be the Total Asset Swaps.

But, regardless of the vehicle by which the positions are taken, the logic is similar.

The process begins by a few institutions taking a very risky position, due to, say, the pegged exchange rate regime. The resulting higher than normal returns make the position spread to other institutions. This fuels some type of property price rise, which in turn helps sustain the risky positions further. After a while, the system as a whole has moved to the risky position and has become "too big to fail." The initial mispricing becomes very difficult to change, since the risk is now systemic. The process continues further.

Such effects reduce the overall risk of these positions which in fact were very risky at the micro level. This equilibria lasts until some shock hits the economy.

The case of Thailand

Consider the data below related to the banking system positions for Thailand during the period 1994–1997.[14]

---

14. After devaluation in July 1997, the Thai baht exchange rate went from 26 to 28.5 baht/USD.

Year	1994	1995	1996	1997 (July)
Thai commercial bill rate	14.4	16.3	15.3	14.9
Thai baht per USD	25.1	26.3	25.9	26.0
US. short rates	4.2	5.5	5.1	5.6
Japan short rates	1.9	1.0	0.3	0.5
Japanese yen/USD	102.2	94.1	108.8	117.0

We now use the data shown in this table. Suppose a player takes either one of the following two positions:

• Position A: Beginning of 1994 borrow $100 million worth of yen. Invest in Thai commercial bills until July 1997. Unwind the position at .225 baht per yen.

• Position B: Beginning of 1994 borrow $100 million in international markets. Invest in Thai commercial bills until July 1997. Unwind the position at the devalued rate 28.5 baht per USD.

What would be the yearly return of these positions during the period 1994–97? We perform this calculation below.

Annual Net Return

Year	1994	1995	1996	1997
Position A return in yen	2.5%	17.3%	25%	12.5%
Position B return in USD	11.2 %	10.7%	10.2%	8.2%

The table above gives net returns in USD and in yen of the two positions. If one subtracts from these numbers a "normal" return for Thailand, one in fact obtains the excess reruns component of the variable m that we introduced above.

Looking at the table, we see that the returns in dollars are systematically high during the entire period 1994–1997. Returns in yen on the other hand are even *better*. For example, $100 million worth of yen borrowed in 1994 from international capital markets would have generated a net income of $69 million. The same investment started by using funds in USD provides a net income of $47 million in 3.5 years.

Note the following points.

To secure such an investment all one needs is a banking or financial company license, a phone, and a secretary. Hence these numbers mentioned above may in extreme cases indeed be viewed as net earnings.

But of course there are risks. The main risk of these positions is the currency exposure. The borrowing and the lending are done in different currencies. If the baht is devalued and the currency collapses, losses would be severe and insolvency might result.[15]

---

15. The Thai government's exchange rate policy was as follows. The baht was pegged to a basket of currencies dominated by the dollar. The basket was composed of 80–85% USD, 8–10% yen, 4–10% DEM, and 0–2% Sterling. Hence, the currency was essentially pegged to the dollar. But still there was some flexibility in the adjustment process. After the devaluation, the baht was let to float.

One may also have a maturity mismatch of the loans. The borrowings would usually be with floating one year or six month terms. The lending could be with somewhat longer term fixed interest rates.

Yet, within the context described in this paper these risks may not appear as "big" to the local players. It turns out that the currency peg is the main building block of these strategies. As long as the players see the peg holding for a reasonable period of time, they may even find these short positions "riskless." For example, the players may think that there are enough reserves available to allow them to unwind their positions, albeit at somewhat unfavorable rates. But since the whole position is unusually profitable, these last minute "costs" would be regarded as tolerable. They may even be factored in the strategy, ex ante.

In fact, the expectation of a typical player may be as follows:

"The peg will hold at least for the next few weeks. We borrow yen, lend baht, secure 20% annual net return. In case currency starts to collapse, we unwind the position, or simply hedge ourselves in the forward market."[16]

One must also factor in the well-known high growth of Asian economies. In an economy experiencing high growth for years, the risk of entering in a severe financial crisis may indeed seem very remote. This also reinforces the *one-way bet* view of the situation.

Moral hazard aspects

There is more to the above explanation. In fact, there are significant moral hazard aspects of the above positions, aspects that *reduce* the risk of collapsing currencies. These moral hazard aspects play a crucial role in the building of the risky positions because they essentially make the positions A or B *one way* bets, for a rather lengthy period of time.

It turns out that once most players start following the same strategy and the balance sheet of the system moves into positions such as A and/or B, then the authorities cannot afford to change the peg anyway. Instead, they will try to resist any speculative attacks until the end. Most players would then have ample time to unwind their positions.[17]

In the event of a significant and sudden collapse which leaves the players unable to cover their positions, this aspect of the problem will make the government step in and bail out the biggest players. In the extreme case that this does not happen, the government will eventually assume the liabilities of foreign banks or of domestic depositors and the domestic players will just walk away from their

---

16. In Thailand, for example, such forward markets did exist and were utilized for about $22 billion.

17. Needless to say, some players would still be non-liquid at the time of the collapse given the maturity of the loans that they made. For example, in Thailand the stress period before the devaluation lasted about eight–ten months. If a player had issued a one year loan in September or October 1996, he or she would still not be liquid enough to unwind the position by July 1997, when the currency was allowed to float. Also, often such loans were callable.

obligations. Assuming that the mispricing continues a reasonable amount of time, and given that no significant initial capital was invested in the "bank," the players may make money even under such severe conditions. So, regarded from this angle, the positions are not very risky. Or, more correctly, ex ante they may not appear very risky to each player.

There are some minor points that we would like to emphasize. First of all, the analysis above gives the net incomes after the initial float (devaluation) of the Thai baht during July 1997. The returns *before* the devaluation are 10% higher for the year 1997.[18]

Second, it should be noted that the returns shown for Thailand are systematic. In spite of the Mexican crisis, and the ensuing Tequila Effect, players who took these positions were *gainers* consistently. Due the exchange rate regime, the spreads remained "excessive" throughout the 3.5-year period.

Third, if these funds in yen were invested in Thai property directly, the returns during the period 1994–1997 would be significantly higher. Thai property prices at some point were increasing at rates of 20% to 30%. However, such investment is at the outset significantly more illiquid and risky than the positions A and B outlined above. Of course, to the extent the eventual borrowers from the banks were real estate speculators, the short-term nature of the bank lending was meaningless, because during a period of stress the real estate speculator could default on its loan regardless of the maturity of his or her commitment.[19]

Finally, there is an additional cost that we need to add to the figures in the table. The so-called Thailand premium that banks may have to pay during this period was between 95 basis points and 50 basis points during the interval under consideration.

The dynamics

We can now summarize the dynamics of the financial markets under the conditions described in this paper and in the event the players start taking positions A and B.

Phase 1

One or two big local banks start taking the relevant positions on or off-balance sheet. These institutions do this hesitatingly, because they know it carries high risks. They are the only ones to do so. Initially, other institutions look at their decisions skeptically.

----

18. Several weeks before the devaluation the players had the opportunity to unwind their positions. The Thai central bank was on the other side of the deal and sold about $20 billion of foreign reserves and FX forwards.

19. Some numbers: in Thailand after the crisis, 56 finance companies, two-thirds of the sector, were closed by the government. These companies had assets totaling $20 billion, of which a third is real estate loans gone bad. Because this property has not been liquidated, the Thai property market has not really collapsed yet.

But, when regarded from the point of view of the whole banking system in the aggregate, the position is small. Also, there is the factor of corrupt administrations. Hence, the position remains unnoticed by local or international regulators. In fact, the position from the point of view of the whole system does not carry much risk. It certainly does not necessitate a change in the exchange rate regime.

Phase 2

Initially the high risk was born by a few pioneering institutions. But there was no crisis and the institutions end up realizing high returns. In fact their profits are significantly higher than the local competition. But this is an environment where the banks are owned by individuals or by families and these individuals have close relations. Hence, other banks and investors notice quickly this difference in profits and compare these returns with their own. The number of institutions taking the same position starts to increase.

After two or three years, the "true" balance sheet of the banking system has moved towards the risky positions in the *aggregate*. In general, the system is short in some foreign currency and long in some high-yielding local (Indonesian, Thai) asset.

Phase 3

Eventually the *whole system* could move in these short positions. Under these conditions, even if they have the intentions, the administrators will be incapable of acting, due to a systemic risk. Namely, any major policy decision that goes against the position may cause a sudden collapse of currency (or, for example, in property) prices. So, they will try to defend the *peg* as long as possible. They will use reserves or other rationing mechanisms available to prevent the collapse of the currency.

This will give enough time to shrewd speculators to unwind their positions.

Obviously the dynamics are unstable and will eventually collapse. Crisis is only a matter of time, but as always, it is impossible to forecast when this collapse will occur. Yet, this fragile state of affairs may continue much longer than an outside observer might think.

An example

In this section, we discuss a numerical example that illustrates the dynamics of ever enlarging exposures to FX risk in the balance sheet of the financial sector. We intend to provide a rationale for two hypotheses:

1. That the large devaluation risk premium built in domestic currency assets such as bonds, O/N or repos can persist for many years even in the presence of significant capital inflows.

2. That these risk premia will lead to increased FX exposure and to the eventual collapse of the exchange rate regime. Yet, the increased likelihood of the collapse may provide, paradoxically, some sort of insurance against an early collapse for a surprisingly *long* period.

In providing the rationale behind these assertions we will emphasize three necessary conditions. First, we need some sort of a pegged exchange rate regime.

Second, we need a current account deficit. A third possible necessary condition is the existence of some kind of deposit insurance. Yet, the presence of unwritten rules such as "too big to fail" will also lead to the same conclusion.

The example below uses overly simplified balance sheets to illustrate the main points. We assume that there are three balance sheets in the economy. That of households (HH), that of the central bank (CB), and the balance sheet of the financial sector (FS).

In the following, all numbers are expressed in USD. The symbol e is the local currency price of the USD.

Phase 1

The household sector will not play an important role in the example. It is assumed to have the following balance sheet that will not change during the process[20]:

Assets		Liabilities	
Real Assets (USD)	100	Equity	100

The central bank has the following initial balance sheet:

Assets		Liabilities	
Reserves	0	Notes	0

The financial system has the following initial balance sheet:

Assets		Liabilities	
Domestic currency assets	0	Loans	0

Clearly, these balance sheets can be complicated in many ways. But, for the arguments below we don't need to do that.

Phase 2

In the second phase, some players in the financial sector decide to open their FX positions and take an FX exposure. In particular, they increase their USD borrowing in international markets, sell the dollars to the central bank, get domestic currency and lend these at high real rates either to the government, to realtors, or to the business sector.

The high *real rates* obtained from these loans would be around, say, 10% to 15% per year because they incorporate the domestic currency risk premium.

Yet, although these exposures are risky, the CB has the USDs and is ready to defend the exchange rate policy by selling the dollars back to the market. Hence, looked at closer, the "high risk" FX exposures are in fact not risky at all. Local and

---

20. This can certainly be modified. The household sector can start by taking speculative positions as well. For simplicity, we assume these away.

international players know this. In addition, there is no reason, at this point, for the CB to change the exchange rate policy and devalue the currency. The economy grows, the current account deficit is manageable, and the exposures are not excessive.

Hence, the banks that opened their FX positions will realize high profits, while others will perform poorly. The treasurers of the latter will be "penalized" for their conservative policy.[21] This will lead to further financial institutions joining the policy of open FX positions. After one or two years the system's balance sheet will start to change. The new balance sheet will be as follows.

Households are assumed to have the same balance sheet since they don't join in opening FX positions, although this assumption can easily be modified.

Assets		Liabilities	
Real Assets	100	Equity	100

The financial system has borrowed USD and has lent domestic currency:

Assets		Liabilities	
Dom. cur. Loans	$e100$	Loans	100

The central bank has purchased the USD sold by the financial institutions:

Assets		Liabilities	
Reserves	100	Notes	$e100$

Note that the money supply must have increased. Shouldn't this lower the domestic interest rates, lower the returns in USD terms, and eventually stop the process of opening positions? Not necessarily. In fact, the financial system is now carrying significant FX exposure and the devaluation risk premium may increase somewhat. As result, the effects of a looser money supply may be compensated by a higher risk premium.

But the situation does not have to lead to a crisis at this point, because the central bank can always sell the reserves back to the financial sector and the FX positions can easily be closed.

Phase 3

In this phase we need some sort of effect that will lower the central bank reserves. This can happen in many ways. But one way or another the existence of a current account deficit is required. Whether financed by foreign borrowing or by CB reserves, the effect of this deficit will not be very different. So we assume that the central bank spends 25% of the reserves to finance the current account deficit.

---

21. Note that if the banking system is immature, or if modern risk management is not very well understood, it may be extremely difficult to explain to the owners of these banks, returns such as 7-8% while their competitors have been displaying performances of 10-15%, two or three years in a row.

The new balance sheets will look like this.
Again the household balance sheet has not changed.

Assets			Liabilities	
Real Assets (USD)	100		Equity	100

The financial system has borrowed even more USD and has increased domestic currency lending, because given the weaker balance sheet of the CB, a devaluation will now lead to a financial crisis. Hence, paradoxically, the exchange rate policy will in the short run be even less likely to change. Also, given the increased risks, risk premium must have increased and the real returns would go up to ranges such as 15 to 25%. This could very well lead to new players entering the game.

Assets			Liabilities	
Dom. cur. Loans	e200		Loans	200

The central bank has purchased and sold some USD in order to finance the current account deficit. At the end the balance sheet may look like:

Assets			Liabilities	
Reserves	150		Notes	e150

Note that any demand by the financial sector to reverse the FX positions will immediately lead to an insolvency of the financial sector and hence to a financial crisis. This is because the USD liabilities of the system are now greater than the available reserves of foreign currency. Hence the CB now is *obligated to maintain* the exchange rate regime as long as it can. This will be seen as some sort of *short-term* insurance by other market players, who may join the process.

Clearly, the devaluation risk premium must also increase. It is more profitable to open positions as long as there is no imminent danger of a devaluation.

CONCLUSIONS

The example above can be complicated many ways. In fact, one interesting complication is to differentiate between two types of open positions: those that finance domestic currency O/N investment, and others that finance longer term maturities.

It can be shown that as long as the central bank has enough reserves to meet the reversals of O/N positions, there will be no real danger of an imminent financial crisis. On the other hand, given that O/N positions are earning high returns, there is no need to reverse them either, since they can be reversed at any time. Finally, given that O/N positions are not reversed, the longer maturity domestic currency positions will never be reversed either.

Thus, the amount of central bank reserves necessary to maintain the temporary "equilibrium" may in fact be much smaller than the foreign exchange liabilities of the banking system. A stock of reserves that exceeds O/N, or weekly repos may be sufficient to keep the players away from unwinding any positions.

The "equilibrium" will continue as long as it can. And this may be many years.

REFERENCES

Cavalleri, L., and C. Corsetti. 1997. "Arbitrage Mechanisms Leading to Currency Crises: A Theoretical Perspective." Manuscript.

Claessens, S., and T. Glaessner. 1997. "Are Financial Sector Weaknesses Undermining the East Asian Miracle?" The World Bank.

Corsenti, G., P. Pesenti and N. Roubini. 1998. "What Caused the Asian Financial Crisis?" Manuscript.

Flood, R., and N. Marion. 1998. "Perspectives on the Recent Currency Crisis Literature." NBER.

Risk Magazine.1997. *Asian Risk*, November.

World Economic Outlook. 1997. Interim Assessment, December.

12
• • •

The Three Routes to
Financial Crises
The Need for Capital Controls

*Gabriel Palma**

> *We will never use capital controls: we want to be a First World Nation.*
> F. H. CARDOSO

> *People usually prefer to fail through conventional means rather
> than to succeed through unconventional ones.*
> J. M. KEYNES

LIKE CALIFORNIA's "Proposition 13" in 1978, Chile's imposition of capital controls in 1991 will probably one day be seen as an economic and political landmark.

It is not that other countries did not have capital controls before (like India or China), or since (like Malaysia and Colombia), but of all the countries applying capital controls in recent years, the case of Chile in the 1990s has turned out to be the most ideologically influential one within the "mainstream." This is

---

*Faculty of Economics and Politics, University of Cambridge. An earlier version of this paper was presented at a workshop on "The New World Financial Authority," organized by the Center for Economic Policy, New School University, New York, July 6-7, 1999. I should like to thank the Center for its financial support, and the participants at the workshop, particularly John Eatwell, José Antonio Ocampo and Lance Taylor for their helpful comments. Participants at other conferences and seminars in Bangkok, Bilbao, Cape Town, Kuala Lumpur, London, Paris, Santa Cruz, and Santiago, particularly Edna Armendáriz, Daniel Hahn, Arturo O'Connell, Jonathan Fox, Carlota Pérez, and Bob Sutcliffe also made useful suggestions. The usual caveats apply.

probably the result of the fact that Chile was the first country that implemented capital account regulations *after* having fully liberalized its economy; i.e., with its neo-liberal credentials intact (as until then it had followed the whole spirit and the letter—including the small print—of the liberalization and reform programs). It also did so explicitly as a *temporary* measure (as opposed to what Keynes always recommended[1]), necessary to deal with (what was expected to be) a temporary phenomenon of "excess" capital inflows. That is, Chile implemented capital controls in 1991 clearly not in any way as part of a fundamental questioning of the classical "efficient-market" theory, but simply as a mechanism for tackling some short-term strains caused by what they believed to be an otherwise efficient international financial flow system.[2]

However, as soon as it became evident that these controls had been particularly effective in helping the Chilean economy to weather the so-called "Tequila effect" (following the 1994 Mexican crisis), they suddenly began to attract an enormous amount of attention—and one that (oddly enough) has not been shared by other equally interesting experiments in inflow-controls, such as those of Colombia (1993) and Malaysia (1994).[3]

As is well known, after California's "Proposition 13," the neo-liberal tide started gathering pace, soon becoming not just a tide but a tidal wave with Reagan's and Thatcher's Jihad against the public sector, government regulations, and the Keynesian welfare system in general.[4]

However, major financial crises in Mexico, East Asia, and Brazil seem eventually to have had the effect of slowing down the seemingly unstoppable advance of this neo-liberal tidal wave. They certainly have not stopped it, let alone turned the tide back, but at least they have dented the fundamentalist way in which some in the markets-always-know-best brigade thought about certain crucial policy issues. Suddenly, views such as those expressed by Summers just a few years before felt as if they belonged to a different era:

> The ultimate social function [of financial markets are] spreading risks, guiding the investment of scarce capital, and processing and disseminating the information possessed by diverse traders [...]. Prices will always reflect fundamental values [...]. The logic of efficient markets is compelling (1989, p.16; quoted in Davidson, 2000, 1117).

---

1. Well, at least from his "Economic Consequences of Peace" onwards.

2. This would include Chile's capital controls within the family of policies that Paul Davidson has called "liquidity plumbing solutions"; i.e., solutions designed simply to patch up short-run macroeconomic stresses (see, for example, 2000).

3. For the experience of Colombia, see especially Ocampo and Tovar (1999), and Ocampo (2000); for that of Malaysia, Rodrik and Velasco (2000). For other experiences, such as India and China, see Joshi (2000), and Bhalla and Nachane (2001). For some of the growing literature on capital controls, see also Fisher et. al. (1998); Calvo and Reinhart (1999); and Eichegreen (2000).

4. Other influential events at the time were the rejection of Stalinist-style planning, and the embracing of market economics, by the 1978 Congress of the Chinese Communist Party (under the leadership of Deng Xiaoping), the elimination of exchange controls in Britain in 1979, and the first major privatization by the Thatcher government in 1981 (British Aerospace).

In fact, Chile's capital controls became the first real issue in the last third of a century in which some segments of the "mainstream," and some important figures in the "Washington Consensus," have conceded (often reluctantly) that in at least one important sphere of LDCs' economic life the normal market interactions of intelligent, rational, self-interested, and "maximizing" economic agents may not lead to an "equilibrium," neither a "global" nor even a "local" one.

Specifically, it is increasingly acknowledged that in the dynamic which lead to these three major financial crises, these market interacting agents somehow lost their capacity to assess and price their risk properly, ending up accumulating far more risk than was privately (let alone socially) efficient.

Of course, these mainstream economists have not gone nearly as far as agreeing with Keynes' "liquidity preference" theory—that international financial markets can *never* be trusted to deliver liquidity in an *orderly* fashion, in either the short or the long term—but they have made a significant departure from more extreme views of the classical efficient-market theory.

This does not mean that there are not still a large number of diehard neoliberals insisting that these financial crises were entirely and exclusively the result of "exogenous" market interferences, which affected the (otherwise efficient) behavior of these "maximizing" market interacting agents, and the (otherwise efficient) resource allocation mechanisms of financial markets. As is well known, the three main issues identified by this vast literature in their search for culprits that would explain why prices did not always reflect fundamental values are governments' deposit insurance, IMF-led rescue operations, and the allocation of financial resources in many LDCs according to non-market criteria (i.e., two "moral hazards" and a system of resource allocation characterized as "crony capitalism").[5]

Although these issues are obviously part of the story, fortunately, most of the debate in the financial and development literatures has recently begun to put them into some perspective, moving away from the tiresome insistence on negative "exogenous" interventions and into a more illuminating analysis of the dynamic that led to these financial crises. In this new journey, the necessity and effectiveness of some government intervention in financial markets, such as whether Chilean-style controls on inflows and Malaysian-style controls on outflows can be effective mechanisms for avoiding (or at least for mitigating) the effects of financial crisis, are attracting a good deal of attention.

One of the main issues discussed in this new literature regarding Chilean-style inflow-controls is whether they have been more effective in dealing with the *levels* or with the *composition* of capital inflows; regarding outflow-controls the new literature discusses in particular both their short-term effectiveness in stopping outflow-stampedes, and their long-term effects on growth and financial stability.

Of course, the need for capital controls is not a new issue in economic theory. For example, Keynes' work on the matter (and his insistence on integrating them

---

5. See my chapter on Brazil in this volume for a more detailed discussion of these issues.

in the Bretton Woods institutions) is well known, as is the work of those of his contemporaries who deal with these matters, such as that of Nurkse.

However, the more recent debate was sparked not by the issue of capital controls proper, but by a related controversy started by Tobin with regards to his proposal for a small tax on foreign exchange transactions (intended to slow down flows of "hot-money" without interfering significantly with currency transactions related to trade and productive investment). Some of the issues related to this so-called "Tobin tax" were later taken up by such influential figures as Stiglitz and Krugman, and eventually the debate moved on to the issue of capital controls proper.[6]

The aim of this paper is to study both the need for inflow-controls in developing economies that have liberalized their capital accounts at times of high, volatile and mostly unregulated international liquidity, and the effectiveness of these controls in the countries that have implemented them.

The first part of the paper will tackle the first issue, trying to show that no matter how hard financially-liberalized LDCs have tried in the last quarter of a century to deal with the problem of sudden and massive surges in capital inflows, they have ended up in a financial crisis. Among crisis-countries the paper will identify three different forms through which these LDCs have tried unsuccessfully to deal with the difficult problem of absorbing these sudden inflow-surges, and will conclude that each of them led to financial crises via a different route; these are best exemplified by the Mexican, the Korean, and the Brazilian experiences. In order to do so, this first part will study the period between financial liberalization and financial crisis in each of these three paradigmatic countries.

These three routes (from now on called "route 1" for Mexico, "route 2" for Korea, and "route 3" for Brazil) will contain the experiences of other countries that have also ended up in a financial crisis after the liberalization of the capital account of their balance of payments led to a surge in inflows, as for example the Chilean case leading to its 1982 crisis ("route 1"), and those of Malaysia and Thailand leading to their respective 1997 crises (a combination of "route 1" and "route 2").

The second part of this paper will study the possible effectiveness of capital controls. Special attention will be paid to the experiences of Chile and Malaysia.[7] In the case of Chile, this country first introduced (price-based) capital controls on inflows in 1991 and then strengthened these controls in 1995. These controls, however, were later progressively lifted as a result of the difficulties that this country was experiencing in obtaining the additional international finance needed to pay for its large current account deficit after the turmoil in international financial markets following first the East Asian, then the Russian, and

---

6. See Tobin (2000), Stiglitz (1998 and 2000), and Krugman (2000). One use made of this tax that Tobin did not anticipate is to be found in Latin American countries in which income tax collection is very difficult; here a Tobin tax on domestic financial transaction was implemented not as a mechanism to limit financial market volatility by increasing financial transactions costs, but simply as an effective revenue mechanism.

7. For the Colombian experience, see footnote 4 above.

finally the Brazilian crises. In the case of Malaysia, this country had a (often ignored) short but radical experience of inflow-controls in 1994, which (as opposed to the Chilean and Colombian cases) concentrated on quantitative restrictions on inflows. These controls were imposed at the beginning of 1994, but were then progressively lifted towards the end of that year because Malaysian policy makers began to worry that they were "overshooting" the reduction in private inflows.

THE THREE ROUTES TO FINANCIAL CRISES

Figure 1 shows the key issue at stake: the extraordinary surge in capital inflows following financial liberalization in all crisis countries.

FIGURE 1.

LATIN AMERICA and EAST ASIA: aggregate net capital flows before financial liberalization and between financial liberalization and financial crisis

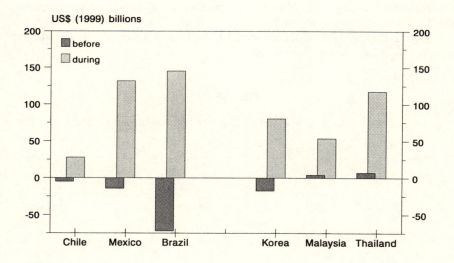

In each case the period "during" covers the years between financial liberalization and financial crisis—Chile, 1975-82; Mexico, 1988-94; Brazil, 1992-98; and Korea, Malaysia, and Thailand, 1988-96. "Before" covers a period of similar length, but including the years before their respective financial liberalizations; in the case of East Asia, however, as the period "before" would have included years preceding the 1982 debt crisis, I decided only to include years from 1983 onwards (i.e., 1983-87 versus 1988-96).
SOURCE: IMF (2000b). Unless otherwise stated, this source, together with IMF (2000a and c), World Bank (2000a and b), ECLAC Statistical Division and ECLAC (2000) will be the sources for all graphs in this paper.

The turnaround is extraordinary: in the case of Brazil the difference between the two periods amounts to about $220 billion, in Mexico $150 billion, and in the three East Asian countries $260 billion (all figures at constant 1999 values).

The principal component of these surges in capital inflows is clearly its private component. In Brazil, for example, this turnaround is close to $190 billion, and in the three East Asian countries well over $200 billion.

These surges are even more impressive in relative terms; in Chile, for example, net capital inflows before the 1982 crisis achieved a level similar to total exports; in Malaysia, net private inflows reached a massive 25% of GDP; and in Korea inflows went on to exceed an annual figure of $1,200 per capita.

In fact, some of these countries even began to be important players in the newly developed derivatives markets; for example, according to the IMF, in the "Asia Pacific" market, the "notional principal amount outstanding" for selected derivative financial instruments grew from just under $1 billion in 1986 to $2.2 trillion in 1996 (equivalent to an average annual rate of growth of 38%), reaching a level equivalent to over three-quarters of that of Europe, and 45% of that of the United States.

Key question: why did so much foreign capital fly into these countries?[8] Twofold answer: [i] there was a lot of liquidity in international financial markets, and [ii] some LDCs produced (often artificially) strong magnetic attractions for this liquidity.

Figure 2 shows one aspect of factor [i], the extraordinary expansion in international liquidity during this period.

FIGURE 2.

G7: assets of institutional investors (nonbank financial sector), 1988 and 1986

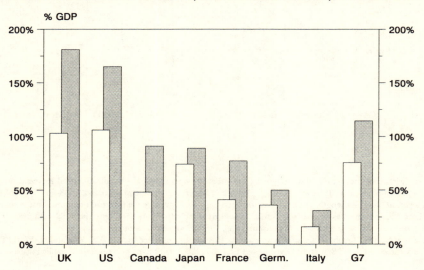

Looking at just this aspect of the growth of international financial markets, (according to IMF data) the increase in the value of assets of institutional investors between 1988 and 1996 is quite extraordinary, especially in the United Kingdom (where the growth in this period is equivalent to as much as 80 percentage points of GDP) and in the United States (60 percentage points). The average increase for the G7 is equivalent to 40 percentage points of GDP. Needless to say, these are large numbers![9]

Figure 3 shows another part of answer [i]: the transformation of international financial markets and, in particular, the development of new financial instruments also contributed massively to this increase in international liquidity.

FIGURE 3.

Derivaties Markets: notional values of outstanding "over-the-counter" interest rate, currency and exchange-traded derivative contracts, end-March 1995

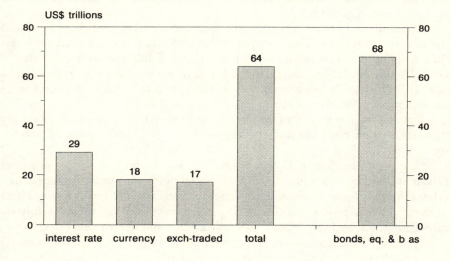

Bonds, eq & b as=aggregate value of all bonds, equity and bank assets of the G 17 (G7 plus smaller European countries).

This figure shows that (again according to IMF data) the "notional" value of outstanding "over-the-counter" derivative contracts (interest rates, currency, and exchange traded derivatives) reached $64 trillion in 1995; this amount is similar

---

8. Of course, one had to remember that it is not really all "foreign"; in some cases domestic capital leaves only to return again as "foreign," to enjoy benefits!

9. A related problem is that the LDC-exposure of these institutional investors was proportionally so small, that often they (wrongly) believed that it did not pay to invest properly in information about these LDCs; so, normal problems of "asymmetric" information were exacerbated.

to that of the aggregate value of all bonds, equity, and bank assets of the G17 group of countries.

By now the legendary case of the LTCM exemplifies both the extraordinary recent changes in international financial markets, and the resulting added degree of financial vulnerability.[10]

However, while massive international liquidity may be a necessary condition for increased inflows to LDCs, it is certainly is not a sufficient one. So, why did the capital flow to (a few) LDCs? Three main reasons: [i] LDCs have usually played the role of "market of last resort," in particular when an increase in international liquidity comes together with slow growth in OECD economies[11]; [ii] the high expectations placed on economic reforms in LDCs, partly resulting from the massive "spin" put on them by their advocates, particularly those to be found circling around the "Washington Consensus"; [iii] magnetic attractions (often artificially created), such as undervalued asset markets (in particular stocks and real estate), high interest rate spreads,[12] and the expectation of real appreciation of exchange rates.[13]

As mentioned before, the key issue facing these LDCs was how to absorb the sudden surges in inflows—in particular when they reached extreme levels such as being equal to the total value of exports (Chile), or to one-quarter of GNP (Malaysia). It is in the different forms in which these countries tried to deal with this specific problem of inflow-absorption that the three routes to financial crises began to emerge.

Figure 4 clearly shows a first movement in two opposite directions among these crisis-countries—the first encompassing "route 1" and " route 2," and the second "route 3."

One response ("route 1" and "route 2") was to ride out the surge in net private inflows by unloading them into the economy via credit expansion, the other ("route 3") was precisely the reverse, to try to stop the expansionary effect of these surges in inflows via placing an "iron curtain" around them (mainly via increasing reserves, high degrees of sterilization, and high interest rates).

However, if the main similarity between the way that "route 1" and "route 2" dealt with the surge in inflows is through credit expansion, their main difference (as will be discussed in more detail below) is in the use made of this credit expansion—

---

10. For the extraordinary case of the LTCM, described by the *Washington Post* as "the biggest financial misstep ever to hit Wall Street," or by *The Financial Times* as "the fund that thought it was too smart to fail," see especially Dunbar (2000). *The Wall Street Journal*, which sometime likes to play the role of the Pravda of the US financial markets, had more affectionate words to describe this institution; according to them, it was only "one of [Wall Street's] most aggressive offspring."

11. See Palma (1998).

12. For detailed data in this respect, see Palma (1999b).

13. Brazil's Finance Minister, Pedro Malan, tells us with disarming candor how one of the aims of economic policy was precisely "artificially" to create the need for foreign capital via the appreciation of the exchange rates: according to him "The logic of the exchange rate policy is to [...] increase imports and the current account deficit and, therefore, make the country import capital again" (statement made on October 24, 1994, quote in Saad Filho, 2000, p. 15).

FIGURE 4.

EAST ASIA and LATIN AMERICA: credit to private sector between the
beginning of financial liberalization and respective financial crises

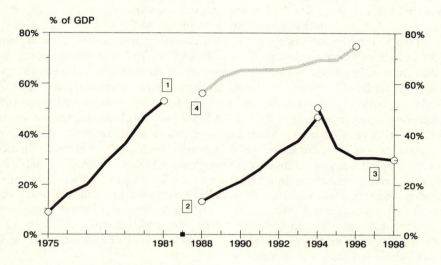

[1] = Chile; [2] = Mexico; [3] = Brazil; and [4] = Korea.[14]

"route 1" directs this additional credit mainly towards increased consumption and
asset speculation, "route 2" directs it mainly towards corporate investment.

In other words, if the similarity between these two routes was credit expansion, the crucial difference was the "magnetism" that attracted these inflows in
the first place—in one case, "route 2," it is mainly a matter of an "endogenous
pull" for additional finance to sustain high levels of investment, in the other, it is
rather an "exogenous push" movement of foreign capital into these countries,
which then has to "create" a need for itself.[15]

From this point of view, "route 1" countries could be viewed as a rather peculiar case of Say's Law, in which "supply creates demand" through fuelling expectations and optimism regarding the future prospects of the economy. This circle, of
course, reinforces itself, becoming (for a while) a self-fulfilling prophecy. Easy

---

14. In order to cover all four major financial crises of the last 20 years, events leading to the
Chilean 1982 financial crisis are also included in the graphs of this section, even though the Chilean case clearly belongs to (the Mexican-type) "route 1." Finally, the important cases of Malaysia
and Thailand, as they are a combination of "route 1" and "route 2," will not be included in the
graphs, but will be discussed throughout this section.

15. This, of course, is not a new phenomenon; the most insightful work on this matter is that
of Kindleberger (see especially 1996).

access to credit fuels expectations regarding the performance of the economy, performance that is improved by the additional expenditure brought about by the extra borrowing and availability of foreign exchange. That is, "overlending" and "overborrowing" are not only the result of a closely interrelated process, but one that has a clear direction of causality: the propensity to "overlend" is a crucial factor that leads to the propensity to "overborrow." [16]

Finally, the cases of Malaysia and Thailand are characterized by having one foot in each of these two camps ("route 1" and "route 2"). Their surges in inflows were so large, and the credit to the private sector increased (even for the high standards set by "route 1" countries) by such an extraordinary amount—in Malaysia, between financial liberalization and financial crisis, credit to the private sector grew from 67% of GDP to 135%, and in Thailand from 64% to 142%!—that they ended up following both routes simultaneously. First, they followed "route 2" in the sense that they needed high levels of external finance for their ambitious private investment programs—Malaysia actually doubled its share of private investment in GDP, from 15.4% in 1988 to 30.5%, while Thailand brought its own to 34.1% of GDP. But second (as opposed to Korea), because inflows surpassed even the financial requirements of these ambitious investment drives, there was enough credit to spare for them to follow at least *one element* of "route 1" too—this "excess" credit fuelled a Latin American-style asset bubble in their stock markets and real estate.

In fact, what is extraordinary is that in these two countries massive credit expansion did not only not fuel an increase in the share of consumption in GDP, as it did in Latin America, but it was actually associated with a *drop* in this share; in Thailand, for example, during this period the share of consumption in GDP fell from 56.7% to 54.8%, and in Malaysia from 49.4% to 45.9%—no sign of "route 1" here . . .

One of the problems facing these countries is that they found themselves in rather uncharted territory. They had had few previous experiences of sudden surges in inflows, let alone of these levels and composition (see below). Historically, the norm for these LDCs was to have difficult access to international finance, and having to live with a constant foreign exchange constraint on growth and aggregate expenditure. But in this case, it did not rain but poured!

Furthermore, one of the (many) peculiar features of economic theory is that it has rarely been concerned with the effects of "shocks," let alone this specific one. There are, of course, exceptions like Keynes' constant concern with the effects of autonomous changes in private investment and "animal spirits." Also, starting with Prebisch and Singer, Latin America's Structuralist School did some analysis of the effects on LDCs of sudden changes in the terms of trade of primary-commodity exporting countries. The "Dutch Disease" literature also studied the related issue of the effects of sudden increases in the price of commodity exports, and "long-wave" theorists (like Freeman and Pérez) have been concerned with the effects of

---

16. For a more detailed analysis of this issue, see Palma (1998).

sudden changes in the "technological paradigm." But these are the exceptions rather than the norm.

This bias in economic theory is certainly true in matters relating to the effects of shocks brought about by sudden surges in capital inflow. There are, of course, exceptions like (again) Keynes, Kindleberger, and Minsky.[17] Among them, Kindleberger is the one that has been most concerned with this issue.

In sum, LDCs that had these surges in capital inflows were faced with two basic alternatives: one, following the beliefs of the classical efficient-market theory and the first law of Welfare Economics, they could allow markets to sort out the resulting problem by themselves[18]; the other, to try to contain the expansionary effect of surges in capital inflows via placing an "iron curtain" around them. Figure 5 shows the resulting different levels in interest rates.

FIGURE 5.

LATIN AMERICA and EAST ASIA: domestic real lending rates between the beginning of financial liberalization and respective financial crisis

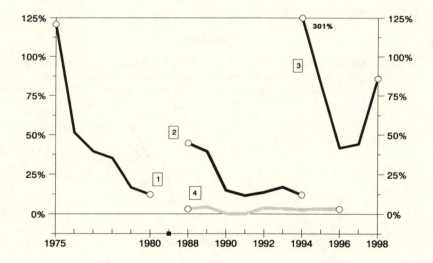

[1] = Chile; [2] = Mexico; [3] = Brazil; and [4] = Korea.

---

17. Galbraith is also another exception; see, for example, (1994).

18. This is sometimes called the "Lawson law," following the British Chancellor's famous statement that when imbalances are the result of private transactions, no matter how large they are, governments should not intervene.

In "route 1" countries (Chile and Mexico), real interest rates start at a high level due their stabilization policies, but as soon as these are successful in conquering inflation, they allow interest rates to fall to international levels (plus a relatively small spread). "Route 2" countries, like Korea, are characterized by long-term policies of particularly low real interest rates, which continued during this period. However, in the case of Brazil, real interest rates not only start at a much higher level than other Latin American countries, but (for reasons discussed in detail in the chapter on Brazil in this volume) they are never allowed to fall anywhere near the values of "route 1" countries (let alone "route 2" countries).

The case of Brazil is very important from the point of view of a critique of mainstream "moral-hazard-type" crisis analysis. According to the McKinnon and Pill approach to financial crisis, for example, the main cause of agents losing their capacity to assess and price their risk properly is that internal and external moral hazards lead to "artificially" low interest rates; these, in turn, gave a false incentive to agents to accumulate excessive amounts of risk.[19] However, in Brazil high interest rates did not seem to have been able to avoid a financial crisis either.

Figure 6 shows a first crucial difference between "route 1" and "route 2"; even though in both cases the credit to the private sector grew rapidly, the use made of this credit was rather different.

FIGURE 6.

LATIN AMERICA and EAST ASIA: imports of consumer goods between
the beginning of financial liberalization and respective financial crisis
(base year=100 in each case, constant US$ values)

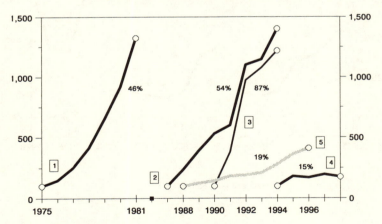

Percentages written in the graph are average *annual* rates of growth.
[1] = Chile; [2] = Mexico; [3] = Argentina; [4] = Brazil; and [5] = Korea.[20] Source: United Nations (2000).

---

19. See McKinnon and Pill (1997); for a critique of this position see Palma (1999c).
20. Argentina is included in this graph just to reinforce the point of the extraordinary increase in imports of consumer goods in non-Brazil Latin America, following their processes of trade and financial liberalization.

In "route 1" countries the expansion of imports of consumer goods is truly extraordinary; this is not the case in "route 2" countries, where the additional credit was directed towards investment. The corresponding figures for Malaysia and Thailand are also low (annual rates of growth of these imports are 16% and 19%, respectively), as these countries direct their additional credit towards investment (their leg in "route 2") and asset bubbles (their other leg in "route 1"), but not to consumption (a crucial characteristic of "route 1").

In the case of Brazil, mainly as a result of its interest rate policy (in part implemented after the Mexican crisis *precisely* in order to avoid following "route 1") and a more cautious policy of trade liberalization, imports of consumer goods did not grow anywhere near as quickly as in Chile or Mexico. In this sense, they succeeded in this aim, but at a huge cost in other areas of the economy (see the chapter on Brazil in this volume).

Figure 7 shows one element of the other main characteristic of "route 1," how the easy access to credit transformed itself into an asset bubble in the stock market, "tulipomania"-style.

FIGURE 7.

LATIN AMERICA and EAST ASIA: annual stock market indices between
the beginning of financial liberalization and respective financial crisis
(base year=100 in each case, constant US$ values)

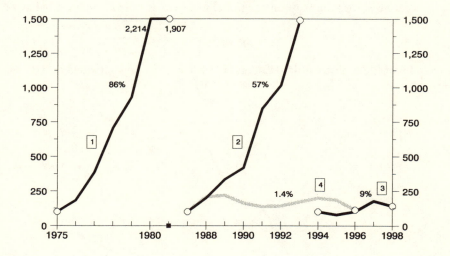

The percentages written in the graph are average *annual* rates of growth (the figure for Chile refers to 1975-1980).
[1] = Chile; [2] = Mexico; [3] = Brazil; and [4] = Korea.
SOURCE: Datastream.

Again, the difference between countries in "route 1" and the rest is extraordinary. While the Dow Jones and the (Datastream dollar-denominated) aggregate indices for the European and Asian markets grew by between 2 to 3-fold between 1975 and 1980, the stock market in Chile grew 22-fold in dollar terms.

Although the stock market in Chile in 1975 was still depressed as a result of the turmoil during the Allende government, the 1973 coup, and the subsequent stabilization program, it is difficult to argue that a 22-fold jump in U.S. dollar terms is simply prices reflecting changing fundamentals (no matter how much investors' expectations of future performance of the economy were excited by ongoing reforms). The massive crash of this index in the early 1980s confirms the fact that the foundations of the previous surge were rather hollow.

A similar argument can be advanced for Mexico; although economic reforms and NAFTA can, from the average investor's point of view, justify some life in the Mexican stock market, a 15-fold surge belongs to a different story—one of a typical Kindlebergian "mania." Again, the subsequent panic and crash are part of the same story.[21]

As mentioned above, Malaysia and Thailand did follow "route 1" countries in this respect, but their stock markets' bubbles were small in comparison with those of Chile or Mexico even if one compares the change between the lowest quarterly point in these countries' indices vis-à-vis the highest one—in Malaysia the increase is *6-fold* (between the second quarter of 1988 and the fourth quarter of 1993), while in Thailand the corresponding jump is *5.4-fold* (between the first quarter of 1988 and fourth quarter of 1993).

Figure 8 shows the resulting regional differences in stock market behavior.

FIGURE 8.

LATIN AMERICA, EAST ASIA, USA and EUROPE: stock market indices, 1987–98
(US$ terms, 1987=100)

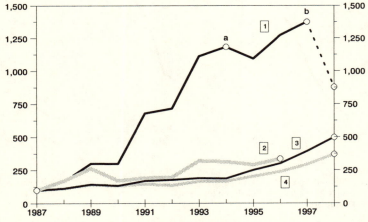

[1] = Latin America (a = Mexican crisis; b = East Asian crisis); [2] = Asian emerging markets; [3] = US (S&P); [4] = average of European markets. SOURCE: IFC (1999).[22]

Figure 9 shows the other asset bubble of "route 1" countries, that of real estate.

FIGURE 9.

LATIN AMERICA and EAST ASIA: real estate price indices between the beginning of financial liberalization and respective financial crisis
(local currencies, base year=100 in each case)

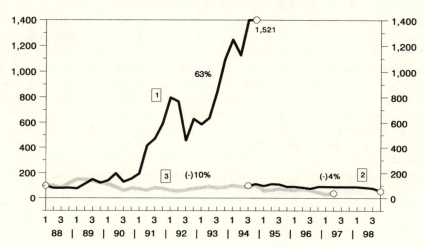

The percentages written in the graph are average *annual* rates of growth (for Mexico between the last quarter of 1988 and the last of 1994, for Korea between mid-1988 and mid-1997, and for Brazil between mid-1994 and mid-1998—i.e., before the Russian crisis; this index falls even further in the last two quarters of 1998).
[1] = Mexico; [2] = Brazil; and [3] = Korea.
SOURCE: Datastream. This source unfortunately does not provide information on Chile between 1975 and 1981.

The contrast could not be more pronounced: another Kindlebergian "mania" in Mexico and Chile,[23] and an actual fall in the indices of Korea and Brazil.[24]

Also, again, Malaysia and Thailand are in this respect much closer to countries in "route 1" than "route 2." In the case of Malaysia, the index between mid-1988 and mid-1997 grows (a Latin American) 12.3-fold (32% average annual rate of growth), while Thailand does so only 1.7-fold (6%) during this whole period. However, as Figure 17 in the Brazil chapter of this volume shows, if one

---

21. For a more detailed analysis of this phenomenon, see Palma (1995 and 1998).

22. See this source for countries included in each series.

23. Chilean Central Bank statistics (Chile 1988), although using a different methodology, show an increase similar to that of Mexico; however, due to the difference in methodology used for calculating this index to that of Datastream, the Chilean data are not included in the graph.

24. The Brazilian average is a mixture of some increase in Rio de Janeiro, stagnation in Sao Paulo, and a fall in Brasilia.

takes the highest and lowest points of the Thai index during these years (first quarter of 1988 and the third of 1994), the increase jumps to a more "route 1"-level of almost 8-fold.

It should come as no surprise, then, that countries on "route 1" were characterized by a large increase in the share of private consumption in GDP and a falling one in savings. In Chile the former grew from 65% to 75% of GDP and Mexico's from 66% to 78% in their respective periods; the latter in Chile had a dismal level of 1.7% of GDP the year before the 1982 crisis, and in Mexico the share of private savings in GDP fell from 20% in 1988 to just 10% the year before the 1994 crisis. In the meantime, the share of private investment in GDP in "route 1" countries reached a maximum of just 15% in their respective periods. Furthermore, as the real effective exchange rates were revalued by about half in both countries in their respective periods (see Figure 2 in the Brazil chapter), this, together with the other issues already discussed, not only rapidly increased their deficit in the current account (to a level equal to 96% of exports in Chile in 1981, and 41% in Mexico in 1994) and transformed the growth-path of these countries into the "postmodernist" scenario in which "export-led" growth is characterized by falling shares of exports in GDP (see Figure 3 in the Brazil chapter), but also, and very importantly, distorted the composition of what little investment there was towards its non-traded components.

FIGURE 10.

MEXICO: investment in residential construction, infrastructure, and machinery and equipment, 1981–94
(constant 1980 prices, 1981=100)

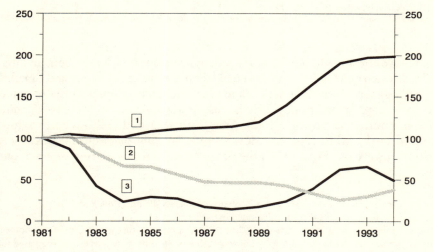

[1] = investment in residential construction; [2] = in infrastructure and business construction; and [3] = in machinery and equipment.
Source: Hofman (2000).

In this graph the starting point is 1981 because this year represents the peak of the previous (ISI) cycle.[25] While residential construction doubled in these 13 years, investment in machinery (despite its recovery in 1991-92) fell in all by half, and that in infrastructure and business construction fell by an even higher level. In other words, the distortion in relative prices (mainly brought about by the huge revaluation of the currency), the easy access to credit, and the asset bubble in real estate set in motion a "Kusnetz cycle" of rather large relative dimensions.

This is a rather odd picture for countries that explicitly seek to transform their economies into export-led ones. For the reasons discussed above, these "route 1" economies ended up switching the engine of growth away from their desired aim—domestically financed private investment in tradable production—towards private consumption, asset bubbles, and externally financed private investment in non-tradable production (and services).

Figure 11 reinforces what has been said above regarding the key difference between "route 1" and "route 2" countries. The large capital inflows and massive expansion in private credit in "route 2" is used mainly to finance the ambitious investment plans of the corporate sector.

FIGURE 11.

SOUTH KOREA: sectoral surpluses of the corporate,
household, public, and foreign sectors, 1982–96
(current prices, % of GNP)

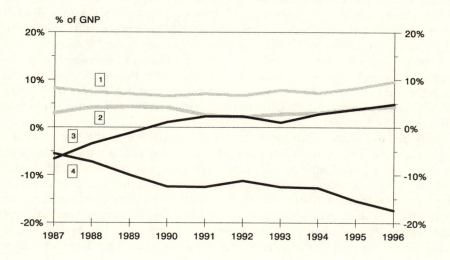

Sectoral surpluses are the respective differences between savings and investment. [1] = household sector; [2] = government sector; [3] = capital account of the balance of payments; and [4] = corporate sector.

---

25. According to this source, Chile presents a similar picture.

As discussed in detail in the Brazil chapter of this volume, and mainly due to declining profitability (a decline which had little to do with the Krugman-type of critique of the development path of these countries, and a lot to do with collapsing prices in the microelectronic industry[26]), the corporate sector has to finance its continuous high levels of investment switching from its own profits to external finance.[27] This process absorbs all the increase in the surplus of the "foreign sector." This is the key characteristic of the "route 2"-style of foreign inflows-absorption, and what most distinguishes this style from that of "route 1."

Malaysia and Thailand, with some added peculiarities, basically share this characteristic with Korea. In the case of Malaysia, this country *doubled* its share of private investment in GDP during this period, from 15% in 1988 to 30.5% in 1995; and despite the fact that it also doubled its share of private savings in GDP to 20% (and in the process reduced its share of private consumption in GDP to 45.9%), it still has an increasing savings-investment gap to finance. Thailand, meanwhile, increased its share of private investment in GDP to an even higher level, 34%, while maintaining the share of private savings (at about 22%, while reducing that of private consumption marginally to 55%); so, again, another savings-investment gap to finance.

The case of Brazil is discussed in detail in the companion chapter in this volume; basically, and in an apparently odd development, little seems to have happened on all of these fronts. While the share of private investment in GDP was maintained at about 15% (despite massive inflows of foreign direct investment), that of consumption increased by little (from 62.7% in 1994 to 64.4% in 1998, a much lower level than "route 1" countries), and private savings also fell by a smaller share than "route 1" (from 18% to 14% between 1995 and 1998). The "iron curtain" placed by the economic authorities around the surge in net private inflows—precisely in order to avoid a repetition of a Mexican "route 1"-style of inflow-absorption—seems to have succeeded in this respect; however, as is argued in the Brazil chapter, it did so at a huge cost, which ended up being hardly different in magnitude (although very different in composition) from that of "route 1" countries.

To end this section showing the characteristics of the three routes to financial crises, it is important to emphasize that they also have significant elements in common. Figure 1 already shows their similarities in terms of surges in net private inflows following their respective processes of financial liberalization. Figures 12 to 16 now indicate that these countries also share common elements that added to their growing financial fragilities; i.e., no matter how different their processes of absorption of these surges in inflows are, they have to face at least three further similar problems. One is the constant changing composition

---

26. The D-Ram price per megabyte fell from $26 in 1995 to $10 in 1996 and US$ 4 in 1997; see *The Financial Times*, May 8 1999.

27. At the time of writing this paper, Daewoo was being crushed by the weight of its $80 billion debt.

of these large net private capital inflows; the next is the progressive shortening of their term structure; and the last is that in a financially liberalized economy there is also a constant danger of an attack from "within."

Figure 12 shows the first of these issues for the case of Mexico.

FIGURE 12.

MEXICO: composition of net private capital inflows (WB), 1970–94

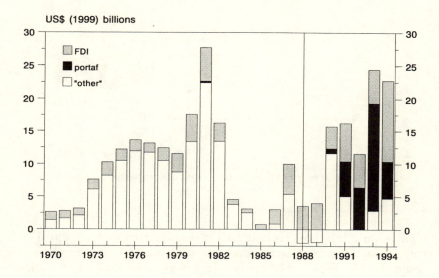

FDI = foreign direct investment; portaf. = portfolio inflows; and "other" = other inflows.
SOURCE: World Bank (2000b); see this source for definition of components.

In the case of Mexico, as in Brazil (Figure 1 in the Brazil chapter) and Korea (Figure 13 below), only foreign direct investment grows in a relatively stable manner—although even this more "stable" component of net capital inflows more than doubles in one year in Mexico (from $5 billion in 1993 to over $12 billion in 1994; similar jumps are found in Brazil). However, net private portfolio inflows are all over the place, growing in Mexico from less than $1 billion in 1990, to more than $5 billion in 1991, to jump again from $6 billion in 1992 to US$ 16.5 billion in 1993, then falling to less than $6 billion in 1994 (all at 1999 values)—i.e., it changes from less than 1% of net private inflows in 1990, to over one-third in 1991, and from about half in 1992 to over two-thirds in 1993, to fall to just one-quarter in 1994. The share of "other" net capital inflows also changes rapidly. Figure 13 shows the picture for Korea.

FIGURE 13.

KOREA: composition of net private capital inflows (WB), 1970–97

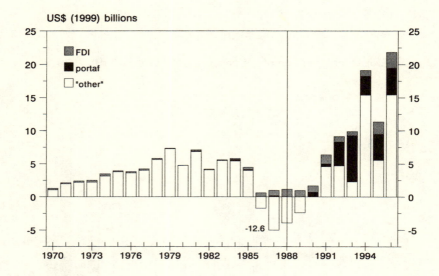

Sources and definitions as in Figure 12.

There are at least four issues related to this changing composition. The first is that, although it is common to all countries, it has a larger magnitude in "route 1" countries. This is probably related to the large and unstable asset bubbles in these countries. The second is that, although *volumes* of net capital inflows in the 1970s also changed rapidly, particularly in Mexico, the constantly changing *composition* of inflows is a phenomenon of the 1990s.

The third is a methodological issue that is important for the next section of this paper; if composition of net private inflows is changing continuously and to such a degree in countries that did not impose capital controls, is there any way of knowing with any certainty whether controls really did affect composition by themselves?[28]

The fourth and most important issue is that this changing composition made the already difficult matter of absorbing massive inflows even more complicated, and one that was bound to create even more financial fragility within these countries

---

28. In an econometric exercise (that we do not have space in this paper to report), I found that if Mexico had imposed capital controls at the same time as Chile did (1991), and these had had no effect at all on the actual composition of net capital inflows (i.e., net private inflows in Mexico would have been exactly the same), one could still "prove" statistically that these (nonexistent) controls did have a "significant" effect on composition, as this composition changed so much in its own right (so to speak).

(fragility in a "Minskian" sense—i.e., that augments the weight of "speculative" and "Ponzi" finance).

Finally, the term structure of the net inflows of foreign capital is also changing during this period, but in a different form from the composition of inflows: the movement is in one direction (unless controls were imposed, as will be discuss below). Obviously, this adds further fragility to an already difficult situation.

FIGURE 14.

LATIN AMERICA and EAST ASIA: ratio of short-term debt to total debt between the beginning of financial liberalization and respective financial crisis

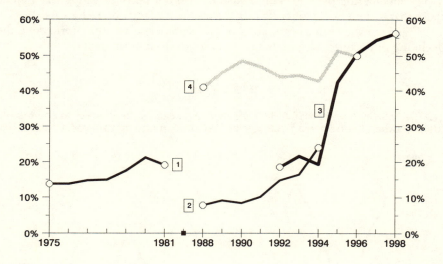

[1] = Chile; [2] = Mexico; [3] = Brazil; and [4] = Korea.
SOURCE: IMF (2000c).

Comparing first "route 1" and "route 3" countries, there is a clear increase in the share of short-term debt as time goes by. Mexico starts in 1988 with a share of short-term debt in its total foreign debt of 8%, to end up with a 24% share in 1994, at the time of its financial crisis; then Brazil takes over with a relatively similar share as Mexico's in 1994 (20%), and ends up with one of 56% in 1998. IMF statistics (2000c) show a similar progressive increase in this share over time for most Latin American countries.

What is important to note here is that the major increase in Brazil's share of short-term debt happened in 1994-95, when this ratio more than doubled (from 20% to 42%); and this was a time when most of Brazil's fundamentals still were (deceptively) exemplary!

Turning now to "route 2" countries, what is really extraordinary is that they had high shares of short-term debt much earlier than Latin America—and when problems blew up in 1997, they paid a high price for this. Logic would suggest that this should have been the other way round, because in the late 1980s and early 1990s (according to any available risk assessment) the likelihood of a financial crisis was so much higher in Latin America than in East Asia. So, why did East Asian countries have such a high share of short-term debt?[29] The answer is as obvious as it is extraordinary. East Asian countries, especially Korea, had implemented a system of financial regulation that gave a huge incentive to the corporate sector to borrow "short." Basically, there was a lot of red tape for any form of long-term borrowing and very little for short-term borrowing. That is, it was the Korean government that gave the incentive to Korean corporations to borrow short, as opposed to the international financial system imposing short-term debt on them! This is an amazing phenomenon that so far had not been properly picked up by those that make a hobby of criticizing government regulation in East Asia!

Figure 15 shows one of the consequences of increasing short-term debt: the declining ratios of foreign exchange reserves to short-term debt.

FIGURE 15.

LATIN AMERICA and EAST ASIA: ratio of foreign exchange reserves to short-term debt between the beginning of financial liberalization and respective financial crisis

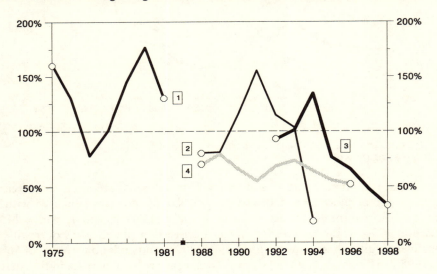

[1] = Chile; [2] = Mexico; [3] = Brazil; and [4] = Korea.

---

29. In 1991, for example, while 70% of BIS reporting banks' assets in Korea and Thailand were in short-term maturities, the corresponding figure for Mexico was less than 40%, for Argentina just over 40%, and for Brazil 45%; see BIS (1999).

First, in terms of "route 2" countries, Korea's main weakness in 1997—that made it so vulnerable to events in Thailand and Malaysia; i.e., so vulnerable to what these days people like to call the "contagion" effect—was precisely its low ratio of reserves to short-term debt. Figure 15 indicates that Korea's reserves could cover only half its short-term liabilities; and what this Figure does not show is that, in fact, they were not enough even to cover foreign liabilities with 90 days maturity or less! Again, as in the case of a large "voluntary" share of short-term debt in total foreign debt, Central Bank authorities in Korea seemed to have had a misguided sense of security, operating "voluntarily" with low levels of reserves, which compounded the short-term debt problem: they paid dearly for this in 1997.[30]

This is obviously an issue that needs further investigation because the Korean authorities seemed to have had a sort of schizophrenia vis-à-vis economic planning and regulation: in matters relating to the real economy and some aspects of domestic finance, they felt the need for strong and detailed intervention (particularly in the form of trade and industrial policies, and tight financial domestic regulation in areas relating to the household sector), but in areas relating to the capital account and monetary policy, they seemed only to have been interested in long-term capital movement, exchange rate stability, and in keeping interest rates as low as it was feasible; this left unchecked what turned out to be two "suicidal" tendencies in the economy: that of the corporate sector to accumulate truly extraordinary amounts of short-term debt, and that of the Central Bank to operate with low levels of reserves.

In terms of "route 3" countries, Brazilian authorities had a mixed policy on these issues. First, as the Cardoso quotation at the beginning of this paper shows, they were against intervening in the capital account to reduce the share of short-term foreign debt (they were against instruments such as capital controls). However, they did make a serious and continuous attempt to increase the level of reserves; but, as Figure 15 shows, this seems to have given them a false sense of security because short-term debt grew even faster and, as the "fundamentals" deteriorated rapidly, the economy was left extremely vulnerable to a sudden collapse of confidence and withdrawal of finance.

Finally, of course, in a financially liberalized economy, the "attack" could also just as easily come from "within."

In the 1990s, none of the three paradigmatic countries seemed to have had significant defenses against internal attacks on their exchange rates.[31]

In sum, "route 1" countries, after massive surges in capital inflows, followed a path to financial crisis led by an explosion of credit to the private sector, low levels

---

30. See Palma (1998). Recent statements by new Central Bank authorities in Korea have shown that they certainly learned this lesson: now the stated policy is to aim at a ratio of two between foreign exchange reserves and short-term debt (i.e., a ratio four times higher than that of 1997).

31. In a separate paper I analyze some of the political consequences of this "internal" vulnerability of liberalized economies, in particular vis-à-vis internal political distributional conflict; see Palma (1999a).

FIGURE 16.

LATIN AMERICA and EAST ASIA: ratio of foreign exchange reserves to M2 between the beginning of financial liberalization and respective financial crisis

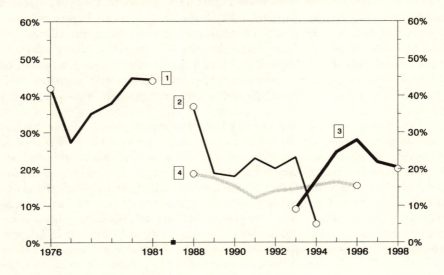

[1] = Chile; [2] = Mexico; [3] = Brazil; and [4] = Korea.

of interest rates (after stabilization), and a rapid revaluation of their real exchange rates. All these produced consumption booms, assets bubbles in the stock exchange and in real estate, a reduced level of savings, a massive deterioration of current accounts, and distorted the already low levels of investment towards residential construction. In the meantime, the level of foreign debt grew out of control, while its term structure deteriorated. It did not take much for this route to encounter some problem which led to a sudden collapse of confidence and withdrawal of finance, leading to major financial crises.

In turn, "route 2" countries, particularly Korea, again after massive surges in capital inflows followed a path to financial crisis also led by an explosion of credit to the private sector, and by particularly low levels of interest rates. But this credit, instead of being used for consumption booms or asset bubbles, was used to sustain high levels of investment in a situation of declining profitability and rapid technological change in a world (particularly that of electronics) where there were collapsing prices, but life only at the cutting-edge of technology. This ended up producing corporate debt/equity ratios that reached heights that even for this part of the world should have produced serious feelings of vertigo. Added to this there were incomprehensive policy incentives to the corporate and financial sector to borrow abroad short and a central bank that seems to have enjoyed the thrill of living dangerously with low levels of reserves. Again—and despite the extraordinary growth record of Korea, its remarkable degree of competitiveness, and having fundamentals that although not perfect were the envy of "route 1" and "route 3" countries (and most other LDCs)—it did not take much for this route also to encounter problems that lead to a sudden collapse of confidence and withdrawal of finance, leading to major financial crises.

As far as Malaysia and Thailand are concerned, they followed a mix of "route 1" and "route 2." Again after massive surges in capital inflows, they followed a path to financial crisis also led by an (even higher) explosion of credit to the private sector, but without the revaluation of exchange rates, consumption booms, declining savings and distorted investment of "route 1." The mix included the asset bubbles of "route 1" and most of the problems of "route 2" as well, but also with the added problem that they were reaching a point in their process of development where not only was further upgrading of exports to higher value-added products becoming increasingly difficult (in particular to break away from a "subcontracting" type of industrialization), but also where China was becoming a formidable competitor in many of the markets that were crucial to these second-tier East Asian NICs. Again—and also despite their strong growth record, their growing degree of competitiveness, and having fundamentals that although worse than those of Korea, were still better than those of "route 1" and "route 3" countries (and of many LDCs)—it was not long before this "mixed" route also encountered problems (in this case in the form of voracious fund managers, eager to profit from long-standing but only abruptly acknowledged peccadilloes of these economies) that led to a sudden collapse of confidence and withdrawal of finance, leading to major financial crises.[32]

Finally, "route 3." As discussed in detail in the Brazil chapter of this volume, this third route to financial crisis also started with a massive surge in capital inflows. The scene was soon dominated by high interest rates, initially necessary for price-stabilization, but later becoming stubbornly permanent to avoid another Mexico and to respond to external shocks. These high interest rates were successful in avoiding a repeat of "route 1," but soon created massive domestic financial fragility in the banking system and in the public sector finance. These rates, which became systematically higher than both the growth in public revenues and the returns on foreign exchange reserves, led to an increase in the stock of public debt via government rescue activities and this public debt exploded. In the meantime the real economy imploded because of those rates, which affected the growth of public revenues even further. High interest rates became even more necessary as a (poor) substitute for missing public sector reforms and political stalemate, and to defend the "peg" in order to avoid both further domestic banking crises due to high foreign-exchange banking liabilities

---

32. One common element to all these financial crises is the way in which international financial markets, Washington institutions, and the financial press have interpreted economic news from these LDCs; this interpretation has repeatedly gone through a three-stage cycle: in the first, good news is exaggerated and bad news is simply ignored (the "turning a blind eye" stage); in the second stage, bad news cannot be ignored any longer but it is believed that there isn't anything that can't be handled (the "omnipotent stage"); and in the third, there is a sudden turn towards panic, when bad news is not only properly acknowledged, but it is exaggerated, sometimes grossly, often by a seemingly insignificant event (the "hysterical stage).

and a stampede by restless international fund managers. The "Ponzi" finance in the public sector ballooned out of control. Again, it did not take much for this route too to have a sudden collapse of confidence and withdrawal of finance, leading to a major financial crisis.

So, the moral of the story of the "three routes" is that no matter how LDCs facing sudden and massive surges in capital inflows have handled their absorption, they have ended up in major financial crises. Of course, with hindsight one can always think of theoretical ways in which the worst excesses in each of these three routes could have been avoided, but the fact is that the economic (and political) dynamic created by these surges in capital inflows is one that has proved extraordinarily difficult to control.

CAN CAPITAL CONTROLS HELP? AND BY HOW MUCH?

Keynes once wrote that economics would only be successful if economists had the same ability as dentists to address and solve practical problems. Well, here LDCs are faced with a practical economic problem if ever there was one: how to live with a liberalized capital account, in a world with an already high, rapidly expanding, ever more volatile, and practically unregulated financial liquidity.

The previous section of this chapter was crucial for placing capital controls within the context of the extraordinary mess they were expected to deal with. No matter how optimistic one could be regarding their effectiveness, after section two one could hardly expect too much from them; at best one could expect capital controls to be just one component in a complex package for dealing with these issues.

This section will briefly study the inflow-controls experiences of Chile and Malaysia. Beginning with the case of Chile, price-based capital controls were established in 1991; capital inflows were subject to a flat rate foreign-currency deposit in the Central Bank, reaching a peak value of 30%. This was originally meant to last for only a three-month period, but was later extended to 12 months.[33] There was an alternative to this deposit (also used in Colombia), which was to pay the Central Bank a sum equivalent to the opportunity cost of the deposit—this made it into a "Tobin-type" tax, as it was equivalent to a fixed cost for external borrowing. By Tobin tax standards, however, this tax was very high (about 3% for one-year loans during booms in the capital market),[34] and tended to

---

33. In the relatively similar case of Colombia (created in 1993), as Ocampo (2000) explains, this deposit requirement applied only to credits with maturities below a specified term (initially 18 months, but this was later lengthened to between three and five years); the amount to be deposited was inversely proportional to the term of the credit. Because of its greater complexity, this system was replaced by a simpler one in 1997 that was more similar to the Chilean scheme, the main difference being that the deposit (originally 30% for 18 months) is made in the local currency and is therefore not protected from devaluation. For reasons of space, and because the subject has been dealt with thoroughly by Ocampo, the Colombian case will not be discussed here.

34. According to Ocampo, the level for Colombia was even higher—average level of 13.6% for one-year loans and 6.4% for three-year loans (during 1994–1998).

fluctuate in response to changes in certain macroeconomic factors, such as international interest rates.[35] This tax was aimed at having a counter-cyclical role, which is why it has been raised during periods of rapid expansion, and lowered (even to a zero rate in both countries) when necessary (for example, in the aftermath of recent financial crises).

Furthermore, controls on capital inflows have not been limited to reserve requirements; for example, until very recently all inflows (including direct investment and portfolio flows) were subject to a one-year minimum stay requirement. There were also numerous regulations regarding minimum sums and ratings for bond and ADR issues on the external market.[36]

Figure 17 shows the level and composition of net private capital inflows in Chile before, during, and after capital controls.

FIGURE 17.

CHILE: composition of net private capital inflows (WB), 1988–97

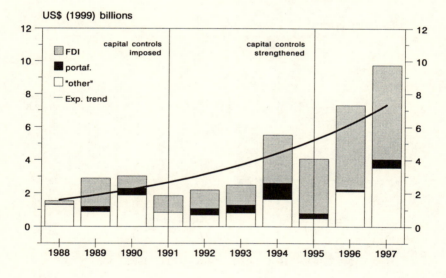

Exp. trend = simple exponential trend.
As Figure 12 for source and definitions of components of inflows.

---

35. For the case of Colombia, domestic interest rate and devaluation expectations also played an important role.

36. In Colombia, the Superintendent of Securities could also regulate the operations of portfolio investors in the country and bond or ADR issues made by Colombian firms on foreign markets. Although trade loans were exempt from reserve requirements, other types of regulation have been used to control this type of borrowing.

As is fairly evident from the graph, in terms of *levels*, capital controls in Chile seem to have had a significant but rather short-term effect. By 1994 the 1991 reduction seems to have evaporated, and the reduction brought about by the 1995 strengthening of controls seems only to have lasted for one year.[37] Of course, we will never know what levels these inflows would have reached had it not been for these controls, but the evidence seems to indicate that private inflows did bounce back after having been affected briefly by the imposition of controls. So, in terms of volume, then, these controls seem to have had the effect of "speed bumps" rather than speed restrictions, although in terms of composition there is a clear increase in the share of foreign direct investment.[38] This phenomenon is even clearer in Figure 18.

FIGURE 18.

CHILE: net equity securities and "other" investment (IMF), 1988–97

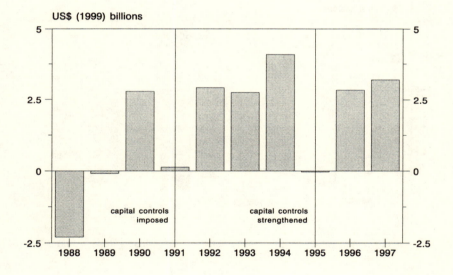

Source: IMF (2000b). See this source for definitions.

---

37. The empirical literature that tries to test whether controls in Chile were effective, and whether they had more effect on levels or on composition is extensive; see for example Valdés-Prieto and Soto (1998).
38. But the increase in the share of FDI is also found in countries that did not impose controls, such as Brazil; see the relevant chapter in this volume.

In terms of volume, net equity securities and "other" investments, which up to 1995 represented a major component of total net private inflows, reacted quite extraordinarily to the imposition and strengthening of controls; in fact, they actually vanished from the scene altogether. However, in both instances, these disappearing acts lasted for just one year!

So, the basic evidence on the effect of controls in Chile in terms of *volume* of inflows seems to tend towards significant but short-term effects. Of course, this phenomenon is not independent from the level that these price controls actually reached (which, as mentioned above, although high for a standard Tobin-tax level, were lower than those of Colombia, and, in practice, much milder than Malaysia's controls in 1994); unfortunately, there is no sufficient data from which to construct a proper measurement for the relevant elasticity.

Furthermore, these controls not only seem to have had little effect on levels, but were also fairly ineffective in tackling two crucial problems facing the Chilean economy at the time (see Figure 19).

FIGURE 19.

CHILE: real effective exchange rate and foreign exchange reserves, 1988–98

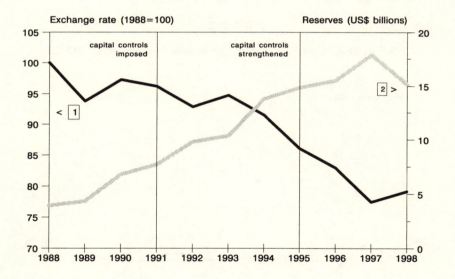

[1] = real effective exchange rate; and [2] level of foreign exchange reserves.

One should not forget that the immediate reason for the Chilean Central Bank imposing controls in 1991 in the first place was both the continuous pressure on the peso to revalue beyond the permitted "band," and the ever growing levels of reserves. These phenomena not only forced the bank to implement increasingly costly amounts of sterilization, but were also threatening to seriously imbalance an economy that was growing extremely quickly and in clear danger of overheating. However, as Figure 19 shows, controls were particularly ineffective in dealing with either problem; the level of reserves continued to increase and the revaluation of the peso in fact gathered pace.

As it happened, the 1997 East Asian crisis "succeeded" where capital controls failed, by quickly reversing both trends (see Figure 19). In this respect, one of the main stylized facts of the Chilean economy in the 1990s was the contrasting effect of the 1994 Mexican crisis and the 1997 East Asia crisis; and this contrast, of course, was not independent of these ineffective aspects of capital controls (at least at the levels that they were applied in Chile at the time) in dealing in particular with the problem of the continuous revaluation of the peso. As a result, while the "Tequila effect" that swept Latin America in 1995 found the Chilean economy with a balanced current account (which, obviously, helped the Chilean economy enormously to weather this crisis), the 1997 East Asian crisis found the Chilean current account not only in the red, but already at a level equal to 20% of exports.[39]

Well, then, is there anything really positive that can be said for Chilean-style, and levels, of price-based capital account regulations? The answer is yes, and starts in Figure 20.

FIGURE 20.

CHILE vs BRAZIL and THAILAND: short-term foreign debt, 1989–98

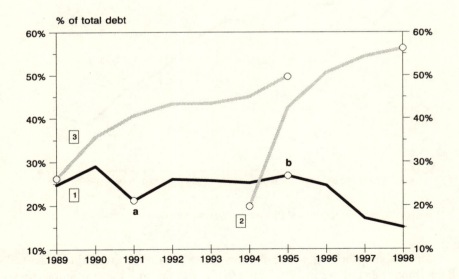

[1] = Chile; [2] = Brazil; and [3] = Thailand.
Source: IMF (2000c).

Figure 20 highlights one of the main econometric problems of studying whether controls were effective in Chile in terms of affecting the share of short-term debt in total foreign debt. The question is which one is the counterfactual? Is it a matter of controls being effective because they reduced this share vis-à-vis *its own trend*, or were they effective because they helped Chile not to follow the trend *of other LDCs* that did not impose controls (like Thailand or Brazil)? If, for example, Chile's share had increased, but not by as much as these other two countries, could this increase be taken as a sign of failure or of success of its capital account regulations?

As it happened, *vis-à-vis its own trend*, capital controls seem to have had little long-lasting effect in Chile until 1995, but a significant one after the strengthening of controls in that year.[40] However, if the comparison is made vis-à-vis the trend followed by countries that did not impose controls, such as Thailand and Brazil, then controls in Chile seem to have had quite an extraordinary effect *from the very beginning*. For example, though Thailand and Chile had the same level of foreign debt in 1989, by 1995 Thailand had a share twice as large as Chile's.

Furthermore, at the beginning of the *Plano Real* and full-blown financial liberalization in Brazil in 1994, Chile actually had a share of short-term debt five percentage points higher than that of Brazil; however, by 1998, Brazil's share was nearly four times higher than Chile's. Moreover, by 1996, when the financial press only had praise for Brazil's economic reform program (i.e., when it was still in the "turning the blind eye" stage), Brazil's share of short-term debt had already more than doubled that of Chile (which had just strengthened its capital account regulations).

So, in terms of flows, Chilean-style (and levels of) capital account regulations seem to have had little long-lasting effect in controlling the *volume* of inflows, but probably some in helping to shift the composition of flows towards a larger share of foreign direct investment. However, in terms of stocks, they seem to have had a major influence in restraining the share of short-term debt in the total.

Added to this, and as opposed to what most of the relevant literature does, the effectiveness of capital controls should not only be tested vis-à-vis the changes in the external accounts of a country, either in their flows or stocks, but also regarding the effects on the macro-economy in general. Figure 21 looks at one of these important effects.

---

39. And as this crisis affected Chilean exports badly both in volume and prices—Chile had the highest share of exports going to these markets in Latin America, and prices of many commodities exported by Chile fell sharply after this crisis—by 1998 Chile's current account deficit had increased further, to 25% of exports.

40. In fact, according to Chile's Central Bank balance of payments statistics, after 1995 this share fell even further than is indicated by the IMF source used in this graph—from over 18% in 1994, to 16% in 1995, 12% in 1996, and less than 5% in 1997. According to IMF data, both in Colombia and Malaysia the share of short-term debt in the total also fell significantly; from 22% in 1995 to 13% in 1998, and from 25% in 1993 to 18% in 1994, respectively.

FIGURE 21.

CHILE: quarterly stock market index, 1989–99
(US$ terms, 3/89=100)

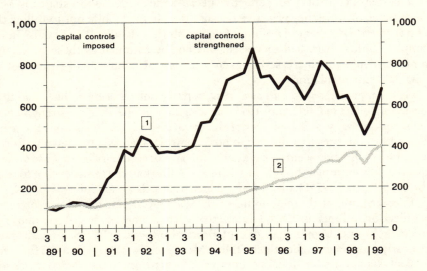

[1] = Chile's quarterly stock market index in US dollar terms; and [2] Dow Jones.
SOURCE: Datastream.

As is clear from the graph, Chile was again experiencing an asset bubble in its stock market in early 1991—in the four quarters preceding the first imposition of controls the index used in Figure 21 had jumped by as much as 3.3-fold; seven quarters after the introduction of these controls, the index was still stuck at the same level. However, as in the *levels* of net private inflows studied above, this effect soon ran its course and together with the huge new increase in inflows in 1994, this index jumped again, this time 2.3-fold (following eight quarters). Then the strengthening of controls in 1995 had an immediate impact on this new bubble, bringing the index down considerably; and when it began to re-cover again in early 1997, with the new increases in inflows, the mid-1997 East Asian crisis put also a stop to that (as had happened with the revaluation of the exchange rate and increases in reserves).

Something similar, but even more pronounced, took place in real estate after 1995 (see Figure 22).

FIGURE 22.

CHILE: quarterly real estate index, 1989–99
(local currency, 3/89=100)

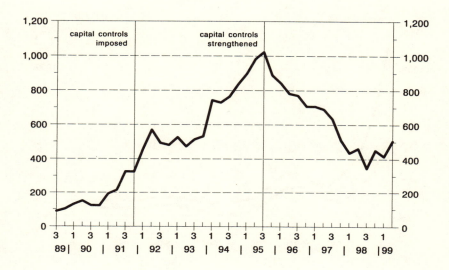

SOURCE: Datastream.

In this market Chile is facing another bubble when capital controls are imposed in 1991. In this case, the (short-term) reduction in net private inflows that
came with inflow-controls did not have such an immediate effect as in the stock
market, but seems to have had a significant delayed one; by then (mid-1992),
this index had already increased 4.7-fold in just six quarters. However, as in the
stock market, the respite is also temporary, and this index doubles again between
the end of 1993 and the strengthening of capital controls in the third quarter of
1995, following the renewed increase in inflows. The subsequent fall is remarkable—as in the stock market these new controls seemed to have had the effect of
starting a process that took all the life out of this market (even though the economy
continued to grow rapidly until 1998).

Finally, Figure 23 shows another related aspect of the Chilean economy that,
at least in timing, is associated with the imposition of capital account regulations.

From the perspective of the variables included in Figure 23, between 1975
and 1997 the Chilean economy can be clearly classified into three sub-periods;
from liberalization to crisis, from crisis to capital controls, and from the imposition of capital account regulations to the East Asian crisis. Of course, from 1991
onward there were more things happening in the Chilean economy than capital
controls, not least the return to democracy, the change in the economic team (away
from the "Chicago boys"), tighter and more effective regulation and supervision

FIGURE 23.

CHILE: credit to the private sector and real interest rates, 1975–97
(3-year moving average, %)

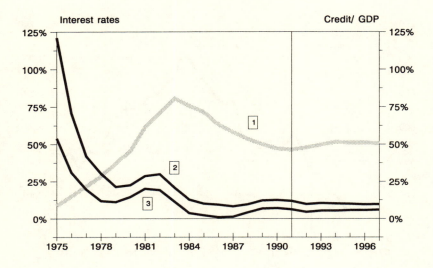

[1] = credit to the private sector; [2] = real lending rates; and [3] = real deposit rates.

of the domestic financial system,[41] and the large post-Pinochet degree of consensus behind the economic model. But for the reasons discussed above, the weight of the evidence seems to support the hypothesis that capital account regulations can rightfully claim to have played at least a part in the more macrostable post-1991 story.

Turning now briefly to the Malaysian case, as Figure 24 shows, the surge of net private capital inflows, in relative terms, could probably claim a place in the Guinness Book of Records.

In fact, it is even difficult to imagine how one can run an economy that is facing this kind of surge in capital inflows. Facing this problem, the Malaysian authorities decided to impose strict controls on capital inflows at the beginning of 1994. Unlike the Chilean and Colombian experiments with capital account regulation, the key characteristic of these controls is that they were quantitative in nature; in particular, strict controls on foreign exchange exposures were placed on Malaysian banks and large corporations. Also, deposit interest rates were reduced drastically—real deposit rates fell from an annual average of 4.2% in 1993

41. Another positive aspect of price-based capital controls in Chile (which there is no space in this chapter to expand on), is that they seem to have mixed well with better regulation of the domestic financial system (which by nature, takes more quantitative forms).

FIGURE 24.

MALAYSIA: net private capital inflows (IMF), 1988–96

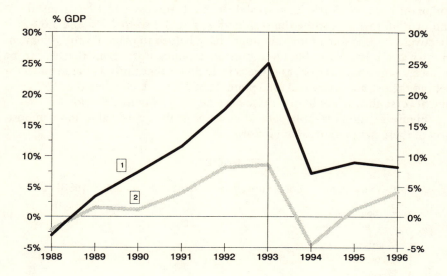

[1] = net private capital inflows; and [2] = their short-term component.
SOURCE: IMF (2000b); includes "errors and omissions"; see this source for definition of "short-term" flows.

to one of minus 0.93% in 1994, and real lending rates from 6.2% to 1.8%, respectively; this was done in order to reverse arbitrage flows, both "passive" and "active" ones. Also, there was some relaxation of financial restrictions on residents.

As these measures were so drastic, and as they included such an strong quantitative component, the effect was not only immediate, but also dramatic; so much so that as early as September of the same year, some of the controls were already beginning to be lifted, and by the end of the year most had disappeared: the Malaysian authorities seem to have developed some "overshooting" anxiety.

In fact, net private inflows fell in one year by no less than 18 percentage points of GDP! These measures seem to have been particularly effective vis-à-vis short-term flows, which fell by more than 13 percentage points of GDP in one year; and, although these recovered after 1994 with the lifting of controls, total net private inflows did not, at least in relative GDP terms, continuing at just under 10% right up until the 1997 crisis. This quantitative short-sharp-shock seems to have had rather more long-lasting effects than the continuing (and strengthening) Chilean price-based controls. Maybe when drastic action is needed, as was clearly the case in Malaysia in 1994, quantitative controls are to be preferred.[42]

---

42. This point is supported by Tobin, who advocates a system in which "[...] governments should limit the hard currency exposure of banks and business" (2000, p. 1104).

However, not all elements of the inflow-control package were dismantled at the end of 1994; low interest rates were maintained as part of residual policy package to disincentive a possible rapid return of private capital inflows after the end of quantitative restrictions—real deposit rate increased in 1995 to just 0.9% and in 1996 to 1.8%, while the real lending rate did so to 2.5% and 3.6%, respectively. This is something that might have helped to maintain the volume of inflows at a relatively stable level, but was a policy instrument that was to be seriously regretted later on, as there is little doubt that this was the main factor behind the extraordinary real estate bubble of 1996, which made the 1997 crisis much worse than it would otherwise have been (see Figure 28 below).

Figure 25 shows what happened in terms of the actual value and composition of these net private capital inflows.

FIGURE 25.

MALAYSIA: composition of net private capital inflows (IMF), 1988–96

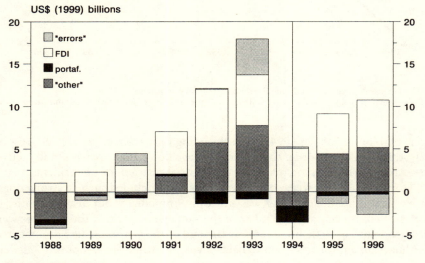

SOURCE: as Figure 24.

As the majority of the harsh quantitative controls lasted for even less than a year, and the 1997 crisis came so soon after the imposition of (and lifting of the majority of) controls, we will never know whether this "short-sharp-shock"-type of control could have had more long-term effects on the levels and/or composition of net private capital inflows; i.e., whether they made international fund and bank managers restless in a more permanent way. As it happened, the reduction of private inflows in 1994 was substantial—other than in FDI—and the recovery in 1995 and 1996 (after the lifting of most controls) was relatively slow—at least compared with the recovery of net private inflows in Chile after 1995, when there was a particularly rapid recovery, despite the fact that the price-based controls were not only still in place, but that they had just been strengthened.

Figure 26 shows the changes in non-FDI inflows to reinforce the point.

FIGURE 26.

MALAYSIA: net "other," portfolio investment, and "errors" (IMF), 1988–96

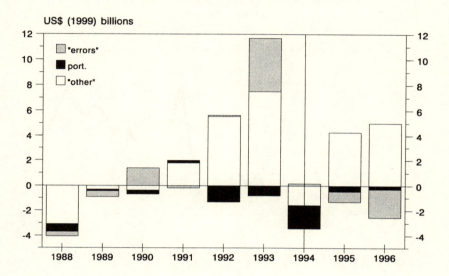

According to Figure 26, non-FDI inflows had increased by about $16 billion between 1988 and 1993; the 1994 controls reversed this whole increase in just one year. Moreover, the recovery after most controls were lifted took place only in "other" inflows, leaving net portfolio inflows still in a net negative figure; finally, "errors and omissions" changed from a large positive to a large negative net figure.

One of the main peculiarities of the Malaysia case is the large size of the balance of payments item "errors and omissions." This phenomenon is relevant not only because it reveals pre-1994 deficiencies in Malaysia's Central Bank accounting practices, but also because with controls in place they first disappear, and then, become negative. The relevance of this is that one of the most repeated criticisms of controls is that they would tend to be ineffective because capital will always find ways of bypassing them. Well, in Malaysia it seems to have been the other way round; with controls came a successful tightening of procedures of recording inflows, and a massive reduction, rather than an increase, in this item.[43]

---

43. The negative figures for this item in 1995 and 1996 probably reflect capital flight by Malaysian citizens. If this was the case, like their counterparts in Mexico before their December 1994 crisis, maybe they predicted trouble with better foresight than international fund and bank managers did.

Finally, Figures 27 and 28 show that in Malaysia, as in Chile, even if capital account regulations only led to temporary reductions in net private inflows, these seem to have enough capacity to pierce asset bubbles, helping to keep macrostability within the economy.

FIGURE 27.

MALAYSIA: quarterly stock market index, 1988–97
(US$ terms, 1/88=100)

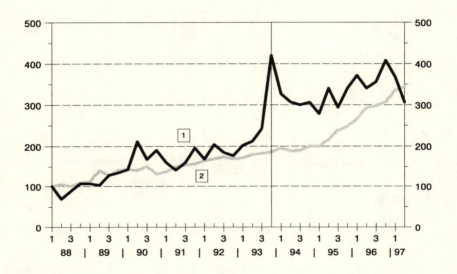

[1] = Malaysia's dollar denominated index; and [2] = Dow Jones index.
Source: Datastream.

Figure 27 shows the remarkable jump in stock prices at the time of the surge in inflows in 1993. Before the imposition of controls, this index jumped 2.4-fold in just four quarters. However, during the three-quarters that these controls lasted in full, this index fell by 30%; it then began to recover somewhat erratically, almost reaching the previous peak again in the last quarter of 1996.[44]

Figure 28 shows the extraordinary behavior of real estate prices in Malaysia.

First, as in the stock market, there was a rapid bubble developing in real estate prices before the imposition of controls; the jump in the index in the four quarters before the imposition of controls was equivalent to a 2.6-fold increase. Second, as in Chile, the piercing of this bubble was not as immediate as the one in the stock exchange. Third, as opposed to Chile, the return of inflows in 1995

---

44. The crash after the mid-1997 crisis was equally remarkable; by the third quarter of 1998 the local currency denominated index had fallen to just 38% of its early 1997 level.

FIGURE 28.

MALAYSIA: quarterly real estate index, 1988–97
(local currency, 1/88=100)

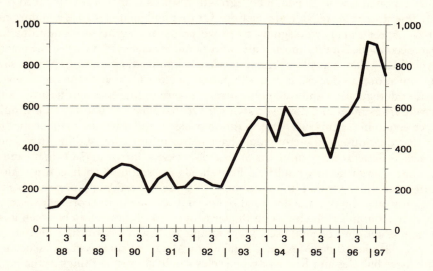

SOURCE: Datastream.

pushed this index back up with a vengeance; of course, the difference was in the levels of interest rates. As mentioned above, Malaysia may have lifted most of the quantitative controls on inflows towards the end of 1994, but kept the low interest rate part of the residual control package. The return of inflows, extremely low deposit rates and little life in the stock exchange (by pre-crisis standards), together with low mortgage rates, set in motion a new real "route 1"-style estate bubble: in just four quarters the index jumped 2.6-fold again. Together with the usual serious destabilizing effect that any asset bubble of this kind tends to have, this one set in motion a Kusnetz cycle that could compete with any of the Chilean or Mexican ones.

Of course, as is often the case, the crash was even more amazing; the trough level of this index (in the third quarter of 1998) was equal to just 9% of its pre-crisis peak!

CONCLUSIONS

Who was the economist who said that prices always reflect fundamentals? And particularly so in financial markets? And certainly in financially liberalized LDCs? Or that estimates of today's objective probabilities, calculated from an observed dataset, can provide statistically reliable information about the conditional probability function that will govern future outcomes? So that the key economic problem is not any longer the uncertainty that surrounds future outcomes? And who were the Nobel prize winners who said that LTCM could not fail? Or that (in economies like Chile or Mexico) trade and financial liberalization were going to switch (in a fairly automatic way) the engine of growth towards domestically financed private investment in tradable production? Or that budgetary balance and unregulated market signals were going to prove practically sufficient conditions for macroeconomic equilibrium and microeconomic efficiency? Or that, at the macro level, fiscal balance would necessarily release significant amounts of private savings for more productive uses in the private sector? Or that at the micro level, market deregulation and trade liberalization were to increase significantly both private investment and domestic savings? Or that financial liberalization would place economic agents in a better position to assess and price their risk properly? Or that the household sector would have better information and incentives not to accumulate excessive amounts of risk via reckless borrowing? Or that capital account liberalization would help households to "smooth" their consumption paths over time? Or that (in economies like those in East Asia) financial liberalization would impose much needed financial discipline in the corporate sector? Or that economies which run on the basis of a close relationship between governments and the corporate sector are unique to "Asian despotism"? Or that (in economies like Chile, Mexico, Thailand, or Malaysia) sharp swings associated with asset bubbles and Kusnetz-type cycles would almost be things of the past? Or that in a financially liberalized economy there would be no room for populism, and that governments (like Brazil's) would have no option but to keep their fiscal accounts in order?[45]

Sorry, I forgot, I suppose it is all the fault of moral hazards and crony capitalism. Or, more likely, as Stiglitz asks:

> Are international policies in this area [financial liberalization] being designed on the basis of the best available economic theory and evidence, or is there another agenda, perhaps a special interest agenda, seemingly impervious to the effects of such policies, not only on growth, but on stability and poverty? If that is the case, is there a more fundamental problem in the international economic architecture going [...] to issues of accountability and representativeness? Do those making decisions that affect the lives and livelihood of millions of people throughout the world reflect the interest and concerns, not just of financial markets, but of business, small and large, and of workers, and the economy more broadly? These are the deeper questions posed by the crisis through which the world is just emerging. (2000, p. 1085)

Another (probably deeper) question that needs to be added to Stiglitz's, is why, at best, did it take massive crashes before policy makers in some LDCs (like Chile) realized some of these problems and began implementing these types of policies (even if still not based in the best available economic theory and evidence)

---

45. And if, as argued in this paper, there are such different "routes" to financial crisis, what is the econometric point, so fashionable at the moment, of mixing data from such different experiences in order to find empty "averages"?

in a less dogmatic way? And only then were previously untouchable issues, such as capital account regulations, taken seriously.

But at least some policy makers in a few countries have learned at last—which cannot be said for the majority of international fund managers who do not seem to have learned anything from their mistakes and continue to act as if these crises have never happened, and there is nothing in this world but the end-of-year bonus.

In this world of already high, rapidly growing, extremely volatile, and almost totally unregulated international liquidity, capital controls can, of course, be of some help; but one cannot expect them to be able to hold the fort on their own![46]

---

46. This is particularly the case in small countries—small vis-à-vis not only to international financial markets in general, but even to the position-taking capacity of a small number of hedge funds; in them, theory and evidence suggest that they need to follow fundamentally different policies than larger ones, not just as a temporary measure but in the steady state (see Eichengreen, 2000, p. 1105).

REFERENCES

Bhalla A. S. and D. M. Nachane. 2001. "The Economic Impact of the Asian Crisis on India and China," in Chang, H-J, J. G. Palma and H. Whittaker.

BIS. 1999. "The BIS Consolidated International Banking Statistics," November.

Chang, H-J, J. G. Palma, and H. Whittaker. 2001. *Financial Liberalisation and the Asian Crisis*, Forthcoming, Macmillan.

Chile. 1988. *Indicadores Economicos, 1968-86*, Banco Central.

Davidson, P. 2000. "Is a plumber or a new financial architecture needed to end global international liquidity problems?" *World Development*, Vol. 28, No. 6.

ECLAC. 2000. Statistical Survey of Latin America, ECLAC.

Eichengreen, B. 2000. "Taming capital flows." *World Development*, Vol. 28, No. 6.

De Gregorio, J., S. Edwards and R. O. Valdes. 2000. "Controls on capital inflows: do they work?" *Journal of Development Economics*, Vol. 63.

Dunbar, N. 2000. *Inventing Money: the story of Long Term Capital Management and the Legends Behind it.* John Willey & Son, Ltd.

Galbraith, J. K. 2000. *A Short History of Financial Euphoria*, Penguin Books.

Hofman, Andre A. 2000. "Standardised capital stock estimates in Latin America: a 1950-94 update." *Cambridge Journal of Economics*, Volume 24, Number 1, January.

Howell, M. 1998. *Asia's "Victorian" financial crisis*, mimeo. Cross Border Capital.

IFC. 1999. *Emerging Stock Markets Factbook*.

IMF. 2000a. *International Financial Statistics*. Databank.

——. 2000b. *Balance of Payments Statistics*.

——. 2000c. *World Economic Outlook database*.

Joshi, V. 2000. "*Capital account convertibility and the national advantage—Has India got it right?*" mimeo. Oxford.

Kindleberger, C. 1996. *Manias, Panics, and Crashes: a History of Financial Crises.* John Wiley & Sons.

Krugman, P. 2000. "Curfews on capital flight; what are the options?" http://www.mit.edu/krugman.

Kuczynski, M. 1998. "How Asian has the Asian crisis been?" mimeo. *Adenauer Stiftung.*

McKinnon, R., and H. Pill. 1997. "Credible economic liberalizations and overborrowing," *American Economic Review*, 87 (2).

Ocampo, J. A. and C. Tovar. 1999. "Price-Based Capital Account Regulations: The Colombian Experience." *Financiamiento del Desarrollo Series*, No. 87, ECLAC.

Ocampo, J. A. 2000. "Developing Countries, anti-cyclical policies in a globalized world," mimeo. ECLAC.

Palma, J. G. 1995. "UK Lending to the Third World from the 1973 Oil Shock to the 1980s Debt Crisis: on financial manias, panics and (near) crashes," in P. Arestis and V. Chick, eds., *Finance, Development and Structural Change: a Post-Keynesian Perspective.* Edward Elgar Publishing.

———. 1998. "Three and a half cycles of mania, panic and [asymmetric] crash: East Asia and Latin America Compared." *Cambridge Journal of Economics*, November.

———. 1999a. "Why does Latin America have the worst income distribution in the world?—on changing property rights, distributional coalitions and institutional settlements," mimeo. Cambridge.

———. 1999b. "Spin-doctoring or preventive medicine? The role of the World Bank in economic reform in Latin America," in J. Pincus and G. Winters, eds., *Reinventing the World Bank*, forthcoming. Cornell University Press.

———. 1999c. "The over-borrowing syndrome: structural reforms, institutional failures and exuberant expectations. A critique of McKinnon and Pill." Paper presented at the American Economic Association Meeting—1999, 3-6 January 1999, New York, mimeo, Cambridge.

———. 2000. "The Magical Realism of Brazilian Economics: How to Create a Financial Crisis by Trying to Avoid One," in J. Eatwell and L. Taylor, eds., *International Capital Markets: Systems in Transition*, forthcoming. OUP.

Rodrik, D. and A. Velasco. 1999. "Short-term capital flows," mimeo. Harvard.

Saad Filho, A. 2000. "The Brazilian economy in the 1990s: counting the cost of neo-monetarism," mimeo. SOAS.

Stiglitz, J. (1998). "Sound finance and sustainable development in Asia," mimeo, Manila.

———, (2000). "Capital market liberalization, economic growth, and instability," *World Development*, Vol. 28, No. 6.

Summers, L. H. and V. P. Summers, (1989). "When financial markets work too well: a cautious case for a securities transactions tax," *Journal of Financial Services*, vol. 3.

Tobin, J. (2000) "Financial globalization," *World Development*, Vol. 28, No. 6.

Valdés-Prieto, S. and M. Soto (1998). "The effectiveness of capital controls: theory and evidence from Chile," *Empirica*, No. 25.

United Nations (2000). *Comtrade database.*

World Bank (2000a). *World Development Indicators CD-ROM.*

——— (2000b). *Global Development Finance CD-ROM.*

13

· · ·

"Asian Capitalism" and the Financial Crisis

Ajit Singh

WITH THE ECONOMIC crisis in East Asia and a continuing boom in the United States, American triumphialism is in the air. The latter is perhaps not unexpected and probably does no harm. But what is more questionable is the view held in the highest circles in the U.S. government and international financial organizations in Washington which causally links the so-called Asian model of capitalism to the economic and financial crisis which is currently engulfing the hitherto highly successful economies of East and Southeast Asia.

Thus, Mr. Greenspan, the highly respected chairman of the U.S. Federal Reserve, in testimony before the Senate Foreign Relations Committee suggested that, in the last decade or so, the world has observed "a consensus towards, for want of a better term, the Western form of free-market capitalism as the model which should govern how each individual country should run its economy. . . . We saw the breakdown of the Berlin wall in 1989 and the massive shift away from central planning towards free market capitalist types of structures. Concurrent to that was the really quite dramatic, very strong growth in what appeared to be a competing capitalist-type system in Asia. And as a consequence of that, you had developments of types of structures which I believe at the end of the day were faulty, but you could not demonstrate that so long as growth was going at 10% a year."[1] Mr. Larry Summers, the former U.S. Treasury Under Secretary, puts the matter in slightly different terms. *The Financial Times* (February 20, 1998) reports him as arguing that the roots of the Asian financial crisis lie not in

---

1. Quoted in the *International Herald Tribune*, February 13, 1998.

bad policy management but in the nature of the economies themselves. Summers states: "(this crisis) is profoundly different because it has its roots not in improvidence but in economic structures. The problems that must be fixed are much more microeconomic than macroeconomic, and involve the private sector more and the public sector less." Similar views have been expressed perhaps in more measured terms by the Managing Director of the IMF, Mr. Michel Camdessus.[2]

A central aim of this paper[3] is to systematically assess the validity of this influential and important thesis, i.e., the paper will explore to what extent, if any, the so-called "Asian model" is responsible for the present crisis in countries like Thailand, Indonesia, Malaysia, and Korea. This question is also important in part because in economic terms until very recently this model seems to have been exceptionally successful. It is no exaggeration to say that the industrialization and economic development of the Asian newly industrializing countries (NICs), as well as Japan in the post-World War II period, has been the most successful example of fast economic growth in history. Moreover, the "Asian model," in addition to its economic achievements, has also had a number of attractive qualities from a social point of view, e.g., poverty reduction, lifetime employment for employees in large firms, and a relatively equal income distribution.

In view of these economic and social merits of the Asian model, it is important to ask whether the model also entailed some long run hidden costs. Was it, for example, likely to lead to the kind of crisis which descended suddenly and almost simultaneously on several of the hitherto highly successful economies? Such an analysis will obviously involve, inter alia, an assessment of other factors which may have been responsible for the crisis.

From the practical policy perspective, the central issues for the affected East Asian countries are the appropriateness and the effectiveness of the IMF remedies. Will these measures enable these economies to adjust quickly so that they can go back to their long-term trend growth path? Or will the world witness another "lost decade" of the kind experienced by Latin America in the 1980s under IMF tutelage following the debt crisis?

The paper is organized as follows. The first section reports on the economic and social achievements of the leading East Asian NICs and of the Asian model over the last three to four decades. As we shall see, Joseph Stiglitz, former Chairman of the U.S. Council of Economic Advisers and now Chief Economist at the World Bank, and an eminent but dissident member of the Washington Establishment, is quite right to observe that "no other economic model has delivered so much, to so many, in so short a span of time." The next section outlines the essential characteristics of the Asian model. These have been the subject of an intense debate in the past, but as will be shown below, current events appear to be leading to a consensus on the broad contours of the system. Section three examines al-

---

2. See, for example, Mr. Camdessus' speech to Transparency International reported in the *IMF Survey*, February 9, 1998.

ternative theories of the current financial crisis, paying particular attention to the idea that the Asian economic system itself is the main cause of the financial turmoil. The fourth section reviews the evidence bearing on these issues. Section five analyzes the IMF policy programs in East Asia including, inter alia, the extent, if any, to which these may have contributed to the crisis. The last section sums up the analytical conclusions of the paper and comments on their policy implications.

INDUSTRIALIZATION AND CATCHUP IN ASIA, 1955–1995

The Asian model of "guided" capitalist development originated in and is epitomized by the post World War II experience of Japan, especially in the high growth period between 1950 and 1973. In the early 1950s, after the economy had recovered from the war and at the end of the period of U.S. occupation, the Japanese economic situation was not much different from that of a developing country. The total value of Japanese exports in 1952 was less than that of India's (Krueger, 1995); exports consisted mainly of textiles and other labor intensive products. In 1955, Japan produced only 5 million tons of steel and 30,000 automobiles. U.S. production at that time was 90 million tons of steel and nearly 7 million cars. Japan possessed few natural resources for producing steel or other heavy industrial products, and indeed the Japanese costs of producing steel were at that time considerably greater than the prevailing world prices. Nevertheless, disregarding short term comparative advantage and against almost all economic advice, the Ministry of International Trade and Industry (MITI) deliberately encouraged and orchestrated the development of heavy industry in Japan. The rest is history. By the mid-1960s, Japan emerged as the lowest cost steel producer in the world and was outselling the U.S. steel industry in the United States itself. By early 1970, it was producing as much steel as the United States By 1975, Japan had overtaken Germany as the largest exporter of automobiles in the world. By 1980, Japan produced more automobiles than the United States. Looking back on this phenomenal growth, this incredible catchup occurred over the relatively short space of 30 years.

One might argue that Japan was a special case because it had been undergoing industrialization since the Meiji Restoration in 1870. However, Korea, which consciously followed the Japanese economic strategy, was unequivocally backward in industrial development in the 1950s. In 1955 Korea's per capita manufacturing output was only $8 compared with $7 in India and $60 in Mexico.[4] It was then a largely agrarian economy with agriculture accounting for more than half of GDP and with 70% of the population living in rural areas. Korea's domestic savings rate was one of the lowest in the world (close to zero). Less than

3. This is a revised and updated version of Singh (1998a). The editors of the volume and the author are grateful to the ILO for permission to reproduce here material from that paper.
4. The source of these figures is Maizels (1963), quoted in Amsden and Hikino (1993).

four decades later, Korea has become an industrially developed economy. It competes with advanced economies in a wide range of industrial products. Next to the United States, it is the second most important country in the world in electronic memory chip technology (DRAM). By the year 2000, Korea was expected to become the fourth largest producer of automobiles in the world.

The Japanese and Korean development models have been followed to varying degrees in Taiwan and Singapore but, more significantly, also in Malaysia, Indonesia, and Thailand. There are important differences in aspects of industrial strategy followed by these five countries compared with that of Japan and Korea. The second group of countries has, for example, relied much more on FDI compared with the first group. Nevertheless, all these countries have followed the basic model of guided capitalist development rather than relying on free competitive markets.

The outstanding economic success of this group of East and Southeast Asian countries, together with Hong Kong, is widely acknowledged. These countries have been able to industrialize quickly and grow very fast over the last three decades (see Tables 1 and 2). Indeed, since 1980, this part of the world has emerged as the most dynamic region in the world economy (Table 1). Between 1980–1995, developing East Asia was growing at three times the rate of growth of the world economy.

TABLE 1. Trends in GDP growth:
Selected developing regions and industrial countries
1965–1996 (average annual percentage growth)

	1965–1980	1980–1989	1990–1996
Low-income economies (excluding China and India)	4.8	2.9	1.4
China	6.8	10.2	12.9
India	3.6	5.8	3.8
Middle income economies	6.3	2.2	0.2
Latin America	6.0	1.7	3.6
Sub-Saharan Africa	4.2	1.7	0.9
South Asia	3.6	5.7	3.9
East Asia and Pacific	7.3	7.9	9.4
All low and middle income economies	5.9	3.1	1.9
High income economies	3.8	3.2	1.7
United States	2.7	3.0	2.5
Japan	6.6	4.1	1.2
Germany	3.3	2.2	1.1
World	4.1	3.1	1.8

SOURCE: World Bank (1992, 1996); IMF (1996).
NOTE: The World Bank defines income groups according to GNP per capita in 1994 as follows:
(i) Low income $725 or less
(ii) Middle income $8955 or less
(iii) High income $8956 or more

TABLE 2. GDP Growth East and Southeast Asian NICs
1970–1996 (annual average percentage growth)

	1970–1979	1980–1989	1990–1996
Hong Kong	9.2	7.5	5.0
Singapore	9.4	7.2	8.3
Taiwan	10.2	8.1	6.3
South Korea	9.3	8.0	7.7
Malaysia	8.0	5.7	8.8
Thailand	7.3	7.2	8.6
Indonesia	7.8	5.7	7.2
China	7.5	9.3	10.1

Source: *The Economist*, March 1, 1997.

Significantly, fast growth was accompanied by low inflation as is indicated by the data for the affected Asian countries in Table 3. Moreover, World Bank (1993) notes "… For the eight HPAEs (high performing Asian economies), rapid growth and declining inequality (in income distribution) have been shared virtues, as comparisons over time of equality and growth using Gini coefficients illustrate."[5] In addition, as Stiglitz rightly emphasizes, one of the most important achievements of Asian countries during this period was an enormous reduction in poverty. Stiglitz (1998a) observes: "In 1975, six out of 10 Asians lived on less than $1 a day. In Indonesia, the absolute poverty rate was even higher. Today, two out of 10 East Asians are living in absolute poverty. Korea, Thailand and Malaysia have eliminated poverty and Indonesia is within striking distance of that goal. The USA and other western countries, which have also seen solid growth over the last 20 years but with little reduction in their poverty rates, could well learn from the East Asian experience."[6] Indonesia's success in reducing poverty is particularly remarkable. In 1970, 60% of the population was living below the official poverty line. By 1996, the proportion had fallen to 12%, while during this period the population had increased from 117 to 200 million. (*IMF Survey* 16 August 1997.) Table 5 shows changes in social indicators of development for selected Asian countries between 1970 and 1994.

There is still further evidence which suggests that these high performing economies, most of which were working under some version of the Asian model, not only achieved fast growth for the last three decades, but that this growth was widely shared. Between 1980 and 1992, real wages in the fast growing Asian NICs rose at a rate of 5% a year, whilst at the same time employment in manufacturing increased by 6% a year. Some of these hitherto labor surplus economies began to experience a labor shortage and imported labor from neighboring

---

5. The World Bank's conclusion of declining income inequality in East Asian economies is, however, subject to important qualifications. See further, Singh (1995a, 1997a) and UNCTAD (1997).

6. "Restoring the Asian Miracle," *Wall Street Journal*, Europe (February 3, 1998, p. 4).

TABLE 3. Key Indicators for Asian Crisis Economies
Malaysia, Indonesia, Thailand and Korea
(percent of GDP unless otherwise noted)

	1975–82 (avg.)	1983–89 (avg.)	1990–96 (avg.)	1995	1996	1997 (f)
Malaysia						
real GDP growth	7.1	5.4	8.8	9.5	8.6	7.0
inflation (a)	5.3	2.0	3.5	3.4	3.5	3.7
domestic saving	21.6	29.4	32.1	33.5	36.7	37.0
fixed capital formation	29.4	28.5	38.3	43.0	42.2	42.7
current account	-2.0	-0.7	-6.0	-10.0	-4.9	-5.8
fiscal balance	-6.3	-4.0	0.0	3.8	4.2	1.6
external debt service	3.8	9.0	6.0	6.6	5.4	8.4
Indonesia						
real GDP growth	6.2	5.5	8.0	8.2	8.0	5.0
inflation (a)	15.0	8.1	8.6	9.4	7.9	8.3
domestic saving	19.3	23.2	28.9	29.0	28.8	27.3
fixed capital formation	19.8	24.3	27.4	28.4	28.1	26.5
current account	-1.2	-3.5	-2.6	-3.3	-3.3	-2.9
fiscal balance	-2.6	-1.3	0.3 (c)	0.8	1.4	2.0
external debt service	3.5	6.8	8.6	8.5	9.0	10.5
Thailand						
real GDP growth	7.0	8.1	8.6	8.7	6.4	0.6
inflation (a)	9.0	3.1	5.1	5.8	5.9	6.0
domestic saving	19.6	25.4	34.2	34.3	33.1	31.8
fixed capital formation	23.6	27.7	40.4	41.8	40.8	35.8
current account	-5.6	-3.2	-6.9	-8.0	-7.9	-3.9
fiscal balance	-5.8	-3.0	2.8	2.6	1.6	-0.4
external debt service	3.8	5.8	4.5	5.0	5.4	7.1
Korea						
real GDP growth	7.0	9.6	7.7	8.9	7.1	6.0
inflation (a)	17.6	3.8	6.4	4.5	4.9	4.3
domestic saving	25.7	32.7	35.0	35.1	33.3	32.9
fixed capital formation	29.4	29.4	36.7	36.6	36.8	36.6
current account	-4.6	2.5	-1.9	-2.0	-4.9	-2.9
fiscal balance	-2.7	-0.3	-1.0	0.0	0.0	0.0
import cover (b)	n.a.	1.4 (d)	2.2 (e)	n.a.	n.a.	n.a.

SOURCES: IMF.1997. *World Economic Outlook: Interim Assessment*. December, World Bank.

(a) average annual percent change of consumer price index
(b) gross international reserves in months of import cover
(c) 1991 and 1994 data unavailable
(d) 1980–1990
(e) 1995 figure
(f) IMF estimate

TABLE 4. Key Indicators of Comparator Countries
Brazil, Mexico and India
(percent of GDP unless otherwise noted)

	1970–80 (avg.)	1980–90 (avg.)	1990–94 (avg.)	1995
Brazil				
GDP growth	8.6	2.3	1.0	3.0
inflation (a)	36.6	557.8	1840.5	84.5
savings (b)	19.2	18.1	18.7	19.9
investment (c)	21.8	20.9	20.4	21.9
current account	-4.4	-1.9	-0.1	-2.6
fiscal balance	0.0	-8.1	-3.3	n.a.
external debt	21.9	37.0	30.1	23.1
import cover (d)	n.a.	2.8	5.9	7.9
Mexico				
GDP growth	6.7	2.4	1.4	-7.2
inflation (a)	16.8	65.2	16.3	35.5
savings (b)	17.8	n.a.	n.a.	15.0
investment (c)	20.7	20.2	19.7	15.7
current account	n.a.	-1.2	-5.9	-0.3
fiscal balance	-3.5	-9.0	n.a.	n.a
external debt	23.7	52.8	37.6	66.3
import cover (d)	n.a.	2.1	2.3	2.1
India				
GDP growth	3.3	5.9	4.3	6.1
inflation (a)	8.2	9.1	10.2	10.1
savings (b)	19.4	20.7	21.7	22.7
investment (c)	16.8	20.8	22.4	23.7
current account	-0.4	-2.3	-1.5	-1.8
fiscal balance	-4.6	-7.5	-6.7	-5.4
external debt	14.0	19.3	33.9	28.9
import cover (d)	n.a.	4.9	4.1	5.2

SOURCE: World Bank.

(a) average annual percentage growth of consumer price index
(b) gross national savings as percentage of GDP
(c) gross domestic fixed investment as percentage of GDP
(d) gross international reserves in months of import cover

countries. Overall, in Southeast and East Asia, there was a vast improvement in the standards of living of literally hundreds of millions of people, especially if China is also included in this group of countries.[7]

The above highly positive East Asian record stands in striking contrast to that of large parts of the developing world in the recent period. In relation to

---

7. Although China has a different political system, there is evidence that during the last two decades of the relative liberalization and marketization of the economy, the country has attempted to emulate the East Asian model. See further, Nolan (1995) and Singh (1996a).

TABLE 5. Selected Asian Countries:
Social Indicators of Development, 1970–1994

	1970	1980	1994
Infant Mortality Rate			
(per thousand births)			
Indonesia	119	90	53
Malaysia	46	30	12
Philippines	67	52	40
Thailand	75	48	35
Life Expectancy			
(in years)			
Indonesia	48	56	64
Malaysia	61	68	71
Philippines	57	62	65
Thailand	60	65	69
Adult Illiteracy Rate			
(percent of population;			
above 15 years)			
Indonesia	43	33	16
Malaysia	42	26	17
Philippines	17	17	5
Thailand	21	12	6

SOURCE: *IMF Survey*, vol.26, no.16, August 18, 1997, p.263.

Latin America, for example, ILO (1995) reports that during the 1980s and the early 1990s there was a steady fall in modern sector employment, with paid employment falling at a rate of 0.1% a year. This reversed the trend of the previous three decades, when steady economic growth had led to a significant expansion of modern-sector employment. Tokman (1997) reports that there has been a huge "informalization" of the labor force in Latin America since the debt crisis of the early 1980s, that is, four out of five new jobs that have been created during the last 15 years are low quality, informal jobs paying low wages. The average real wage in Latin American manufacturing in 1995 was still below its pre-debt crisis level.

THE EAST ASIAN MODEL

Before any causal connection can be established between the Asian model of capitalism and the current financial crisis in the South East and the East Asian countries, it is important to be clear about the precise nature of this model of development. In this connection it is interesting to observe that, in the 1990s, the international financial institutions' (IFIs) theses—specifically the World Bank's—concerning (a) the basic characteristics and (b) the effectiveness of the Asian model have undergone a number of distinct changes.

At the first stage, in a seminal contribution,[8] World Bank (1991) claimed the East Asian countries were successful because they followed a "market-friendly" strategy of development and integrated their economies closely with that of the world economy. In order for the term not to be a mere tautology, the Bank's economists to their credit defined "market-friendly" in a fairly precise way as follows:

1. "intervene reluctantly," i.e., the government should intervene in economic activity only if the private sector is unable to do the tasks required

2. interventions should be subject to checks and balances

3. interventions should be transparent. This characterization essentially suggested a "night watchman" state, the main task of which was to provide the legal framework and the infrastructure necessary for private enterprise to flourish.

These propositions concerning the East Asian economies could not however be sustained as they were greatly at variance with facts. Critics pointed out that all the evidence suggested that the governments in countries like Japan and Korea did not "intervene reluctantly." Rather they pursued a vigorous industrial policy, the basic purpose of which was to change the matrix of prices and incentives facing private enterprise in the direction preferred by the planners. Similarly, students of the subject pointed out that neither Japan or Korea, for instance, closely integrated their economies with the rest of the world. Although both countries were export-oriented, both of them made extensive use of selected import controls to protect specific industries.[9] Moreover, both countries discouraged rather than promoted inward foreign investment.

At the second stage, in response to these criticisms, in another seminal publication in 1993 (*The East Asian Miracle*), World Bank economists significantly changed their characterization of the East Asian model. The fact of enormous government interventions in these economies was now fully acknowledged. The *East Asian Miracle* stated:

> Policy interventions took many forms—targeted and subsidized credit to selected industries, low deposit rates and ceilings on borrowing rates to increase profits and retained earnings, protection of domestic import industries, the establishment and financial support of government banks, public investment in applied research, firm- and industry-specific export targets, development of export marketing institutions, and wide sharing of information between public and private sectors. Some industries were promoted while others were not.

At a theoretical level the *East Asian Miracle* represented a path-breaking advance for Bank economists in their analysis of economic development (see further Singh, forthcoming). The Bank provided a sophisticated discussion of coordination failures in market economies and introduced several new concepts to

---

8. The significance of this contribution is discussed in Singh (1995a).

9. As late as 1978, long after Japan had become a member of the OECD and had greatly reduced or abolished most formal import restrictions of the earlier era, its manufactured imports were only 2% of GDP. The comparable figures for countries like France, Germany, and Britain were at that time five to six times as large. See Singh (1994).

reconcile the East Asian experience with economic theory. To illustrate, the concept of deliberation councils was used to describe a significant aspect of government-business relationships in these economies and their positive merits in addressing coordination failures were addressed (see further Singh, forthcoming). Nevertheless, at a policy level the results were disappointing. The Bank argued that, although the government did intervene heavily, these interventions were more measured and in tune with market forces than was the case in other developing countries. The *East Asian Miracle* concluded:

> What are the main factors that contributed to the HPAE's (high performing Asian economies) superior allocation of physical and human capital to high yielding investments and their ability to catch up technologically? Mainly, the answer lies in fundamentally sound, market-oriented policies. Labor markets were allowed to work. Financial markets … generally had low distortions and limited subsidies compared with other developing economies. Import substitution was … quickly accompanied by the promotion of exports. … the result was limited differences between international relative prices and domestic relative prices in the HPAE's. Market forces and competitive pressures guided resources into activities that were consistent with comparative advantage …

It was therefore suggested that the Bank's traditional policy conclusions—that countries should seek their comparative advantage, get the prices right, have free markets as far as possible—are still valid.

Now, in the wake of the current financial crisis in Southeast Asia, the IMF in particular is suggesting that important characteristics of the East Asian model are dysfunctional.[10] Especially singled out for criticism are: (a) the close relationship between government and business, and (b) various distortions to competitive markets. The relationships under (a), which include the deliberation councils which were positively regarded in the *East Asian Miracle* study, are now being portrayed as creating crony-capitalism, leading to corruption and myriad inefficiencies in resource allocation. The inference is that these countries should go back to the World Bank (1991) prescription of a "night watchman" state and an economy which is closely integrated with the world economy.

The Bank's critics vigorously dispute its theses on the lack of effectiveness of interventions in the East Asian economies.[11] There is, however, now much greater agreement between the two sides on the broad description of the model as outlined in the first of the two quotations from World Bank (1993) above. Based on my own previous research and that of other scholars, there would be more or less agreement on the following important characteristics of the East Asian model in its "ideal form":[12]

---

10. As indicated earlier, the World Bank's former Chief Economist, Professor Stiglitz, takes a rather different view of the crisis than that of the Fund. However, as Wade and Veneroso (1998) suggest, the position of Bank staff is closer to that of the IMF than to that of their Chief Economist.

11. For comprehensive critical analyses of the World Bank (1993) theses, see the contributions in Amsden (1994); see also Singh (1995a).

12. See Singh (1995a, 1997a, 1998b); see also Okimoto (1989), Tsuru (1993), Amsden (1989), Wade (1990), and Amsden and Singh (1994).

1. The close relationship between the government and business where the government does not do anything without consulting business and vice versa.

2. Many interventions are carried out through a system of "administrative guidance" rather than through formal legislation.

3. The relationship between the corporation and the financial system in countries like Japan and Korea has also been very different from that of the United States and the United Kingdom. The former countries have followed, for example, the so-called main bank system which involves long-term relationships between the corporations and the main banks. This enables Japanese or Korean managers to take a long-term view in their investment decisions. The managers are not constrained by the threat of hostile takeovers on stock markets as is the case in the Anglo-Saxon countries.

4. There are differences in the internal organization of East Asian corporations compared with those of the United States and the United Kingdom. The former involve cooperative relationships between management and labor, epitomized by the system of lifetime employment. This implies considerable imperfections in the labor market.

5. As for the competition in product markets, such competition is not regarded by the East Asian authorities as an unalloyed good. Unlike in countries like the United States, economic philosophy in the East Asian countries does not accept the dictum that "the more competition the better." The governments in these countries have taken the view that, from the perspective of promoting investment and technical change, the optimal degree of competition is not perfect or maximum competition. The governments have therefore purposefully managed and guided competition: it has been encouraged but also restricted in a number of ways.[13]

6. Following this basic economic philosophy outlined above, the East Asian governments have sought not "close" but what might be called "strategic" integration with the world economy, i.e., they have integrated up to the point where it has been useful for them to do so. Thus during their high-growth, developmental phases, Japan (between 1950–1973) and Korea (1970s and 1980s) integrated with the world economy in relation to exports but not imports; with respect to science and technology but not finance and multinational investment.

As noted above, this is a characterization of the East Asian model as an ideal type. Not all countries, or even Japan and Korea have followed the model exactly at all times in the postwar period. As far as the government-business relationships are concerned there is a continuum with the closest relationship to be found in Korea, and the least close in Thailand. Malaysia and Indonesia fall in between. Similarly, the main bank system worked differently in Korea compared with Japan. Unlike Japan, where the "main banks" were by and large private entities, in Korea for much of the period these were directly state-controlled. Only in the recent period have they been privatized. Thus, although at one level each country has specificities that are important, there is considerable truth in

13. For a fuller discussion, see Amsden and Singh (1994).

the view that the Asian way of doing business and the institutional structures it has generated are considerably different from those of countries like the United States and the United Kingdom as well as other developing regions.

CAUSES OF THE CRISIS

Table 6 outlines the salient financial facts concerning the crisis in the East and Southeast Asian countries between July 1997 and February 1998. In the worst affected country, Indonesia, the stock market fell by more than 80% and the exchange rate of the rupiah against the dollar by almost 75%. This implies that a foreign investor who invested $100 in a company quoted on the Indonesian stock market would have seen the value of the investment fall by 96% during the half year. By the same token, it also means that if a foreign corporation had to pay $100 to acquire an Indonesian company in July 1997, it could in principle purchase it now for only $4. This is of course not just a theoretical possibility, but as Krugman (1998) notes, there may be a "fire sale" of East Asian assets in the wake of the financial crisis.[14] The twin crises of the stock and currency markets have also resulted in corporate and financial sector bankruptcies with huge losses of production and jobs.

Those who attribute the crisis to the failings of the Asian model suggest that, while there may have been various immediate triggers—a property price bubble, macroeconomic imbalances, a fall in the rate of growth of exports, or a

TABLE 6. Southeast and East Asian Countries
Percentage Movements in Equity Markets and Exchange Rates
(July 1, 1997–February 18, 1998)

Country	Equity Markets (against US$)	Exchange Rate
Indonesia	-81.2	-73.5
South Korea	-32.3	-48.1
Thailand	-47.9	-43.2
Malaysia	-59.0	-33.3
Singapore	-45.0	-13.2
Hong Kong	-36.6	pegged to US$

SOURCE: *Financial Times*, February 20, 1998.

---

14. Krugman reports that in the case of South Korea, the price of its corporations to foreign buyers essentially fell by 70% during 1997. Thus, the stock market value of Korean Air Lines with a fleet of more than 100 aircraft at the end of 1997 was only $240 million. This is approximately the price of two Boeing 747s. However, any acquirer would also have to take on the Korean Air Lines debt of $5 billion.

regional contagion effect—the underlying causes were structural and an integral part of the Asian model of capitalism. The crisis manifested itself in the form of "overinvestment" (see further below), misallocation of foreign capital inflows, and severe problems in the financial sector. The financial structure of the corporations and the banks, as well as other deficiencies of the state-guided or state-directed financial systems in Asian countries, made these economies very fragile. IMF (1997, p. 14) points to the following specific structural weaknesses of the most affected economies:

• In Korea, the industrial structure has been heavily influenced by government intervention, including, as well as directed credits, regulations and explicit or implicit subsidies. The resulting lack of market discipline has contributed to the problem of unproductive or excessive investment that has played a role in the buildup of the recent crisis.

• In Indonesia, trade restrictions, import monopolies, and regulations have impeded economic efficiency and competitiveness, and reduced the quality and productivity of investment.

• In Thailand, political disarray at various times during 1996–97, including in the wake of the November 1996 general election, delayed the implementation of necessary policy measures. In these and other cases, the power of special interests has often appeared to have had considerable influence on the allocation of budgetary resources and other public policy actions.

• In a number of countries, uncertainty has been increased and confidence adversely affected by inadequate disclosure of information and data deficiencies, particularly with regard to extra-budgetary fiscal transactions, the quasi-fiscal activities of the central bank, directed lending, the problem loans of financial institutions, official foreign exchange reserves and their management (including reserve-related liabilities), and private sector short-term debt. There has also often been a lack of transparency in policy implementation, such as with the decisions regarding public infrastructure projects and ad hoc tax exemptions.

The failure of the Asian model thesis has powerful proponents including Mr. Greenspan, Mr. Summers, and the IFIs. But it is by no means the only significant available theory with respect to the financial crisis. Many Asian political leaders have put forward an entirely different perspective. They are prone to blame the whole of the crisis on the activities of foreign speculators and reject the view that the crisis was essentially "home grown" (to use the phrase of the IMF Deputy Managing Director, Mr. Stanley Fischer).

A more sophisticated version of this "external factors" view is contained in the recent academic literature spawned by the Mexican crisis of 1994.[15] These contributions, based on careful theoretical and empirical analyses, show that it is entirely possible for a financial crisis to occur even when a country's fundamentals are totally sound. It may arise because of changes in investor sentiment or

---

15. See for example Calvo and Mendoza (1996), Sachs, Tornell and Velasco (1996), Cole and Kehoe (1996), Krugman (1998).

perceptions which may be triggered off entirely by external events such as changes in interest rates or equity prices in advanced countries. Some of these theories suggest that such crises of confidence can be self-fulfilling prophecies. Other models use the analogy of the classic panic-induced run on the banks to describe the present financial crisis in East Asian countries.

A third important theory ascribes the crisis to liberalization of the global financial markets, and particularly to the deregulation of the capital account which many Asian countries had undertaken in the preceding period. It is suggested that the latter was the main cause of the crisis rather than any structural factors connected with the Asian development model. Indeed, it is argued that if these countries had continued to follow the Asian model of state-guided investment and state direction of the financial system, there would not have been a crisis at all in the first place. The crisis occurred directly as a result of deregulation and liberalization when the governments relinquished controls over the financial sector as well as corporate investment activities. This led to misallocation (towards, for example, the property sector) of investment as well as overinvestment.

As these theories are central in determining the choice of remedies for the crisis, it is clearly important to know which of them is more congruous with the facts. The events are too close to be able to provide anywhere near a definitive explanation of the crisis, but the following section will review the evidence.

EVIDENCE ON THE THEORIES CONCERNING THE CRISIS

The survey below of available evidence bearing on the alternative theories of the present financial crisis in Southeast and East Asian countries is organized around the following themes:
   (a) the role of fundamentals;
   (b) the proximate cause of the crisis—the capital supply shock;
   (c) the role of structural factors; and
   (d) financial liberalization.

Fundamentals

The most important point to note here is that all the affected countries prior to the crisis had for a long time enjoyed strong "fundamentals." This is evident from our earlier discussion in Section II and from the more detailed data presented in Tables 1–3. Thailand, Indonesia, Malaysia, and Korea had all recorded extraordinarily strong economic growth for many years; their inflation rates were usually in single figures and much below the developing country average. These countries also had high domestic savings rates, indeed considerably greater than those of other developing countries including Brazil, Mexico, and India (the three countries for which data is provided in Table 4 for comparative purposes.)

Moreover, the crisis countries had healthy fiscal positions. The public sector finances were either in surplus or had small sustainable deficits. The fiscal position of these countries compared very favorably with the average of developing countries as well as with that of Brazil, Mexico, and India.

A potentially significant blemish on this generally positive pre-crisis long-term economic record was the position of the current account balance in the some of the affected countries. Thailand and Malaysia have experienced huge current account deficits, which in the 1990s amounted to nearly 6.9% of GDP in the case of Thailand, and 6% of GDP for Malaysia. In 1996 the Thai current account deficit was almost 8% of GDP while that of Malaysia had fallen to 4.9%. Nevertheless, it is also the case that both those countries had a relatively low debt service to exports ratios throughout the 1990s—4.5% for Thailand, and 6% for Malaysia. The comparable average figures for the Latin American countries was almost three times as high. Furthermore, in the case of Malaysia, as Table 7 on external capital flows indicates, the high current account deficit was to a considerable extent financed by a strong net inflow of foreign direct investment.

The Korean current account deficit in 1996 was 4.9% of GDP, an unusually high figure for Korea. Korea was not, however, a persistent offender—its average deficit during the 1990s was less than 2% of GDP. The larger 1996 deficit was caused by special circumstances, notably the collapse of prices of semiconductors of which Korea was a major exporter. However, this sharp increase in the current account deficit was a temporary phenomena, as one would expect from a highly diversified export-oriented economy. Indeed, in the last quarter of 1997 the Korean economy recorded a huge current account surplus of $3 billion. Indonesia's current account deficit during the 1990s averaged 2.6% of GDP; in 1996 it was 3.3%, an entirely sustainable figure on the past record of the economy. The only country where the current account deficit could be regarded as a real problem was Thailand. This is mainly because the deficit was being financed by bank borrowings (see Table 7).

It is also relevant to observe that, as late as September 1997, the Korean debt had a high rating from western rating agencies. Similarly, until almost the eve of the financial crisis in August 1997, the IMF was praising the Indonesian government for its successful management of the economy as well as for its achievements in reducing poverty.[16]

To sum up, all the affected Asian countries had strong "fundamentals" in the sense of a proven record of being able to sustain fast economic growth. In view of their export orientation, they also had the ability to service their debts in the long term. They did, however, suffer to varying degrees from short term imbalances such as overvalued exchange rates, as well as short term liabilities of the financial sector which exceeded the value of the central bank's reserves. This required some macroeconomic adjustments and restructuring of debts. In other words, these countries had problems of liquidity rather than solvency. In this

---

16. See *IMF Survey*, vol. 26, no. 16, August 18, 1997.

TABLE 7. Capital Flows to Asian Crisis Economies (a)
Malaysia, Indonesia, Thailand and Korea
(in percent of GDP)

	1983–88(b)	1989–95(b)	1992	1993	1994	1995	1996	1997(c)
Malaysia								
Net private capital flows (d)	3.1	8.8	15.1	17.4	1.5	8.8	9.6	4.7
Net direct investment	2.3	6.5	8.9	7.8	5.7	4.8	5.1	5.3
Net portfolio investment	n.a.	n.a.	n.a.	n.a.	n.a.	n.a.	n.a.	n.a.
Other net investment	0.8	2.3	6.2	9.7	-4.2	4.1	4.5	-0.6
Net official flows	0.3	0.0	-0.1	-0.6	0.2	-0.1	-0.1	-0.1
Change in reserves (e)	-1.8	-4.7	-11.3	-17.7	4.3	2.0	-2.5	3.6
Indonesia								
Net private capital flows (d)	1.5	4.2	2.5	3.1	3.9	6.2	6.3	1.6
Net direct investment	0.4	1.3	1.2	1.2	1.4	2.3	2.8	2.0
Net portfolio investment	0.1	0.4	0.0	1.1	0.6	0.7	0.8	-0.4
Other net investment	1.0	2.6	1.4	0.7	1.9	3.1	2.7	0.1
Net official flows	2.4	0.8	1.1	0.9	0.1	-0.2	-0.7	1.0
Change in reserves (e)	0.0	-1.4	-3.0	-1.3	0.4	-0.7	-2.3	1.8
Thailand								
Net private capital flows (d)	3.1	10.2	8.7	8.4	8.6	12.7	9.3	-10.9
Net direct investment	0.8	1.5	1.4	1.1	0.7	0.7	0.9	1.3
Net portfolio investment	0.7	1.3	0.5	3.2	0.9	1.9	0.6	0.4
Other net investment	1.5	7.4	6.8	4.1	7.0	10.0	7.7	-12.6
Net official flows	0.7	0.0	0.1	0.2	0.1	0.7	0.7	4.9
Change in reserves (e)	-1.4	-4.1	-2.8	-3.2	-3.0	-4.4	-1.2	9.7
Korea								
Net private capital flows (d)	-1.1	2.1	2.4	1.6	3.1	3.9	4.9	2.8
Net direct investment	0.2	-0.1	-0.2	-0.2	-0.3	-0.4	-0.4	-0.2
Net portfolio investment	0.3	1.4	1.9	3.2	1.8	1.9	2.3	-0.3
Other net investment	-1.6	0.8	0.7	-1.5	1.7	2.5	3	3.4
Net official flows	0	-0.3	-0.2	-0.6	-0.1	-0.1	-0.1	-0.1
Change in reserves (e)	-0.9	-0.8	-1.1	-0.9	-1.4	-1.5	0.3	-1.1

SOURCE: IMF. 1997. *World Economic Outlook, Interim Assessment.* December.
   (a) Net capital flows comprise net direct investment, net portfolio investment, and other long- and short-term net investment flows, including official and private borrowing.
   (b) Annual averages
   (c) IMF estimates
   (d) Because of data limitations, other net investment may include some official flows.
   (e) A minus sign indicates an increase.

context Wolf's (1998) observations concerning Indonesia are pertinent:

Dwell for a moment, on Indonesia: its current account deficit was less than 4 percent of GDP throughout the 1990s; its budget was in balance; inflation was below 10 percent; at the end of 1996 the real exchange rate (as estimated by J.P. Morgan) was just 4 percent higher than at the end of 1994; and the ratio to GDP of domestic bank credit to the private sector had risen merely from 50 percent in 1990 to 55 percent in 1996. True, the banking system had mountains of bad debt, but foreign lending to Indonesian companies had largely bypassed it. Is anyone prepared to assert that this is a country whose exchange rate one might expect to depreciate by about 75 percent? Some exchange-rate adjustment was certainly necessary; what happened beggars belief.

The Capital Supply Shock

It is generally agreed that the proximate cause of the crisis in all the four affected countries was the capital supply shock—the sudden interruption and reversal of normal capital inflows into these economies. Table 8, which provides aggregate financing figures for these countries plus the Philippines, indicates that their net external capital inflows more than doubled between 1994 and 1996—from a little over $40 billion to more than $90 billion. The latter figure greatly exceeded the combined current account deficits of these countries, allowing them to build sizeable reserves. In 1997, however, there was a huge capital supply shock: the net inflow of $93 billion in 1996 turned into a net outflow of $12 billion in 1997, a turnaround of $105 billion. The latter figure is equivalent of 10% of the pre-crisis GDP of these countries (Wolf 1997). The decomposition of the capital inflows in Table 8 suggests that the most volatile item was commercial bank lending which turned from a positive figure of over $50 billion in 1996 to a negative figure of $21 billion in 1997.

What the above evidence on the "fundamentals," as well as the analysis of section II on the long-term supply-side capabilities of these economies suggests is that, whatever the trigger for the crisis (whether external macroeconomic imbalances or the liabilities of the financial institutions), the foreign commercial banks grossly overreacted, giving rise to a classic panic induced bank-run. Such behavior on the part of the banks, although rational within its own terms, makes default or a major IMF bailout a self-fulfilling prophecy.

Structural factors

Turning to the "structural factors" connected with the Asian model, which the IMF and others implicate in the crisis, we first consider the issue of "transparency." It is suggested that, because of the nature of the Asian corporations (involving extensive cross-subsidization of subsidiaries) and their close, non-arm's length relationship with banks, and similar relationships between banks and gov-

TABLE 8. Five Asian Economies, External Financing (a)
(billions of US dollars)

	1994	1995	1996	199(b)	1998(c)
Current account balance	-24.6	-41.3	-54.9	-26	17.6
External financing (net)	47.4	80.9	92.8	15.2	15.2
Private flows (net)	40.5	77.4	93	-12.1	-9.4
Equity investment	12.2	15.5	19.1	-4.5	7.9
Direct equity	4.7	4.9	7	7.3	9.8
Portfolio equity	7.6	10.6	12.1	-11.6	-1.9
Private creditors	28.2	61.8	74	-7.6	-17.3
Commercial banks	24	49.5	55.5	-21.3	-14.1
Non-bank private creditors	4.2	12.4	18.4	13.7	-3.2
Official flows (net)	7	3.6	-0.2	27.2	24.6
International financial institutions	-0.4	-0.6	-1	23	18.5
Bilateral creditors	7.4	4.2	0.7	4.3	6.1
Resident lending/other (net) (d)	-17.5	-25.9	-19.6	-11.9	-5.7
Reserves excluding gold	-5.4	-13.7	-18.3	22.7	-27.1

SOURCE: *IMF Survey*, Vol. 27, No. 3, 9 February 1998, p. 35.

(a) The countries are: Malaysia, Indonesia, Thailand, Korea, and the Philippines.
(b) estimate
(c) forecast
(d) including resident net lending, monetary gold, and omissions

ernments, the markets did not have enough information about the true financial status of the corporations and the banks. This is regarded as being one important reason for the overreaction by the markets.[17]

However, in relation to this proposition, the following observations are relevant. First, as Stiglitz (1998a) notes, following financial liberalization there have been similar banking crises in the early 1990s even in the Scandinavian countries. These countries would be regarded by many as being at the top of any international transparency league: the availability of reliable information was evidently not adequate by itself to prevent financial panics. Secondly, it is specifically claimed that international banks did not have accurate and timely information on the shortening maturity of bank claims on Asian countries. This complaint is also controversial. As Professor Alexandre Lamfalussy, the former chief economist at the Bank of International Settlements noted in a recent letter

---

17. Thus Mr. Camdessus (1998): "In Korea, for example, opacity had become systemic. The lack of transparency about government, corporate and financial sector operations concealed the extent of Korea's problems—so much so that corrective action came too late and ultimately could not prevent the collapse of market confidence, with the IMF finally being authorized to intervene just days before potential bankruptcy."

to the *Financial Times* (February 13, 1998):

...the Bank for International Settlement is encouraged to speed up the publication of its statistics on international bank lending...The suggested improvement will surely do no harm but it will not do much good either as long as market participants and other concerned parties fail to read publicly available information or to draw practical conclusions from it.

In the summer of 1996 the BIS reported in its half yearly statistics that by end-1995 the total of consolidated bank claims on South Korea, Thailand, Indonesia, and Malaysia reached $201.6bn. It reported in January 1997 that by mid-1996 the figure rose to $226.5bn and six months later, that by end-1996 it reached $247.8bn—an increase of 23 per cent in one year. For each of these dates the maturity breakdown was available. It was therefore known by midsummer 1996 that bank claims maturing within one year made up 70 per cent of the total for South Korea, 69.4 per cent for Thailand, 61.9 per cent for Indonesia, but "only" 47.2 per cent for Malaysia.

Professor Lamfalussy goes on to add:

Moreover, in its Annual Report published on June 10 1996, the BIS did not hesitate to use strong words describing developments that had taken place already in 1995: '. . . By year end, Thailand had become the largest bank debtor in the developing world. . . .'

Thirdly, in relation to this argument about transparency and information, it is also pertinent to note that international banks lent huge sums of money to merchant banks in South Korea. Most of the latter did not have a long enough track record, being less than two years old (Chang 1998). Many would regard such lending practices to be highly imprudent, if not reckless.

Turning to other structural features of the Asian model which it has become customary to blame for the crisis, we consider first the questions of overinvestment and misallocation of investment in countries like Thailand to the nonproductive property sector. Here the IMF's critics are quite right to say that, if in the process of financial liberalization, the governments of countries like Korea and Thailand had not eschewed control over their financial sector and corporate investment activity, such overinvestment and misallocation would not have occurred. Indeed, until financial liberalization, the Thai government had regulated investment going into the property sector. It was therefore not the Asian model but the abandonment of one of its essential features which was directly responsible for the observed weaknesses that came to the fore.

Another structural characteristic of the Asian model which is the subject of much adverse comment in orthodox analysis of the current crisis pertains to corporate finance. As is well known, the typical corporation particularly in Japan, Korea, or Thailand is heavily geared, i.e., has a high ratio of debt to the equity capital of the shareholders. The Korean *chaebol* enterprises which spearheaded that country's extraordinarily successful industrialization drive and the continuous technological upgrading of its exports over the last three decades are typically family owned. They are however very big—11 South Korean companies are included in *Fortune* magazine's top 500 in the world. To put this figure into perspective, it may be useful to note that Switzerland, a far more developed economy, also has only 11 companies in the world's top 500.[18] In order for the families to be able to own such huge corporations, the equity component of the total invested corporate capital tends to be small relative to debt. Table 9 shows the debt-equity ratios of leading Korean corporations. Table 10 provides a comparative analysis of the debt equity ratios of the largest quoted companies in nine emerging markets in the 1980s and 1990s. It clearly indicates that the Korean companies are relatively very heavily geared with a median value of 4.3 between 1980 and 1994. However the bottom two parts of the Table indicate that between the early 1980s and the early 1990s, this ratio fell from 5.48 to 3.96. The Table also reveals that the Asian corporations, including those from India, have considerably higher debt-equity ratios than those of the Latin American corporations.

However, the important point to note is that such corporate financial arrangements have been functional within the traditional Asian economic system.

TABLE 9. Debt-Equity Ratios of Korean *Chaebol*

Company	Total assets	Debt (billion won)	Debt/Equity ratio (billion won)
Samsung	50,856.4	37,043.6	268.2
Hyundai	53,183.7	43,319.3	439.1
Daewoo	34,205.6	26,383.2	337.3
Lucky-Goldstar	37,068.4	28,765.6	346.5
Hanjin	13,904.5	11,787.7	556.9
Kia	14,161.9	11,890.9	523.6
Ssangyong	15,807.2	12,701.4	409.0
Sunkyong	22,726.6	18,040.3	385.0
Hanwha	10,967.7	9,718.8	778.2
Daelim	5,793.3	4,586.5	380.1
Kumho	7,398.0	6,117.9	477.9
Doosan	6,402.0	5,594.0	692.3
Halla	6,626.5	6,320.8	2,067.6
Sammi	2,515.4	2,593.3	3,329.0
Hyosung	4,124.4	3,252.8	373.2
Hanil	2,628.1	2,231.8	563.2
Dong-Ah Construction	6,287.9	4,905.8	355.0
Kohap	3,653.6	3,123.6	589.4
Jinro	3,940.5	3,895.2	8,598.7
Dongkuk Steel	3,697.5	2,536.4	218.4

SOURCE: *Financial Times*, 8 August 1997.

---

18. See further Amsden and Hikino (1994), Singh (1995).

TABLE 10. Top Listed Manufacturing Corporations in Nine Developing Countries
Distribution of their Average Gearing Ratios
(Gearing is the ratio of total liabilities divided by shareholders' equity)

Gearing	Argentina	India	Jordan	Korea	Malaysia	Mexico	Peru	Thailand	Zimbabwe
Whole Period	1991–95	1980–92	1980–94	1980–94	1983–94	1984–94	1991–95	1987–94	1980–95
Mean	0.70	3.24	1.04	5.22	1.03	0.60	0.67	1.23	3.86
Standard deviation	0.66	10.90	1.08	4.98	1.96	1.61	0.60	0.98	57.35
Minimum	0.02	0.31	0.05	0.42	0.03	-1.94	0.04	0.00	0.07
First quarter	0.29	1.50	0.43	2.53	0.32	0.16	0.30	0.60	0.47
Median	0.53	2.28	0.67	4.30	0.64	0.32	0.51	1.00	0.68
Third quarter	0.84	3.16	1.16	6.39	1.11	0.61	0.79	1.52	1.04
Maximum	4.70	259.41	7.49	61.97	29.12	24.49	4.24	6.78	1090.44
Range	4.68	259.10	7.44	61.55	29.10	26.43	4.21	6.78	1090.37
Early Period		1980–83	1980–83	1980–83	1983–86	1984–87		1987–90	1980–83
Mean		3.44	1.13	6.90	1.04	0.95		1.27	0.87
Standard deviation		14.46	1.26	5.84	2.14	2.04		1.00	0.55
Minimum		0.31	0.05	1.47	0.03	0.04		0.03	0.07
First quarter		1.47	0.43	4.30	0.31	0.32		0.62	0.52
Median		2.37	0.74	5.48	0.62	0.52		1.03	0.78
Third quarter		3.13	1.24	7.81	1.12	0.84		1.62	1.14
Maximum		259.41	7.49	61.97	29.12	24.49		6.78	4.95
Range		259.10	7.44	60.51	29.10	24.45		6.76	4.88
Late Period		1989–92	1991–94	1991–94	1991–94	1991–94		1991–94	1992–95
Mean		3.06	0.98	3.38	1.02	0.13		1.18	6.97
Standard deviation		6.03	0.92	2.87	1.74	0.35		0.95	81.91
Minimum		0.50	0.13	0.42	0.06	-1.94		0.00	0.08
First quarter		1.53	0.45	1.81	0.33	0.03		0.59	0.45
Median		2.21	0.62	2.62	0.68	0.16		0.97	0.63
Third quarter		3.19	1.13	3.96	1.09	0.27		1.41	0.92
Maximum		83.38	4.17	27.56	22.42	1.53		6.56	1090.44
Range		82.88	4.04	27.14	22.36	3.47		6.55	1090.35

SOURCE: Glen, Singh and Matthias (forthcoming).

This is in part due to the continuous monitoring of the corporations by "main banks" with whom they have long term relationships, as well as to the close oversight by the government over the banks. These arrangements were particularly useful during Korea's industrialization drive, as the corporations were induced by the government to enter into new technological areas involving huge risks. Left to themselves, the corporations may not have been able to undertake such risks, but with the government becoming in effect a copartner through the banking system, such technological risks were "socialized." Following the work of Williamson (1976), Lee (1992) has characterized this system as essentially constituting an internal capital market. In view of the well known weaknesses of free capital markets (e.g., a tendency towards short termism and quick profits) such an internal capital market may in fact be more efficient than the former.[19]

However, such a corporate system became dysfunctional when, for example, in Korea the government undertook during the last few years a process of financial liberalization (under pressure from the U.S. government and the IFIs, but see the discussion in Section VII). Korea resisted allowing nonresidents to buy majority stakes in its corporations. However, its mistake was to implement other components of capital account liberalization by permitting Korean companies and banks to raise money abroad without the traditional supervision and control. So, in that sense, it was again financial deregulation (i.e., the dismantling of a fundamental aspect of the previous system) which rendered the system dysfunctional and fragile.

It is interesting in the above context to consider the case of India. As Table 10 indicates, the Indian corporations are also very highly geared. Moreover, India's fundamentals, as Tables 3 and 4 (discussed earlier) indicate, were much weaker than those of the East Asian countries. Nevertheless, India has not had a financial crisis. At a time of deep turbulence in the currency markets of its South East and East Asian neighbors, the Indian currency market has almost been a model of stability. Why? Most observers would agree that the main reason for this is that India has extremely limited capital account liberalization. It does not allow its corporations or banks to borrow or lend capital abroad without government approval. It has carried out some liberalization by allowing nonresidents to purchase shares directly on the Indian stock markets, but they cannot become majority shareholders. This limited, cautious openness, the relatively small size of foreign portfolio inflows as well as that of the stock market itself have been helpful to the Indian economy. The Indian currency is consequently much less vulnerable to changes in investor sentiment or speculative attacks from outside.

THE IMF POLICY PROGRAM AND THE EAST ASIAN CRISIS

As the financial crisis deepened in East Asia during the last six months and more and more countries became involved, the IMF assembled large financial packages to bail out the affected countries. However this aid was available only in return for draconian conditionality. Apart from their usual policies of demand restraint (cuts in money supply, high interest rates, fiscal retrenchment, etc.) the IMF went further. It demanded far-reaching changes in the economic and social systems of these countries. These changes included still more liberalization of the financial sector (including permitting hostile takeovers of domestic firms by nonresidents); changes in the system of corporate governance, in labor laws, in government business relations, and in competition policy. Such measures were

---

19. There is a large literature on these issues. For a fuller discussion, see further Aoki and Patrick (1996); Singh (1996b); Singh and Weisse (1998).

insisted on because it was believed (erroneously as we have seen above) that the root cause of the crisis was the "dirigiste" institutional structures and policies of these countries.

The IMF policy programs for the affected Asian countries have been heavily criticized by leading economists from both inside and outside the economic establishment.[20] Taken as a whole, the critics' case is formidable and telling. The main points may be summarized as follows:

1. The IMF's traditional policy program of demand restraint etc. is typically designed to deal with countries with persistent current account disequilibria, fiscal deficits, and overheated economies. For the Asian economies, however, except perhaps to some extent for Thailand, the problem has been one of capital account disequilibrium rather than that of current account imbalances. Moreover, as we have seen earlier, the public sector finances in these countries have been by and large in equilibrium and it is the private sector which is in severe disequilibrium. In these circumstances, the large fiscal austerity demanded by the IMF's original programs for these countries would have made matters worse rather than better, pushing the countries deeper into recession, and thereby exacerbating the private sector financial disequilibria.

2. The high real interest rates entailed by the IMF programs would have similarly deleterious effects on the private sector's viability. Such rates will lead to the bankruptcy of a large part of the sector, deepening the depression of the real economy. In response to this criticism, the IMF has argued that higher interest rates are required for restoring international confidence in the countries' policies. Stiglitz's counter argument is that there is little empirical evidence to support the view that high interest rates improve confidence. He goes on to add that one could perhaps make a case for an increase in interest rates for a brief spell, but countries like Indonesia and Thailand have had real interest rates of 20% or more now for nearly nine months.

There is some truth in both these contentions. Evidence from the financial crisis in the various parts of the world suggests that higher interest rates help before a crisis has occurred (i.e., they may forestall the crisis), but once the crisis has taken place, increasing interest rates is often regarded by the market as a sign of weakness and is therefore counter-productive.

3. The IMF is quite right to stress the importance of prudential regulation and supervision of the financial sector. Certainly, financial liberalization by the affected countries without such regulations was a serious mistake. However, to forestall the crisis, the IMF should have discouraged financial liberalization by these countries until the appropriate regulatory regime was in place. This the institution did not do, presumably because of its own strong commitment to external account liberalization. Further, it is a moot point whether under a regime of free capital flows, prudential regulation of the domestic financial sector, without that of international banks as well, would have been enough to prevent

---

20. See among others Sachs (1997); Stiglitz (1998a, 1998b); Feldstein (1998 a, b); Wade and Veneroso (1998); Amsden and Euh (1997); Akyuz (1997).

a financial crisis (Akyuz, 1997; Stiglitz, 1998).

4. The misdiagnosis of the crisis by the IMF (that it has been due to the dirigiste model of the Asian capitalism rather than being caused by internal and external financial liberalization) has had serious adverse short as well as long term consequences for the affected countries. It is certainly arguable that the Fund's emphasis on what it perceived to be the fundamental structural difficulties of the Asian model (crony capitalism, corruption, etc.), panicked foreign investors still further, and thereby worsened the crisis (Feldstein, 1998a, b).

5. As the evidence outlined earlier (the strong fundamentals, the large inflows of private capital from abroad, and IMF's own seal of approval for economic management of these countries until the eve of the crisis), suggests the East Asian crisis was originally one of liquidity rather than solvency. In these circumstances, it would have been preferable for the Fund to have acted as an intermediary to help bridge the gap between lenders and borrowers over the mismatch of maturities. Instead, the institution raised huge sums of money for bailouts and imposed far-reaching conditionalities on the crisis countries which could be interpreted as signalling a deeper solvency rather than a mere liquidity crisis.

6. Professor Feldstein [1998 a, b] makes an important point of political economy concerning the IMF programs which deserves serious consideration by the international community. He notes that the IMF is an international agency whose purpose ought to be to provide technical advice and, as appropriate, the financial assistance necessary to help countries overcome a balance of payments crisis with as little loss of output and employment as possible. It may also wish to ensure that the country continues to follow the right economic policies so that, as far as possible, the situation does not reoccur. However, he suggests that the IMF "should not use the opportunity to impose other economic changes that, however helpful they may be, are not necessary to deal with the balance-of-payments problem and are the proper responsibility of the country's own political system."

Professor Feldstein proposes the following three-point test for the structural aspects of the IMF conditionalities:

> In deciding whether to insist on any particular reform, the IMF should ask three questions: Is this reform really needed to restore the country's access to international capital markets? Is this a technical matter that does not interfere unnecessarily with the proper jurisdiction of a sovereign government? If the policies to be changed are also practised in the major industrial countries of Europe, would the IMF think it appropriate to force similar changes in those countries if they were subject to a fund program? The IMF is justified in requiring a change in a client country's national policy only if the answer to all three questions is yes. (Feldstein, 1998b)

Unfortunately, the answers to none of the three questions above for Korea, for example, is in the affirmative. The structural reforms the IMF has asked for include labor regulations, corporate governance, the relationship between government and business. These clearly involve deeply political matters. Apart from the questions of morality and national sovereignty, even in practical terms insisting on such far-reaching conditionalities would not appear to be a good idea at all for resolving a financial crisis. Few governments can deliver such reforms in a short space of time and this unnerves the markets, making the resolution of the crisis more difficult.

ANALYTICAL CONCLUSIONS AND POLICY IMPLICATIONS

Analytical conclusions

The main analytical arguments of this paper may be summarized as follows. Firstly, the current widely held and highly influential thesis that the root cause of the present financial crisis in South East and East Asian countries lies in the *dirigiste* model of Asian capitalism pursued by these countries is seriously mistaken. The analysis of the paper suggests that the fundamental reason for the crisis is to be found not in too much, but rather in too little government control over the financial liberalization process which these countries implemented in the recent period.

Secondly, in view of the rather different circumstances of the Asian countries (compared with the kinds of countries that usually face financial difficulties), the IMF staff appears to have misdiagnosed the crisis. They have therefore proposed inappropriate remedies (for example, further financial liberalization, large fiscal austerity, a steep rise in real interest rates) which are likely to deepen the crisis. Moreover, market confidence, which was of critical importance in the evolution of the crisis, is unlikely to have been helped by the IMF's emphasis on the ostensible fundamental structural weaknesses of these countries and requirement that they should implement far-reaching reforms in their economic and social systems. All these factors contributed to turning what was essentially a liquidity problem into one of solvency.

Thirdly, as explained in the previous sections, the governments of the affected countries made serious errors by not controlling the financial liberalization process. Although it is true that the IMF as well as the U.S. government have been urging capital account liberalization for these countries, it is also the case that a growing domestic constituency also supported such liberalization. Thus, for example, prior to the crisis, Thailand and Malaysia were vying with one another as well as with Hong Kong and Singapore to assume the role of regional financial center. This necessarily entailed considerable financial liberalization. In the euphoria accompanying the large inflows of capital during the 1980s and 1990s, the benefits of becoming a regional financial center were readily seen (the development of the financial services industry, skilled employment,

---

21. Chang (1998) notes that a major ambition of the previous South Korean government was for the country to become an OECD member during its own term of office. In pursuit of that ambition the government was willing to forsake important parts of the Asian model, particularly control over investment activity and the financial transactions of large firms and banks.

etc.). However, the governments seemed oblivious to the potential costs.[21]

In addition to the pursuit of financial liberalization without proper institutional controls, the governments of some of the crisis countries (particularly Thailand) might also have made some macroeconomic mistakes, for example, not adjusting the exchange rate and relying on short-term capital to finance a large current account deficit. Nevertheless, a central argument of this paper is that, although these government policy errors may have initiated the crisis, this was compounded by other factors: the lack of coordination between banks and the desire of each bank not to renew its short-term loans following the crisis of confidence; the herd behavior of international investors which was partly responsible for the "contagion" throughout the region; and, as suggested above, the inappropriate policy response from the IMF to the confidence crisis. Thus a liquidity problem has been transformed into a far more serious solvency problem.

Policy implications

What are the policy implications of these conclusions? The basic policy issues which are closely interlinked are as follows:

1) How to restore investor confidence so that normal capital flows in the region are resumed;

2) How to ensure that long-term growth in the real economy is restored as quickly as possible; and

3) How to provide immediate assistance to the millions of people who are likely to become unemployed or pushed back into poverty once again.

The importance of the last issue cannot be exaggerated. This is not just for humanitarian reasons but, as indicated in the previous section, it is also necessary for maintaining social peace. To provide such assistance effectively and on an adequate scale will require not only considerable imagination but also a large expansion in government activity and often direct intervention in the market processes. Such emergency safety net programs may include wider subsidies, food for work schemes, and public works projects, including the kind of labor intensive infrastructural projects which the ILO has pioneered in countries like Indonesia.[22] How to pay for these measures within the limits of fiscal prudence, let alone within the IMF fiscal austerity programs, will be a major issue of political economy for these countries.

Turning to the first policy issue, the most important requirement for achieving a resumption of normal capital flows to the affected countries are economic policies which are credible and have wide domestic political support. Such credibility is much more likely to be achieved if there is political unity in the country and if there is close cooperation not only between government and business but also labor and civil society organizations in a national program to resolve the economic situation. This would inevitably mean that the burden of adjustment would

---

22. For a fuller discussion of these short-term measures see Singh (1998a).

need to be equitably shared by all sections of society. Thus, the traditional Asian model of capitalism essentially based on corporatism becomes all the more essential if the present acute economic crisis is to be overcome.

The first best approach to resolving the present crisis of confidence is for the IMF and the affected countries to cooperate closely on the essential and immediate narrow task of restoring their access to the international capital markets. For this purpose, the IMF should act as an intermediary between the international banks and other major creditors on the one side and the private sector debtors on the other, in order to achieve a rapid restructuring of the debt. In this role, the institution needs to reiterate to investors and creditors the healthy fundamentals of these countries, their proven strong supply-side potential, their export orientation and therefore their ability in the medium to long term to service their debts. It is significant and most encouraging that in response to the criticism of its policy programs, the IMF has already made some important changes such as softening the strong demand restraint measures required of Thailand and Korea. Although somewhat late in the day (rather than before the crisis began) the Fund has also been participating in discussions to facilitate the rescheduling of the debts. However, the institution needs to go a great deal further in the direction of its critics. For the long term, the IMF should seriously reexamine its whole project of promoting capital account liberalization in developing countries.[23]

_____

23. For a fuller discussion of the issues concerning capital account liberalization see further Singh (1997), Singh and Weisse (1998).

REFERENCES

Akyuz, Y. 1997. "The East Asian Financial Crisis: Back to the Future?," unpublished paper.
Amsden, A., ed. 1994. "Reviews of World Bank, 1993," *World Development*, vol.22, no.4.
Amsden, A. 1989. *Asia's Next Giant: South Korea and Late Industrialization*. Oxford: Oxford University Press.
Amsden, A., and Y-D. Euh. 1997. "Behind Korea's Plunge," *New York Times*, November 27.
Amsden, A., and T. Hikino. 1993. "Innovating or borrowing technology: Explorations in paths to industrial development," in R. Thompson, ed., *Learning and Technological Change*. London: Macmillan.
Amsden, A., and A. Singh. 1994. "The optimal degree of competition and dynamic efficiency in Japan and Korea," *European Economic Review*, vol. 28, pp. 941–951.
Aoki, M., and H. Patrick, eds. 1994. *The Japanese Main Bank System: Its Relevance for Developing and Transforming Economies*. Oxford: Clarendon Press.
Calvo, G., and E. Mendoza, 1996. "Mexico's balance of payments crisis: A chronicle of a

death foretold," *Journal of International Economics*, vol. 41, Nos. 3/4, November, pp. 235–264.

Camdessus, M. 1998. "Good governance has become essential in promoting growth and stability," address to Transparency International, *IMF Survey*, vol.27, no.3, February 9, 1998.

Chang, H-J. 1998. "Reform for the long-term in South Korea," *International Herald Tribune*, February 13, 1998.

Cole and Kehoe. 1996. "A self-fulfilling model of Mexico's 1994–1995 debt crisis," *Journal of International Economics*, vol.41, Nos.3/4, November, pp.309–330.

Feldstein, M. 1998a. "Trying to do too much," *Financial Times*, March 3, 1998.

———. 1998b. "Refocusing the IMF," *Foreign Affairs*, March/April 1998.

Glen, J., A. Singh, and R. Matthias (forthcoming). "How Intense is Competition in Emerging Markets? An Analysis of Corporate Rates of Return from Nine Emerging Markets," forthcoming as IMF Working Paper.

ILO. 1995. *World Employment Report*. Geneva: ILO.

IMF. 1997. *World Economic Outlook: Interim Assessment*. Washington, D.C.: IMF (December).

Krueger, A. 1995. "East Asian Experience and Endogenous Growth Theory," in T. Ito and A. Krueger, eds., *Growth Theories in Light of the East Asian Experience*. Chicago: The University of Chicago Press.

Krugman, P. 1998. "What Happened to Asia?" (unpublished).

Lee, C.H. 1992. "The Government, Financial System and Large Private Enterprises in Economic Development in South Korea," *World Development*, vol. 20, no. 2, pp. 187–197.

Maizels, A. 1963. *Industrial Growth and World Trade*. Cambridge: Cambridge University Press.

Nolan, P. 1995. "Large Firms and Industrial Reform in Former Planned Economies: The Case of China," DAE Working Papers, Amalgamated Series No.9516. University of Cambridge, Department of Applied Economics.

Okimoto, D.I. 1989. *Between MITI and the Market*. Palo Alto, California: Stanford University Press.

Ros, J. 1997. "Employment, structural adjustment and sustainable growth in Mexico," Employment and Training Papers 6. Geneva: ILO.

Sachs, J. 1997. "IMF orthodoxy isn't what Southeast Asia needs," *International Herald Tribune*, November 4.

Sachs, J., A. Tornell, and A. Velasco, 1996. "Financial Crises in Emerging Markets: The Lessons from 1995," *Brookings Papers on Economic Activity*, No.1, pp. 147–215.

Samuelson, P. 1997. "Wherein do the European and American models differ?," address to the Bank of Italy, October 2, 1997.

Singh, A. forthcoming. Review of Aoki, Kim and Okuno-Fujiwara, eds., *The Role of Government in East Asian Economic Development. Journal of Development Economics*.

———. 1998a. "Financial Crisis in East Asia: 'The End of the Asian Model?'," Issues in Development, Discussion Paper no. 24. Geneva: ILO.

———. 1998b. "Savings, Investment and the Corporation in the East Asian Miracle," Journal of Development Studies, vol. 34, no. 6, August, pp. 112–137.

———. 1997a. "Catching up with the West: A Perspective on Asian Economic Development and Lessons for Latin America," in L. Emmerij, ed., *Economic and Social Development into the XXI Century*. Washington, D.C.: Inter-American Development Bank.

———. 1997b. "Financial Liberalisation, Stockmarkets and Economic Development," *Economic Journal*, vol. 107, no. 442, May, pp. 771–782.

———. 1996a. "The Plan, the Market and Evolutionary Economic Reform in China," in A. Abdullah and A.R. Khan, eds., *State, Market and Development: Essays in Honour of Rehman Sobhan*. New Delhi: Oxford University Press.

———. 1995a. "The Causes of Fast Economic Growth in East Asia," *UNCTAD Review*.

———. 1995b. *Corporate Financial Patterns in Industrializing Economies: A Comparative International Study*, Technical Paper No. 2. Washington, D.C. IFC.

———. 1994. "Openness and the Market Friendly Approach to Development: Learning the Right Lessons from Development Experience," *World Development*, vol. 22, no. 12, pp. 1811–1823.

———, and B. Weisse, 1998. "Emerging Stock Markets, Portfolio Capital Flows and Long-Term Economic Growth: Micro- and Macroeconomic Perspectives," *World Development* (forthcoming).

Stiglitz, J. 1998a. "Restoring the Asian Miracle," *The Wall Street Journal*, February 3, 1998.

———. 1998b. "More instruments and broader goals: Moving toward the post-Washington consensus," WIDER Annual Lecture, January 7, 1998. Helsinki, Finland: WIDER.

Tokman, V. 1997. "Jobs and Solidarity: Challenges for Post-Adjustment in Latin America," in L. Emmerij, ed., *Economic and Social Development into the XXI Century*. Washington, D.C.: Inter-American Development Bank.

Tsuru, S. 1993. *Japan's Capitalism: Creative Defeat and Beyond*. Cambridge: Cambridge University Press.

UNCTAD. 1997. *Trade and Development Report*. Geneva: UNCTAD.

Wade, R. 1990. *Governing the Market: Economic Theory and the Role of Government in East Asian Industrialization*. Princeton, N.J.: Princeton University Press.

Wade, R., and F. Veneroso. 1998. "The Asian financial crisis: The high debt model and the unrecognized risk of the IMF strategy," Working Paper No. 128. New York: Russell Sage Foundation.

Williamson, O. E. 1975. *Markets and Hierarchies: Analysis and Antitrust Implications*. New

14
...

The Triumph of the Rentiers?
The 1997 Korean Crisis in a Historical Perspective

Ha-Joon Chang and Chul-Gyue Yoo*

THE CAUSES OF THE 1997 Korean financial crisis, together with those of the recent crises in other Asian countries, have been, as we all know, hotly debated. Especially in the early days of the crisis, many commentators argued that the crisis was caused by fundamental institutional deficiencies of the Korean economy that encouraged inefficiencies and excesses by systematically protecting the investors from the negative consequences of their poor decisions.[1] However, others, including surprisingly many mainstream economists, have argued that the crisis was largely the result of a premature and ill-managed financial liberalization (and the dismantling of other "traditional" policies) in the context of an increasingly volatile international financial market.[2]

The present paper aims to shed some new light on this debate from a historical perspective by comparing the three episodes of foreign debt crisis in modern Korean history (1970–72, 1980, 1997) and the evolution of the country's financial system before and after these crises. Through this comparison, the paper shows

---

*We thank Ilene Grabel and Kyung-Rok Kim as well as the participants at the first workshop in July for their useful comments in the first version of the paper. A shortened and less academic version of the paper will appear in the November–December 1999 issue of *Challenge*.

1. Examples include Krugman (1998a, 1998b), Frankel (1998), Brittan (1997), and McKinnon & Pill (1998).

2. The mainstream works that argue along this line include Corden (1998), Furman and Stiglitz (1998), Radelet and Sachs (1998), and Stiglitz (1998). Non-mainstream works along this line include Kregel (1998), Singh (1998), Taylor (1998), and Chang (2000).

that the 1997 crisis is distinguished from the previous crises in many ways, but most importantly in the way it has been managed in the interests of the financial rentier class, rather than of industrial capitalists. It is argued that the changes in the country's financial system and corporate governance system that have been made during the crisis management process are likely to dampen, rather than enhance, Korea's future growth dynamic.

The paper is organized in the following manner. The next section describes the main characteristics of the "traditional" Korean financial system that was behind the country's economic success until the late 1980s. The following section discusses and compares the three episodes of foreign debt crisis. The fourth section describes the institutional "reforms" following the 1997 crisis, which aim for an even greater degree of financial liberalization and opening-up and analyses (and speculates about) what this means for the future of the Korean economy. The final section sums up the discussion and concludes.

THE KOREAN FINANCIAL SYSTEM DURING THE HIGH-GROWTH PERIOD

As it is well known by now, one of the most striking features of the Korean economy during its high-growth period was the "repressive" and closed nature of its financial system. The main elements of the financial policy regime that lasted until the early 1990s (although in a more muted form since the late 1980s) were the following.

First of all, financial policy was run as an accessory to industrial policy. Although the Korean government had a great aversion to running public debt, it ran a relatively loose monetary policy in order to maintain a generally expansionary macroeconomic environment. Expansionary macroeconomic policy was regarded as crucial in sustaining the "investors' confidence" necessary for continued investments, which in turn were regarded as crucial for industrial upgrading (Chang 1993). In this process, the interests of the financial rentier class were "repressed," as reflected in the low profitability of financial institutions, and as most dramatically exemplified in the government-declared moratorium on curb market loans in 1972 (see section 3.1).

Underlying such a regime of "financial repression" was the view of the then ruling elite, who came to power through the 1961 military coup, that a financial rentier class was at best a "necessary evil" and at worst a parasitic group damaging "genuine" entrepreneurs engaged in production. Such a view is well reflected in the following commentary on the pre-1961 financial system made by the official Summary of the First Five Year Plan (published in 1962):

> [O]nly the privileged few who had access to bank credits were able to enjoy profit from production activities .... Instead of making creative and honest efforts to improve management and techniques of production, many entrepreneurs went into unsavory league with politicians and bureaucrats seeking to amass easy fortunes. . . . Industries were compelled to resort to high interest private loans,

and, consequently, usurious lending activities flourished. . . . The degradation of banking not only discouraged development but also distorted or corrupted the ideals underlying national institutions and distorted the sense of social justice. (pp. 11-12; translation by Kim 1995).

Although such a view softened over time and eventually (from the late 1980s) gave way to monetarist thinking, which essentially puts the interest of the financial sector before that of the industrial sector, it will be difficult to make sense of Korea's financial system before the mid-1990s without recognizing that the government basically saw finance as a servant to industry.

Secondly, the country's financial system was a "bank-based" one, and a government-dominated variety of it at that. In the 1962 revision of the central bank act, the Bank of Korea Act, the Minister of Finance was made the head of the Monetary Board (later renamed the Monetary Policy Committee) of the Bank of Korea, thus depriving the central bank of its independence.

Moreover, the banks were, regardless of their ownership status, practically run as public enterprises. A substantial proportion of the banks were "special purpose banks" that were 100% owned by the government - such as Korea Development Bank, Korea Exchange Bank, Korea Housing Bank, and the Bank for Small and Medium-Sized Firms. Even in the case of the other banks, where the government did not have the majority stake, the government maintained its absolute control through the "temporary" law introduced in 1961, which limited private shareholders' voting rights, and subsequently through the 1981 provision in the Banking Act that replaced the "temporary" law, which set a 8% ceiling on bank share ownership for any individual or a group of related shareholders.

Thirdly, through its control of the banking system, the government implemented various directed (and usually subsidized) credit programs, known as "policy loans." As it is well known, these loans were the key instrument in the industrial policy regime of Korea.[3]

The regime of policy loans was perfected when the Korean-style "main bank" system was introduced in May 1974, following the 1970–72 crisis (see section 3.1), on the recognition that a tight monitoring is necessary in order to ensure efficient use of policy loans (and the foreign debts that usually accompanied them). By appointing one of the largest lending banks to each of the *chaebols* (which took the lion's share of policy loans) as its "main bank," the government made sure that there was someone who took an active interest in supervising the use of policy loans. If the main bank was not satisfied with the performance of the recipients of its policy loans, it had to report it to the government, which then would decide on the punishment for the lax performance (e.g., refusal to extend new loans).

---

3. The importance that was attached to policy loans is testified by the fact that, even in times of macroeconomic stabilization, the amount of policy loans was actually *increased* at the expense of other loans (see Itoh 1982).

Fourthly, and probably most importantly for the purpose of the present paper, a tight capital control existed—on both inflows and outflows.

Unlike Japan or Taiwan, which have had "structural trade surplus" since the 1960s, Korea suffered from a chronic foreign exchange shortage.[4] And when combined with the structural political uncertainty due to the presence of North Korea, a very tight control on capital outflow was seen as absolutely necessary for maintaining economic stability—those who engaged in capital flight could be sentenced to death in extreme cases. Central to this regime of control were the so-called Foreign Exchange Concentration System, under which all foreign exchange had to be surrendered to the central bank, and the Foreign Exchange Management Act, which put severe restrictions on the use of foreign exchange (e.g., limits on overseas remittances, on overseas real estate acquisition, or even on expenditure on foreign tourism, which was severely restricted until the late 1980s).[5]

At the same time, the Korean government almost fully controlled foreign borrowing and the use of the borrowed capital through the Foreign Exchange Management Act (1961) and the Law for Payment Guarantee of Foreign Borrowing (1962). In 1966, the Law for Payment Guarantee of Foreign Borrowing was merged with the Special Law to Facilitate Capital Equipment Imports (1962) and the Foreign Capital Inducement Law (1960) into the Foreign Capital Inducement Law, in an attempt to improve the effectiveness of the guarantee procedures for foreign borrowing so that what the government considered "unnecessary" or "wasteful" uses of scarce foreign exchange could be prevented.[6] Government control of foreign borrowing meant that the government could control not only capital inflow at the macro level but also the destinations of investment at the micro level, given the critical importance of imported capital goods in investment in late-developing countries.[7]

---

4. Between 1945 and 1997, the country recorded trade surplus only for three years. It will have posted trade surplus for two years by the end of 1999. However, the two periods of trade surplus are very different from each other because the latter is due to a massive collapse of imports following the 1997 crisis, while the former was achieved amidst the biggest economic boom in the country since the mid-1970s.

5. As we shall see later, this system of foreign exchange control began to be relaxed from the late 1980s (see section 3.3).

6. In the case of foreign *public* borrowing, the borrowing proposal had to be considered first by the relevant ministries, after which the Ministry of Finance had to conduct economic and feasibility studies. The proposal then had to be approved by the Economic Planning Board, which would make it sure that it is consistent with the Five Year Plan and the budgetary plans, and eventually by the Parliament. Only then the borrowing will be approved and government payment guarantee granted. In the case of foreign *commercial* borrowing, the proposal had to satisfy the Guidelines for Commercial Borrowing (issued by the Ministry of Finance) and get passed the Ministry's Foreign Capital Project Committee in order to get the government approval and guarantee.

7. The fact that the Korean government provided payment guarantees to all foreign borrowings during this period has been frequently criticized for creating "moral hazard" on the part of the borrowers. However, especially for a developing country, whether or not foreign borrowings had

THREE EPISODES OF FOREIGN DEBT CRISIS

Since the early 1960s, the Korean economy has experienced three episodes of big surges in foreign borrowing, all of which eventually ended up in a debt crisis. The first episode of debt crisis that happened during 1970–72 was the result of the introduction of a McKinnon-Shaw-style financial reform in 1965. The second episode that occurred during 1980–82 was the outcome of the Heavy and Chemical Industrialization (HCI) program launched in 1973, which was financed by the cheap oil money following the First Oil Shock and severely hit by the world recession following the Second Oil Shock. The third crisis that broke out in 1997 was the result of the large-scale financial liberalization and capital market opening since the mid-1990s that financed excessive and duplicative investments in the industrial sector.

In this section, we discuss in some detail the causes and the resolution (still ongoing in case of the 1997 crisis) of these three episodes of foreign debt crises, so that we can understand the current crisis better by putting it in a historical perspective.

The Unknown Crisis: the late-1960s to the early-1970s

Korea introduced a McKinnon-Shaw-style financial reform in 1965, which, among other things, raised real interest rates to an unprecedented level. The real interest rate on deposits rose from –6.4% on average for the 1960–64 period to the average of an astonishing 26.9% during 1965–9 (calculated from Dornbusch and Park 1987, 419, table 14). This naturally created a huge interest rate gap between domestic loans and foreign loans, generating a very strong incentive to contract foreign loans, especially cash loans that enabled the borrower to re-lend the money in the curb market, which paid even higher interest rates. The result was a rapid rise in foreign debts. As we can see from Table 1, between 1964 and 1967 Korea's total foreign debt rose 3.7-fold (from $177 million to $645 million) and the debt/GNP ratio rose 2.5-fold (from 6.1% to 15.1%).

In the face of such rapid foreign debt accumulation, the government announced the Rationalization Measure for Foreign Capital Inducement in December 1967. The Measure set ceilings on foreign borrowing, especially cash loans, with a view to contain the debt-service ratio at below 9% (it was already 10.7% in 1966). It also raised the ratio of domestic fund reserve required for the

---

been formally guaranteed by the government or not, a foreign debt crisis compels the government into providing ex post payment guarantees to foreign lenders. The best example that illustrates this point in the Korean context is the current financial crisis, where the government was forced to provide such *ex post* guarantees despite the fact that, in the building up of foreign debts during the 1990s, the government did not provide any formal ex ante payment guarantee for foreign loans. If the government has to provide ex post payment guarantees once a debt crisis breaks out, it may be better for it to provide ex ante guarantees while trying to minimize moral hazard in the system by tightening the loan approval and monitoring procedure.

approval of foreign borrowing. However, foreign debt kept on growing. It nearly doubled between 1967 and 1968, and the debt/GNP ratio rose by over 50% (from 15.1% to 22.9%).

As a result, the government introduced even stronger measures (most of them in 1969) in order to "improve the quality of foreign loans," which meant encouraging public loans and discouraging private loans, especially cash loans. They included the strengthening of the qualifications needed for the grant of government payment guarantees, the imposition of ceilings on commercial loans, the prohibition of cash loans other than borrowing by public corporations or borrowing from international institutions, and the introduction of new guidelines for the management of insolvent firms with foreign debt.

Thanks to these measures, for a few years after 1969, the growth of foreign debt slowed down. During the three years between 1969 and 1971, total foreign debt grew by 62.3% (recall that it nearly doubled between 1967 and 1968), and the debt/GNP ratio rose by less than 15% (from 27.2% to 31.2%), whereas it rose by over 50% between 1967 and 1968.

However, domestic financial problems accumulated in the meantime. High economic growth starting in the mid-1960s enhanced the optimism of the Korean firms, leading to an investment boom during the second half of the 1960s. Gross domestic investment ratio, which averaged only 13% between 1960 and 1965, rose to an average of 23.5% between 1966 and 1969. However, the high interest rates that prevailed after the 1965 liberalization squeezed corporate profitability, thus prompting many firms to borrow even more to meet their interest payments obligations.

As the current account deficits started swelling from a very small positive balance in 1965 to the equivalent of 10% of GDP in 1966 and 15% of GDP in 1967, and then finally to 27% and 26% of GDP in 1968 and 1969, respectively, the IMF intervened with an orthodox adjustment program in 1969. The program demanded, among other things, the devaluation of the local currency (won), the abolition of export subsidies and import restrictions, ceilings on foreign borrowings, and the tightening of the monetary supply. Initially, the Korean government objected to the program, but in 1970 it finally had to accept it (except for the demand for the abolition of export subsidies), because the IMF and the U.S. government made the continuation of U.S. government loans conditional on the acceptance of the program.

The combination of devalued currency, high interest rates, and tight money supply following the IMF program naturally resulted in a sharp fall in the profitability of nonfinancial firms and a rapid piling-up of non-performing assets in the banking sector. Interest payments as a proportion of net sales in the corporate sector rose from the average of 3.9% during 1963–65 to the average of 5.6% during 1966–68, and then to 7.8% in 1969 and 9.2% in 1970, and finally to 9.9% in 1971. Given the tight monetary policy, many firms had to increase their reliance on the informal financial market (the so-called curb market) for their survival, which increased their long-term financial burden even more. By 1972, the consequent increase in corporate bankruptcy pushed the country closer and closer to a full-blown foreign debt crisis, as many of the bankrupt firms had

TABLE 1. Korea's Foreign Debt Profile, 1960–97

Year	Total Debt (millions of dollars)	Share of Short-term Debt (%)	Foreign Debt to GNP (%)	Debt Service Ratio (%)
1960	83	1.2	3.9	0.4
1961	83	n.a.	3.9	0.4
1962	89	n.a.	3.8	0.7
1963	157	14.0	5.8	0.9
1964	177	5.6	6.1	2.6
1965	206	1.5	6.9	5.0
1966	392	1.8	10.7	2.9
1967	645	10.2	15.1	5.2
1968	1,199	7.4	22.9	5.2
1969	1,800	10.8	27.2	7.8
1970	2,245	16.6	28.1	18.2
1971	2,922	16.4	31.2	20.4
1972	3,587	17.8	33.9	18.4
1973	4,257	16.5	31.5	14.2
1974	5,933	20.9	32.0	11.2
1975	8,443	28.5	40.5	12.0
1976	10,350	28.9	36.7	10.6
1977	12,649	29.4	33.8	10.2
1978	14,823	21.3	28.5	12.1
1979	20,287	26.9	32.5	13.6
1980	27,170	34.5	44.4	13.3
1981	32,433	31.5	49.0	14.3
1982	37,083	33.5	52.0	16.2
1983	40,378	30.0	50.8	15.7
1984	43,053	26.5	49.5	16.5
1985	46,762	23.0	52.1	18.7
1986	44,510	20.8	42.3	20.8
1987	35,563	26.1	27.6	29.6
1988	31,150	31.4	18.0	13.8
1989	29,368	36.8	13.9	9.7
1990	31,700	45.3	13.3	8.0
1991	39,135	44.0	13.9	4.6
1992	42,819	n.a.	n.a.	n.a.
1993	43,870	43.7	12.7	n.a.
1994	56,850	n.a.	14.2	n.a.
1995	78,439	n.a.	16.1	5.4
1996	104,695	58.3	20.2	5.8
1997	120,800	n.a.	25.5	n.a.

SOURCES: Economic Planning Board and Bank of Korea

foreign debts, and prompted the Korean government into implementing a series of extraordinary measures.

The most important of these measures was the President's Emergency Decree on Economic Stability and Growth announced on August 3, 1972 (the so-called "August 3 Decree"), which bailed out debt-ridden manufacturing firms by declaring a moratorium on the payments of all corporate debt to the curb market lenders for three years—probably the most extreme example of "financial repression" in recent world history.[8] It was declared that, after the end of the moratorium, all curb market loans were to be converted into five-year loans at the annual interest rate of 16.2% (at the time, the curb market interest rate was more than 40%). An extensive rescheduling of bank loans at a preferential rate was also implemented, with the central bank supporting the rescheduling by accepting the special debentures issued by the commercial banks.

A total of 210,000 cases and 357.1 billion won of curb market loans were reported by the creditors and 345.6 billion won by the debtor firms. The amount was equivalent to around 42% of total bank loans. As a result, the interest payments burden of the firms (measured by the ratio of interest payments over net sales) was reduced from 9.9% in 1971 to 7.1% in 1972 and to 4.6% in 1973 and 4.5% in 1974. This ratio stayed constant at 4.9% between 1976 and 1978.

The August 3 Decree, of course, raised the fear among the Korean policy-makers that the rescued firms would become lax in management, believing in continued government support. The trouble that it had to go through in sorting out the financial troubles of a number of major firms with foreign debt in 1969 (through essentially government-mediated takeovers) must have made it realize that there needed to be a more systematic approach to corporate governance.[9] Consequently, the government introduced a series of policy measures intended to improve corporate governance in the aftermath of the August 3 Decree.

The main pillar of these measures was the Presidential Directives on the Inducement of Public Listing and the Sound Management of Private Enterprises (announced on May 29, 1974). These Directives included the following five major elements (the details are from Kim 1997): (i) measures to expedite public listing of corporations; (ii) an information system regarding the credit and taxpaying status of non-listed firms and of their major shareholders; (iii) strengthening of credit restrictions to large firms in order to reduce their dependence on bank credit; (iv) provisions to force highly-leveraged firms to sell part of their businesses when they enter a new business; (v) strengthening of tax collection mechanisms and of outside auditing on enterprises and their major shareholders.

The Directives were accompanied by a few more implementational measures to provide the Office of Bank Supervision with the authority to extensively scrutinize the financial state of the business conglomerates (the *chaebols*), which were the main recipients of policy loans and foreign borrowing. According to these measures announced on May 30 and 31, 1974, the Office was given the authority to scrutinize, at any time, the state of bank debts, assets, the distribution of share ownership, and foreign debts of the *chaebols*. The Office also had the power to control the amount of new bank credits to the *chaebols*. Also, the

---

8. However, it should be noted that a substantial proportion of the loans in the curb market was in fact made by large industrial firms, as it made perfect sense for those firms with surplus cash to loan it in the curb market.

9. The details of the 1969 enterprise restructuring program, which was managed by a special task force answerable only to the President, has never been made public.

Bankers' Association agreed to discriminate against *chaebols* with weak financial status in their lending decisions.

The measures taken to resolve Korea's first debt crisis, while highly unconventional, set the stage for a renewed growth in the following years. The profitability and the financial health of industrial corporations were restored through a brutal confiscation of the financial rentier class as well as through a series of government-mediated corporate restructurings. In addition, the corporate governance system was improved by strengthening the banking system's monitoring and sanction mechanism over the *chaebols*.

The Notorious Crisis: the late 1970s to the early 1980s

With corporate profitability restored through the August 3 Decree and associated measures, the Korean economy started to accelerate once again. In 1973, the government announced the famous (or notorious, if you are a mainstream economist) Heavy and Chemical Industrialization (HCI) program, with an emphasis on six strategic industries—steel, nonferrous metal, shipbuilding, chemical, electronics, and machinery. The government provided supports to the firms in the strategic industries through preferential bank loans, government investment and loan programs, tax exemptions, accelerated depreciation allowances, cuts in import tariffs for capital and intermediate goods, the establishment of industrial estates by state expenditure, and so on (for further details, see Chang 1993).

After experiencing a minor decline in growth rate during 1974 and 1975 in the aftermath of the First Oil Shock—the GDP growth rate slowed down from 12.8% in 1973 to 8.1% and 6.6% in 1974 and 1975, respectively—a major investment and growth spurt started. Gross Fixed Capital Formation grew in real terms by 21% in 1976, 28.7% in 1977, and an astonishing 34.4.% in 1978. And GDP grew at 11.8%, 10.3% and 9.4% in 1976, 1977, and 1978, respectively.

By late 1978, the economy was showing signs of strain. Major investments were made in the HCI industries, but many projects naturally had some way to go before they could turn profitable. Above all, many of them were suffering from very low capacity utilization ratios, because many plants were (correctly from a long-term point of view) built on scales that needed to export in order to be profitable, but major inroads into export markets were yet to be made. The government made some attempt in 1979 to stop or scale down some of the duplicative investments, but had little success in the face of unstoppable optimism in the private sector (for more details, see Chang 1987).

The Second Oil Shock in 1979 and the subsequent introduction of monetarist macroeconomic policies in the US and other major industrial economies pushed the Korean economy into an unprecedented crisis. The import bill was skyrocketing with the quadrupling of oil prices, the major export markets were in serious recession, and above all, the hike in interest rates resulted in a crushing foreign debt repayment burden. Foreign debt/GNP ratio rose from 25.8% in 1978 to 44.4% in 1980 and 49% in 1981 (see Table 1). Financial costs as a proportion of manufacturing value added increased from the average of

16.5% between 1974 and 1978 to 19.2% in 1979, to 28.7% in 1980, and eventually to 32.4% in 1981 (Chang 1987).

In the face of the macroeconomic instability and corporate distress, the Korean government announced a stabilization program with an IMF support in January 1980. However, the tight monetary policy wreaked havoc on the corporate sector, and by June 1980, the Korean government moved away from the monetarist macroeconomic policy stance.[10]

In addition, the 1980 crisis management also included an "industrial restructuring" program, which imposed forced mergers and market segmentations in 6 industries which were most seriously suffering from overcapacity: power-generating equipment, passenger cars, diesel engines, heavy electrical machinery, electronic switching systems, and copper smelting (for details see Chang 1987).[11] Some financial liberalization measures were also implemented—bank privatization, a partial liberalization of entry by foreign banks, increase in the number of industries that were allowed to borrow from abroad, re-allowance of cash loans in certain "key" industries—but the government maintained a strong grip on the financial sector. Strong capital control that had characterized the Korean financial system was maintained[12] and the government regulations over foreign debts were strengthened (see Amsden and Euh 1990, for further details).

Subsequently, between 1985 and early 1988, the government once again took up the task of restructuring the overseas construction and the shipping industries, which were the main sources of non-performing assets in the 1980s, and some other "sunset" industries.[13] The Industrial Policy Deliberation Council was set up to select industries as targets for "rationalization" and approve the merger plans submitted by the main lending banks and the overtaking firm. The Law on Tax Deduction and Exemption was revised in 1985 so that, when firms in industries designated for rationalization merged with other firms in the same industry or sold their assets in order to enter into new (promising) lines of business, they were given tax privileges (e.g., partial exemption of capital gains tax or acquisition tax).

---

10. A similar macroeconomic policy U-turn was observed during the current crisis, but the damage done by high-interest policy in the 1997 was greater as the initial credit squeeze was much more severe (see section 3.3).

11. This is the precursor of the so-called "Big Deal" industrial restructuring program implemented after the 1997 crisis, but with more coherence and more direct government mediation than the "Big Deal." See section 3.3.

12. It was no coincidence that there was virtually no capital flight from Korea around the early 1980s international debt crisis—a major contrast with some Latin American debtor countries during the time (Sachs 1984).

13. The popular view is that it was mainly the HCI industries that produced all those non-performing assets in the Korean banking system, but the main sources of non-performing loans were in fact overseas construction and shipping industries, which were not really objects of industrial policy. Amsden (1994) reports that about 60% of non-performing assets of the Korean banks in the mid-1980s were accounted for by the construction industry alone.

By 1985, the 1980 crisis was largely resolved and the Korean economy entered a new economic boom accompanied by unprecedented trade surpluses between 1986 and 1988. The resolution of the 1980 crisis did not involve direct attacks on financial rentier interests as in the early 1970s crisis, but still bore the hallmark of the pre-1990s Korean economic system. Despite the initial credit squeeze, the pro-investment stance of macroeconomic policy was sustained, and the state control over finance—especially capital control—was largely maintained. The state-mediated corporate governance system was also very much in evidence, as seen in the industrial restructuring exercises (the 1980 industrial restructuring program and various "rationalization" exercises during the second half of the 1980s). This recurrent pattern, however, breaks down in the management of the 1997 crisis, which we shall turn to in the following section.

The Misunderstood Crisis: 1993 to 1997

As we mentioned above, some financial liberalization measures were taken in the immediate aftermath of the 1980 crisis, but the basic nature of Korea's financial system did not change until the late 1980s. Since then, however, there were a number of structural changes that created pressures for more fundamental changes in the financial system.

First of all, the importance of nonbank financial institutions (NBFIs) started to increase rapidly from the mid-1980s, and by the late-1980s, their importance in the financial system started to outweigh that of the banks.[14] Given that these institutions were subject to much less strict governmental regulation (in the case of the now-infamous merchant banks, it was virtually nonexistent), the government's grip on the financial system weakened as never before. The *chaebols* were especially keen to acquire NBFIs, as their ownership of banks was strictly controlled.

Secondly, the large trade surplus generated between 1986 and 1989 made the existing mechanisms of capital account control problematic. Given the Foreign Exchange Concentration System, under which all foreign exchange had to be surrendered to the central bank, the large trade surplus generated excess liquidity in the system, prompting the government to relax restrictions on foreign exchange use. Although trade surplus disappeared subsequently, the surge of capital inflow in the 1990s provided the justification for the continued raising of the ceilings on foreign exchange holdings until the system was finally reduced to near insignificance in 1995.

Thirdly, the increased credit ratings of Korean corporations and banks in the international financial markets meant that the government's grip on the financial sector was diminished even more. By the late 1980s, the private sector seems to have started regarding government involvement in their foreign exchange

---

14. The share of commercial bank assets in total assets of financial institutions fell from 80% in the first half of the 1970s (average for 1971–76) to 73% by the early 1980s (1979–81 average). By 1985, this ratio fell to 59% and then finally below 50% in 1988 (48%). The fall slowed down since then, and the ratio stayed at 42% during the mid-1990s (1993–96 average).

transactions as a burden rather than a necessity—as we mentioned, previously they simply had not had the creditworthiness to borrow in the international capital market without government guarantees.

By the early 1990s, the above-mentioned "structural" pressures towards financial liberalization were becoming very strong. Meanwhile, since the late 1980s, the US government started to put enormous pressure on the Korean government to open up the financial market. The agreement from the March 1992 bilateral talks with the US subsequently formed the basis for the 1993 financial liberalization program. The decision of the Kim Young Same government made in 1993 to apply for membership of the OECD also subjected Korea to further external demands for financial market liberalization.

A series of liberalization and opening-up measures taken in the early 1990s finally resulted in a fundamental change in the Korean financial system. As we can see from Table 2, the changes included, among other things, interest rate deregulation, abolition of "policy loans," granting of more managerial autonomy to the banks, reduction of entry barriers to financial activities and, most importantly, capital account liberalization, something that Korea's previous plans of financial liberalization had characteristically failed to include.

As it is well known, the result of this financial liberalization was the accumulation of a huge amount of short-term foreign debts, which led to the 1997 financial crisis. Foreign debt nearly trebled from $44 billion in 1993 to $120 billion in September 1997. This debt buildup was almost twice as fast as that during 1979–85, the period of the country's second foreign debt crisis following the 1982 Mexican default—Korea's foreign debt grew at 17.8% per annum during 1979–85, while it grew at 33.6% per annum during 1994–96. While Korea's overall foreign debt was *not* at an obviously unsustainable level,[15] the overall debt figures do not tell us the problem with its maturity structure. As we can see from Table 1, the share of short-term debts in total debts rose from an already high 43.7% in 1993 to an astonishing 58.3% by the end of 1996. The magnitude of this problem can be better comprehended if we recall that during the times of the country's two earlier crises, this figure never rose above 20% and 35%, respectively (see Table 1).

As the downfall (and the related corruption scandal) of the new major steel company, Hanbo, and the bankruptcy and the subsequent nationalization of the third largest car manufacturer, Kia, battered international confidence in Korea during the first half of 1997, the financial crisis in Southeast Asia broke out, dragging the country into the whirlpool. Once the international lenders lost confidence in the economy, it did not matter whether their view was justified or

---

15. The World Bank considers countries with debt/GNP ratios under 48% as low-risk cases, but Korea's debt/GNP ratio was only 22% in 1996, and was still around 25% on the eve of the crisis. The corresponding figures at the end of 1995 were 70% for Mexico, 57% for Indonesia, 35% for Thailand, 33% for Argentina, and 24% for Brazil (World Bank 1997). Also, in terms of debt service ratio, Korea on the eve of the 1997 crisis was well below the World Bank 'warning' threshold (18%) at 5.4% in 1995 and 5.8% in 1996. These compare very favorably with those of countries like Mexico (24.2%), Brazil (37.9%), Indonesia (30.9%), and Thailand (10.2%) in 1995 (World Bank 1997).

TABLE 2. Major Financial Liberalization Measures in Korea during the 1990s

1) Interest rates deregulation (in four stages: 1991 to July 1997)
By 1997, all lending and borrowing rates, except demand deposit rates, were liberalized

2) More managerial autonomy for the banks and lower entry barriers to financial activities
Freedom for banks to increase capital, to establish branches, and to determine dividend payments (1994)
Enlargement of business scope for financial institutions (1993)
continuous expansion of the securities business of deposit money banks (1990, 1993, 1994, 1995)
freedom for banks and life insurance companies to sell government and public bonds over the counter (1995)
permission for securities companies to handle foreign exchange business (1995)
Abolition of the limits on maximum maturities for loans and deposits of banks (1996)

3) Foreign exchange liberalization
Adoption of the Market-Average Foreign Exchange Rate System (1990)
Easing of the requirement for documentation proving "real" (i.e., nonfinancial) demand in foreign exchange transactions (1991)
Setting up of foreign currency call markets (1991)
Revision of the Foreign Exchange Management Act (1991)
changing the basis for regulation from a positive system to a negative system
Introduction of "free Won" accounts for nonresidents (1993)
Allowance of partial Won settlements for the export or import of visible items (1993)
Foreign Exchange Reform Plan (1994)
a detailed schedule for the reform of the foreign exchange market structure
A very significant relaxation of the Foreign Exchange Concentration System (1995)

4) Capital market opening
Foreign investors are allowed to invest directly in Korean stock markets with ownership ceilings (1992)
Foreigners are allowed to purchase government and public bonds issued at international interest rates (1994), equity-linked bonds issued by small and medium-sized firms (1994), non-guaranteed long-term bonds issued by small and medium-sized firms (Jan. 1997), and non-guaranteed convertible bonds issued by large companies (Jan. 1997)
Residents are allowed to invest in overseas securities via beneficiary certificates (1993)
Abolition of the ceiling on the domestic institutional investors' overseas portfolio investment (1995)
Foreign commercial loans are allowed without government approval in so far as they meet the guideline established (May 1995)
Private companies engaged in major infrastructure projects are allowed to borrow overseas to pay for domestic construction cost (Jan. 1997)
Liberalization of borrowings related to foreign direct investments related (Jan. 1997)

5) Policy loans & credit control
A planned termination of all policy loans by 1997 is announced (1993)
a step-wise reduction in policy loans to specific sectors (e.g., export industries and small and medium-sized firms)
Simplifying and slimming down the controls on the share of bank's loans to major conglomerates in its total loans

SOURCE: Chang et al. (1998)

not. International lenders stopped rolling over Korean debts from the fall of 1997, and the country finally had to go to the IMF for a rescue package in December 1997 (for a more detailed chronology of the crisis, see Chang 1998).

Under a most comprehensive and tough IMF program, with stiff macroeconomic conditions and unprecedented demands for institutional changes (especially regarding corporate governance), the economy contracted to an unprecedented degree. In a country where 5% growth had been considered a "recession," the economy shrank by 5.8% in 1998, recording the biggest contraction in output since the Korean War (1950–53). Industrial production was especially adversely affected and fell by 7.5%.

The virulence of the 1997 crisis may be put into a clearer perspective by comparing it with the 1980 crisis, which resulted in the biggest fall in output before the 1997 crisis (–2.7%).

According to the figures released by the Bank of Korea, gross fixed capital formation fell by 21.2% in 1998, whereas in 1980 it recorded a 10.7% fall. Particularly hard hit was machinery and equipment investment, which fell by a staggering 38.5% (a particularly large fall, given that it already fell by 8.7% the previous year). The corresponding fall in 1980 was 24.6% (and at that after a very large positive growth in 1979—23.3%). Exports in 1998 fell by 2.8% (in value terms) for the first time since 1958, whereas they grew at 16.3% in 1980.

Unemployment rose from 2.5% just before the crisis (and from the trough of 2% in 1996) to the height of 8.7% in February 1999 (it is reported to have fallen since March 1999), in contrast to the rise from 3.8% in 1979 (or from the trough of 3.2% in 1978) to 5.2% in 1980. Income inequality also worsened markedly following the crisis—the ratio of the income of the top quintile to that of the bottom quintile rose from 4.49 before the crisis to 5.38 by 1999 (*Joongang Daily Newspaper*, June 18, 1999) and the ratio of the income of the top 10% to that of the bottom 10% rose from 7.1 in the first quarter of 1995 to 9.8 in the first quarter of 1998 and 10.2 in the first quarter of 1999 (*Daehan Maeil Newspaper*, June 25, 1999). The worsening of income inequality in the aftermath of the 1980 crisis was not very significant, if at all.[16]

It is not simply its virulence but also its management that sets the 1997 crisis apart from the earlier crises. In the management of the 1997 crisis, the traditional anti-finance/pro-industry stance of the Korean government was abandoned. In the management of the 1997 crisis, credit squeeze was much greater than in the two earlier episodes of crisis—loans by deposit money banks *fell* by 0.1% in 1998, whereas they *grew* by about 28% during 1970–71 and by about 36% in 1980. Especially important in creating the credit squeeze during the 1997 crisis was the newly introduced BIS capital adequacy standard, whose pro-cyclical nature only amplified the crisis (see section 4 for further discussion). Even the fall

---

16. Of the five estimates of trends in income inequality reviewed in Ahn (1996), two showed a small fall in Gini coefficient between 1980 and 1982 (from 0.389 to 0.357 and from 0.409 to 0.393) and three showed a small rise during the same period (from 0.386 to 0.406, from 0.356 to 0.385, and from 0.337 to 0.376).

in exports following the 1997 crisis, which contrasts with the continued rise in exports after the 1980 crisis, owed significantly to the squeeze on export credits, rather than to an overvalued currency or to the depressed world market conditions (the world economy was in a deep recession in the early 1980s, whereas it has remained relatively buoyant since 1997).

As the credit squeeze crushed the economy, the IMF belatedly took a U-turn and allowed the Korean government lower interest rates and (in the face of continued aversion of the Korean government to budget deficits) pushed it to increase its budget deficit (the fourth agreement in May 1988—see Table 3). And largely as a result of this U-turn, the speed of contraction of the economy slowed down from the fourth quarter of 1998, and by the end of the first quarter of 1999, the economy started to recover rapidly. Some are now even predicting an 8% growth for 1999.

What do we make out of this rapid recovery? Does it prove that the IMF policy was a success, as the IMF and its supporters claim? Our contention is that it does not.

First of all, the recovery is largely a natural reaction to the easing of the initial macroeconomic policy that was excessively tight and unnecessarily shrank the economy. The fact that the financial markets did not stabilize until May 1998, when the IMF abandoned its earlier policy (see Figure 1) suggests that the country could have recovered much more quickly and much more strongly, had the IMF policy not been so restrictive.

Secondly, the quality of the recovery is not as impressive as it looks. Even an 8% growth in 1999 will mean that the economy is only 1.7% larger than what it was in 1997. In contrast, in 1981, the year after the country's worst crisis before the current one, the economy recorded a 6.2% growth following a 2.7% contraction in 1980, which meant that Korea's 1981 GDP was 2.1% higher than that in 1979. The current recovery looks even less impressive when we consider its performance in terms of unemployment and inequality (see above).

More importantly, it is questionable whether the recovery is sustainable in the medium term. The current phase of recovery has been led by consumption rather than investments. What is worrying is that the rise in consumption seems to be largely fuelled by the wealth effect created by an overly inflated stock market, which in turn was the result of the excess liquidity created by the easing of monetary policy (since the third quarter of 1998) in the face of a dramatic collapse in real investments. The stock market price index, which fell below 300 (297.9, to be precise) in the second quarter of 1998 went up to 562.5 by the fourth quarter of 1998, broke the 1,000 barrier in July 1999, and since then has been moving around 900 (at the time of writing).

In theory, the increase in consumption through wealth effect may eventually lead to an increase in investments, which should make the recovery sustainable, but it is questionable whether the stock market will be buoyant for a long enough period of time, especially given the imminent large-scale correction (or collapse?) in the US stock market.

What is more worrying, however, than the medium-term sustainability of the recovery is that the changes in the country's institutional configuration that

TABLE 3. Changes in the Contents of the IMF Program during the 1997 Crisis

	Macroeconomic Targets for 1998	Monetary policies	Measures for promoting domestic demand
First Memorandum (Dec. 3. 1997, revised Dec. 24, 1997)	Growth rate (GDP): 3% Inflation: 5% Trade surplus: $4.3 billion Central government deficit: balance or surplus Unemployment rate: 3.9%	Tight monetary policy High interest rate policy Financial sector restructuring Interest rate over 30% Elimination of upper limit in interest rate	Emphasis on tight fiscal policy rather than promotion of domestic demand
Jan. 7, 1998 Agreement	Growth rate: 1–2% Inflation: 9% Trade surplus: $3 bil. Usable reserves: $24 bil. (1st quarter) Unemployment rate: 5%	Establishing foundation for interest rate stabilization Monetary base: 14.9% (1st quarter)	Inevitable fiscal deficits allowed
Feb. 7, 1998 Agreement	Growth rate: 1% Inflation: 9% Trade surplus: over $8 billion Usable reserves: $20 billion (1st quarter), $30 billion (2nd quarter) Unemployment rate: 6–7%	Cautiously Permit lowering interbank call rate conditional on the market situation Increase in money growth rate target monetary base: 13.5% (1st quarter), 14.1% (2nd quarter)	Allow fiscal deficit up to 0.8% of GDP Reduction in luxury goods tax
May 2, 1998 Agreement	Growth rate: –1% or less Inflation: less than 10% Trade surplus: $21–23 bil. Usable reserves: $32 bil. (2nd quarter)	Pursue a continuous fall in interbank call rate	Fiscal deficit allowed up to 1.7% of GDP Increase in support for small and medium sized companies
July 24, 1998 Agreement	Growth rate: –4% Inflation: 9% Trade surplus: $33–35 bil.	Lower interest rate by flexible monetary control	Fiscal deficit allowed up to 5 % of GDP
Oct. 29, 1998 Agreement	Growth rate: –4% Inflation: 8% Trade surplus: $ 37bil.	Eliminate the limit on the growth rate of reserve money	
Nov. 13, 1998 Agreement	Growth rate for 1999: positive Inflation: 5% Current account surplus: about $20 bil. (7% of GDP) Usable reserves (targeted to reach $41 bil. at end-1998): already reached $45 bil. at end-October and expected to rise moderately in 1999	Maintain the easy monetary stance, consistent with achievement of the inflation target and stability of the exchange rate BOK intervention in exchange rate: limited to smoothing operations	Fiscal deficit: around 5% of GDP in 1998 Direct social safety net outlays: to increase from W5.7tril. in 1998 to W8.2 tril. (about 2% of GDP) in 1999 Public works programs: W2 tril. Outlays for job training: W0.8 tril. in 1999

Mar. 31, 1999 Agreement

Growth rate for 1999: over 2%	Continuing a flexible interest rate policy	Fiscal deficit allowed up to 5% of GDP for 1999
Inflation: around 3%	Broad money (M3) growth expected at 13–14% in 1999	Import financing for small- and medium-sized enterprises: at least $1 bil.
Current account surplus to narrow significantly but remain substantial		
Usable reserves, which reached $48.5 bil. at end –1998, to rise further in 1999	BOK intervention in exchange rate will be limited to smoothing operations	BOK rediscount of export bills for small- and medium-sized enter- prises: $0.3 bil.

SOURCES: KIEP(1998), *Adjustment Reforms in Korea since the Financial Crisis (Dec. 1997–June 1998)*
MOFE(1998), *The Agreement Between Korea and the IMF for Fourth Quarter*
MOFE(1999), *The First Letter of Intent Agreed between Korean Government and IMF in 1999*
Samsung Economic Research Institute (1998), *One Year after the IMF Bailout: A Review of Economic and Social Changes in Korea*

FIGURE 1. Trends in Financial Market Variables

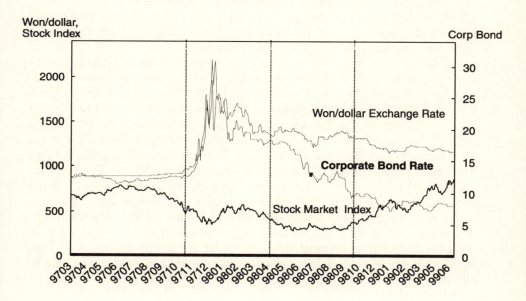

SOURCES: BOK, MOFE, Major Economic Statistics

were made in the process of crisis management, especially the ones regarding the financial system but also regarding the corporate governance system, are likely to have negative effects on the long-term dynamism of the economy—an issue that we wish to discuss in the following section of the paper.

INSTITUTIONAL CHANGES AFTER THE 1997 CRISIS—
WHAT FUTURE FOR KOREA?

The policy package that was adopted in order to manage the (still-unresolved) 1997 crisis was not entirely in the mould of the standard IMF package and still showed some traditional Korean streaks. For the most important example, the Korean government pushed the *chaebols* into a "voluntary" industrial restructuring program involving mergers and business swaps in eight industries (semiconductors, automobiles, power-generating equipment, naval diesel engines, aircraft, petrochemicals, petroleum refining, and railway carriages)—the so-called "Big Deal." Although this program is not part of a coherent long-term industrial policy as in the case of previous industrial restructuring programs, it is similar to its earlier counterparts in its spirit.

However, in general, the crisis management package implemented since 1997 has resulted in institutional changes that are likely to significantly transform the nature of the Korean economy. Are these changes for the better or for the worse? Important changes were made in other areas too (e.g., employment institutions, bureaucratic recruitment and appointments), but, given the nature of the paper, we will confine our discussion to institutional changes that concern the financial system and to a lesser extent the corporate governance system, and discuss what they mean for the future of the Korean economy.

First of all, the "pro-finance" policy stance, which characterized the macroeconomic policy in the early days of the current crisis, was subsequently institutionalized through a series of legal changes in the financial system. To begin with, the role of the central bank was redefined into a fundamentally monetarist (i.e., pro-finance) one. In the old central bank act, the Bank of Korea (BOK) Act, the BOK was supposed to maintain the "soundness of the banking and the financial system" (which can mean a lot of things in practice) as well as price stability. The new Act that took effect in April 1999 specifies that price stability should be the sole aim of the BOK. This change, while appearing minor, has profound implications for the Korean financial system, as it de-legitimizes the kind of pro-investment, pro-growth monetary policy that characterized the Korean financial system up to now. Moreover, the banking law and other financial laws were revised in a way that strengthens the shareholder interest in the running of the banks, thus making it possible and, more importantly legitimate, to defend financial interests at the cost of industrial interests (something that was not allowed before).

The second important institutional change in the Korean financial system that followed the current crisis was the introduction of the BIS standard on capital adequacy ratio into the financial system. The BIS standard has certain merits (e.g., simplicity, transparency), but one important problem with it is its procyclical nature as proven by the recent Korean experience—in recession, increased bankruptcy, and falling asset prices shrink the banks' asset bases, which makes them withdraw their loans in order to meet the standard, thereby making the recession even worse.[17] Moreover, the very way in which the BIS standard is defined encourages the holding of liquid assets and therefore a strict enforcement of the standard, to which the Korean government claims to be committed, will make the banks reluctant to lend to industrial projects that involve large sunk costs.

The third important institutional change made after the current crisis was a radical capital market liberalization and capital account opening, including the full-scale liberalization of corporate borrowing from abroad (which makes government regulation of foreign debts much more difficult) and the complete opening of the stock and bond markets to foreigners. As shown in Figure 1 above and Table 4 below, these changes have increased the volatility in the financial market, which is not conducive to long-term investments and therefore harmful for the country's investment-growth dynamics. Table 5, which charts the changes in the average holding periods and the turnover ratios for different types of investors in the Korean stock market between 1996 and 1999, shows that what lies behind this worrying trend is the dramatic shortening of the duration of financial asset holding as a result of the radical liberalization of the financial market.

TABLE 4. Volatility of Financial Market Variables

	Mean	Standard Deviation	Coefficient of Variation	Volatility*
KOSPI (stock market index)				
Jan. 1993–Nov. 1997	830.19	130.06	0.1567	0.00538
Dec. 1997–Sep. 1998	538.17	210.71	0.3915	0.01260
Oct. 1998–Sep. 1999	676.09	204.61	0.3026	0.01176
Interest Rate**				
Jan. 1993–Nov. 1997	12.73	1.10	0.0861	0.00337
Dec. 1997–Sep. 1998	12.69	5.23	0.4118	0.01040
Oct. 1998–Sep. 1999	8.86	0.94	0.1059	0.00656
Won/Dollar Exchange Rate				
Jan. 1993–Nov. 1997	815.47	49.84	0.0611	0.00200
Dec. 1997–Sep. 1998	1,319.23	155.28	0.1177	0.00854
Oct. 1998–Sep. 1999	1,216.29	50.03	0.0411	0.00202
May 1998–Sep. 1999***	1,256.69	80.46	0.0640	0.00280

*The standard deviation of log-differenced values.
**Yield of corporate bond with 3-year maturity.
***This periodization is used on the ground that the exchange rate stabilized markedly from May 1998.

Also problematic is the demand made on the *chaebols* that they bring down their debt-equity ratio from above 400% to 200% by the end of 1999, which made them cut down on new investments as well as engage in "distress selling" of their existing assets. The short-run effect of this change was to create a downward investment spiral. But more importantly, in the long run, if they continue to meet this demand, the Korean corporations are unlikely to be able to mobilize the funds necessary for the kind of aggressive investment strategy that they have

---

17. It should also be noted that the introduction of the BIS standard in Korea was done at the worst time—in the middle the deepest recession in the country's modern history.

traditionally pursued. The hope held by the policy makers who introduced this rule is that the deregulation of the stock market will lead to a greater reliance of the *chaebols* on direct financing. However, given the well-known short-term orientation of the stock market, which is markedly worsening in Korea at the moment (see Table 5), it is unlikely that the Korean firms are going to be able to mobilize through the stock market enough "patient" funds needed for the investments in large-scale industries.

TABLE 5. Stock Holding Periods (months) and Turnover Ratios (monthly, %) of the Different Groups of Investors

Year	1996	1997	1998	1999 (January–July)
Foreign Investors	22.3 months 54%	14.4 months 83%	11.5 months 104%	9.3 months 129%
Domestic Investors	12.3 months 97%	—	—	2.6 months 466%
Individuals	5.8 months 207%	—	—	1.2 months 1,041%
Investment Trusts	11.2 months 107%	—	—	2.4 months 502%
Banks	46.8 months 26%	—	—	6.6 months 183%

Source: Korea Stock Exchange

CONCLUDING REMARKS

The present paper has tried to put the 1997 Korean crisis into a historical perspective by comparing the three episodes of foreign debt crisis in the country's postwar history (1970–72, 1980, and 1997).

The 1997 crisis signifies an important watershed in modern Korean economic history. It is not simply that it was the result of the disintegration of the "traditional" economic system, where industrial interests dominated financial rentier interests. What is more important is that the crisis has been managed in the interests of financial rentiers, rather than for the industrial interests as in previous crises—through monetarist macroeconomic policy, full-scale financial liberalization, and capital account opening, among other things. More importantly, it has brought about institutional changes that are likely to end the dominance of industry over finance that has characterized the Korean economic system.

In contrast, the 1970–72 crisis, although its origins also can be found in a radical financial liberalization, was resolved through a most dramatic instance of "financial repression" in the interest of industry (the August 3 Decree) and the introduction of more, and not less, financial regulations. In the case of the 1980 crisis, financial liberalization did not play a role in its making, and its resolution involved only relatively mild and mostly formalistic financial liberalization measures.

Is this transition to a new economic system desirable? We have shown that it is unlikely to be so. We pointed out that the short-term performance of this new system in resolving the crisis has been much poorer than that of the traditional system. And this was despite the fact that the external economic conditions have been much more favorable than in the two earlier crises—they were followed, respectively, by the First Oil Shock of 1973–74 and the Monetarist world recession of the early 1980s. From the longer-run perspective, we argued that the institutional changes made in the Korean economic system following the 1997 crisis are likely to dampen the economy's investment dynamism by making the financial system much more volatile and "conservative" than before, thus making long-term, patient capital much more scarce.

REFERENCES

Ahn, G. S. 1996. Trends in Korean Income Distribution: Conflicting Estimates and Their Evaluations in J.W. Lee et al., *Industrial Relations and the Lives of the Workers in Korea* (in Korean), Seoul Institute of Economic and Social Studies, Seoul.

Amsden, A. 1994. Why isn't the Whole World Using the East Asian Model to Develop?: Review of the World Bank's *East Asian Miracle Report*, *World Development*, vol. 22, no. 4.

Amsden, A. and Y. Euh. 1990. Republic of Korea's financial reform: What are the lessons?, Discussion Paper, no. 30, United Nations Conference on Trade and Development (UNCTAD), Geneva.

Bank of Korea (BOK). Various years. *Economic Statistics Yearbook*, Bank of Korea, Seoul.

BOK 1999. *1998 National Accounts (preliminary)*, Bank of Korea, Seoul.

Brittan, S. 1997. Asian Model R.I.P., *Financial Times*, 4 December 1997.

Chang, H. J. 1987. Crisis of Capital Accumulation in South Korea, 1979–1982, unpublished M.Phil. dissertation, Faculty of Economics and Politics, University of Cambridge.

_____. 1993. The Political Economy of Industrial Policy in Korea, *Cambridge Journal of Economics*, vol. 17, no. 2, pp. 131–157.

_____. 1998. Korea: The Misunderstood Crisis, *World Development*, vol. 26, no. 8, pp. 1555–61.

_____. 2000 (forthcoming). The Hazard of Moral Hazard—Untangling the Asian Crisis, *World Development*.

Chang, H.J., H. J. Park, and C. G. Yoo. 1998. Interpreting the Korean Crisis: Financial Liberalisation, Industrial Policy, and Corporate Governance, *Cambridge Journal of Economics*, vol. 22, no. 6, pp. 735–746.

Corden, M. 1998. Sense and Nonsense on the Asian Crisis, The Sturc Lecture, delivered on 8 November, 1998, at the Paul H. Nitze School of Advanced International Studies, Johns Hopkins University.

Dornbusch, R. and Y. C. Park. 1987. Korean Growth Policy, *Brookings Papers on Economic Activity*, no. 2.

Frankel, J. 1998. The Asian Model, the Miracle, the Crisis and the Fund, a speech delivered at the US International Trade Commission, 16 April.

Furman, J. & Stiglitz, J. 1998. Economic Crises: Evidence and Insights from East Asia, a paper presented at the Brookings Panel on Economic Activity, 3–4 September, 1998, Washington, D.C.

Itoh, K. 1982. Development Finance and Commercial Banks in Korea, *The Developing Economy*, vol. 20, no. 4.

Kim, P. J. 1995. *Financial System and Policy, 1961–79*, Korea Institute of Finance, Seoul.

_____. 1997. Financial Policies and Institutional Innovation, in D.S. Cha, K.S. Kim & D. H. Perkins (eds.), *The Korean Economy 1945–1995*, Korea Development Institute, Seoul.

Kregel, J. 1998. Yes, "It" Did Happen Again—the Minsky Crisis in Asia, a paper presented at the conference on the "Legacy of Hyman Minsky," December, Bergamo.

Krugman, P. 1998a. What Happened to Asia?, mimeo, Department of Economics, Massachusetts Institute of Technology.

_____. 1998b. Fire-sale FDI, a paper presented at the NBER Conference on Capital Flows to Emerging Markets, 20–21 February.

McKinnon, R. and H. Pill. 1998. International Overborrowing—A Decomposition of Credit and Currency Risk, *World Development*, no. 7.

Radelet, S. and J. Sachs. 1998. The East Asian Financial Crisis: Diagnosis, Remedies and Prospects, *Brookings Paper on Economic Activity*, 1998, no. 1, 1–90.

Sachs, J. 1984. Comments on C. Diaz-Alejandro, "Latin American Debt: I Don't Think We Are in Kansas Anymore," *Brookings Papers on Economic Activity*, 1984, no. 2.

Singh, A. 1998. Financial Crisis in East Asia: "The End of the Asian Model?," Issues in Development Discussion Paper, no. 24, International Labour Office, Geneva.

Stiglitz, J. 1998. Sound Finance and Sustainable Development in Asia, a speech delivered at the Asian Development Forum, 12 March, 1998, Manila, the Philippines.

Taylor, L. 1998. Capital Market Crises: Liberalization, Fixed Exchange Rates and Market-driven Destablization, *Cambridge Journal of Economics*, vol. 22, no. 6, pp. 663–676.

World Bank. 1997. *Global Development Finance*, World Bank, Washington, D.C.

15

...

The Magical Realism of Brazilian Economics

How to Create a Financial Crisis by Trying to Avoid One

*Gabriel Palma**

IN THE LAST two decades there have been four major financial crises in the Third World: the 1982 debt crisis (affecting particularly Latin America, with the Chilean economy the worst hit in the region); the 1994 Mexican crisis (and its repercussions throughout Latin America, especially Argentina, commonly known as the "Tequila effect"); the 1997 East Asian crisis, and lately the Brazilian one (in 1999). The main common characteristic of these financial crises is that the economies most affected were those that had previously undertaken radical processes of financial liberalization. Furthermore, these countries had not only liberalized their capital accounts and domestic financial sectors, but had done so at times of both high liquidity in international financial markets, and slow growth in most OECD economies; i.e., at times when a rapidly growing, highly volatile, and largely under-regulated international financial market was anxiously seeking new high-yield investment opportunities.

*Faculty of Economics and Politics, Cambridge University. An earlier version of this paper was presented at a workshop on "The New World Financial Authority," organized by the Center for Economic Policy, The New School University, New York, July 6–7, 1999. I should like to thank the Center for their financial support, and the participants at the workshop, particularly John Eatwell, José Antonio Ocampo, and Lance Taylor for their helpful comments. Participants at other conferences and seminars in Bilbao, Cambridge, Chicago, Santiago, and Trento, particularly Marcelo Abreu, Edna Armendariz, Paul Davidson, Jorge Fodor, Daniel Hahn, Michel Kuczynski, Murray Milgate, Angela Montes, Bob Sutcliffe, and especially Paul Cammack and Arturo O'Connell also made useful suggestions. The usual caveats apply.

These recurrent financial crises, which repeatedly took most business and academic observers by surprise, have generated a heated debate on fundamental issues of finance, economics, and economic policy making in general. In fact, the only issue on which there seems to be some agreement is that before these crises, international and domestic financial institutions had overlent, and that in the crisis-countries the government, corporations, and/or households had overborrowed—in both instances, "over" refers specifically to the fact that lenders and borrowers ended up accumulating excessive amounts of risk.

However, there are several related issues regarding these financial crises, which are among the most controversial topics in economics today. The most controversial one, as in so many other areas of economic theory that deal with crises and market failures in general, is whether the dynamic that led to these events was set in motion by "exogenous" or "endogenous" factors. That is, did borrowers and lenders accumulate more risk than was privately (let alone socially) efficient due to exogenous market interference, which distorted their otherwise rational and efficient behavior? Or did they do so because specific market failures within financial markets led them to be unable to assess and price their risks properly?

In other words, did artificially created factors, such as "moral hazards" or "crony capitalism," interfere with the incentive mechanisms and resource allocation dynamics of financial markets? Or did the combination of a particular type of international financial market with a particular form of financial liberalization lead to the creation of an economic environment in which the interaction among intelligent, self-interested, "maximizing" economic agents certainly did not lead towards some sort of "equilibrium" (local or global)? Did this particular combination produce incentives that led to the failure of this maximization-cum-equilibrium process because it created a situation characterized by factors such as excess liquidity (through a massive growth in inflows), and increased financial fragility (via augmenting the weight of "speculative" and "Ponzi" finance)? Did this particular combination also make significantly worse other common economic problems, such as asymmetric information by, for example, liberalization being so sudden that it led to the interaction, on one side, of international financial institutions with very little knowledge of the institutional dynamics of emerging markets and, on the other, of still inexperienced domestic financial players?[1]

This paper attempts to answer these questions regarding Brazil's 1999 financial crisis. It does so mainly from an "endogenous-failure" perspective. It argues that the general mechanisms that led to this financial crisis were in essence endogenous to the workings of financial markets when they operate with overabundance of liquidity and become overdependent on highly volatile capital flows. However, it will also argue that there was a very specific "Minskian" feature in the Brazilian crisis, which made it different from previous financial crises. In Brazil, the absorption of the massive increase in inflows, and the dynamic that

---

1. Among the large literature on the role of "moral hazards" in financial crises, probably the best exposition is that of McKinnon and Pill (1997). Literature related to most of these issues can be found at http://w.w.w.stern.nyu.edu/~nroubini/asia/AsiaHomepage.html

this process generated, were uniquely conditioned by an economic environment characterized by particularly high and unstable interest rates, and the particular financial fragility they tend to create.

Although these high interest rates were initially devised as an essential component of the successful price-stabilization program, it was clearly expected by markets and the government that soon afterwards they would be able to fall significantly, as had happened before in similar experiments of stabilization-cum-financial liberalization, such as those in Chile, Mexico, and Argentina (see Figures 13 and 14 below). After inflation had been conquered, the new and lower levels would be determined (as in the other countries) by international interest rates with some added "normal" risk premium. In Brazil, however, each time that this began to happen, interest rates stubbornly kept bouncing back to extraordinarily high levels, becoming at the end a permanent rather than a temporary feature of the Real Plan (see Figure 11 below). This was mainly the result of three unexpected factors. Firstly, after its successful price-stabilization the Brazilian economy was hit by three external shocks (those created by the Mexican, East Asian, and Russian crises), and after each of them, the economic authorities chose to increase interest rates sharply as a mechanism both to avoid capital flight and to slow down the economy (mainly to improve the rapidly worsening balance of payments). Secondly, the new Brazilian economic authorities soon learned that the main lesson from the Mexican crisis was that financial liberalization could easily lead to very destabilizing processes—especially rapid credit expansion, consumption boom, meteoric rises in imports of consumer goods, and asset bubbles (see Figures 15 to 18 below); so higher interest rates were then also chosen in Brazil as the main mechanism for avoiding a repeat of these phenomena. Thirdly, Cardoso's economic team did not expect that it would be so difficult to get through Parliament the necessary (and endlessly promised) fiscal reforms, so this failure also made higher interest rates necessary.

One of the main arguments of this paper is that these high and volatile interest rates, coupled with the peculiar way in which the government dealt with the inevitable domestic financial fragility that these rates created, were at the heart of the process that led to Brazil's 1999 crisis in general, and the public sector to sleepwalk into an ever growing "Minskian Ponzi" in particular (i.e., having to capitalize increasing amounts of its interest payments). By struggling to avoid three types of financial crisis (a "Kindlebergian" Mexican-type one, an external or internal shock creating an East Asian-type sudden loss of confidence and panic-withdrawal of funds, and a domestic banking collapse), the Brazilian authorities ended up creating a different type of crisis—it seems that in Brazil solutions to difficult problems cannot be done without a magical realist hint to them.

From this perspective, one of the most interesting features of the Brazilian experience is that it contradicts one of the key propositions of the traditional literature that uses "moral hazards" as its main explanation for financial crisis. As is well known, this literature tries to explain in particular the Mexican and East Asian crises by associating exogenous market interference (like deposit insurance and the international financial markets' expectations that, as in an old Western, they could always count on the cavalry arriving in the nick of time in the form of a vast international IMF-led rescue operation) with "artificially" low interest rates; and, then, these low rates with lenders and borrowers ending up accumulating excessive amounts of risk. What the Brazilian case shows is that the opposite scenario is equally dangerous: "artificially" high interest rates (i.e., significantly higher than international interest rates plus any possible reasonable risk premium)—and with high volatility adding on top an important element of uncertainty—can lead just as easily to financial fragility. This is done via the problems it creates both in the domestic financial system (mainly due to under-performing banking assets), and in the public sector (due to the high cost of servicing its debt). Of course, these problems can be compounded, as happened in Brazil, if a government chooses to create a vicious circle between the public sector fragility and the private sector one by adopting a policy of absorbing the resulting bad debt of the domestic banking system in a continuous and indiscriminate manner. In this way the Brazilian authorities not only added a crucial new "moral hazard," but also a very costly one because then the private sector's financial fragility helped push the public sector one to levels that became unsustainable by rapidly increasing both the stock and the flows of the public debt.

Thus, one of the key lessons of Brazil's financial crisis is to show that the traditional "moral hazard" literature only looks at one side of the story. Even though it discusses important issues in this respect, it seems crucially to forget that financial liberalization in emerging markets is a far more complicated phenomenon than the problems created by "artificially" low interest rates. As will be discussed in detail below, the crucial issue seems to be that when this liberalization is done in a context of high, volatile and unregulated international liquidity, it creates speculative activity of the sort which generates "damned-if-you-do, damned-if-you-don't" choices in relation to interest rates.

This paper concentrates on the period between the beginning of Brazil's experiment with financial liberalization and economic reform proper and the outbreak of its financial crisis—i.e., between the start of the Real Plan in mid-1994 and the financial crisis of January 1999. However, some attention will also be given to the previous period, between the 1990 New Brazil program (or "Collor Plan") and the 1994 Real Plan, as it was with this initial plan that some of the key components of the reforms began to be implemented. Throughout the paper, the 1994–1999 period will be compared and contrasted with similar periods preceding other financial crises, in particular in Latin America (Chile between 1975 and 1982, and Mexico between 1988 and 1994), and in East Asia (Korea, Malaysia and Thailand between 1988 and 1997).

FINANCIAL LIBERALIZATION AND ECONOMIC REFORM IN LATIN AMERICA

Brazil, like the rest of Latin America, was badly affected by a series of negative external shocks at the end of the 1970s and the beginning of the 1980s, which found the countries of the region in a particularly vulnerable position due to their enormous stock of foreign debt, and their large deficits on current accounts. Firstly, international interest rates began to rise rapidly in 1979 (following Paul Volcker's tightening of monetary policy at the Fed). Secondly, the terms of trade of most countries in the region began to decline rapidly from 1980 onwards. Thirdly, with Mexico's default in 1982, voluntary lending to Latin America stopped abruptly in the second half of that year. Fourthly, the whole process of rescheduling foreign debt after 1982 became institutionally cumbersome, politically degrading, and economically very expensive. Finally, recession and growing protectionism in most of the North complicated still further the economic environment within which Latin American economies had to regain their internal and external macro-equilibria during the 1980s.

All these problems placed the whole model of state-led development under considerable strain throughout Latin America—in Brazil, this was compounded by the economic and political difficulties of the transition to democracy; and as had already happened in the 1930s, a massive and persistent external shock, that found Latin America in an extremely vulnerable position both politically and economically, not only brought about the need for a very painful internal and external macroeconomic adjustment, but also laid the foundations for a radical change in economic thinking. The resulting ideological transformation of the 1980s, and the extraordinary changes in world politics at the time, eventually led to a generalized change in the economic paradigm of the region. In this case, it was characterized by a profound move towards trade and financial liberalization, wholesale privatization and market deregulation. Therefore, a key element in understanding Brazil's reforms (and those of the rest of Latin America), and in particular the rigid way in which they were implemented, is recognizing that they were carried out as a result of the perceived economic weakness of the previous model of development, not as a mechanism for improving and strengthening the existing development process—in essence, it was a desperate attempt to reverse capital flight, finance the exploding foreign debt, reduce runaway inflation, and come out of recession. This contrasts sharply with the way in which these reforms were understood and implemented in other parts of the world, especially in East Asia, where the main aim of the reforms was instead to strengthen their existing development path, by helping to tackle some emerging constraints of their existing economic strategies.

As I have argued elsewhere (Palma 1999a), East Asian economies implemented their economic reforms in part out of necessity, and in part out of mounting external political and financial pressure from the U.S. government, the Bretton Woods institutions, and international financial markets. As is well known, the East Asian economies had integrated their economies into the increasingly complex world division of labor in a very different way to those of Latin America. Instead of accepting their static, exogenously given comparative advantages, they struggled to gain a different type of endogenously created comparative advantage, mainly via a "flying geese" pattern of production and upgrading. Following Japan's example, this was achieved through an increasing export penetration of OECD markets for manufactured goods, within a process of the regionalization of production. Their extraordinary success was based on several factors—mainly the openness of OECD markets, especially the United States, to their manufactured exports (this openness was clearly not extended to Latin America, and especially not to Brazil); their high rate of expansion of exports in these goods; their ability to produce manufactures that could compete globally; the continuous upgrading of their exports through the above-mentioned "flying geese" path (which helped them to remain competitive as wage levels began to increase); their being able to generate the high levels of savings and investment required for this upgrading; and their achieving an effective coordination of this investment through different forms of trade and industrial policy.

However, important problems for the East Asian economies emerged in the late 1980s and early 1990s. One of the most important was a result of their own success: some of their most important exports, particularly electronics, began to experience excess supply and rapidly falling prices. In part this was also a result of the increased standardization (or "commoditization") of inputs to the electronics industry, in which many of these economies had concentrated their exports. As a response to this, their corporate sector massively expanded investment in new productive capacity to try both to remain competitive, and to turn falling prices to their advantage via increased market shares. In fact, the combined result was to exacerbate the global excess supply and to put further downward pressure on prices.[2] An obvious casualty of this increased struggle for market shares was profitability. This led to a rapidly changing composition of the finance for investment, away from internally generated profits and towards (domestic and foreign) debt. This was clearly reflected in rising debt/equity ratios, which (particularly in Korea) were reaching heights that even for this part of the world should have produced serious feelings of vertigo. This necessity to have access to an ever-growing amount of finance was clearly one of the key domestic pressures behind the drive towards external and domestic financial liberalization.

Another problem was that in the same period China became a formidable competitor in many of the markets that were crucial to the second-tier East Asian NICs, a process that also affected their profitability and led to an increased need for external finance. At the same time, given the changing international division of labor, some of these economies, particularly Thailand and Malaysia, were reaching a point where further upgrading of exports to higher value-added products was becoming increasingly difficult. In particular, it was becoming more and more complicated to break away from a "subcontracting" type of industrialization, and to advance further along the path towards the form of industrial development that characterized the first-tier NICs. So these economies increasingly looked towards financial liberalization as a way of continuing to accelerate their ambitious growth strategy.

---

2. For example, in 1996, in part as a result of new investment in Taiwan, the price of a 16-megabyte memory chip fell to about one-fifth of its 1995 price; Korea was particularly affected since a significant amount of its exports consisted of this type of microchip.

In Latin America, however, the economic environment in which the reforms were being implemented was very different. It was one characterized by an attitude of "throwing-in the towel," vis-à-vis their previous growth strategy of import-substituting industrialization. As a result, a kind of "born-again" neo-liberalism emerged, which sought to reverse almost every aspect of their previous growth strategy. So the reforms were viewed from a "fundamentalist" perspective; for example, it was taken for granted that trade and financial liberalization were going to switch, in a fairly automatic way, the engine of growth towards domestically financed private investment in tradable production; that budgetary balance and unregulated market signals were going to prove practically sufficient conditions for macroeconomic equilibrium and microeconomic efficiency; that, at the macro level, fiscal balance would necessarily release significant amounts of private savings for more productive uses in the private sector; and that, at the micro level, market deregulation and trade liberalization were to increase significantly private investment and domestic savings.

So far, as the Brazilian crisis showed yet again, this process of reform has turned out to be far more complex than predicted, and its results more mixed. As Figure 1 shows for the case of Brazil, one of the main achievements of the new policies in the period between liberalization and the subsequent financial crises was a drastic reversal of capital flight—from a net outflow of over $3 billion the year before the "Collor Plan" (this outflow would have been significantly higher had it not been for endless rescheduling of existing foreign debt), to a net inflow of $50 billion the year before the crisis.[3]

This rapid increase in inflows relaxed almost completely the external financial constraint to increased expenditure. They also made possible extraordinary reductions in inflation (like the one that followed the implementation of the Real Plan), and were an important stimulus to the resumption of growth (although in Brazil the latter turned out to be short-lived). There was also a rapid increase of foreign direct investment (particularly in Brazil), often directed towards the privatization of utilities, leading in some cases to gains in efficiency. Exports of many primary commodities increased significantly and, except for Brazil, there were sharp reductions in public deficits.

However, these reforms also had many negative effects. In particular, financial liberalization not only greatly increased the likelihood of shocks, but (as it was often implemented simultaneously with drastic stabilization programs; i.e., in the wrong "sequencing") it altered the fundamentals in a way that threw the export-led growth strategy off course. In particular, those countries that shifted their domestic imbalances into the external sector by using the nominal exchange rate as a price "anchor" have been the ones where the positive results of this process of adjustment and policy reform have proved to be most costly to sustain. As Figure 2 shows, their exchange rate policy produced a substantial appreciation of their currencies, which distorted the whole of the export-led growth strategy.

---

3. From now on US$ will be expressed as $ and billion as b. Also, dollars at 1999 prices will be shown as $ (1999).

FIGURE 1.

BRAZIL: net private capital inflows and their composition (WB), 1970–99

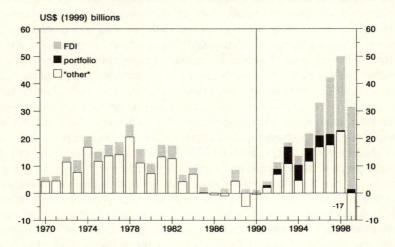

Nominal dollars were transformed to dollars at 1999 prices using the US GDP deflator. The same will be the case for other graphs in this paper.

Source: World Bank (2000). See this source for the definition of the three components of capital inflows.

FIGURE 2.

LATIN AMERICA and EAST ASIA: real effective rate of exchange between the beginning of financial liberalization and respective financial crisis
(base year=100 in each case)

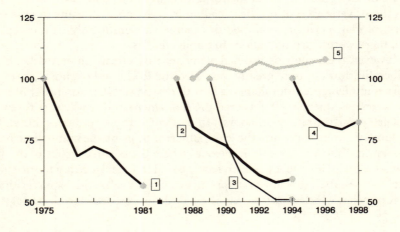

A decrease in the index signifies a revaluation.

[1] = Chile; [2] = Mexico; [3] = Argentina; [4] = Brazil; and [5] = average of Korea. Malaysia and Thailand.

Source: For Latin America, ECLAC Statistical Division; for East Asia, IMF (2000a and b).

These extraordinary exchange-rates revaluations in Latin America (which in fact was lower in Brazil than in the other countries of the region due to a much faster decline in inflation and a program of small nominal devaluation), and the massive increase in inflows switched the engine of growth away from the desired aim—domestically financed private investment in tradable production—and towards private consumption and externally financed private investment (often directed towards non-tradable production and services; see Palma 1998). Figure 3 shows the resulting "post-modernist" picture of export economies with a *declining* share of exports in GDP.

This phenomenon, coupled with clearly overoptimistic expectations of future performance of these economies (set in motion not only by the usual "expectation-augmenting" easy access to credit, but also by the massive "spin" put on these reforms), had many serious negative effects, particularly on the balance of payments, national savings, nonresidential investment and employment—and, though only in Brazil, also in the public sector accounts (see Palma 1998). As a result, the Latin American economies in general, and Brazil's in particular, ended up being more vulnerable to financial crises and external shocks than at any time since the 1920s.

FIGURE 3.

BRAZIL, MEXICO and CHILE: imports and exports as a share of GDP between the beginning of financial liberalization and respective financial crisis

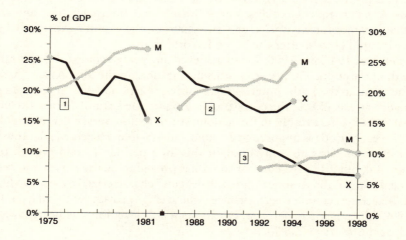

Ratios of nominal values. M = share of imports in GDP; X = share of exports in GDP.
[1] = Chile; [2] = Mexico; [3] = Brazil.
SOURCE: ECLAC Statistical Division.

THE BACKGROUND TO THE BRAZILIAN REFORMS

Although the country already had a substantial manufacturing sector before the depression of the 1930s, the determining factor for the Brazilian economy during the 20th century was the fact that it turned decisively towards industrialization after this depression made the economic and political elite finally lose faith in the growth potential of its coffee-based export sector. For six decades thereafter, governments of all kinds pursued fairly successful state-led industrial development through often-unorthodox interventionist policies. As a result, Brazil emerged as a major industrial power in the Third World (e.g., by the end of the 1970s it was already producing one million vehicles per year), and by the late 1980s it had become the 10th largest economy in the world. In fact, according to an international comparison drawn by A. Maddison, in the period between 1900 and 1987 Brazil's economy grew more rapidly than any other in the whole world.[4]

Despite bouts of selective economic nationalism, foreign capital was generally welcomed into the manufacturing sector, beginning in particular in the 1950s. However, the state frequently insisted upon stringent requirements relating to the source of capital, the transfer of technology, and joint ventures (often with state, rather than private, capital). One of the key stated aims of the 1990s reforms was to reverse this pattern of state-led development in favor of the deregulation of the economy, financial and trade liberalization, and the integration with Argentina, Paraguay, and Uruguay into a regional common market, Mercosul—Mercado Comum do Sul (Southern Common Market)—or, more familiarly, in Spanish, Mercosur.

A striking feature of state-led development was a massive building of productive capacity, particularly in the areas of energy, heavy industry, and capital goods. As a consequence of this, and of Brazil's large internal market and abundant and extraordinarily varied natural resources, the country experienced particularly rapid growth after the Second World War.

Between 1947 and 1980, Brazil achieved an average compound real rate of growth of output of 7% per year—this puts it more in the East Asian "growth-league" than in the Latin American one during this period—as Argentina's performance attests (2.8%; the corresponding figure for Latin America, excluding Brazil, is 4.6%). As a result, in Brazil domestic output increased nearly tenfold in this 33-year period (as opposed to 2.5-fold and 4-5-fold, respectively). However, the 1982 debt crisis not only brought this long period of rapid growth to an abrupt end, but also marked what so far has proved to be the permanent return of Brazil to the Latin American "growth-league," characterized by low and highly volatile average economic performance—the average growth for Brazil from 1980 to 1999 fell to just 2% per year, but its standard deviation was nearly twice as much as this average (3.8%).

---

4. For a discussion of these and other data, see Palma (1999b).

FIGURE 4.

BRAZIL and ARGENTINA: gross domestic product, 1940–2000

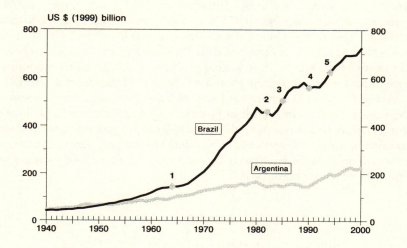

The original data, expressed in 1980 prices, were transformed into 1999 values as in Figure 1. Data for 2000 is a forecast of 4% growth for the year for Brazil and 2% for Argentina.

[1] = coup d'etat; [2] = 1982 debt crisis; [3] = end of military rule; [4] = beginning of the reforms with the "Collor Plan"; and [5] = beginning of the *Real Plan*.

SOURCE: As Figure 3.

Before the Real Plan Brazil had three perennial economic problems: high inflation, growing foreign debt, and high income inequality. In terms of inflation, until this 1994 Plan attempts to halt periodically rampant inflation since the 1982 debt crisis experienced only brief success. With the rate of increase in consumer prices at over 200% per year when the military left power in 1985, it was then held at close to zero for nine months, from February 1986, by President José Sarney's Cruzado Plan. Under this Plan the *cruzeiro* was replaced by a new currency, the cruzado, which was equivalent to 1,000 units of the old currency, and a briefly successful price "freeze" was instigated. Inflation resumed later in the year, however, due to the collapse of the balance of payments—the sudden price stabilization created such an expansionary effect that, as it was implemented at a time when Brazil had little access to external finances (and massive external obligations), it used practically all available foreign exchange reserves. The annual rate of inflation accelerated rapidly again, to reach 1,900% by 1989. In March 1990, with an annual rate of inflation threatening to reach 5,000%, the new President, Fernando Collor de Mello, introduced his New Brazil program or "Collor Plan." Its most contentious measure was the temporary freezing of virtually all financial assets, totalling about $110 billion, with limits of $1,000 on bank and savings account withdrawals (but, this being Brazil, by the middle of the year this was already subject to increasing evasion, and was therefore subsequently abandoned). It also restored the cruzeiro as the currency and implemented a set of measures that did manage to reduce price rises to a monthly rate of around 10% within six months. Inflation was held at just under 3,000% for the year as a whole, then fell to 473% in 1991, but increased again thereafter with the collapse of the Collor government, to reach nearly 2,500% in 1993. This was the main problem that the Real Plan had to tackle immediately.

In terms of the second long-lasting problem of the Brazilian economy, the balance of payments and growing foreign debt, one of the key characteristics of the postwar Brazilian economy has been its long-term export weakness—even by the standards of Latin American postwar export deficiencies, Brazil's stands out for its failure to balance its trade account, let alone generate a surplus to pay for its existing foreign obligations.[5] This, added to the long period of easy access to international finance it enjoyed before 1982, led to a rapid increase in its foreign debt since the mid-1960s.[6]

FIGURE 5.

BRAZIL: total long-term foreign debt (WB), 1979–98

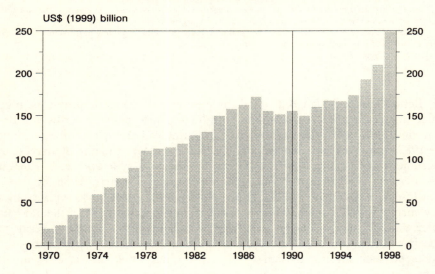

Sources: As Figure 1.

---

5. See Ffrench-Davis, Muñoz and Palma (1994).

6. Brazil was one of the few Latin American countries that had access to significant amounts of international finance before 1973. In fact, when the military took power in 1964 Brazil's foreign debt was only $2.4 b, but by the time of the first oil crisis it had already grown to $20 b (in 1999 prices, this is equivalent to an increase from about $12 b to $60 b).

In February 1987, with a debt-service ratio that in 1986 had reached over 90% of exports of goods and services (see Figure 6), and little access to "new money" in international finance, the government had little option but to declare a moratorium on payments on its medium- and long-term debt, by then worth more than $120 billion.

FIGURE 6.

BRAZIL: foreign debt service and profits remittance on FDI ratios (BP), 1984–99

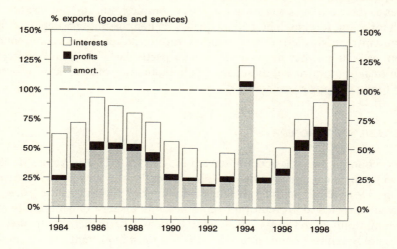

BP = Balance of payment definition.
SOURCE: Central Bank statistics (reproduced in Boletim MACROMETRICA, No 168, April 2000).

Early in 1992 President Collor de Mello negotiated a partial rescheduling with the IMF, by which time total foreign debt had already reached $136 billion. By the time of the Real Plan this debt had reached $150 billion. With little access to additional resources in international financial markets after the 1982 debt crisis, and with a need to generate massive external resources for the payments on external debt, Brazil had to produce large trade surpluses after 1983, reaching $16 billion in 1988 (goods and services); this effort was greatly helped, no doubt, by the rapid fall in the price of oil imports. Although this surplus fell afterwards, it still maintained a very useful level at the time of the beginning of the Real Plan in 1994 (between January and July 1994, Brazil had accumulated an $8 billion trade surplus).

As regards the third long-lasting problem of the Brazilian economy, its huge income inequality, as is well known, Brazil's increasing wealth under the military was accompanied by a rapidly worsening pattern of wealth and income distribution. In particular, the share of the richest 10% of the population in national income had leaped from 39% in 1960 to 46% in 1970 and to about half of the total in 1980. This brought Brazil into a position among the countries with the worst income distribution in the world. At that time, for example, the income share of the richest 10% in Brazil was about *double* those of the richest 10% in Korea and Taiwan—countries with a comparable income per capita, economic dynamic, and run by similarly authoritarian governments. If Brazil's economy had significantly improved during the military rule, the lot of the majority of its people certainly had not.

In sum, the long period of military rule saw the completion of a process that was already well underway before the 1964 coup. This was the emergence of Brazil as a major world industrial power. However, the legacy left by the military regimes to their civilian successors was a very complex one, and not just because of high inflation, foreign debt, and inequality. When the military departed from government they also left a widespread culture of political and economic corruption, as well as what has proved to be a particularly weak and ineffective institutional framework. All these have made economic policy making a particularly difficult enterprise ever since.

THE BRAZILIAN REFORMS

Brazil's economic reforms actually started in March 1990, well before the Real Plan, when the incoming president, Collor de Mello, announced his New Brazil program. Despite the political weakness of his short presidency, the extraordinary events that led to his removal from office, and his unsure handling of macroeconomic policy, the initiatives Collor launched permanently changed the direction of Brazil's economic development. The most important announcements of his New Brazil program were the removal of subsidies for exports, and phased reductions in tariffs. The latter were set to halve in three years, with no tariff exceeding 35% by the end of that period. Of equal moment was the commitment to remove the cumbersome system of import licensing.[7] The beginning of the privatization program, the deregulation of the fuel market (ending years of massive state support for ethanol production), and the announcement of the dissolution of the coffee and sugar trading boards followed in 1991.

The program of privatization was initially intended to raise $18 billion from the disposal of 27 state companies. Privatization eventually began in October, with the sale of the USIMINAS steel mill, after delays arising from a legal challenge.[8]

---

7. This system was partly responsible for Brazil being named, in 1989, under the "Super 301" provisions of the 1988 US Trade Act.

8. Although the sale raised $1.2 billion, more than the $1 billion reserve, this was a rather peculiar "privatization" in that other state companies took a majority stake in the new company (especially CVRD—Companhia Vale do Rio Doce, SA—and the pension fund of the state-owned Banco do Brasil). Also, the sale allowed SIDERBRAS (Siderúrgia Brasileira, SA), a holding company that previously owned a large share, to redeem a significant proportion of its public debt, as USIMINAS shares were accepted by the government in return for SIDERBRAS debt. Of the shares on offer foreign investors took up only 6%.

Over the following months further privatization took place in smaller concerns, but receipts tended to fall far short of the target. The government of President Fernando Henrique Cardoso gave another impetus to privatization, which resulted in receipts quadrupling in 1996, to $3.7 billion. In the first half of 1997 just two privatizations produced receipts totalling twice as much as the 1996 figure.[9] This process continued in the second half of 1997, and increased rapidly in 1998, particularly due to the sale of about 20% of TELEBRAS stock for $19 billion (a rather well-timed privatization as it happened only days before the Russian devaluation and the subsequent Third World "paranoia" in international financial markets).

A related policy initiative of the Collor government was the creation in March 1991 of Mercosul, the already mentioned common market with Argentina, Brazil, Paraguay, and Uruguay. Trade between Brazil and Argentina grew by 45% in the first year alone; in all, exports to Argentina grew 4.5-fold between 1991 and 1998, and imports from Argentina by five-fold. In 1998, 17% of exports (and about one-quarter of manufactured exports) and 16% of imports were with Mercosul countries. However, the recent economic problems of Brazil and Argentina have raised doubts whether harmonization of tariffs and economic integration can continue apace. In fact, intra-Mercosul trade, after having grown by 20% in 1997, fell by 3% with the worsening economic situation of 1998, and then fell again in 1999, this time by a massive 24%.

In 1992 escalating corruption charges and unbelievably bizarre private scandals led to the resignation of President Collor de Mello. His deputy, Itamar Franco, became Acting President in September and President in December. Economic policy continued very much unchanged during the first year of President Franco's government, with its principal objectives being the liberalization of most prices, control over public expenditure, and a strict monetary policy through high interest rates (the average real lending interest rate for the year reached 197%). However, political uncertainty continued and inflation exploded again in late 1992.

In May 1993, after several changes of finance minister, President Franco appointed senator (and world-famous sociologist) Fernando Henrique Cardoso to the position. Together with a group of highly skilled economists, including Edgar Bacha and Pedro Malan, Cardoso devised an all-encompassing Real Plan, which began operations on 1 July 1994 (it took its name after the new currency, which it introduced, the real). The main characteristic of this new Plan was that, as opposed to most of its predecessors, it intended to avoid "shock treatments" (such as price freezes, the withholding of financial assets, or surprise announcements). The Plan took a long time to be prepared and was announced in all of its details several months in advance of its implementation. It was basically an attempt to reduce inflation by three interconnected means: firstly, by reducing inflationary expectations (mainly through the real being initially fixed at a rate of one real to the dollar—but, crucially, not rigidly "pegged" to the dollar as in

---

9. These were the sale of 40% of CVRD for $3.2 billion, and the sale of the concessions for cellular telephones for about $4 billion.

Argentina); secondly, by reducing inflationary "inertia" (via dismantling a complex system of indexation); and, thirdly, by a progressive achievement of internal and external macroeconomic equilibria.

The Real Plan was implemented in three stages between March and July 1994. In so far as monetary policy was concerned, instruments and rules were devised to guarantee price stability. Quarterly quantitative goals were established for the monetary base to indicate the government's intention of not utilizing inflationary financing. To keep consumption to levels compatible with price stability, special attention was to be paid to credit expansion. New reserve requirements were imposed on the banking system, including those affecting additional demand deposit to 100%. A relatively fixed exchange-rate system was introduced, in which the Central Bank would intervene to avoid destabilizing speculation with the new currency. Several measures were adopted which were aimed at attaining fiscal balance, such as the Federal Securities Debt Amortization Fund. Furthermore, the system of guarantees and endorsements granted by the national treasury was to be discontinued. However, the real strength of this new Plan was political: the fact that it succeeded in gathering an overwhelming degree of consensus and public support. Its initial successes in mid-1994 helped Cardoso's campaign for the presidency, in the pursuit of which he had resigned from the government in March.

In terms of these above-mentioned long-lasting problems of the Brazilian economy, inflation, foreign debt and inequality, the Real Plan succeeded in tackling the first, but made the second significantly worse, and had little impact on the third; furthermore, it has added another one that now rivals any of the others in magnitude, the ever-growing domestic public debt.

In terms of inflation, following full implementation of the Real Plan, the monthly rate of inflation, which had reached nearly 50% in June 1994, fell to 1.8% in August and 1.4% in September. As a result, while the average rate for the 12 month period between July 1993 and June 1994 had reached 5,000%, that from July 1994 to June 1995 fell to 27%. Inflation continued to fall, posting a rate of 9.6% for 1996, 5.2% for 1997, and only 0.4% for 1998. Furthermore, a unique feature of Brazil's 1999 financial crisis was that the substantial devaluation of the real in January 1999 had a very limited inflationary effect, with the rate of inflation for the whole year reaching just 8.4% (as measured by the consumer price index). This low inflation has continued during the first half of 2000, with an overall increase of 2.5% for the period from January to July (though with some acceleration towards the end, with the figure for the month of July reaching 1.3%). As will be discussed in more detail below, several factors help to explain this apparent enigma.

In terms of its impact on the balance of payments and foreign debt, the Real Plan was certainly not as successful as with inflation. In part due to an extraordinary worsening of the trade and current accounts, as shown by Figure 5 above, foreign debt increased by half in just four years (1994–98), with its private component nearly doubling during this short period; this added another $82 billion to the total, which reached a level nearly five times that of exports of goods and services. In turn, Figure 6 shows how the service of this foreign debt more than trebled between 1995 and 1999 (from 36% of exports of goods and services in 1995 to 120% in 1999—or, if profits remittances on foreign direct investment are included in this ratio, from 41% to 138%, respectively).[10]

In all, during the five-year period between the beginning of 1994 and the end of 1998, $220 billion left Brazil on account of these three items (amortization and interest payments of foreign debt, and profit remittance)—and if the whole 15-year period since the deepening of the debt crisis is taken into account (1984–98), this figure rises to $583 billion, equivalent to *four-fifths* of all exports of goods and services of these years.

Also, bad as these meteoric rises in the level and service of the foreign debt were, the problem was compounded by a rapidly deteriorating maturity structure of this debt: according to the IMF's World Economic Outlook databank, the share of short-term debt increased from just 20% at the start of the Plan in 1994 to 56% before the January 1999 crisis (a level higher than even those of Korea and Thailand, let alone Malaysia, before their respective crises).

Finally, in terms of the effect of the Real Plan on inequality, despite the abrupt price stabilization, radical economic reforms and all the economic upheaval, recent studies have shown that during the years of the Plan income distribution remained relatively unchanged. The latest figure for the income share of the richest 10% of the population still places it at 48% (and the Gini inequality-index at 60%)—a rather surprising phenomenon given all the events that have taken place.[11] However, according to the World Bank's latest World Development Indicators, this level of inequality is certainly enough not only to place Brazil among the five countries with the worst income distributions in the world (by now even worse than South Africa), but also as clearly the worst among those with similar income per capita (with Chile a close second).[12]

As mentioned above, besides these three main perennial problems of Brazil's economy, if the Real Plan has succeeded in removing that of inflation, it has added another, that of the domestic debt. Of course, this is not a new problem, but now it has grown to such levels that it has changed in nature to a totally different dimension; furthermore, this change is not only related to the extraordinary rate of growth of this debt, but also came about because in a financially open economy the differences between the foreign and domestic debts have become blurred.

The federal deficit was another casualty of the 1982 crisis; first it deteriorated to an average of about 4% of GDP between 1985 and 1988, and then it moved up to 7% in 1989 (at the time of the Cruzado Plan). With the failure of this Plan, economic policy making became paralyzed until the inauguration of a

---

10. In 1994 the extraordinarily large increase in amortization to $ 50 b (a one-off), equivalent to more than all exports of goods and services for the year (103%), reflects that the immediate reaction of foreign capital to Brazil's full opening of the capital account was rather paranoid!

11. See Rocha (2000); Ferreira et al. (1999); Neri and Camargo (1999); and Paez de Barros (1997) .

12. See World Bank (2000), and Palma (1999c).

new president in 1990. One of the most ambitious aims of President Collor's New Brazil program was not only to eradicate this deficit, but also to transform it into a surplus of 2% of GDP. This was to be achieved by a mixture of tax increases, expenditure reductions and the beginning of the privatization program. Although a budget surplus was reached in 1990 (equivalent to 1.3% of GDP), the government was not able to sustain this achievement, and this figure changed to a deficit of 1.4% in 1992.

Like the "Collor Plan," the Real Plan had only short-lived success as far as the public accounts are concerned; it managed a public sector surplus in 1994, equivalent to 1.4% of GDP. However, by 1995 this had already turned into a massive deficit of 4.9% of GDP, to reach 8% of GDP in 1998 (see Figure 7)—and still neither the government nor Parliament seemed to have the sense of urgency, or the nerve, to pass the long-awaited budget reform.[13]

FIGURE 7.

LATIN AMERICA and EAST ASIA: public sector deficit between the beginning of financial liberalization and respective financial crisis

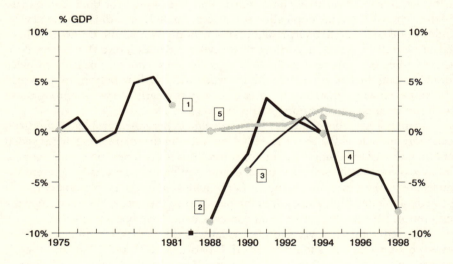

[1] = Chile; [2] = Mexico; [3] = Argentina; [4] = Brazil; and [5] = average of Korea, Malaysia and Thailand.
Sources: As Figure 2.

_____

13. A well-known Brazilian economist summarized the main problem of the economic team during this period as one of constantly "waiting for Godot"—waiting for Cardoso and Parliament to finally agree on the fiscal reforms (at the time of writing this paper in mid-2000, they, like the characters in the play, are still waiting).

As already mentioned, this unique Brazilian problem among crisis economies was mainly the result of high interest rates becoming a permanent rather than a temporary feature of the Real Plan, the way in which the public sector dealt with the financial fragility brought about by these high interest rates, and the endless delays in implementing the budget reforms.

As a result, "net" internal public debt (that is, total internal public debt minus related public assets) increased 3.4-fold in dollar terms between 1993 and 1998— from $82 billion in 1993 to $280 billion in 1998 (and by then there was no inflation to help reduce the real value of the stock of internal debt, as had happened before the Real Plan).[14] Figure 8 shows this increase in real dollar terms.

The federal government and central bank component of the "net" internal debt was the main source of this increase, going from $8 billion in 1993 to $164 billion in 1998—an 83% average annual rate of growth (see Figure 19 below).

FIGURE 8.

BRAZIL: "net" internal debt of the public sector, 1992–98

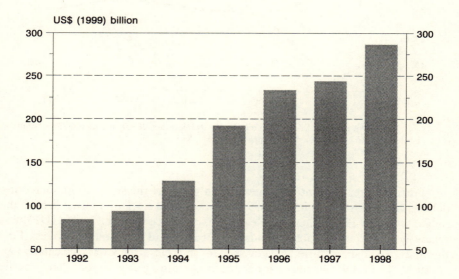

SOURCE: Official government statistics reproduced in Boletim MACROMETRICA, No 168, April 2000.

---

14. These figures, moreover, are probably even larger because in this "net" figure there are some dubious deductions of overvalued related public assets.

HOW TO SLEEPWALK INTO A PUBLIC SECTOR "PONZI" FINANCE.

What is really extraordinary about the dynamic that led to such an increase in the internal debt is that throughout this period the "primary" accounts of the public sector were in either in surplus or roughly in balance (See Figure 9).[15]

FIGURE 9.

BRAZIL: financial requirements of the public sector, 1993–98

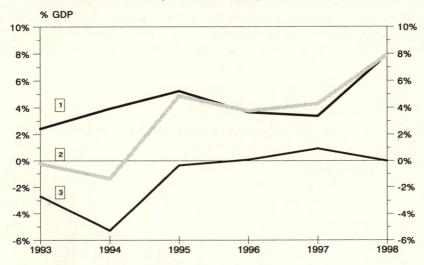

[1] = Interest payments (calculated in real term); [2] = public sector deficit/surplus; and [3] = "primary" deficit/surplus. A positive figure is a deficit, a negative is a surplus.
Source: As Figure 6.

Furthermore, high interest rates are only part of the story of the increasing debt service ratios shown in Figure 9, since the initial stock of internal debt of the public sector in 1993, when the Real Plan was conceived (18.5% of GDP), was relatively low by international standards (particularly Latin American ones). Furthermore, the share of the federal government and central bank was particularly low, at just 1.8% of GDP. Obviously, for Brazil to run into a public sector "Ponzi" of the dimensions that they did, they not only had to violate some of the most important financial "golden rules" of public finance—by, for example, systematically hav-

---

15. As is often the case, one of the main casualties in the fight to keep the "primary accounts" in balance was public investment in physical and human capital (the latter being public expenditure in health and education). In all, the share of these two types of investment in total public expenditure fell by *half* between 1993 and 1998—from 34% to 17%, respectively. In the meantime, interest payments on public debt went up 2.7-fold (from 7% to 19%, respectively).

ing both interest rates paid on public debt higher than the growth of public revenues, and interest payments on liabilities (sterilization of foreign inflows) larger than revenues from related assets (foreign exchange reserves; see Figures 20 and 21 below). They also should have had an initial stock of debt somewhat higher than they did. So, how was it that the Brazilian public sector sleepwalked into a "Ponzi" finance, something that previous crisis economies managed to avoid?

During the first months of the Plan growth accelerated rapidly, reaching a peak of 10.4% in the first quarter of 1995.[16] The main growth-stimuli were the expansionary effect of the sudden disappearance of the "inflationary tax," the massive increase in foreign inflows, and a large reduction in the "primary" surplus of the public sector (equivalent to five percentage points of GDP; see Figure 9 above).[17]

FIGURE 10.

BRAZIL: quarterly GDP growth, 1993–2000
(% variation vis-a-vis same quarter previous year)

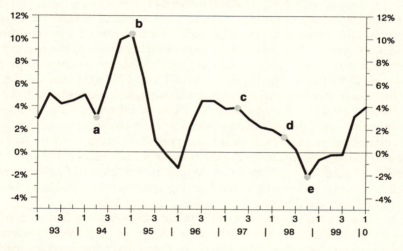

[a] = beginning of the Real Plan; [b] = Mexican crisis; [c] = East Asian crisis; [d] = Russian crisis; and [e] = State of Minas Gerais' default.
SOURCE: As Figure 8.

This initial extraordinary expansion of output soon proved unsustainable due to both external and internal constraints. The external one hit almost immediately, just six months after the full implementation of the Real Plan, with the so-called "Tequila effect" which followed the Mexican financial crisis of December

16. From now on, all quarterly growth figures refer to rates vis-à-vis the same quarter the year before.
17. For figures on the growth of consumption during this period, see Dornbush (1997), and Palma (1998).

1994. The panic in financial markets that followed this crisis threatened Brazil's future access to international finance—the corner stone of the new economic policies. Under these conditions, for example, the rapid deterioration of the trade balance (brought about by increased expenditure, the revaluation of the real and trade liberalization) was not sustainable[18]; nor would Brazil be able to keep payments on its foreign debt. The internal reason was the fact that the public sector deficit began to deteriorate rapidly. However, if the first problem was a fairly straightforward one of excess aggregate demand, changing relative prices and a high debt service ratio, the second one was rather more complicated.

Normally one would expect that rapid growth would actually help the public accounts via increasing revenues; however, in this case old rigidities in the public finances (in particular the complex way in which Parliament approves the budget) made it more difficult for the government to take advantage of this. Furthermore, from its beginning, the Real Plan saw the origin of the meteoric rise of the internal public debt, especially that of the federal government and central bank. There were many factors involved in this, which will be discussed in detail below.

With these mounting external and internal problems, the government tightened monetary policy and took a series of other measures to ensure a sharp decline in the rate of growth of private expenditure, which proved to be very effective in the short term. In fact, not only foreign capital returned to the country very rapidly, but also, in just one year, output growth fell by no less than 12 percentage points (between the first quarters of 1995 and 1996). However, the very effectiveness of this first package of restrictive measures seems to have deluded the government into believing that the urgent fiscal reforms did not have to remain at the top of the political agenda. The main consequence of this, and in particular of the persistently high interest rates (that, at least in part, had to be implemented as a substitute for the always soon-to-be-realized, but never actually achieved fiscal reforms), was the buildup of further financial fragility throughout the economy, particularly in the banking system and the public sector; this financial fragility has haunted the Brazilian economy ever since.

After such a fall in output growth (in fact, the economy had entered into recession in the first quarter of 1996, with a figure of –1.4%), the government could ease monetary policy and the economy began to recover, reaching a growth rate of 4.5% by the last quarter of 1996, to continue growing at nearly 4% during the first half of 1997. But then it was the turn of the East Asian crisis of July 1997 to force the same cycle all over again (see Figure 11). Economic policy had to be tightened again immediately (with the interest rate paid on government debt jumping to over 40%), and growth fell steadily to reach just 1.4% in the second quarter of 1998 when the Brazilian economy was hit, yet again, by a massive external crisis (this time the one unleashed by Russia's devaluation and default). This new external crisis, although less damaging for the world economy

---

18. The 1994 $8 billion January–July trade surplus had changed into a $4.2 billion trade deficit during the same period in 1995 (with imports doubling in respective periods).

and financial markets than either the Mexican or East Asian ones—by then the Yeltsin government had lost so much political and economic credibility that any crisis coming from Russia, anticipated by financial markets or not, could be more easily "discounted"—proved to be much more damaging for Brazil due to its growing financial fragility in both the public and the private sector finances. In a rapid response, the government tightened economic policy again (the interest rate on government paper back to over 40%), and the economy back in recession again (with growth falling to a low point of –2.2% in the last quarter of the year).

This scenario, and the general uncertainties prevailing both in the country itself and in international financial markets vis-à-vis the real health of the Brazilian economy (in particular the government's capacity to sort out its own finances, the banking sector fragility, and its growing deficit in the balance of payments) was obviously not helped by the default declared towards the end of the year by the Minas Gerais state governor (former President Itamar Franco) on the state debts to the central government. Although the amounts involved were small, it was feared that other state governors (many of them belonging to opposition parties and with heavy debts to the central government) would follow suit; and monetary policy had to be tightened for the fourth time in four years. The resulting roller-coaster-shaped interest rate path (a roller coaster in more sense than one) is shown in Figure 11.

FIGURE 11.

BRAZIL: nominal interest rate paid on internal public debt, 1994–2000
(annualized monthly rates, %)

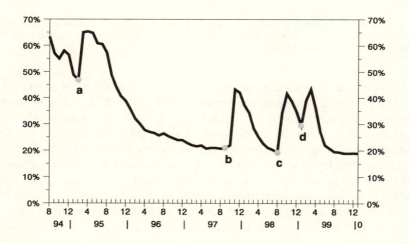

"Selic" rate (rate was paid on internal public debt; the graph shows the annualized monthly rates).
Interest rate increase due to [a] = the Mexican crisis; [b] = the East Asian crisis; [c] = the Russian crisis; and [d] = the State of Minas Gerais' default.
SOURCE: As Figure 8.

The continuous changes in deposit rates were obviously reflected, and augmented, in the extraordinary levels (and volatility) of nominal lending rates both for working capital and consumer credit (see Figure 12). With these rates, and an economy with practically no inflation (for real rates see Figures 13 and 14 below), it is hardly surprising that the banking system had problems due to nonperforming assets.

FIGURE 12.

BRAZIL: nominal lending interest rates, 1994–2000
(annualized monthly rates, 3-month moving average)

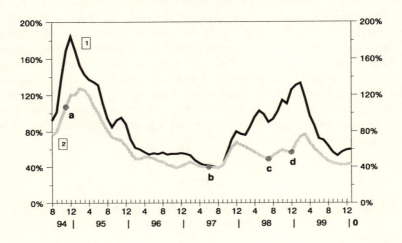

[1] = consumer credit; and [2] = credit for working capital (the graph shows the annualized monthly rates).
Interest rate increase due to [a] = the Mexican crisis; [b] = the East Asian crisis; [c] = the Russian crisis; and
[d] = the State of Minas Gerais' default.
SOURCE: As Figure 8.

However, the increases in interest rates at the end of 1998, even to the levels that they did reach—those on government debt got to 42%, those of working capital to 61%, and those on consumer credit to 118% (and with no inflation at all to help reduce their real value)—proved to be one set of increases too many. Although they did succeed in bringing the economy even deeper into recession, by then they had lost their previous nearly magical touch to calm down financial markets (and help avoid a stampede by jittery international fund managers). It soon became obvious that they were unable to stop the fears of a repeat of an East Asian-1997-type uncontrolled devaluation and full-blown financial crisis. Furthermore, by this time not only high interest could not do the trick, but also the easy reelection of Cardoso to a second four-year term, Brazil being prepared to accept for its internationally issued bonds a yield spread of up to 1,500 basic points above U.S. Treasury bonds (August–September 1998), or even a new dollar-indexed instrument developed in despair by the central bank, could not do it either.[19] When by the turn of the year the Central Bank had lost about half its huge reserves, the choices open to the government became relatively narrow: either to continue defending the currency, Argentinean-style, bringing with it a recession and a financial crisis probably larger in scale than that of Argentina in 1995 (because of the potential explosive effect of a failure on the public debt), or to risk a devaluation (and hope that this would not bring about a collapse like that of East Asia in 1997). The second choice was taken, and the government allowed the real to float in January 1999.[20]

Following what had happened in relatively similar circumstances in the past, especially in Chile (1982), Mexico (1994), and East Asia (1997), most observers expected that as a result of this devaluation and financial collapse, Brazil would enter a period of acute recession, increased inflation, and exchange rate volatility. In fact, and not for the first time, the Brazilian economy surprised everybody because almost the opposite happened. First, the economy actually posted a small growth in the first quarter of 1999 (0.2%), then entered into a short and mild recession (-0.5% and -0.2% in the following two quarters), to rebound rapidly in the last quarter of 1999 (with growth of 3.8%). In all, the economy actually had a 1% growth rate for the year (and this recovery was still continuing at the time of writing this paper in mid-2000, with most projections expecting growth of 4% for the year as a whole). Second, the consumer price index increased by only 0.7% in January, and 1.3% both in February and March, to end the year with an overall increase of just 8.3% (the wholesale price index increased more rapidly, but still by less than expected—1.6%, 7%, 2.8%, and 28.8%, respectively). Finally, the real, after falling from an average of 1.21 per dollar in December 1998 to one of 2.06 in

---

19. This new instrument, the "swan song" of the Real Plan, was a Tesobono-type of bond—real-denominated but dollar-indexed, with an otherwise lower interest rate than the non-indexed bonds. As this bond was created when there was already a panic-buying attack on Brazil's foreign exchange reserves (i.e., at a time when most observers thought that a devaluation or a foreign exchange crisis was imminent), one can only think that it was implemented either as a sort of "suicide pill" by the more "fundamentalist" wing of the economic team (whose jobs were also on the line, like the President of the Central Bank), or as a timing device by Cardoso to delay the crisis. The former would have wanted to make a devaluation impossible with this new bond—in fact, if this was the case, they nearly succeeded in that if the devaluation had been delayed a bit longer, allowing more existing debt to mature and be switched to this new bond, a devaluation would have been really suicidal from the point of view of the public debt. As it happened, if the latter was the case (a timing device), it succeeded in that the devaluation took place only a fortnight into Cardoso's second term as Brazil's president (and this new bond was quickly abandoned after that). Today it ranks high among the many instances that will only be remembered for their costly additions to the public debt.

20. This critical decision, as so many others in Brazil, could not be done without a magical realist hint to it. Just days after the inauguration of his second term, Cardoso took the most traumatic decision of his political career, speaking on a mobile phone from a public lavatory at Rio de Janeiro's international airport (where he had taken refuge from the media); in this call, made on January 12, Cardoso ordered his finance minister to prepare to devalue the real the next morning.

Now it is known that some domestic financial institutions knew about the devaluation sufficiently in advance so as to be able to make huge profits from it; so either this call was intercepted, or there was a leak by an "insider."

February, almost immediately stabilized at a rate just below 2 reais per dollar for the rest of the year (a relative stability that has continued in 2000).

The fact that Brazil entered its financial crisis (January 1999) already in a recession (i.e., at the point in the cycle where a devaluation is likely to be least inflationary and more expansionary), not only made this country the exception among those that have experienced major financial collapses in the Third World in the last 20 years,[21] but helps to explain both the low inflationary effect of this devaluation, and the speed of the subsequent recovery. Of course, the fact that in Brazil imports represent only 10% of GDP; that Cardoso had recently been reelected with a large majority; that the Central Bank still had $35 billion worth of reserves after the crisis (more than Korea had before its crisis); that the IMF had agreed a rescue package well before the January crisis; and that the IMF (apparently having learned from its mistakes in East Asia) was prepared to be much more flexible in its conditionality, also helps to understand this apparent enigma. Finally, and very importantly, international financial markets clearly did not panic as much as had been expected—in particular, foreign direct investment continued to flow into the country (see Figure 1)—because by then they also seemed to have learned from the East Asian crisis (and the Mexican one before that) the "moral hazard" lesson that both the IMF and the U.S. government were prepared to provide any amount of liquidity necessary to crisis countries, like Brazil, in order to keep the capital account of the balance of payments open; so, no matter how bad the domestic situation could become, they would always count on being able to exchange their reais for dollars.

So, in order to respond to external shocks, try to avoid capital flight, manage aggregate demand, try to stop the worst excesses that led to the Mexican crisis, and to compensate for the lack of proper fiscal reforms, the Brazilian government used interest rates in a clearly active and aggressive way. If a comparison of *real* interest rates is made between the countries involved in the four financial crises mentioned above, this policy is what most distinguishes the Brazilian period between financial liberalization and financial crisis (see Figures 13 and 14).

As has been discussed in detail above, and at a huge cost, these higher Brazilian rates were successful in one respect—controlling economic activity and, up to the second half of 1998, in avoiding capital flight after continuous external shocks. However, in another respect, these rates were also costly but successful— in helping Brazil to avoid the worst excesses that had characterized other experiences of financial liberalization, particularly those in Chile (before 1982), and Mexico and Argentina (before 1994). In short, in these other countries the absorption of the massive amounts of foreign capital attracted by their financial liberalization and economic reforms had led (mainly via increasing expectations, declining interest rates and currency appreciation) to a Kindlebergian

---

21. In the year before its financial crisis Chile was growing at 4.8% (1981), Mexico at 4.6% (1994), Argentina at 8.5 % (1994), and Korea at 7.1%, Malaysia at 8%, and Thailand at 6.4% (all 1996); in all these countries output fell massively after the financial crises.

FIGURE 13.

LATIN AMERICA and EAST ASIA: domestic real deposit rates between the beginning of financial liberalization and respective financial crisis

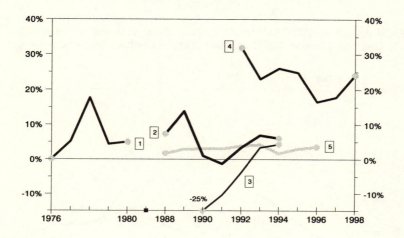

[1] = Chile; [2] Mexico; [3] = Argentina; [4] = Brazil; and [5] = average of Korea, Malaysia, and Thailand.
SOURCES: As Figure 2.

FIGURE 14.

LATIN AMERICA and EAST ASIA: domestic real lending rates between the beginning of financial liberalization and respective financial crisis

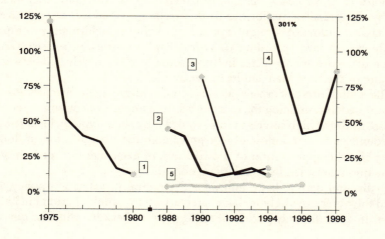

[1] = Chile; [2] Mexico; [3] = Argentina; [4] = Brazil; and [5] = average of Korea, Malaysia, and Thailand.
SOURCES: As Figure 2.

mania-type credit expansion, and through this, to an unsustainable consumption and imports boom, and asset bubbles in the stock exchange and in real estate.[22]

FIGURE 15.

EAST ASIA and LATIN AMERICA: credit to the private sector between the beginning of financial liberalization and respective financial crisis

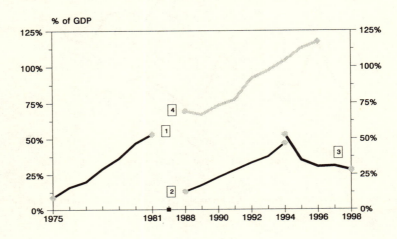

[1] = Chile; [2] Mexico; [3] = Brazil; and [4] = average of Korea, Malaysia, and Thailand.
SOURCES: World Bank (2000).

Figure 15 shows how successful Brazilian interest rates (and other measures taken by the Brazilian authorities in this respect; see above) were in averting their massive inflow of foreign capital from being transformed into a private credit boom. In fact, according to World Bank statistics, in relative terms to GDP, credit to the private sector in Brazil actually fell by nearly half between the beginning of the Real Plan and its financial crisis.

This control of credit expansion and a more moderate trade liberalization policy also succeeded in restraining the rate of growth of imports of consumer goods.

Also, in Brazil high interest rates avoided a Kuznets-type cycle: in the other crisis countries a large inflow of foreign capital, the liberalization of domestic finance, and the appreciation of the real rate of exchange did set in motion a construction mania, led by a real estate boom.

Finally, and despite large inflows and a radical privatization policy, Brazil avoided the other asset bubble that characterized the similar period in Chile and Mexico. In fact, the only period of rapid growth, between the first quarter of

---

22. For an analysis of this cycle see Kindleberger (1996), and Palma (1998).

FIGURE 16.

LATIN AMERICA and EAST ASIA: imports of consumer goods between the beginning of financial liberalization and respective financial crisis

(base year=100 in each case, constant US$ value)

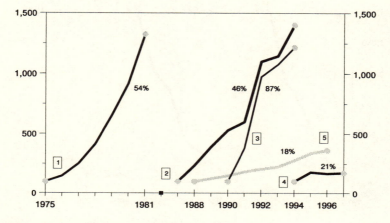

Percentages written in the graph are average *annual* rates of growth.
[1] = Chile; [2] Mexico; [3] = Argentina; [4] = Brazil; and [5] = average of Korea, Malaysia, and Thailand.
SOURCES: United Nations Comtrade databank.

FIGURE 17.

LATIN AMERICA and EAST ASIA: real estate price indices between the beginning of financial liberalization and respective financial crisis

(local currencies, base year=100 in each case)

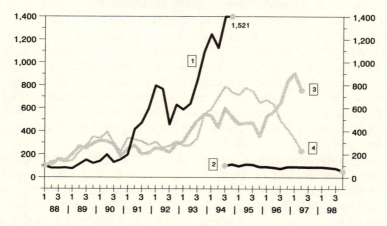

[1] = Mexico; [2] = Brazil; [3] = Malaysia; and [4] = Thailand.
SOURCE: Datastream. This source does not have data on Chile between 1975 and 1982. However, Chilean Central Bank statistics (1988), although using a different methodology, show an increase similar to that of Mexico (due to the difference in methodology, these data are not included in the graphs).

FIGURE 18.

LATIN AMERICA and EAST ASIA: real estate price indices between the beginning of financial liberalization and respective financial crisis
(US$ terms, base year=100 in each case)

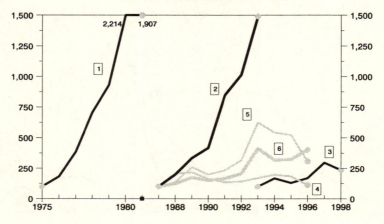

[1] = Chile; [2] Mexico; [3] = Brazil; [4] = Korea; [5] = Malaysia; and [6] = Thailand.
SOURCES: IFC (2000).

1996 and the second quarter of 1997, was almost entirely led by just one sector (telecommunications).[23]

So, Brazil's experiment of liberalization and reform with "artificially" high interest rates seemed to contradict at least one part of the McKinnon and Pill-type of argument—by their nature, "moral hazards" lead to artificially low interest rates. However, indirectly, it tends partially to support at least one other aspect of this argument—low interest rates lead to excessive credit expansion, and this to expenditure booms and asset bubbles. Regarding the first issue, in Brazil not only were all the traditional "moral hazards" clearly in place—the government did give deposit insurance, and everybody certainly expected the IMF and the U.S. government to bail out big international institutional investors in the event of a major crisis—but they also added several new ones (already discussed above). However, these accumulations of "moral hazards" did not by any stretch of the imagination lead to low interest rates (let alone "artificially" so).

Regarding the other part of the "moral hazard" argument, although Brazil's high interest rates did help to absorb high inflows without developing many aspects of a Kindleberger mania-type credit expansion (which in particular characterized other neo-liberal experiments in Latin America), they certainly did not help agents (both domestic and foreigners) to be able to assess and price their risk

---

23. See Datastream.

properly (which would have prevented them from accumulating more risk than was privately efficient). The recurrent problems in the domestic financial system and in the public sector accounts attest to that. These rates may have helped the financial system to reduce the *quantity* of their credit exposure to the private sector, but they certainly did not help them to improve the *quality* of this exposure; nor did they help the financial strength of the public sector.

The latter is the final issue to be discussed in a more detailed way; in particular, which were the dynamics that trapped the public sector in its "Ponzi" finance? We know that, other than for a small deficit in 1997, the "primary" accounts of the public sector were in surplus throughout the period, and that it was high interest payments that brought the public sector into deficit (Figure 9). However, the problem is far more complex than that. First, in the Brazilian case it is the service of the *internal* debt that accounts for most of these interest payments (while the external net debt of the government fell by more than half between 1993 and 1998, from 14.4% of GDP to 6.3%, the internal net debt doubled, from 18.5% to 36.1%, respectively). Secondly, within the internal net debt, it was its federal government and central bank component that was booming (see Figure 19).

Now, the reasons for the growth of the net debt of the federal government and central bank are not at all obvious. As there was no "primary" deficit that required to be financed, and as this sector had practically no stock of debt at the

FIGURE 19.

BRAZIL: net internal debt of the federal government and central bank, and state governments, municipalities and publiccorporations, 1992–99

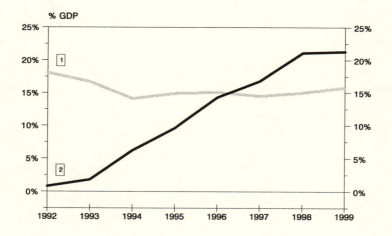

[1] = State Governments, Municipalities and public corporations; and [2] = Federal Government and Central Bank.

SOURCE: As Figure 8.

beginning of the Real Plan, it is difficult immediately to blame high interest rates for this extraordinary growth. Obviously, in order to get into a "Ponzi" one needs to have a significant amount of debts to start with. This is the crucial issue that needs to be explained: where did this "primary" stock of debt of the federal government and central bank come from—from where the interest rates-related "Ponzi" took off?

The answer to this key question has already been advanced: the Real Plan also added indirectly to the stock of public debt by being associated with a series of banking crises, the first as early as 1995. The government took the crucial decision of absorbing substantial amounts of this bad debt, arguing that this was the only way to avoid financial panic. However, this decision not only created what turned out to be a very costly new "moral hazard," but also avoided serious investigations of these banking crises, which would have opened a Pandora's box of corruption and mismanagement involving important figures in the Brazilian political establishment (and in one case, even a government minister[24]). Figure 20 shows one of the peculiar ways in which the banking system in Brazil fought

FIGURE 20.

LATIN AMERICA and EAST ASIA: spread between lending and deposit rates between the beginning of financial liberalization and respective financial crisis
(as % of deposit rates, 3-year moving averages)

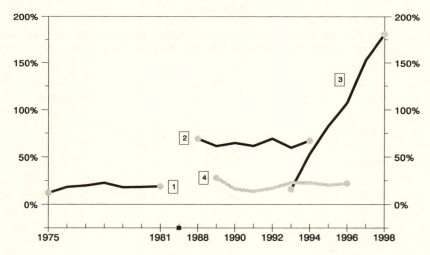

[1] = Chile; [2] Mexico; [3] = Brazil; and [4] = average of Korea, Malaysia, and Thailand.
SOURCES: As Figure 2.

---

24. In 1997, for example, the Banco Banmerindus, owned by the then Minister for Commerce and Industry, went bust in a very "untransparent" way, leaving a shortfall of about $5 billion. The government took over this bad debt without ever doing a proper investigation; then, it sold what was left of the bank to the Hongkong & Shanghai Banking Corporation.

back trying to regain lost profitability; however, by its very nature, this hasty rise in spreads ended up only exacerbating the vicious circle between the high cost of borrowing, under-performing assets, banking crises, government rescues, and growth of internal public debt.

The debt of the federal government and central bank also increased because the government had to spend large sums re-capitalizing some state banks.[25] These banking difficulties, and those of other sectors of the economy (state governments in particular), which rapidly added to the stock of the internal debt of the federal government and central bank, certainly were related to the high interest rates policy of the federal government itself.

The key issue at the end is that in a financially liberalized economy, the government constantly has to face "damned-if-you-do, damned-if-you-don't" types of choices in relation to interest rates. As In Mexico, if they choose a low interest rate policy, they seem to soon end up in the scenario described by Figures 15 to 18. But if as in Brazil, they choose a high interest policy to begin with, this tends to overvalue the currency; then, so long as this overvaluation is expected to continue (for example, through commitment to a "peg"), this becomes an incentive to substitute borrowing in domestic currency with borrowing in foreign currency. Soon, there are domestic exposures that require interest rates to come down, but there are also external exposures that require the currency to remain overvalued (i.e., require that interest rates stay up). So, from the point of view of the domestic financial system, interest rates are soon stuck between the needs of banks' foreign-currency liabilities, and those of the banks' domestic assets. In the case of Brazil, policy makers opted for trying to avoid bankruptcies on banks' foreign-exchange exposures, at the cost of having to accept bankruptcies on banks' domestic assets exposures—and then they opted for footing the bill of the latter. It is the problem of the choosing one type of bankruptcy against the other; and in Brazil's political and economic environment, one type of government rescue operation against the other. Either way, the public sector debt would swell—and, given the character of the present international financial market, from there onwards the economy is just one step away from speculative activity of the partly self-fulfilling, partly truth-telling type that tends to end in financial crisis.[26]

In sum, a financial liberalization with low interest rates seems to unleash a private sector credit explosion, leading to an unsustainable consumption and imports boom and asset bubbles; another that tries to avoid this via high interest rates seems to destabilize the domestic financial system in a way that leaves the government having to chose between a rock (absorbing large amounts of bad debt created by under-performing banking assets) and a hard place (allowing the collapse of the domestic financial system because of its foreign-exchange exposures). The

---

25. This was not only due to high interest rates also affecting the performance of state banks' assets, but also because in a financially liberalized economy even state banks need to have a minimum of capital base and other financial requirements which before they could just ignore.

26. See especially Kuczynski (1999).

Brazilian government chose the route of high interest rates, and high financial sector bad debt absorption.[27]

Added to this, of course, there is another crucial factor fuelling the financial fragility: in Brazil, financial liberalization was implemented with a particularly grossly inadequate system of regulation and supervision of the domestic financial sector. Furthermore, the federal government deliberately exacerbated this problem by overlooking and covering up cases of wrongdoing and corruption in financial institutions, particularly when they were owned by political *caudilhos* that were crucial for the survival of its weak political coalition.

And once the "primary" stock of debt of the federal government and central bank began to swell, the "Ponzi" finance related to high interest rates took over (see Figure 21).

FIGURE 21.

BRAZIL: interest rates paid for internal public debt
and growth of public revenues, 1994–99
(domestic currency)

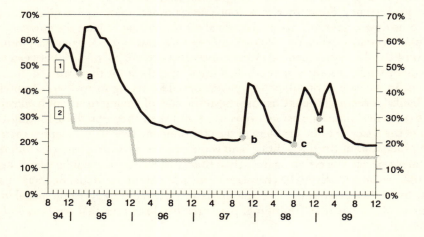

[1] = interest rate paid for internal public debt (annualized monthly rates); and [2] = growth of public revenues (annual rates).

[a] = Mexican crisis; [b] = East Asian crisis; [c] = Russian crisis; [d] = State of Minas Gerais' default.
SOURCE: As Figure 8.

Figure 21 shows two crucial phenomena of the public sector "Ponzi" finance. First, there was the violation of one of the most important financial "golden rules" of public finance: interest rates paid on public debt were systematically higher

---

27. For a chronology of the Brazilian government's absorption of the domestic financial sector bad debt, see ECLAC (1999).

than the growth of public revenues. Second, each external and internal shock made this problem worse. Given the even much higher levels of lending rates (see Figure 12), these phenomena must have repeated themselves in the household and corporate sector. In "Minskian" terminology, all these turned the public sector finances into a "Ponzi"; and, inevitably, also some private sector finance from "hedge" into "speculative," and some "speculative" into "Ponzi"—thus fuelling a growing financial fragility in the Brazilian economy.

Finally, Figure 22 shows the other side of the public sector "Ponzi" finance.

FIGURE 22.

BRAZIL: interest rates paid for internal public debt and received for foreign exchange reserves, 1994–99
(annualized monthly rates, domestic currency)

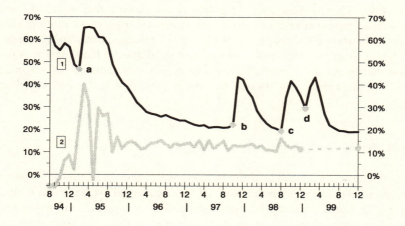

[1] = interest rate paid for internal public debt (annualized monthly rates); and [2] = interest rate (in domestic currency) received for foreign exchange reserves (in this series 1999 is not included, other than for the last observation, due to an initial large monthly variation due to the devaluation.

[a] = Mexican crisis; [b] = East Asian crisis; [c] = Russian crisis; [d] = State of Minas Gerais' default.
SOURCE: As Figure 8.

Again, until the January 1999 crisis, interest payments on liabilities (sterilization of foreign inflows) were systematically larger than revenues from related assets (foreign exchange reserves).

There were, obviously, other problems with the public finances (and the banking sector) which we cannot expand on here due to problems of space. The most important ones were the peculiar effects of the initial rapid price stabilization on banking profitability and public finance, and the delicate political balance between central and state government finance. Regarding the first, as Brazilian hyperinflation lasted for a long time, the banking and public sectors had adjusted to it in a way that made them vulnerable to a sudden decline in the rate of inflation—the first mainly via declining nominal spreads, the second via loss of a complex system of "asymmetric" indexation between revenues and expenditure. Regarding the second, part of the increase in the federal government's stock of debt was also due to a complex process of renegotiation and rescheduling of state government debts (in particular because their budgets could not cope with prevailing interest rates, especially with the sudden surges in rates shown in Figure 11).[28]

In sum, high interest rates, initially necessary for price stabilization, led to domestic financial fragility. First, via loss of inflation-related profitability in the banking system and loss of "asymmetric" indexation in the public sector finance and, soon afterwards, via problems in banking assets made worse by ever increasing spreads and problems in state government finance. This led to an increase in the stock of public debt via government rescue activities, and this public debt exploded due to high interest rates becoming permanent and systematically higher than both the growth in public revenues and the returns on foreign exchange reserves. In the meantime the real economy imploded because of those rates, which affected the growth of public revenues even further. High interest rates became permanent not only to absorb external shocks, avoid another Mexico, and as a substitute for the missing public sector reforms, but also to defend the "peg." The latter in order both to avoid further domestic banking crises due to foreign-exchange banking liabilities and to avoid a stampede by restless international fund managers. The "Ponzi" finance in the public sector ballooned out of control.

CONCLUSIONS

One of the difficulties faced by those working under the "Washington Consensus" paradigm in explaining previous financial crises to Brazil's is that crisis countries, especially in Latin America, had opened up their economies and implemented economic reform more or less by the book, and at the same time their public sector had managed to keep their accounts in order. Under these conditions it was not easy to explain why the private sector had run wild, creating large private macroeconomic imbalances, with both borrowers and lenders accumulating much more risk than was privately (let alone socially) efficient—making a financial crisis almost inevitable. Fanciful theories of the "rational" bubbles-type had little explanatory power and credibility. As a result they seem to have had little option but to fall back into well-rehearsed arguments of "exogenous" market interference by governments and international institutions—thus not only switching the whole debate towards traditional issues such as "moral hazards" and "cronyism," but also blowing them out of all proportions (as if they had never existed before, and now they could only be found in crisis economies).

Brazil's financial crisis, however, seems to be the exception; finally, there was, apparently, one crisis easy to explain—the growing public sector deficit provided a

---

28. See ECLAC (1999).

familiar way out. Under these conditions reforms could not possibly be "credible"; if governments did not understand that they have to be serious about the way in which they implement their reforms, and make the necessary efforts to do so, there could be little chance of success.[29] "Populist" governments are not only easy to dismiss, but also are not an attractive subject for economic research.[30]

This paper has shown that the legacy left by the military regimes to their civilian successors was a complex one (to say the least). The Brazil of 1985 was very different from that of 1964. Brazil's economy had improved significantly, but the lot of its people certainly had not. The first more democratic government (under Sarney) proved unable either to alleviate even the worst of the social problems afflicting rural and urban areas or to deal with the pressing problems of debt, inflation, slow and uneven growth, and inequality. President Collor de Mello's attempt to bring about a significant shift in the character of the economy and its external relations, and to put a gradual end to over 50 years of state-led development clearly failed. Short-term economic problems and the emergence of massive corruption and bizarre private scandals as major issues in 1992 revealed the fragility of his political base. This threatened not only his liberalization program, but also the survival of the administration itself. After his enforced resignation, his successor (Itamar Franco) also proved unable to deal with Brazil's major political and economic problems, but achieved some recognition in the last year of his government with the appointment of Fernando Henrique Cardoso as his finance minister. President Franco allowed Cardoso and his top-class team freely to devise and implement what seemed to be the best planned and most ambitious stabilization program in Latin America since the 1982 debt crisis. The Real Plan succeeded in dramatically reducing inflation and resulted in the election of Cardoso to the presidency (but, being Brazil, only ex-President Franco, now elected governor of the State of Minas Gerais, to become his worst enemy; as mentioned above, the January 1999 devaluation was detonated by Governor Franco's default on his state debt to the federal government).

However, although by the end of 1998 the stabilization plan had hitherto succeeded in its inflation objective, it was at a growing cost. The exchange rate was massively overvalued; there was a fast growing deficit in the trade and current accounts of the balance of payments; foreign and domestic debt were increasing at an accelerating pace; domestic interest rates were high and volatile; unemployment remained high; and levels of public investment were absurdly low. Finally, Brazil had an ever-growing public sector deficit, to which the government seemed oblivious—as far as the economy is concerned, Cardoso has certainly proved to be better as Minister of Finance than as President.

One of the strengths of the Brazilian economy for many years had been that its economic authorities (of very different political persuasions) did not allow

---

29. See, for example, World Economic Outlook (May, 1999)

30. Although there is an overabundance of literature on other financial crises, especially on the Mexican and East Asian ones, there is very little on the Brazilian neo-liberal experiment. See the relevant sections in http://w.w.w.stern.nyu.edu/~nroubini/asia/AsiaHomepage.html.

inflation, interest rates, public finances, exchange rate, and external balance to become a constraint on economic growth. As this policy finally ran its course, and ended (after the 1982 debt crisis) in "hyper-stagflation," the present economic authorities reversed it into the opposite policy, in which economic growth, interest rates, public finances, and external balance were not allowed to become a constraint in the fight for price and exchange rate stability.

Although inflation was controlled very successfully—even more impressively after the January devaluation[31]—this created major economic problems, not least the "Ponzi" finance of the public sector. These problems were exacerbated by the fact that the *Real Plan* was being implemented simultaneously with trade and financial liberalization, in a highly volatile international environment, and with an unsuccessful attempt at fiscal reforms, pension reforms, and a general restructuring of the public sector.

A deregulated, but badly supervised, domestic financial market, closely linked to a highly liquid, but under-regulated and unstable international financial market, coupled with a domestic economy characterized by large imbalances, a weak state, and an even weaker government coalition, made a sudden collapse of confidence and withdrawal of funds a real possibility. Events show that this seems not to have been fully realized by Brazilian policy makers—perhaps because Chile, Mexico, and Argentina, on the one hand, and East Asia, on the other, had followed different routes to their financial crises. The important issue, as the experience of Latin American countries had demonstrated, was that using the nominal rate of exchange as the main anti-inflationary "anchor," coupled with allowing abundant but volatile foreign finance to dominate the balance of payments and monetary policy, could all too easily lead to economic crisis in more ways than one (via low or via high interest rates).

As soon as hyperinflation was conquered by the end of 1995, or the beginning of 1996, a comprehensive fiscal reform, a tight regulation and supervision of the domestic banking system, some exchange controls on short-term flows (like in Chile, Colombia, or Malaysia, which have proved to be particularly useful as an external shock-absorber[32]), a managed real devaluation, and a decrease in interest rates were the sensible options. However, as often happens in politics, risk-averting inertia took over (made worse in this case by the uncertainties created by financial crises in other countries). So, an initial extremely successful set of economic policies (the Real Plan) that conquered a hyperinflation that had defeated so many other plans, was kept rigidly in place after it had accomplished its objectives, and run its full course. As a result, the same policies that were the solution to the original problem (hyperinflation) began to be the causes of the problem in the new cycle; and the longer they were kept, the more difficult their change became. Part of the problem was that massive foreign inflows first gave

---

31. So much for those warning that an economy like Brazil could not possibly function without the nominal exchange rate as a price "anchor."

32. See Palma (2000).

the appearance of being unlimited, and then seemed to have the capacity to solve almost everything (as if they had the Midas touch); and when in 1998 the time came for the government to stop prevaricating with its fiscal reforms, it was unfortunately an election year when (in the country which practically invented populism) it was unlikely that the authorities would take such a controversial initiative as this seriously.

Finally, and very importantly, the Cardoso government basically squandered the unique advantage it had of taking power at a time in which the Brazilian people, after years of economic upheaval (in fact, since the 1982 debt crisis), had an enormous disillusionment with previous development and economic policies, and were really desperate for hyperinflation to stop. Although this had been the ultimate condition for the initial success of the Real Plan—i.e., for the success of a radical economic change in a (relatively) democratic society—by 1998 the government still hoped that it was political capital from which they could continue endlessly to depreciate. The price of this complacency paid so far has been extremely high. History shows that some of the worst populists are those disguised as "technocrats."[33]

---

33. A good example of this, and of the political "mania" (so often) brought about by power, is the extraordinary statement made by President Cardoso, about a year into his first mandate: "Brazil is such an easy country to govern."

REFERENCES

Boletim Macrometrica, various issues, Rio de Janeiro.
Dornbush, R. 1997. Brazil's incomplete stabilization and reform, mimeo.
Chile. 1988. *Indicadores Economicos, 1968–86*, Banco Central.
ECLAC. 1999. "La Economia Brasilera ante el Plan Real y su Crisis" (paper written by P. Sainz and A. Calcagno). *Serie Temas de Coyuntura*, No. 4.
IFC. 1999. *Emerging Stock Markets Factbook*.
IMF. 1999. *World Economic Outlook*, May.
_____. 2000a. *Global Development Finance* CD-ROM.
_____. 2000b. *International Financial Statistics* Databank.
Ferreira, F., P. Lanjouw, and M. Neri. 1999. "A new poverty profile for Brazil using PPV, PNAD and census data," mimeo.
Ffrench-Davis, R., J. G. Palma, and O. Muñoz, 1994. "The Latin American Economies, 1950–1990," in *Cambridge History of Latin America*, Vol. 6. Cambridge University Press. Also published in Spanish in *Historia de América Latina*, Vol. II, Crítica.
Kindleberger, C. 1996. *Manias, Panics, and Crashes: A History of Financial Crises*. John Wiley & Sons.
Kuczynski, M. 1998. "How Asian has the Asian crisis been?," mimeo, *Adenauer Stiftung*.
McKinnon, R., and H. Pill. 1997. "Credible economic liberalizations and overborrowing," *American Economic Review*, 87 (2).

Minsky, H. 1982. "The Financial Instability Hypothesis: Capitalist Processes and the Behaviour of the Economy," in C. Kindleberger and J. P. Laffargue, eds., *Financial Crises: theory, history and policy*, CUP.

Neri, M. and J. M. Camargo. 1999. "Structural Reforms, Macroeconomic Fluctuations and Income Distribution in Brazil," ECLAC, *Serie Reformas Economicas*, No. 39.

Paez de Barros, R., ed. 1997. *Inequality in Brazil: facts, determinants and policies*, IPEA, mimeo.

Palma, J. G. 1998. "Three and a Half Cycles of 'Mania, Panic and [asymmetric] Crash': East Asia and Latin America Compared," *Cambridge Journal of Economics*, November.

_____. 1999b. "An Overview of Brazil's Economy and the January 1999 Crisis," in *Regional Surveys of the World: South America, Central America and the Caribbean*, 8th Edition. Europa Publications Ltd.

_____. 1999a. "How to Turn Flying Geese into Sitting Ducks? The 1997 East Asian Financial Crisis," UNESCO.

_____. 1999c. "Property Rights, Institutional Constraints and Distributional Outcomes: Why Does Latin America Have the Worst Income Distribution in the World?" mimeo.

_____. 2001. "Capital Controls on Short-term Flows; the Experiences of Chile, Malaysia and Colombia," in J. Eatwell and L. Taylor, eds., *International Capital Markets*, forthcoming. OUP.

Rocha, S. 2000. "Pobreza e desigualdade no Brazil: o esgotamento dos efeitos distributivos do Plano Real," IPEA, *Texto para Discussao* N 721.

United Nations. 2000. *Comtrade database*.

World Bank. 2000. *The World Development Indicators*. CD-ROM.

PART V

Regulatory Questions

16

...

Synthetic Assets,
Risk Management,
and Imperfections

Salih N. Neftci

FROM A RISK management point of view, individual instruments in a balance sheet have no meaning by themselves. Most large financial institutions carry a large number of instruments on their balance sheets. Even a careful *visual* analysis of these financial tables and balance sheets cannot pinpoint the exact exposures a financial institution is facing. Application of financial engineering methods and the resulting synthetic assets cannot be reconstructed by outsiders using a conceptual analysis.

Similarly, regulatory and taxation policies cannot rely on an analysis of financial tables and balance sheets. Using replicating portfolios and Special Purpose Vehicles (SPV) institutions can reconstruct all the instruments that they would like to buy or sell, in principle. Hence, policies such as capital controls and stamp duties, witholding taxes, etc., may end up having unexpected results if the financial engineering dimension is ignored.

In this paper we illustrate these points of view by using a simple yet powerful method that develops *contractual equations* for some basic instruments. We show, using these methods, how even the basic instruments can be replicated in many *different* ways.

We also argue that using quantitative methods of risk management is the only cost effective way of assessing the potential losses institutions may face in case of financial turbulence. We discuss why this is so, and introduce the difficulties of managing risks and conducting regulatory policy using non-quantitative approaches.

Hence the paper makes a number of major points. First, we would like to illustrate how financial derivatives can be used for reconstructing in a practical way any cash flow that one needs to replicate. This means that any regulatory and taxation policy needs to take into consideration the multiple ways cash flows can be generated and hence the policies can be circumvented.

Second, we make the point that although linear market risk and optionality can be successfully hedged using the logic of synthetic asset creation, the existence of stochastic volatilities can fundamentally change this and make some risks very difficult to replicate at least within the present market environment.

Finally, we summarize and then illustrate how current risk management methods can indirectly handle these issues. It turns out that although these methods can *measure* the risks reasonably well, they are mostly incapable of helping the policy maker in deciding on important policy issues such as capital controls and taxation.

The paper is organized as follows. First, we introduce the notion of a synthetic asset. The next section obtains the so-called contractual equation used in the paper. To motivate the discussion, we utilize the case of imposing a witholding tax on interest income from bonds. Yet, the same equation can be obtained in much more general settings as well. Section three discusses the case of some regulatory policies and illustrates how a bank can generate synthetic loans. The fourth section deals with capital controls. In particular we see that the use of replicating portfolios may end up being much more limited than the case of a witholding tax. Section five discusses an important issue that is especially relevant for turbulent markets. We claim that if volatility is stochastic, static or dynamic replication may not be possible. Hence policy will be more potent in this case. The next section is the summary of current risk management methods and shows how risks can be measured even in the presence of replicating portfolios. The final section concludes.

SYNTHETICS AND RISK MANAGEMENT

In order to motivate the discussion we will look at a very specific setting. We consider a local currency denominated emerging market bond and try to analyze the final risks that such a position might entail. Our purpose is to obtain a *contractual* equation that can be applied in many other settings as well. In fact, we intend to use this equation to discuss the ways capital controls and other market oriented policies might be circumvented.

We use very simple cash flow diagrams, which are nevertheless very effective in making some points. The situation is shown in Figure 1.

The top portion of the figure shows the cash flows of a pure discount bond. By itself, a local currency default-free pure discount bond has the following cash flows. (1) At time t one pays 80 to buy the bond. (2) At time T the bond matures and pays 100 units of local currency.

From the point of view of a player in the local markets, what are the risk factors? At the outset it appears that the only risk is the interest rate risk r_T, where this latter denotes the rate on maturity default-free deposits or loans.[1] Yet, this way of looking at these positions is incomplete; it may even be erroneous.

In fact, the main strategy in buying these local currency bonds is due to the exchange rate policy that these economies have adopted. A liquid market for these bonds is possible only when there is ample supply of such instruments. Yet, the important point is that for small economies such large bond stocks will exist only if in the short run the FX risk is made *predictable*, and if the government is running large budget deficits.[2] Both of these imply that governments of such economies must have recourse to some sort of fixed exchange rate policy. But as soon as this is adopted, the following strategy will be put in place.

A typical player will fund the position in local currency emerging bonds by borrowing foreign exchange, for example, dollars, and then selling these in the spot market to get the local currency needed to buy these bonds.

This situation is shown in Figure 1. The borrowing yields the needed dollars to buy 80 units of local currency, which in turn is used to buy the bond.

The important point is the following. When we add the three cash flow diagrams in the top portion of the graph we see that the negative and positive dollar cash flows cancel at time *t*. The same is true for the negative and positive local currency cash flows. At the end, at time *t* no net cash changes hands. Yet, at time *T* there are two cash flows remaining. According to these last cash flows the player makes a foreign currency denominated cash payment and receives a local currency denominated cash flow. This is shown at the bottom of Figure 1.

It turns out that we can recognize this last diagram as the cash flows generated by a forward FX contract. It is as if that the player is selling dollars forward, at time *t*. Thus, the *final* risks of the positions involving local currency emerging market bonds are quite different than what one might think at the outset. These positions entail *three* risks. (1) The local T-maturity interest rate risk r_T, (2) the foreign T-maturity dollar interest rate risk, R_T, and (3) the spot exchange rate risk e.

This is a first example of the point that we are making; that looking at the instruments individually may end up giving a very misleading impression of the true underlying risks. The regulator has to combine the items on the balance sheet *in a specific way* in order to understand the final positions taken by the player. Yet, how could one do this if the balance sheet contains thousands of instruments in many different parts of the world? Clearly, the knowledge of *how* to combine these instruments is not going to be information available to regulators. Such information is in general available only to the traders concerned with these positions and their supervisors.

---

1. We are assuming that there are no bid-ask spreads throughout this paper.
2. See for example Neftci (2000).

FIGURE 1. A Local Currency Bond Position

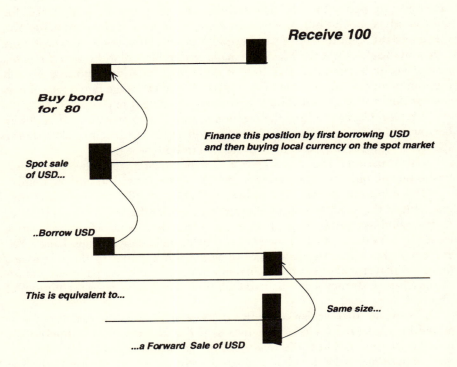

Receive 100

Buy bond for 80

Finance this position by first borrowing USD and then buying local currency on the spot market

Spot sale of USD...

..Borrow USD

This is equivalent to...

Same size...

...a Forward Sale of USD

WITHHOLDING TAX ON INTEREST

The above discussion of funding a local currency emerging market bond leads us to a much more general result. In fact, in the section above we succeeded creating a synthetic for *any* T-maturity discount bond with price $B(t, T)$ at time t.

In this section we can use this synthetic to show how some market related economic policies can be thwarted by the use of financial engineering methods. As an example, we consider imposing withholding taxes on interest income from bonds.

Suppose a discount bond with par value $100 and maturity 12 months is sold at a price of 95. The interest income is subject to 20% withholding tax. That is to say, the bond holder will receive only 99 at redemption.

We immediately use the logic shown in Figure 1 to form a synthetic for the bond. The situation is shown in Figure 2. In particular, the top diagram in Figure

2 shows the cash flow of a discount bond on which there is a withholding tax. We see that an identical cash flow can be produced by taking *three* independent positions.

In fact, (1) we can buy the as-yet unspecified asset X with \$95, (2) deposit the asset at time t until the date T,[3] and (3) at the same time, sign a forward contract to sell the proceeds of this deposit at time T.

FIGURE 2

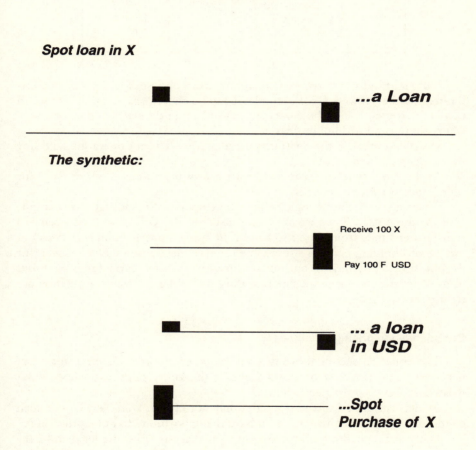

Spot loan in X

...a Loan

The synthetic:

Receive 100 X

Pay 100 F USD

... a loan
in USD

...Spot
Purchase of X

---

3. This deposit could yield an interest or may simply be a storage.

Thus we have obtained a very important *contractual* equation. We see that the discount bond is equivalent to a portfolio of a spot sale, a deposit and a forward contract. In other words we have:

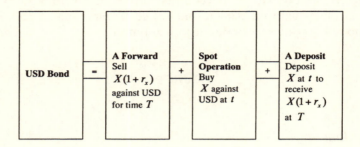

Note that in this contractual equation we can choose X in a practically unlimited number of ways.[4] For example, it can be chosen as any other 12 month bond in currency X with the same maturity of 12 months *and* issued in a country where there is no withholding tax.

We then exchange the $95 into currency X with a spot operation, and buy this X-denominated bond.

At the same time we write a contract a forward purchase of our $100 for time T, against the currency X.

There is a very simple logic behind these operations that may look complicated at the outset. Since we are being taxed on the USD bond, we prefer to transfer our funds from time t to time T by using another bond that does not carry a withholding tax. But at the same time we make sure that we recover our $100 at time T, by buying our dollars forward. In brief, carry funds *over time* using other means, but make sure that the entry and exits from the position are tightly secured at time t.

Contractual vs. pricing equations

The equation shown above is a *contractual* equation. This does not mean necessarily that the *value* of the two sides is the same. Thus, as such we don't necessarily have a *pricing* equation.

In fact, either one of the two sides may not *exist* in a market. Under such conditions, the market may not even have the opportunity to put a price on it.

With such equations, all we are saying is that the risks, the legal and contractual attributes of the two sides are the same. Yet, the market value of the two sides of the equation may differ due to several considerations, such as liquidity, transaction costs, existence of markets, and others.

---

4. Good choices for X should in principle have the following characteristics. (1) The X should not be subject to withholding tax. (2) It should be liquid. (3) It should not carry credit risk. (4) It should have minimal transaction costs.

However, if there is no credit risk, no transaction costs, and if the markets are liquid, then we expect that *arbitrage* will make the *value* two sides of the contractual equation equal to each other. This in fact is how static arbitrage positions are taken and are used to find arbitrage-free prices.

SYNTHETIC LOANS

The contractual equation above can be used to manufacture synthetic loans in any currency. This is the case since a loan and a bond have the same cash flow diagrams. This means that shorting a bond creates the same cash flow diagram as a loan obtained from a bank.[5] In other words, we can immediately write:

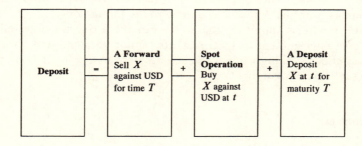

Or, reversing signs:

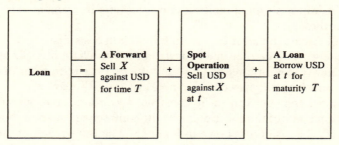

Suppose for a certain reason (regulatory or credit line problems?) a bank has difficulties in borrowing in currency X. Then by forming the following portfolio:

Portfolio = {Borrow USD, sell the proceeds spot against X, forward purchase the USD.}

the bank can create the same loan synthetically.

Here again we see that the need to transfer funds from time t to time T is carried through by using the USD as an intermediate tool. Obviously this intermediate tool should be chosen as the most convenient, least cost, and liquid currency.

---

5. We are always assuming zero default risk.

All this brings us to the main point of this section. We see that policies such as taxing transactions or imposing withholding taxes on interest is not likely to be very effective. It is true that such policies might "throw sand" into the engines of a fast moving market and slow down capital flows. But this is highly unlikely given the rapid globalization of well-functioning financial markets.

Also, with recent technological changes, executing orders across the world is in the process of converging towards some minimal costs. Improvements in legal and regulatory environments also augment the number of possible markets where one can implement such synthetic replications.

In fact, the main effect of such taxes and fees that a policy maker may introduce can end up resulting in a migration of capital and jobs from the economy. Given that synthetics will often use foreign instruments that are similar in characteristics to the local ones one is trying to recreate, the replication effort will shift resources from the domestic economy to the foreign one.

Yet, we should also point out that to the extent the transparency, reliability, and the legal environment of local markets cannot be duplicated abroad, the players may choose willingly to pay the taxes, instead of moving to less transparent or less reliable environments.

Capital controls

Several countries have, at different times, applied capital controls. We can use the same methodology developed above to discuss this issue. In fact, suppose a government imposes capital controls, can synthetic instruments be created to circumvent these?

We will discuss the ideal case of no transaction costs first.

Suppose we assume that in a country, a spot purchase of USD against the local currency X is prohibited. Banks cannot lend or wire transfer in USD and hard cash cannot be purchased in the (non-existing) FX market.

A financial engineer can easily construct a synthetic spot operation, since this operation is one of the constituents of the contractual equation shown above.

Consider the cash flow shown in Figure 3. The top portion of the diagram displays a spot purchase of USD against currency X. The lower part of the figure shows how we can recreate the identical cash flows by using three operations. (1) We take a loan in USD. (2) We make a deposit in local currency X. (3) We forward sell USD against X at time t. Now, these contracts are signed at time t and hence all the prices are known. Under the conditions of no credit risk, the sum of these three contracts will be identical to the spot purchase of USD.

This can also be seen from rearranging the contractual equation discussed above.

This gives a synthetic instrument that replicates a spot FX transaction. Hence, at least *in theory* capital controls can be circumvented easily by using local and foreign loans.

However, in practice, the situation is more complicated. The player intending to replicate the spot FX transaction needs to make what is known as "parallel

FIGURE 3

**Spot Purchase
of USD**

The synthetic:

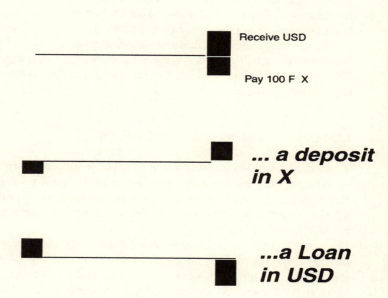

Receive USD

Pay 100 F X

**... a deposit
in X**

**...a Loan
in USD**

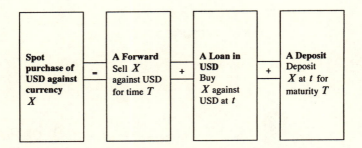

loans" or "back-to-back loans" with a foreign player. Finding a sufficient number of such players who are willing to enter into *back-to-back loans* may not be possible. This means that the replication of such synthetic spot FX transactions may indeed be somewhat reduced by imposing capital controls.

Yet, the approach above indicates that at least the "big players" in the markets, that is to say those with the ability to borrow externally, will not be affected very much by capital controls. This however may not be visible in the collected data, or for that matter from a cursory analysis of the balance sheets, because back-to-back loans are made using the foreign subsidiaries (or SPVs) of involved institutions.

Accordingly, the imposition of capital controls could lead to a two-tier market where the small players are indeed prevented from transactions in the spot FX market, but where the big players, though paying a somewhat higher price, are still being able to conduct them.

NON-LINEAR POSITIONS AND VOLATILITY

The simple examples given above in terms of replicating some *basic* positions are deceivingly simple but are also very powerful. In fact, they suggest that a financial engineer can replicate almost any basic positions using practically an infinite number of strategies. This complicates regulatory and taxation policies directed towards financial markets.

Yet, the positions considered above are all in terms of *linear* assets, for which there are liquid markets. Options are highly non-linear, and they were not treated above. Can we apply the same methods to options? In fact, we can also ask a more general question. Are there situations or instruments for which static replication methods cannot be exploited? The answer to this question is positive.

First, there may be cases where required *liquid* instruments for replicating a *linear* product may not exist. Then, one cannot apply the contractual equations shown above in practice. However, as long as *some* similar liquid instruments exist, by modifying the method and by adopting *dynamic* replication strategies one can again construct synthetics albeit by rebalancing the replicating portfolios periodically. This is both (1) more complicated and hence, (2) more expensive. Thus, although one can circumvent policies and/or capital controls this would be more difficult and open to fewer players in the markets.

The real complication occurs with volatility products. Obviously, options can be replicated by dynamic hedging involving the underlying instrument. Today, this is a straightforward exercise in financial markets. Yet, the case when volatility becomes *stochastic* is different.

Stochastic volatility complicates option hedging significantly. If volatilities of risk factors contain independent sources of disturbances, then the markets will in general be *incomplete* and it would be impossible to form replicating instruments even if one used dynamic methods. Thus, to the extent that noise trading magnifies volatility, and to the extent that big players have significant exposures to volatility surprises,[6] then regulatory measures that reduce the noise trading may indirectly "complete" the markets and make dynamic hedging of these positions easier. Otherwise, the behavior of noise traders may magnify the volatility during critical periods and due to incompleteness of markets the hedging of the Vega risk will become more difficult. [See for example Musiela and Rutkowski (1988).]

SOME RISK MANAGEMENT CONCEPTS

The examples above show that a visual analysis of balance sheets will eventually fail to discover the correct risk exposures. That is the reason why current methods of risk management have adopted a different approach. The approach of current risk management methodologies consist of the following principle:

It is literally impossible to determine the exposures faced by institutions to various types of risks by looking at and analyzing their balance sheets. As shown above, the instruments on the two sides of a balance sheet can be combined in too many different fashions and may result in completely different exposures, to make a visual examination impossible. The current risk management metholodologies acknowledge this and approach measuring risks not by trying to recognize the final exposures that a balance sheet contains, but by calculating the *sensitivities* of all the elements of the balance sheet and then trying to measure the money that can be lost in case of some extreme turbulence in the markets. In this section we provide a short summary of the major concepts used in risk management.

Risk management can be seen as having two broad branches. The first, and the one that we are mainly concerned with in this paper, is *market* risk management. The second, and equally important, is the *credit* risk management.

Market risk has to do with losses that may be caused by the changes in these market risk factors such as interest rates, exchange rates, equity prices, and commodities. There are three major ways in which changes in risk factors can affect the value of a portfolio.

The first effect is the portfolio or asset's Delta. The yield R_T of a default free discount bond $B(t, T)$ with maturity T is a random variable and it will change by

---

6. That is to say, if they have significant Vega exposure.

DR_T as time passes. This change can be "large" and may cause significant drops in the value of the bond. Taking the standard derivative, the change in the value of the bond can be written as:

$$\Delta B(t,T) = -\left[T\frac{100}{(1+R_T)^{T+1}}\right]\Delta R_T$$

The losses are proportional to increases in R_T. This proportion, called the Delta of the instrument, will be greater, the longer the maturity of the bond, that is to say, the T:

$$Delta = -\left[T\frac{100}{(1+R_T)^{T+1}}\right]$$

Delta is the first order price risk of a bond portfolio, and this is clearly caused by the random movements in the risk-free yield.

The secondary effect of movements in risk factors is the Gamma effect. An institution that is long (short) the bond, or some other instrument, can hedge the Delta risk. This can be done by selling (buying) T-bond, Tbill, or other appropriate interest rate futures. But in some cases[7] the futures price is a *linear* function of interest rates, whereas the bond price is a non-linear function of R_T as can be seen from the formula above. Thus, the institution may have exposure to the second derivative with respect to yield:

$$\Delta B(t,T)^2 = \left[100\frac{T^2+T}{(1+R_T)^{T+2}}\right]\Delta R_T^2$$

This risk is called the Gamma risk and is created by the inability of a linear instrument to hedge fully for the non-linear effects of random changes in the risk factor R_T. Notice that in this particular case the Gamma risk is of the opposite sign to the Delta risk. Hence if one has exposure to a particular Delta, ignoring the Gamma risk will be equivalent to adapting a conservative approach.

The third category of market risk is somewhat more complicated. Suppose the yield R_T remains the same. Hence the price $B(t,T)$ does not move from one period to another:

$$DB(t,T)=0$$

Yet, suppose the *volatility* of R_T changes. Then although the price of the bond remains the same, the price of the corresponding options may move adversely. Letting $F(R_T,t)$ denote the price of these options at time t we have:

---

7. Such as the Eurodollar futures.

$$DF = F_s\, Ds_T$$

where s_T is the volatility of the yield R_T.

This is another major form of the market risk called the Vega risk, where the Vega is given by:

$$Vega\text{-}F_s$$

This illustrates the main forms of market risk which consist of the changes in the first and the second order movements of market risk factors as well as by *random* changes in the volatilities associated with these market risk factors. Hence, there may potentially be *two* sources of randomness, one emanating from the market risk factors, the other from the corresponding volatilities. This distinction is subtle and non-trivial for an institution with options books, even though the two sources of randomness will eventually be present in a history of observed data on market risk factors.

Once one defines these broad classes of risk, the next step becomes one of measuring the effects of extreme movements in these risk factors. Here the main notion is the Value at Risk (VaR), which consists of estimating the amount of money an institution can lose in case of extreme variations in some predefined risk factors.

Hence let $\{dx_1,\ldots,dx_n\}$ be n risk factors possibly affecting the k, instruments $\{V^1,\ldots,V^k\}$ on the balance sheet. We can then calculate the *first order* VaR of a balance sheet P by using the following steps. First we get the variation of the balance sheet as the sum of the variations in all positions.

$$dP = dV^1 + \ldots + dV^k$$

Next, we represent each increment using the Delta (Gamma, Vega) sensitivities. For example for the i'th asset we have:

$$dV^i = V^i_1 dx_1 + \ldots + V^i_n dx_n$$

Finally, we calculate the VaR by approximating the extreme changes in dx_j with the a'th percentiles:

$$VaR = \sqrt{\left[\sum_{i=1}^{k}[V^i_1 d\hat{x}_1 + \ldots + V^i_n d\hat{x}_n]]\right]^2}$$

with each extreme movement in the risk factor, $d\hat{x}_j$ being approximated by:

$$d\hat{x}_j^2 = L^a s_j^2$$

and

$$d\hat{x}_j d\hat{x}_i = L^a r_i j$$

where the L^a is the a-percent threshold at the tail (usually selected as 1%). The $r_{l}j$ is the covariance between the j'th and l'th risk factors.

The VaR number calculated this way can be repeated by including second order and Vega related risk factors as well. The inclusion of Gamma would in principle improve the approximation of the sensitivities for non-linear assets, whereas the Vega effects will be relevant in case one has reasons to believe that the volatilities have independent sources of randomness and that they change over time.

It is important to realize that this way of measuring risks does not try to record the types of exposures one has in balance sheets by looking at individual positions. These positions themselves may look very risky, yet when put together with other positions may in fact show no risk at all. The opposite may be true also. A position that may not look risky at all when considered individually may end up being very risky when put together with other positions. Instead, VaR calculations consider the combined effects of some calculated "extreme" movements in risk factors on the *whole* balance sheet or portfolio. We see that the use of Delta, Gamma, and Vega type sensitivities and then calculating the implied VaRs circumvents the attempts to reconstruct exposures entirely.

CONCLUSIONS

This paper showed, using simple examples, that methods of financial engineering may thwart many of the regulatory and taxation policies directed towards financial markets. At the least, policy considerations should carefully investigate the possibilities of replicating the instruments under consideration. If these policies are implemented blindly, they may be, at best, ineffective, and at worst, may lead to flight of jobs and capital.

Yet, under some conditions, regulatory policies may also reduce the underlying risks. This is especially the case where noise trading may cause violent volatility movements, which in turn will make large volatility positions non-hedgeable.

REFERENCES

Musiela, M., and M. Rutkowski. 1998. *Martingale Methods in Financial Modeling.* Springer-Verlag.
Neftci, S., *An Introduction to Methods of Financial Engineering.* Preliminary manuscript.
Neftci, S., *Local Currency Emerging Market Bonds.* Forthcoming, Revistas Economico.

17

...

The Role of Derivatives in the East Asian Financial Crisis

Randall Dodd*

DERIVATIVES PLAYED a key role in the East Asian financial crisis of 1997. Their use developed alongside the growth of capital flows to those developing economies in the 1990s. Derivatives facilitated the growth in private capital flows by unbundling the risks associated with investment vehicles such as bank loans, stocks, bonds and direct physical investment, and then reallocating the risks more efficiently. They also facilitated efforts by some entities in raising their risk-to-capital ratios, dodging regulatory safeguards, manipulating accounting rules, and evading taxation. Foreign exchange forwards and swaps were used to hedge as well as speculate on the fixed exchange rate regimes, while total return swaps were used to capture the "carry business" of profiting from the interest rate differential between pegged currencies. Structured notes were used to circumvent accounting rules and prudential regulations in order to offer investors higher, though much riskier, returns. Viewed at the macroeconomic level, derivatives first made the economy more susceptible to financial crisis and then quickened and deepened the downturn once the crisis began. This analysis of the East Asian crisis offers several policy lessons. Financial regulations should contain reporting requirements, capital requirements should be updated to reflect the market risk of derivatives, regulations governing the holding of assets and liabilities should be updated to reflect that they often have attached derivatives, and regulatory

*The author would like to express his appreciation for comments and suggestions from seminar participants at the Economic Policy Institute, American University, the Center for Economic Policy Analysis, and the InterAmerican Development Bank.

incentives should be structured so that derivatives are used to facilitate capital flows and not be used to increase risk-to-capital ratios by out-maneuvering government regulations.

ROLE OF DERIVATIVES IN THE EAST ASIAN FINANCIAL CRISIS

Derivatives and capital flows

Although many factors contributed to the East Asian financial crisis, this paper focuses on the role of derivatives. There are many studies that focus on other sources of the crisis, and their conclusions usually fall within the following range. There was too much hot money or short-term foreign bank lending. There was too much investment, and this led to excess capacity. There were too many bad investments that led to too many bad loans and later bankruptcies. There were overvalued exchange rates that were defended for too long. There was too much corruption or crony capitalism. This might be summed up with the words of the great wit and sage Yogi Berra, "They made too many wrong mistakes."

This study is not designed to reaffirm or refute these points, but to add to the overall level of understanding of the crisis by adding an analysis of the role of derivatives. And while this study focuses on the role of derivatives, it will address issues of overall financial market regulation and the composition of foreign capital flows in the form of bank loans, securities, and physical investment.

It should be pointed out at the beginning that this study is limited by the lack of data available on over-the-counter (OTC) derivatives markets.[1] Unlike derivatives trading on exchanges, transactions in OTC markets are neither registered nor systematically reported to the public in detail, and so information on them is scarce.[2]

The old way. The financial crisis that engulfed developing economies in the 1990s was significantly different from that which struck in the 1980s. While both crisis periods involved some degree of over-lending, unproductive investing and corruption, there are two key differences between the two crises that provide the more important policy lessons. The first is the different forms of foreign capital that flowed to developing countries during the two periods, and the second is the emergence of derivatives as an integral part of capital flows in the 1990s.

The private foreign capital flows that led up to the crises of the 1980s were largely in the form of dollar denominated, variable interest rate, syndicated commercial

---

1. Derivatives are said to be traded either on exchanges, where trading is public, multilateral, and closely regulated by governments and the exchanges themselves, or in over-the-counter markets where trading is non-public and largely outside government regulation.

2. Most data comes from the Bank for International Settlements, the U.S. Office of Comptroller of the Currency, some Bloomberg and Reuters quotes, and Swaps Monitor.

bank loans to sovereign borrowers. The loans from private sources were issued by the major U.S. and European banks that were in the process of recycling "petro-dollar" deposits from OPEC surpluses.[3] The formation of syndicates to under-write these loans helped to bind lenders together, and together with cross-default clauses[4] in the loan contracts, it greatly reduced banks' credit risks. In order to reduce the banks' exposure to market risk, these loans were issued as variable interest rate loans (usually priced as a spread above LIBOR or some short-term interest rate that reflected banks' funding costs), and they were denominated mostly in dollars and otherwise in other G-5 currencies (which reflected the currency denomination of the banks' funding sources).

Foreign capital flows in this form shifted most of the market risk into the hands of the borrowers. The borrowers bore both the foreign exchange risk as well as the interest rate risk. Lending banks in the advanced capital markets, whose liabilities were mostly short-term and denominated in the same curren-cies as their loans to developing countries, bore little market risk. Their expo-sure was almost entirely credit risk, and this was substantially mitigated through the syndication of the loans and the inclusion of cross-default clauses.

This distribution of risk laid the foundation for the crisis that began in Au-gust of 1982. The crisis began to build when the U.S. central bank decided to increase short-term dollar interest rates. Higher dollar interest rates, which served as the basis for payments on adjustable rate loans, both increased the dollar pay-ments on loans and increased the cost of obtaining those dollars by pushing up the value of the dollar against other currencies in global foreign exchange mar-kets. Together this increased the non-dollar currency cost, especially the local currency costs of debtor countries, of servicing these dollar bank loans. Initially, debtor countries increased their borrowing in order to reduce the burden of servicing higher debt costs. When they were no longer able to increase their borrowing, they were forced into crisis. This was signaled in August of 1982 by the Mexican government's announcement of its inability to make its scheduled foreign loan payments.

Once the crisis was apparent, the developing economy governments, major money center banks, and the IMF and World Bank began developing post-crisis recovery policies. The initial policy solution was to reschedule existing debt, arrange new lending, and require the developing economy governments to imple-ment austere fiscal and monetary policies to make possible the eventual repay-ment of the still growing debt burden.

---

3. Goodman, Laurie. "Bank Lending to Non-OPEC LDCs: Are Risks Diversifiable?" Fed-eral Reserve Bank of New York Quarterly Review. Summer 1981. Dodd, Randall. "The Rise of Syndicated Eurocredits in North-South Lending." Working Paper, Dept. of Economics, American University. 1989.

4. Cross-default clauses mean that a default against one lender is treated as a default against all lenders and thus prevent borrowers from selecting lenders for default.

TABLE 1. Composition of Private Capital Flows to
Developing Countries
(percentage of total private and public flows)

Type of flow	1973–81	1990–97
Bonds	3.5%	15.2%
Bank Lending	63.9%	11.7%
Foreign Direct Investment	16.8%	50.3%
Portfolio Equity	0.3%	16.4%

SOURCE: World Bank. Global Finance Report, 2000.

The new way. The foreign private capital flows that preceded the 1997 financial crisis were of a substantially different character. Firstly, these flows went to private entities in East Asia and not just sovereign borrowers. Secondly, commercial bank loans, measured as a percentage of total foreign capital flows, were substantially less important than in the earlier period. Instead, capital flows to East Asia were in a myriad of forms that ranged from direct foreign investment to portfolio equity investment (meaning less than 10% ownership), corporate and sovereign bonds[5] as well as structured notes, repurchase agreements, and also bank loans to public and private borrowers. (See Table 1.)

This more diversified flow of foreign capital (diversified in the sense that various vehicles were used to channel the capital flows) generated a different distribution of risks. Compared to the bank loans of the 1970s and early 1980s, this more diversified flow of capital tended to distribute risk towards investors in the advanced capital market economies. Stocks and bonds investments shifted market risk and credit risk to foreign investors who bore the risk of changes in interest rates, securities prices, and exchange rates. Direct foreign investment in physical capital and real estate similarly shifted market risk and credit risk to foreign investors. Even dollar denominated bonds issued by East Asian governments shifted interest rate risk, as well as credit risk, to foreign investors. The effect was to potentially reduce the developing economies' exposure to the risk of changes in the U.S. interest rates or the relative value of the dollar.

Derivatives trading grew up alongside these new forms of capital flows as part of an effort to better manage the risks of global investing. In doing so, derivatives facilitated this new composition of capital flows by unbundling risk and redistributing it away from investors who did not want it and towards those more willing and able to bear it. At the same time, derivatives created new risks that were potentially destabilizing for developing economies. The following is an analysis of how derivatives played a constructive role in channeling capital from advanced capital markets to developing economies, and how at the same time they played a potentially destructive role in laying the foundations of the crisis.

---

5. The growth of bond issuances was discussed in Ismail Dalla and Deena Khathkate, "The Emerging East Asian Bond Market," IMF-World Bank Finance and Development, December 4, 1997.

Facilitating flows. Derivatives facilitated capital flows by unbundling and then more efficiently reallocating the various sources of risk associated with traditional capital vehicles such as bank loans, equities, bonds,[6] and direct foreign investment. Foreign currency loans expose the foreign investor to credit risk and the domestic borrower to exchange rate risk. A fixed interest rate loan exposes the foreign lender to interest rate risk and a variable rate loan exposes the domestic borrower to interest rate risk. A long-term loan exposes the foreign lender to greater credit risk and a short-term loan exposes the domestic borrower to refunding risk (sometimes called liquidity risk). Equities expose the foreign investor to credit risk along with the market risk from changes in the exchange rate, market price of the stock, and the uncertain dividend payments. Notes and bonds expose the foreign investor to credit risk and market interest rate risk, and in the case of hard currency bonds expose the domestic borrower to exchange rate risk. The financial innovation of introducing derivatives to capital markets allows these traditional arrangements of risk to be redesigned so as to better meet the desired risk profiles of the issuers and holders of these capital instruments.[7]

Facilitating unproductive activities and lowering safeguards. While the risk shifting function of derivatives serves the useful role of hedging and thereby facilitating capital flows, the enlarged presence of derivatives also raises concerns about the stability of the economy as a whole. The use of derivatives can lead to lower levels of transparency between counterparties and between regulators and market participants. They can be used for unproductive activities such as avoiding capital requirements, manipulating accounting rules and credit ratings, and evading taxation. They can also be used to raise the level of market risk exposure relative to capital in the pursuit of higher yielding—and higher risk— investment strategies.

In the event of a large change in the exchange rate or other market prices, the greater the amount of market exposure—possibly created by open positions in derivatives contracts—the greater will be the pace and depth of impact on the financial sector and economy as a whole. In this context, the use of derivatives to reduce the amount of capital that acts as a buffer to market turbulence raises the risk of systemic failure and heightens doubts about the stability of the financial sector and the economy as a whole.

Derivatives used in East Asian economies

Derivatives are unlike securities and other assets because with the exception of foreign exchange swaps, no principal or title is exchanged. In their essence, nothing is owned but pure price exposure. They are purely pricing contracts. Their price is derived from an underlying commodity, asset, rate, index, or event,

---

6. The term bond is used here to mean any securitized credit instrument whether it be a short-, intermediate-, or long-term fixed rate security, a floating rate note, or a structured note.

7. A good, short exposition of this point is made by John Chrystal (1996).

and this malleability allows them to be used to create leverage and to change the appearance of transactions. Derivatives can be used to restructure transactions so that positions can be moved off of the balance sheet, floating rates can be changed into fixed rates (and vice versa), currency denominations can be changed, interest or dividend income can become capital gains (and vice versa), payments can be moved into different periods in order to manipulate tax liabilities and earnings reports, and high yield securities can be made to look like convention AAA investments. The following describes several of the key derivative instruments used in East Asia, and how they were used for hedging (risk shifting) as well as for taking on additional risk in the pursuit of higher returns on capital.

FIGURE 1. Forward Contract

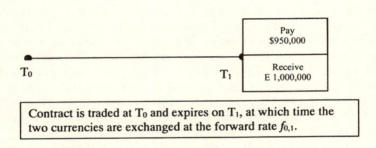

Foreign exchange forwards and foreign exchange swaps

Foreign exchange forwards and swaps are an integral part of the global foreign exchange market. Together with spot transactions, foreign currency swaps, and foreign exchange options, they make up a market whose daily volume is estimated at $1.5 trillion. Of this total, $578 billion is in spot transactions, $130 billion is in forward transactions, $734 billion is in foreign exchange swaps, $10 billion is in foreign currency swaps, and $87 billion is in foreign exchange options.[8]

A foreign exchange forward is a contract in which counterparties are obliged to exchange specified amounts of foreign currencies at some specified exchange rate on a specified future date. The forward exchange rate is the price at which the counterparties will exchange currency on the future expiration date. The forward rate is negotiated so that the value of the forward contract at the time it is traded is

---

8. Bank for International Settlements, *Central Bank Survey of Foreign Exchange and Derivatives Market Activity*, 1998.

zero; in other words, the contract is traded at par. As a result, no money need be paid at the commencement of the contract, although the counterparties may agree to post collateral in order to insure each other's performance of the contract.

For example, party A enters a 180-day forward contract to buy 1,000,000 Euros at the exchange rate of $0.95. In 180 days party A must deliver $950,000 to party B who will in turn deliver Euro 1,00,000. In this way, currency is said to be "delivered" in the fulfillment of the terms of the contracts.

Trading in "non-deliverable" foreign exchange forward contracts emerges when cross-border transactions cannot occur due to government restrictions or market failure. A non-deliverable forward market would likely emerge in order to avoid currency transactions taxes such as the "Tobin tax" because there is no exchange of foreign currencies. Non-deliverable forwards are contracts to exchange not the two currencies but instead an amount of the available currency, for example dollars, based on the change in the exchange rate over the term of the forward contract.

For example, party A enters a 180-day non-deliverable forward to sell 1 million baht for U.S. dollars at $0.050 (20 baht to the dollar). If the baht were to depreciate to $0.045 (22 baht to the dollar) when the contract expires in 180 days, then party A would receive the dollar value of 1 million baht times the change in the exchange rate calculated at the new spot rate of $0.045—or in other words 1,000,000 times $0.050 - $0.045 or $5,000. The result is equivalent to taking delivery on a normal forward contract and then converting the gains, which are realized in baht, back into dollars at the exchange rate of $0.045.

A foreign exchange swap is simply the combination of a spot and forward transaction (or possibly two forwards). The start leg of the swap usually consists of a spot foreign exchange transaction at the current exchange rate, and the close leg consists of a second foreign exchange transaction at the contracted forward rate. For example, party A enters a foreign exchange swaps of baht against the dollar in which it buys 1,000,000 baht today at $0.050, and contracts to sell 1,000,000 at $0.045 in 180 days. Party A first receives 1 million baht (in exchange for paying $50,000), and then upon the swap expiration date pays 1 million baht (in exchange for receiving $45,000). This 10% loss in dollar terms is due to the depreciation of the baht against the dollar (or appreciation of the dollar against the baht) and reflects the fact that the rate of return from investing in baht is considerably higher then investing in dollars.

Forwards and foreign exchange swaps are not always highly collateralized (measured as a percentage of the principal). Collateral is less likely to be used for trading between the major market dealers, and collateral is lower for less volatile financial instruments such as currency. This exposes foreign exchange derivatives counterparties to credit risk. The largest source of credit losses in the derivatives markets in recent years were due to defaults on foreign currency forwards in East Asia and Russia (Swaps Monitor, 1999).[9]

---

9. The largest source of credit loses by ACM derivatives dealers in 1997 and 1998 were on dollar-ruble foreign exchange forwards made with Russian firms.

FIGURE 2

Foreign Exchange Forward: I
(Deliverable)
Investor sells baht forward at $0.05 (20 baht to $1)

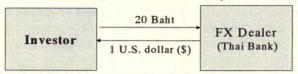

The LDC investor has sold baht forward, and is thus
said to be short baht in the forward market.

Foreign exchange forwards and swaps were potentially used in East Asia by
both foreign and domestic investors to hedge foreign exchange risk. Foreign
investors from advanced capital markets who purchased securities denominated
in local East Asian currencies could use foreign exchange forwards and swaps to
hedge their long local currency exposure. Similarly, foreign direct investments
in physical real estate, plant, or equipment were exposed to the risk of local
currency depreciation. Local East Asian investors who borrowed in dollars, yen,
or European currencies and invested in local currency assets were also exposed
to foreign exchange risk.

Of course foreign exchange forwards and swaps were also used for speculation in these East Asian currencies. Derivatives enabled speculators to leverage
their capital in order to take larger positions in the value of local currencies. It
also meant that East Asian central banks had to watch the exchange rate in two
markets, the spot and forward, in order to maintain their fixed exchange rates.

Swaps

The term swap is sometimes used to refer to OTC derivatives in general.
This no doubt arose from the fact that the vast majority of OTC derivatives are
swaps of one form or another. The precise meaning of the term, used throughout
this chapter, refers to a particular method of structuring a derivatives contract.

While the above section described the foreign exchange swap as a contract
for the sale and repurchase (or alternatively the purchase and resale) of foreign
currency, this section will describe the structure of interest rate swaps and total
return swaps.

Vanilla interest rate swaps. The basic interest rate swap, called a vanilla
interest rate swap, is an agreement between two parties to exchange the net of

two series of payments. One series of payments is based on a fixed interest rate applied to a notional principal, such as 6% on $1 million, and the other series of payments is based on a floating rate, such as three-month LIBOR, applied to the same notional principal. In order to simplify payments and other clearing issues, most swap contracts allow the two parties to pay (or receive) only the net or the difference between these two series on each payment or "drop" date. This is illustrated in Figure 3.[10]

A borrower with a variable interest rate loan can hedge his interest rate risk with a swap in which he receives the floating rate and pay the fixed rate (i.e., buy a swap) and thereby swap his floating rate payments for fixed rate payments.

Consider the following example of a short swap position. Every year for the length or tenor of the contract, the swap pays the net of a fixed rate of 6% less a floating interest rate applied to a notional principal of $1,000,000. If the floating rate were 5%, then the floating payment would be $50,000, the fixed payment would be $60,000, and the net payment to the fixed rate receiver would be $10,000. If the floating rate were to rise to 6%, then the next payment would be zero. If the floating rate were to rise to 8%, then the fixed rate receiver would make a net payment of $20,000 to the fixed rate payer. This is alternatively illustrated in Figures 4 and 5.

FIGURE 3

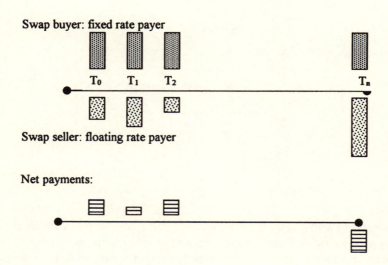

10. The party whose position is to pay the fixed rate and receive the floating rate is considered long the swap, and the party whose position is to receive the fixed and pay the floating rate payment is the short position or the swap seller. This is opposite from the convention in the credit market where the party receiving the fixed bond or loan payments is considered the long position.

Swap agreements often include provisions for collateral. Collateral arrangements usually require that collateral be posted in the form of G-5 currencies or government securities (excluding Japanese government securities). The initial amount is determined by the variance on the instrument, and an adjustment is made for when the position moves out of the money. This reduces counterparty credit risk to the winning side, and thereby reduces the winning side's requirement to hold capital against that credit risk.

Swaps are traded by negotiating a fixed swap rate that will make the present value of the fixed payments equal to the expected present value to the floating payments. The swap rate has traditionally been expressed as a spread above the yield on U.S. Treasury securities or the relevant benchmark instrument to that currency's interest rate. For example, a swap dealer's bid/ask quote of 45/53 basis points on a two-year swap means that the fixed interest rate that will enable this swap to trade at par or "at the market" is 45 basis points above the two-year Treasury note rate if the dealer is to make the fixed payment, and 53 basis points if it is to receive the fixed payment. In the past two years, dollar interest rate swaps have come to be quoted as all-in rates, reflecting their ascendancy in U.S. financial markets.[11]

FIGURE 4

SWAP: I

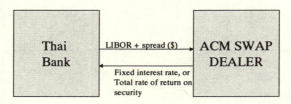

Total return swaps. A total return swap (TRS) is a contract in which at least one series of payments is based on the total rate of return (change in market price plus interest or dividend payments) on some underlying asset, security, or security index. The other leg of the swap is typically based on a variable interest rate such

---

11. Fleming, Michael J. 2000. "The Benchmark U.S. Treasury Market: Recent Performance and Possible Alternatives." Economic Policy Review, Federal Reserve Bank of New York, Vol. 6, No.1, April 2000.   Pesek, William, Jr. 2000. "Swapping Curves." Barron's, September 4, 2000.

as LIBOR, but may be a fixed rate or the total rate of return on some other financial instrument. Based upon what is known about the pre-crisis situation in East Asia as well as Mexico, the total return swaps in those situations usually swapped LIBOR against the total rate of return on a government security.

A total return swap replicates the position of borrowing at LIBOR in order to finance the holding of a security or security index. The returns are the same, but unlike the actual cash market transaction, it does not involve ownership or debt. Instead the only capital involved in a TRS is the posting of collateral. In addition to the reduction in the need to commit capital to the transaction, a TRS also has no impact on a firm's balance sheet and not be subject to regulatory restrictions on foreign exchange exposure. It would incur a capital charge only if it were to move into the money. In short, TRS allow financial institutions and investors to raise their risks, and potential returns, relative to capital.

One of the uses of total return swaps in East Asia was to capture the gains from the carry trade or carry business. A profitable carry trade exists where exchange rates are fixed and interest rate differentials persist between the two economies. Then it is possible to borrow in the low interest rate currency and lend in the high interest rate currency with no risk other than that of a failure in the fixed exchange rate.

In the case of East Asia, the money center banks were willing to lend the major currencies, and the East Asian banks were eager to capture carry profits from the interest rate differential of borrowing and lending. The profitability of the activity, and ultimately the solvency of the financial institutions conducting this carry business, depended upon the East Asian central banks' ability to maintain the exchange rate peg or at least prevent it from depreciating by more than the interest rate differential.

FIGURE 5

SWAP: II

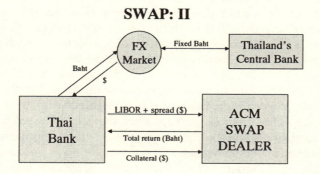

There were a couple of factors that limited the amount of this profitable carry trade activity. The combination of foreign borrowing and domestic lending created a foreign exchange mismatch on financial institutions' balance sheets. Financial market regulations either strictly limited the extent of this mismatch or they required additional capital charges in proportion to the exchange rate exposure. Other limits came from the limits on how much foreign banks were willing to lend to any one East Asian financial institution, and the disincentive for borrowers to swell their balance sheets (which lowered the reported earnings on assets).

In this context, TRS were appropriate that financial institutions could avoid prudential regulations by taking their carry positions off balance sheet.

Consider the following example. A Thai financial institution borrows dollars for six months, which cost LIBOR plus some spread to cover the lender's credit risk, and uses the proceeds to invest in higher yielding six-month Thai baht assets. This borrowing in dollars and lending in baht, however, creates a foreign exchange mismatch—i.e., a short forward position in dollars—on the Thai institution's balance sheet. This exchange rate exposure, which is the risk of the government failing to maintain the fixed exchange rate, is the cost of capturing the interest rate differential.

In order to avoid government financial regulations, which discouraged this activity by either assessing a special capital charge on excess foreign exposure or expressly restricting the amount of foreign exchange imbalance, a developing economy investor would use a TRS to move this activity off its balance sheets. This is illustrated in Figure 5 entitled "Swap II."

The use of TRS altered the form of capital flows to developing countries. If banks engaged in the carry business by borrowing abroad, then the capital flows were in the form of short-term, hard currency bank loans. If banks pursued the same profit opportunities by using TRS, then it would generate indirect capital flows as swaps counterparties, usually ACM swaps dealers, bought the underlying asset as a hedge against their own position in the TRS. (This point is illustrated in Figure 6.) As a result, the capital flow was in the form of a local currency denominated security instead of a dollar bank loan. However, the local currency security did not have the effect of shifting foreign exchange risk to advanced capital market investors. Instead, it functioned in conjunction with the TRS to leave the local developing country investors holding the foreign exchange risk (the short dollar position) much like a hard currency bank loan. Not only is the developing economy's foreign exchange exposure the same, but the TRS carry strategy exposes it to even greater surges in foreign currency than with short-term bank loans. The bank loans, except when there are attached puts, are certain for the maturity of the loan. However, the collateral arrangements on the TRS can result in a large immediate surge, overnight if not intraday, in foreign currency transfers. If short-term bank loans are considered hot money, then payments to meet margin and collateral requirements are microwave money.

The use of TRS also increases the likelihood of contagion. They often involve cross-currency assets and payments and are therefore more likely to transfer disruptions from one market to another. Neftci (1998) claims that one reason that Korean banks engaged in so many Indonesian total return swaps was that they were seeking higher rates of return in response to a rise in their funding costs. "But, note that at the end of this process, Korean banks are being exposed to Indonesian credit. This however, is not visible on their balance sheets. This situation not only creates the possibility for contagion, buy may also make the contagion unpredictable and severe."

FIGURE 6

SWAP: III

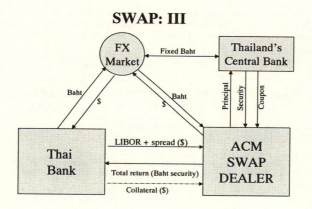

Structured notes

Structured notes, also known as hybrid instruments, are the combination of a credit market instrument, such as a bond or note, with a derivative such as an option or futures-like contract. Structured notes were part of the new wave of innovation in capital flows to East Asia in the 1990s. They offered issuers and investors either better yields than similarly rated securities, or better combinations or bundles of risk characteristics. In some cases, structured notes were designed to circumvent accounting rules or government regulations so as to allow lower capital charges, greater foreign exchange exposure, or greater overall risk to capital.

Hybrid instruments include such conventional securities as convertible stocks, convertible bonds, and callable bonds. These have long been among the set of traditional securities regularly issued and traded in U.S. financial markets. There is also a history of less conventional hybrids instruments. An early example of structured notes comes from the Treasury of the Confederate States of America. It attached various types of derivatives features to its bonds in order to enhance its borrowing power. In one instance, it structured a bond so that it contained an option that allowed the investor to be paid the principal and interest in either

Confederate dollars or New Orleans Middling Grade Cotton. Another more creative Confederate issue was designed as a tri-valued instrument that paid upon maturity, at the purchaser's option, the higher of 100 pounds sterling, 2500 French francs, or 4000 pounds cotton (Markham, 1994).

FIGURE 7

Structured Note
PERL - Principal Exchange Rate Linked Note

Principal and interest payments are denominated in dollars, but the value of payments is linked to a futures or option position on a foreign currency exchange rate. Enhanced yield is return for holding foreign currency risk exposure.

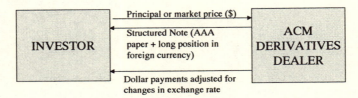

Benefits to investor include regulatory and capital treatment as dollar denominated asset and higher yield than similarly rated dollar asset.

The structured notes used in East Asia were usually structured so that their yield was linked to the value of one or more of the currencies or stock indices in the developing economies. The issuers of these structured notes were financial institutions from advanced capital market economies and the investors were often East Asian financial institutions and investors who were more willing to hold their own exchange rate risk or that of their neighboring developing countries. One reason given for this is that they are more knowledgeable of their economies and markets than investors from advanced capital markets. An additional reason is that they are inherently long their own currency—long in the sense that if the fixed exchange rate regime were to collapse, then the whole economy would contract—and therefore the cost of perceived cost of additional foreign exchange exposure is small.

Financial institutions from advanced capital markets were interested in issuing these instruments in order to create long-dated futures and options positions in developing country currencies and securities. Foreign exchange forward and swap markets are short-term markets; the vast majority of transactions in these markets have a maturity of one year or less. The 1998 BIS report on foreign exchange markets showed that only 1.4% of foreign exchange swaps and 3.9% of forwards had maturities in excess of one year, and that the majority were for seven days or less.[12] Faced with the absence of other alternatives, these hybrid instruments were designed to create such a multi-year foreign exchange derivative. The issuer held a long-term short position in a developing country currency for the cost of the 100 or 200 basis points per year on the principal.

The most widely known of these derivatives is called a PERL—principal exchange rate linked note. These instruments were denominated in dollars, but the value of their payments was linked to a long position in the value of a developing country currency.[13] (See Figure 7.) The compensation or premium for holding this exchange rate exposure was a higher than normal yield in comparison to a similarly rated dollar denominated note. If the foreign currency exchange rate remained fixed, or did not decline too far in value, then the higher yield would be realized. A devaluation or a substantial depreciation, however, could cause the return of the note to fall below the norm, and in the event of a major depreciation the structured note might realize a negative return.

Financial institutions in developing countries were interested in buying these hard currency denominated assets because they needed hard currency assets to match their hard currency liabilities on their balance sheets.

While it has been noted that derivatives have generally facilitated capital flows to developing economies, in this case they encouraged the reverse. When a developing economy investor or financial institution purchases a high yielding structured note such as the above example of PERLs, then the capital flow is reversed and principal is transferred to the advanced capital markets.

"Putable" debt

The largest threat to financial market stability that did not directly involve foreign exchange exposure was the use of embedded derivatives, called put options, in loan and bond debt contracts. These put options on the debt principal enabled lenders to recall their principal in the event of economic trouble. The effect was to drain the development country financial markets of liquidity just at the time it was most urgently in need.

In is not unusual for credit instruments to have attached options. Callable bonds are familiar financial instruments in advanced capital markets. They are the combination of a conventional bond and a call option that allows the issuer to recall the principal on the bond at a specified value (usually par) after some future date. Callable bonds are used by borrowers to reduce the risk that they will be locked into higher than market rates of interest on their outstanding debt. Until the 1980s, the U.S. Treasury issued callable 30-year bonds in which the principal was callable at par after 25 years. The Treasury exercised its option on several series of these bonds in the early and mid-1990s.

In the case of East Asian debt, the attached options were usually puts rather than calls. This granted the lenders, not the borrowers, the right to reclaim their

---

12. Bank for International Settlements, Central Bank Survey of Foreign Exchange and Derivatives Market Activity, 1998.

13. This long position could be in the nature of a futures contract or a short-put position.

principal. Foreign lenders attached put provisions to loans and bonds in order to reduce their risk of adverse macroeconomic conditions or other circumstances which would reduce the ability of their borrowers to repay their debts. It also reduced their exposure to increases in dollar or other hard currency interest rates. Yet another motivation involved outflanking tax and regulatory requirements because the putable loans could be treated like long-term debts even though they potentially functioned like short-term ones.

These put options were in the form of "hard" and "soft" puts. Hard puts, usually attached to a note or bond, gave the lender the right to demand principal repayment after a certain date, e.g., a five-year note might be put-able after one year. Soft puts, usually attached to loans, gave lenders the right to reschedule the terms of their credit in the event of certain adverse "events."

TABLE 2. Putable Bonds Issued from East Asia

	$ million due in 1999 or 2000
Hong Kong	$2,642
Indonesia	963
Korea	3,986
Malaysia	1,730
Thailand	<u>1,313</u>
Total	$10,634

Most of the "hard" put options were closer to the European rather than the American style option. In these cases, option holders were granted the right to exercise the option only on specific days or perhaps semiannually; in only a very few cases were the options exercisable on a continuous basis like American options.

These attached put options facilitated lending by lowered costs to borrowers and by giving lenders the assurance of obtaining some lending alternatives in the event of adverse market disruptions.

This put-able debt instrument was used widely in the rapidly growing East Asian bond market. The IMF estimated in 1999, using available public databases, that there were $32 billion in debts putable through the end of 2000 for all emerging countries. Of the total, $23 billion of this was from East Asian issuers, and $8 billion was from Brazil.[14] Of this $23 billion, $10.6 billion was in the form of bonds issued from the East Asian countries listed in Table 2.

Table 3 shows a very similar picture for the case of put options on loan contracts.

Of course a great deal has probably already been put to the borrowers since the crisis began about two years ago. Of this East Asian debt putable through 2000, $11.5 billion are notes and bonds, and $12 billion is in loans. An estimated 90% of the total putable debt was issued by private, as opposed to government, borrowers.

---

14. IMF, 1999. Involving the Private Sector in Forestalling and Resolving Financial Crises. Policy Development and Review Department. Washington, D.C. Note that the disaggregated figures in the tables do not add to $23 billion due to rounding and the exclusion of non-crisis countries such as Vietnam.

According to an IMF memo written in the summer of 1997, there were instances of the use of *both* call and put options on bond principal and coupons in East Asia. The issuer held the call option in the event that interest rates fell, and the investor held the put option in the event of a decline in the credit rating of the issuer.[15] Of course it is the put rather than the call options that pose potential problems to financial market stability in emerging economies.

TABLE 3. Loans with Put Options Issued from East Asia

	$ million due in 1999 or 2000
Hong Kong	$1,549
Indonesia	2,876
Korea	3,263
Malaysia	547
Philippines	75
Singapore	532
Thailand	1,680
Total	$10,522

*IMF, 1999. Involving the Private Sector in Forestalling and Resolving Financial Crises.

The presence of put-able debt in lending to developing economies raises several policy concerns. First, the attached put lowers the borrowing costs and this in turn encourages more borrowing and lending. Second, the tax and regulatory treatment of putable debt often incorrectly treats it as long-term debt even though it functions like short-term debt. Third, it creates liquidity shortages in the event of a financial disruption, and it does so just at the time in which liquidity is crucial for the successful functioning of the financial sector. In sum, put-able debt tends to increase indebtedness and does so in a manner that exacerbates financial disruptions.

New risks and regulatory concerns

The above sections described various derivative instruments and how they were used to facilitate capital flows to developing economies. This section analyzes their more conflicting and problematic roles.

Reducing transparency

Derivatives lead to transparency problems in two basic ways. One, they distort the meaning of balance sheets as the basis for measuring the risk profile of firms, central banks, and nation accounts. Two, when traded over-the-counter, derivatives lack adequate reporting requirements and government surveillance.

---

15. IMF Office Memorandum on private market financing for emerging markets: developments for the second quarter of 1997, July 17, 1997.

In the absence of off-balance sheet transactions like derivatives, a firm's balance sheet provides a basic picture of its risk exposure. The differences between the maturities of assets and liabilities define interest rate risk, and the differences between the currency denomination of assets and liabilities define foreign exchange rate risk. Credit risk is measured as the creditworthiness of borrowers, customers or clients with payment obligations (i.e., receivables), issuers of securities held, and counterparties to other assets.

The introduction of derivatives drives a wedge between total risk exposure and that reflected by balance sheets. Off-balance sheet exposure can reverse, exaggerate, or dwarf the risk exposure indicated by balance sheets.

For instance, a Korean corporation's balance sheet may show equal amounts of dollar assets and liabilities reflecting a neutral or balanced dollar foreign exchange position, and yet it may have derivatives that create substantially large short dollar positions off-balance sheet. The result is a delinking of an entity's risk exposure from that reflected in its balance sheets or official reports.

Accounting rules are used to calculate profits and losses, designate assets and liabilities, and determine tax liabilities and capital requirements. A recent survey of U.S. businesses reveals that 42% use derivatives primarily to "manage reported earnings" by moving income from one period to another.[16] In this case the lack of transparency results in distorted market information.

The lack of transparency caused by off-balance sheet positions is also a problem for the economic public in their efforts to assess a central bank's ability to intervene in the foreign exchange market. The ability to intervene is critical in the context of a fixed exchange rate regime, but it is also important in the context of a floating rate system in order to stabilize the economy following a speculative attack or other financial market disruption. The problem arises when a central bank accurately reports the value of its foreign reserves, but does not report the amount it has contracted to sell in the future through foreign exchange forward and swaps contracts.

This delinking of total risk exposure from balance sheets also occurs in regards to a nation's balance sheet, i.e., its balance of payments accounts. A country's actual exposure to market risk was once reflected in the maturity and currency denomination of its foreign assets and liabilities in its capital account. That is no longer the case. The currency denomination of assets and liabilities such as foreign loans can be changed with foreign exchange derivatives. Interest rate swaps can alter the interest rate exposure on assets and liabilities. Long-term loans can become short-term ones if attached "put" options are exercised. Even the form of capital or the investment vehicle can be transformed with derivatives. Total return swaps can make short-term dollar loans (liabilities) appear as portfolio investments. Also, the requirement to meet margin or collateral calls on derivatives may generate sudden, large foreign exchange flows that would not be indicated by the amount of foreign debt and securities in a nation's balance of payments

---

16. Cited in Woolley, Scott. "Night baseball without lights." *Forbes*, November 1, 1999.

accounts. As a result, the balance of payments accounts no longer serve as well to assess country risk.

David Nussbaum (1977) explains that one of the "main challenges facing the IMF due to the spread of derivatives is how to restructure the balance of payments accounting systems of its major member countries." He paraphrases David Folkerts-Landau as saying that "cross-country derivatives positions have played havoc with the balance of payments data" and that "one internal [IMF] estimate has off-balance positions potentially warping emerging market economic data by as much as 25%."

Derivatives also create transparency problems in other ways. The lack of reporting and government surveillance limits the government's and market participants' ability to assess the amount of open interest in the market, large positions held by single entities, and the adequacy of collateral and capital. This prevents a dependable assessment of the stability of these markets as well as the markets to which they are linked.

In these ways the presence of derivatives can make it difficult for firms to make an accurate assessment of their counterparties' creditworthiness. Similarly, the lack of information and data on OTC derivatives means that regulatory authorities cannot detect and deter manipulation in the immediate or related markets. In addition, the regulatory authorities cannot know outstanding positions—whether measured gross or net—of their financial sectors or major participants in the financial sector. Thus they cannot know how much risk their financial markets are exposed to in comparison to the capital on hand. As a result, it is difficult for government regulators or supervisors to track the sensitivity of the economy to changes in certain key market variables such as interest rates and exchange rates. The World Bank's Chief Economist put it very well, stating "The increased use of derivatives [in developing economies] is increasingly making the full disclosure of relevant information, or at least the full interpretation of the disclosed information, even more difficult." (Stiglitz 1998).

Outflanking regulatory safeguards

Investors sometimes use derivatives in order to outflank prudential regulations. Derivatives are used to manipulate accounting to rules in various ways, to dodge restrictions on foreign exchange exposure on financial institutions' balance sheets, and to lower required capital holdings.

Accounting rules distinguish different types of assets and receivables by their creditworthiness or credit rating. These rules assign capital charges according to their credit risk, and in some cases government regulations prohibit financial institutions from holding certain classes of assets. For example, structured notes are sometimes designed to manipulate accounting rules so that high yield notes can be treated like top rated credit instruments for the purpose of assigning capital charges. The result is that foreign exchange exposure is not treated as such for regulatory purposes. These types of structured notes have been also used to outflank U.S. regulations that prohibit institutional investors such as pension funds and insurance companies from holding foreign currency assets.

Some tax provisions are designed to enhance regulatory safeguards by raising the relative costs of certain financial activities deemed to be less productive. For instance, long-term capital gains may be taxed at a lower rate that short-term gains in order to raise the reward on long-term investing. Using derivatives, payments, receipts, and income can be shifted from one period to another. Transactions can be restructured so that they appear to occur as capital gains instead of interest payments (or vice versa), or as long-term capital gains instead of short-term ones. This problem is doubly important for developing economies whose tax bases are not well established, and where threats to their tax bases can put fiscal pressures on the government that can lead to monetary expansion or greater foreign borrowing.

The use of derivatives to circumvent or outflank prudential regulation has been acknowledged by the IMF, World Bank, and the OECD amongst others. The IMF's David Folkerts-Landau stated, "Financial restrictions on such positions [domestic equity markets] are being circumvented through derivatives transactions."[17] The World Bank's Global Development Finance 2000 stated it in the following way, "Brazil's complex system of prudential safeguards was easily circumvented by well-developed financial market and over-the-counter derivatives." The point was similarly stated in an OECD Economics Department Working Paper by Blondal and Christiansen, "The expansion of financial derivatives, which regulators have found difficult to control, has also seriously undermined prudential controls on currency exposure."

Another problem is the tendency for derivatives to be used to raise the level of risk relative to capital. This can occur even within the regulatory structure. Derivatives are designed to create price exposure so that risk can be transferred from one party to another without the expense of transferring title and principal as required to buy or short-sell. If the initial payment is thought of as equity or capital, then the size of the notional principal in comparison to capital is the degree of leverage in the derivative instrument. This leverage allows investors to assume far greater degrees of risk per dollar of capital than would be available by purchasing the asset outright or even borrowing in order to purchase the asset outright.

Leverage is a double-edged sword. Leverage enables derivatives to offer a more efficient use of capital for hedging or investing, and at the same time it reduces the amount of capital backing a given amount of price exposure (i.e., the size of a position). Raising the risk-capital ratio weakens the stability of each investor, and in turn it increases everyone else's exposure to the repercussions from investor failure. In short, it increases system risk.

In order to illustrate the point, consider an example of a Thai bank choosing between an outright $100 million purchase of a Thai corporate security (financed by borrowing abroad) or entering a $100 million total return swap in which the same security's return is swapped against LIBOR. The purchased securities would be treated as an asset on its balance sheet and receive a capital charge. At a capitalization rate of

---

17. Quoted in David Nussbaum, "Seeing is Believing." *Institutional Investor*, September 1997.

8%, this would require $8 million in capital. Alternatively, the swap, which takes the same investment position off-balance sheet, would not be assessed a capital charge. Off-balance sheet items are assessed a capital charge based on their market value. Swaps are initially transacted "at the market" or at par which means their present value is zero; therefore they are neither in the money[18] nor out of the money. At the market value of zero, swaps are assessed no capital charge. Once a swap moves into the money, a firm would be required to hold capital against the amount of its fair market value. However, the capital charge would only reflect the degree to which it moved into the money. If the position increased in value to $10 million dollars (10% of its notional value), then the capital charge would be $0.8 million compared to the outright purchase which would now be worth $110 million and its capital requirement would amount to $8.8 million.

A more subtle illustration can be drawn from the above example of structured notes called "PERLs." The note would have a rate of return above a similarly rated AAA dollar note because the attached derivative position amounts to the sale of a put whose premium pays for the higher yield. The investor captures a higher yield on the same principle, but from a public interest concern the firm has taken on more market risk without a commensurate change to its capital requirement.

Increasing systemic risk by raising the risk-capital ratio throughout the financial system and the economy as a whole is matter of public concern and provides the economic basis for government's regulatory role to protect the national peace and security. Even if a government were to reject policies of protecting foolish investors from themselves, that government would not be acting inconsistently to be concerned with protecting everyone else from the fools.

This concern has come to the attention of the IMF. An IMF report from 1999 stated, "Third, the growing use of OTC derivatives and structured notes is increasing the ability of institutions to leverage up capital positions. The high levels of leverage may be creating financial systems that are capable of making costlier mistakes during periods of euphoria (exacerbating the boom) and that can magnify the adverse consequences of a negative shock or a reappraisal of risk."[19]

Threatening the stability of fixed exchange rate systems

The presence of a market for foreign exchange derivatives can undermine the stability of a fixed exchange rate system in several ways.

Derivatives provide greater leverage (lower capital costs) and lower transactions costs for investors taking a position against the success of the fixed exchange rate. Such investors are often referred to as speculators, attackers, or hedge fund operators. Lowering the costs of betting against the fixed exchange rate will only encourage this behavior and strengthen the effects those efforts. The greater the volume of positions that are short the currency, i.e., against the

---

18. The term "in the money" means a positive fair market value of the position.
19. IMF, International Capital Markets. 1999.

fixed rate regime, the greater the necessary size of central bank intervention or interest rate hikes needed to defend the currency peg.

The presence of foreign exchange markets means that the central bank is faced with the greater task of having to peg the exchange rate in two markets: the spot markets, and the forward or swap market for foreign currency. Whereas the spot market is generally large in relation to the amount of foreign reserves at the central bank, and thus the central bank's potential for intervention is small in regards to the overall size of the market, the size of the derivatives market is unlimited. Together they increase the critical size for a successful central bank intervention.

Another problem posed by the presence of foreign exchange derivatives markets is that price discovery process in those markets will, under many circumstances, indicate a future devaluation. There are two reasons for this. First, interest rates in developing countries are in most circumstances higher than in advanced capital market or developed economies. This interest rate differential means that the equilibrium forward or swap rate will always be higher than the spot rate—thus indicating that the currency will depreciate at the same rate as the interest rate differential. Second, if the credit market in the developing country is not perfectly efficient, then foreign exchange market makers will not provide forward and swap contracts at rates that do not include a market risk premium.[20] If a market risk premium is added to the interest rate differential, then the forward and swap rates will indicate a greater rate of depreciation.

Quickening and deepening the crisis

In the event of a devaluation or a sharp downturn in securities prices, derivatives such as foreign exchange forwards and swaps and total return swaps function to quicken the pace and deepen the impact of the crisis.

Derivatives transactions with emerging market financial institutions generally involve strict collateral or margin requirements. East Asian firms swapping the total rate of return on a local security against LIBOR were posting U.S. dollars or Treasury securities as collateral; the rate of collateralization was estimated at around 20% of the national principal of the swap.

If the market value of the swap position were to decline, then the East Asian firm would have to add to its collateral in order to bring it up to the required maintenance level. Thus a sharp fall in the price of the underlying security, such as would occur at the beginning of a devaluation or broader financial crisis, would require the East Asian firm to immediately add U.S. dollar assets to its collateral in proportion to the loss in the present value of its swap position. This would trigger an immediate outflow of foreign currency reserves as local currency and other assets were exchanged into dollars in order to meet their collateral requirements. This would not only quicken the pace of the crisis, it would also

---

20. Market makers use the credit market to create synthetic short positions in order to lay off their exposure in offering short forward and swap positions in the market. They borrow in the local currency, buy the hard currency with the proceeds, and they invest in hard currency assets for the maturity of the forward or swap.

deepen the impact of the crisis by putting further downward pressure on the exchange rate and asset prices, thus increasing the losses to the financial sector.

As an indication of the potential magnitude of these collateral outflows, Garber and Lall (1966) cite the IMF and "industry sources" which reported that Mexican banks held $16 billion in tesabono total return swaps at the time of the devaluation of the Mexican peso. The authors calculated that the initial peso devaluation depressed the value of tesabonos by 15%, and that this would have required the delivery of $2.4 billion in collateral the next day. This would explain about half of the $5 billion dollars of foreign reserves lost by the Mexican central bank the day after devaluation. In this way, collateral or margin calls on derivatives can accelerate the pace of a financial crisis, and the greater leverage that derivatives provide can also multiply the size of the losses and thereby deepen the crisis.

Increasing systemic risk and the risk of contagion

The Bank of International Settlement's report known as the "Lamfalussy Report" defined systemic risk as "the risk that the illiquidity or failure of one institution, and its resulting inability to meet its obligations when due, will lead to the illiquidity or failure of other institutions."[21] Similarly, contagion is the term established in the wake of the East Asian financial crisis of 1997 to describe the tendency of a financial crisis in one country to adversely affect the financial markets in other, and sometimes seemingly unrelated, economies. It is the notion of systemic risk taken to the level of national and international markets. The term "contagion" amounts to a more dry, clinical variation of the term "tequila effect" which was used to described the spreading effects of the 1994 Mexican peso crisis.

The presence of a large volume of derivatives transactions in an economy creates the possibility of a rapid expansion of counterparty credit risk during periods of economic stress. These credit risks might then become actual delinquent counterparty debts and obligations during an economic crisis.

The implication is that even if derivatives are used to reduce exposure to market risk, they might still lead to an increase in credit risk. For example, a bank lending through variable rate loans might decide to reduce its exposure to short-term interest rate variability, thus the volatility of its income, by entering into an interest rate swap as the variable rate receiver. If short-term rates were to rise, then the fair market value of the bank's swap position would rise, and thus would increase the bank's gross counterparty credit exposure above that already associated with the loans which were being hedged.

In so far that derivatives increase counterparty credit exposure throughout the economy, they increase the impact of one entity becoming unable to fulfill its obligations. And to the extent that derivatives are not used to reduce firms' exposure market, then the greater leverage brought to speculative investments

---

21. Bank for International Settlements (BIS). Report of the Committee on Interbank Netting Schemes of the Central Banks of the Group of Ten Countries. Basel, 1990.

increases the likelihood of such a failure. In this way derivatives contribute to the level of systemic risk in the financial system.

The presence of derivatives can also increase the global financial system's exposure to contagion through two channels. Regarding the first, derivatives can spread the stress or crisis in one country to another because of the international nature of markets. Many derivatives involve cross-border counterparties, and thus losses of market value and credit rating in one country will affect counterparties in other countries. The second channel of contagion comes from the practice of financial institutions responding to a downturn in one market by selling in another. One reason firms sell in other markets is because they need additional funds to purchase liquid G5 currency denominated assets to meet collateral or capital requirements. In order to obtain these assets,[22] firms will make a portfolio shift and sell securities in other markets. This demand for collateral assets can be sudden and sizable when there are large swings in financial markets, and thus this source of contagion can be especially fast and strong. Neftci (1998) discusses how OTC derivatives such as total return swaps contribute to contagion in this way.

Complicating post-crisis policy making

The process of policy formation was much more straightforward in the wake of the 1980s' debt crisis. The borrowers were mostly governments, and the private lenders were the large money center banks. This meant that a single representative borrower for each debtor country[23] was therefore represented by a single borrower, and the key lenders could be gathered into a single room. Together with the relevant multilateral institutions, all the parties could negotiate a plan to restructure debt payments.

The policy making process became much more complicated in the 1990s. There were many different private and public debtors and issuers of securities. There were many investors and many different types of claims on parties in the effected developing countries. Capital flows in the form of stocks, bonds and structured notes meant that there were hundreds of major investors and millions of lesser investors. These claims were all the more complicated because of derivative contracts. Derivatives added to both the number of potential counterparties and raised problems as to who held the first claim on outstanding debts and other obligations.

Moreover, losses on derivatives are not the same as late payments on loans. Debt payment problems do not necessarily have to result in losses to either side. Some loan payment problems are short-term liquidity problems that can be solved by merely restructuring the loan payment schedule. Derivatives losses, in contrast, are already lost and cannot be mitigated. These loses must be paid immediately, although the payments can feasibly be financed by acquiring additional

---

22. Collateral for OTC derivatives is generally required to be in the form of G5 currencies or their Treasury securities, except for Japanese Treasury securities.

23. In some countries, such as Mexico, part of the foreign debt was owed by local or regional governments. However the national government assumed responsibility in debt negotiations.

debt. What is more, changes in market interest rates and exchange rates can cause derivatives losses to occur more suddenly, accumulate more quickly and sum to greater magnitudes than the losses associated with dollar denominated variable rate bank loans.

Summary and lessons

Derivatives play a two-fold role in the economy. They provide a useful role in hedging and risk management so as to facilitate capital flows to developing economies. At the same time, however, they create the conditions for the possibility for raising risk in relation to capital through leveraging and by dodging prudential regulatory safeguards. They can also make fixed exchange rate systems less stable, and then later quicken the pace and deepen the impact of a devaluation once it occurs. This functions to increase the systemic risk in financial markets and raises the possibility of spreading contagion amongst economies. In the wake of the crisis they can make the process of post-crisis recovery policy making even more difficult.

There are several policy lessons for financial market regulation. The accounting rules, capital requirements, and risk-management requirements of financial institutions must be updated to address the potential role played by derivatives in undermining their intended goal of functioning as regulatory safeguards in the financial system. This means that credit evaluations should consider market risk as well as credit risk. The capital requirement for off-balance sheet items should reflect their market risk and not simply their credit risk. The restriction on foreign exchange exposure should apply equally well to off-balance sheet items as to items on the balance sheet. Derivatives markets, both exchange traded and over-the-counter, must become more transparent by reporting requirements for transactions (price, volume and contract type), open interest (especially large open positions), and collateral and margin standards. Overall, the implication for regulatory policy is that derivatives regulations must contain provisions that shape the structure of the incentives for derivatives trading so that they will be used in proper ways to facilitate capital flows without their being used in destructive ways to increase risk-to-capital and out-maneuvering government safeguards.

REFERENCES

Bank for International Settlements (BIS). 1990. *Report of the Committee on Interbank Netting Schemes of the Central Banks of the Group of Ten Countries* (known as the Lamfalussy Report). Basel, May.

_____. 1996. *Central Bank Survey of Foreign Exchange and Derivatives Market Activity 1995*. Basel, May.

_____. 1998 *Central Bank Survey of Foreign Exchange and Derivatives Market Activity 1998*. Basel.

Bank for International Settlements (BIS). 1998. *OTC Derivatives: Settlement Procedures and Counterparty Risk Management*. Basel (September).

Bloendal, Sveinbjorern, and Hans Christiansen. 1999. "The Recent Experience with Capital Flows to Emerging Market Economies." OECD Working Paper #211 (February).

Bodnar, Gordon M. and Gunther Gebhardt. 1998. "Derivatives Usage in risk Management by US and German Non-Financial Firms: a Comparative Survey." NBER Working Paper #6705.

Brown, Stephen, J. Goetzmann, and James Park. 1998. "Hedge funds and the Asian Currency Crisis or 1997," NBER Working Paper 6427 (February).

Chew, Lillian. 1996. *Managing Derivatives Risk*.

Chrystal, John. 1996. "Using Derivative Products to Lower Borrowing Costs." *Latin Finance, Latin Derivatives Supplement* (January/February).

Clow, Robert. 1998. "Risk Rediscovered." *Risk Magazine* (October).

_____.1999. "Safety First." *Institutional Investor* (February).

Cole, Harold and Timothy Kehoe. 1996. "Self-fulfilling Debt Crises." Federal Reserve Bank of Minneapolis, Staff Report 211 (December).

Corsetti, Giancarlo, et al. 1998. "What Caused the Asian Currency and Financial Crisis?" manuscript (September).

_____. 1998. "Paper tigers? A Model of the Asian Crisis." manuscript (September).

Dalla, Ismail & Deena Khathkate. 1997. "The Emerging East Asian Bond Market," IMF-World Bank Finance & Development (December 4).

Edwards, Franklin. 1994. "System risk in OTC Derivativs Markets: Much Ado About Not too Much." Columbia University Business School Working Paper 94–17..

Eichengreen, Barry and Donald Mathieson. 1998. "Hedge Funds and Financial Markets: Implications for Policy," in Eichengreen et al., *Hedge funds and Financial Market Dynamics*. IMF Occasional Paper 166. IMF, Washington D.C..

Figlewski, Stephen. 1997. "Derivatives Risks, Old and New," in Robert E. Litan and Anthony M. Santomero, eds., *Brookings-Wharton Papers on Financial Services*. Washington, D.C.: Brookings Institution Press.

Folkerts-Landau, David. 1994. *The Wild Bear of Derivatives*. Oxford Press.

Folkerts-Landau, David, and Peter Garber. 1997. "Derivative Markets and Financial System Soundness," in Charles Enoch and John Green, eds., *Banking Soundness and Monetary Policy*, IMF, Washington, D.C.

Garber, Peter. 1996. "Managing Risks to Financial Markets from Volatile Capital Flows: the Role of Prudential Regulation," *International Journal of Economics*, Vol. 1 (July).

_____. 1998. *Derivatives in International Capital Flow*, NBER Working Paper #6623 (June).

Garber, Peter and Michael Spencer. 1995. "Foreign Exchange Hedging with Synthetic Options and the Interest Rate Defense of a Fixed Exchange Rate System." IMF Staff Papers, Vol. 42, No. 3 (September).

Garber, Peter and Subir Lall. 1996. "Derivative Products in Exchange Rate Crises," in Reuven Glick, ed., *Managing Capital Flows and Exchange Rates: Perspectives from the Pacific Basin*, Cambridge University Press. (Prepared for Federal Reserve Bank of San Francisco conference.)

Goldstein, Morris, David Folkerts-Landau, Liliana Rojas-Suarez, and Michael Spencer. 1993. *International Capital Markets*, Part I. IMF (April).

Gordon, Gary and Richard Rosen. 1995. "Banks and Derivatives." NBER Working Paper 5100.

Grant, Jeremy. 1998. "Concern: Hidden risks in Credit Derivatives." *Financial Times* (November 2).

IMF memorandum. 1997. *Private Market Financing for Emerging Markets: Developments for the Second Quarter 1997.*

Jordan, Bradford and Susan Jordan. 1991. "Salomon Brothers and the May 1991 Treasury Auction: Analysis of a Market Corner." *Journal of Banking and Finance.* Vol. 20, No. 1, pp. 25–40.

Kregel, J. A. 1998. "East Asia is Not Mexico: The Difference Between Balance of Payments Crises and Debt Deflations." Jerome Levy Economics Institute Working Paper 235.

_____. 1998. "Derivatives and Global Capital Flows: Applications to Asia." *Cambridge Journal of Economics*, Vol. 22, No. 6, pp. 677–692 (November).

Lall, Subir. 1997. "Speculative Attacks, Forward Market Intervention and the Classic Bear Squeeze." IMF Working Paper (June).

Lee, Jang-Yung. 1997. "Sterilizing Capital Flows." IMF Economic Issues No. 7.

Loomis, Carol. 1995. "Cracking the Derivatives Case." *Fortune* (March 20).

Markham, Jerry W. 1994. "'Confederate bonds,' 'General Custer,' and the Regulation of Derivative Financial Instruments." Seton Hall Law Review.

McClintock, Brent. 1996. "International Financial Instability and the Financial Derivatives Market." *Journal of Economic Issues* 30(1) (March).

Neftci, Salih N. 1998. "FX Short Positions, Balance Sheets and Financial Turbulence: An Interpretation of the Asian Financial Crisis." CEPA Working Paper #11 (October).

Nussbaum, David. 1997. "Seeing is Believing." *Institutional Investor* (September).

Partnoy, Frank. 1999. *F.I.A.S.C.O.: The Inside Story of a Wall Street Trader.* New York: Penguin.

Rotberg, Eugene. 1995. "Derivatives: The Ultimate Freudian Slip-Up." Lecture at the Jerome Levy Institute (April 7).

Saunderson, Emily. 1997. "Derivatives Aid Development." *Institutional Investor*, September.

Smithson, Charles W., Clifford W. Smith, Jr., and D. Sykes Wilford. 1995. *Managing Financial Risk.* Irwin, New York.

Stiglitz, Joseph. 1998. "Sound Finance and Sustainable Development in Asia." World Bank Group, keynote address to Asia Development Forum (March 12).

Swaps Monitor, edited by Paul Spraul.

Thorbeeke, Willem. 1995. "Financial Derivatives: harnessing the Benefits and containing the Dangers." Jerome Levy Economics Institute Working Paper 145 (August).

World Bank. 1998, 1999, 2000. "Global Development Finance Report."

18

. . .

Procyclicality of
Regulatory Ratios?

*Philip Turner**

"PROCYCLICALITY" HAS BECOME something of a buzzword in recent discussions about regulatory ratios. The feeling that banks have accentuated economic cycles in the emerging markets has been nurtured by the experience of recent crises. Massive increases in bank lending fuel rapid and unsuitable growth and, when the recession comes, the machine goes into reverse. In almost every recent crisis in the emerging markets, sharp contractions in bank lending appear to have made bad recessions worse. This note looks briefly at one aspect of this: how far the bank regulatory system contributes to this procyclicality. Four distinct aspects are identified for consideration.

The question of the procyclicality has several aspects. One concerns the timing of any tightening of capital rules—usually after a crisis when bank lending is in any case being curtailed. A second possible element is a supposed regulatory bias in favor of short-term lending, rather than long-term lending—which means that emerging markets are more vulnerable in a downturn. Another concerns the inherent cyclicality of any invariant minimum capital ratio. A final aspect is that capital ratios themselves could move in a procyclical way—the proposed use of credit rating agencies could

* The opinions ventured in this note do not necessarily reflect the views of the BIS. Thanks are due to Pierre Cailleteau, Bill Coen, Karl Cordewener, Craig Furfine, John Hawkins and Bill White for helpful comments and to Emma Warrack for an orderly document.

lead to this. A key philosophical question that lies behind the whole issue of cyclicality is how far financial institutions (and those who supervise them) should use discretion in following current (and cyclical) market prices.

TIMING OF TIGHTENING CAPITAL RULES

The timing of measures to tighten capital or loan classification rules is bound to be controversial. It has been argued that regulatory rules should not be tightened when macroeconomic conditions are adverse because the very sharp change in reported bad loans that would result might undermine confidence. In practice, most countries allow a phase-in period for the tightening of prudential ratios or in dealing with generalized problems. For instance, U.S. money center banks whose loans to heavily indebted countries exceeded their capital in the early 1980s were allowed several years to adjust—but there was no doubt that they would have to adjust. The Basel Accord itself, published in July 1988, envisaged a transitional period to the end of 1992 (backed up with an interim standard to be met by the end of 1990). Following the recent crisis, several Asian countries have established timetables for meeting specified capital standards or for adopting realistic rules for loan-loss provisioning. In Thailand, for instance, tighter requirements for loan-loss provisioning are being phased in over a two-to-three year transitional period. As each deadline during this period is reached, additional capital can be required.

One consideration that often tells against tightening capital rules too abruptly is the reluctance to take banks into state ownership—which in effect occurs if the full and immediate recognition of losses wipes out a bank's capital and the government injects new equity. In countries with efficient state institutions that are not susceptible to corruption and with a well-established tradition of keeping economic activity in the private sector, a temporary state takeover of a private bank may work well (as in Sweden, for example). But in countries where these preconditions are not satisfied (or in countries which have only recently managed to privatize their banks), it may be better to leave the bank with the original owners who may be more likely than government-appointed administrators to implement the necessary restructuring, ensure that loans are extended on commercial criteria, and keep up the pressure to collect on bad loans. If so, there may be a tactical case for not forcing shareholders to fully or immediately write down the losses incurred.

None the less, it is important to make clear that any departure from normal prudential norms decided upon in exceptional times is temporary. There should be a commitment to meet normal standards according to some explicit timetable. And because temporary forbearance can be effective only if it does not damage confidence, it must be accompanied by measures that build confidence in the long-run viability of the banking system. For instance, any protection granted to the stronger banks should be accompanied by urgent measures to close or restructure the weakest banks.

REGULATORY BIAS TOWARDS SHORT-TERM LENDING?

Under the present Accord, international interbank lending of up to one year maturity has a 20% risk-weight irrespective of country. As interbank lending of more than one year to non-OECD countries carries a 100% risk weight, short-term lending to non-OECD countries may be encouraged at the expense of long-term lending. One possible consequence of this distinction is that bank lending to emerging markets is "too" short-term, and thus more subject to cyclical forces. While a lower risk weight for short-term lending than for long-term lending may make sense for the lending of an individual bank (which is the focus of the supervisors), it makes less sense if *all* banks lend short-term so that the borrower is vulnerable to a sudden loss in liquidity. In other words, the systemic (or macro) considerations may to some extent run counter to supervisory (or micro) considerations.

How important this effect has proved in practice is open to question. Simple calculations suggest that the rule is unlikely to add more than 100 basis points to the charge for a long-term loan over a short-term loan.[1] A second consideration is that a bank that holds capital above the regulatory minimum need not be constrained by officially-imposed risk weights—it may attach a lower risk weight for short-term lending on the basis of its own risk procedures. Informal enquiries made of banks and empirical studies have not resolved the question of the quantitative importance of the 20%/100% distinction.

At any event, the consultative document proposes to considerably soften this distinction. Under one option (where risk weighting depends on the rating of the bank rather than the sovereign risk rating), claims on banks of short original maturity (e.g., less than six months) will receive a risk weight one notch lower than for longer maturities.

PROCYCLICALITY ARISING FROM MINIMUM CAPITAL RATIOS

The third aspect concerns the possible procyclicality of capital ratios. Loan losses tend to rise in a recession. To the extent that they are not covered by loan provisions (and in practice these usually prove inadequate), such losses will lead to capital write-offs. If capital ratios then fall near or even below the required minimum, banks will have to raise new capital or reduce assets with high risk weights, especially loans. Because raising capital is difficult in a recession, banks are likely

---

1. For example, if a bank borrows at 4% and has a cost of capital of 20% (to choose a number at the high end of the range), then the additional cost of a longer-term loan is $0.08*(1-0.2)*(20-4) = 1.02\%$. (This assumes banks would not set aside more capital of their own accord for longer-term lending.) Bonte et al. (1999, p. 24) compare the proportion of lending with maturity under one year to OECD economies with that to non-OECD economies with similar ratings. This suggested there was some effect among higher-rated borrowing economies but little among lower-rated ones (but it is based on a fairly small sample).

to choose the second option and cut lending. There is strong evidence that banks do indeed act in this way.[2]

One ad hoc response to this problem is to set the required capital ratio higher when output is above trend. In practice, of course, it is often very difficult to identify the true cyclical position.[3] Furthermore, it would be even more complicated to translate it to cyclically adjusted ratios for individual banks because banks lend to various sectors and thus have different exposures to cyclical conditions. For these reasons, any rigid rule relating capital to cyclical position is probably not feasible. But something could be done in more flexible ways. For instance, the supervisory review pillar proposed in the Basel Committee's consultative document could encourage banks to take account of cyclical influences in assessing their capital adequacy needs.

The ideal response to procyclicality is for provisions made for possible loan losses (i.e., subtracted from equity capital in the books of the bank) to cover normal cyclical risks. If done correctly, provisions built up in good times can be used in bad times without necessarily affecting reported capital.[4] To ensure this, and because all loans have some risk of loss, it is important to maintain some general provisioning that applies to all loans. But there are some possible impediments when it comes to the practice.

The first stumbling block is that tax laws often severely limit the tax deductibility of precautionary provisioning and may insist on evidence that losses have actually occurred. This is important because loan loss provisions increase internal funding for the bank only to the extent that they reduce taxes. This problem is complex (ministries of finance generally view any narrowing of the tax base with scepticism), but does require attention.

A second possible stumbling block may be the securities laws. For example, the SEC in the United States has argued that precautionary provisioning distorts financial reports and may mislead investors. These are legitimate concerns. Allowing banks to build up reserves to cover possible losses that are not foreseen in any detail may prove difficult to square with the demands of having well-documented accounting because the decision on how much reserves to set aside is inherently judgmental. Too much discretionary accounting would allow banks to smooth earnings over time and perhaps delay the revelation of developing problems.

A third possible stumbling block is that the management of banks may be too eager to report strong improvements in earnings during booms (and so too

---

2. See Jackson et al. (1999). It might, however, be noted that capital requirements do incorporate one significant aspect that makes capital ratios less procyclical: the fact that loans to the private sector carry a 100% risk weight while government bonds have a 0% risk weight. In a recession, banks tend to replace some loans with government bonds which lowers the measure of risk-weighted assets and so reduces the capital required.

3. Japan's problems in the 1990s dramatically illustrate this point. The weakening of growth in early 1992 was at the time regarded as a cyclical downturn in an economy with an underlying growth rate of around 4%. With the benefit of hindsight it was the early stage of a decade when growth would only average 1½% a year.

4. Under the Basel Capital Accord, loan loss provisions can count as tier 2 capital.

reluctant during good times to make adequate provisions for losses). The present wave of takeovers in the banking industry may accentuate this eagerness: good reported earnings and high share prices serve to fend off takeovers.

PROCYCLICAL CAPITAL RATIOS: DANGER OF USING CREDIT RATING AGENCIES?

The 1988 Capital Accord is under major review. Under that Accord, the risk weight for sovereign entities is basically decided by OECD membership, and this approach is also reflected in the risk weights for banks. All corporates receive a single risk weight of 100%. These ratings were not cyclically sensitive—indeed one frequent criticism of them is that they are not sufficiently risk responsive.

The recent consultative paper (Basel Committee, 1999) envisages a major overhaul of this approach based on greater reliance on "credit assessment agencies"—a deliberately broad expression to encompass export insurance agencies, credit registers, and market data, as well as credit-rating agencies. But it is credit-rating agencies that have attracted the most attention. The possible risk weights for *sovereigns* (based on S&P's ratings) are shown in Table 1. The risk weighting for *banks* will, under one possible option, be one notch higher than the weighting of its home country. Top-quality *corporates* will receive a 20% risk weighting, while corporates with a very low rating will receive a 150% weighting. All other corporates will continue to be weighted at 100%.

Most would be wary of putting too much emphasis on the assessment of credit-rating agencies. Their performance during the Asian crises certainly suggests a marked cyclicality: while they did not downgrade Asian countries pre-crisis (when imbalances were developing), their downgrades in the midst of the crisis—especially when they brought Korean, Indonesian, and Thai bonds to non-investment grade—made the crisis worse. Perhaps the most damning criticism is that the rating agencies were *backward-looking* rather than *forward-looking* in their assessments. For instance, there is evidence that credit ratings of countries exhibit a strong negative correlation with the real effective exchange rates.[5] This means that depreciation in the wake of a crisis typically leads to a downgrade—whereas a *forward-looking* approach (e.g., as applied in much of the recent work on indicators of vulnerability) would recognize a more competitive exchange rate as a source of medium-term strength, not weakness.

One particular danger of reliance on external credit assessment agencies is that developing countries that are downgraded in a crisis would be hit twice: once via higher risk-weights used by international lending banks and secondly via higher risk-weights for domestic bank lending to major corporations which also may be downgraded in a crisis. A second reservation is that making greater use of ratings could tempt the raters to be more lenient. Finally, the development of corporate

---

5. Monfort and Mulder (1999).

TABLE 1. Risk weightings for emerging economies

Credit rating	Risk weight	Unchanged* 1997–99	As at June 97	As at June 98	As at Dec. 99
AAA to AA-	0%	Singapore Taiwan	Korea		
A+ to A-	20%	Chile Czech Rep. Hong Kong	Malaysia Thailand	Malaysia	
BBB+ to BBB-	50%	China Colombia Hungary Poland	Indonesia Colombia	Thailand Colombia	Korea Malaysia Thailand
BB+ to B-	100%	Argentina Brazil India Mexico Peru Philippines South Africa Turkey	Russia	Korea	Colombia
below B-	150%			Indonesia	Indonesia Russia

*In some cases, the rating has changed by a notch or two but not enough to imply a change in risk weighting.

Sources: Basel Committee (1999), Standard & Poor's.

ratings is quite uneven across countries—and because there may be a tendency to rate newly-rated entities conservatively (i.e., on the low side), those without a history of credit rating may be placed at a transitional disadvantage.

Nevertheless, the recent proposals represent a major improvement on present practice which is rather arbitrary. The aim should be to rely on credit assessments that have a long-term focus (i.e., "see through" economic cycles) and which can therefore exert a stabilizing influence. It is possible that export insurance agencies and the official credit registers that exist in some countries do indeed have a more appropriate long-term focus. As Bonte et al. (1999) have observed, an expanded regulatory use of external ratings needs to be carefully researched.

One subject for reflection is how quickly a change in credit rating should be reflected in the regulatory risk weight. On the new proposed scale, for instance, loans to the Korean government would have gone from a zero risk weight in 1997 to a 100% risk weight in 1998 only to go back to 50% in 1999 (Table 1). However, it is sometimes overlooked that there is nothing in the Basel Committee's consultative document to say that changes in credit ratings have to be immediately reflected in risk weights. Indeed, the need to mitigate procyclicality might suggest a case for phasing in very gradually any change in risk weights resulting from a change in credit ratings. If the phase-in period were long relative to the length of the economic cycle, then procyclicality might be mitigated. But there is of course a trade-off: such smoothing devices weaken the link between risk and capital weights—yet the whole point of the recent proposals is to make Basel Accord rules more risk sensitive. And it is not clear how effective these devices would be in practice. Expectations are important, and the knowledge that a country's "ultimate" risk weighting has gone up might have an immediate impact on banks' decisions irrespective of any phase-in period and might, in addition, affect the market value of the exposed bank.

Perhaps an added danger of a reliance on any small number of credit assessors (e.g., a credit rating agency) in assessing risk is that it could narrow the diversity of opinions and so could increase the degree and spread of procyclicality. For instance, a downgrade by a major agency could trigger sudden and simultaneous attempts by all banks to cut their exposure. If instead very many banks are independently assessing risk, the chances of imposing progressive discipline on a country running into trouble—rather than provoking a sudden discontinuous drying up of foreign inflows—are greatly enhanced. For this reason, the fragmentation of risk assessment across many different banks and other institutions may help the market mechanism to work more smoothly.[6]

These considerations suggest putting greater reliance on banks' own internal rating mechanisms, as the Basel Committee has recently proposed. Internal ratings are of course easier to apply to corporations where there are data on credit history (so that default probabilities can be calculated) than to sovereigns. The greater use of internal ratings may well offer one of the more promising avenues for avoiding putting too much weight on rating agencies.

FOLLOWING THE MARKET VERSUS DISCRETION: A FUNDAMENTAL DILEMMA

However, lurking behind widely-held reservations about the performance of credit rating agencies is a still more fundamental problem—the fact that market prices are themselves cyclical. Asset prices rise and credit spreads typically narrow with the cycle. If lending institutions "follow the market," their behaviour will also be procyclical. Moreover, the time horizon for banks' credit assessments tends to be rather short, with the probability of default on a loan being calculated over a near-term horizon (e.g., over one year) rather than over the whole cycle. And many quantitative models of credit risk tend to extrapolate recent history (so that low current rates of default tend to lead to low expected default rates). This

---

6. A similar conclusion is reached by Morris and Shin's (1999) analysis of market mechanisms where outcomes depend on what others do, which can in simple models lead to multiple equilibria. They argue that when there are disparities in the information available to participants, the indeterminacy is largely removed.

can be made worse by the "herding" of financial institutions, all using very similar risk management techniques.

This raises a key dilemma for both the private and the public sectors. In making judgments of valuation and risk, how closely should a financial institution follow the dictates of the market? How much discretion should it apply? It is important to understand that the various mechanisms that are often proposed to address the dilemma in effect replace (partially or completely) current market prices by some other prices: (1) Value collateral at a discount on current market prices (perhaps at a cyclically adjusted discount—some supervisory authorities, for instance, reduce loans-to-value ratios during a boom). (2) Credit risk models could put greater emphasis on variables covering macroeconomic or financial overextension and the consequent threat to current prices. (3) The time horizon for default calculations could be extended, perhaps involving the calculation of the present discounted value of future expected losses. (4) Use could be made of stress tests that allow for unfavourable scenarios ("how will this loan look in a recession?"). These techniques are easy to state, but are hard to implement in practice because macroeconomic developments are uncertain, borrowers are affected differentially by cyclical developments, and so on.

Once the dilemma is stated in this way, the complexity of the issue becomes evident. The main cause of procyclical behaviour by financial institutions lies in the procyclicality of markets. Correcting this, while ensuring that financial institutions respond to market signals (essential for efficiency), is a formidable challenge. What might help is to intensify supervisory oversight during booms, rather than during recessions (when the problems are usually revealed). In addition, those responsible for the oversight of the financial system as a whole need to monitor carefully any instances of "herding" when financial institutions all take on the same exposures—e.g., real estate, high-tech companies—and thus magnify the aggregate risks.

CONCLUSION

The question of the procyclicality of regulatory ratios is an important one, to which there is no easy answer. It is clear that financial markets are themselves cyclical. The financial system can amplify shocks of all kinds, including cyclical ones, and can do so irrespective of the regulatory system in place. A question to ask of any supervisory framework is whether it exacerbates or lessens this potential amplification of shocks. The issues that have been raised in this note can be distilled into four sub-questions, to which only partial answers can be given.

1. Do rules decided on micro grounds make sense on macro grounds? Supervisors have much experience in designing effective "micro rules"—that is, for individual institutions. Such rules can be refined from long experience with many thousands of enterprises. But there is an aggregation problem: a rule that makes sense for an individual institution may not make sense in aggregate. Taking account of macro aspects is therefore one key challenge.

2. Do rules introduce destabilizing discontinuities? One well-known example is risk weight matrices which mean a small change in credit standing can lead to a large jump in capital requirements. If a change of ratings moves a borrower across one of these thresholds, then a sudden withdrawal of funds can be triggered, even though the change in underlying risk assessment is rather modest. The answer to this is to construct more sophisticated approaches that allow the smooth graduation of risk assessment and measurement.

3. What can public policy do to encourage diversity of opinion among financial institutions? This old issue (Keynes's beauty contest metaphor) has been given new life by the rise of rating agencies and quantitative risk management techniques. The public sector should be wary of doing anything that encourages blind reliance on rating agencies, value-at-risk models, or indeed any specific formula that could encourage "herding" among financial institutions. Proper risk assessment requires judgment, and differences of perspective are healthy.

4. Are other public policy interests blocking reforms that would make the financial system safer? Any prospective adjustment of the regulatory system has to face the fact that there are several distinct public policy interests whose perspectives on potential reforms can differ. In some cases, desirable reforms may be blocked or unnecessarily delayed. This paper noted several such impediments to the frequently proposed response to procyclicality that banks should build up general provisions in good times to be drawn down in bad times. Resolving such conflicts is never easy because it involves the balancing of several (possibly conflicting) objectives. In the international arena, however, the creation of the Financial Stability Forum should help by ensuring different public policy interests "talk to each other" about contentious issues. This is a major step forward.

Yet the complexity of addressing procyclicality should not be underestimated. There is no reason to think that the public sector is any more able to forecast the cycle than is the private sector. At the same time, the market has many shortcomings. Market prices are themselves procyclical. Market participants often tend to copy each other ("herding"). In the face of uncertainty, diversity of opinion (and of action) is more likely to be stabilizing than is uniformity. Such desirable diversity could well be favored by the increased reliance on banks' own internal ratings mechanisms that is envisaged by the Basel Committee.

REFERENCES

Basel Committee on Banking Supervision. 1999. "A New Capital Adequacy Framework" Paper No 50. June. (www.bis.org)

Bonte, R., et al. 1999. "Supervisory lessons to be drawn from the Asian crisis" Basel Committee on Banking Supervision Working Paper No 2. June. (www.bis.org)

Jackson, P., et al. 1999. "Capital requirements and bank behaviour: the impact of the Basel Accord." Basel Committee on Banking Supervision Working Paper No 1. April. (www.bis.org)

Monfort, B., and C. Mulder. 2000. "Using credit ratings for capital requirements on lending to emerging market economies—possible impact of a new Basel Accord." IMF working paper 00/69. March (www.imf.org)

Morris, S., and H. S. Shin. 1999. "Risk management with interdependent choice." *Oxford Review of Economic Policy*. Vol. 15, No. 3, Autumn pp.52–62.